£2.50

THE CELTS – ARTISTS AND STORYTELLERS

THE CELTS – ARTISTS AND STORYTELLERS

Grange BOOKS

A QUANTUM BOOK

Published by Grange Books
an imprint of Grange Books Plc
The Grange
Kingsnorth Industrial Estate
Hoo, nr. Rochester
Kent ME3 9ND

1-84013-112-8

This book is produced by
Quantum Books Ltd
6 Blundell Street
London N7 9BH

Project Manager: Rebecca Kingsley
Project Editor: Judith Millidge
Designer: Wayne Humphries
Editor: Andrew Brown

The material in this publication previously appeared in
An Introduction to Celtic Mythology

QUMCA&A
Set in Times
Reproduced in Singapore by United Graphic Ltd
Printed in Singapore by Star Standard Industries (Pte) Ltd

CONTENTS

INTRODUCTION

For centuries, the art and myths of the Celts have exerted a powerful influence on our own culture. In the eighteenth and nineteenth centuries the Romantic poets and artists, with their love of mist, mystery and magic, glorified the Celtic past, finding in it a nostalgic escape from the Industrial Age to a fantastic and mysterious moonlit world, ruled by nature and spirits, and peopled by heroic warriors, fair-skinned maidens and white-robed druids performing strange rituals and brewing potions. We, too, require our fantasies and Celtic culture continues to attract us today. Celtic design, particularly in jewellery, seems to have a near-universal appeal. With its abstract patterns, curvilinear forms and intertwining lines, it appears to hold the secrets of an unknown pagan age. Celtic literature weaves a similar spell: the storyteller takes us from a world of seemingly real people and transports us to an incredible fantasy land of fairies, wizards, heroes and monsters; his skill is such that not only we do not notice the transition, but also the fantastic tales seem to be so believable. It is easy to be bewitched by such a culture. Without a doubt our view of the Celtic past is itself a myth, coloured by the Romantic 'Celtomania'. But if we are to learn about Celtic society through its art and mythology we must first of all rid ourselves of our own modern ideas of the Celts.

WHO WERE THE CELTS?

We can not think of the Celts as a single race, like the Greeks or Romans, but as a number of diverse peoples who, despite coming from various ethnic origins, all displayed certain common characteristics. They had sufficient shared features, for example in language, in social and religious institutions, and in their general way of life, to mark them as a recognizably distinct nation. The earliest references to the Celts occur in Greek literature around 500 BC. By then the Celts had already expanded from their original homeland, which comprised southern Germany and part of Bohemia, and were inhabiting a wide geographical area, ranging from the upper reaches of the Danube in eastern Europe across to France and Spain in the west. Archeological dating of Celtic finds not only confirms the accounts of the ancient Greek writers, but also informs us of the prehistoric Celtic past. We can tell from discovered remains, for example, that a recognizably 'proto-Celtic' culture existed around the upper Danube in 1000 BC.

Right: The Gundestrup Cauldron, Denmark (first century BC). This interior silver panel represents a divinity and warrior grappling with a wheel. The god could be any one of a number of Celtic sky divinities. The wheel is a solar symbol in Celtic art, and the griffins that appear across the bottom of the panel were traditionally associated with Apollo.

However, some archeologists now argue for a widespread and gradual 'Celticization' of cultures which already existed in Bronze-Age northern and western Europe: thus, 'Celtic' Britain might be said to date back to as early as 1500 BC, when the so-called Wessex culture had the 'heroic' social features which conform with the early Irish Celtic myths.

THE CELTIC DOMINANCE OF EUROPE

Towards the end of the fifth century BC the eastern European Celts were exploiting iron for tools and weapons and expanding their territories, firstly across Europe to France and the Iberian Peninsula, as the early Greek historians affirm. This migration was towards the end of the period of prehistory which archeologists call the 'Hallstatt' era. This period is named after a prehistoric site in Austria, some 225 kilometres southwest of Vienna, which was discovered in 1846. The discovery revealed hundreds of artefacts, including weapons and armour, statues and engravings and everyday objects such as clothes, mirrors, wine sieves and drinking vessels. It was clear that at this time the site was a busy commercial centre, probably the result of the salt mines located nearby. Similar items have since found at other sites in Germany, Austria and France, evidence of the spread of the Hallstatt culture across eastern and central Europe. While these objects may not be instantly recognizable as Celtic in their design, they display many various artistic elements that would later come to together to form the distinctive Celtic style.

By about 400 BC Celtic tribes had made incursions into Etruscan and Roman Italy, and having almost succeeded in besieging Rome in 387 BC, finally settled in the Po valley. The Celtic culture of this period is known as 'La Tène', after a site discovered near the

Opposite: 'Tristan and Isolt' (tempera on canvas by John Duncan; 1912). The story of Tristan and Isolt, who have an adulterous love affair, has undergone many transformations since it first appeared in pagan Celtic times. Hundreds of different versions have been written since the medieval period, culminating in Wagner's opera Tristan and Isolde. *Artists have been inspired by the tale, too. In the manner of the Pre-Raphaelites, John Duncan has here used the white priming of the canvas to produce a gleaming, jewel-like image of the two lovers. He chose the turning-point of the story, with the two unknowingly about to drink the magic love-potion. Celtic patterns are employed to give authentic details of dress and wood-carving.*

Left: Iberian bronze female figurine, from Aust-on-Severn, Gloucestershire, England (c. fourth to third centuries BC) Similar objects are known to have been made in Spain. The glass-eyed figure was probably imported from Iberia along the trade-routes of the Atlantic coast.

northern end of Lake Neuchâtel, Switzerland, in 1857. After thorough excavations, archeologists unearthed hundreds of spears and swords, jewellery and human and animal bones deposited underwater. It was once thought that the site was a prehistoric arsenal, but it is now believed to have been a sacred place, where precious objects and human and animal sacrifices were thrown into the water as offerings to the gods. Many archeologists see La Tène as the first truly Celtic culture, during which Celtic art as we know it today truly blossomed. Certainly, these are the people referred to from now on as Celts by the classical historians. Their military presence in northern Italy in the late fifth and early fourth centuries BC is attested by Roman mythical accounts of the Gallic siege of Rome, which was apparently frustrated by the warning cackles of sacred geese; and some Etruscan funerary relief sculptures depict battles with Celtic warriors.

By this time most of Britain had also been conquered by the Celts. It is thought that the earliest Celtic immigration into the British Isles occurred in the fifth century BC, another took place in the third century BC, while the final major influx was in the early first century BC. It is not clear exactly when Ireland was first occupied by the Celts but archeological remains show that they were definitely inhabiting the island by the third century BC. These Celtic peoples are described as insular Celts to distinguish them from the continental Celts of mainland Europe.

A further Celtic expansion took place in the fourth century BC and was directed towards southeastern Europe, the Baltic, and western Turkey. We find Alexander the Great receiving Celtic ambassadors at his Macedonian court; and in 279 BC we hear of

Celtic tribes attempting to loot the Greek sanctuary at Delphi, defied by a miraculous fall of snow sent by the god Apollo. In the following year Celtic tribes originally from Gaul crossed into Asia Minor and established themselves in the region that still bears the name Galatia. The Greeks distinguished between these oriental Celts, whom they called *Galatoi*, and the Celts of western Europe, whom they called *Keltoi*. The Romans made a further distinction by naming the French Celts *Galli* (Gauls) and the British Celts *Belgae* (originally from what is now Belgium) and *Britanni* (Britons).

THE FALL OF THE CELTS
Although in the early part of the third century BC the Celts controlled a vast area of Europe, from Galatia in the east to Britain and Ireland in the west, they were ill-equipped to establish an enduring empire or confederation as

the Greeks had done and the Romans were about to. They lacked any real form of central organization and, although they shared a common culture, common social and religious customs, common language and common artistic traditions, they had little sense of cohesion or political unity. They were divided into aristocratic tribes, ruled by chieftains who appear to have been constantly fighting one another rather than working together. In some areas the Celts were a ruling minority, surrounded by an often hostile indigenous population. Long distances weakened lines of communication between the Celtic tribes, encouraging further disintegration. By the end of the third century BC the Celts' influence of Europe was in decline. Before long they were being threatened on several sides: in the north by the Germans, in the east by the Dacians, and in the south by the Romans, all of which probably fomented tribal divisions among the

Above left: The coast at Harlech, Wales. This west-facing stretch of the northwest coast of Wales provides the ideal setting for the tale of Branwen, one of the 'Four Branches' of the Welsh collection of myths, the Mabinogion. *Shallow beaches provided landing places along the coast for ancient ships, while the mountainous hinterland encouraged the building of strongholds, from prehistoric camps to medieval castles.*

Opposite top: A map of Celtic Britain and Ireland showing tribal territories and key settlements and sites.

Opposite bottom: The extent of the Celtic world from the early Hallstatt era to the period of Celtic dominance in the third century BC.

Celts to facilitate their own invasions. Within a hundred years no more than a fraction of the former Celtic territories remained under their control. Only in Gaul and Britain did the Celts preserve their independence and their separate identity.

This was not to last long, however. In the first century BC Gaul was invaded by Emperor Julius Caesar, renamed Gallia and incorporated into the Roman Empire. A century later, in AD 43, Emperor Claudius conquered Britain and renamed it Britannia. Over the next four centuries the Romans steadily destroyed the Celtic civilization in both lands. By the time the Roman Empire collapsed in the fifth century AD the Celtic language in Gaul had been almost wiped out. In Britain the Celts had been driven to the furthest extremes of the land: Scotland, Wales and the southwest of England. When the Roman presence in Britain came to an end at the end of the fifth century, it was followed by that of the Anglo-Saxons. From then on the area of Celtic speech and sovereignty gradually got smaller and smaller. In a bid to escape complete eradication some Celtic tribes emigrated from southwest England and settled in Brittany.

Meanwhile, Celtic Ireland had enjoyed almost complete security from invasion. As a result its culture, traditions and language, which linguists call Goidelic and which in its modern form is known as Gaelic, survived for much longer than had been the case elsewhere in the Celtic world. In fact the Celtic Irish social order remained virtually intact long

after Ireland had officially become a Christian country and Irish adopted as the written language. For this reason Irish artists and storytellers, more than any other Celtic artists and storytellers, have preserved the early, prehistoric Celtic culture in vivid detail.

The pagan Celts spoke an Indo-European language which relates them in prehistory to the Greeks, Romans and Hindus. However, no record exists of their ancient languages, except brief dedicatory inscriptions that occur throughout the territories occupied by the Romans, and references in the classical authors' writings to Celtic names. When the Celtic myths were finally written down, from the end of the sixth century AD onwards, they were not in their original Celtic language; instead the languages varied according to the writer's country of origin: thus the Irish myths were recorded in Gaelic, which would have been impossible to understand by the contemporary Welsh writers. It would appear that by the time of the Roman invasion any former cultural unity provided by a single Celtic language had all but disappeared: the Irish Celts were speaking Goidelic, while the British Celts were speaking 'Brythonic'. The Brythonic language seems to have been distantly related to that spoken by the Gauls. Around the fifth century AD there were invasions and population movements in the western Celtic lands which led to linguistic changes: the Irish Goidelic language entered Scotland, later to become Scottish-Gaelic, while the Anglo-Saxon 'English' language entered southern Britain, pushing the Brythonic language across the sea to Brittany.

Left: Gaulish prisoner (c. first century BC). This Roman bronze depicts the Celt as the stereotyped heroic enemy, with his hands tied behind his back.

Left: Thracian rider god on a gilt-silver helmet from Romania (c. fourth century BC). Thracians, like the Celts, were considered hostile barbarians by the Greeks and Romans. Their culture was also one of aristocratic warriors in which the horse and rider symbolized hero or god.

ANCIENT CELTIC SOCIETY

The Celts did not write their own histories. Therefore we must learn about their civilization from the works of contemporary Greek and Roman writers such as Posidonius and Julius Caesar, from interpreting Celtic mythology, and from archeological remains.

Most classical authors, however, had no first-hand knowledge of the Celts. Instead, they derived their information from earlier sources, and many of their accounts were based on the assumption that the Celts were uncivilized barbarians. Even Julius Caesar, who had a better opportunity than most to become

Above: The Turoe Stone, County Galway, Ireland (c. first century BC). The shape suggests a sacred fertility stone: it is similar to the World-Navel stone in ancient Greek Delphi. The carved decoration with its curvilinear stylized foliage is typical of Irish La Tène art.

Right: Bronze boar statuette (Hounslow, Middlesex, England; first century BC to first century AD). The figure was found together with a wheel, which were perhaps votive offerings to a sun god at a Celtic shrine. Like other Celtic boars, its dorsal spine is emphasized: the animal was a symbol of virility, which was signified in myth and reality by the warrior's bristling hair.

acquainted with Celtic customs in Gaul, did not rely entirely on his own experience and observation. Classical evidence must therefore be treated with some caution. However, many of the ancient descriptions of the Celtic customs have been corroborated by archeological discoveries and surviving Irish literature. Archeology has confirmed, for example, that Celts performed human sacrifice and indulged in head-hunting.

The Celts were primarily a warrior society ruled by brave warrior kings, queens and aristocrats. Their enemies respected them as superb horsemen and fierce, volatile fighters who could ride for miles on end and then fight long and hard. The ease and extent of the Celtic tribes' conquests in Europe demonstrate that at the height of their power they were ruthlessly efficient in war. Both historical accounts and myths reflect the Celtic pride of dressing up for battle. In *Gallic War V* Caesar wrote 'The Britons dye themselves with blue woad in order to appear more terrifying in battle.

They wear their hair long, and their bodies shaven except for the head and upper lip.' Diodorus of Sicily, a contemporary of Caesar, described the Celts as 'tall and muscular, with pale skin and blond hair which they highlight artificially by washing it in lime-water; they gather it back from the forehead to the top of the head and down to the nape of the neck … therefore the hair becomes so heavy and coarse that it looks like the mane of horses.' Another Roman writer, Herodian, who was writing in the third century AD, added: 'As they are not used to clothes, they wear iron ornaments about their waists and necks, which they consider to be both decorative and a sign of wealth … they tattoo their bodies with abstract patterns and all sorts of animals.' Classical marble sculptures showing Celtic soldiers and prisoners conform with these literary stereotypes and archeologists have found tattoos on preserved Celtic flesh.

As well as being excellent warriors, the Celts were also accomplished farmers. They grew

Above: Bull-headed terminal of iron fire-dog, Capel Garmon, Denbigh, Wales (c. first century BC). One of a pair used to support roasting spits over a fire, the bull was a Celtic symbol of virility and would have been a fitting decoration at a warrior banquet.

Left: 'The Holy Well' (William Orpen; tempera on canvas, 1916). The Irish symbolist artist has depicted the 'beehive' huts of a Late Celtic Arran community. The islanders are being converted to Christianity in the waters of their pagan well; Orpen's artist friend Sean Keating stands above the well, apparently unconvinced by the new religion. The deserted crofter's hut in the background and the shamefully naked 'Adam and Eve' in the centre reinforce Orpen's criticisms of cultural change in Celtic places.

corn, cultivating fields on a regular basis with ox-drawn ploughs instead of manual implements. They also depended on extensive trade, and learnt the use of coinage from the Greeks and Romans. As noted by Herodian, the Celts placed great importance on visual displays of wealth. This fact is reflected in the eye-catching quality of their art. Celtic artists and craftsmen produced not only some of the most intricate jewellery and the finest ornaments of all the early civilizations, but also some of the most decorative functional and everyday objects, such as buckets, cauldrons, and chariots, and some of the most stunning battle dress, including helmets, swords and shields. Their ability to create beautiful and ornate objects from rough and simple metals, stone and wood was considered almost magical by the other Celts. Consequently, artists and craftsmen enjoyed privileged positions in Celtic society. The smith, for example, was given special burial rites.

Similarly, the storyteller, or bard, had a special place in Celtic society. Throughout the Celtic world learning, literature and religion rested upon a highly organized system of three professional classes: the druids, the bards and, between these two, an order of soothsayers, known as *vates* in Gaul and *filidhs* in the Irish tradition. An essentially identical system also probably existed in Galatia, too. The druids had the highest social status, being considered semi-divine. They conducted a system of education, enforced legal decisions and officiated at religious ceremonies. The Celts were an intensely religious nation, and worshipped a whole host of gods and goddesses. Their religious rituals played an important role in reinforcing the sacred power of the druids, and in maintaining the social hierarchy of chieftains and tribes. The *vates* carried out many of the druids' functions and in many respects were a subordinate order of the druids. The bards were the class concerned with literature, and appear to have been held in almost equal respect to the druids.

Above left: 'The Riders of the Sidhe' (John Duncan, tempera on canvas; 1911). The Sidhe (Shee) were the Irish fairies, ancient heroes who lived in the Otherworld.

Top: Celtic bronze torc from Dumfriesshire, Scotland (c. first century AD). The taut abstract designs are found on many types of object in La Tène art.

Bottom: Beard-pullers and beasts from the Book of Kells (Irish; eighth to ninth centuries AD). The Christian scribes illustrated their texts with motifs and styles from the pagan Celtic past.

CELTIC ART

Previous page: Bronze belt hook from the German Tyrol (fourth century BC). Early La Tène artists used running tendril patterns; here 'dragons' (or stylized horses?) and a human figure are depicted in such a pattern. Whatever the subject matter, it appears to symbolize the power of man (or god?) over beast, and would therefore have been fitting decoration for the aristocratic warrior.

Above: The Trundholm Chariot (from a fen in Denmark; c. 1300 BC). The religious themes, artistic styles and materials of Iron-Age Celtic art have their roots in the Bronze-Age Hallstatt culture. This bronze model of a horse and gold-plated disc probably symbolized the sun: horse and sun symbols appear together on later Celtic coins.

According to several classical authors the Celts were a proud people, fond of displaying their wealth and status. In particular they had an obsession with gold. To some Roman and Greek writers, this was their major weakness. The Greek geographer Strabo, for example, wrote about what he called the Gaulish Celts' childish 'love of decoration. They wear ornaments of gold, torcs on their necks and bracelets on their arms and wrists, and their nobles adorn themselves with dyed garments sprinkled with gold. It is this vanity which makes them so unbearable in victory and so downcast in defeat ....'

Below: Human head on a large bronze cauldron from Rynkeby, Denmark (first century BC). He wears a warrior torc, and his stylized features are typical of Celtic representation. Heads of oxen also decorate this cauldron, and may have signified its use as a ritual container for animal sacrifice.

The eye-catching quality of Celtic art reflects a society which placed great importance on visual displays of its wealth. The distinctive Celtic style is at its most characteristic in the abstract La Tène curvilinear patterns used as ornamentation on a wide range of objects. The early Celtic craftsmen established a basic repertoire of attractive decorative patterns. These patterns, though to our modern eyes 'abstract' and therefore without obvious meaning, must have provided the ancient Celts with a powerful visual sign of cultural identity: the same patterns and motifs are found throughout the Celtic world.

The remarkable resilience of this decorative style to external changes in Celtic culture can be gauged by its survival through time. The unmistakable taut, curving lines of Celtic art can be traced in an unbroken tradition from the eighth century BC with the early Hallstatt culture in eastern Europe. The style appeared in Britain in the third century BC with the La Tène culture, and survived some fourteen hundred years through to the Norman conquests. Various chronological changes in the basic style of Celtic art as well as regional variations have been identified by art historians, although the most important themes,

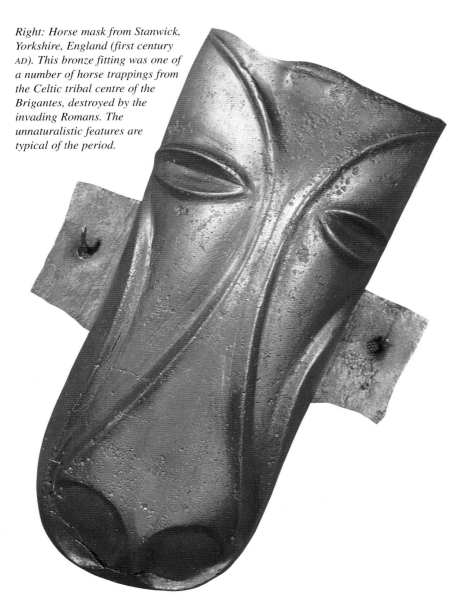

Right: Horse mask from Stanwick, Yorkshire, England (first century AD). This bronze fitting was one of a number of horse trappings from the Celtic tribal centre of the Brigantes, destroyed by the invading Romans. The unnaturalistic features are typical of the period.

symbols and motifs remain constant. The style never completely disappeared from artistic and craft production in those areas which retained a strong sense of their Celtic past. Ireland and Scotland have been particularly successful in reviving the art at different times of their post-Norman history, and nineteenth- and twentieth-century metalworkers have continued a thriving market for Celtic jewellery designs.

The Celtic artists and craftsmen seem to have left storytelling to the poets, and there is little that can be called 'narrative' in Celtic art. In place of the representation of heroic adventures found for example in ancient Greek art, the Celtic artists attracted the eye with what were often highly intricate interwoven linear forms: these forms range from simple threaded lines through to complex fantasies drawn from the natural world. Vegetal and floral patterns consisting of tendrils, lotus buds, palmettes and flowing wreaths abound. When human or animal forms do appear, the naturalistic representations of classical western art are ignored, and nature is interpreted in a strikingly stylized, even distorted manner. They are often half-concealed amid the surrounding foliage. Also unlike their classical counterparts, Celtic artists avoided the straight line at all times and only rarely produced symmetrical designs.

The fantastical and sometimes bizarre abstract forms of this art should be seen in the overall context of Celtic culture. The sheer time and skill involved in creating such complex forms in stone, wood and metal provided the tribal leaders with visible signs of their wealth and dominant position in Celtic society. The rich men and women who wore and handled these exquisite art objects also commissioned the storytellers, and the myths themselves rely on a similar interweaving of plots and subplots to hold the listener's attention; likewise, mythical narratives are peppered with marvellous incidents and occasional shocks. The mysteries of druidic religious ritual were at the core of Celtic thought, and this also must have affected the artistic tendency to avoid the direct and perfectly naturalistic representation of humans and animals.

The pagan Celts took their most treasured possessions into the grave and the finest examples of Celtic art have been discovered in aristocratic tombs. Clothing accessories for both men and women, such as brooches, neck collars, torcs and armlets, were of rich metals. Gold, silver and bronze were cast in flat moulds and sometimes plaited to create more complex forms; some torcs consist of hollow tubes. Colour was provided by enamel inlays. Bronze hand-mirrors have been mainly found in women's graves, their backs incised with Celtic designs. Finely decorated metal horse-tackle, drinking bowls, swords, shields and helmets reflect the fighting and feasting of the myths.

Religious shrines and sanctuaries are also important sites for rediscovering lost Celtic art. The most important sacred places for the Celts were those near water. They saw water as a supernatural dwelling, where gods, giants and monsters all lived, and from where they occasionally emerged. Throughout the Celtic world, archeologists have found remains of religious activity near wells, springs,

Right: Teutonic gilt-bronze brooch from Denmark (c. AD 500). The Teutonic tribes were probably originally close to the Celts of Eastern Europe. Similarities of style and subject matter can be seen in this brooch, with its decorative spirals, frontal wide-eyed faces and monster/human oppositions.

streams, rivers, and lakes. In the north of England, for example, there are many dedications and stone carvings near wells in honour of a Celtic water deity named Coventina. Although we can not be certain of what forms the religious ceremonies took at these sites, the discovery of large ornamental bronze horns suggests that music may have played a part in Celtic rituals.

We do know, however, that the Celts threw many different objects into sacred streams, rivers, lakes and seas as offerings to the water gods. Bronze helmets and shields, stone carvings and bones from animal sacrifices have all been recovered from a number of sites, including the River Thames at Wandsworth, London, and the River Witham near Lincoln, northern England. Several sacrificial wells containing similar items have been unearthed in Denmark, while a collection of wooden sculptures have been found in marshes at the mouth of the River Seine in France. These not only included animals and whole human figures, both male and female, but also torsos, heads, limbs and even internal organs. The goddess of the source, Sequana, from whom the river's name is derived, was associated with healing, and these sculptures were probably votive offerings to the deity. Objects were

Above right: Bronze shield-boss from the River Thames at Wandsworth, London, England (second to first centuries BC). The Celtic La Tène style is evident in this rich votive offering to the water gods by a warrior aristocrat: the taut curvilinear foliate patterns are imperceptibly combined with bird forms. The repoussé designs were hammered from behind the bronze plate; fine details were then engraved onto some of the resulting shapes to give them texture.

Above: Ornamented 'Q', the first letter of St Luke's Gospel (illuminated manuscript of the Gospels of Lindisfarne, Northumbria, England; c. 698). Christian monks working in Celtic areas often ornamented their manuscripts in a Celtic style: pagan monsters and human figures appear among the interwoven patterns.

Right: Base of the Cross of Cong (bronze and oak; twelfth century). The Viking invaders influenced late Celtic Irish art with its interweaving tendrils and dragons. The use of a beast to support the cross symbolizes the triumph of Christianity over nature.

Left: 'The Children of Lir' (tempera by John Duncan, 1866–1945). This painting depicts the characters from one of the Irish Celtic Three Sorrowful Tales of Erin. *In the story the children metamorphose from human to animal form, a common ability of the Celtic gods. Silver chains link the swan-children, a token of their fairy status.*

also thrown into springs to invoke the gods to bring harm to an individual. In Bath, southwest England, for example, curses were written on lead tablets and thrown as an offering to the water goddess Sulis.

A LIVING TRADITION

The work of Celtic craftsmen under Roman rule kept the artistic tradition alive: Celtic and Roman artistic styles can often be identified in the same art object. The Romans never penetrated Ireland and it is perhaps ironic that the 'golden age' of Celtic art occurred not under the patronage of pagan chieftains but within a Christian context. New metalworking techniques of filigree and granulation were learnt by the Irish artists in the seventh century AD. The old pagan interlaced designs now appeared on objects of Christian ritual – crosses, chalices and patens for Communion; reliquaries for the bones of saints; bishops' crooks as signs of the new spiritual leaders; and decorative letter-headings in Christian manuscripts, such as the famous *Book of Kells*. The richest Celtic brooches are also from this late period.

In terms of Celtic visual art, the most recent revivals occurred mainly in the works of the late nineteenth-century Scottish painters such as John Duncan. They incorporated the old Celtic patterns into the clothing and furniture of scenes from the Celtic myths. These artists tended to romanticize the myths, according to the taste of their day. In the more recent Celtic revival, the artwork of the Devon painter Alan Lee has provided the new romantic evocations of the ancient Celtic world in his book-illustrations of Welsh and Arthurian myths. Lee, like Duncan, has drawn on the decorative patterns of earlier Celtic artists to imbue his more realistic images with an authentic Celtic flavour.

Above: 'Branwen' (watercolour by Alan Lee; 1981). The artist has painted one of the heroines from the Welsh Celtic Mabinogion *collection of myths. Here she is sending her starling to Wales bearing the message of her dishonour at the hands of the Irish.*

Right: Silver torc from Trichtingen, Germany (c. second century BC). Decorated in a more linear, Eastern style, the bull-head terminals are symbols of the strength and virility of the Celtic warrior.

JEWELLERY

For the Celts the most prestigious of all jewellery was the torc. Worn around the neck, this was a heavy metal collar worn by the most important figures in Celtic society, such as nobles, warriors and druids. Torcs were also thought to have magical properties, offering some kind of protection to the wearer. The Celtic warrior would sometimes go into battle completely naked, save for his weapons and his torc. They had divine associations, too: Celtic deities are often shown wearing or holding them. The Celts also often offered torcs to the gods. At Snettisham in Norfolk, England, a hoard of sixty-one such torcs dating back to the first century BC were discovered between 1948 and 1990. According to classical sources, this area was the tribal territory of the Iceni, who were led by Queen Boudicca. The Roman writer Cassius Dio records that Boudicca wore a gold torc when she led a rebellion against the Romans in AD 61.

Celtic torcs were made in a variety of sizes and materials. Some were made from a hollow tube and were light and pliant enough to be pulled open. Others, on the other hand, were made of thick twisted strands of gold and silver wires, and were so large, heavy and lavishly decorated that they were only used for ceremonial purposes. Perhaps the most magnificent of all torcs discovered by archeologists was the one which was buried in the tomb of the princess of Vix, Côte d'Or, France, in the late sixth century BC along with many other items of jewellery. It is 96 per cent pure gold and weighs some 480g. Like most torcs the decoration is concentrated on the terminals, which are formed from large globes

attached to lions' paws. Winged horses also spring from the terminals.

The most popular piece of jewellery worn by the Celts was the brooch. Worn by both men and women, they were at once practical clothes fasteners and magical talismans. Brooches were valued for their decoration. The most striking examples took the form of stylized animals or occasionally humans. One bronze example was found at Parsberg, Oberfalz, Germany, which was decorated with a moustached face with large, round popping eyes. On the top of the brooch is another face with catlike ears, which spreads out to form two griffins. Like many brooches, this piece may have been coloured with enamel or inlaid with precious stones.

The Celts also produced a variety of other ornamental objects, such as gold bracelets, armlets and ankle rings, often produced in matching pairs. Animal motifs were commonly used, especially snake forms or exotic sphinxes and winged griffins.

Celtic craftsman also created highly decorative clasps, buckles, amulets, belt loops and other items associated with clothing and jewellery, such as combs and mirrors. Bronze mirrors were particularly popular in Britain, and some of the finest examples have been found in Northamptonshire. The backs of these mirrors were usually delicately engraved with complex, near-symmetrical curvilinear designs. Although there is evidence that the craftsmen sometimes drew their designs freehand, in most cases they used compasses and tracers. Occasionally the mirrors were also covered with basketry hatching ornament. The use of compasses was a common technique in Celtic art. The technique was later used in the Christian period in the design of illuminated manuscripts.

WEAPONS

The Celts spent a great deal of time and effort decorating their weapons and armour, to which they had a reverential attitude. In

Above: Electrum torc from Snettisham, Norfolk, England (first century BC). Eight twisted wires make up each of the eight main strands; these were soldered onto the terminals, which were decorated with curving La Tène style ornaments. The British Celtic artists developed an increasingly insular version of the continental style.

Left: Irish silver penannular brooch (seventh century AD). This type of brooch was exported from pre-Roman Celtic Britain to Ireland. By the early medieval period the Irish Celts were making their own extremely rich examples.

Left: Gold amulets, from Szarazd-Regoly, Hungary (c. 100 BC). These fine examples of miniature Celtic metalwork are formed from embossed gold-leaf with filigree and granulated decoration. The wheel symbolized the sun god and was used in burials as a protective talisman against the forces of darkness.

Below: Gilt-silver brooch from Ardagh, County Limerick, Ireland (c. eighth century AD). The meticulous golden filigree and granular decoration of this late Celtic penannular brooch would have signified a high degree of wealth and social status in the wearer.

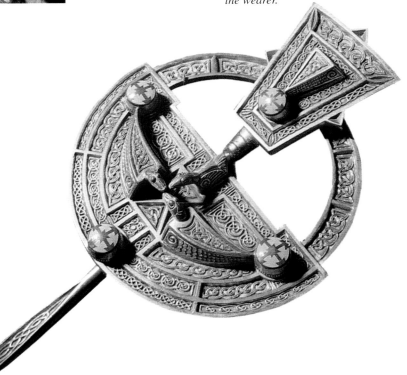

Celtic legend the finest weapons were magical pieces with their own personalities. Warriors wield mighty swords that are powerful enough to slice through hill-tops, while other characters have shields that scream aloud when the master is in trouble. Celtic chieftains would have been very familiar with such mythic weaponry, and may have given names to their own weapons.

Archeologists have discovered two distinct kinds of Celtic arms and armour. There are those items that were designed to be used in fighting, and there are those ceremonial items that were clearly intended for ritual use, such as being offered to the gods or being buried with a high-ranking figure. The former are usually found battered and bearing the scars of battle, while the latter are often relatively intact. Many swords, shields and helmets have been discovered in rivers and other waters.

The principal weapon of the Celts was the heavy, long-bladed sword. The large size of the blade dictated a substantial hilt, and it was here that artists and craftsmen concentrated

27

Right: Bronze armlet from Pitkelloney, Tayside, Scotland (c. first century BC). This massive piece of warrior ornament was originally polished and shining like all other Celtic bronze objects, with additional colour provided by red and yellow inlay.

Below: Warrior fights monster (bronze matrix for making decorative helmet plaques, from Torslunda, Sweden; eighth century AD). The Teutonic warriors of pre-Viking Sweden, like their Celtic neighbours, decorated their helmets with scenes of power. Here, a warrior with an axe confronts a wild beast.

their decorative energies. Handles were sometimes inlaid with precious materials such as ivory and amber, or else coloured with enamel. Occasionally the handle was designed in the shape of a stylized human figure, the head forming a fearsome pommel, the torso acting as a handgrip, and the projecting arms and legs providing some protection to the swordsman's hand. Scabbards were often decorated with soldiers, horsemen and figures turning a wheel – a common motif in Celtic art – or else covered with flowing tendril and floral patterns. Sometimes these patterns contained traces of animal and bird forms.

Celtic shields tended to be long and flat, although a few circular pieces have also been found. Usually they were bronze, but some were also gilded. Craftsmen often decorated the front of ceremonial shields with elaborate, fluid and swirling La Tène designs. They also sometimes studded it with coloured glass

or enamel. In some cases only the central boss has survived, suggesting that the main shield was originally made from wood or leather.

The use of expensive materials and elaborate designs was even more widespread in the manufacture of helmets. These were often produced in the jockey-cap format, consisting of an iron or bronze hemispherical cap, hinged cheek-flaps, a neck guard and usually a fitting on the top for a plume or crest. This crest often took the form of a boar, which was symbol of power and strength in Celtic society. Geometric curvilinear patterns, such as triskeles and s-curves, normally decorated the entire helmet, which was also occasionally covered with gold leaf and studded with pieces of coral or coloured glass. Some helmets were less ornate but had more elaborate shapes. These include the sharp pointed helmets common in Gaul in the fifth century BC, and the twin-horned bronze helmet from the first century BC, found

Below: Bronze helmet with decorated neck-guard (British; first century AD). The Celtic warrior's helmet was often highly decorated depending on his rank. This is a relatively restrained example with decoration in the taut curvilinear La Tène style: however, the holes on the crown might have held a plume or other fixture. Artistic representations of Celtic warriors depict them wearing animal crests, such as birds or boars; horned helmets were also worn.

Above: Bronze shield from the River Thames at Battersea, London, England (c. first century AD). Such fine objects appear to have been deliberately thrown into rivers by Celtic warriors as votive offerings to the water gods. The shield has the curvilinear La Tène designs which become abstract faces in the central roundel. Colour was applied in the form of red glass.

Right: Bronze fittings on a wooden bucket from Aylesford, Kent, England (first century BC). The helmeted head on the handle mount suggests that the bucket was used in a warrior ritual. The wide-eyed and angular facial features are typical of La Tène art, as are the spiralling patterns on the hoop.

Far right: Gold boat model from Broighter, County Derry, Ireland (first century BC). This miniature boat, complete with benches, mast and oars, was part of a hoard of gold jewellery and may have been an offering to a water deity, such as the Irish sea god Manannán mac Lir.

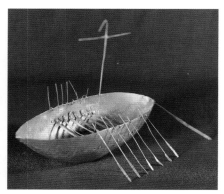

in the River Thames by Waterloo Bridge. Horns symbolized virility and aggression, making them the ideal addition to a warrior's armour.

EVERYDAY AND CULT OBJECTS

The Celts liked ostentatious display of skilful craftsmanship in all things, and some of the most common of everyday household items were decorated with remarkable creativity. Pins, coins, vases, flagons, buckets, horse tackle and chariot fittings are just some of the many ordinary objects that are enlivened with stylized heads and masks, charming depictions of animals and spiralling La Tène curvilinear patterns. Some may also have been inlaid with enamel and coral. One splendid example is a bowl dating from the sixth century BC which was discovered at Hallstatt. The vessel is surmounted by a cow and its calf: the cow stands on a platform extending over the interior of the bowl while the calf clambers up the side. These figures may have been the result of the *cire perdue* technique, whereby a wax model of a figure is encased in clay to create a mould. The bowl is also covered in geometric patterns. Also at Hallstatt, ducks appear to swim up the side of another bowl,

which is also embossed with ducks and wheels. The bowl may have been used in religious ceremonies: the waterfowl may represent an association with water deities while the wheel was a long-established symbol of Celtic sun gods. Birds also adorn a flesh hook found in Dunaverney Bog, County Antrim, Ireland. Here swans are accompanied by ravens, all of which are sacred in later Celtic mythology: swans are solar symbols, while ravens are associated with battle.

One of the most important everyday objects in Celtic life was the cauldron. It was not only used for ordinary domestic activities, such as boiling meat and heating water, it was also employed in druidic religion. The importance of the cauldron is reflected in the fact that the vessel is frequently mentioned in Celtic mythology. In Irish legend, for example, the cauldron was the attribute of the druid-god Daghdha, who was the legendary father of the Irish gods and of all the Irish people. The cauldron was a symbol of abundance, and in the Otherworld each feasting hall would have its own vessel, which would provide an endless supply of food. Cauldrons were also associated with death

and regeneration. In Welsh mythology, for instance, there is reference to a magic cauldron which could restore dead warriors to life. This association with death was echoed in real life, too: the Celts often used cauldrons in their funerary rites, and sometimes placed one in the burial chamber to sustain the deceased in the Otherworld. Some cauldrons were used to hold offerings to the gods – one was found deposited near a sacred spring containing more than 2,000 items of jewellery.

In other cases, the cauldron itself was the offering. In 1891, a large bowl was found in a peat bog at Gundestrup, Denmark. Probably dating to the first or second century BC, the bowl is one of the most famous and splendid of all Celtic treasures. It is made of thirteen plates of solid silver, originally covered with gold foil, and is richly decorated in embossed high relief on the outside with a number of torc-wearing deities, and on the inside by various smaller, mythological scenes. Perhaps the most important plate depicts a cross-legged figure with antlers, surrounded by a number

Left: The Gundestrup Cauldron, Denmark (first century BC). On this silver inner panel of the gilt-silver ritual vessel, the artist has depicted warriors going into battle, preceded by a ram-horned snake. The figures on the right blow carnyxes, or war-trumpets; some of the warriors have bird and boar crests, or horns, on their helmets; on the left, a god dips a human sacrifice into a bucket.

Below: 'Flesh-hook' from County Antrim, Ireland (c. sixth century BC). The birds are represented in the taut geometric style of Hallstatt art. The function of the object is debatable: water-birds often appear in Celtic art and myth in both sacred and warrior contexts. Therefore such decorations would be apt on banquet or ritual equipment.

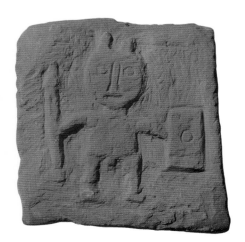

of creatures. This figure is normally identified as Cernunnos, the Celtic god of animals, nature and fertility. He was the most represented of all Celtic gods and was worshipped throughout the Celtic world.

The Gundestrup cauldron was probably a cult cauldron used by a druid as a ritual vessel in which to mix potions. It had been deliberately dismantled before being abandoned in the bog, probably as an offering to the water gods. Similar cauldrons have been uncovered at a number of religious sites. One such container, found in a bog at Brå, Jutland, and dating from the third century BC, had been smashed before being offered to the gods. Another, found at Rynkeby, Denmark, but thought to be Gaulish in origin, was decorated with heads of bulls, perhaps signifying its use

as a ritual vessel in animal sacrifice. The bull was one of the most potent of all Celtic symbols, representing among other things strength. The animal was a common sacrifice for all the Celts. Other vessels have been found in tombs and sacred sites, too. The Vix Krater, for example, discovered in the tomb of the princess of Vix, is a bronze wine-mixing bowl decorated with a procession of soldiers on foot and on horseback.

One of the ways the Celts worshipped their gods and goddesses, was by carving wooden, stone or bronze representations of their deities or sacred animals, such as boars and bulls. They would then either worship these carvings themselves or give them as an offering to the gods and cast them into the water at sacred spring, stream or river shrines. Wooden figures were usually small, plain and cheaply made. They were deposited in the water to invoke the healing powers of the gods. Sometimes, the donor making the offering might deposit a wooden representation of a diseased limb or organ in the hope that the gods will restore the real bodily part to health. Similarly, the Celts might carve the image of a warrior in wood or stone and offer it to the gods so that the deities will look favourably on him when he goes into battle. The Celts also offered more valuable and ornate objects to the gods. Earlier this century, a decorated bronze pony cap was found in a drained lake in Kircudbrightshire, Scotland, while a delicate, miniature golden boat has been discovered in County Derry, Ireland.

Above: Horned warrior from Cumbria, England (Romano-British). This naive and roughly incised image represents a naked horned warrior. His virility is emphasized by the horns and erect phallus.

Right: Wooden figure from County Cavan, Ireland (c. first century BC). Before they learnt stone-carving techniques, the Celts carved wooden figures. This one originally had a phallus and may be a fertility god.

CELTIC MONUMENTS AND ARCHITECTURE

As well as making small, intricate statues, ornaments, jewellery and other delicate decorative pieces, the Celts also created much larger and more permanent works of art. The most remarkable are the massive land figures that can be found on a number of sites throughout the Celtic world. These figures, which are often carved on the side of a chalk hill, can be several hundreds of feet in length. One of the most famous chalk carved figures is the Uffington White Horse in Oxfordshire, England. This 111-metre (364-feet) figure was probably carved by the local Dobunni Celts close to a pre-existing Iron-Age hill-fort, either to signify the tribe's territory or as an offering to their patron deity, the Celtic horse goddess Epona.

Right: Dolmen at Kilclonely, County Donegal, Ireland (c. 2000 BC). The dolmen (or cromlech) type of prehistoric tomb was originally covered with an earth mound. Many folk-tales surround these structures which, like other Neolithic and Bronze-Age sites, were often reused, misinterpreted or mythologized by later Celts.

Previous pages: Uffington White Horse, Oxfordshire, England (chalk-carved figure; c. first century BC to first century AD). This may represent the horse goddess Epona, the patron deity of the local Dobunni Celts.

This goddess, from whose name the word 'pony' is derived, was one of the most represented of all Celtic deities. She was associated with fertility, but also with death. Sometimes she was shown as a horse with a woman's head, or else she was portrayed simply as a human riding on the back of a horse. Carving such a figure must have been a huge undertaking, requiring the industry and skill of many hundreds of people. Only a close community with a strong sense of common purpose would have been able to organize themselves to complete such a demanding and complex project. Some other famous carved chalk-figures also represent horses, while some show human warrior-like figures instead.

MONUMENTS

All over the Celtic world large standing stones are scattered across the landscape. Many of these stones, some of which stand singly, in lines, or in circles, had been erected by earlier civilizations to mark burial places or boundaries. But they were often misinter-

preted, mythologized and revered by the Celts as sacred topographical 'focuses' of worship or memorials of famous legendary events. The famous stone circle at Stonehenge in the south of England could have been one such centre. Irish Celtic tradition often ascribed prehistoric grave stones, tombs and tumuli to the activities of supernatural beings, or goddesses known as *caillecha*, 'hags'. They were seen as passages to the Otherworld.

As well as venerating pre-existing standing stones, known as *galláin* in Irish, the Celts also erected their own monuments. Some of the stones were nothing more than plain slabs set in the ground. Many others were carved with runic inscriptions or dedications written in ogham text, an ancient Celtic form of writing. There are more than 300 surviving ogham stones in Ireland alone, and more than fifty in Britain, mostly in Wales. Other stones, such as the domed granite Turoe Stone in County Galway, were carved with intricate incised or relief abstract patterns or recognizable human, animal and plant shapes. One of the earliest and most ornate examples of such a stone is the four-sided, tapering pillar found at Pfalzfeld in the Rhineland. On each side a pear-shaped human face with a leaf-crown headdress stares out, surrounded with stacked s-scrolls and stylized floral patterns. Originally the pillar was surmounted with a head, but this had been broken off by the seventeenth century. Some stones were actually carved into lifesize human figures, often to represent a dead warrior or a deity.

The Celts used their standing stones in a number of various ways. Most were probably set up in shrines, as stone versions of a sacred tree. They may have been seen as having talismanic properties, or else the stones themselves were the focus of ritual cult

Above: Irish cross-base inscribed with ogham and runic letters (Killaloe Church, County Clare, Ireland; c. AD 1000). The earliest Irish writings were in ogham script and date back to about the fourth century AD. The oghams (right) read: 'A blessing upon Thorgrimr'; the runes (left) read: 'Thorgrimr carved this cross'.

Left: 'Ossian's Grave': a neolithic grave, County Antrim, Ireland (c. 2500 BC). The monumental graves of earlier cultures were revered as sacred by the Celts.

worship. Some were used to swear oaths, while others were used in healing and fertility rites. Many stones took the form of pillar-statues and were placed on the summits of ancient burial mounds, or barrows. One such monument is a lifesize naked figure found near a tomb at Hirschlanden in Germany. Dating back to the late sixth century or early fifth century BC, the sandstone statue originally stood atop the grave and probably represents and glorifies the dead person lying below. The figure's attributes – a helmet, a heavy torc, a dagger and an erect phallus – all symbolize a heroic warrior. Twin-headed Janus figures, with their ability to look out in two directions at once, were often placed on the tops of barrows, too. Traditionally, such figures had a watchful and protective function, and this may be their role here. They also emphasized the tomb's status as a boundary between the natural and supernatural worlds.

Other stones were claimed to have incredible properties. According to Irish legend, on the Hill of Tara in County Meath, the mystical centre of Ireland, stood the Stone of Fál, a 'stone penis' which cried out whenever it was touched by the man destined to be king. Other legendary stones were used in the ritual selection of Celtic kings, too. One of the several ordeals to test a candidate's fitness for the crown involved two sacred stones, with just a hand's width between them, which opened up to allow the chosen candidate's chariot to pass through.

Early Christian missionaries to the Celtic areas attempted to appropriate the tradition of standing stones by carving Christian symbols such as the cross on them. According to legend this practice had been started by St. Patrick himself. Later, sometime in the sixth century AD, Celtic stonemasons were erecting the first of the famous Celtic crosses seen all over

Far left: The 'Swearing Stone' (Castledermot Churchyard, County Kildare, Ireland). Folk memory carries traditions from the Celtic past, and prehistoric standing stones were probably used in pagan healing and fertility rites. This would explain why the Christians gave them evil names such as the 'Devil's Arrows', but their original sacred properties have survived in local superstitions: this one is still employed in the binding of oaths.

Left: Pagan Celtic stone figures (Boa Island, Lough Erne, County Fermanagh, Ireland; c. fifth to seventh centuries AD). The double-sided figures stand in a Christian graveyard but retain the stylized, staring features of pagan Celtic images.

Ireland and parts of Scotland. These normally combined the Christian cross with the wheel, an ancient Celtic motif associated with a number of Celtic solar deities. Other Celtic symbols also frequently appear on these otherwise Christian monuments, too, such as the crouching figure of the horned-god Cernunnos, the master of the animal kingdom and the most represented of all Celtic gods.

Above left: The 'Drosten' Stone (Pictish cross-slab from St. Vigeans, Scotland; ninth century AD). The late Celtic art of the Picts continued earlier themes and styles. On the shaft of this Christian cross are the age-old subjects of mastery of animal over animal, and man over beast: an eagle clutches a salmon, while a hunter shoots at a wild boar. The spiralling lines of the decorative and representational figures are continuing Celtic elements, expressed in a vigourous and naive manner by the Pictish sculptors.

Above: The 'Ossian's Grave': a neolithic grave above Glen Aan, Country Antrim, Ireland (c. 2500 BC.) The monumental stone graves of earlier cultures were revered as sacred by the Celts. The attribution of this grave to the Irish hero 'Ossian' (Oisin) was probably made under the influence of James Macpherson's spurious eighteenth-century Gaelic romances of the bard Ossian.

Above: Horsemen drinking (Pictish stone from near Dundee, Scotland; ninth century AD). Horses were status symbols in all Celtic societies; here, the rider drinks from a horn which, with its eagle-headed terminal, is a further symbol of power.

Right: Reconstruction of Iron-Age huts at Butser Hill, Hampshire, England. Archeology has provided evidence of sizes, shapes and materials used in building Celtic dwellings. The Butser Ancient Farm has also launched experiments with Celtic farm animals, crops, cooking and pottery methods.

CELTIC BUILDINGS

Very little Celtic architecture has survived to this day. Most has been destroyed either by invading armies or simply by the onslaught of time. This means that in many cases we have to rely on classical sources to discover what kinds of buildings the Celts constructed. But these literary accounts by Greek and Roman authors present an external and generally biased view of Celtic society which needs to be balanced by the objective research of modern archeology. Scientific excavation of physical Celtic remains can often tell us more about the Celts than the witness and hearsay of the classical authors. However, because of the lack of Celtic literary sources and the fragmentary nature of the material evidence – there is no Celtic 'Pompeii', for instance – archeological controversies abound.

In his account of the Gallic Wars, Julius Caesar, writing in the first century BC, tells us that the Gaulish Celts lived in *oppida* or small townships. Some of these oppida have been identified with the three thousand or so Iron-Age hill-forts of southern Britain and similar townships throughout continental Europe and Galatia. Remains from these sites show that the settlements probably consisted of few small houses, all located relatively close to one another. These were generally circular or rectangular houses with wooden walls and thatched roofs. Archeological evidence has also allowed archeologists to reconstruct the *oppida* dwellings. Among the most famous reconstructions are those recently built at Butser Hill in Hampshire, England. Opinions vary among archeologists as to the exact function of these hill-forts: it is not known for certain whether they were permanent villages or temporary shelters. Other sources suggest that later Celtic communities lived in stone beehive-shaped huts, although once again archeological evidence is scarce. These relatively primitive houses would have provided

Left: Din Lligwy, Anglesey, Wales (c. fourth century AD). A well-preserved native British settlement from the late Roman period. The old Celtic cultural traditions survived in such remote areas, the circular and rectangular huts contrasting vividly with the contemporary luxurious Roman villas of southern England.

Below: Iron-Age settlement, Chysauster, Cornwall, England (c. first century BC to third century AD). The well-preserved remains of nine 'courtyard houses' at Chysauster reveal a stone-paved passage leading into an open courtyard, off which open several small rooms. Originally with thatched roofs, the houses had drains and terraced gardens.

a vivid contrast to the luxurious villas of the Romans occupying southern England. The influence of the Roman construction methods was soon felt on native settlements, however. There is evidence that by the first century AD Celtic townships in England had relatively sophisticated drainage and water-supply systems, stone paving and terraced gardens. The remains of a Celtic township at Din Lligwy, Anglesey, a small island off the northwest coast of Wales, reveal a small fourth-century AD settlement of two circular and seven rectangular stone dwellings with thatched roofs, all located around a central courtyard and surrounded by a limestone wall. Two of the buildings contained evidence of iron smelting in their hearths.

From a number of Celtic myths, it would seem that the Celts also built large banqueting halls in which to hold their great feasts. For example, in the Saga of CuChulainn from the Ulster Cycle, which was first written down

in the seventh century but which had existed for centuries before that, a magnificent feast is held in a 'beautiful house designed specifically for the occasion.' The narrator of the tale goes on to tell us that opposite the house was a cottage with large glass windows, suggesting that the material was known to the early Celts. However, we must not take this definitive proof: the mention of glass may equally have been an adaptation of the original myth by the seventh-century writer. Another feast mentioned in the saga takes place in a house which has an exterior courtyard, suggesting a large, relatively sophisticated building or perhaps even a complex of buildings. Other myths indicate that Celtic feasting-halls were rectangular, although once again this may have been a later adaptation of the original stories.

Many Celtic myths speak of citadels and forts with strong defensive walls, gatehouses and watch towers. The Celts in Britain certainly built a number of permanent defensive strongholds on sites of particular strategic importance, especially hills. At Maiden Castle in Dorset, southwest England, the Durotriges Celtic tribe built a large hill-top stronghold. The only access to the main entrance of the fort was a remarkable winding path that slowly twists its way up the side of the hill, providing plenty of time and opportunity for the castle's defenders to repulse any attackers. The approach proved little defence, however, when the Romans stormed the site in the first century AD.

One of the finest surviving examples of an Irish Celtic stone fort lies on Inishmore, the biggest of the Aran Islands. Dun Aonghusa is a massive fort that may date back to the fifth century BC. Local tradition has it that the fort was built by the Fir Bholg, one of the

Above: Aerial view of Tintagel, Cornwall, England. The Lower Ward of the thirteenth-century castle is visible on the mainland (centre left). A modern bridge leads to a steep cliff-path which climbs up to the castle's Island Ward. On the summit of the Island are remains of medieval Christian chapel. Archeologists have found evidence of an earlier, wealthy post-Roman stronghold on the Island contemporary with the 'Arthurian' Age (c. AD 450–600). Local medieval legends associated the site with the birth of Arthur, while others saw it as King Mark of Cornwall's castle and the setting for the Tristan and Isolt tales.

earliest tribes to inhabit Ireland. Another large stone fort stands on the summit of Grianán Ailigh, a 245-metre (800-foot) hill in County Donegal. It was once the royal seat of the powerful Northern Uí Néill family. Despite these examples, hill-forts are relatively rare in Ireland in comparison to Britain. The most common settlements in the country have been identified as *raths* (earthen ringforts), *crannógs* (lake dwellings) and the occasional *souterrain* (underground 'earth-houses').

Perhaps the most famous of all the mythical Celtic forts is Tintagel Castle in Cornwall. Since the Middle Ages this site has been referred to as the legendary birthplace of King Arthur, who first appears in written Welsh folktales in the tenth century. Tintagel was its medieval name, meaning 'The Fortress of the Constriction' and taken from the Celtic words *din* (fort) and *tag* (obstruct or construct). Until recently, however, there was no archeological evidence to associate the site with King Arthur, and many archeologists believed that it was once a monastery. But a fire in the 1980s revealed further features and finds which showed it to have been an important community in the late Roman period. More excitingly from the Arthurian point of view, the site appears to have developed into a powerful post-Roman stronghold and centre of trade in the fifth and sixth centuries. However, a separate medieval folk tradition presented Tintagel as the palace of the legendary King Mark of Cornwall. Such is the power of myth and legend to impose itself on landscape.

RELIGIOUS SITES

The Celts also used hill-top sites for religious worship and other ritual activities. The Hill of Tara, for example, rises some 90 metres (300 feet) over the surrounding landscape, and

Left: Door column of the Church of St Mary and St David, Kilpeck, near Hereford, England (twelfth century AD). Late Celtic warriors are interlaced with dragons in the pagan decorations of the church exterior.

commands extensive views across the central plains of Ireland. Early myths describe a large complex of buildings on the site, including the great *Tech Midchuarta*, 'The Hall of Mead-circuit'. This extravagant banqueting hall was the scene of the new king's marriage-feast, the *Feis Temhra*, by which the status of the king was confirmed and his union with his kingdom solemnized.

Most of the Celts' religious sites have long disappeared, and our knowledge of ritual activities is mainly limited to the monumental sanctuaries of the Roman period. However, a few earlier places of worship have been discovered. One of the most famous to have been unearthed is the Gaulish shrine of Roquepertuse in Provence, southern France, which was excavated in the 1920s. Archeologists found a number of religious artefacts in the shrine, which probably dates from the sixth century BC, which together reveal a great deal about Celtic religious practices. Their discoveries included traces of animal paintings, a series of carved birds, statues of two cross-legged figures and a frieze of horses' heads across the lintel of a portico. This latter find suggests that horses were probably associated with the deity honoured at the shrine. Limestone Janus heads were also discovered at the sanctuary. The fact that these heads, which were originally painted, have no modelling on the sides, suggesting that they were not be seen from that angle, means that they were probably designed to be placed over a doorway. Like many Janus figures, they have slightly different facial features: one is frowning rather more than the other.

The grisliest find of all was discovered at the entrance of the shrine. Here stood a portico consisting of three limestone pillars, each furnished with niches in which were nailed human skulls. A similar portico was discovered at the nearby shrine at Entremont. These skulls were probably the remains of defeated enemies. Classical writers record that the Celts would often cut off the heads of their slain enemies and take them home as battle-prizes. However, these severed heads were no mere

Far left: Figurative corbels on exterior of Kilpeck Church, near Hereford, England (twelfth century AD). The pagan fertility deity (top) Sheela-na-gig (Irish for 'Sheelagh of the Breasts') is probably apotropaic, being used to ward off the 'evil eye'. The gaping head (bottom) performs the same function. The large, staring eyes and wedge-shaped noses are traditional in Celtic representation.

Left: Reconstructed portal to a Celtic shrine (Roquepertuse, Bouches-du-Rhône, France; third to second centuries BC). Niches in the columns contained the human skulls of fit young men, probably head-hunted in battle.

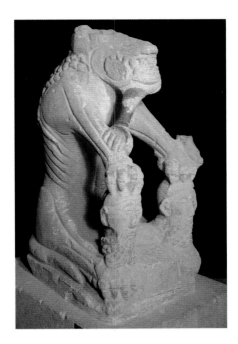

Above: The 'Monster of Noves', Bouches-du-Rhône, France (c. fourth century BC). Monsters devouring human bodies symbolized the triumph of death and the Otherworld over living creatures. A victim's limb protrudes from this Gallic monster's jaws and his claws clasp severed heads, which were often used by the Celts for ritual purposes.

trophies. The Celts also venerated them, believing them to be sacred. The Celts thought that severed heads contained magical properties and that they were a source of beneficial energy. They functioned as a symbol of the divine and the supernatural, warding off evil from the individual and the tribe. They was also associated with healing, fertility, prosperity and

Above: Head from Msecke Zehrovice, Czechoslovakia (limestone; c. third to second centuries BC). This eastern Celtic head was discovered beside a religious shrine and was probably an offering to a god, but whether it represents a deity or a worshipper is uncertain: the torc, symbol of a warrior chieftain, would suggest the latter. The staring eyes and stylized curvilinear features are typical of La Tène art.

43

Above: Foundations of the Hayling Island temple. The stone foundations of the Roman building can be seen around the gullies of the earlier British structure. The radial sliced wedges are archeological trenches which gradually revealed the various layers of the building's past. The central pit was possibly for holding a ritual stone.

youth. The Celts sometimes offered heads of the enemy to warrior-gods, and the shrines at Roquepertuse and Entremont were probably devoted to such worship. Stone carved heads probably had similar ritual significance. Some were hollowed out to hold healing libations. Celtic coins have been found with images of gods wearing severed heads dangling on chains

around their necks. Stone reliefs of severed heads appear at shrines and sanctuaries throughout the Celtic world. These often have no mouths and are shown with their eyes closed, emphasizing the fact that they are dead.

From the time of the Romans onwards, the Celts built more permanent places in which to worship. At Maiden Castle, England, for

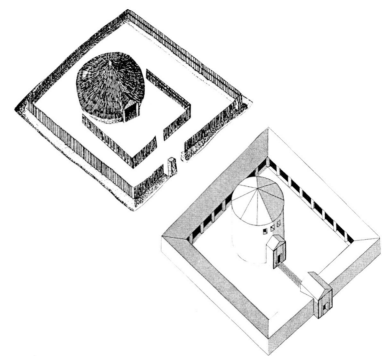

example, the Celts built a circular timber temple in the first century AD, after the Romans had stormed the site. In the fourth century the temple was rebuilt as a stone building.

This temple was probably very similar to that revealed by archeological excavations at Hayling Island in Hampshire, England, in the late 1970s. In 1975–76, excellent weather conditions for the discovery of new archeological remains occurred, when drought caused crops growing over buried walls to receive less water than usual and to become stunted. These variations in height appear as darker areas or 'crop-marks' when seen from above. Aerial photographs of Hayling Island revealed a rectangular walled enclosure of some 40

square metres (48 square yards) surrounding a circular structure. Early this century archeologists had interpreted the site as a Roman villa with a fish-pond at its centre, a most unusual plan which was further called into question by certain features in the aerial photographs. New excavations were undertaken between 1976 and 1981, and as the modern layer of topsoil was gradually removed and various investigatory trenches were dug, further clues as to the history and function of the site were brought to light.

The circular structure was found to have had two quite different building periods. The earliest had post-holes sunk into an inner circular gully with two larger post-holes at the

Far left: Excavating the Hayling Island Celtic temple. The site was stripped in order to recover every available piece of evidence, however small. The polythene sheeting sealed moisture in the unexcavated area, so that soil colour variations were retained: these provided pointers to the subsurface remains.

Above: Reconstruction of the temple and sacred enclosure at Hayling Island. In the first century BC the sanctuary appears to have been a fairly temporary structure of wood and thatch. Later a more substantial stone building was constructed.

Above: Bent spear from the Hayling Island site. The rectangular courtyard contained votive burials of intentionally damaged military equipment, including spearheads, swords, and chariot decorations. These suggest that the cult activity was in honor of a warrior-god. Pig and sheep bones provide evidence of animal sacrifice.

earliest had post-holes sunk into an inner circular gully with two larger post-holes at the entrance, suggesting that the original building was a typical Celtic "roundhouse" dwelling, probably roofed with thatch and a doorway on its eastern side. However, excavations in the surrounding courtyard revealed the true function and approximate date of this early structure. The finds included votive offerings often grouped around burned areas: sheep and pig bones; Celtic coins (dating the first building and subsequent ritual activity to around

50 BC onward); horse equipment and weapons.

All this material evidence suggested that the "roundhouse" was actually a Celtic temple, typically oriented toward the rising sun, in use during the period of early contact. Contemporary literary sources help explain the wider context of the discoveries. Caesar tells us that the Celtic Gauls used to bring piles of booty from the battlefield to their sacred places, where they would dedicate them to a war god and accompany the ritual with animal sacrifice. Among the Hayling Island votive

weapons were spearheads, intentionally bent during rituals to signify the defeated enemy. The sanctuary was in a region of intertribal warfare until the Roman invasion, so there was ample opportunity for such victory dedications.

Far from being destroyed after the Roman invasion in AD 43, this potent architectural symbol of Celtic religion was added to; a second building was put up by the Romans soon after the Claudian invasion. It was a larger and more permanent stone version of the Celtic temple, and apparently even more imposing. The width and depth of the surviving foundations suggest a high tower surrounded, like many Romano-Celtic temples, by a covered portico. Roof tiles and eye-catching red wall-plaster were found that would have covered the temple's exterior, and an entrance porch had been built. There was no evidence to identify a specific deity worshiped there, but a similar site in Gaul included an inscription to the Romano-Celtic war god, Mars Mullo.

It is interesting that there were far fewer votive offerings from the Roman period, suggesting that the site was now intended as a symbol of the dominant Romano-Celtic culture rather than as a place for native British religious ritual. This important evidence from Hayling Island not only confirms Celtic religious architecture and ritual, but also indicates the apparent continuation of Celtic religious activity during Roman domination.

Left: Temple of Vesunna (?), Perigueux, Dordogne, France (late first to third centuries AD). This rare Romano-Celtic temple was originally 24 meters (79 feet) high and had an ambulatory: the holes for its roof beams can be seen 11 meters (36 feet) up. It was oriented eastward and had a large galleried portico.

Above: Green Man: capital door column of the Church of St Mary and St David, Kilpeck, near Hereford, England (twelfth century AD). The pagan fertility god was used to scare away 'the evil eye' in many medieval Christian churches. His staring eyes and the tendrils emerging from his mouth demonstrate the continuing stylistic traditions of Celtic art.

Right: South door of Kilpeck Church (twelfth century AD). A rare example of Late Celtic art in medieval England. Interlacing tendrils, dragons and warriors decorate the columns. The door was restored in the nineteenth century with Celtic revival ironwork.

CELTIC STORYTELLERS

Most of our knowledge of the early pagan Celtic storytellers and poets comes mainly from the recorded observations of their Greek and Roman contemporaries. Diodorus of Sicily, for example, who was writing in the first century BC, tells us that among the Gallic Celts were 'lyric poets called bards, who accompany their songs with instruments similar to lyres: these songs include praise poems and satires'.

Below: Robin Williamson. The Scottish songwriter and storyteller often accompanies his singing with music on the Welsh harp. Williamson creates sung and spoken versions of a number of Celtic myths and legends. He has also written music and lyrics for a play of the Mabinogion *collection of Welsh myths.*

According to Diodorus, the bards played an important social role: they would be hired to write poems praising their patrons, but also to pour scorn on the patron's enemies. They would also relay the myths of legends of aristocratic Celtic society during the feasting, dancing and love-making that normally followed a day of hunting and fighting. Like the early Greek poets, the bard was considered to be a kind of priest, passing religious mysteries on to future generations. This may account for the many 'unexplainable' aspects of the myths. Diodorus recorded that that the bards 'converse with few words and in riddles, mainly using obscure hints to refer to things and saying one word when they mean another; and they tend to use superlatives to boost their own achievements and put down those of others.' The evidence of surviving myths confirms the exclusive nature of the bards: poets often sing songs of praise that only other poets can understand. Unlike their classical counterparts, the Celtic bards did not record their myths and poems in writing but passed them down orally from teacher to pupil.

In the medieval period the bards were highly paid and socially respected, often working in the households of surviving Celtic nobility. There were also wandering minstrels, who usually received small payments for their songs, but who certainly helped to keep the oral tradition alive by carrying poems and

myths across Britain and Europe. It was in this period also that the first written versions of the myths were made, although since the scribes were usually monks, the stories were often heavily Christianized. Finally, there were storytellers, who since time immemorial have told both heroic myths and folk-tales wherever people listen, such as around the domestic hearth or in a corner of the pub. They still exist today in the remoter Celtic areas, and their feats of memory are legendary. A fisherman in Barra, Scotland, is recorded as saying that when he was a boy he listened to the same storyteller every night for fifteen years and that he hardly ever heard a story repeated twice.

THE SURVIVAL OF CELTIC MYTHOLOGY

Celtic myths have been preserved in two main traditions: some have stayed alive in the oral folk traditions of surviving Celtic areas, while others were recorded by Christian writers. Gaulish literature, being purely oral, vanished with the disappearance of the Gaulish language. As a result Gaulish mythology is lost beyond recovery. There is a similar lack of material from other former regions of the Celtic world, although Celtic themes can often be observed in existing European folk-tales.

It is the Irish tradition that has left us the greatest surviving record of Celtic mythology. The writing down of Irish literature had already started by the end of the sixth

Right: King Arthur riding a goat (mosaic from Otranto Cathedral, Italy; twelfth century). The British hero first appeared in the Mabinogion *and is found in medieval art from all over Europe. Here he features in a southern Italian mosaic which incorporates biblical and pagan figures.*

51

*Above: A scribe writing a book
(Anglo-Saxon ivory). Monastic
scribes were the only literate men with the
time and ability to record the oral Celtic
myths in written form.*

century, but only a few fragments of manuscript survive from the period before AD 1100. The earliest substantial survival of Irish mythology is a manuscript called *The Book of the Dun Cow*. Its Christian writer was a certain Maelmuri, whom historians know was murdered by Viking raiders in his cathedral at Clonmacnois in 1106. The curious title derives from a lost earlier manuscript of the seventh century AD which had been written by St. Ciaran on the hide of his pet cow.

There is evidence to suggest that the Celts in Britain also inherited a rich mythological tradition, although it is poorly documented in comparison to Irish literature. British mythology is now best known from the *Mabinogion*, which was the title given by Lady Charlotte Guest to her 1849 English translation of a collection of eleven Welsh tales preserved in earlier manuscripts: these are the *White Book of Rhydderch* of around 1300–25 and the *Red Book of Hergest* of around 1375–1425. *Mabinogi* means, broadly speaking, 'a tale of childhood': this was a mythical account of the conception, birth and early training of a Celtic hero. Lady Guest's word *Mabinogion* (which she incorrectly thought was the plural form of *Mabinogi*) therefore implied that all eleven tales were of this genre. In fact only the first four tales, or 'branches', are from an original *Mabinogi*. They abound in mythological themes, motifs and the gods of ancient Britain.

THE NATURE OF CELTIC MYTHOLOGY

Just as the Celts were not a single, united race, but rather various tribes that shared common characteristics, so too their mythology is not a close unity. In fact it is as diverse and varied as the tribes themselves. That said, it is nonetheless true that the Celtic

learned classes had a highly developed sense of affinity, based on a common cultural inheritance. Even though Celtic myths had endless narrative variants, and characters of varying names and physical features, the basic themes were largely constant and common throughout the Celtic world.

The Irish Celts themselves classified their myths by theme: plunderings, battles, voyages, adventures, elopements, etc. But they can also be divided into three broad categories: miscellaneous tales associated with the reigns of various kings, the cycle of the Ulaidh, or 'Ulstermen', and finally the cycle of Fionn mac Cumhaill and the roving bands of warriors known as *fiana*. As well as this collection of varied tales, the Irish Celts created a number of pseudo-historical works.

Above: The Atlantic coast and the Ring of Kerry mountains, Ireland. Mild winters encourage continual vegetation and pasturage throughout the year here; Mediterranean trees grow in some parts. Kerry was on the prehistoric migration and trade routes and has many surviving remains of its ancient past. It is easy to see how such landscapes could be mythologized into paradises.

Among these is the *Leabhar Gabhála Éireann*, 'The Book of the Conquest of Ireland', commonly known as *The Book of Invasions*, which is said to describe the several invasions of Ireland from before the time of the Great Deluge.

Recurrent themes in Celtic mythology tell us a great deal about their civilization. Like all Celtic mythology, ancient Irish literature records the exploits of its warrior heroes. Tribal warfare and individual strength and bravery are its preoccupations. The Celtic bards were teachers as well as entertainers, and the behaviour of their mythical and legendary characters provided living Celts with ideals, thus ensuring the continuity of the warrior society. These stories served as an education for young Celtic noblemen, the vivid heroic characters providing them with models of youthful warrior behaviour.

A love of beauty and bodily display is evident throughout the myths: when warriors go into battle, for example, their brightly coloured clothing, glowing jewellery and bristling hair are visual symbols of their heroic status. And heroines signify their own high and leisured status by wearing their hair in time-consuming intricate plaits, and by setting off their white unweathered skin with rich jewellery.

The world of nature was an unexplained and alien place to the Celts: therefore magical happenings tend to occur outside the stronghold; talking animals and birds feature in many of the stories; and Celtic divinities often represent the forces of nature. It is most likely that some of these stories were originally mythical explanations of religious mysteries or quests. So visits to the Otherworld, for example, might reflect an original rite of passage in which Celts passed from childhood to adulthood by

Above: Distant view of Tintagel, Cornwall, England. The legendary birthplace of King Arthur was also believed in local folklore to have been the fortress of King Mark. The place's medieval name, meaning 'The Fortress of the Constriction' and taken from the Celtic words din (fort) and tag (obstruct or construct), is an apt description for the dramatic manner in which the Island meets the mainland.

means of a ritual period of absence outside the community. The druidic philosophy encouraged a belief in immortality and the myths celebrate this idea: love persists beyond the grave in the form of intertwining trees on burial mounds; heads of dead heroes retain supernatural powers. Such beliefs were a great consolation to the warrior society, where the hero's greatest glory was to die in battle.

Neither the myths nor the classical writers discussed the lower classes of Celtic society. Similarly, they had little to say about Celtic women, except that they were 'shared between groups of ten or twelve men'. To the Romans and ourselves this would have appeared barbaric, but it may well imply a matriarchal system in which women had the social privilege of a number of lovers. Certainly high-ranking Celtic women enjoyed a degree of power unknown to their classical counterparts: witness the warrior queen Boudicca, also known as Boadicea, who led her Iceni tribe in a first-century AD rebellion against the Roman invaders. Although we must bear in mind that the Celtic myths were probably always told from a male viewpoint, the human female characters in Celtic mythology are rarely the downtrodden or faceless figures of Greek myths, which might also suggest that, unlike in classical Athens, women formed part of the bard's audience.

THE ART OF DESCRIPTION IN CELTIC MYTH

As is evident from the following extracts, Celtic storytellers were experts in the vivid description of imaginary worlds, fantastic animals and superhuman characters. Bright colours and meticulous details of landscape, human appearance and dress are the main characteristics of Celtic descriptive passages, mirroring a similar manifestation of rich colour and detail found in the Celtic visual arts. Descriptions of women tend to be highly voyeuristic and unrealistic, reflecting the male gender of the storyteller, and for the same reason, storytellers glamourized the warrior aspects of their male characters.

FANTASY LANDSCAPE:
THE DISCOVERY OF PARADISE ON EARTH

'The storm was over and the wind blew gently now; the sea-warriors hoisted their sail and the boat took in less water. A stillness fell upon the wide ocean, the waves were smoothed and it was bright and calm. Birds of different kinds never seen before filled the air round about with their singing. A land of graceful shape and fair shores came into view ahead of them; the sailors rejoiced at the sight of it. They sailed closer and entered a beautiful estuary, its green breasts hanging above silver-pebbled beaches, and in the clear waters the splendid deep purple of the handsome salmon flashed; and they looked about them and were pleased by the lovely streams running through woods tinged with purple.

'Tadhg the Irish Prince of Munster stood at the bow and addressed his men: "This is surely the island of our dreams, my fighting men; it is blessed with fruit and all things most lovely; we shall make for the beach, haul up the boat and give it time enough to dry out after its storm-battering." Twenty stout warriors went on ahead with Tadhg, leaving twenty behind to guard the boat; and the wonder of it was that though they had come through wind and hard rain and the extremes of cold and hunger, they felt no desire for food and the camp fire in that place. It was enough and more than enough to breathe in the incense of the trees, glowing with purple flowers about them.

'Tadhg led them into the wood beside their path and they soon came to an orchard of

Above: Restaurant signboard, Alderley Edge, Cheshire, England. Local legend tells of a farmer who is travelling to the market to sell a white mare. He is waylaid on the Edge by a strangely dressed man who offers to buy the mare. The farmer refuses, expecting a better price in the market. To his surprise, no one buys the horse, but on the way home the wizard reappears and the farmer accepts his offer. The wizard takes him into the hill and shows him the sleeping knights, one of whom was lacking a horse. The farmer receives magic jewels as payment.

Above: 'The Four Queens find Lancelot Sleeping' (Frank Cadogan Cowper, oil on canvas; 1954). Cowper (1877–1958) was one of the last British painters to be influenced by the Pre-Raphaelites. Even in this late work their influence can be seen in the choice of medieval subject and late Romantic style. The scene is from Malory's La Morte d'Arthur: *four British queens find the Arthurian hero asleep beneath an apple tree. The sorceress Morgan le Fay attempts to make him take one as a lover, but he remains faithful to Guinevere.*

glorious purple-fringed apple trees and oaks with leaves of lovely hue and hazels teeming with nuts of bright yellow. "What a wonderful thing occurs to me", said Tadhg to his warriors. "It is winter back home, yet summer reigns here."

'There was indeed no end to the lovely places they discovered in that land. Leaving the orchard, they came upon a wood without shadows, with round purple berries the size of men's heads giving off wonderful scents; and the birds that fed on the berries made the men blink and look again, for they were white birds with purple heads and golden beaks. They sang the songs of minstrels as they ate their fill of berries, and their music was plaintive and yet so soothing, that it would have lulled wounded warriors to sleep ….'

Anonymous Irish author of the fourteenth or fifteenth century

FANTASY WOMAN:
A VISION OF ETAIN THE FAIRY

'The men could see a woman besides the spring. In her hand glinted a comb of silver with decorative work in gold and she was about to wash her hair in a bowl of beaten silver with reddish-purple gems glittering on its rim and on its sides four inlaid golden birds could be seen as she turned the bowl. The woman wore the fleece of a fine shaggy sheep dyed purple, and on the shoulders of this cloak were silver brooches worked in twisted filigree with golden ornament. Beneath the cloak she wore, stiff yet smooth, a tunic of green silk with a long hood, embroidered with reddish-gold thread; they could see the interlacing of exotic animals worked into the tunic in gold and silver running over her breasts, shoulders and shoulder blades. The gold gleamed in the sunlight against its green silken background.

'Her golden-blond hair was arranged in two long tresses; each tress was made up of four plaits, and at the end of each plait hung a bead. To some men her hair was the colour of the yellow flag iris which grows by summer water; others thought it like ruddy polished gold.

'She began to untie her hair for washing, her arms reaching out from the openings in her dress. The arms were straight yet soft, their tops as white as a fall of night snow before the sun rises; the skin of her face was clear and her cheeks blushed red like the foxglove on the moor. Like the black beetle's wings were her eyebrows; like a spray of pearls were her teeth; like the brilliant blue starry flowers of borage were her eyes; of bright red vermilion were her lips. Her soft, smooth shoulders stood high and white; of the purest white were her fingers, long and slender as were arms; and long, slender and soft as pliable wool were her white sides, like the foam on the wavecrest. Smooth, shiny and sleek were her warm white thighs; her small, firm knees were white and rounded; white shins she had, short and straight. She stood straight and even on her heels, which looked lovely from behind; if a straight rule were placed along her feet, no fault would be found, unless the skin or flesh were made to bulge by pressing too hard.

'The bright blush of the rising moon glimmered in her noble face; her smooth forehead was high and dignified; the beams of eroticism shone from her royal eyes; her cheeks bore the dimples of her sport which flushed now with a purple as red as the blood of the frisky calf and now the white brilliance of snow. Her voice was noble and gentle; she walked as befits a queen, stepping steadily and stately. She was the most perfect woman in the world to behold, as fair and lovely as

Left: 'The Failure of Sir Gawaine' (Edward Burne-Jones, wool and silk woven on cotton warp; 1895–6). Burne-Jones (1833–1898) was also influenced by the medievalism of the Pre-Raphaelites, of which he was a late member. In the last decade of his life his interest in Malory was revived and he created a series of tapestry designs for his industrialist patrons on the Grail theme. Here Sir Gawaine and Sir Uwain are refused entrance to the Chapel of the Holy Grail because of their sinful natures. The treatment of space and natural detail is intentionally medieval.

they could ever hope to see; the men agreed that she must have been a fairy ….'

Anonymous Irish author of the ninth century

FANTASY MEN: SOME HEROES FROM THE COURT OF KING ARTHUR

'Morfran son of Tegid, was so ugly that he was thought to be an evil demon; therefore he was avoided in Arthur's last battle at Camlan. He was as hairy as a stag. Sandde Angel-Face was also left unharmed at that battle, but for a different reason: he was so beautiful that he was thought to be a heavenly angel.

'There were three men, all sons of Erim, best known for their magical speed. Henbeddestr could run faster than any other man, even when they were on horseback; Henwas the Winged could run faster over even the shortest distance than any man or four-footed beast; and Scilti the Nimble-Footed was often sent as a messenger by Arthur, for he would not bother with roads, but take the shortest route, touching the tree-tops and skipping the bog-rushes on the mountain slopes. Scilti was so light of foot that he never once bent or broke the rushes that he stepped on.

'Teithi the Elder, son of Gwynham, who barely escaped when his lands were covered by the sea, had come to Arthur's court. Some magic curse was on his knife, so that no haft could be found to fit it; and therefore he lived a life of disease and misery, and died of it.

'Drem the son of Dremidydd had eyes that could see the gnat in the rising sun's light as far away as Penn Blathon in Scotland from Cellig Wig in Cornwall.

'Cynyr of the Beautiful Beard – some say that Cei was his son – once said to his wife, "If there is anything of me in your son, my girl, he will be touched by a magic which removes the warmth from his heart and makes him headstrong. He will have other magical abilities: no one, from in front or behind him, will ever be able to see what he is carrying, however large or small it is; he, more than anyone, will be able to face fire and water; he will be the most loyal page and court official."

'Then there was Gwallgoig, who used to keep whole towns awake with his bodily requirements when he was staying overnight: no one could sleep.

'Osla of the Great Knife, who carried a short broad weapon at his side, used to be a boon to Arthur whenever he came to a torrent with his army. Osla's knight in its sheath would be placed across the narrowest point above the raging steam so that a bridge was formed broad enough to take the army of the three lands of Britain and its three offshore islands (England, Wales and Scotland, Anglesey, the Isle of Man and the Isle of Wight).

'Gilla Stag-Legs was the champion of Ireland at long-jump: three hundred acres were his in one bound.

'There were three more great heroes: Sol, who could stand on one foot for a day; Gwaddn Osol, who could level a mountain by standing upon it; and Gwaddn of the Bonfire, a boon to Arthur when the armies encountered woody obstacles: the sparks from his metal-studded soles were as large as pieces of red-hot iron drawn out of the forge.

'There were the two great eaters, Hir Erwm and Hir Atrwm. On feasting days they would get their supplies by raiding three hundred towns. Then they would eat till noon and drink into the night; they would not stop eating in bed but would bite off the heads of the rats. When invited to another man's feast they would polish off the meat, be it lean or fat, hot or cold, sweet or sour, fresh or salted. Another eater was Huarwar, son of Halwn,

Above: Tintagel Castle, Cornwall, England. Remains of the thirteenth-century castle can be seen overlooking the high cliffs (centre right). The modern bridge from the mainland to the Island is also visible (bottom right).

who only smiled when he was full. One of the Three Great Plagues of the West Country was caused by his demands to be given his fill from Arthur as a present.

'There were a number of curious heroes. Sugn, son of Sugnedudd, had the ability to suck up the sea from beneath as many as three hundred ships, leaving only the dry sea-bed; he used to get red-hot heartburn. Cachamwri, one of Arthur's serving men, could work his way through a barn containing the crops of thirty ploughed fields: he would thresh around with his iron flail until the wooden posts, rafters and cross-beams were lying in as many bits on the floor as there were oats. When Gwefl, son of Gwastad, had the sulks, his lower lip would hang down to his navel and he would pull the upper lip over his head for a cap. The beard of Uchdryd Cross-Beard was so long that he had to throw its bristly red strands across the fifty rafters of Arthur's hall when he came to visit him.

'Others had wonderful senses. You could have buried Clust, son of Clustfeinad, seven fathoms underground, but he would still have heard an ant getting up in the morning fifty miles away. Medr, son of Medredydd, could stand at Celli Wig in Cornwall and shoot through the legs of a wren standing at Esgeir Oerfel in Ireland. Gwiawn, 'Eye of the Cat', could cut the lid from a gnat's eye without damaging the eye.

'Cei, whom I have already mentioned, was able to hold his breath underwater for nine days and nine nights; his sword-cut could be cured by no doctor; he could extend his height to look out over trees; his body-heat was such that, when it was pouring with rain,

Below: Sunset beach at Harlech, Wales. In the distance are the hills of Lleyn Peninsula, some of which bear evidence of Celtic occupation. This area is rich in ancient remains: it was protected by the mountains of Snowdonia from over-exposure to the Romans and later invaders, yet it invited contact with prehistoric Mediterranean and Irish cultures. A perfect setting for the tale of Branwen in the Mabinogion, *with its Welsh and Irish topography.*

Above: Madron Well, Cornwall, England. Sources of water were revered by the Celts for their religious powers, and many of these sacred springs and wells continued to be visited for spiritual healing in the Christian era, often dedicated to saints. Madron was also a site of a baptistry. Sick people still drink these waters and hang votive rags on the surrounding trees.

whatever he was holding would stay dry; and when his companions were freezing he was the kindling to light their fire.'

Anonymous Welsh author of
the tenth century

FOLKTALES AND SONGS FROM AROUND THE CELTIC WORLD

Although, with the advent of television in even the remotest areas of the Celtic world, the oral folk tradition is dying out, many Celtic folktales and poems still survive today thanks to the traditional storytellers and singers all over the former Celtic areas. The 'high' bardic tradition has survived in the annual Welsh Eisteddfod meetings, but there is also an attempt to revive it in less formal surroundings. The Scottish singer and harpist Robin Williamson, for example, performs and records the Celtic hero-tales in spoken and sung poetry to the accompaniment of his 'Celtic' harp, and the Breton artist Alan Stivell similarly recreates the Celtic myths of Brittany. The pioneer in the English folk-song and tale revival is the singer and guitarist Martin Carthy, who has recorded a number of traditional British and Breton songs. While some of these folk-tales and poems are simply good stories told by and for the rural community, there are also many which preserve the 'high' myth and legends of the ancient Celtic ruling class. The Celtic storytelling tradition is therefore still very much alive for those who wish to experience it.

CORNWALL

Cornwall was a stronghold of Romano-Celtic culture until the Saxon invasions and not surprisingly it is the birthplace of many Arthurian legends, including that of Tristan and Isolt. Until recently, the River Tamar was regarded by the Cornish people as a cultural boundary between the Cornish and English. The Cornish language was related to Breton, but was extinct by the nineteenth century. However, Cornish folk-singers such as Brenda Wooton have kept the poetic language alive, and recently there have been attempts at revival. This poem appeared in the Cornish language in the seventeenth century. It originates in an earlier English folk song. Strawberry water was once a favourite skin toner. The bold replies of the girl are characteristic of the Celtic mythological tradition of feminine pride.

'Where lies your path, lovely girl,' he said,
  'with your flaxen locks, and your face
so pale?'
  'I go to the spring, kind sir,' said she,
'with strawberry leaves,
  I'll never fail.'

May I come too, lovely girl,' he said,
  'with your flaxen locks, and your face
so pale?'
  'If that is your wish, kind sir,' said she,
'with strawberry leaves,
  I'll never fail.'

'And what if I lay you on the grass,
  with your flaxen locks, and your face
so pale?'
  'I'll rise up again, kind sir,' said she,
'with strawberry leaves,
  I'll never fail.'

'And what if you find yourself with child,
  with your flaxen locks, and your face
so pale?'
  'I'll carry that child, kind sir,' said she,
'with strawberry leaves,

I'll never fail.'

'What man will be there to hold the child,
  with your flaxen locks, and your face
so pale?'

  'You'll be the father, kind sir,' said she,
'with strawberry leaves,
  I'll never fail.'

'With what will you clothe this child
  of yours, with your flaxen locks,
and your face so pale?'

  'From the father's thread, kind sir,'
said she, 'with strawberry leaves,
  I'll never fail.'

SCOTLAND

The original Celtic inhabitants of Scotland north of the rivers Forth and Clyde were known by the fourth century AD as Picti ('Painted Ones'). The Picts were probably given this nickname by the Roman soldiers guarding Hadrian's Wall to describe their tattooed bodies. Archeologists have found tattoos on preserved Celtic flesh and ancient writers tell us that they painted their bodies. The Scotti ('Irishmen') came to Argyll from the kingdom of Dalriada in Antrim, Ireland, bringing their Irish Gaelic language to Scotland. In the ninth century the Scots took over the Pictish areas and it is their Gaelic language which still survives in parts of the Highlands and Hebrides. The land of Scotland features in many of the ancient Irish myths and legends and the Scottish folk-tales and local legends which have survived are mainly from the later Gaelic tradition. The following folk-tale looks back to the ancient period.

'Some say that the Picts knew the recipe for the brewing of heather-ale. The secret was passed down from father to son for many centuries, but was finally lost when the Scots invaded the Pictish kingdom in the ninth century. The story goes as follows. The Scots loved the heather-ale, which they imported from the Picts, and they longed to have the secret recipe. The family who guarded the recipe lived in the Mull of Galloway in the far west of the Pictish kingdom. One day father and son were captured in battle and the Scots had them brought out onto the open moor high up above the sea where the purple heather used for the famous brew was growing all around them. The Scots demanded the recipe, threatening and torturing the old man and his young son until they were on the point of death.

The sea-gulls were mewing as dusk began to fall. "I shall tell you what you want to know," spoke the old man, "but only on the condition that you first kill my son, so that he does not have the pain of witnessing his father bring dishonour and shame to our people." The weary Scots raised a cry of victory and the boy was put to the sword. "Now, old man," they said, "tell us the recipe."

"Ha!" said the father, "do you really think

Below: Alderley Edge, Cheshire, England. Arthurian myths and legend are present in most areas of Celtic Britain. At Alderley Edge, local legend and folklore tells of a king and his warriors who sleep in a cave beneath the hill: one day they will be awakened to defend us against invaders. Such legends occur elsewhere in Britain and Europe and are often associated with Arthur. The summit of Alderley Edge commands a sweeping view of the Cheshire Plain, where the peat-preserved body of a murdered or sacrificed Celt was discovered in Lindow Moss.

Above: Christy Moore. The Irish singer/songwriter continues the tradition of the Celtic bards by heroizing the modern freedom-fighters of Ireland and Central America. He has sung with the Irish group Planxty as well as with Moving Hearts, one of the earliest bands to combine folk, rock and jazz styles. Here he is playing the Irish bodhran, a hand-held drum.

I would tell a Scot the secret of heather-ale? My son was about to divulge the recipe, for he still had many years to live and would not readily give up this beautiful world of sea-birds, high cliffs and the sounds of the foaming sea. Therefore he had to die; and the secret of heather-ale dies with him, for you will never have it from me!"

The Scottish chieftain was furious. "Take him," he cried, "and hurl him from the highest cliff. Let him be smashed to pieces on the sharp rocks below, and may the sea mourn him forever more with her salty tears."

Thus the old man died, and now shares the secret of heather-ale with the sea.'

THE ISLE OF MAN

The island's position in the Irish Sea between Ireland and Scotland has ensured it a place in Celtic mythology and tradition. It may have been considered one of the Isles of the Blessed, ruled over by the Irish god of the sea, Manannán mac Lir. The Manx language, closely related to Scottish Gaelic, was thought to be extinct by the 1950s, but there have been recent attempts at revival. An oral tradition of law, which might reflect the original druidic practice, had precedence, over written laws. Post-Celtic man was governed by Vikings until Scottish rule began in the thirteenth century. The following Manx folk-song has Christian references, but its themes of love vows, curses and powerful natural elements are those of Celtic mythology.

'I first met my truelove at the Christmas ceilidh; we sat while the fiddler played and began our courting. For seven whole years we met and made love, and her unfaithful tongue swore that she would never leave me. On the Sunday before Ash Wednesday I visited my truelove; she placed her hands over mine and swore that she would marry only me. I came home in ecstasy, everything was roses; on the Wednesday I heard she had married another. I cursed her for courting me for so long a time; when she found she had no love for me she should have said so. But I cannot speak wickedly of her or call for bad luck; may she make her new friends glad, though love has made a fool of me. No one knew about our love save the old walnut tree; it cannot speak for me though it knows my lover false. On St. Patrick's Day I shall visit the fair in my young man's clothes, I'll walk right by her, pretending not to notice. At the fair I'll take my pick from all the best girls; but she has no second chance with her deceitful new husband. I walked the long winding road and grew weary of the slopes, but whenever I rested I thought of my love. I wish that the wind would bring me news of my love; I wish she would cross the steep highlands to greet me by the shore. How happily I would run to the shore if she were there; how happily my hand would make a pillow for her hair. I wish that the sea would run dry and let me have my way; but the white snows of Greenland will sooner run red of roses before I forget my truelove.

IRELAND

For historical reasons the Celtic tradition has survived better in Ireland than in any of the other Celtic areas. Modern Irish Gaelic is a close descendant of the ancient Celtic language; it is still spoken in the southwest and was recognized as an official language by the Republic of Ireland in 1921. Many Celtic myths and legends have come down to us in Irish, and the Irish folk-tale tradition is equally strong. The following traditional ballad was first sung at the time of the mass emigrations to America by young Irish men and women seeking work after the Great Famine of the 1840s. This relatively modern song is addressed to the legendary heroes of Ireland, a typical use of myth to conjure up a distant Golden Age. The emigrations themselves have now become legendary and the mythical power of the song remains relevant in a country still affected by emigration; it was recently recorded in 1983 by the Irish band Planxty.

You brave Irish heroes
   wherever you be,
I pray stand a moment and
   listen to me,
Your sons and fair daughters
   are now going away,
And thousands are sailing to
   Americay.

So good luck to those people
   and safe may they land,
They are leaving their
   country for a far distant strand,
They are leaving old Ireland,
   no longer can stay,
and thousands are sailing to
   Americay.

The night before leaving they
   are bidding goodbye,
And it's early next morning
   their heart gives a sigh,
They do kiss their mothers
   and then they will say
'Farewell, dear old father,
   we must now go away.'
Their friends and relations
   and neighbours also,
When the trunks are all
   packed up, all ready to go,

O the tears from their eyes
   they fall down like the rain,
And the horses are prancing
   going off for the train.

So good luck to those people
   and safe may they land,

Above: Fight of the Red and White Dragons (The St. Alban's Chronicle, Lambeth Palace Library, London, England; fifteenth century AD*). The manuscript illustration depicts a red dragon (representing Celtic Britain) defeating the white one (the invading Saxons).*

They are leaving their country
   for a far distant strand,
They are leaving old Ireland,
   no longer can stay,
And thousands are sailing to
   Americay.
When they reach the station,
   you will hear their last cry,
With handkerchiefs waving,
   and bidding goodbye,
Their hearts will be breaking
   on leaving the shore
'Farewell, dear old Ireland,
   will we ne'er see you more?'
O pity the mother that rears
   up the child,
And likewise the father
   who labours and toils,
To try to support them he
   will work night and day,
And when they are older
   they will go away.

So good luck to those people
   and safe may they land,
They are leaving their country
   for a far distant strand,
They are leaving old Ireland,
   no longer can stay,
And thousands are sailing to
   Americay.

BRITTANY

In the fifth century several noble Welsh families fled the Saxon invasion of their country and landed in France. The area later became known as 'Little Britain' or Brittany. The Bretons brought their Celtic language and mythology with them, but many of their stories have been lost owing to the French government's past ban on speaking Breton. Only folk-tales and songs have survived in the Breton tongue: the Breton singer and harpist Alan Stivell has led the recent revival. The following traditional ballad contains a reference to the Virgin Mary, but the common ancient Celtic theme of the sea as a setting for miraculous tales involving women is present in the song. It was collected from the singing of Janet ar Gall of Kerarborn in 1849.

It was the first of November when the English reached Dourduff. They beached at Dourduff and snatched a young girl.

They snatched a lovely maiden and took her to their ship.

Her name was Marivonnik and she came from Plougasnou. As they carried her away, she cried at her father's door:

'Fare thee well dear mother and father, for I'll never see you more. Fare thee well dear brother and sister, for we'll never meet on earth. Fare thee well kinsmen and friends, for I'll never see your world again.'

And young Marivonnik wept, with no one there to comfort her. No one was there to comfort her save the big Englishman, he comforted her. 'Do not cry, my Marivonnik, your life is not at risk; Your life is not at risk, but I cannot save your honour.'

'Sir Englishman, my honour means more to me than all your ships at sea; Tell me then, shall I lose my honour to more than you alone?'

'To me and to my cabin boy, and to the sailors if they want you. To my sailors if they want you, every one hundred and one.'

'Tell me then, Sir Englishman, may I walk with you on the bridge?'

'You may walk up on the bridge, but take care not to drown.'

Young Marivonnik cried, whilst walking on the deck: 'Help me Mary Virgin, shall I end it all by drowning?

'It is for you, dear Virgin Mary, so as not to offend you.

'If I shall fall into the sea, then drowned I shall be; if I stay I shall be killed.'

Young Marivonnik was guided by the Virgin and dived into the sea.

She was brought back to the surface by a small fish.

The big Englishman then called to his sailormen: 'Sailors, sailors, rescue her and five hundred crowns are yours!'

And later that day he told young Marivonnik: 'You should not have done this, Marivonnik, for you were to be my wife.'

Above: Martin Carthy. The English solo singer and guitarist also performs with the Watersons, Dave Swarbrick and John Kirkpatrick, all of them pioneers in the revival of English folk songs and dance.

THE STUBBORN
SCOTSMAN

THE STUBBORN
SCOTSMAN

DON RITCHIE

WORLD RECORD HOLDING
ULTRA DISTANCE RUNNER

First published 2016 by DB Publishing, an imprint of JMD Media Ltd,
Nottingham, United Kingdom.

ISBN 978-1-78091-546-3

Printed and bound in Great Britain by Marston Book Services Ltd, Oxfordshire

PREFACE

Don Ritchie is justifiably regarded by many as one of the greatest ultra runners of modern times. With track World Best Performances at 50km (twice), 40 miles, 50 miles (twice), 100km, 150km, 100 miles and 200km, plus world road bests at 100km and 100 miles he has an unparalleled record in the sub 24-hour events. Added to this is his excellent competitive record both at home and abroad. He has numerous Continental 100kms wins to his credit, (including setting a world road best), and a 100 mile road best in the USA. In 1990 he won the IAU International 24-hour Championship and in 1991 he produced the best 24 Hour performance of the year, some fourteen years after setting his first world track best.

It is rare for a top class runner to have a long career. The sustained stress of pushing one's body to the limit usually results eventually in career-ending injury. Don Ritchie did have significant injuries, but he came back from these to add further laurels to his already distinguished list of achievements.

Don's longevity as a runner allied to his ability to push himself to the limit; to sustain a pace, only very slowly giving way to inexorable fatigue, makes him virtually unique amongst ultrarunners. His autobiography will be an invaluable resource both for those who would seek to emulate his achievements and for those who wish to document the remarkable sport he has served so well.

Andy Milroy, (statistician of the RRC and IAU.)

ACKNOWLEDGEMENTS

I am very grateful to my Mum and Dad for their love, guidance and encouragement during my formative years and their continuing support thereafter. Early in my running career I was very fortunate to meet Peter Duffy, who 'took me under his wing' and became a good friend and early mentor. Alastair Wood inspired me to try marathon running and encouraged me to join Sunday training runs from his home and took over mentoring when Peter moved on. Early in my development, regular training runs for several years with Steve Taylor and Mel Edwards were always challenging, but beneficial.

My wife Isobel has given me love, support and encouragement in training and racing over three decades, which is very much appreciated. My thanks are also due to Isobel for undertaking tedious but necessary scrutinising of my text.

The late (Magic) Malcolm Morgan kept me training and racing by providing diagnosis and appropriate and very prompt physiotherapy treatment. He was a marvellous practitioner and I had absolute faith in him. He took a week's leave to accompany me on my first LEJOG attempt. I was extremely grateful to Malcolm for his friendship and expertise.

My thanks are also due to, initially Moray district education department and later the management of Moray College, for granting me leave of absence to participate in international races and other important events.

In my attempts to run LEJOG and JOGLE I was delighted to have help in planning and implementation from: Graham Milne, Peter Chalmers, Malcolm Morgan, Mike Francis, Donald Gunn, John Diffey and Glen Elliot. I am very grateful to the Rotary Clubs, who provided accommodation along the route of my LEJOG and the following sponsors: 'The Macallan', Arthur Duthie organisation, Evan Young, McRae & Dick, 'Baxter's' and 'Fine Fare' (now Asda). 'The Macallan' provided excellent sponsorship for my JOGLE.

My thanks also go to the trustees of the 'Ritchie Foundation': Noel McPartlin, John Diffey, Glen Elliot, Graham Milne, Peter Chalmers and Mike Francis, for their help with charity fund raising and establishing the Speyside Way 50Km race.

I was thankful to receive running shoes and apparel from the following: Karhu, Nike, Reebok and Asics. Thanks are also due to 'United Distillers' and later 'Neways' and the Scottish Co-op for their sponsorship of the 'Ritchie Foundation Speyside Way 50Km race'.

Finally, many thanks to my long-time running pal, Colin Youngson, for editing the text and making appropriate helpful suggestions.

CONTENTS

EARLY DAYS

I was born on the sixth of July 1944 and at this time my parents were living in a tenement flat at 4 Copland Road Govan, Glasgow, which was close to Clydeside and subject to enemy bombing, since it had already suffered a 'Blitz'. Because of this danger, expectant mothers from this area were taken to safer regions to give birth and my mum was taken to the emergency hospital located in Haddo House in Aberdeenshire and this is where I first saw the light of day. One side of the Haddo estate borders the river Ythan and is close to the village of Methlick, so my birth is recorded in the parish of Methlick.

My full name is Donald Alexander Ferguson Ritchie. The Alexander and Ritchie are from my Father (Alec); and Ferguson is from my mother (Rachel or Rae), who was a Ferguson. I was called Donald after mum's older brother Donald Ferguson, who was 'lost' (missing, presumed dead) during the war. He was a flight engineer in the R.A.F. in Wellington Bombers.

After the war Dad wanted to return to the country and farming, so we moved to Inverlochy Farm and this is the first home I remember. It was a cottage near the West Highland Railway Bridge over the river Lochy and opposite the decaying Inverlochy Castle. Our cottage had an upstairs but no electricity, bathroom or toilet, the latter being a pail in a narrow wooden pillar-box like structure. I cannot remember if we had running water or had to carry the water in, but we seemed to be OK. There was a rain barrel at one end of the cottage to collect rainwater from the roof and I managed to fall headfirst into it when trying to retrieve a toy I had accidentally dropped in. Thankfully, I managed to extricate myself and avoid drowning.

Mum's parents had a railway house; the 'Red House', which was alongside the west Highland Railway line just before Inverlochy village and only about six hundred yards from our cottage, so Mum and I used to visit regularly. The house got its name because it was constructed from red bricks and unusual for the region.

On the 20th of June 1948 my sister Anne was born in the hospital at Inverness and both Mum and baby were well. When they returned home our minister came to visit to offer his congratulations and just before leaving asked me teasingly, where he could get such a beautiful baby, to which I am told that I said, 'If you get sick and go to hospital you can get one too'.

A short time after Anne's birth we moved from the cottage into a modern house, with electricity, a bathroom and toilet, at the farm and we occupied the upstairs part. I had another potentially fatal accident there when trying to climb to the top of an oak wardrobe. It toppled from the base unit containing drawers and luckily it was prevented from crushing me when it hit Anne's cot, which arrested its fall. Fortunately, Anne was not in the cot at the time. We had a lodger, a German, who was a prisoner of war and who had been working on the farm during the war and had decided to delay his return to Germany.

Our next home was in the east of Scotland at a farm on Fetternear Estate close to the River Don and two miles from Kemnay in Aberdeenshire. There were many wooded

Mum, Dad and me aged about two.

Anne and me in 1951.

areas and hundreds of rabbits around, so with the help of a dog, which befriended me, many rabbits were caught, at least four on each outing, which Mum made into tasty dinners.

I began my primary School education at Kemnay and at the end of the first day set off home in the wrong direction with my shoes on the wrong feet. Mum, who had come to collect me, intercepted me, before I had gone too far astray. Our only form of transport then was walking or taking the bus for longer journeys, so occasionally on my Dad's monthly weekend off we would walk to Kemnay and catch a bus to Aberdeen, for extra shopping. On one occasion, for some reason, we missed the last bus to Kemnay and had to take the Inverness bus and get off at the junction of the road for Kemnay and walk home from there, which must have been at least six miles. It must have been after 10pm when we started, with Mum and Dad taking turns to carry Anne, so it was quite a challenge for us and seemed to take a very long time to reach home.

Every afternoon after School, one of the farm workers would ask; '*Weel did yi get the Tag (strap) the day?*' and always I had said no, but on one occasion I had to answer yes because, of bad behaviour, I had received the strap or belt, which seemed to amuse him.

After a couple of years at Fetternear, Dad accepted a position as a dairy cattleman at a farm called Little Ythsie and we moved, or 'flitted' there. The normal method of moving families of farm workers in those days was by livestock lorries, known as 'cattle floats'. Furniture and other possessions were loaded into the part normally allocated to cattle or sheep and the family, cat and dog sat in the cab with the driver. Our new home was in a row of two cottages, with each cottage providing two family homes, so I suppose it would be described as semi-detached now. It had two bedrooms, a living room, a bathroom and a small kitchen at the back and there were two sheds outside. There was a large garden at the front of the house with a path at the side leading to the 'midden', which was for our rubbish and this was emptied every six months. On a lower level below the midden was a grassy area with clothes poles. There was a field in front of this and beyond, were the farm buildings and more fields.

There was no electricity supply, so cooking was by liquefied natural gas and a burner, while water heating was by a coal or wood fire in the living room and other heating was provided by Paraffin heaters. Our lighting was provided by a 'Tilley' lamp and we acquired a 'portable' radio which had a high-tension battery and a lead-acid battery, known as an accumulator. The accumulator, which provided current for the thermeonic valve heaters, required recharging quite frequently and was taken to the cycle shop in our nearest village; Tarves. Two accumulators were required so that the radio could be used while the other was on-charge. I remember trying to listen to 'Dan Dare' on Radio Luxembourg while the accumulator was becoming depleted so the signal faded away.

My new School was 'Tarves Public School', which was the inscription on the stonework above the entrance, but Aberdeenshire Education department ran it. Because I had learned to talk in Inverlochy and Kemnay, my accent was quite different to the 'Doric' spoken by the local children and this led to some difficulty integrating with them and I was not keen to get involved in fights over it. A mini bus used to do a round picking up children under a certain age and transporting them to school and I qualified for this service for a few years. The Grieve at the farm and his wife had seven children at that time so the mini bus was well used. After a year of this I got a bicycle so I was able to cycle the two and three-quarter miles there and the same back. I did not find school very stimulating and one teacher appeared to take a dislike to me, so I did not make much progress in her classes. Mum used to insist that I completed any school homework before being allowed out to play, so I often rushed homework to escape.

There was always snow during winter and if a blizzard began during the school day, farmers would send a tractor and a cart with a tarpaulin covering it to collect the children from school and take them safely to their homes. The roads would get filled with blown snow up to the level of the dry-stone dikes, so we could not attend school until the roads were cleared by snow ploughs. This could take several days after a severe snowstorm and on one occasion we had two weeks off school.

The importance of the 'eleven plus' examination was not emphasised by our teachers and I had not been encouraged to prepare for it. As a result of this I was recommended to have a 'Junior Secondary' education, while three of my classmates were recommended to attend Ellon Academy. The secondary education was more interesting than primary and I enjoyed science, maths, metal and woodwork and gardening subjects. We had a peripatetic teacher for the woodwork and metalwork, who was an excellent teacher and known as 'Kipper', I think because of his dark complexion. The Headmaster, the 'Dominie' took the gardening lessons, from which we all benefited.

He also taught maths and on one occasion became exasperated with a pupil who could not solve an algebra example and said, '*You won't need algebra to pu neeps*', by which he was assuming that this pupil would work on a farm and lifting turnips would not require algebra. We also had a peripatetic music teacher called Mr Spears, who did not manage to teach me anything because there was no continuity in his lessons. He kept reminding us that he had 'Gone to war for you shower'. However, he did manage to get a choir together to sing at the annual prize giving. By third year at school I began to enjoy learning and produce good results, leading me to be runner-up to the Dux award.

During my school years I had joined the 'Life Boys' and then the 'Boys' Brigade (B.B), which I thoroughly enjoyed. The leader of both was our Welsh science teacher, Trevor Hollyoak. These groups met on one evening each week and had occasional activities on Saturdays and of course, church on Sundays. Our 'Brigade' went on summer camps where we slept in bell tents on sacks filled with straw, which we made up the first day. Camps were well away from home in farm fields at Grantown-on-Spey, Arbroath and St Andrews. There we indulged in a variety of activities some of which would not be allowed in today's 'health and safety/risk analysis' society. At evening meetings, we did PE and worked towards various badges.

Me in Boys Brigade uniform 1958.

The B.B diary we each received had a lot of information in it, including track running records, so I decided to try and run a hundred yards as fast as possible to find out how I compared. There was a flat field near the burn with a track made by cows in it, where the grass was worn down leaving the earth surface, so I paced out what I thought to be a hundred yards, marking each end. I then ran as fast as I could over it several times, timing myself using the second's hand on my wristwatch. I was deluded into thinking that I had almost equalled the world record and was inspired to keep trying to improve on this in the following weeks.

School sports were held once a year and included the usual events like the sack race, tattie and spoon race, wheelbarrow race with a partner, slow cycle race, two running races and the high jump. The running races were the short one, from the bottom goalposts up the field to the top posts and the long race was the short one then around the top posts and back to the bottom posts. Most times I won the long race and also did quite well in the high jump using the scissors technique. On one occasion I volunteered for the school football team and played in a match against Methlick School, but the verdict of the Gym teacher in charge of the team was 'that I was 'as much good as a post on the field'. It appeared that I had no aptitude for football and that was the end of my football playing.

Once a year there were inter B.B company sports in Ellon where competition was arranged in age groupings and I used to run in the 100 yards and 220 yards and participate in the high jump. I discovered in an old BB diary the cardboard shield badges awarded at these events for the first three: red for first, white for second and yellow for third. I appear to have shown some promise at running as I had a selection of these badges.

During my school days I used to fish in the nearby Yowlie burn, at every opportunity, which was most weekends and several evenings a week in late Spring, Summer and Autumn. There were brown trout to be caught and I usually caught at least one per outing; I would keep trying until I caught one. When the burn was in spate, sea trout would occasionally make their way up and I once caught a two and three-quarter pounds' specimen, which was a great thrill and is still the largest fish I ever caught. Thanks to my fishing efforts, brown trout could be added to our diet fairly regularly. According to my 1957 diary, the most trout that I caught in one day totalled forty-three.

I also developed an interest in bird watching, following the gift of the 'Observer's Book of British Birds', from my Auntie and Uncle, Dolly and Archie Ross in Keith. Uncle Archie had a collection of bird's eggs and encouraged me to start one also, which I did, not realising at the time that this was not an ethical pursuit.

As we had no car we relied on a mobile grocer's van for provisions and this visited the cottages every Monday evening. On Saturday evenings a fish van called and during the summer months an ice cream van called on Sunday evenings. The milk tanker driver, who came from the creamery in Aberdeen to collect the milk, used to bring 'The Sunday Post', by arrangement, to my Dad.

A highlight of the year was the annual 'tattie (potato) holidays' when the school closed for a week in October to allow children to work on the farms picking tatties. It was hard work but good fun and we got ten shillings a day for our efforts. There would also be work at the weekends doing this on some farms. We were also employed in planting the tatties during the Easter holidays and this involved walking in the prepared drill with a box of seed tatties and placing one every two and a half to three feet.

Playing 'conkers' with horse chestnuts on strings was popular at school during conker time, but as there were very few horse chestnut trees around our area, the nuts were highly sought after. There was a tree in the garden of the farmhouse at North Ythsie, some in Haddo House estate and one in the garden of the house where the doctor lived and held surgeries. It was from this tree that I fell when the branch I was standing on, while collecting conkers, broke and I came down on the fairly hard driveway. When I tried to ride my bike home I found that my left arm would not work properly and had become rather swollen so it was not possible to ride my bike. I walked to the doctor's house, knocked on his door and explained my predicament. After examining my arm, he suspected that I had a fractured wrist and drove me home and ordered an ambulance. An X-ray taken in hospital in Aberdeen confirmed his diagnosis, so my arm was plastered and I was kept in hospital overnight.

Our best neighbours in the dairyman's house were a family from West Hartlepool called Bushnell. There were four boys in the family and I became good pals with Alistair, who was my age. The oldest boy, Edward joined the RAF and then the fire service and in due course became chief fire officer for the city of Aberdeen. Our families kept in touch when they left and I visited them in their next home, Drumoak on Deeside and also later in West Hartlepool.

As Anne and I grew older we were given separate bedrooms, which meant that Mum and Dad had to get a bed-settee, which was made up each evening in the living room. Dad had to rise at 4am each morning to prepare for the first milking of the forty milk cows for which he was responsible. After the milking and feeding the cows, he would return for breakfast and a short sleep. The second milking was in the late afternoon and this was followed by 'mucking out', providing more bedding and feeding. I used to help after school but not regularly. During the summer months the cows were outside on grassy fields and only inside for milking, but for about six months they remained inside the byre. When the clocks changed by an hour in Spring and Autumn, this change had to be phased in, to allow the cows to adjust.

It was a seven-day week job and so very tiring for Dad and, although he did get every fourth weekend off, it appeared to be a hard life to me. He had extra responsibility at calving time, when he would often have to return at night to deliver calves when the mother was having difficulty or the calf was coming the wrong way. He was always pleased when it was a female calf as these would be kept and grow into milking cows.

In 1958 a supply of electricity, via overhead cables on a line of poles, was delivered to the cottages, which were wired for electric lighting and with appropriate outlet sockets. The 'Tilley' lamp could be retired and we could enjoy instant illumination. This also allowed us to use our 'mains' radio and purchase a television set and become the proud owners of a seventeen-inch GEC receiver. During harvest time, when the grain dryer was operating the voltage supply would fall to such a low level that the television picture would fade, shrink and disappear, which was rather annoying.

During our summer holidays from school we would go on our annual holiday of one or two weeks. We might go to Keith to stay with relations there and visit others. Auntie Carrie and Uncle Bill lived above Keith Laundry and had gas lighting, but their toilet was outside the back down at ground level and reached by wooden stairs. I never liked using these when I was young because of the frequent venting of steam near them.

On one occasion Mum took us to Liverpool by train to visit her sister Lexie and her family. Her husband, Jack Malone, met us at the station with his motorbike and sidecar to transport us to their home. Jack had been in the commandos during the war and did training around Spean Bridge and Fort William, where he met Lexie, who was working in the Laboratory of the British Aluminium works there.

Most summer holidays, however, were spent at my grandparents' house. By then they were living in Caol near Fort William. To get there we would have to walk about two miles to the main road where the bus stop was, catch a bus to Aberdeen, and from there take a bus to Inverness, where we would arrive in early afternoon. Following a brief meal, while we waited for the next stage, we boarded the MacBrayne's bus for Fort William and, after about an hour of being wobbled around on the twisty road down Loch Ness side and beyond, I would vomit into some improvised sick bag. Unfortunately, this happened every time on this stage of the journey. Finally, we would reach Fort William and complete our journey by taking a local bus to Caol and arrive feeling rather worn out.

On most days there was low cloud so one could not see much of Ben Nevis or it was raining. I used to ask Granddad to take me up Ben Nevis, but he always managed to persuade me that it was not a good idea just yet. In Loch Linnie, on several occasions, I tried unsuccessfully to teach myself to swim.

One summer, when I was fifteen, I decide that I would cycle to Fort William for our holiday and back at the end, so I made my way across to the A96 and on to Keith. There I had a brief rest at Auntie Carrie's before continuing to Inverness and down Loch Ness side. I cycled through the night and arrived at Caol at around 7:30 am, much to the relief of my parents and Anne who had arrived by bus the previous evening. At the end of our week I cycled back, but this time I went by: Loch Laggan, Newtonmore, Kingussie, Aberlour and Keith, arriving home at 2am the following morning. My bike was the one that I had used for cycling to and from school and had the normal three gears Sturmey Archer mechanism built into the rear wheel so my average speed was probably around ten miles per hour. I suppose that this illustrated that I had some ability at an endurance event and had a sense of adventure.

In June 1959, I left school with the intention of joining the RAF. My uncle Ian, who was Mum's younger brother, had also served in the RAF, so there was a family tradition developing. I had applied for the apprenticeship programme, but did not achieve the necessary educational standard, so I applied for the 'Boy entrant scheme'. After an interview, aptitude tests and assessment at RAF Cardington, Bedfordshire, I was offered parachute folding or alternatively, motor transport driver, neither of which appealed to me, so I declined the offers. I did pass the medical examination, which was reassuring for my parents, because I had suffered all the usual childhood illnesses around then, including a week in hospital with Scarlet Fever.

I obtained work in Henderson's sawmill on the outskirts of Ellon and would cycle there in the morning and back at night. I was allocated work with the sawyer, who had only three fingers on his left hand and smoked a clay pipe. We had to roll tree trunks onto the saw bench, which was mounted on rollers, and then push the aligned trunk into the large circular saw to cut the required beams, battens, posts, pit-props or planks as required.

There were five of us working there and one man kept ferrets and used these to catch rabbits, which were very plentiful then, before the disease, myxomatosis, killed millions. The technique was to put small nets, attached to pegs driven into the ground, over rabbit holes in a warren and then let the ferret go into the warren, down one of the burrows. If there were rabbits present, there would be some bumping noises before the rabbit or rabbits bolted out and got trapped in the nets. The ferret would then emerge and had to be retrieved and put safely back in his box. I was keen to try this for myself, so I built a hutch and acquired two ferrets from my fellow worker in January 1960. One was an albino while the other was light brown and they were used to being handled.

At weekends Jimmy Sinclair, one of the Greave's sons, would come ferreting with me and once we had a potato sack full of rabbits we would take them to the butcher in Ellon, who would buy them from us at two shillings and sixpence per gutted rabbit. We had to carry a spade with us so that we could dig out the ferret if it did not come out of the warren. On one occasion, however, I could not locate the brown ferret so he escaped to the wild and probably found a stoat as a mate. The white ferret suffered a similar fate on a rainy day a few months later and that was the end of my ferreting days. I used to send the skins of the rabbits we ate, to Horace Friend in Wisbech, Cambridgeshire, for processing and received some payment for these. On one occasion we persuaded Mrs Cameron, whose husband Charlie looked after the pigs on the farm, to lend us his four-ten shotgun, to try shooting some wood pigeons in a nearby wood, with the idea of selling these to the butcher in Ellon. We only succeeded in downing one pigeon before returning the weapon to Mrs Cameron, having found ferreting more productive.

THE SIXTIES

1960

Because of the negative outcomes from my RAF applications I decided to try to improve my education so I started a correspondence course, now called distance learning, in maths and English with Skerry's college in Glasgow and I think this probably helped me improve a little.

I had developed a strong interest in Radio and sent away for a kit, which I assembled. I decided that I would like to work in this field and started to look for an apprenticeship in this sort of work. With the aid of a youth employment officer I obtained the addresses of all the businesses carrying out radio and television repair work in Aberdeen and went around each, enquiring if there were any possibility of being employed as an apprentice. This proved a fruitless exercise, but a position did become available at 'Grants' in Union Street, which I applied for, but did not get. I then heard through the youth employment officer that A.M. Mackie's in Inverurie were looking to start an apprentice. I was interviewed by Mr Mackie on the 6th of February 1960 and was offered the position on a trial basis and started there on the 22nd of February, much to my delight. Mackie's was a shop on 10-12 West High Street, Inverurie, which sold all electrical goods and records, but also had a large electricians' business in workshops behind the shop. A condition of being taken on was that I should live in digs in Inverurie to avoid travel problems during the winter.

After a week's work, on Friday evenings I would cycle the 12 miles to my parents' home in Little Ythsie, near Tarves, and then cycle back to Inverurie on Sunday evening, to be ready for the next workweek. During the light evenings of May, June, July and August I used to cycle through the surrounding area, which was very interesting. In September I started attending evening classes in Aberdeen at Marywell Street for the City and Guilds and Radio Trades Examination Board certificate in radio and television servicing. This was a five-year course as was my apprenticeship. After work on Wednesdays I would catch a bus to Aberdeen for the class, which lasted two and a half hours and following class I would catch the Inverness bus back to Inverurie. I often fell asleep, but usually wakened by instinct just before Inverurie; however, on one occasion I woke as the bus approached Pitcaple, some six miles beyond Inverurie, so I had a long walk back to my lodgings and made sure that this did not occur again.

One of my responsibilities at work was recharging the lead-acid batteries that customers with non-mains radios brought in. The bench had a lead covering to protect it from sulphuric acid spills and I had to connect the batteries in series to the charger and adjust the output voltage to suit the number of batteries. Despite taking care, small holes began to appear in some of my clothing where some acid must have reached them. Other work included helping to repair domestic electrical items such as kettles, toasters, lamps, irons and heaters.

In 1960 I participated in my first walking race, which had become popular because of the publicity surrounding the Lands End to John o' Groats walk undertaken by Dr Barbara Moore. On the evening of the 12th of August there was a walking race from Oldmeldrum to Fyvie and was part of the 'Oldmeldrum Sports', which was mainly an 'Agricultural Show', to be held on the 13th of August. There were 45 starters in this seven miles walking race along the A947 and I finished a tired 5th, like others wearing my working clothes and shoes. In the following year the race was from Kintore to Oldmeldrum, a distance of 10 miles, and I participated again, completing the walk in two hours in 24th place from the 67 starters. I noted that two girls had finished ahead of me, so I would need to train if I wished to improve my race walking ability. I did this walking race again the following year.

1961

Occasionally I would go out with an electrician called Jim Morrison to wire extra outlet sockets in houses, which was interesting. I was the one who had to crawl under floors pulling cables or carefully crawl through small and dirty loft spaces to run a cable. I found out then that I did not suffer from claustrophobia, but sometimes it was impossible to turn around and I had to wriggle backwards to get out, once the cable was in place.

One of the electricians at work suggested that I should get some motorised transport and that he had a friend who had a Raleigh moped for sale. I duly visited his friend with him and was persuaded to purchase this moped, which was like a cross between a heavy bicycle and a motorbike, so that you could pedal it or use the engine. This turned out to be a bad decision because the engine, which was a 50cc two stroke, would cut out very frequently and refuse to restart, so I pedalled a lot. I never found the reason for this frustrating fault, so with help from my friend Leslie (Les) McAllan I traded it in, receiving £9, as part of the purchase of a second hand, Triumph 'Terrier' 150cc motorbike for £20, from Furneau's in Aberdeen in September 1961. I lacked skill in driving a motorbike at this stage and, on my second outing, the bike collided with the verge and I flew over the dry stone dyke into the field beyond. Fortunately, neither the bike nor I were damaged. However, in due course, I passed my driving test for the motorbike in Inverurie.

1962

Now that I had a reliable motorbike, Les, who had a Norton 'Jubilee' 250cc twin cylinder machine, and I used to go for runs on our bikes. Les was from Glen Buchat up on Donside, so I visited there and also his cousin in Kinellar. We became good pals and went out most weekends and even went to dances in village halls on our bikes, which was rather inconvenient because of our cumbersome motorcycle gear, which had to be removed and stored somehow.

That July, Les, Davie, Gordon and I decided to go on a motorcycle-touring holiday, pitching our tents wherever we could find a suitable location. We covered quite a distance, going to Inverness, Fort William and down to Ayr, because Gordon wanted to visit a girl at 'Butlins' Holiday Park. We camped on the beach there for several days and enjoyed the area around, including Ayr itself.

Although I had always enjoyed being outdoors during my boyhood, as well as taking exercise – helping with farm work, walking, cycling, running and jumping at the annual school sports – I was eighteen years old when my running career really began. I was living in Inverurie at the time, 16 miles from Aberdeen.

In order to give a real impression of my early development and struggles, and to give a flavour of the Scottish running scene at the time, the forthcoming account of races and training from 1962 to 1966 will be very detailed

Someone showed me an article in the 'Press and Journal' on Aberdeen Athletic Club, saying that they would welcome new members. I contacted the club coach Colin Donald, who was identified in the article and he arranged to take me in to Aberdeen for a club night. Colin and his younger brother Roy had a farm called 'Parkhill' on the outskirts of Oldmeldrum, so I drove there on my motorbike and got a lift with them to Linksfield Stadium, off King Street for a training night. As a result, in September 1962, aged 18, I joined Aberdeen Amateur Athletic Club (AAAC), the membership fee for the year being fifteen shillings.

At that time the Monday evening session was at Fredrick Street School Gym for circuit training followed by a three-mile run down to the prom and around a loop. I gave Adam Aitken, the other runner in Inverurie, a lift on my motorbike for training nights. On Thursday evenings we had track training at Linksfield Stadium.

An extract from my training diary indicates what I was doing on Club evenings: *'to date (9/12/62) I have not missed a training session, although I have been late due to mishaps with my motorbike. My circuit on Monday evening is as follows: 17 step ups, 16 curls, 24 jumps, 6 press ups, 22 back lifts, 14 burpees. Between each circuit I take 2 minutes' rest. I found it hard for a start, but last week I managed 8 circuits; the sweat was pouring off me. On Thursday evenings we run 220 yards Paarlaufs, usually sixteen. In these we formed two groups and one group would run the half lap around the bend and when the lead runner reached the group waiting there they would set off running around the far bend. The first group then have to jog across to the other side of the track and get ready to run off again when the lead runner from this second group arrives and the sequence is repeated. At first I only managed half that, but gradually worked up to sixteen, and after six weeks I managed to take the lead on the last one'.*

My first race for the club was on 20th October in the Kingsway four-man road relay race in Dundee (2.75 mile laps). I was in the 'C' team and on the last leg, taking 19:10 for my lap and I felt very ill afterwards. Unfortunately, due to my inexperience, I was still in my tracksuit bottoms when my teammate came in to hand over; he was annoyed.

My first cross-country event was a North East League race in St Andrews on 1st of December and, as we were short of time, we got changed on the ferry across the Tay, and began warming up on the deck! We got some strange looks from fellow passengers. The race start was delayed 15 minutes to 3:15pm for us. It was a 6-mile cross-country race, which I enjoyed. The fellow in front of me took the wrong way and I followed him, which cost us a few minutes. I completed the course 38:12 in 41st place, out of 46 starters, so there was little sign of natural ability in this performance.

By mid December I started to do some training each night in addition to the club nights, so this would be, typically, a one-mile warm-up followed by a three-mile run. My mileages for my first three months were: October-18 miles, November-18 miles and December-56.5 miles.

1963

My first experience of championship races was on 23rd of February 1963, when we went to Hamilton for the Scottish National Cross Country Championships, held on the Racecourse for horses. On arrival we got changed in the bar, which had a wet stone floor and the shelves were covered in dust. The lavatories were frozen and the smell was overpowering. My event, the Junior race, was over 5 miles and I finished second last in 100th place, hardly a thoroughbred performance. There were no showers only some drinking troughs for horses so we decided to go home unwashed.

In March 1963, I joined the Garioch Hill Walking Club, which was based in Inverurie and had outings once a month to climb mountains in the Cairngorms. My first walk was up the Munro, Beinn a' Bhuird, from Deeside. I was rather ill equipped, as I had no hill-walking boots or appropriate clothes, so I walked about 10 miles in Wellington boots and a raincoat over my normal clothes. By the next outing I had acquired suitable boots and an anorak. On some outings we would climb four Munros, which are mountains over 3000 feet high, and walk 15 miles. As well as being enjoyable and satisfying, I regarded this as part of my endurance training.

Also in March, Colin Donald the AAAC club coach suggested that I start doing repetition 220yds in an attempt to improve my speed for 440 yards races. I started to do sessions of 12 times an estimated 220yds or 12 times an estimated 110yds on a fairly flat section of road near my home. These were done in the evening, on non-club nights, when I returned from work, wearing gym shoes (gutties), which had no cushioning, just a solid rubber sole. Around this time, I noticed that my urine was very dark and cloudy especially after doing these sprints on the road. On 18th March I did 12 times 220 yards on the road and afterwards when I went to the toilet to urinate I received a nasty shock: blood came out, so I had to seek advice, as this seemed quite worrying.

I consulted my local GP, Dr Laing, who asked for samples of 'normal' urine and a sample of the dark cloudy version. On a follow up consultation he informed me that he had never come across this before and would write to a consultant in Aberdeen for a second opinion as he suspected that it was something to do with my kidneys. On my next appointment with Dr Laing on 1st April he thought that I had haemoglobinuria, a very rare condition affecting young males between 12 and 20 years old, and that one should grow out of it. He explained that it was not blood that was passing through, but the red blood pigment from the blood cells, which had broken down, and this was making my urine the dark colour. He would send my samples and my story to a consultant in Aberdeen for a second opinion. The consultant might be able to tell me what to do as regards sprinting, which caused the condition. In the meantime, I had to avoid sprinting on the road.

On 17th April I attended Woolmanhill Hospital, where a lady doctor, performed various tests, asked many questions and examined me. After she had finished another doctor, who read the report she had written, then discussed it with her. They wanted me in Hospital for a couple of days to do some tests, including injecting some sort of radio-active tracer into a vein to establish if my kidneys were functioning correctly. I was not looking forward to going into Hospital but the Senior Doctor said that he thought my problem was not serious.

From 23rd April to the 27th of April I was in Forrester Hill Hospital, Aberdeen for a battery of procedures and tests, 25 in all. One of the more unusual procedures was that I had to drink two glasses of water and then sit with my feet in a basin of water with ice cubes in it, for 15 minutes and then blood samples were taken for analysis. Another was I had to drink two glasses of cold water then go for a run; my kit consisted of: my string vest, a pair of rather long shorts which they found from somewhere, a pair of suitable gym shoes, and a pullover. As I passed some nurses on the way out they burst into laughter! I did 5 times 220 yards and 7 times 50 yards sprints. My urine was OK after this session, so I drank another two glasses of water, gave another blood sample and set off to run again. I ran into a nurse while doing 12 times 220 yards and then gave another blood sample and my urine sample was dark so the doctor was highly delighted and five more samples were collected every 15 minutes following the run.

Bobby Duncan, a member of AAAC and a good distance runner, was a technician in the lab there so he gave me a visit and said that he could find nothing wrong in the blood samples. Next I had an enema in preparation for an X-ray next day. I just made it to the lavatory seat before exploding into the bowl and I was there for some time. Next day I had two injections of tracer liquid into a vein to show kidney function; I was strapped to the bench during the X-ray, which lasted 1hr 15 minutes.

Between procedures I read Volumes One, Two and Three of Radio and Television Servicing by G N Patchett, to prepare for the City and Guilds Intermediate examination in Radio and Television Servicing, which was due in May. This proved to be good revision time as I passed the exam comfortably.

On the 16th of May I attended Woolmanhill Hospital to hear the results of the tests performed during my recent stay in Foresterhill Hospital. The Doctor reaffirmed that it was the blood red pigment that was coming through with my urine, and was due to violent physical exercise. He thought that most people would experience this if they ran hard enough. He did not know how the pigment got into the urine or why it was so marked in my case. He said that I should continue running and that the condition was not harmful, so I was mildly reassured.

On the 27th of May I became a club quarter miler on the basis of a couple of runs at Linksfield track. An extract from my training diary records the occasion: '*after six laps warm up I ran in the club Junior 440 yards championship. There were two heats, and in my heat there were four of us, with me in the outside lane. I was second and moved into the final, which had six runners. I was given a loan of John Dixon's spikes, which were a big help. I took the lead and maintained it until the last bend, where Graham passed me. My legs became stiff, like running in a dream, but I managed to finish second in 58 seconds. Everybody was excited by my run; I was very sore and my mouth was so dry that I could not swallow. I vomited twice soon after and had a thumping headache. After about 45 minutes I began to feel better and managed a shower.*' John later sold these spikes to me and on the 5th of June he gave me a loan of his copy of "Run to the Top" by Arthur Lydiard and Garth Gilmore. I read this book very carefully and I was inspired by it. I tried to adopt some of the ideas in it, but I was not ready for 100 miles per week, and I only accumulated 83.5 miles that June.

John Dixon (who went on to run for Scotland in 1966 with a personal best of 49.1 seconds) and I became the regular quarter milers representing Aberdeen AAC in inter club matches. My times did not improve very much, and I got stuck at around 53 seconds, but the tracks were often grass and five or six laps to the mile, with the occasional 440 yards cinder track.

During the summer, apart from inter-club matches, I ran in Highland Games at Alyth, Forres, Dingwall and Aberfeldy. Usually I ran in the handicap quarter and half miles and at Dingwall in the AAAC four by 110 yards relay and although I won few prizes, I enjoyed the atmosphere at these gatherings

By September 1963, the cross-country and road relay season was underway and I purchased a pair of Reebok ripple shoes, which I used for road running and cross-country races. Initially they hurt my right heel and on investigation I found some nails, which were part of the heel construction, sticking up through the heel, so I hammered them down which solved the problem.

My Triumph Terrier motorbike began to get unreliable, breaking down on several occasions and this could involve a long push home. I always managed to repair it once back at the house, but I decided to trade it in, receiving £15, for a newer bike, a Velocette 'MAC' 350cc (CRG885) which cost £100 and had a characteristic 'fish tail' silencer. This was a much heavier bike and considerably faster than the Triumph so this reduced my commuting time to and from work and on trips to Aberdeen.

By late September I started running twice a day on Mondays, Wednesdays and Fridays, if my mum could get me out of bed. Mum was always up early as Dad had to get up for the first milking, which I thought was a hard life. So, before breakfast and driving to Inverurie, I would run 4 miles or 5.5 miles on roads. At night before tea I would run the same distances, so now I was training seven days a week and accumulating around 46 stamina-building miles a week.

On Saturdays I began driving to Hazlehead Park in Aberdeen to train with Bob Duncan, Innis Mitchell and Bill Livingston, who Bob was coaching. I used to get changed in the toilet or just by my bike when they were closed. Later I combined these journeys to Aberdeen with motorcar driving lessons, before the training sessions. I received instruction from a chain-smoking Aberdeen Corporation double-decker bus driver, so the running afterwards appears to have negated the effects of passive smoking during lessons.

By mid October I was beginning to show some improvement in fitness and at the Kingsway road relays in Dundee, running in the Aberdeen AAC 'C' team I was 2-30 faster over the 2.75 miles lap than last year, but I still lost seven places.

My mileage for the month of October was 209 miles, which was the most I had achieved to that date and by the end of 1963 my total mileage for the year was 1499.5 miles.

1964

The winter weather in December 1963 and January of 1964 was rather severe with lots of snow, gales, ice and blocked roads, so my running was restricted on quite a few occasions. On the last Saturday in February the Scottish National Cross Country Championships were again at Hamilton Racecourse. In the Junior race Mel Edwards from Aberdeen won and I was 45th out of 168, which was a pleasing improvement over the previous year, but I was not satisfied with my performance.

By April I was again running quarter miles in inter-club matches as second string to John Dixon. In May we had a match against R.N.A.S. Lossiemouth where I ran in the half-mile and finished third in 2-09.5, with the winners – Les Anderson from our club and a Navy runner – dead-heating in 2-08, so I was pleased. I also ran in the mile and finished third again in 4-51. A.A.A.C. won the match. Later in the month I improved to 2-06, but club coach, Colin Donald said that I needed more speed work, and that I should not be doing it on road, which is advice I agreed with.

However, before I acted on this advice I arranged to have my two weeks summer holiday early, from the 8th of June to the 21st of June and did no running during this time. I drove my motorbike the 230 miles to Ardrossan and embarked with it on the ferry to Douglas on the Isle of Man. I had planned this trip to coincide with the TT races and I was amazed at the huge number of motorcycle enthusiasts who had brought their bikes over for this event: there seemed to be 'bikes' everywhere. I rode around the course before the roads were closed and then found a suitable vantage point to watch the first race, which was for 50 c.c. machines. I was shocked by the speed achieved by these twelve-gear, high-revving bikes, which bore no resemblance to the 50cc moped I had previously owned. Over the next few days I watched the races for the other bike classes and was suitably impressed by the skill and bravery of the riders. Following the TT races, I toured the island, visiting all the places suggested by my Bed and Breakfast hosts in Douglas. On consulting my diary, I see that I rode 1213 miles between leaving home and returning there.

By mid-summer I had implemented Colin Donald's advice and I was doing sessions like: 22 times 110 yards in 15s with a 30s recovery jog or 12 times 220yds in 30s to 32s, jogging 220yds between, or 6 times 440yds in an average of 59s. As a result, my weekly mileage was around 25 miles.

In August I ran in the Club 6 mile Championships and finished 5th and last in 35-12.5, but this was 2-17.5 faster than last year. I might have gone faster if my spikes had been in better shape, as one burst, allowing cinders into my shoe, so I got a great red blister along the side of the big toe on my right foot, and the ball of the same foot was painful and tender. Next week I purchased replacement spikes, at a cost of two pounds, eight shillings and three pence and these helped me to reduce my half-mile time to 2-04 by late August.

At the Glenurquhart Highland Games on the 29th of August, after finishing second in the handicap half-mile and finishing last in the mile, I decided to run in my first hill race. At the top we got a rubber stamp on the back of our hand as proof of being there, and in my inexperience I took a direct route down and had some difficulty with the cliff, but after that I belted down through the brambles. However, when I reached the tarred road I took the wrong turn and had to be called back, losing two places, which I managed to regain and finished 4th. When I stopped I noticed that my legs were bleeding due to the brambles and everyone was cut somewhere. I noted in my training diary: *It was a strange race; a test of skill in climbing and descending hills. Only on the first and last parts of the race could you run properly.*

As a result of this race my quads were extremely painful on the following three days.

I was quite attracted to hill running; so my next hill race, on the 19th of September, was the six miles Knockfarrel Hill race at Strathpeffer. Our team: Peter Duffy who was second; Roy Donald who was third; and myself fifth, won the team race. We each received a Pyrex dish for the team prize. Alastair Wood retired from the race when he lost a shoe in the muddy section. After the race we had tea in the village hall, which was a very pleasant end to an enjoyable event. My weekly mileage around this time was typically 45 miles.

Back at the Kingsway road relays in Dundee I was now in the AAAC "B" team and my time was 61 seconds faster than in 1963, so this was a marginal improvement and I finished quite strongly.

At work my apprenticeship was progressing and I had more responsibility for fault finding and repairing radios, record players, domestic electrical appliances and some televisions. At that time manufacturers were introducing portable transistor radio receivers and any that came in for repair were given to me to fault-find, as I was dubbed the 'transistor kid'. I had learned the theory of transistor operation and their circuits, thanks to my enthusiastic teacher, Alick Smith, in evening classes for the City and Guilds Intermediate Certificate in Radio and television servicing. The British manufacturers were using Germanium (Ge) transistors from suppliers such as Mullard or Ediswan, in the construction of their sets and produced some very good models. Later, although we did not sell them, small compact and much cheaper radio receivers started coming in for repair. These were from Japan and Hong Kong and their small size was due to a printed circuit construction with very high component density on which it was difficult to find faults. They also used Silicon transistors, which were not yet available in Europe.

Television receivers all relied on thermeonic valves for signal amplification and signal processing and were 'black and white', (monochromatic) on the 405 lines standard. Changes to the 625 lines standard and colour television were being planned, but implementation was still several years in the future. Mackie's sold 'Murphy' television receivers, which had a unique construction and styling, but later other brands such as: Bush, Philips, Ferranti, Decca, Pye and GEC were sold to customers. However, many other brands came into the workshop for repair.

I appeared to have sensitive feet, prone to blistering and subsequent infections; and in October I required medical treatment to lance an infected blister and a course of antibiotics to stop the infection. Later in the month I had an injury in the muscle which joined the thigh to the pelvis, for which some anti-inflammatory tablets were prescribed, along with the advice not to run more than one mile a day for a week!

My running training in November and December was usually steady running of around nine miles in one session, so I would typically achieve around 55 miles in a week. My total mileage for 1964 amounted to 2013 miles, which is a weekly average of 38.7 miles, so that could be regarded as fairly moderate training.

1965

At the end of February 1965, I was back at Hamilton Racecourse for the Scottish Cross Country Championships. Our team in the junior race finished 8th and my place at 65th, which was 20 places worse than 1964, so I was not happy with that and started to look for possible reasons. I came to the conclusion that I had not done sufficient appropriate training over the winter.

On Sunday the 25th of April I ran in my first ten miles road race in a North East District League match in Dundee. I finished 8th out of twelve in 58-52 and I quite enjoyed it, although I found the hills tough.

After the next North East District Athletics match, where I finished fifth and last in the half-mile in 2-06, Colin Donald advised me to try 12 times 110yds in 13s to 14s with a 75s rest between, to see if this would improve my speed. However, I had doubts about pursuing a running career as a quarter miler or a half miler as my basic speed was not fast enough. I did take Colin's advice and included two of these sessions each week in May, June and July, but this produced no improvement in my times.

During my annual summer holiday, I decided to tour part of Ireland on my motorbike. On the 18th of July, I drove to Ayr, stayed overnight and next morning continued to Stranraer and caught the ferry to Larne. From there I drove through Northern Ireland to Londonderry and then into the Republic of Ireland, visiting: Letterkenny, Donegal, Ballyshannon, Sligo and Westport. While in Westport I joined pilgrims walking to the summit of 'Croagh Patrick' at 762 metres. I made my way back from the west coast to Larne on the east to catch the ferry back to Stranraer. I observed that in the Republic there were rather a lot of damaged vehicles compared with home, perhaps a reflection of the relaxed attitude of the people there. I arrived home on the 27th of July, having covered 2008 miles since departing on my tour. I had used bed and breakfast accommodation mainly and only used my tent on one occasion.

In August in the Club one-mile championships at Linksfield, despite falling on the first lap, I finished second in 4-41, which was an improvement. Three days later at RNAS. Lossiemouth our club had a match against the North of Scotland and I ran in the half mile and won in 2-9.3, on a soggy grass track. I also ran the 440yds and finished last and then ran a leg of the four by 110yds relay.

In the Club 6 miles championship, later in August, I finished third, in a personal best of 33-18, so I was very pleased with my performance. This race probably indicated that I had more potential at longer distance events than quarter-miles and half-miles.

A week later I ran in my first Ben Nevis race and completed the course in 2-10-21, starting and finishing in King George V Park in Fort William. My diary entry for the race included: *We lined up at the start after being checked. There was a false start, but we got underway on the second attempt. It was a fast start, and I also started quickly, being up with Peter Duffy until the car park. After we started on the mountain path I lost a lot of places; I was extremely tired and soon had to walk. My back ached from stooping. I kept to the path all the way to the top where it was misty. There we were given a marker on a string, which you put around your neck. I made up quite a few places on the way down, although I had to take care not to lose control, as this could be very dangerous. As I was nearing the bottom the man in front of me fell, so I stopped and asked if he was okay. He said that he was so I continued; my legs felt queer when I started to run on the road again. I was soon back, in the field where we had started, glad to be finished. We were given lemon squash and a seat in the first aid tent. We got showered in the British Aluminum Hostel, and then had high tea at K.K. Cameron's. I enjoyed my day.*

On the following weekend I met Peter Duffy in Inverurie Square, and we set off for Strathpeffer, stopping at Kennethmont Distillery where Peter did some work as part of his employment as a customs and excise officer. We continued on our way and arrived in Strathpeffer for the Knockfarrel hill race. On finishing I was informed that I was second which was rather surprising, since I thought that I was fifth; it seems that a marshal near the bottom of the hill had directed the leaders the wrong way. Peter received first prize – a silver teapot and jug – and I got a canteen of cutlery for second. We also won the team prize, with Dave McFarquhar being our third man and each received a tea set.

Peter invited me to come to his home in Aberdeen next day to train with him and I readily accepted this kind offer. So I went to Peter's house, got changed, and set off running with him, Alastair Wood, Ken Ballantyne, Innis Mitchell, and a navy chap. I began to fall back after about an hour; I was very tired, and my legs felt like lead, but I completed the 14 miles course in about 1 hour 25 minutes. After this, I became a regular member of this Sunday training group and gradually improved so I could get further on the run before losing contact with the rest. Peter's wife, Rita, who was from Orkney, provided excellent home baking and coffee after the run, which I always enjoyed. Peter 'took me under his wing', so to speak, taking a supportive interest in me and became my mentor and also a very good friend indeed as did Rita.

The next race on the calendar was the Alves to Forres 6 miles race along the A96, which is the main road between Aberdeen and Inverness. Health and safety, along with risk analysis were perhaps less of a priority then, but the volume of traffic using the road was also much less than nowadays. Ron Coleman from Dundee Hawkhill Harriers won in 30-18, from Ian Mackenzie of Forres Harriers and I was 10th in 33-50. Next weekend we were back at the Kingsway road relay in Dundee and that year I had been selected for the 'A' team and I ran as hard as I could, which made me feel nauseous. Our team finished in sixth place. Next on 30th October I competed as a guest in the Aberdeen University Hare and Hounds cross-country trial over their home course. Bill Ewing won in 35-20 from Peter Duffy and I was surprised to come in a very tired third. It was clear that I was making some progress.

I was selected for the AAAC team to run in the prestigious Edinburgh to Glasgow Road Relay, which was the highlight of the winter season for many club runners. The rivalry between the twenty invited participating clubs was intense and this event had a special and memorable character. I was given Stage Three, taking over in ninth and gaining two places but then losing one, to hand over eighth – I found out later that I was seventh fastest on the stage. Dennis Whiting moved up to seventh on the next stage and Alastair Wood moved us up to sixth on the long stage and the rest of our team maintained this position to the finish. I did not think that this would be the first of thirteen efforts in this event, my last being in 1983. The magnificent Edinburgh University team won in a new course record time. Afterwards high tea was provided for all runners and officials in the 'Cadora' restaurant, the team medals were presented and results sheets issued and scrutinised to see how our team members' stage times ranked.

During the winter months the club met for training at Linksfield stadium on Tuesday evenings, so I used to drive there on my motorbike from work in Inverurie. We usually did an interval session on the track such as 14 X 330 yards, with 110 yards recovery jog. On other days I would sometimes run five miles on the road in the morning before driving my bike to work or on returning from work I would run 8 miles or sometimes 11 miles on roads, before having my evening meal. On Saturdays I often drove my bike to Collieston, got changed, and ran on the beach and sand dunes to the River

Ythan estuary and back twice, which was about 14 miles. On Sundays I drove into Aberdeen to train with Peter and Alastair and whoever had joined the group that day and we usually covered 13 miles. My weekday runs from home in Little Ythsie during the winter months were completed in the dark, which was okay as one's vision adapted, but I did fall on three occasions when I could not see the ice on the road.

That November my Vellocet motorbike required a major engine repair, so I went for the option of trading it in for £172, as part of the purchase of a second hand 1960 Austin A35 van with 30568 miles recorded, so I said goodbye to the joys of motorcycling. This van was a faithful servant for several years and had the additional advantage of providing a sleeping space in the back when necessary.

By the end of 1965, having endured some icy roads, snow and slush, my training and racing mileage for the year amounted to 2556 miles.

1966

My five years' apprenticeship as a radio and television servicing technician with A.M Mackie's in Inverurie had been completed in July 1965 and, after five years of evening classes in Aberdeen, I had passed the City and Guilds of London final certificate in radio and television servicing and Radio Trades Examination Board examinations. I was ready to move on and I applied for a post as an electronics laboratory technician in Robert Gordon's Institute of Technology (RGIT) in Aberdeen and was successful, beginning work there in January 1966. This meant a longer drive to and from work, but I could then train at lunchtimes in daylight, which was a benefit and also train again after work. Typically, during my one and a half hours' lunch break I would drive to Kings College and get changed in the Hare & Hounds dressing room and run through old Aberdeen, Seaton Park, over the Bridge of Don and out onto Murcar golf course and back, covering around eight miles, mixing steady running and fartlek. My weekday runs after work would usually be five miles steady on roads again from Kings before going home to Little Ythsie.

AAAC participated in the North East cross-country league, so I ran in all the available league races in Aberdeen, Dundee and St Andrews. The club entered teams in the East District and National cross-country championships.

The 1966 East District championships were in Kirkcaldy on a frozen rutted course, where I finished a disappointed 27th. Our highest placed runner was Ian Mackenzie in 7th (2nd Junior). In the National Senior Championships, again at Hamilton racecourse I finished 44th and our best-placed runner was Alastair Wood in 12th, running in bare feet. Unfortunately, we did not have enough runners to have a team placing.

In the week beginning the 7th of March I reached 100 miles of running in a week for the first time and I noted in my training diary: *I feel that this level of training saps one's strength, as indicated by increased times for training runs during the week.* The next time I reached this level again was in the week beginning 4th of April, since I had intended to prepare for a possible marathon race.

After the cross-country season, on the 17th of March the club entered a team in the popular Perth North Inch, four-man road relay. I ran the first leg of three miles followed by Alastair, Steve Taylor and Bill Ewing. I was very happy to be part of such a strong team and we finished second behind Victoria Park, but ahead of Edinburgh University Hare and Hounds.

On the first of April, Alastair, Ian Mackenzie and I, travelled by train to Glasgow and on to Motherwell for the Law to Motherwell 'Tom Scott Memorial' 10 miles road race. Andy Brown won in 48-06, 49 seconds ahead of Jim Alder. Alastair was 4th in 49-46. Ian was 9th in 51-01 and I was 30th in 53-35, so we were third team. Next day I joined the Garioch hill-walking club on their monthly outing, walked 21 miles and climbed two Munros.

In my training I was including three interval sessions a week such as 24 x 220 yards in 30s - 32s with a 220 yards recovery to allow my pulse rate to drop back to 120 before the next effort, or 12 X

440 yards in 65s–70s with a 440 yards recovery jog of 3 minutes, or 6 X 880 yards in 2-25 to 2-30 with 880 yards recovery. Our Scottish National athletics coach, John Anderson, convinced us that a session of repetition 220 yards, with recoveries sufficient to allow one's heart rate to fall back to 120 beats per minute, was the best way to improve fitness.

FIRST THREE MARATHONS

I had always wanted to run a marathon, as I had been inspired by the marathon running of Alastair Wood. The previous July (1965), I became 21 years old, which was the minimum age at which Scottish Athletics would allow one to participate in a marathon, so I was now able to give marathon running a try. There were three marathons in Scotland then: Shettleston, the Scottish Championship event and the Inverness to Forres. As the Shettleston marathon was the first of these, on the 23rd of April I entered, along with Alastair. I was apprehensive about what might happen during such a long run, because the furthest that I had done in training was a 17 miles road run on the 26th of March. My training diary entry was: *Saturday: I rose at 05:30, had some breakfast and drove to Aberdeen to pick up Alastair and drove to the train station where we caught the 07:10 train to Glasgow. After spending two hours in Glasgow, we caught the bus to Shettleston, where we got changed and set out on the marathon at 2.19pm. I reached 10miles in 59-00 and passed 20miles in 2-2-45, by which time the day was warm and my feet hurt very badly. I splashed through any convenient puddles to try and cool my feet and gladly took all the sponges offered. At 23miles I was 6th and feeling quite good apart from painful feet and a rubbed groin and nipples. With only three-quarters of a mile remaining I passed Alistair Matson of Edinburgh University, who had slowed greatly. My time was 2-43-25, which pleased me. After I stopped my legs were tingling and it was easier to jog than walk. I arrived home at 11.55pm.* I remember Andy Forbes asking me during the first lap, 'Are you going all the way son?' to which I replied 'I hope so'. Alastair won in 2.24.00. After finishing I did <u>not</u> think to myself 'never again', so I was keen to run more marathons!

My next race was the Scottish Amateur Athletics Association (SAAA) 10 miles track championships on the 6th of May at Seedhill track in Paisley. I drove down in Mum's Morris Minor with Mum and Dad and I left them visiting relations in Paisley while I went to the race. I ran reasonably well to 4miles but after this got slower and slower and finished 7th in 57-14, my lap times ranging from 76s to 93s. Lachie Stewart won in 48-44 and my club mate, Peter Duffy ran an excellent race to place second in 53-43.6. During this race I ran my fastest 3 miles and 6 miles on the track. My poor performance was probably due to driving a good part of the way from home and driving through Glasgow. Also my warm-up was rather short and I wore spikes rather than racing flats.

The following Saturday I travelled to Edinburgh with club mates Ian Mackenzie and Mike Scott to run in the Edinburgh University 10. Andy Brown won in 50-04, ten seconds ahead of Alex Wight. Ian finished 8th in 52-15, I was 15th in 54-42 and Mike was 27th in 58-02, so we did not gain any team award. Next day I ran in the three miles in the North East Athletics League meeting at Linksfield and finished 5th in 15-16.5, 1.5s behind Peter Duffy, with Alastair gaining maximum points for our club by winning.

My second marathon was the SAAA Marathon Championships on the 28th of May, from Westerlands track in Glasgow. I travelled down with Alastair, who was prepared to race if a serious contender for selection to the Scottish team for the marathon in the Commonwealth Games was also there, but as Jim Alder was not running he decided against taking part and instead would concentrate on running well, probably in the Polytechnic marathon. Alastair showed me his training schedule in preparation for this marathon, which I valued. My training diary entry for that day was: *Saturday: I travelled with Alastair to Westerlands in Glasgow for the SAAA Marathon Championships. Alastair did not run, as he wanted to run in the Poly marathon instead. Despite the very warm day, I felt fine until the turn, after which I began to slow and was passed by two chaps. The weather was so hot that the tar on the road was melting and you could feel your shoes sticking to it. I was seriously considering abandoning the race; the last six miles seemed to take an age to pass. I was never so glad to finish a race in my life before: it was the hardest most painful race I have* ever run. *My time was 2-45-58. On removing my shoes and socks I found four blisters on my right foot and one burst blister on my left foot. I had a nauseous feeling, which lasted until about 9.30 p.m., but I was not actually sick. My neck and arms were sunburned, as there was not a cloud in the sky during the race. I passed 10miles in 58-26 and 20 miles in 2-01-00.* Charlie McAlinden won in 2-26-31, Gordon Eadie ran 2-28-19 and Andy Fleming finished in 2-32-47. This was my first experience of how hard a marathon can be, but despite this, I did not think 'never again'.

A week later in the Dundee Sports at King George V. Stadium, Caird Park, I ran in the 13 miles road race and kept up with Ron Coleman, for about four miles, but by the end he was out of sight. I was pleasantly surprised to finish second, in a time of 69-12 and I felt quite good at the end. Mike Scott of Forres Harriers and Aberdeen AAC, was third. My prize was a bathroom scales. Two days later I supported my club in a match against the Teacher Training College, running in the one-mile race, finishing 4th in 4-39; and 3rd in the half mile in 2-10.7.

Our next North East Athletics League match was in Dundee on Sunday the 19th of June, so I went to Aberdeen, to the arranged rendezvous. Because we were short of transport I agreed to take four girls from the Club, in my van to Dundee. One had the passenger seat, but three were in the back, which could not have been very pleasant, rattling around in the back especially as there were, no windows and no seats. One of the girls became travel sick on the way, which was upsetting for us all, poor girl. I ran in the one mile and I stuck with the leaders until the last lap, where I was unable to accelerate enough to stay in contact. Fergus Murray won in 4-26, from Hunter Watson and I finished sixth in 4-36.

On the following Friday evening I ran in the SAAA six miles track championships at Meadowbank in Edinburgh and finished 9th in 31-13, one second ahead of Peter Duffy.

Our next adventure was on the second of July 1966, at the Kinlochleven Highland Games where we were invited to participate in the two miles team race. Jim Alder won on the six laps to the mile grass track in 9-07 and, from our team, Ian Mackenzie was fifth, I was tenth and Alastair was eleventh. I was surprised to beat Alastair. I was ahead of him for 9 laps, but he passed me on the 10th, so I stuck with him and sprinted past on the last lap. He felt pretty bad after the race. I was delighted to see Peter Duffy winning the Mamore Hill race by a large margin. We stayed in Kinlochleven on Friday and Saturday nights, so we had a pleasant social evening after the Games.

Next Saturday, the 9th of July, Forres Highland Games would be held, so I travelled up to Inverness with Alastair for the Inverness to Forres marathon, which was part of the Games. Weather conditions were ideal: a cloudy day, with a following wind. My training diary report on this race was: *Alastair led, followed by: Ron Coleman, Peter Duffy, Donald Ritchie and Hugh Mitchell. By 10 miles Alastair was well away and Coleman had got away from Mitchell, who in turn had pulled away from Ritchie and I had a gap on Peter. My time at 10 miles was given as 50-05, which seemed very fast. We had a refreshing shower of rain, which lasted for about 30 minutes, between 10 and 20 miles. My time at 20 miles was given as 1-53-30 and from there I could see Hugh pass Ron. About three quarters of a mile later Ron stopped for a drink and then started jogging. I passed him soon after this and the sun broke through, making the temperature rise considerably so that conditions became very hot. We left the A96 at Brodie, crossed the railway line and followed a minor road, before re-crossing the railway to rejoin the A96. By this point I was really feeling grim and felt like I needed to stop for a serious call of nature. However, I managed to keep going and the feeling passed. I was some two miles from Forres and gradually it got closer. There are two nasty little hills as you enter Forres, which I felt hard. I was very glad to see the sports field in Grant Park and I was soon on my last lap. Alastair's time was a great 2-13-45, the fastest in the world that year. Hugh Mitchell ran 2-25-16 and I achieved 2-29-08, with Brian Goodwin 4th in 2-38-21 and Peter finishing 5th of the 11 starters. I had two blisters on my right foot.*

A month later a hill race caused a blister so bad that it became infected and I had to go to hospital for an operation under general anaesthetic! Then my Achilles tendons became painful; but before long the racing continued as frequently as ever.

REVIEW

Three marathons in less than two and a half months! Looking back at my diary, I can see that the pattern had been set for the next few years. Only ultra-marathons remained to be tackled. I had a voracious appetite for racing nearly every weekend. Cross-country, road, track and hill racing – the surface mattered little to me in the mid-60s. However, it also seemed clear that my attempts to be a sprinter were in the past; my training involved considerably increased mileage as well as faster running; and already there were hints that the longer the race (particularly on the road), the better result might be achieved.

Six years earlier, during my last year at secondary school I started to enjoy learning and began to produce some good results, but I had left this urge to study rather late. I decided while working at my electronics technician job at R.G.I.T. that I wanted to extend my education to degree level in electrical or electronic engineering. The first step on this road would be obtaining the required 'Higher' subjects and grades to allow entry to a BSc. A route to this end by evening classes would take several years, so I decided to go into full time education, which should give me access in two years. I worked my notice at R.G.I.T. and finished there in late August. I was fortunate to be given a yearly Further Education Bursary of £259 by Aberdeen City Education Committee, to support me during my proposed two years of study.

I enrolled at Aberdeen College of Commerce in Holburn Street in late August and my 'O grade' subjects were to be: English, Mathematics, Chemistry, Physics and Modern Studies.

At the Glenurquhart Highland Games at Drumnadrochit on 27th August I ran in the half-mile handicap and in the one-mile handicap, finishing 7th and 3rd respectively. I then ran in the hill race and recorded my diary: *In the hill race I ran easily with the leaders and was 3rd at the top and still in contact. I took the lead, from Mike Davis of Reading and Ian Grant on the descent and led onto the path, but by the road, Ian had taken the lead. I passed him and kept ahead back to the Games field, where I piled on the pace on the track so that I could not be caught. There were 19 in this race so I was pleased with my victory.*

In the Ben Nevis race the following Saturday, I wrote in my diary: *went off quite hard from the start to get up with Mike Davis, who I had decided to follow. As we ascended the path I was surprised that I found it relatively easy, compared to last year. I was able to run well and got past some runners. At the 'Red Burn', where there is a choice of route, I chose the path in preference to the scree, which Davis and a few others chose. I was still going surprisingly well and at the top I was 9th. I stopped to put my shoe on properly as my heel had come out. On the way down I was passed by, about five runners, while I only passed one. I fell once but managed to continue and passed another fellow only to be re-passed further down. When I got back to the road my legs felt very queer and I was tired. I closed on the chap ahead but did not catch up. I finished thirteenth in 1-54-34: an improvement of 36 places and 15-47 over last year. Peter Duffy was 2nd at the top and finished eighth in 1-51-01, his best ever. If I try this race again I require to get stronger, to be able to run up faster and also practice running downhill. I think that I will stick to the path going up. After my shower I had my cuts cleaned by a Red Cross lady. The coffee made with milk was very good.*

Alan McRae of Lochaber AC won in 1-43-49, from Bobby Shields of Clydesdale Harriers (1-45-49) and there were 117 finishers. Next day I was a little stiff, but not nearly as bad as the previous year, but my arms were very painful and so were my shoulders and ribs.

On 24th September in the Nairn to Inverness road relay along the A96, I ran the first stage and handed over in the lead to Alastair. He set a new second stage record of 18-03 and handed over to Mel Edwards, who then handed over to Duncan Davidson, who set a new record for this last stage. We were all pleased that our A.A.A.C team won in a new course record. Aberdeen University Hare & Hounds were second and Dundee Hawkhill Harriers third.

Once I had settled into the College of Commerce I trained at lunchtimes from there, changing in the college gym changing rooms, running routes down to the Bridge of Dee and out the South Deeside road and back or to Inverdee football pitches for repetition 220 yards or 440 yards. Alternatively, I would run up to Hazlehead and around the pony track. Once or twice a week I would drive to Kings College and run intervals on the grass there, usually with company. I also went to Linksfield stadium to run sessions of 40 X 220 yards with the usual 220 yards recoveries. These sessions were rather tedious and I began to question their benefit. After classes finished in the afternoon I ran my second session, unless it was a club night, when I waited and trained at Linksfield with company.

In preparation for the Edinburgh to Glasgow relay on Saturday the 19th of November we travelled down to Edinburgh the evening before and booked into Pirie's Hotel. I did not sleep well for some reason and at breakfast I made the mistake of having porridge followed by two poached eggs and then coffee, which was not appropriate as I was to run the first stage. I had a horrible run, feeling ill and struggled to the changeover in 16th. Alastair Wood ran next and was 5th fastest, gaining 7 places. Graham Reid was 12th fastest on stage three and lost two places. Bill Ewing was 2nd fastest on stage four and improved 4 places. Steve Taylor ran next, recording the third fastest time and improved three places. Mel Edwards was fastest on stage six and picked up one place. Ian Mackenzie ran a great seventh stage, finishing 2nd fastest and moving us to second team, a magnificent performance. Innis Mitchell ran the last stage and was 8th fastest. Poor Innis went the wrong way at a turning and lost 3rd place, which was very disappointing.

I wrote in my diary: *I feel like a thief as I virtually stole the medals from the Aberdeen team with my bad run. It was very unfortunate that I ran poorly in such an important race, when others are depending on you.*

When Peter Duffy moved from Aberdeen to Wishaw in October 1966 because of his work with the Customs and Excise, Alastair Wood suggested that I should train from his home in Cairnaquheen Gardens on Sundays and I readily agreed to this. Every run from there had an uphill start on Kings Gate before continuing to Hazlehead Park and then much further on paths and roads, usually for fifteen miles or more. After the run, being conservationists, or supporting the Aberdonian myth, we shared the bath water. Alastair would go first and then it was my turn and I could add some more hot water as necessary. His wife Jean would give me a welcome cup of coffee and a biscuit before I drove back to Little Ythsie.

I had decided to enter the Morpeth to Newcastle 13-mile race to be held on the last day of 1966, and in preparation averaged 94 miles for three weeks, with one at 100 miles, mainly steady runs, but with one interval session a week. On Friday the 30th of December I drove down to West Hartlepool to stay overnight with old neighbours, the Bushnells.

Next morning, I met Joe Clare at the rail station and we headed off for the race start. This was the largest race in which I had participated and there were an estimated 60,000 spectators along the route. I finished 42nd in 1-12-44, which was 3-16 inside the Road Runners Club (RRC) first class standard. I finished ahead of Hugh Mitchell, which pleased me. Mel Edwards was 4th and Joe Clare was 137th. Afterwards Joe came with me to West Hartlepool, where he too stayed overnight with the Bushnells.

During 1966 I had run and raced a total of 3867 miles (1300 more than 1965) at an average of 72.4 miles per week.

1967

On New Year's Day we ran 6 miles, accompanied by Alistair Bushnell in his van. Then I drove back to Aberdeen with Joe. Unfortunately, the heater in my van was not functioning and the weather was rather cold, so Joe's and my teeth were chattering well before the Scottish border. Poor Joe was quite miserable by the time we reached Aberdeen.

A week after the 3rd northeast cross-country league race on the 14th of January 1967, we travelled to the East District Cross Country Championships from Newcraighall Baths in Edinburgh. Bob Jenner, our driver had to drive at up to 75 miles per hour between Dundee and Edinburgh to get there before the start. I enjoyed the varied course and had a good run to finish tenth. Mel Edwards won from Bill Ewing, Ian Mackenzie was sixth and Steve Taylor was eighth. We won the team trophy from Edinburgh University, by 32 points.

The final northeast cross-country league race in St Andrews was my best cross-country race yet, when I finished fourth behind Ian Mackenzie, Peter Duffy and Alastair Wood, who finished only two seconds ahead of me.

On the 18th of March we were back again at the North Inch road relays. I ran the first leg and had one of my best ever runs, hanging onto Jim Wight and Don McGregor and handed over in 5th place, ahead of Don and two seconds down on Wight. Ian Mackenzie ran next, followed by Bill Ewing, who brought us up to 2nd place. Mel Edwards ran the last lap in 13-43 to set a new lap record and was just two second behind Ian Young of Edinburgh University at the end. Edinburgh University Hare and Hounds won this exciting race by two seconds from Aberdeen A.A.C, with last year's winners Victoria Park AC third.

On the first of April in the Tom Scott memorial 10 miles road race from Law to Motherwell, Alastair ran very well finishing 5th in 48-44, I was in 18th in 51-07, Ian Mackenzie was 20th in 51-34 and Peter Duffy finished 22nd in 51-44. I noticed that I produced dark urine afterwards. Lachie Stewart won in 46-41, from Ian McCafferty and Andy Brown. We were third team behind Motherwell YMCA and Edinburgh Southern Harriers.

By mid March I had started running a 20 miles road and country loop from College at lunchtimes on Mondays as my timetable allowed this. On other weekdays I would run nine miles on roads at lunchtimes and then after classes run a second session, which could be a steady run or intervals such as: 12 X 440 yards with 440 yards jog recovery or 30 X 220 yards with 220 yards recovery jogs in 90 seconds. Occasionally I would also include a session of 8 or 6 X 880 yards with the same distance or less recovery jog. Because of this volume of running my weekly mileage was passing 100 miles fairly frequently from then on.

On the sixth of May I was back at Seedhill track in Paisley for the SAAA track 10 miles championships. In pouring rain I finished 8th in 53-36, with Peter Duffy 10th in 53-45. Lachie Stewart won from Don Macgregor.

A week later I travelled with Alastair in his car to Shettleston for the marathon on a cool day with a N.E wind. I went with the leaders, passing 5 miles in 27-23 and 10 miles in 54-55, 15 miles in 1-22-25, 20 miles in 1-52-31 and finished third in 2-29-59 on very painful feet – this was the worst that I had felt after a marathon. Alastair won in 2-23-02 from Hugh Mitchell, who finished in 2-26-11. My prize was two 'Downie' blankets, plus a pair of pillowcases. I was rather nauseous on the journey back to Aberdeen, probably due to dehydration.

In June I ran well in our club three miles championships at Linksfield Stadium. Alastair won in 14-6.9 and I finished second in 14-42, two seconds ahead of Joe Clare. I covered the first mile in 4-40 and two miles in 9-45, which was a personal best, as was my three miles time, so I was pleased.

My next marathon was the Scottish Marathon Championships from Grangemouth Stadium on Saturday the 24th of June. I had tapered by not running on Thursday and Friday and on Friday afternoon I drove to Wishaw to stay with Peter, Rita and their daughters, Sheila and Sharon.

My diary entry for that day read: *I felt good and decided to go with Alastair and Hugh Mitchell. Unfortunately, we were misdirected by an incompetent marshal and had run about 25 yards before he realized his mistake and called us back. As a result of this we ran an extra 50 yards and found ourselves at the tail of the field. Alastair and I worked up to the front and ran together passing five miles in 26-12 and ten miles in 52-50. We eventually reached the turn and were given the time of 1-11. Alastair was displeased with this and started to push on. We met the rest of the field, who were approaching the turn and I was pleased to see such a large gap to Hugh, who was third. Shortly after 14 miles I had to let Alastair go and struggled on at my own pace. The miles passed slowly and my feet became more painful. Peter Duffy and his family were watching the race, and gave me*

Alastair shouting on Donald. Rita Duffy cheering beside him, holding her daughters' hands.

encouragement, as did Hugh, who had dropped out at 18 miles. As I went down by the canal-side I almost choked because of phlegm stuck in my throat. Eventually the stadium was in sight and I was soon struggling around the track, in lane six as directed, to the finish and received a sizeable cheer from the spectators. I was very thankful to be finished although my feet were in quite good condition despite their pain. The presentation was held at about 5 p.m. and we had to climb onto a rostrum to receive our medals. It was a proud moment for me — my first Scottish championship silver medal. Alastair got a cup and a laurel wreath on his head. Many people warmly congratulated me and I felt great. I also felt proud when running with Alistair at the front of the race.

Results: 1) A Wood 2-21-26, 2) D Ritchie 2-27-48, 3) A Wight 2-29-36, 4) B Goodwin 2-29-56, 5) G Eadie 2-30-44, 6) J K Wight 2-34-34

I spent a very pleasant weekend with Peter, Rita and family. Peter and I worked on Peter's car on Saturday night and again on Sunday after our easy five miles run.

At Alyth Highland games the following Saturday I ran in the handicap half-mile, finished well back and next ran in the handicap one-mile and finished second to Ian Mackenzie. I just managed to stay in front of Alastair. My prize was many cans of soup, beans, peas, sauces and pickles!

On the 8th of July, I drove from home to Inverness with Peter Duffy for the Inverness to Forres marathon. Alastair won in 2-16-00 with me a very poor and tired second in 2-35-00. My training diary report was: *Peter dropped out at 13 miles because of a blister, which allowed a Shettleston runner to take third place. I have never felt so bad in a marathon before. I went with Alastair for about 5 miles, but found it very hard and had to let him go. I felt that I was running fairly well until 13 miles, when I began to experience restricted breathing and extremely painful legs. I struggled on shuffling along at jogging pace. The miles passed painfully and I felt like giving up many times. Eventually I reached Forres and Grant Park. I felt that I was almost walking around the track lap at the finish. I was extremely relieved to have finished this race.*

To run two good marathons in two weeks was impossible for me at that stage and a poor three miles track race at the Inverness Highland Games the following week emphasised that I required more than a week to recover from a marathon race.

On Monday the 17th of July I started my summer job with my old firm, A.M Mackie's in Inverurie. A second television channel, Independent Television (ITV) was now becoming available, being transmitted from a mast in Kincardineshire at Durris. The signal was fairly good around Inverurie, so there was a demand for this additional channel, but this required an additional 'Band 3' aerial. Over that summer I drove to aerial installation jobs in Inverurie and around the local area in an Austin mini-van, which was great fun to drive, with my 'Loon' (apprentice) Jake. Usually the aerial could be installed in the house loft-space, but sometimes an outside aerial would be necessary, but whatever the location the signal from it was 'matched' with the signal from the BBC1 'Band 1' aerial to the down-lead to the television receiver. Once the new aerial was pointing in the correct direction, towards Durris, I would 'tune in' the receiver to receive the new channel and then the aerial direction would be adjusted slightly if necessary to obtain the optimum picture quality. Sometimes the signal strength was low and the resulting 'picture' was rather 'snowy', but customers accepted that that was the best we could do.

During my lunchtime in Inverurie I would fit in a training session and then train again on returning home. An example of a training day then was: 22 X 220yds in the Park in Inverurie after running up from the workshop. At night I ran 2 X approximately 660yds in; 95 seconds and 102 seconds taking 4 minutes rest between. I finished with 2 X 220yds run at full speed.

One Sunday in August I went for a training run up and down Ben Nevis while my Grandfather timed me and found that my time from the car park to the top and back was 2 hours. I was very tired indeed and stopped three times for drinks from streams. On the way down I became dizzy and had to stop and rest for some seconds. I tried a different descent and was quite pleased about it.

At the Glenurquhart Highland Games at Drumnadrochit I ran in the hill-race and finished first in 20-44, beating Mike Davis from Reading. I took an early lead and flogged myself up the hill and reached the top first. There I was delayed as a woman from the Civil Defence insisted on signing her name on my race number. She presumably delayed the others by a similar length of time. I managed to stay in front on the downhill section and, reaching the road, pushed on and finished about 100yds ahead of Davis, feeling ill from my effort.

Monday the 28th of August I returned to Aberdeen College of Commerce, to study Higher English, Maths and Physics. I went training with Mel Edwards but soon felt the pace too fast and by about 8 miles I felt grim and could hardly walk, let alone run. I finished the 14 miles road circuit in 1-29 as opposed to Mel's 1-21.

On the 2nd of September I was back at 'The Ben' race and finished 11th; my diary entry was: *I felt easy for a start and ran with the leaders, but as we reached the hill I began to slow slightly and then ran with Peter Duffy for a while and felt quite good. Shortly before half way up we were enveloped in mist and it became bitterly cold as wind and a mixture of sleet and rain blasted us. By the time I was reaching the top, my hands and feet were numb. As I turned at the top I began to shiver as I faced the blast and could not stop shivering and could not run fast. My head began to feel light and I had difficulty staying upright. I strayed off the path on the way down and as a result lost some time. I began to feel warmer as I got lower, but I fell once. Eddie Campbell passed me going at a great pace, giving me a shock. I reached the road and managed to pass one runner and reduce Eddie's lead from half a mile to 22s at the end. I was disappointed at missing 10th place, which is the last of the medals. My time was 4-27 slower than last year due to the bad conditions. I was, however, only 2-22 behind Peter Duffy who finished in 8th place, the same place as he occupied last year. Mike Scott finished 30th, My club-mate, Brian Craig, after reaching the top, collapsed on the way down and was taken down on a stretcher suffering from exposure. He was taken to the Belford Hospital where he was given a warm bath to bring back the heat to his body.* I had given Brian a lift through from Keith, so I was responsible for getting him back. He was released from Hospital at about 9pm so we reached his home in Keith at about 12-30 and I reached home at 2am.

Bobby Shields had won the race in 1-41-11 from Mike Davies who finished in 1-45-07. There were 131 finishers in this classic race that year.

In the Knockfarrel hill race I finished second, 41 seconds behind John Linaker of Pitreavie AC and 15 seconds ahead of Peter Duffy. I felt that I was running strongly and was pleased with my performance and time, which was 1-16 faster than last year. We were beaten by one point in the team race, which went to Forres Harriers.

In mid-November I was part of a strong Aberdeen AAC team in the Edinburgh to Glasgow Road Relay. Bill Ewing ran the first leg in 27-26 and arrived in second place behind Jim Alder, who ran 26-54. Mel Edwards went next and took us into the lead with the fastest stage time of 29-14. Joe Clare was on stage three and ran very well, keeping the lead and running the second fastest time on this stage of 22-09. Although I felt that I was running fast on stage four I dropped two places. I hung on to the Shettleston runner for about three quarters of a mile before he got away. My time of 31-44 was 7th fastest. Steve Taylor went next and recorded the fastest time on the 5th Stage of 28-03, moving us to second. Alastair was 6th fastest on stage 6, with 33-48 and dropped to third again. Ian Mackenzie maintained third with the third-fastest time (29-39) on stage 7. Terry Baker ran brilliantly, setting a new stage record of 23-17 and moved to joint second. Actually, near the finishing line, a taxi prevented him from overtaking the Shettleston runner. A dead heat was announced, which met with general approval. I was the weakest runner in our team, but it was a very good team performance. The special race medals were sponsored by 'The News of the World' and showed Edinburgh Castle on one side and Glasgow's George Square on the other.

In December I was quite pleased to finish 6th in the northeast cross-county league race in Aberdeen. Also that month our team of Alastair Wood, Joe Clare, Terry Baker and I finished second in the 'Fernieside' road relays in Edinburgh, behind Victoria Park AC, but ahead of Edinburgh Southern Harriers (ESH).

At the end of 1967 I had a total training and racing mileage of 4372 miles and November was my highest month with 531 miles, so my training volume was gradually increasing, because I was doing longer road runs and fewer interval sessions and also some of my Sunday runs with Alastair were twenty miles long.

1968

On New Year's Day 1968, after staying once more with the Bushnells in West Hartlepool, I ran in the Morpeth to Newcastle 13-mile race and finished 26th in 1-11-11, which was 1-33 faster than the previous year. I was disappointed, as I had hoped to do better. Joe Clare finished in 17th place in 1-10-14. I might have run a better time if I had tried to run an even pace race instead of going too quickly over the first two miles.

In February we were back at Hamilton Park Racecourse for the Scottish cross-country championships, where I did not run particularly well, finishing 48th. I felt very tired and my calf muscles were very painful. I found that I was slipping and wished that I had worn my studs rather than the 'tiger cubs' I was wearing. Our team was narrowly beaten into second by Edinburgh University, with a total of 93 points compared to our 94 points. Mel Edwards was 9th, while Bill Ewing, Peter Stewart, Alastair Wood, Steve Taylor and Joe Clare all finished close together between 14th and 20th place. Terry Baker was about 33rd and Peter Duffy was about 36th. Tom McCook was somewhere in the fifties. Tom McCook, formerly of Inverness Harriers and AAAC, was by then working in Birmingham and had joined Birchfield Harriers. He had suggested to his very talented club-mate Peter Stewart, whose father was Scottish, from Musselburgh, that he run in this championships for Aberdeen AAC.

A snowy NE League race, January 1968). R to L in finishing order: Bill Ewing, Steve Taylor, Alastair Wood and Donald Ritchie.

At the North Inch road relay in Perth in March, our AAAC team of Bill Ewing, Steve Taylor, Joe Clare and I finally won this event in 57-33. Victoria Park AC finished second in 58-42 and Edinburgh University Hare and Hounds were a close third in 58-55. Gareth Bryan Jones of Edinburgh University ran 13-36, which was a new record for the course.

I had applied to Aberdeen University for a place on the BSc Electrical Engineering course and received provisional acceptance. I was classed as a 'mature' student and I had to achieve two 'B' grades and a 'C' in the Higher subjects that I was studying at College, so I now knew the minimum standard required of me. I never considered applying to another University.

In the Scottish Track Ten miles championships at Seedhill track, Paisley in May, rain poured throughout the race and there was an annoying wind blowing. I decided to go with Joe Clare and did this for 4.5 miles, after which I began to lose contact with him. I lapped Innis Mitchell and Peter Duffy and was lapped myself by Lachie Stewart on the second last lap. Joe finished second in a time of 51-15, only 25s behind Lachie who recorded 50-50 and I was third in 52-19. I wrote in my diary: *I was pleased at getting third as I now have Scottish championship bronze and silver medals. All I need now to complete the set is a gold medal. My one-mile times ranged from 5-05 to 5-22, my 5 miles time was 25-36 and 6 miles was 30-57. My fastest lap was 76 seconds and my slowest, the 39th, was 84 seconds.*

A week later I ran in the Shettleston marathon on a course that had been altered because of road alterations and this, I believe, had made the course more difficult because of the extra hills included. I went with Alastair Wood from the start, as did Gordon Eadie and we passed through 10 miles in 55-25, about 40yds behind Alastair. I could not understand why the times were so slow as I felt that the effort I was putting in justified faster times. I ran with Gordon until 14 miles, at which point he began to draw away. I reached 20 miles in the poor time of 1-54-49, feeling very weak and could barely get up small hills. I noticed that Gordon was slowing down and I gradually drew nearer to him and reduced the gap to 15yds with half a mile remaining. As we reached the track he increased his pace and the gap between us. I was glad to be finished, as usual, but very disappointed with my poor time of 2-34-13. Alastair was first in 2-25-27 and Gordon finished in 2-34-04 and Peter Duffy was fourth in 2-35-24, so we won the team race. There were 24 starters but only 10 finishers. On the drive home with Alastair I had to request him to stop three times to allow me to vomit.

At the East District Athletics Championships at Pitreavie track, Dunfermline, towards the end of May, I ran in the three miles, finishing 5th in 14-47.4. I was disappointed at not running a faster time, but I suppose that it was reasonable in the strong wind.

In the Dundee 13 miles road race the following weekend I finished 3rd in 65-23-00, behind Don Macgregor, 62-29 and Alistair Matson, 64-40, with Dave McLean 4th, 65-40. Rain poured throughout the race so our clothes were sodden.

Four days later on Wednesday evening, I ran in the Club 6 miles track championship at Linksfield, improving my personal best to 30-32.4 in finishing 3rd behind Alastair and Steve.

Three days later I picked up Alick Howie in Aberdeen, Ian Mackenzie and Duncan Davidson in Forres and continued to Fort William for the Spean Bridge to Fort William 9 miles road race. Ian Mackenzie and I ran stride for stride, mile after mile. At the top of the small hill, opposite the Aluminium Factory entrance, I made a break and got clear of him and went on to win in 45-35, which was 2-09 faster than last year. Ian ran 46-13 and Duncan Davidson was third in 46-59. To my surprise, AAAC won the team prize from Forres Harriers by two points, with Charlie Greenlees, who had not wanted to run because of a cold, finishing 4th with Alick 6th.

ANOTHER SCOTTISH CHAMPIONSHIP SILVER

My next marathon was the Scottish Marathon Championships from Grangemouth Stadium on the 22nd of June: I decided to go with Alastair Wood and we went through one mile in 5-10. We passed five miles in 26-03. I began to feel that I was running too fast and I indicated this to Alastair, who adjusted his pace slightly and said that we would run together to 10 miles. We passed the ten miles point in 53-01. Alastair reached the turn in 69-08 and I turned at 69-55. On the return journey we had to face a fairly stiff headwind and I do not run very well into a wind at any time and found myself slowing right down. I reached 20 miles in 1-52-00 and struggled over the last painful six miles. Alastair Matson had dropped out, but Don Turner was gaining on me. I felt a muscle in my right leg cramping and I could not straighten or bend it. On reaching the track I was 80yds ahead, but by the finish it was down to 60yds. I was very glad to be finished and began vomiting after drinking a cup of tea. Alastair won in 2-21-18, I was second in 2-32-25 and Don Turner was a close third in 2-32-42.

At the Forres Highland games in the Grant Park two weeks later, on my 24th birthday, in the North of Scotland AAA 2 miles championships, Alastair Wood won in 9-18.6 and I was second in 9-32. The grass track was seven laps to the mile. I was pleased with my time, which was a personal best. Later I ran in the handicap mile off scratch, which meant I ran the full distance and finished 6th in 4-32.

On Tuesday the 9th of July I started a summer vacation job as a television service technician at Clydesdale TV service workshop in Aberdeen. I was surprised to find that the manager was David Leslie a friend from TV servicing days in Inverurie. By now colour television transmission was underway so I got the opportunity to see some of the colour television receivers, which was a new experience for me. I had to adjust my training schedule to accommodate this work. At lunchtimes I ran to Westburn Park and did interval sessions on the grass there and in the evening I would run my 9 miles road route.

On Friday evening the 26th of July, I started my journey to Cwmbran in South Wales for the AAA marathon championships, which were also the selection race for the Great Britain Olympic team members. I caught a train from Aberdeen at 7:15pm, which arrived in Edinburgh at 11:15, then the 12:05pm sleeper train to Birmingham, which was a new experience for me. I was surprised how small the sleeper compartment was and how warm it was; I could feel the sweat running off me at times. In Birmingham I boarded a train to Newport at 08:15 and arrived there at 10:15 and made my way to the bus depot, caught a bus to Cwmbran and arrived there at about 11:10. I walked to the Sports Centre and left my kit there and set out to find the guesthouse where Alastair was staying.

I found this and there met Mel Edwards, Dunky Wright (Sports Journalist), Jim Alder and Ron Hill assembled there. Ron made some comments on my long journey, as did Jim. My Diary entry was: *We all had tea together and I was keenly interested in the conversation they had. We rested for a while and at 2 p.m. we made our way to the stadium. The entry of 106 runners included all the best marathon runners in the country and at 3:15 we were underway. I planned to run a steady race aiming for a 10 miles time of 54-30 and the next ten in 55-00. After running two miles I began to get the impression that it was a terrifically long way between mile markers. At 5 miles I was still running quite well in a bunch, which included Ron Franklin. By six miles I could feel my feet burning as the heat from the road got through to my tired feet.*

I learned later that the temperature during the race was between 73°F and 75°F and we were subject to direct sunshine most of the way. By 7 miles I was feeling like dropping out as I realised that I was flagging and had no drive at all. I reached 10 miles, very tired indeed in 56- 00. The course was three laps with a great many sharp turns, was hilly and with only about 4 miles of flat in all. The temptation to drop out was great, but I resisted and struggled on for long mile after long mile to reach 20 miles in 1-59-something. My only aim then was to finish the course and I was helped in this respect by the encouragement of the many spectators, but those last six miles seemed never-ending. At last I reached the track and finished in the poor time of 2-44 in 33rd position. I made my way to the changing rooms and sat there, feeling ill and too exhausted to move for about 45 minutes. My upper arms were white and rough with crystallised salt due to sweating. This is the first marathon in which I drank liquid during the race. I found that water was best, as diluted squash left a horrible aftertaste. I came to the conclusion that taking drinks had no beneficial effect on me and so was unnecessary. I drank some Lucozade and then some milk and vomited it up about 30 minutes later.

I met Tom McCook and informed him that I was mad to spend £13 to come down here to run another marathon. I had buzzing in my ears and I could not hear myself, so I suppose that I must have sounded rather strange.

Alastair was 6th in 2-20, Mel 7th in 2-21 and Joe Clare 14th in 2-24-50. I went by taxi with Alastair, Mel and Joe to the railway station and caught a train for Crewe at 7:35pm. I felt rotten on the train and had to vomit again. Later, I began to feel better and managed to get a compartment to myself, where I slept until Crewe. Here I had a 1 hour 45 minutes wait for the Edinburgh train, which was crowded, and as a result we were allowed to use the first class carriages, so I got a compartment where I was able to sleep until Edinburgh. I got a train to Aberdeen, arriving there at 11:15 a.m. and then drove home.

I realized later that I was quite badly dehydrated and also that it was necessary to try to replace lost water and electrolytes during a marathon, but electrolyte replacement drinks with glucose (ERG) had not been invented then.

In my Diary I reflected: *I do not understand why I cannot run a good marathon this year. I have been doing a greater volume of running and have been improving over the shorter races. I have been training differently, however, omitting repetition 220yds and 660yds. I feel it is my stamina that has diminished. Before this race I cut down on my mileage, so I cannot be over-trained, which I thought might be the case at the Scottish marathon. At the moment training seems more of a mystery than ever.*

In September I competed in the Ben Nevis race and finished a tired 65th, having driven to Caol near Fort William to stay with my Grandfather Ferguson and Margaret the night before. By the Red Burn I felt completely drained of energy and my body seemed to refuse to exert itself. I struggled on, with runners passing me continuously as I felt sick and weak. Eventually I reached the top and started my careful descent so that many less cautious runners passed me. On the lower slopes I discovered some blaeberries and I paused to pick and eat some. My time of 2-16-42 was my slowest ever.

Mike Davis won by almost six minutes in 1-39-29. I wrote in my diary: *I am disappointed, but realize that if I want to do well in this race I must train regularly on hills/mountains and spend at least two weeks running on the Ben prior to the race. Also I would have to throw caution to the wind on the descent in the same way I used to. I now have the fear of a serious accident on the descent, so in view of this I have decided to give the 'Ben' race a miss in future.*

A week later at the Knockfarrel Hill race I was pleased to win in 40-11, ten seconds ahead of Peter Duffy who was just eight seconds ahead of Joe Clare. Next day I discovered that I had an injury to a ligament under the instep of my right foot, which caused a lot of discomfort.

ABERDEEN UNIVERSITY

Having achieved the required grades in the higher exams I enrolled at Aberdeen University to begin my BSc Electrical Engineering degree course. During fresher's week (for First Year Students) I joined the Hare and Hounds club and put an application in to join the University Air Squadron. After my first run with the Hare and Hounds club, Colin Youngson, the club captain, teased by referring to me as 'the greatest middle-aged Fresher' when I was first in the cross-country 'team trial' race, reducing his fresher's record by four seconds.

My Mum and Dad were in a 'tied' house at Little Ythsie Farm, as was normal practice for farm workers. The farmer, as part of the employment deal, provided the house and this meant that some provision would have to be made for when my parents retired from work. Mum arranged to purchase a top storey one bedroom flat at Number 22 Howburn Place, off Holburn Street in Aberdeen for their retirement. My sister Anne and her friend Dorothy Watson, both of whom worked in Aberdeen were able to stay there, until my parents required it.

Some time after I started my course at Aberdeen University I began to stay in Aberdeen, which saved me a lot of driving to and from Aberdeen from Little Ythsie. Mum and Dad had bought a larger flat on the ground floor at 89 Willowbank Road, so I was able to share this with Anne and Dorothy. Once I moved to Willowbank Road I used to run to Steve Taylor's home, which was only four minutes away in the right direction towards Alastair's, meet him and then we would run, sometimes racing each other, up to Alastair's for the 'Sunday run'. The number on these runs varied, with the minimum being Alastair, Steve and I, but could be as many as 7. Usually the pace picked up and gradually runners began to drop behind, including me on several occasions.

I had my first race representing Aberdeen University Hare and Hounds in the Kingsway road relay, Dundee; and my second the following Saturday in an Inter-University cross-country race at Westerlands in Glasgow. John Myatt of Strathclyde won in 36-42, I finished second in 37-17, with Colin Youngson third in 37-43. I had to stop and ask directions at one point as I had lost sight of Myatt and this lost me some time.

Following my interview to join the Aberdeen University Air Squadron I received a letter offering me a place and I readily accepted this opportunity. Since I was a young child I had always had a very keen interest in aircraft and as noted earlier I had applied to join the Royal Air Force on leaving school. The University Air squadron was one means of promoting the RAF and recruiting suitable graduates into the service. Squadron Leader Jack Butcher was in command, assisted by two flight lieutenants, an airman and a civilian called Kitty Morris, who looked after the office. Later I found out that Kitty's son Graham was on the same electrical engineering course as I was. I began my two-year engagement on the twelfth of December 1968, with the rank of 'Pilot officer' with service number, A2621016 and part of the RAF Volunteer Reserve. Our Mess was at Fairfield House and was run like an officers' mess at any RAF station, so I was introduced to mess bills, formal dinners and drinks receptions. We attended Fairfield House for lectures on meteorology, flight, engines and navigation. Following this there would be a short film about some aspect of RAF operations and then we would adjourn upstairs to the Bar. The upstairs lounge and bar were available for use on Saturday evenings, but I was not able to take advantage of this because I was racing somewhere most Saturdays and there was always a hard run to look forward to on Sunday morning.

Learning to fly took place at Dyce airport, now called Aberdeen International Airport, where the Air Squadron had a Hut left over from the previous RAF presence there. There were very few commercial flights to and from Dyce, probably just two each day then – North Sea oil developments were several years ahead. De Havilland Mark 10 Chipmunks, made in Canada, were the trainer aircraft we were to learn to fly with the aid of our instructor, who sat in the back seat. I was surprised to find that one's parachute was to provide the cushion for the metal seat. Squadron leader Butcher was my instructor and we got on very well together. Wednesday afternoons ('Sports Afternoon') and Saturdays were 'flying days', so I was not able to give total commitment to this because of Hare and Hounds 'club runs' on Wednesday afternoons and races on Saturdays. Running had skewed the direction of my life again.

At the East District Cross-country relay championships at Hazlehead in early November, our team of Colin Youngson, Charlie Macauley, Bob Anderson and I finished fifth, which we all thought was rather good.

The following Saturday we held the Hare and Hounds half marathon, which was two laps of our cross-country course. Bill Ewing's student record for this was 70-00, so I was well pleased with my time of 70-31. Colin Youngson was second in 71-07, closely followed by Jim Maycock with 71-18. I was awarded the Sawfish Trophy to retain for a year. This was the long flattish snout (of a large Ray) with regular 'teeth' sticking out along both edges.

In the Edinburgh to Glasgow road relay the following Saturday I ran for the AAAC team. Ian Mackenzie ran the first leg and finished in 7th place, but quite close to the leaders. Alastair Wood went next and ran brilliantly to set a stage 2 record of 28-32 and handed over to Peter Stewart, who was 2nd fastest on Leg 3. Joe Clare was on stage 4 and was overtaken by Dick Wedlock of Shettleston Harriers, who was fastest on that stage. Steve Taylor ran stage 5, but made no impression on Bill Scally's lead. Ian Stewart ran stage 6, the longest leg, and lost some time to Lachie Stewart. I ran stage 7, was second fastest but still lost 8 seconds to Les Meneely, who maintained the lead for Shettleston with the fastest stage time. Bill Ewing ran Stage 8 and ran very well to take 23 seconds off the previous record to secure our 2nd place.

On the following Saturday my parents were moving to Folla Rule near Rothienorman, so that morning I was occupied loading furniture into a cattle float (truck) from about 8am. Unloading was completed by 1:15 pm but in this process, because my arms and fingers were exhausted, I dropped a very heavy oak wardrobe on my foot. Not unexpectedly I ran fairly poorly in the Scottish Universities team trial over our cross-country course that afternoon, compounded by having arrived fifteen minutes before the start. I could only struggle on as best as I could to finish 7th to gain selection for the team to run against the Scottish Cross Country Union (S.C.C.U) team. John Myatt was first in a new course record of 33-26 and Colin Youngson ran well to finish fourth.

In the second North East cross-country league race the following Saturday, over the Aberdeen University course, Joe Clare and Steve Taylor dead heated in first. I finished 3rd after a race long tussle with teammate, Colin Youngson, who was just 7 seconds behind me at the finish.

The last race of the year was the SCCU versus the Scottish Universities annual match on the 14th of December at Camperdown Park in Dundee. I finished fifth counter for the university team in 14th place after a terrific battle with Harry Gorman, of the SCCU, who finally beat me by 5 seconds. Alastair Wood was 10th and Colin Youngson 21st.

My Dad, as he became older, wanted a less demanding job than that of a dairy cattleman and accepted a job looking after mainly young cattle at a farm at Folla Rule and my parents moved into a cottage there on the 23rd of November 1968. I stayed there once the Christmas break from University arrived and I enjoyed finding out new training routes. The weather was bitterly cold, a lot of snow fell and chilling winds blew it into huge drifts, some up to twelve feet high. I found the disused railway line from Banff to Turriff and on to Inverurie and it was fun, at least for the first thirty minutes, running through the snow and observing nature's 'snow sculptures' extending from some banks.

On totalling my training and racing miles in 1968 I found that this amounted to 4130 miles, which was an average of 79.5 miles per week.

1969

By the third of January 1969, the weather was beautiful, with the snow gone and I enjoyed a memorable rambling run: *From Folla Rule I ran over country, roads and woods, to the hill of Foundland, which I ran up. From the top I got a terrific view and could see the coast at Banff and the 'Prop' (hilltop tower) at North Ythsie.*

Two days later the snow was back and I had a difficult time on a road loop run. As the weather was not cold when I started, I wore no gloves or oil on my legs or a hat. With about 7.5 miles remaining, snow began falling, with big flakes the size of florins, very thick and wet, so within minutes I was plastered with snow. I pushed on, getting colder and colder as the wind drove this wet snow onto my body. I began to worry that I might succumb to exposure before I could reach home. The snow occasionally would blind me and my legs, face and arms became numb. Eventually I got home and staggered to the bath, having difficulty keeping my balance. In the bath I was shivering despite the hot water and my fingers went completely white. I was still shivering although sitting in front of a fire with plenty of clothes on for several minutes. I suppose that I must have been suffering from a mild case of hypothermia.

In the East District cross-country championships at Musselburgh, on the 18th of January, Adrian Weatherhead won, just 3 seconds ahead of Don McGregor, who in turn was 14 seconds ahead of Fergus Murray. Alastair was 6th, Bill Ewing 8th and I finished 10th.

Next day the Sunday run turned into a burn up. Alastair, Steve Taylor, Joe Clare, Colin Youngson and Bob Meadows and I started at a very pleasant pace and after about 50 minutes we were at the foot of Tyrebagger hill. Steve began to up the pace considerably, followed at intervals by the rest of us. The pace was now hard and maintained to Skene, eight miles from Aberdeen and here Steve pushed the pace further, so Alastair, Joe and I hung on. Joe and I managed to keep in contact for about three miles and I held onto Joe for a further half mile. My run had taken 2-00-00, while Bob was out for 2-15-00 and Colin thumbed a lift back to Aberdeen.

A week later our Hare and Hounds club team ran in the Scottish Universities cross-country championships at Heriot-Watt University campus. Dave Logue led me and Andy McKean and was pulling away at about four miles into the race. As we crossed a river and came to a junction, Dave turned left and we followed. Ken Fyffe (Heriot-Watt) of course knew the route and went straight ahead and the marshal at that junction called us back. I felt deflated as I turned after shouting to Dave and finding McKean and Colin Youngson ahead of me. I next discovered that Ian Picken was also ahead, which was very disheartening. I passed Colin and closed on McKean and Picken, but I was tired and could not get close enough to challenge them and the finish was always getting closer. Fyffe produced a good finish to beat Picken, who only just beat McKean. I finished 4th, 3 seconds behind McKean and 9 seconds ahead of probable winner Dave Logue, and Colin Youngson was 6th, 17 seconds behind Dave.

On the 1st of February at the British Universities Sports Federation (BUSF) cross-country championships at Graves Park in Sheffield, before the start, I ran around part of the seven and a half miles course and tried out barefoot running, which seemed okay, so I decided to run in bare feet like Ron Hill and Bruce Tulloh. On starting, however, I realized my mistake, because with so many runners, the ground became muddy and slippery very quickly and I was slipping all over the place instead of running strongly as I intended. After about three-quarters of a mile we had to run down a slippery bank and through a bog and along a short stony path and I lost about 20yds on this section on every lap. On parts of the course where I could get a grip, I ran well, but lost any advantage at corners. If only I had the sense to foresee that this would happen and worn studs instead, I estimate that I would have finished much further up than my disappointing 50th. Andy McKean was 20th and Fyffe 38th, while Colin, who had started far too fast, ended up 74th. Both Dave Logue, who was ill, and Ian Young were behind me. 312 finished the race. Afterwards we caught a train to York, where we all had a good drink in a few pubs while waiting for the overnight train from London to Aberdeen.

The following Saturday, the 8th of February, in the 4th and final northeast cross-country league race at Dundee. Bill Ewing won, ahead of Alastair and I finished 3rd, 11 seconds behind Alastair and 45 seconds ahead of Bob Heron.

A week later in a Seven Scottish Universities cross-country race in Camperdown Park in Dundee I was pleased to finish first, 26 seconds ahead of the Scottish Universities cross-country champion Ken Fyffe.

By the following Friday morning I had a painful throat and by afternoon I could hardly breathe and my chest was very painful and a doctor diagnosed influenza. This was very disappointing, as I had been looking forward to running in the Scottish National cross-country championships next day. This flu was quite severe, so no running was possible for several days and when I did resume running I was very weak.

At the meeting of the Aberdeen University Athletic Association Blues committee on the 12th of March, Colin J Youngson and I were awarded Full Blues for our cross-country running for the Hare and Hounds Club. We were informed that we could now wear Blues tie, scarf, blazer and sweater if we desired to do so. I was very pleased to receive this award but only purchased a blues tie (the blazer was light powder-blue and would have been very embarrassing to wear!)

On Saturday the 22nd of March I hired a minibus and drove with Hare and Hounds club members to see the International Cross-Country Championships at Clydebank, which was inspiring. Gaston Roelants of Belgium won the Senior Men's title after a dramatic battle with England's Dick Taylor. Scotland's Ian McCafferty was a valiant third. Dave Bedford of England won the Junior International title.

On Monday the 14th of April I started a five days detachment to RAF Kinloss, staying in the Officers' Mess. Most days were spent flying in Avro Shackleton Maritime reconnaissance aircraft, sometimes for several hours practising to locate a submerged submarine. It was an interesting five days and I learned quite a lot about life in the RAF at an operational station.

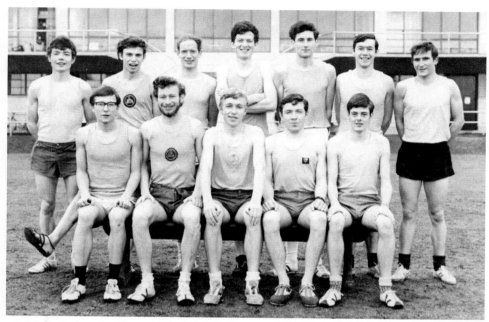

Aberdeen University Hare & Hounds Club, first team, session 1968-69

The Universities athletics season had started and I ran in inter-university track races at three miles and the new metric distance of 5000m. In the Aberdeen University Athletics Club six miles championships at Kings I finished first in 30-53.6 on the very soft grass track. At the Aberdeen University sports at Kings, I was 3rd in the one-mile in 4-41.2 and won the three miles in 14-59. I took my Dad to watch and he was proud to see me running and winning this race.

At the East District Athletics Championships at Grangemouth at the end of May, I ran in the longest track race, which was 5km. Fergus Murray won from Alistair Blamire and Don Macgregor. I finished 9th in 14-48, which was a personal best by 49s. I went through two miles in 9-24, which was also a personal best by 8s and three miles in 14-20, which was an improvement of 22s on my PB. I ran with Steve Taylor and Alastair Wood, who finished 7th and 8th respectively. I assumed that I would improve my 5km race time in some future race, but I never did.

Two weeks later I ran in the BUSF 10Km track championships at Motspur Park in the outskirts of London and made a major mistake in wearing new spikes without socks. My diary entry reminds me of my folly: *I felt quite good despite the heat for about a mile, but then became aware of my feet becoming very painful. I was not wearing socks in a brand new pair of Reebok spikes (K100 challenge at £2-17) and when I looked down I could see blood coming from the rim of one shoe. By about two miles I began to struggle with the pace and as my feet were worse, I had a great desire to drop out. As it would have been a disgrace to drop out of this race after travelling down from Aberdeen, I toddled around at a pace, which was not too severe on my feet. As a result, my time of 33-06 was well below what I was capable of and I was dejected by my performance. On taking off my shoes I counted 14 cuts, two blood blisters and 4 normal blisters and these will probably adversely affect my marathon next Saturday. I should have made sure that the spikes were comfortable and used in training before racing in them.*

The following Saturday, 21st of June, the Scottish Marathon Championship was held over the 1970 Commonwealth Games course from Meadowbank Stadium in Edinburgh. I suffered from more stupidity as I had a new pair of EB marathon racing shoes from West Germany, in which I had punched extra ventilation holes on the sides of the uppers. I did not realise that this would degrade their stability. I ran with Bill Stoddart from the start and at about three miles Jim Wight joined us. By five miles, as I was not wearing socks, I felt the side of my right foot burning and nipping, but I decided to push on and hope that it would get no worse. Jim dropped at about 7 miles and I passed through 10 miles in 54-16 six seconds behind Stoddart, but my right foot was giving me great pain, so at 11.5 miles I stopped to investigate. To my dismay, I found a burst blister of three inches diameter on the sole of my right foot and stopping had allowed the full pain signals to reach my brain. As a result, I could not bear to put my foot down flat to continue running. I returned to Meadowbank by ambulance and very disappointed at having to drop out. This was another mistake that I should learn from. Bill Stoddart won in 2-27-25 ahead of Hugh Mitchell 2-31-20and Peter Duffy 2-37-04.

Two weeks later, in the morning of the 5th of July I drove to Caol near Fort William, where I picked up my Grandfather and continued to Kinlochleven to compete in the Mamore hill race, which is 17 miles in length and is part of the Kinlochleven Highland games. My diary entry was: *At the start I had thoughts of wanting to win this race and ran with the leaders, Ian Leggett and Peter Duffy, for the first three miles up and over the tough ridge. Shortly after this Leggett pushed on, Peter and I resisted going with him, and we were soon joined by Ian Donald and Bobby Shields, both of Clydesdale, who ran with us for a while. Ian set out in pursuit of Leggett and caught him while Shields went away on the rough section around the side of the Mamore. When I reached the top of the route with Peter the leading trio were out of sight and by the time we had made our way gingerly down we were passed by another runner, so there were now three of us fighting for fourth place. On reaching the road my legs felt useless and I was unable to go with the runner who had caught us on the descent when he increased pace. Peter and I just ambled along as best we could, but after about a mile I began to feel my legs were recovering, so I was able to run faster. I left Peter and about two miles later caught the Dumbarton runner who had been with us as we started the road back and also caught Shields. I was now 3rd and could see that I was catching Ian Donald. I caught and passed him and shortly after saw Leggett about 600yds ahead, but I did not think that I had a chance of catching him. However, I realized that I was gaining on him and I felt a cold shiver pass through me when I knew that I could catch him. I caught him sooner than expected, because as I rounded a corner he was walking only 50yds ahead. In the lead I ran harder, determined not to be beaten now and began to feel quite strong over the last section through the town and into the Games field and enjoyed my moment of success. Peter finished 4th. My nipples were bleeding because of my sodden vest rubbing on them causing two great blood stained patches on my vest. The weather was bad with a howling gale and very heavy showers of rain.*

In the Inverness to Forres Marathon the following Saturday I found that I had not recovered from the Mamore race. At about Nairn I felt my strength going and from there I got progressively slower and was just jogging automatically. Just before 20 miles, Colin Youngson came past running well. I was reduced to a walk by 21 miles and had noises in my ears. Peter Duffy, who was walking faster than me, passed and at 23 miles I accepted a lift to Grant Park. Alastair Wood won in 2-27-44 ahead of Hugh Mitchell, 2-38 and Colin Youngson, 2-41-13.

Next day I had great difficulty walking on my right foot because of a blister one inch in diameter on the sole. I travelled down to RAF West Raynham in Norfolk, where our two-week Aberdeen University Air Squadron summer camp was to be held. On Monday my foot was extremely painful, but I did not get a chance to see about it because of the flying training, even though I had to go to the Medical Officer to get a smallpox vaccination. By Tuesday I had developed a swollen and painful gland in my right groin, indicating that the blister on my foot was septic. I went to the station sick bay where I was given sterile equipment with which I lanced my three blisters. The big painful one, when burst, gushed forth a yellow liquid. The Medical officer prescribed Penicillin tablets with instructions to take two every six hours. At 6pm my blister felt better after being lanced so I ran six miles on the roads with a bit of a struggle. On Wednesday after flying until 12:00, I and two other pilot officers went to Kings Lynn rail station at 13:00 to take a train for London and from there take another to Swindon. From there we got transport to RAF Lyneham arriving there at 21:45. There we were to be supernumerary crew on some of the transport aircraft.

On Thursday I flew to Gibraltar and back in a Britannia, a four-turboprop-engine personnel transport aircraft. I was surprised that the seats for the passengers were facing away from the direction of travel, because this was a safer arrangement in the event of an emergency landing.

I resumed training on returning from this short detachment and mixed 220 yards intervals, 440 yards intervals and 10-mile road runs, usually before dinner or at lunchtime, throughout the rest of my time at West Raynham. The weather was rather warm and the temperature reached 81°F on most days, so I sweated a lot into my parachute seat as I practised circuits and bumps under instruction, as I was not ready to 'go solo' yet.

After several days looking for summer vacation work I was pleased to accept a job at Abergeldie farm, which was between Ballater and Crathie on Deeside. This was a dairy farm where the milk produced was bottled on site and sold mainly in Ballater. My job was at about 08:00 each morning, to fill the two large metal sinks with cold water and in the left one add the required amount of sterilising solution and heat the water in the right hand sink to a high temperature by passing steam through it from the steam boiler just outside. Into this hot water I put the returned glass milk bottles along with some detergent for cleaning, about four crates' contents at a time. Next I had to take two bottles at a time and push them onto a three rotating brush mechanism at about chest height on the wall above the sinks and in front of me. Once I judged that the brushes had done their job I placed the cleaned bottles into the left tank. This process continued until the right sink was empty and the left one was full of clean bottles. These bottles were then placed in crates upside down to drip dry and then I would fill the right sink with returned bottles and the cycle was repeated until all the returned bottles had been cleaned and put in crates. These bottles were filled with cooled milk from a storage tank, four at a time in an appropriate apparatus and capped ready for delivery early next morning. I usually finished my work by about mid afternoon.

I stayed with one of the farm worker's family in Abergeldie cottages, so I did my training from there, usually in the early evening after an early evening meal, which was not ideal. I usually ran to Ballater and back, which was about twelve and three-quarter miles on quiet undulating roads. Sometimes I could fit a shorter session before tea, such as: 9 X 1 minute hard followed by 2 minutes easy, then 7 X up-hill sprints, which averaged 45s and had a 90s recovery jog.

On Saturday the 23rd of August I was allowed to finish work at 12:00, so after a rather large, for me, race day lunch I set off for Nethybridge at 12:30. I drove via the Lecht and Tomintoul to Nethybridge and soon got changed and did a warm-up in a nearby forest, where I ate some tempting blaeberries. I felt tired, probably because I had started work in the dairy at 08:00. The hill race I had been expecting was actually a new 7 miles road race to Dulnain Bridge and back. Bruce Jeffries and Joe Clare and I reached the turn together, where a gentleman in a deerstalker hat and tweeds indicated that we had to stop for him to stamp the backs of our hands with his stamp and inkpad. As I was leading marginally I was first to be stamped and waited until Bruce and Joe had been stamped before we resumed racing each other. With about 2.5 miles remaining I made an effort to break away and succeeded in moving 10yds ahead of Bruce with Joe a further 5yds behind. Having made my break, I could not afford to relax, so I pushed on not daring to look back and I had a feeling that the footfalls were getting closer. After an anxious time, I reached the Games field and was soon on my finishing lap, running strongly and now sure of winning. I finished in 35-35 eight seconds ahead of Bruce Jeffries who was in turn seven seconds ahead of Joe Clare, with Bob Meadows fourth. Next I ran in the one-mile and was out-sprinted by Ian Mackenzie in the last 80yds after a gentle first five laps. Then I ran in the relay for Aberdeen AAC and we got second place after the original winners were disqualified for some infringement.

Next Saturday I got my work finished by 12:00 again and after lunch, drove to Glenurquhart and had just enough time for a toilet visit and warm-up before the hill race at 4:00pm. I had quite a tussle with Alan McRae and Mike Davis. Mike passed me on the descent, but I caught him on the road and after a brief pause at his shoulder I pushed on and beat him by 90yds in 21-29. Alan McRae, the winner of the Ben Nevis race in 1966 was third. Alan told me that his training was 20 miles a day and an example was 8 miles in the morning in boots on a soft surface and 12 miles of fartlek on roads at night.

On the first of September I began training twice a day by introducing a 6.5 miles road loop each morning before my work in the dairy. I also increased my Sunday evening run to a 16.5 miles road loop to Ballater and then down the north Deeside road to Crathie, where I re-crossed the Dee by the suspension foot bridge and back to Abergeldie.

On Saturday the 13th of September I again finished my dairy work by midday and drove to Strathpeffer for the Knockfarrel hill race. Thirteen runners and Tom Mackenzie of Inverness Harriers, who was also an official of the North of Scotland AAA, had assembled there, but the organizers, Ross-shire roads, appeared to have forgotten about the race. We decided to have a race anyway and Peter Duffy led along the old railway line until bushes blocked our way. We found an opening leading up to the fields and Peter got out first and was 30yds away by the time I got through and could start running again. On the ridge I lost control and tumbled, which shook and winded me, so Peter pulled further ahead. A quick descent and two better than usual gate clearances brought me to within 10yds of Peter by the farm. I then ran hard to catch him and on doing so ran past trying to look powerful although I was feeling tired and doubted if I could hold the lead to the finish. I managed to hang on to finish in 39-33, which was 15s inside my previous best for this course. Peter was fifteen seconds behind and Joe Clare was third in 42-27. Tom Mackenzie happened to have three plaques in his car, so he presented these to the first three.

The following Saturday I ran the 3rd leg of the Nairn to Inverness road relay for Aberdeen University H&HC and managed to hold the lead that Charlie Macauley had built up through his strong run on leg 2. Colin Youngson had run well on the 1st leg and finished only about 25yds behind Joe Clare. Alastair ran 63s faster than me on the 3rd leg, which I found hard and was glad to reach the finish. Robin Orr, on leg 4 managed to hold on to secure a win (in front of AAAC) for the Hare and Hounds. I also ran the 4th leg as extra training.

On the 27th September, I finished my work at Abergeldie farm and said goodbye to my host family. I had enjoyed the varied experiences there, which included a Ceilidh at Balmoral Castle for the farm workers and their families.

In early October the cross-country season got underway with the first northeast league race at St Andrews, which Alastair Wood won by 3 seconds from Mel Edwards, who was 4 seconds ahead of me and Charlie Macauley, five seconds behind me. Bill Ewing, Colin Youngson and Joe Clare were next to finish in that order. AUH&H beat AAAC by one point!

At the Kingsway road relays a week later our Hare and Hounds club finished 8th, which equalled our best performance in this event. I ran the first leg in 14-05, an improvement of 12 seconds on my best for the course, but only 19th fastest on the day. Colin (14-09), Donald Macintosh (14-39) and Merv McIntyre (15-10) were my teammates.

I had been preparing for the Harlow marathon on the 26th of October, for two months and travelled down by train to London, with Alastair Wood and Joe Clare. I ran with the leading group of about ten for the first five miles, which we passed in 27-01. Shortly after this the pace increased and I decided to let them go. Joe Clare dropped from this group and I managed to regain contact with him and we passed 10 miles in 54-09. I ran with a Blackheath runner and we went through 20 miles in 1-49-35, which was a personal best. A couple of miles later my companion drew away, but I began to catch Joe and Mike Tagg, who I passed at 24 miles. I could not catch Joe or the Blackheath man although I was running quite well. I finished 9th in 2-24-38, which was pleasing and an improvement of 3-10 on my previous best. I did not find this marathon such a struggle as previous ones and my feet gave me no bother. The weather was quite good for running: light rain, but there was a wind. Alastair Wood was first in 2-19-15, seven seconds ahead of George Brockbank, with Ian Macmillan third in 2-20-34. Joe was seventh in 2-23-58 and there were 94 finishers.

Hare & Hounds Christmas 'fancy dress' Handicap 1969.

On Saturday the 13th of December in the Scottish Universities team against the S.C.C.U team at Paties Road, Colinton, I finished a tired 14th a foot behind my club mate Colin Youngson. We were 4th and 5th counters for the Universities team.

Miles run in training and races in 1969 totalled 3852.5 miles, which was an average of 74 miles per week.

DONALD RITCHIE IN THE SIXTIES by Colin Youngson

Having first taken part in the sport in 1962, by the end of 1969, Donald Ritchie had definitely become a good runner. He had: won Scottish Championship medals for the marathon and ten miles track; represented Scottish Universities in cross-country; and participated successfully in road and hill races, as well as reducing his best times considerably in shorter track events.

The man I had come to know as a friendly rival was quiet and soft-spoken, unless post-race beers had made him more talkative. At the age of 25 he was steadily improving as an athlete, due to a number of factors. Looking back over his progress in the Sixties, it is clear that he could not have been more enthusiastic about improving his running (dedicated, obsessive, utterly determined). It is also obvious not only that he never boasted but also that he seldom complained. Injury and pain was tolerated with stoical bravery. The Sixties had been a time for constant experiment in training: speedwork, fartlek, hill repetitions and especially long hard miles. It was no wonder that, while we were both at University, he beat me so frequently – he was three years more mature and often ran twice as hard and far in training.

Yet it seemed certain that Donald had not yet achieved his potential. Would he find the right training balance of speed and endurance? Would he ever learn to give himself adequate time to recover? Already his racing tactics were bold and daring – he often kept up with faster men as long as possible. One day he might defeat them all – but what would be his best events? The Seventies would provide the answer……..

THE SEVENTIES

1970

I began 1970 by running in the Morpeth to Newcastle race, a distance of 13 miles, finishing 18th in 1-11-23, which was 12s slower than my best for this race. Although 18th was my highest position, I was far from satisfied with my run.

Next day I travelled to RAF Colerne in Wiltshire for a detachment with Transport command. On Wednesday the seventh of January I joined the crew of a Britannia transport aircraft, which flew to RAF Akrotiri in Cyprus. There was no accommodation available for the crew on the RAF base so we were taken to a hotel in Limassol and we appeared to be the only guests there. After our dinner I went out with the crew to sample 'Brandy sours' and the nightlife. Next day the other pilot officer from Aberdeen University Air squadron, Ian Struthers, and I explored Limassol and enjoyed the experience. We made arrangements to hire a car and I picked it up early next morning. The car was a Morris 1100, and I set off driving Struthers and myself west to Paphos then followed the coast to the North of the Island. Before reaching the Turkish controlled part I decided that it was time to head south and over the mountain roads to Limassol. Darkness fell quickly and it became quite nerve-wracking driving up the twisting road with big drops off to one side as we made our way up into the mountains. Eventually we reached the summit of the pass near Mt Olympus in the Troodos Mountains and I could start to relax and it was a relief to see the lights of Limassol in the distance far below. We stopped in a village and entered a tavern to get something to eat and were surprised to find locals watching an English football match on TV. We arrived back in Limassol quite late after a full day.

At the East District cross-country championships in Grangemouth on 24th January I was quite pleased to finish 8th. Alistair Blamire won from Fergus Murray and Jim Wight.

In the BUSF cross-country championships at Graves Park in Sheffield the following Saturday I finished a disappointing 49th, having found the course really testing. Team-mate Colin Youngson finished 52nd, but only 3 seconds behind me and Jim Dingwall was 2 seconds behind Colin. Six seconds covered 47th to 52nd places.

The following Saturday at the Scottish Universities cross-country championships at St Andrews Dave Logue won, ahead of Andy McKean, and John Myatt. I finished 4th again and Colin Youngson was 5th and Innis Mitchell 6th.

On Saturday the 14th of February we were on our Harriers 'Irish tour' and our first race was in Belfast, against Queen's University Belfast, Coleraine and Willowfield. I started well, but the course had a steep slippery grassy downhill, a slippery canal towpath, a stile, two closed gates and a steep slippery uphill, which did not suit me in the least. Colin Youngson was our first finisher in fourth and I was fifth four seconds behind. We managed to retain the 'Mursell' Trophy by beating the team from Queen's University. Next day we ran against Trinity College in Dublin, where Colin won and I was second, eleven seconds behind. Donald Macintosh was third and Robin Orr fifth, so we won the match. Our night's accommodation was in the Students Halls inside Trinity Quad and our hosts had obtained a barrel of Guinness for sampling at the post race get-together in one of the rooms, which promoted an enjoyable, memorable event.

In the Scottish cross-country championships at Ayr on the 21st of February, on a very muddy course I lost ground on all the muddiest sections and finished 35th. Jim Alder won from Dick Wedlock and Bill Mullett. On the following Saturday we Harriers had a cross-country match against Edinburgh University over our home course and I was pleased to win ahead of Colin Youngson and Bill Ewing, in a personal best for the course.

Around this time my training consisted of a six miles run on roads at 7am, before breakfast on

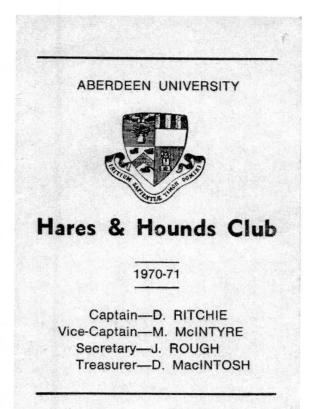

ABERDEEN UNIVERSITY

Hares & Hounds Club

1970-71

Captain—D. RITCHIE
Vice-Captain—M. McINTYRE
Secretary—J. ROUGH
Treasurer—D. MacINTOSH

Mondays to Friday, three road runs of 11 miles, a long fartlek session on Murcar golf course and an interval session such as 5 times 660 yards with 330 yards recovery, on grass at Kings College playing field. Saturday was a race and on Sundays I joined Alastair Wood and Steve Taylor on a long, usually hard run, so my weekly mileage was usually around 90 miles.

The two previous A.U.H&H Club captains had been Colin Youngson and Robin Orr. In early March at the Hare and Hounds AGM, I was narrowly 'promoted' by one vote, from Club secretary to Club captain for season 1970/71, a position that I was proud to accept.

On the 4th of April in the 'Tom Scott' Law to Motherwell 10 miles race, I ran with the leading group until about 1.5 miles before being dropped, but I was pleased to pass six miles in joint fourth in 29-01. I got dropped again at around seven miles and was caught by Eddie Knox at the top of the last hill and he beat me by one second, so I finished seventh in 50-06. Lachie Stewart won in 47-47 from Dick Wedlock and Don Macgregor.

Next weekend was the Shettleston marathon. I tapered by not running on Thursday and Friday to find out if this would be beneficial. My diary record of the race was: *I found that I could easily stay with the leading group, who were: Dick Wedlock, Pat Maclagan, a Small Heath runner and myself as we passed 5 miles in 27-51 and 10 miles in 55-31. Wedlock dropped out at about 11 miles and at about 12 miles Alex Wight caught us and the race started in earnest. Wight was going very fast and I decided to go with him and we pulled away from Maclagan, passing 15 miles in 1-22-03 and we must have been about 80yds clear at 16 miles. Here, however, I could not maintain the pace set by Wight and let him go. MacLagan caught and passed me at about 17 miles and drew away. I passed 20 miles in third place in 1-50-20. Wight ran out of energy near the end and I managed to catch and pass him. My feet were pretty painful after about 15 miles, but I had no blisters.* Pat MacLagan won in 2-22-03, I finished second in 2-25-44 and Alex Wight was next in 2-27-12

The day after, as I had been staying overnight with Peter and Rita Duffy, I went with Peter to the Chevy Chase 20 miles fell race from Wooler in Northumberland. I started off at the back of the field and jogged along and found myself passing runners one by one. It was a tough run and conditions were made difficult by the deep snow, mist and cold wind approaching the summit of Cheviot. I finished 18th of the 50 or so starters in 3-08. The winner recorded 2-44 and Peter, who lost his way at one point finished 12th in 3-04. I did not feel particularly shattered, but my left Achilles tendon was painful; it had been sore before I started this run. I wore my tracksuit during the event and I was glad I had because the snow had a hard crust, which would have cut bare legs when one's feet went through the surface on each step.

Completing this race, a day after the marathon was not a good idea, for my left Achilles tendon, which had been damaged in the marathon, was made worse and on Monday I had a lot of discomfort on trying to jog. I persisted and managed to run once the tightness eased, which was a relief because the Hare & Hounds, seventy-two hours relay at Kings playing fields, for the Students Charities week, was due to begin on Thursday. On Wednesday evening I went to get treatment from Mrs. Coutts ('Ma Coutts') who massaged my tendon and softened the fibrous nodules there, which were rubbing against the tendon sheath. This was quite a painful process, but it seemed to help. She did not charge for the treatment, which was very generous.

I managed to complete sessions of: 25 laps of the Kings field perimeter on Thursday, 30 on Friday, 30 on Saturday and 27 on Sunday. My tendon was extremely painful after each session, but it never became any worse, so next Saturday I was racing again on the track for Aberdeen University Athletic club (A.U.A.C) at Nethercraigs in a match against Strathclyde University. In the 1500 metres I finished 2nd and then won the 5000 metres in a disappointingly slow time due to the strong wind.

CHAMPIONSHIP SILVER AGAIN

On the following Saturday, the 2nd of May, in the Scottish Athletics track 10 miles championships at Scotstoun near Glasgow I finished second in 50-52.2. My diary entry was: *We set out at a steady five minutes per mile pace, but at about two miles Steve Taylor opened up a ten yards gap before I noticed as I was running behind John Myatt and Bill Stoddart. I did not make a determined effort to regain contact with Steve, who had now been joined by Willie Day. I passed Myatt and Stoddart and set a faster pace and hoping that Steve would come back. He pulled away from Day, who I caught and had a terrific duel with before getting away with two miles remaining, but I could make no impression on Steve. There was a wind blowing and I feel that I could have run faster if I had someone to run with near the end, which implies that I should have gone with Steve. I passed 6 miles in 30-17. Steve won in 49-52.6 and Willie Day recorded 51-07.*

Next day at the Aberdeen University sports day at Kings I ran in the 1500 metres, finishing a close 2nd to Colin Youngson. Later I was 2nd to Bill Ewing in the 5000 metres with Colin 3rd. At night I ran 3 miles on the roads to make up my mileage to 101 miles for the week.

On Saturday the 16th of May the Scottish marathon championship, from Meadowbank Stadium in Edinburgh, was the selection race for the Scottish team for the Commonwealth Games marathon to be held over the same course in July. I decided to go with the leaders and we passed 5 miles in 25-50 and 10 miles in 52-21, after which the pace increased so I had to let them go and intended to run steadily for the rest of the race. There had been no wind, when we started, but there was quite a strong wind blowing into our faces on the return leg. Alex Matheson of Morpeth Harriers caught me after the turn and we ran together until I lost contact when I tried to get a sponge at a watering point. I struggled through 20 miles in 1-48 and finished in a disappointing 2-26-28 in eleventh place. I noted in my diary: *My feet were quite painful, especially my right, which felt badly bruised and I had a blister on the sole of this foot, which burst while I was running. On my left foot I had two blisters.* Jim Alder won in 2-17-11 just three seconds ahead of Don Macgregor and Fergus Murray was third in 2-18-25.

Two weeks later, the Sunday morning run was unexpectedly hard and my diary entry was: *I ran up to Steve's and then we ran up to Alastair's, only to find that he had gone 30 minutes earlier. This annoyed Steve, who set a terrific pace for about seventeen minutes from Alastair's to Hazlehead Park, around the zoo and golf course car park to Countesswells Road. Here I decided to run at a less painful pace, but Steve waited for me at the top of the hill and then kept pulling away on hills. We reached the 10 miles point in 52-30, which included two stops by Steve and jogs back. We continued to Maryculter and the Mill Inn and completed the route in 2-03-30, which was 7 minutes faster than three months ago.*

On the 13th of June in the Spean Bridge to Fort William nine and a half miles road race I was first in 45-31, which was 73 seconds slower than Alastair Wood's record. Ian Mackenzie of Forres Harriers was next in 46-36 and Hamish Scott from Perth was eleven seconds behind Ian. The weather was terrifically hot and the roadmen were sanding the roads to prevent the tyres of the traffic from sticking to the melting tar.

Six days later, after my last end of 2nd year exams, I drove my van, with 800 metres runner, Grant Smith as my passenger, down to Durham for the B.U.S.F athletics Championships. When we arrived and made enquiries at Durham Students Union we found that the promised accommodation in the Student Halls had not been arranged. This was rather a shock so we were very pleased when we were very kindly given a bed for the night by the Groundsman and his wife at the Durham University track and playing fields. Next day in the 10,000 metres track championship I finished 5th in 32-38.8. I was not too disappointed with this as I performed better than last year and it was a hot day and quite windy. Andy Holden from Birmingham University won in 30-09 from Frank Briscoe and Doug Gunstone.

Rather than start driving back to Aberdeen I decided that we should stay overnight, so we spent the evening in Durham University Student's Union. We found a common room and once it became quiet, which was quite late, Grant and I slept on the floor behind some couches.

As the university year was finished, after driving back from Durham I went to stay with my parents at Folla Rule for a few days before setting out to drive to R.A.F Coltishall in Norfolk, where the Aberdeen University Air Squadron summer camp was to be held. I drove as far as Wishaw where I stayed overnight with Peter and Rita Duffy; completed the drive next day; and got settled into the Officer's Mess.

Next day I ran in the Mildenhall 10 miles road race and had a disastrous run. The weather was oppressively hot, with the temperature reaching 85°F and a thunderstorm pending. I had set out determined to run well, ignoring the hot conditions. At 2 miles I was with the leader, John Jones of Windsor Slough and Eaton, but I had to let him go and then ran along in joint 2nd after being caught. Shortly after 5 miles I felt extremely tired and my legs stopped working normally. From this point to the end I struggled and was extremely glad to reach the finish in the slow time of 56-49 in 12th place. About 8 minutes after finishing the lightning and thunder started, it became cooler and the rain came down in torrents, so within minutes the gutters were like streams. Jones won by 2-37 in 50-58, which I thought was very impressive in such adverse weather.

On Sunday I travelled to R.A.F Biggin Hill for three days of officer selection testing starting on Monday. I was shocked, when half way through the process I was summoned into an office and informed that I was being rejected. I asked the fellow who was delivering the rejection what the reason was, but he would not tell me, so this left me rather worried. On reflection, it was probably for the best.

Back at R.A.F Coltishall, the home of a squadron of very impressive English Electric 'Lightning' interceptor aircraft, we had flying practice in our Chipmunk trainer aircraft for the 11 days of our 'summer camp'. I was deemed safe to go solo on the third day, which was quite a tense but exciting event. During the following days I became more competent, confident and relaxed, but when an external assessor sat in the back seat I made several errors in the course of the flight, which displeased him and me.

In the late afternoons when flying had finished and before dinner, I used to run around a road circuit of about eleven and a half miles, usually in extremely hot weather. By the 5th run I felt that I was adapting to the hot weather, with temperatures ranging from 76°F to 80°F.

Later in the year while practising solo aerobatics over Aberdeenshire, I received a nasty shock, when I managed to stall the engine. I was practising stall turns, which involves diving as for a loop, but instead of completing the loop one continues vertically and then, on applying full right rudder, the aircraft does a cartwheel and dives back down. On this occasion I left the rudder application too long, so it had no effect, and the aircraft began to fall backwards, stopping the engine and then 'hammer-heading' into a vertical dive with a stationary propeller. I let the speed build up sufficiently to start wind-milling, which restarted my engine and I pulled out of the dive and returned to Dyce still suffering from mild shock.

After driving back from R.A.F Coltishall I had three days at home and completed my 19 miles road circuit each morning. On the 20th of July Colin Youngson and I went to Edinburgh to watch the athletics at the Commonwealth Games until they finished 5 days later. We were sleeping on the floor of Paul Binns, an ex AU Harrier, and his wife's house in Corstorphine. Colin and I had a thoroughly enjoyable time and witnessed some great running performances including: Lachie Stewart's 10,000 metres, Ian Stewart's/Ian McCafferty's 5000 metres duel and Ron Hill and Jim Alder's marathon. We also fitted in some fierce, for me, training sessions.

On Monday the 3rd of August, I started my summer vacation job with 'Deys of Huntly', who do work for distilleries. I was assigned to a journeyman and our first job was to repair a malt-mill in a distillery in Dufftown and on completing the repair we went to the distillery manager's office to inform him that the job was done. He thanked us and poured a dram of the 'good stuff' for us, which we drank as a matter of courtesy. By the time I had walked to our van I thought that I could see violets and roses in the sky. My journeyman, the driver, seemed less influenced by the water of life as we made our way back to Huntly. Probably he had built up a tolerance, as I found that it was customary to receive a dram on completing any job in a distillery, when you go to the manager's office to report completion.

As I was living with my parents at Folla Rule, during the vacation I had to drive to Huntly and back each day, which restricted my training time. I used to run my 19 miles loop after returning home before eating tea, but after 3 days I started running a four and a quarter miles route at lunchtime, which allowed me to reduce my evening run to 11 miles.

At the Huntly Highland Games, I ran in the 3000 metres on a track laid out on the football pitch, with around 14 laps required to achieve the distance. My Aberdeen University teammate, Colin Youngson beat me by 3 seconds after making a break with 2 laps remaining. Later I ran in the handicap 1500 metres off scratch and finished fourth and then ran for 33 minutes on the roads with Mike Scott and Hamish Cameron.

Next week we were in Imperial Distillery at Carron on Speyside, installing metal framework to support three new copper stills. This job was expected to take three weeks to complete, so a squad of 7 of us travelled up and back by a van; 3 in the front and 4 of us sitting on tool boxes in the back.

My lunchtime run there was from Imperial, through Carron, along the road, up a stiff hill to the junction with the A95 and back, which took less than 30 minutes, so I had time for a bite to eat before resuming work. Apart from lunch breaks we had tea breaks, morning and afternoon, synchronised with the distillery workers, so we lined up with them, teacup in hand to receive sustaining drams at 10am and 3pm from the manager. One member of our squad obtained a screw-top glass lemonade bottle of 'clearac', which is clear whisky before it is put into the barrels for maturation. This was then placed in his toolbox to transport home for medicinal purposes. Health and safety considerations stopped this practice some years later. We used to work until 6pm and then on the way back to Huntly there would be a stop in Dufftown at the pub in the main street for a pint of 'dark light' in my case, so it would be around 7pm when we arrived back at Deys workshop. By the time I had driven back to Folla Rule it was a case of: run 11 miles, eat, wash and get to bed to recover for next day's 'adventure'.

On the 16th of August Duncan Davidson from Forres Harriers drove through, in poor weather, from Elgin to meet me at Folla Rule and I drove us down to Perth for the 14 miles road race, organised by Perth Railway A.C. The pace was quite fast from the start and Sandy Keith, Jim Wight and myself passed 5 miles in 25-20. Shortly after this Wight began to drop and at about 6 miles on a steep hill Sandy got away and drew further ahead until the end. I passed 10 miles in 52-42. Sandy finished one minute and thirty-six seconds ahead of me and Hamish Scott was 3rd, while Duncan ran well to place 6th. My prize was a small suitcase. My mileage for the week was 105 miles, so I was happy with my performance.

FIRST ULTRA-MARATHON

On the following Friday, 21st of August in the evening I drove down to Rosyth and booked into the Royal Navy accommodation in the hope of getting a good night's rest before tackling the 'Two Bridges' road race next morning. I had never run further than a marathon, so this would be a step into the unknown and I was apprehensive, wondering how I would 'manage' the extra 10 miles.

Because of my concern about completing the distance, I set out cautiously and ran with a group including John Linaker and Willie Russell. We passed 5 miles in 30-55, 10 miles in 61-03 and 15 miles in 1-31-41 before I lost contact at the drinks station at 18 miles as I slowed to take my drink. My feet became very painful and I had little drive in my legs, so I was more or less jogging from about 25 miles, so my hope to run at 6 minutes per mile all the way was unrealistic. However, I was pleased to finish this classic, 36 miles 183 yards race and to place 7th in 3-50-50. Phil Hampton won in 3-41-18 only 13 seconds ahead of Willie Russell, with Ron Bentley of Tipton Harriers 3rd. In the evening we all enjoyed the 'Social' in the Civil Service Club, where the Tipton Harriers contingent helped the night go with a swing. They demonstrated to me that drinking beer and being a good long distance runner (the term ultra-runner had not been thought of yet) were not mutually exclusive.

A week later was the Inverness to Drumnadrochit 15.5 miles road race, which followed the A82 along by Loch Ness to Drumnadrochit as part of the annual Highland Games. Colin Youngson put in an effort on the first hill and I had great difficulty in trying to increase my pace, so I was soon an isolated 4th as Charlie Macauley and Hamish Scott drew away. I caught the trio as their pace slowed and, due to the strong headwind, no one was keen to take the lead. I tried several times to break away, but each time I tired and was caught again and on my last attempt at 13 miles I almost got away, but I could not sustain my effort and faded. Colin held off Scott to win and 'Hare and Hounds' team-mate Charlie took 3rd place, 5 yards ahead of me. My lacklustre performance may have been due to the Two Bridges race the previous weekend.

After another week of the usual routine of driving, working, running, eating and sleeping I ran in the Ben Nevis race again after vowing not to do so last year. For some reason when the race started I was in the tent taking my tracksuit off, so I had to make up a 60yds deficit before I reached the back of the field and by this time the leaders were 100yds ahead. By the start of the Ben path I was 20th. I was pleasantly surprised at my strength on the climb and reached the top in 11th. If I could have run down with more abandon and my eyes had not been watering, I could have caught some of the runners ahead as they were definitely within catching distance. As it was, I feared becoming badly injured, ran down cautiously and was passed by 13 runners before reaching the road, which was disheartening, although I managed to re-pass 3 on the road to finish 21st in 1-55-02. After this, I decided, definitely, not to run this race again, because my downhill running was not good enough and I did not intend to try to improve this. Jeff Norman won in 1-40-45 from Dave Cannon and Mike Davies.

Our work at Imperial distillery had been completed the previous Thursday, so we moved onto a new job, renovating gravel-sorting machinery at Cloddach sand and gravel quarry, near Elgin. My lunchtime run was now extended to five and three-quarters miles and I maintained my 11 miles circuit at night. By Thursday the post 'Ben' quads pains had subsided, which was a relief, so I felt happier about my prospects in the Knockfarrel Hill race at Strathpeffer on Saturday. *We got off to a fast start and Ian Mackenzie of Forres Harriers led, but on entering the grass fields I began to slip rather badly and fell at one point, losing a good deal of ground to Ian, and others passed me, so I was down to 5th. By the start of the climb I had pulled back to 3rd and then reached the leaders, Ian and Mike Scott (also of Forres Harriers). Although I did not feel great I got to the top first just ahead of Ian. I got away from him on the road section, where I felt that I was running fast, to the finish.* I was surprised to learn that my time of 36-37 was a new course record. Ian was 13 seconds back and Mike Scott was 3rd.

The following Saturday, 19th September, our AUH&HC team of: Colin Youngson, Charlie Macauley, myself and Donald Macintosh won the Nairn to Inverness road relay race (along the A96) from Aberdeen AAC in a time only 17 seconds slower than the course record. Our team all ran well and we were delighted with the result. The day after, I ran in the Aberdeen Corporation '10-miles' race in Duthie Park. Alastair Wood won in 43-41 from Colin Youngson and I finished 3rd. The times indicated that the course was not the stated ten miles and was later found to be 9 miles.

Two weeks later my vacation job was finished and I resumed university life as I began the 3rd year of my course.

The next outing for our H&HC was the Alves to Forres road race, on 3rd October, again on the A96. Alastair Wood won again, but our team ran well, with Colin Youngson finishing 2nd, 4 seconds ahead of me and Charlie Macauley was 5th, so we were 1st team.

The following Saturday in the first North East Cross-Country League race at St Andrews I was a surprised winner after a tough race with Alastair Wood and Don Macgregor, with Colin 4th. I was delighted and celebrated by running about 6.5 miles around a nearby playing field. On Sunday I ran 19 miles with Alastair and Steve Taylor in the morning and 10 miles on roads in the evening, for a weekly total of 134 miles.

In the Kingsway road relay in Dundee the following Saturday our Hare & Hounds team – myself, Colin Youngson, Donald Macintosh and Merv McIntyre finished 3rd from 30 teams, which we all thought was very creditable. Next day, after a twenty-one miles glycogen depletion run in preparation for the Harlow marathon the following Saturday, my cold, which had started on Wednesday, had progressed to my chest. On Monday, because of my glycogen depletion I could only manage 5th in the cross-country race over our home course, for the Mursell Trophy against Queens University, Belfast. Colin won the race and with teammates in 3rd and 4th we retained the trophy for another year.

On Friday 23rd October I travelled with Alastair Wood and Colin Youngson by train to London and on to Harlow. In the Harlow marathon I finished 16th in the disappointing time of 2-30-52. I was determined to go with the leaders, providing that the pace was not completely unreasonable. As it was I found that by 2 miles I was feeling the pace, so I let the leading group go and passed 5 miles in 26-39, 10 miles in 55-28. By this point I had been caught by a group and was running along with them. As the race went on I felt weaker and weaker and knew that I was not going to produce a personal best or even a good time. I reached 15 miles in 83-09 and 20 miles in a slow 1-53-36 on very painful feet. My legs were heavy and my skin was dry and rough with salt crystals. I got passed in the last 100yds over a stony path, which I was negotiating fairly slowly for the sake of my feet. I was bitterly disappointed with this performance because I had trained so long for this race and definitely wanted a good time. The reasons for this failure were difficult to isolate, but might be due in part to my cold as I was coughing up phlegm from my lungs. Other points to consider were: the carbohydrate loading diet (was 77 hours sufficient time to restore my glycogen levels?); or perhaps I had over-trained. However, this did not seem to be the case, as I was running faster than ever in the preceding weeks. There appeared to be no obvious reason to guide me in future preparations, although I suspect the main culprit was the cold I picked up in the week before the race. Alastair Wood won in 2-17-59, a course record, over 2 minutes ahead of Harry Leeming and C Perez of Spain. Aberdeen AAC won the team race, with myself 16th and Colin Youngson 24th in 2-34-49. We returned to Aberdeen on the overnight train from London, enduring this tedious journey as best we could.

Exercise physiologist, Clyde Williams, offered to measure my 'VO2 max', so I did a maximal test on a bicycle ergometer at Marischal College and really felt 'done in' after it. The results of this test indicated that I had a value of 60.7mL/Kg of oxygen uptake, which was not very good.

The second N.E. Cross-Country League race over our AU home course was won by Colin Youngson (34-23) from Steve Taylor, me and Alastair Wood. Up until New Year, Colin showed considerable improvement and became harder for me to beat. This culminated in the low-key but flat-out Christmas Handicap over our own course, when he recorded 33-29 (only three seconds slower than John Myatt's record) in front of me (34-06) and Steve Taylor (34-08). However, I defeated him in important cross-country fixtures after that and won the AUH&HC Championship Trophy for the 3rd time in succession.

My next race with the AUH&HC was in the prestigious Edinburgh to Glasgow road relay. Our team of: Donald Macintosh, Colin Youngson, Charlie Aithie, Charlie Macauley, Jim Rough, me, Robin Orr and Merv McIntyre, performed well to finish a creditable 9th from the 20 invited top Scottish teams. This was to be the AUH&HC best ever placing. I ran the long 6th stage and was 10th fastest, an improvement from 15th fastest last year. Jim Alder was fastest, followed by Don Macgregor and Andy McKean.

Two weeks later in the Scottish Universities versus the SCCU team at Knightswood Park in Glasgow I started well but faded and finished a dejected 15th, 13 seconds behind Frank Clement. Teammate, Colin Youngson ran well again to place 8th and 2nd University counter behind Alistair Blamire. The SCCU team won the match as usual. This race coincided with the end of the University term so I went to Folla Rule to stay with my Mum and Dad and had to run on snow-covered roads on most days from there.

NOS GALAN

On Wednesday the day before Hogmanay I drove a hired Vauxhall car with Hare and Hounds team mates: Colin Youngson, Charlie Macauley, Brian Templeton and Bob Masson, to Kerr Walker's home in Ruthin, North Wales, where we were made welcome by his parents and where we slept overnight on their lounge floor. On 'Hogmanay' we continued to Mountain Ash in South Wales and, after getting changed in the local coalmine pit-baths, we competed in the 'Nos Galan' midnight 4 miles race. 350 ran, including 46 teams. The atmosphere generated, by the watching crowds with a section of burning lanterns on either side of the street, was inspiring. I was quite pleased with my run to finish thirteenth, having worked my way through the field after being obstructed at the start. With Colin ninth and Charlie fifty-fifth we received third team medals, plus top 100 Welsh red Nos Galan vests – a pleasant surprise and a good note on which to finish 1970.

Donald leads Colin at Nos Galan. Note 'The Great Wilson' in fifth place! Cartoon by Donald Macintosh.

Charlie, Lord Mayor, Colin and Donald with Third Team trophies on the Nos Galan rostrum.

After the presentation of awards, we adjourned to the building floor provided to sleep in, and started our New Year celebrations. Someone suggested a morning run, so at 06:30, in a tipsy state, seven of us went for a meandering 'training run' of about one mile. In the afternoon after driving to Kerr's home, we ran up a hill near Ruthin in a series of hard efforts. Next day after a long drive we arrived safely from our 'adventure' back in Aberdeen.

My mileage for 1970 was 4866.75 (so precise!), an average of 93.59 miles per week – the highest yearly total I had ever achieved until then. Training had been twice a day, Monday to Thursday, once on Friday if racing on Saturday and twice if not. I usually raced on Saturday – cross-country, track, road or hill, depending on the season. Sunday was a long run with Ally Wood and the gang. During the week I would include at least two effort sessions: intervals at Kings or fartlek on Murcar Golf Course or efforts incorporated during a road run.

1971

On Wednesday the 6th of January, I drove an Aberdeen University Minibus full of Hare and Hounds teammates to Stranraer for the start of our 'Irish Tour'. Several weeks earlier I had written to the British Amateur Athletic Board to get permission for our team to compete in Dublin against Trinity College. I duly received a letter granting permission signed by the Honorary Secretary of the Board, Arthur Gold.

Dublin the following day, we raced against a combined Trinity College and University College Dublin (UCD) team at Belfield over a four and a half miles cross-country course. After a dour struggle with Colin Youngson I finally detached myself on the downhill stretch near the end to finish 14 seconds ahead of Colin, with McDermott of UCD third a further 28 seconds behind.

Two days later, we raced in Belfast against Queens University and some non-counters from Achilles and Willowfield. I made an early break to get to the footpath by the canal first and then hung on to the lead ahead of Colin and Cyril Pennington of Queens University.

Next morning, I drove our minibus to team member Merv McIntyre's parents' home near Magherafelt in Northern Ireland. In the afternoon Colin and I ran along the cliff paths by the Giant's Causeway and then back along the road, before heading off to catch the overnight ferry to Stranraer. By Monday evening we had arrived in Aberdeen and I returned the faithful and thankfully undamaged minibus.

In the 3rd North East Cross-country League race at Hazlehead the following Saturday Alastair Wood won 2 seconds ahead of me. Colin Youngson and Innis Mitchell were 3rd and 4th. Alastair's time was a new course record and all four of us were inside the old record.

In the East District Cross-Country Champs at Heriot-Watt University in Edinburgh on the 23rd of January, Adrian Weatherhead won from Fergus Murray and Gareth Bryan Jones, while I finished a dissatisfied 11th. With Colin 12th, Charlie Macauley 17th, Don Macintosh 19th, Merv McIntyre 25th and Charlie Aithie 50th - AUH&H were happy to finish 3rd team.

The Scottish Universities Cross Country Championships, at Cambuslang in Glasgow, were held the following week on a muddy slippery course. At the turn the leaders, Andy McKean and Alistair Blamire lost about 80 yards by going off-course, but they soon made this up. McKean lost a shoe in a muddy patch and stopped to retrieve it. Blamire won from A Partridge and Frank Clements, who was a frustrating 3 seconds ahead of me. Innis Mitchell, Colin Youngson, Charlie Macauley and McKean were next. Our team was third behind Strathclyde and Glasgow but in front of Edinburgh, St Andrews, Heriot-Watt and Dundee.

Our next race was the B.U.S.F cross-country championships at Guildford on the 6th of February. After travelling down to London by 'sleeper train' on Friday night we walked around London in the morning and saw the Houses of Parliament and Westminster Abbey. Following this walk-about, we caught a train to Guildford and made our way to the race location. Jack Lane won from Frank Briscoe and Andy Holden and I finished a disappointed 38th. I observed that Birmingham University's third counter, who finished 9th, had been behind me in the Nos Galan race.

The following Wednesday in the H&HC cross-country half marathon I retained the Sawfish Trophy with my best time for this annual event, only 16.5 seconds shy of Bill Ewing's course record.

In the Scottish National Cross-Country Championships in Bellahouston Park, Glasgow on the 20th of February 1971, I had a surprisingly good run to finish 14th, which was my best cross-country race to date.

Next week in the five universities cross-country match at Camperdown Park in Dundee I was pleased to improve Adrian Weatherhead's course record. Colin Youngson and Charlie Macauley followed me, so it was a good day for Aberdeen University Hare and Hounds.

Our next team event the following Saturday was the Edinburgh University 10 miles road race from Kings Buildings, Edinburgh. Andy McKean won from Alastair Johnston and Jim Wight. I was pleased to finish 5th in 50-08 and received the prize of a fine umbrella. With Colin 7th and Charlie Macauley 17th we were 3rd team behind Edinburgh Athletic Club (EAC) and Edinburgh Southern Harriers (ESH).

Two weeks later, the 20th of March, we were back at the Perth North Inch road relay, where I ran the last lap for the AAAC team, where we finished 2nd to Victoria Park AC, with Springburn Harriers third. I was pleased to get the 3rd fastest lap time overall, behind Doug Gunstone and Mike Bradley.

There was no race on the weekend beginning, 27th of March; so I ran 44 miles in back-to-back long runs on Saturday and Sunday to give me a weekly total of 156 miles, which was more than I had ever run in one week before.

On Saturday the 3rd of April, in the Tom Scott Memorial 10 miles road race from Law to Motherwell I had a disappointing run after going with the leading group of six. I could not sustain my pace, lost contact by two miles and faded to finish tenth in 49-52. Colin was 8th in 49-38. On reflection, I was probably suffering the effects of excessive mileage the previous week. Andy McKean won from Pat Maclagan and Dick Wedlock.

On Saturday, 24th April, after two 150-mile weeks and then an easier week, it was back to track racing in the Aberdeen University Athletics Championships at Kings playing fields. I arrived late and started the 1500 metres without a warm-up so I seized up and finished 4th. In the 5000 metres I led after a lap and was pleased to maintain this to finish ahead of Colin Youngson and Jim McHardy of Glasgow University.

SILVER AGAIN

My next race was the Scottish Track 10 miles Championships at Scotstoun track in Glasgow on Saturday the 1st of May. My diary entry was: *I set off at a comfortable pace in a group with Colin Martin,*

Willie Day and Colin Youngson: Lachie Stewart having 'bombed' off. We ran together until just after 5 miles, reached in 25-05, when I made a break by going with Lachie as he lapped us. I could only manage about three laps at 70s pace, but I had achieved my objective of breaking clear of the rest and passed 6 miles in 29-55.8. All that was needed then was to stay ahead, which I did by settling down to 75s laps. I was pleased at getting under 50 minutes. My fastest lap was my first at 69.8 seconds and my slowest was 77 seconds. I was pleased to cover my last mile in 4-57. Lachie set a Scottish record of 47-59 and I was pleased with the 'silver' with my best time of 49-54, while Colin gained the bronze with 50-42.

In the Shettleston Marathon which was the following Saturday Steve Taylor, Dick Wedlock and I ran past ten miles in 56-20. Steve and I hammered the next ten miles in 53-30, to pass 20 miles in 1-49-56, which was quite pleasing. Around 24 miles, I felt quite tired and Steve could have pulled away if he had wanted to. At about 25.75 miles as we were entering the field where the track was, Steve said 'here we go', and I thought he had said 'on you go', so I thought that he was going to let me finish first. I increased my pace slightly, which angered Steve, who swore at me as he came past to beat me by 6 seconds in 2-23-25. I was pleased with my time of 2-23-31, an improvement of 67 seconds on my previous best. I noted in my diary: *I am not convinced that the carbohydrate loading (Saltin diet) is all that helpful as I had stiffness in my legs during the second half and was not able to run smoothly. I feel that I did not use up all my supply of glycogen.* My feet were pretty good and I had no blisters. Davie Wyper was third in 2-31-57.

During my lunchtime interval session of 440 yards at Kings on the following Thursday I was averaging 67 seconds until the 7th when I felt a terrific pain in my left calf muscle and almost fell over. I jogged to try and get the muscle to ease off, but it did not, so I realised that it must be a muscle tear and not a spasm so I was very disappointed at becoming injured. By Saturday, with persistence I was able to force myself to walk normally, although I still got more pain when I pushed off with my left foot.

On Sunday I managed to start jogging and walking alternately and eventually I managed to jog eight laps at a slow pace on the grass at Inverdee as the muscle became suppler. This was a relief as I had been selected to represent The Scottish Universities in a 5000 metres track race in a match against the Irish Universities and the University College of Louvain, Belgium, on Saturday the 22nd of May.

On Friday, 21st May, I got a lift to Glasgow airport where our team caught a flight to Dublin and got to our accommodation in Dun Laoghaire on a rainy night, but in time for a couple of pints of Guinness before closing time. Next day, on Saturday, we went to Belfield for the match and as rain was still falling, this spoiled the meeting somewhat. I ran in the 5000 metres and finished 3rd behind Andy McKean and an Irish University man, Baillie. Thankfully my calf muscle did not bother me in the race, but I felt nauseous towards the end and I vomited after finishing the race and then began to feel better. Unfortunately, we had to leave for home in the early evening and so missed out on a social get-together.

In the East District 5000 metres championship at Pitreavie the following Saturday I finished fourth behind Andy McKean, Alex Wight and Colin Youngson.

Two days later on the 31st of May, in the Aberdeen University Athletics Club 10,000 metres championships at Kings, my legs felt weak, my left quads became very painful and I also had pains in my chest. Steve Taylor won in 30-40 from Colin Youngson in 30-49, while I finished a disappointed 3rd in 32-05. In the 5000 metres Colin Youngson won in 14-48 from Alastair Wood (14-59) and I finished 3rd again in 15-13.

On Friday, 11th June, I travelled to Birmingham for the BUSF 10,000 metres championships at Birmingham University track on Saturday. I ran with the leading group of about 8 runners and we passed 5Km in 15-06. I began to struggle at this pace and had to let them go. Andy Holden won in 29-58.6 from Doug Gunstone, while I finished a disappointed 7th in 31-40.

A week after completing my 'finals exams' I learned that I had achieved my BSc in Electrical Engineering and performed sufficiently well to be invited back for the Honours year. I gladly accepted this option to increase my knowledge of the subject and to extend my stay at University for another year, with all its benefits, especially running-related.

On the 26th of June I ran my 15th marathon in the Scottish Marathon Championships from Meadowbank. Pat Maclagan, Don Macgregor and I ran together in joint 2nd behind Bill Stoddart and passed 10 miles in 53-17. I began to weaken at about 12 miles and got dropped and then Willie Day came past as I slowed to reach 20 miles in 1-51 after going off course slightly. At about twenty-three miles I could see Macgregor slowing, but he dropped out before I caught him. Pat Maclagan won in 2-21-17 from Bill Stoddart (2-23-31) and Willie Day (2-26-07), while I finished 4th in 2-28-39 and teammate Charlie Macauley was 5th in 2-32-03. I was disappointed with my time and position, as on form I should have been a close 2nd or 3rd, but appeared to have lost fitness over the last eight weeks.

Around this time Colin Youngson and I were awarded Full Blues, this time for Athletics rather than Cross-Country, in recognition of the good standard of our racing on track and road for Aberdeen University Athletic Club, which was very pleasing.

Two days later on the 28th of June, I started a vacation job as a maintenance electrician at Tait's Paper Mill at Port Elphinstone, near Inverurie.

At the Kinlochleven Highland games, on the 3rd of July, I ran in the 17 miles Mamore hill race in baking hot weather and finished a distant 3rd in 1-49-12 behind Gordon Eadie and Brian Finlayson. I think that I expected too much, hoping to run well in a long hill race a week after a marathon.

At Inverness Highland games in Bught Park on the 17th of July, in the North of Scotland AAA (NSAAA) 5000 metres on the six laps for a mile grass track I finished first in a slow 15-30.9 ahead of Graham Milne of Springburn Harriers and Ian Mackenzie. I was not qualified to accept the NSAAA championship medal, however, as I was not resident in the North District.

I began considering running to and from work, which would be 17 miles each way. Because I had to get to work just after 07:00 for a 07:30 start this would mean a very early start from Willowbank Road in Aberdeen. My first trial of this was on Tuesday the 13th of July, at 05:30 I ran to work in 1-49-30 into a slight headwind. My route from Willowbank Road was up to Mannofield, then across towards Bucksburn, before dropping down to meet the A96 at the bottom of Tyrebagger Hill and from there followed this road through Blackburn and Kintore to Port Elphinstone. At night I got a lift to the square in Kintore and ran home by the reverse of my morning route in 1-29-30, with a following wind. I felt fine and was able to stride out towards the end and added thirty-two miles to my weekly total. Having satisfied myself that this was a practical training session I completed it twice a week on Tuesdays and Thursdays. I used to hang my kit out to dry on an improvised washing line outside our electrician's shed and my 'jock strap' created some amusement among the mill girls as they passed, but they soon got used to it. After a couple of weeks I ran back from work rather than from the square in Kintore making a thirty-four miles round trip. Once the Mill closed for the one-month, annual maintenance schedule, we electricians were working seven days a week servicing motors and installing new equipment so I ran to and from work four times a week. On other days I would run a 9 miles course before driving to work and then fit in a 4 miles hard run along the Kemnay road during my lunch break. My weekly mileage during this period averaged 150 miles and I was feeling good from this and probably the break from racing every weekend.

I arranged to get a weekend off work to participate in an invitation one-hour race in Edinburgh. On Saturday the 21st of August, following 5 weeks of solid training I ran in a one-hour track race, which was part of the twenty-fifth annual Edinburgh Highland Games, at Meadowbank Stadium. I was unsure of myself early on so I sat behind the 2nd group where the pace seemed easy. We passed 10Km in 30-54, a personal best and 10 miles in 49-52.2, also a personal best. I thought that I could achieve 12 miles, but I had to increase my pace, so when Pat Maclagan lapped me I went with him and succeeded in dropping Alastair Wood and Steve Taylor, but Mike Beevor came with me. He and Maclagan pulled away after a couple of laps and left me to battle on alone and I was very disappointed at not reaching 12 miles, which I missed by 78 yards. I noted in my diary that I should have gone earlier and would have, had I realized that the pace of our group was dropping. Jim Alder won with 12 miles 618 yards from Pat Maclagan with 12 miles 315 yards and Mike Beevor was next with 11 miles 1744.5 yards, while I finished 4th with 11 miles 1683 yards.

An athletics match between Great Britain and Belgium was incorporated within in the Highland Games and it was a privilege to witness the 2 miles world record being broken by the Belgian Emiel Puttemans with a time of 8-17.8. Steve Taylor and I were given accommodation in the Edinburgh University Halls of Residence at the Pollock Halls. In the evening, I thoroughly enjoyed the reception and dinner provided by Edinburgh City Council and later attended the 22:30 hrs performance of the Edinburgh Military Tattoo at the Castle.

While driving home from work one evening the following week I lost concentration on North Anderson Drive and collided with a vehicle, which had stopped on the carriageway. This damaged the driver's side front wing on my A40 van, so later I decided to remove this damaged wing and fit a replacement one. While I left my van in this right wingless state it attracted the attention of a zealous traffic warden, which resulted in a fine of £20, for contravening some law about having a vehicle with jaggy bits showing. If I had left the damaged wing on the vehicle it would have been unsightly, but would have avoided the fine

ENSCHEDE, HOLLAND

On Tuesday evening on the 31st of August 1971, Steve Taylor and I travelled to London by overnight train On Wednesday we ran for 62-minutes at Parliament Hills Fields in very warm weather. On Thursday we were travelling by train and ferry to Holland and train again for the 13th edition of the Enschede International marathon race. Steve and I were staying with different host families. We completed a pre-race brisk 25 minutes run in very warm weather, but I felt quite good.

My diary Entry for race day the 4th September was: Much to my dismay the sun broke through the clouds about 20 minutes before the start and the temperature rose, so it became very hot indeed. After marching into the Stadium behind our respective Country signs, we lined up and waited eagerly for the gun to set us on our way. I started slowly and tried to stay close to the kerb on the lap of the track. Once out of the stadium I increased my pace in an attempt to catch up Steve, who was fast disappearing. On and on I went passing runners easily and caught Steve at about 1.5 miles and we proceeded to move through the field, despite Steve's protestations about our zealous pace. We caught Mamo Wolde of Ethiopia and a small bunch after passing 10Km in 31-30 and as the pace felt easy we pushed on dropping Wolde and co. Before the turn we passed Lorenz of the USA and Jansen of Holland to take us to 8th and 9th positions. I began to tire just after the turn, reached in 1-12-00 and had to let Steve go, but I next passed Steve Bagley, who was running for Great Britain. Lorenz passed me, but I recovered and pulled away from him again, as I was running quite strongly despite feeling tired. I next caught the Japanese runner Ohtukt and then Don Faircloth, representing G.B. I was now in 6th place, but finding it increasingly difficult to keep going, despite drinking frequently and taking wet sponges. I was soaked, but still hot. Lorenz came past again and shortly after, I passed Steve, who had run into the ditch after losing his balance and he retired at this 23 miles point. I was becoming very tired and running slowly, so 7 runners passed in the last 2.5 miles. I expect it was the heat or possibly not doing the carbohydrate loading diet that caused me to become depleted of energy at around 22 miles; at least I hope this was the case and not lack of ability. It was a great relief to finish. From a starting field of 262 there were 100 dropouts, because of the difficult conditions. I thoroughly enjoyed running up to the turn when we were pulling in the leaders, which was a good confidence booster. I was pleased to finish ahead of some well-known runners.

Bernie Allen won in 2-16-54 from Eric Austin (2-19-42), both from Great Britain, and Joe Vitale of the USA with 2-20-16. I finished a tired and relieved 13th in 2-28-54, which pleased my host family. For the next four days Steve and I travelled around Holland as tourists, visiting various cities, not attempting to run and staying in bed and breakfast accommodation.

A week after the Enschede marathon on the 11th of September, I ran in the Cairngorm 10 miles Hill Race and managed to lead Sandy Keith by 40 yards at the summit turn. Thankfully I managed to maintain my lead to the finish, despite very painful blisters that developed under my heels from the fast downhill running on the road section. I finished in 1-15-31, ahead of Colin Martin, 1-16-58 and Sandy Keith 1-17-12.

In the Nairn to Inverness road relay, on the 25th September, I ran the 3rd stage for our AUH&HC and was 2nd fastest behind Alastair Wood who set a stage record of 19-23. Times were faster that year, thanks to a following wind. Aberdeen AAC won in a course record and our H&HC team finished 2nd, just under a minute ahead of Forres Harriers.

At the Harlow marathon on the 23rd of October, I started at a steady fast pace with the leading bunch, behind Bernie Allan, who went away very quickly. We were directed off-course and the organizer, Tom Dradey, calculated that we had covered 1.25 miles extra and would adjust the finish accordingly. At about 7 miles I had to ease off and at the first drinks station I had my bottle of glucose and salt in water and lost about 50yds while drinking it. Bernie Allan dropped out at 16.25 miles so I was then fifth and shortly after this I moved to fourth. I felt that I was running quite well, but I must have been slowing quite a lot as two passed me and I finished 6th in the mediocre time of 2-29-13. The weather was hot with the sun shining from a cloudless sky and I later got these details: temp 73°F & relative humidity of 73%. Of the 110 starters only 60 finished. There was some doubt expressed by runners from Harlow, about how much extra we ran by going off-course and some estimated that it was two miles at least. This was my 17th marathon and I did not use the carbohydrate depletion/loading diet for this one. My teammate, Charlie Macauley finished 10th in 2-33-21. Dave Holt won in 2-18-22 from Eric Austin (2-21-36) and R Little (2-27-09).

My well-used Austin A40 van was requiring more repairs than a driver-side front wing, because the engine was burning oil at an unacceptable rate and this would require major work to be done on its engine. In view of this I decided to trade it in for an Italian motor scooter, which I used to get around in Aberdeen.

I cannot remember the reason, but I agreed to run in an inter-universities cross-country race in Leeds along with Newcastle University runners, two weeks after the Harlow marathon. Charlie Aithie was the only teammate willing to come on this adventure, so he and I travelled to Newcastle on Friday afternoon and evening. There we slept the night in sleeping bags on the floor of a student's room in 'Hodgson House' of Newcastle University Halls of Residence. Next morning, we travelled with the Newcastle University runners in their bus to Leeds. Leeds runners Fox and Bird dead-heated to win and I was third, 18 seconds behind, while Charlie finished 20th. I felt that I was running quite well and strongly, so I was not too disappointed.

In the Edinburgh to Glasgow road relay on 20th November I ran the 6th leg of the H&HC, on a snowy day. I took over in 20th place and moved us up one place with 13th fastest time on this stage. Our team maintained this position to finish 19th. Andy McKean was fastest on the 6th stage followed by Dick Wedlock and Alastair Johnston.

A few days later I did an exercise Physiology test with Clyde Williams and the results showed that my maximum oxygen uptake had increased from 65.11 to 66.9 mL/Kg/min and my ventilation had also increased to 4.35l/min.

In the Scottish Universities team cross-country match versus S.C.C.U team on 11th December, at Murchison playing fields, Edinburgh, I had a good run to finish 4th. Andy McKean won from Ron McDonald and Jim Wight. My H&HC teammate from the previous year, Colin Youngson, was running for the S.C.C.U. This performance was my best cross-country race to date.

On the 31st of December I competed in the Nos Galan 4 miles midnight road race again. The start came as a surprise as the starter had refused to start the race until the block of runners who had crept forwards about 10yds had returned to the starting line. I was standing between the two groups of runners when the gun went, so I was not too badly affected, compared to some in the throng behind. I ran hard and moved steadily through the field and finished 15th in 19-11, which was 26 seconds faster than 1970. My team mate Charlie Aithie finished 58th. Tony Simmons won in a course record of 17-41, ahead of Dave Bedford and Bernie Plain.

I finished 1971 with a total of 5120 miles of training and racing and it never occurred to me that I should be spending more time on my studies and running less.

1972

My first race of 1972 was the third North East Cross-country league race at Hazlehead, Aberdeen, on Saturday the 8th of January. I was pleased to finish first 10 seconds ahead of Alastair Wood followed by Steve Taylor and Ian Mackenzie.

Next on the schedule was a mini 'Irish Tour', so on Saturday the 15th of January our H&HC team travelled to Liverpool, where we later caught the ferry for Dublin. After trying to sleep on the floor of a lounge in the car ferry from Liverpool to Dublin, we ran in the 4 teams cross-country match in Phoenix Park. I caught the leader and went into the lead, but I could not extend this because I was relying on the Trinity College runner to shout directions to keep me on the correct route. On reaching the main gates to the park where we had entered I ran hard to the finish ahead of Ian Cotton of the New University of Ulster (NUU). My teammate Charlie Aithie ran well to finish 7th. Our team was beaten by: NUU, Trinity College Dublin and Queens University, Belfast.

The following Saturday, 22nd January in the East District cross-country championships at Dunns, I fell on my back on the slippery mud at the first fence and narrowly avoided being trampled on by the pack. My next misfortune occurred when running down by a hawthorn hedge. I stood on a prickly branch and I felt a thorn going into my foot through the side of my spike. I resisted the temptation to stop and kept going, only to bang my knee on a fence when trying to hurdle it. Sam Downie won from Jim Wight and Willie Day and I finished 6th one second behind Andy McKean and Alex Wight.

Aberdeen University hosted the Scottish Universities Cross-country championships the following Saturday. I benefited from this 'home course' and decided to take the lead going onto the sand dunes and managed to pull away a little, so I had about a five-yard lead coming off the sand. Alastair Wood was at the Bridge of Don shouting encouragement and I managed to maintain a good enough pace to the end winning by 11 seconds from Dave Lorimer and Jim Dingwall. I was delighted to win this title at my 4th attempt. From Aberdeen University, only Alastair Wood (in 1956) had won before me.

On the following afternoon, the 30th of January, I ran my first indoor race at the Bells sports centre in Perth in the Scottish Universities Indoor Athletics championships. This was a 1500 metres (twelve laps) heat, which I won in a time of 4-13.2, which was very close to my outdoor best. In the final Jim Dingwall won in 4-10 and I finished 4th in 4-19 after lying second with only 20 yards remaining. I quite enjoyed the experience of running indoors.

In the B.U.S.F cross-country championships at Graves Park in Sheffield on the 5th of February I had a disappointing run on this testing course and finished 35th. Tony Moore won from Chris Garforth and H Ward and first Scot was Andy McKean in fifth.

Two weeks later on the 19th of February, in the Scottish National Cross-Country Championships at Currie near Edinburgh I finished 13th, which improved my best placing the previous year. I got left somewhat at the start and gradually worked my way through the field, but I never saw the leaders. On one bad stretch of the course I felt something 'go' in my left foot, but I was able to continue. I was very pleased with my performance. Ian McCafferty won from Jim Alder and Alistair Blamire.

My left foot injury appeared to be a strained ligament under the arch and this persisted until I became desperate to get something done. Eventually on Thursday the 22nd of March, four and a half weeks after the occurrence of the injury I went to the casualty department of Woolmanhill Hospital with a letter of introduction from Dr Mercer of the Student Health centre. I had my left foot X-Rayed, which showed that there was no bone damage, so I was given an injection of cortisone and local anaesthetic, which made me squirm with the pain as the doctor covered the region and this seemed to take a long time. When I stood up I felt nauseous and dizzy and fell back to the couch. Later when the local anaesthetic wore off my foot became very painful and I was barely able to walk. I hoped that this would settle my foot problem. I could not run for the next 3 days because my foot was too painful, but on the 4th day I jogged for 10 minutes on the grass at Kings and from then I gradually increased the jogging distance until I was able to resume my training schedule.

During my recovery period I attended potential employment interviews with the Ministry of Defence in Portsmouth, which did not go well and with Plessey Electronics in Ilford, which went very much better.

JOHN O'GROATS TO LAND'S END TEAM RELAY

I had agreed to be part of the Aberdeen AAC 10-man relay team attempting to break the John o'Groats to Land's End, (JOGLE) relay-running record. This was scheduled to take place during the Easter vacation from University, which was convenient, but with 'Finals' exams looming, perhaps I should have considered concentrating on my studies, especially as I was finding electrical power transmission lines, fault analysis and engineering maths level 4 hard going. However, the chance of participating in the JOGLE 'adventure' was irresistible. On Sunday the 9th of April 1972, our team in 5 camper vans set off for John o'Groats. Peter Duffy would be my running partner in van 3 and later I ran my first stint of 3 X 20 minutes, alternating with Peter, as each team of 2 ran a 2-hour stint. I was chosen to run through the Corrieyairack Pass on Monday, I was extremely tired as I had no sleep and the conditions were very bad, with great stretches of snow over the path and snow falling. I was glad to get through and see Peter coming towards me at the other side, eager to take over from me. My next stint alternating with Peter consisted of 4 X 15 minutes plus 8 minutes, with wind assistance, from Creiff to Stirling, a distance of 24 miles. Next day in the early hours I did 4 X 10 minutes plus one mile, and later 6 X 10 minutes and the next session was 6 X 10 minutes again with wind assistance. The following day, Wednesday, I ran: 5 X 10 minutes, then 3 X 10 minutes, 3 X 5 minutes and a stint of 8 X {2 X 5 minutes}. We failed to break Reading AC's record by only half an hour, but learned a lot, which could be incorporated into any future attempt. This had been an exhausting event and all were disappointed at missing the record. (However AAAC, sadly without me, succeeded in: setting a new record in 1973; and in 1982, with me, improving this considerably.)

Towards the end of April, I attended another potential employment opportunity interview with Lucas Aerospace. After travelling overnight by sleeper to Birmingham, I walked from New Street Station to Birmingham University track, where I ran 10 X 800 metres in 2-21 to 2-25, with the usual 400-metre jog in 2.5 minutes as recovery. I finished with 400 metres in 68s. Then I walked back to New Street and there caught a bus to the Lucas factory at Shaftmoor Lane in good time for my interview. Several candidates were assembled there and we were given an introduction and an audiovisual presentation, at which I dozed off, prior to the interviews. However, my interview went well.

Two days later, the 29th of April, Aberdeen University hosted an athletics match at the exposed Balgownie track against Edinburgh and Heriot-Watt universities. I ran in the 800 metres, finishing 6th and later in the 5000 metres led fron the start and won in 15-39.8, which was fairly slow, but I had to battle against the wind each lap.

FIRST TWO MARATHON WINS

My next marathon was the Edinburgh to North Berwick event, organized by Edinburgh Athletic Club, on Saturday the 13th of May 1972. A group of us went through 5 miles in 27-06, 10 miles in

54-57, 15 miles in 1-22-37 and 20 miles in 1-50-05. At about 21 miles I started to increase the pace, as I had been running quite easily up to that point, and established a lead of about 20yds over Davie Wyper. Then I began to slow and he caught me, so I ran with him until just after 25 miles, when I made another effort to get away and was successful. I was very pleased with my finish, taking 6-17 for the final one-mile and 365yds, which is approximately 5-05 for the last mile. My time of 2-24-26 was only 9 seconds ahead of Davie Wyper, who was also satisfied with his run. Cordes from Morpeth Harriers finished 3rd in 2-25-03. I was especially pleased, as at last I had won a marathon race.

Four days later in an evening meeting at the Balgownie track I ran in a 5000 metres race and had a race long duel with Bob Heron, who won by a couple of inches in a track record time of 15-12. My time of 15-12.8 was also inside the previous record.

On the 17th of May, in the Scottish Track 10 Miles Championships at Meadowbank I had an abominable race, finishing 8th in 53-14. I felt comfortable for about a mile, but then I seized up and felt like dropping out. My former H&HC teammate Colin Youngson was 2nd in 50-15 and lapped me twice. I was quite disgusted with my effort, which might have been due to the strain of study and the looming 'finals'. I did not run for several days after this, to concentrate on studying the range of subjects to be examined in our 'finals'.

Final exams began on Monday the 29th of May and were finished on the 7th of June, when all our class went for a post finals celebration/commiseration. I felt that I had performed well in two papers but not so well in several others and knew that I could have done better if I had taken more time to assimilate and fully understand all the information from our various Lecturers.

My sister Anne (Annie) married Robert (Bob) McKenzie on the Saturday the 3rd of June and this provided a two-day study break, which may or may not have been beneficial. I felt exhausted by the strain of these exams and ran poorly in the following BUSF 10,000m; 1500m and 5000m in the second NE Athletics league for AAAC; and in the Scottish 10,000m Track Championships at Meadowbank.

Near the beginning of my summer vacation I drove Mum to her Father's home in Caol, near Fort William and on to her Uncle Donald's home in Carbost, Skye. From there we caught a ferry from Uig to Tarbet in Harris to visit Mum's relations near there.

The results of the degree were published and my fears were confirmed when I saw that I had been awarded 2nd-class, division 2 honours. I was very disappointed and felt like repeating the year to achieve a better degree, but this was not a practical proposition. I graduated and Mum and Dad were able to attend the ceremony, which pleased them.

Having attended the Graduation Ball with Dorothy Watson on Friday evening, 7th July, I ran in the Inverness to Forres marathon sponsored by the North of Scotland Milk Marketing Board the following day. The weather was warm and I took the lead after about a mile and thought that I was running well, but the 5-mile time of 28 minutes was disappointing. Ten miles was passed in 56-15, 15 miles in 104 minutes and I was surviving the heat quite well, but the road surface was very hot and my feet suffered very badly, especially on the newly surfaced sections of road with stone chips. I slowed over the last 2 miles, so I was relieved to reach the Games field in Grant Park and the finish, very pleased to have won. At night I suffered from sunburn on my back and shoulders and my feet were blistered, with raw skin on my big toe and a burst blister on the sole of my foot. I hoped that they would not become infected, despite my cleaning and disinfecting efforts. My time of 2-33-00 was satisfactory for the adverse conditions. Duncan Davidson was second 2-54, followed by Mike Scott 3-01.

FINLAND

The following Wednesday, the 12th of July, Colin Youngson and I set off for Finland. Thanks to Colin's Dad Jim, who worked for 'Burtons' in the Esslemont and Mackintosh clothes store in Aberdeen, we secured a lift in a Burtons van to Newcastle. From there we began hitch-hiking, aiming for

Immingham Docks. We made good progress and after several interesting lifts, made it to Immingham by the following afternoon, where we boarded the overnight ferry to Gothenburg. We were fortunate to meet, on the ferry, a Scot from Edinburgh who was married to a Finnish lady and they gave us a lift across Sweden to Norrtalje, from where we could catch a ferry to Turku in Finland. Our sail across the Baltic Sea on a large vehicle ferry was spectacular as we passed near the Aland Islands over sapphire waters in beautiful sunshine.

After we reached Turku, our Edinburgh couple took us about halfway to Helsinki, before they had to leave the highway to visit her family. As the time was approaching 11pm, we simply selected a suitable spot in the forest and pitched our two-man tent for the night. Wearing Army Surplus kilts, next morning, Sunday, we completed our hitch-hike to Helsinki and on to Charlie Greenlees' flat on the outskirts of Helsinki. The hospitable downstairs neighbour was expecting us, since Charlie had agreed to let us use his accommodation while he was in the UK.

We resumed running that evening, through a forest near Tikkurila; and on succeeding days from the Olympic Stadium in Helsinki, on dirt roads and playing fields. On Wednesday evening we ran for 71 minutes on springy bark-surfaced jogging trails, which were excellent, from the old Stadium in Helsinki, where Paavo Nurmi used to run.

Charlie had arranged a Meeting with Tapio Pekola, the editor of the Finnish running magazine 'Juoksija', and both Colin and I enjoyed his company and also browsing through past editions in his 'Aladdin's Cave' office. Tapio ran with us on Thursday morning for 71 minutes and although I felt tired I managed to keep up. At night I ran again for 30 minutes on roads. Tapio had got permission for Colin and me to run the following Tuesday evening, as guests in the Finnish marathon championships, which was to serve as the selection race for their team for the Munich Olympics, so we began tapering for this. On Monday the 24th of July we had to attend the Olympic Stadium for doping control, which involved giving a blood sample for analysis. I tried to 'carbohydrate-load' by snacking on fructose powder with water most of the afternoon, evening and next day.

On the following afternoon, the 25th of July, we went to the Olympic Stadium in Helsinki and prepared for the marathon start in the early evening. This was on a 14-lap course from the stadium and held in conjunction with an athletics match between Finland, Great Britain and Spain. I started off cautiously, passing 10Km in 34-30. At about this point I began to need a toilet stop urgently (fructose effect?), so I slowed right down to look for a suitable place, but it was a built-up area with no obvious suitable sites. I spotted a lane with a neat hedge on each side so I dashed down it to find that it led to a tennis court, which was being well used, so I entered the pavilion and asked someone where the toilets were. They indicated that they were upstairs, so I went up, found them and got relief. I made my way back and rejoined the race, now in last place and I reckon this stop probably lost me 3.5 minutes. I passed 15Km in 54-51 in 22nd place and 20Km in 1-12-49 and in 21st place and I continued to work through the field and at 35Km I was 10th in 2-07-11. I got up to seventh place and on the last lap I passed 40Km in 2-25-37 before losing one place to finish 8th in 2-33-37, in my 20th marathon. Colin finished 6th in 2-32-18.

Results: 1) R Paukkonen 2-18-49, 2) V Paajanen 2-19-17, 3) O Suomalainen 2-22-25,

We enjoyed seeing the remainder of the evening's races and particularly enjoyed Mario Haro's winning run in the 10,000 metres. On the following evening we saw Lasse Viren win the 5000 metres; and Pekka Vasala the 1500 metres, ahead of Brendan Foster. Later in the evening we were privileged to be invited to the post-match Dinner, where Colin and I shared a table with steeplechasers, Tapio Kantanen and Pekka Paivarinta. (Viren and Vasala both went on to win gold medals in the 1972 Munich Olympics and Kantanen won bronze. Paivarinta became World Cross-Country Champion in 1973 at Waregem, Belgium.)

On the 27th of July, we set out on our travels and walked about 12 miles in kilts, with our packs, while hitchhiking north. Eventually we reached the home of Charlie's long-term, Finnish girlfriend,

Marja, who was staying at her parents for the summer. We introduced ourselves, got fed and pitched our two-man tent on her parents' front lawn. Early next morning we were wakened by her sweet voice and, after a hearty breakfast, we were taken to the family cabin and sauna, reached by rowing across a lake. Colin and I ran for 1-45 through forests and got lost, which could have been dangerous, but thankfully I managed to retrace our route. The following morning, we packed up and continued our travels to Savonlinna where we ran for 32 minutes then ran 400 metres on the track in 60s and I felt a lot better. We stayed another day in Savonlinna before continuing our travels on Monday, 31st of July when we walked 15 miles with our packs, while hitchhiking. I drank a gallon of skimmed milk during the day. On Tuesday, the 1st of August we walked 10 miles with our packs while hitchhiking to Hiekkaharju, outside Helsinki. There we were pleased to accept the hospitality of Tapio's parents, who looked after us well. The following day we ran seven laps of the sawdust track at Helsinki Stadium, which was about one mile per lap. On Thursday went by train to Turku.

On Friday 4th August, after walking for 6 hours in Turku and eating loads of fruit and also having had dinner, we decided at 2 hours notice to run in the 10,000 metres, local district championships in Turku stadium. Colin ran very well to finish 2nd in 30-39, 15 seconds behind Pekka Paivarinta, a Finnish international, who was merely out on a training run before practising his redoubtable sprint! I was about 8th in 33-11, which was faster than I expected. The Turku track of black coal dust appeared to be a 'fast track'. (John Landy had presumably broken Roger Bannister's world mile record there, back in 1954.)

On Saturday we caught the ferry from Turku back to Norrtalje in Sweden and continued hitchhiking towards Gothenburg, which we explored for a couple of days before heading for the ferry and eventually home, on Friday 11th August.

On Saturday, 19th August, I ran for AAAC in the Edinburgh Highland Games 2 miles team race at Meadowbank Stadium and finished last in about 10 minutes, which was rather embarrassing. On 22nd August, after my morning run, I went hill walking with Steve Taylor. We were on our feet for 11 hours and I estimated that we walked about 26 miles and climbed 6 Munros. The following Saturday the 26th of August, I ran in the Inverness to Drumnadrochit 15.5 miles road race, which is part of the Glenurquhart Highland Games programme. Alastair Wood won in 1-18-50, while I finished 2nd three minutes later feeling rather ill, having passed Graham Milne at about eleven miles.

In the Nairn Inverness road relay on 23rd September, I ran the second stage for the AAAC team in 19-34, which was 5 seconds faster than my previous best and 40 seconds outside the stage record. I then continued to run on to Inverness. Our team won, only 10 seconds outside the course record.

In the Knockfarrel hill race from Strathpeffer the following Saturday, 30th September, I eventually finished 2nd to Ian Mackenzie, with Brian Finlayson 3rd. My time was 70 seconds faster than the previous time I had run this race in 1970. Next weekend on the 6th of October in the Alves to Forres road race I had a poor run finishing 4th behind Alastair Wood, Ian Mackenzie and Graham Milne. In the evening I attended a farewell 'do' with my teammates from Aberdeen A.A.C, as I was due to start employment in Birmingham on the following Monday, 8th October.

BIRMINGHAM

Following my pre-graduation interviews I was offered 3 employment opportunities with: Plessey Electronics in Ilford; Westland Helicopters in Yeovil; and Lucas Aerospace in Birmingham. I accepted the position in Birmingham because I knew Tom McCook an ex Inverness harrier and 2nd claim AAAC runner was there. He had persuaded fellow Birchfield Harriers, Ian and Peter Stewart to run for AAAC in the Edinburgh to Glasgow relay, where I had met them. I thought that joining Birchfield Harriers and training with such fine runners would stimulate me to improve my performances sufficiently to make the Scottish cross-country team for the 'International' race next year.

On Monday the 8th of October 1972, I started my employment as an electronics engineer with

Lucas Aerospace. The first week of our graduate apprenticeship was an induction course at a large house called 'Hilver' and accommodation was provided. One of my 9 fellow graduates was Martin Reynolds, a 400 metres runner, who had represented Great Britain in the recent Munich Olympic Games.

At the end of this week on 14th October, in the 20 miles track race at Walton-on-Thames organised by the Road Runners Club (RRC). I did not feel great from the start and began to drop at about 2 miles and just fell further and further behind. Jim Alder won in 1-40-37 and my AAAC club mate Steve Taylor was 2nd in 1-45-40, while I finished last in 1-51-44, which was rather disappointing.

One of our course members was from Solihull and he invited me to stay with his parents on Saturday night until I got accommodation sorted out on Sunday. He telephoned around and I moved into a 'bed-sit' at 4, Cadbury Road, Moseley. My room was one of three on the upstairs floor of a fairly old house, with a shared cooking facility on the landing. The landlord, who appeared to be interested in antiques, lived in the downstairs part. I moved in about mid-morning and in the afternoon, having contacted Tom McCook, I decided to walk to Birchfield Harriers track at Alexander Stadium at Perry Barr. I had rather a long walk of about 7 miles, carrying my running kit from my digs to the Stadium, as they were nearly at opposite sides of Birmingham. I then ran 10 miles, setting off with Ian Stewart and his club mates. I got dropped after about 3 miles, but they waited for me at the turn and then I was dropped again. Next week I had difficulty in motivating myself to run and could only accumulate 44 miles. However, the following week I started running to and from my work in Shaftmoor Lane, about 40 minutes each way and ran with a group of Birchfield Harriers on Tuesday and Thursday evenings.

My sister Annie and her husband Bob drove down for a weekend visit, all the way from Aberdeen in their van with my scooter in the back, which I appreciated a great deal. This allowed me to use the scooter to travel to and from training nights with the club, although initially I made a mistake and ended up on the Aston Expressway, which led to the M6 and panic, until I could get off at the next junction. I only made this error once.

My first race for Birchfield Harriers was the 5th leg of the Bridgenorth road relay on 29th October. Colin Simpson of Small Heath Harriers, who was 43 years old, pulled away from me, so I was not very happy with my debut race. On Saturday, 4th November in the first Birmingham Cross-country league race at Keele I finished 51st, the 7th Birchfield runner home in this high-class field and I felt that I was running quite well. Roy Fowler was first ahead of Ian Gilmour and Ray Smedley.

The following Saturday, Len Cullen, Mal Pickering, Colin Jackson and I drove up to Keswick to run in the Derwentwater 10 miles road race on Sunday the 13th November. We met up with John Orton and his brother in the pub of the hotel where they were staying and we all had a little more than was good for us. In the race I began to have trouble with my insides by about 4 miles and I was forced to slow down at times, until at about six and a half miles I had to make a pit stop. We were 3rd team, with Mal 14th, Colin 21st and me 33rd. I should not have taken the fried breakfast at our B & B.

In the Edinburgh to Glasgow Road Relay the following Saturday, 18th November, I ran the 4th stage for Aberdeen AAC. Graham Milne, on the first stage, handed over in 3rd, to Ian Stewart, who ran brilliantly to set a new Stage 2 record, leaving a lasting impression on all of who witnessed it, as he moved us into the lead. Ian Mackenzie maintained our lead with 2nd fastest time on stage 3, so I took over in the lead – I had no one to chase and felt hunted. I maintained our lead, but my time was only 8th fastest on this stage. Steve Taylor was 4th fastest on stage 5, Alastair Wood was 8th fastest on the long 6th stage, Bob Heron was 2nd fastest on stage 7 and Peter Duffy was 6th fastest on the last stage and brought us home in 2nd place behind Shettleston Harriers.

At the next Birmingham Cross-country League race in West Bromwich on 25th November, Alan Rushmer won from Ray Smedley and Ian Gilmour and I finished 47th.

I was coping fairly well with the transition from University life to working from 8am to 5pm, but running to and from work, going to the club two evenings a week and cooking evening meals did not leave time for much else. Weekends were taken up with racing on Saturdays and 2 training sessions on Sundays.

At work my Graduate apprenticeship progressed as I spent some time in various sections of the aerospace division. The main project was a government contract to build an electronic control system for the Rolls Royce, RB199 engines for the Multi Role Combat Aircraft (MRCA), under development for the RAF and the German and Italian air forces. The MRCA, when it entered service with the R.A.F many years later, was called the 'Tornado'.

My next placement was in the drawing office, where the draughtsmen drew out the required circuit layouts, the 'artwork' for the various modules. This was in the time before 'Computer Aided Drafting' (C.A.D) was developed, so everything had to be done manually.

On Thursday the 21st of December we started on shorter working hours to use less electricity, in response to the miner's strikes, and our Christmas holidays began a day earlier. I headed north on the 22nd, in my old 'Austin Cambridge', which I had bought for £40, and stayed overnight with Peter and Rita Duffy in Wishaw.

Following a morning run with Peter I completed my journey to my Parents' home in Willowbank road in Aberdeen. Over the next week I enjoyed training runs on familiar routes, with my running pals: Alastair Wood, Steve Taylor, Colin Youngson and Graham Milne. My cumulative mileage for 1972 was 4688.5 miles.

1973

Because New Year's Day was not a public holiday in England I had to start my return journey 2 days earlier and again had an overnight stop at Peter and Rita's. I duly arrived back in Cadbury road in time to resume work on the 1st of January 1973. The Warwickshire cross-country championship at Coventry was the first race of the New Year and I had a reasonable race finishing 18th and 2nd counter for the Birchfield team, which finished 3rd team.

A couple of weeks later I travelled up to Scotland for the East District Cross-country championships at Esk Valley College, Dalkeith on the 20th of January. I was rather disappointed with my run, finishing 12th. Andy McKean won from Ian Elliot and Doug Gunstone. Snow began falling heavily as I drove back to Peter's house in Wishaw.

In the third Birmingham cross-country league race at Wolverhampton, on 27th January, I improved to 24th. Alan Rushmer won from Pete Wood and Peter Stewart. Two weeks later, 10th February, in the Midlands Cross-Country championships. I began to feel my right foot painful, under the arch, during the 2nd large lap and by the end of it my foot was extremely painful. I struggled to the finish 44th. We were 4th team and would have been 3rd, had it not been for my foot problem. Dave Black won from Roger Clark and K Hinton. Next day my foot was extremely painful and I was only able to limp about. After work the following evening I got ultrasonic treatment on my right foot from the Edgbaston clinic after the physiotherapists diagnosed a pulled 'spring tendon'. I had follow-up treatments on the following evenings, all at £2 a session. These treatments proved ineffective in relieving my problem and were only effective in generating income for the clinic. I was unable to run for 2 weeks. Later, once I was more knowledgeable about injuries, I came to believe that my foot injury was Plantar Fasciitis.

I began jogging again in early March, but I was compensating for my painful right foot and this caused a blister under the outside of my left foot, which gave me a great deal of pain. I went to the medical centre at work to get some treatment and was faced by a real battleaxe of a nurse, who was rather rude and of little help. She refused to burst the blister, so I did it myself and then she put a dressing on, which later fell off. This blister later became infected and I required antibiotics to clear the infection.

That weekend I travelled to Parliament Hill Fields with some of my club mates to watch the English National Cross Country Championships. The start was a spectacular sight and it was quite a picture to see the long line of runners in their various club colours making their way over the hills. The New Zealand runners ran very well and one of one of them, Rod Dixon, won from Dave Bedford.

In desperation I went to the casualty department of a hospital in Birmingham to try and get some treatment for my foot problem. The Doctor I saw arranged an X-Ray of my foot and after inspecting this prescribed a cortisone injection. I received this and was discharged one and a half hours after entering, which is less than I would wait to consult my local G.P. The cortisone injection did not hurt as much as the last one, so perhaps she had not got it to the right spot.

On Sunday, 15th April, a week after this treatment I ran in the Bulmers Cider 10 miles road race in Hereford and finished 14th in 55-45, which hurt my foot again, so I could only limp around after the race.

I returned to the hospital a few days later and was advised to have physiotherapy and to stop running for a month. The Physiotherapist at the hospital informed me that Lucas had a physiotherapist working in their medical centre at Shaftmoor Lane and put me in touch with her. I began receiving physiotherapy from her that day, the next 2 days and then daily at the end of April and early May for a week. Treatment was then given every 2nd day as my injury continued healing. I heeded the advice to stop running and stopped for three and a half weeks. On Friday the 11th of May I received my last ultrasonic treatment from the Lucas physiotherapist as she and I agreed that the injury had healed. I really appreciated all her help and the fact that Lucas cared enough about its employees to provide this medical facility.

During my injured period I had been attending Hall Green Technical College, for 3 months, along with other newly appointed Graduates on the Lucas Graduate Apprenticeship Scheme. This proved to be a varied and useful course and I learned a lot, including how to use lathes to cut metal shapes, drilling, bending and welding metal, to make a 'G clamp' from the raw metal. We each also had to complete a project. On my last day there, feeling adventurous, having seen 'faggots', which resembled beef olives, on the lunch menu for three months, I decided to try them for lunch that day. The resulting very bad indigestion prevented me from running later in the day, so I decided not to eat these again. The Lucas Graduate training officer Jim Norse coordinated all our apprenticeship training.

A TOUGH 'HOLIDAY' IN SCOTLAND

On Friday afternoon, the 6th of July, my 29th birthday, I began my two-week summer holidays. I drove up to Aberdeen in my 'Hillman Imp' (GST 695F) – which I had bought a few months earlier to replace my decaying Austin Cambridge – with Birchfield team mate, Colin Jackson, affectionately known as 'Jacko the Boot', because of his habit of abruptly increasing the pace in training runs (putting the boot in) as my passenger. He and I had entered for the Inverness to Forres marathon to be run the following day, the 7th of July.

I misjudged the time to drive from Willowbank Road in Aberdeen to the start in Inverness, so I had to drive very assertively, especially after making a wrong turn in Elgin, to get there for the 1pm start. We realised that time was running out, so I stopped in a lay-by between Nairn and Inverness, where we changed in double-quick time into our racing kit beside the car and then pressed on. Luckily, since we arrived at 30 seconds after 1pm, the runners were only lining up and they agreed to delay the start for us. I was completely drained of nervous energy by then. The start was quite brisk and I went with Alastair Wood despite feeling dozy, but after about 3 miles I let Alastair go. I began to feel better and held the gap to Alastair constant for a while and reached 10 miles in 54-25. I was quite pleased with how I felt during the race. Colin was delighted with his run and breaking

2-30. Alastair's won in 2-20-29, I finished in 2-27-10, Colin was next in 2-29-12 and Forres Harrier Duncan Davidson was 4th in 2-49-00. Alastair was convinced that the course was now too long and he estimated that it was 27 miles 680yds, but I do not know what his estimate was based on.

On Friday, 13th July, I travelled to Jura, for the 'Bens of Jura' hill race. This required driving to Kennacraig, by Tarbert on Loch Fyne, where I left my car and caught the ferry to Port Askaig on the isle of Islay. From there I boarded the Feolin ferry across to Jura, then caught the waiting mini-bus to Craighouse. I booked into the Jura Hotel and walked around part of the course, covering about 10 miles.

On 14th of July, I had a very hard time in the 'Bens of Jura' race of 16 miles over 7 mountain summits, including the 'Paps of Jura' for a total of 7500 feet of ascent and descent. My diary entry was: *The course was dreadful and if I had seen it properly before the race I probably would not have started it. On Friday there was a mist so I could not see more than the third hill. I started quite easily and at the first top I was 3rd and within catching distance of the leaders. I maintained this gap until the third top, but when I started the descent from this I had to scramble down a cliff and then 2000 feet of a scree slope. My ankles got badly banged and cut so I could not run down the scree like the others and I lost a lot of ground. I felt exasperated and decided that my aim now, must be to finish in one piece, rather than race for a high placing. I lost a couple of places going up the fourth top, but I had moved back to 4th by the top. The descent from this one was extremely dangerous and I lost more places. We were now climbing the 'Paps of Jura', which had very steep sides and looked a bit like volcanoes but with pointed tops. At the top of the sixth, I was 7th, but the descent from this one was suicidal with a precipice most of the way around the North side. One competitor; John Marstrand started an impressive avalanche as he descended the very steep scree slope. I made my way painfully and slowly down some very steep scree. At the top of the seventh and final hill I was 8th and after stumbling down through the rough boggy ground, to reach the bridge, which was the last checkpoint, I was 9th. On the 3 miles of road to the finish at Craighouse village hall, I passed two and finished 7th in 4-29-13. Bobby Shields of Clydesdale Harriers was first in 3-54. This is a race I will not try again. I was the only non-hill-running specialist participating. At night there was a Ceilidh in the village hall, which we all enjoyed. The summits in the order of climbing were: Dubh Bheinn (1725ft), Glas Bheinn (1839ft), Aonach Bheinn (1636ft), Beinn A'Chaolais* (2407ft), Beinn An Oir* (2571ft), Beinn Shiantaidh* (2477ft) and Corra Bheinn (1867ft) [* indicates the 'Paps of Jura'.]*

I could not run for the following five days because my leg muscles were far too painful.

On returning to the mainland I drove up to John o'Groats, left my car there, and caught a ferry across the firth to Orkney, where I stayed at Rita's Mum's for a couple of days and did some sightseeing. I returned to Elgin by Saturday, 21st of July, to run in the Elgin Highland Games 15.5 miles road race. My legs began to hurt more as Graham Milne and I passed 5 miles in 26-54 and I had to let Graham go as my calf muscles were seizing up. I passed 10 miles in 54-27 and managed to shuffle back, maintaining 2nd place. Graham won in 1-21-46, I finished in 1-24-58 and Stan Stennet was 3rd in 1-26-10. I noted in my diary: *I must avoid hill racing in future as it ruins my legs.*

On resuming work my next apprenticeship placement was at Marston Green near the runway end of Birmingham Airport. This meant longer runs to and from work and I was able to use the canal system in Birmingham to avoid roads, by running along appropriate towpaths for the majority of my runs to and from Marston Green. Following my run to work I used to change from my running kit into my working clothes in the locker room and one morning a group of women workers entered to find me in a state of 'between clothes', which must have upset them because they contacted their shop-steward. He in turn contacted me and asked me to find a more discreet place in which to get changed.

My task there was to look at module circuit diagrams and decide how they would be tested when powered up, following active Laser trimming. Testing was to be by computer-controlled automatic test equipment (ATE). I had to write, after some advice, test programs in 'Automatic Test Language for Avionic Systems' (ATLAS) for modules, which I found satisfying. The circuits were required to function properly over the military specification temperature range of -50°C to 125°C, which was a huge challenge for an analogue system, which our control system mainly was.

By the end of July my training was typically: running to and from work on Monday to Friday with usually hard club runs on road courses, on Tuesday and Thursday evenings. On Saturdays if there were no races I would run a 16.4 miles course and Sundays would be 23 miles on roads in the morning and ten miles with the club on canal towpaths in the afternoon. My weekly mileage would be around 145 miles at this time.

My next race was the Inverness to Drumnadrochit 15.5 miles road race, on Saturday the 25th of August. I felt dreadful after starting and I was intending abandoning the race after crossing the canal bridge because my legs were absolutely dead, presumably as a result of my 580 miles drive from Birmingham the previous day. However, I decided to carry on and use the race as a training run and gradually I picked up places and by 5 miles, I was 5th. By 10 miles, passed in 53-09 I was 3rd and catching Graham Milne. Sandy Keith won in 1-19-10, while I finished 2nd in 1-21-14, which was 1-31 faster than in 1972 and pleasing. Graham was 3rd in 1-22-11.

On Sunday, I ran for 2-40-00 with Graham Milne on roads and forest tracks at quite an easy pace to serve as my glycogen depletion run for the Enschede marathon.

ENSCHEDE AGAIN

I had organized for a group of Birchfield Harriers to run in the Enschede marathon in Holland, so on Thursday the 30th of August 1973, we set off travelling and arrived at Enschede in the late evening and settled in with our host families. Next morning, I ran easily for 3.5 miles to give a total of 583.5 miles in August.

In the 14th International Enschede Marathon on the 1st of September, there were 230 entries with 14 countries being represented. I finished 9th in 2-25-37, but was disappointed with my time as I was hoping to get nearer to 2-20. The weather was warm and there was a wind blowing. I was in the 4th rank at the start and so I was badly boxed and restricted on the 1.5 laps of the track, so on reaching the road I started moving through, from one group to the next but my pace was rather erratic. I got little shelter from the wind in this process, but Colin Jackson did help me by leading me sometimes. My times were slow on the outwards journey and at the turn, reached in 1-13-32, I was 26th. After turning I began to move better and began catching runners, which was encouraging and finally caught and passed Donal Walsh of Ireland on the track. I noted in my diary: *I was pleased at beating runners such as: Joe Keating, Bernie Allen and J Vitale. I will have to learn to run faster in Marathons. My 10Km splits up to 30Km were: 37-08, 32-38, 36-11, 34-06 and the next 5Km to 35Km occupied 17-47.* My Birchfield Harriers teammates were: Roy Tilling, 30th in 2-37-54, Colin Jackson, 37th in 2-41-10, Mike Densley, 72nd in 2-53-34, Len Cullen, 137th in 3-12-47, Brian Roberts, 140th in 3-13-25 and Mal Pickering 151st in 3-17-35. Charlie Greenlees was 107th in 3-03-45. Ron Hill won in 2-18-06 from Hans Jonsson of Sweden in 2-20-05 and Jim Alder in 2-20-41. We had a few days' holiday in Holland, mainly around Amsterdam and at the beach at Zandvoort, before returning to Birmingham.

Ian Stewart had been invited to run in the 'Coatbridge 5' road race, on the 15th of September and to bring a Birchfield team. I volunteered along with Tom McCook, who was married to Carol, Ian and Peter Stewart's elder sister. Ian had arranged for us to stay the weekend with some of Ian's relations in Drumchapel, which was greatly appreciated by Tom and me. Ian won the race and I finished 26th, lacking speed and finding the race hard work. One of Ian's favourite comments was: 'there is more to running than running', by which he meant the planning and type of training and resting, plus the mental aspect of preparing for important races. Another of his often-used comments was: 'It's not the shoes that matter, but who is wearing them that counts'.

Following this short race, I began preparing for the Harlow marathon, but I picked up some sort of infection, which produced flu-like symptoms and swollen lymph glands. My local G.P. prescribed 'Oxytet, 250mg tablets', which I now realise, may have done more harm than good. I felt weak for several weeks afterwards and my black stools were concerning me as I suspected intestinal bleeding. I probably should have stopped running, but instead I maintained my 140 miles a week schedule.

On some Sunday mornings I would jog from Cadbury Road to Ian Stewart's home and run with him and whoever else had turned up, such as Andy Holden or steeplechaser, John Bicourt. We would run an eighteen-mile route. In the afternoon I would run ten miles of fartlek with the club in Perry Barr Parks, trying to keep up with Mary Stewart, Peter and Ian's younger sister and Scottish international runner, so I was rather tired by Sunday evenings.

I got the results of a blood test, which indicated that I was slightly anaemic, so I began a course of ferrous sulphate tablets.

On the 27th of October I started in the Harlow marathon, but I dropped out at 16 miles. I was not distressed and I could have completed the distance, but I was unable to run fast and I would not have broken 2-30. I felt very stiff and heavy; my legs would not move quickly and I also lacked energy, especially on the hills. I just had no 'go' at all. An 'unknown', Ian Thompson, running his first marathon was the surprise winner.

After another prescription of ferrous sulphate tablets, I began to feel less lethargic and in the first Birmingham cross-country league race at Tipton finished 39th of the 109 finishers and was quite pleased with my run, as it showed a good improvement in my form. Ian Gilmour was first ahead of Keith Rollason and Roy Fowler.

Two weeks later on the 17th of November, I ran the 7th leg of the Edinburgh to Glasgow Road Relay for AAAC. Ian Stewart handed over to me in the lead 61 seconds ahead of Don McGregor, so I felt 'hunted' and exposed. Allister Hutton of ESH came up to my shoulder and then he got about 10 yards ahead. This gap remained the same for some time, but then he opened up. My legs were very painful and I could not pull anything back, so I handed over to Tom McCook in 2nd place. My time was 4th fastest behind Greg Hannon, Allister Hutton and Stuart Easton. Our team in running order was: Graham Milne, Sandy Keith, Ian Mackenzie, Alastair Wood, Bob Heron, Ian Stewart, Donald Ritchie and Tom McCook. We finished 3rd in 3-41-33 behind Edinburgh Southern Harriers, 3-39-14 and Edinburgh AC 3-41-23. Once again Tom and I stayed with Ian Stewart's relations in Drumchapel on the outskirts of Glasgow.

The second Birmingham cross-country league race was the following Saturday at Perry Barr, where Ian Stewart won from Andy Holden and Keith Rollason. I was quite pleased finishing 28th of the 121 finishers.

On the 1st of December, I drove down from Birmingham to Bristol, on a very frosty morning, for the Welsh RRC 20 miles track race, organised by Bernard Baldwin. Bernie Plain was first in a new British record of 1-40-35 ahead of Bob Sercombe, 1-40-59 and I was 3rd in 1-46-32.6, which was a personal best. I was quite pleased, but I would have been happier if I had been informed how far I had gone, given intermediate times and told how many laps remained. None of this information was given to runners apart from the 2 leaders, who were well ahead of me.

On Monday the 10th of December my left Achilles tendon became injured, being painful and swollen and became worse in succeeding days of running. Running in 'Gola' racing shoes, which had rather hard soles, may have caused it or it may have been due to running 74.5 miles within 48 hours. I went to my local GP to get a letter authorizing treatment from the physiotherapy department at Lucas. He did this and suggested two weeks off training.

I received treatment from the Lucas Physio, at my work in Shaftmoor Lane, on alternate days and also cut back on my running. On Friday the 20th of December I finished my treatment at the Lucas Physiotherapy department and this treatment had certainly helped, as my tendon felt much better. I drove up to Aberdeen for a week's Christmas holiday and during that week I amassed 178.5 miles, running mostly twice a day, with running pals on at least one session. I finished 1973 with a yearly total of 4858 miles.

On completing my graduate apprenticeship, I was offered a position as an electronics development engineer working on the control system for the RB199 engine to power the MRCA. I was to be based in a 'clean room' at Shaftmoor Lane, actively testing modules as they were produced using automatic test equipment controlled by the ATLAS programs, which I had helped to produce. Because MRCA was to be for Germany and Italy in addition to UK, we had some German electronics engineers join the testing phase, which added to the realisation of the very large scale of this project and the huge financial costs involved. Because of this German aspect, Lucas sponsored Dave Bennett, a fellow testing engineer, and I, to learn 'Conversational German' at evening classes, with a cash incentive to pass the examination, which we both did.

1974

My first race of 1974 was the Warwickshire Cross-country championships at Bedworth on Sunday the 6th of January. The course was very muddy and heavy, but I seemed to run well on it and I was very happy to finish 6th. Birchfield were first team with all 6 counters in by 14th. Ian Stewart won from Ken Bartlett of Coventry and Peter Stewart. This was my best cross-country performance.

On Monday the 7th of January, because of the miners' strike our works began a four-day week, to minimise the requirement for electricity consumption and avoid 'black-outs'. Our working was now: Wednesday, Thursday, Friday and Saturday, so Sunday, Monday and Tuesday were days off. I used my first 'free' morning, running for over 3 hours along the towpaths of the Grand Union canal, heading towards London and in the early evening I ran for 35 minutes and included efforts for a total of 35 miles. It was quite a change for me to be in my bed-sit on a weekday, as I normally left by 06:30 and returned by 18:30.

My neighbours in the two other bedrooms off the landing were fairly transient and I never got to know any of them. For about a month a young couple, an Indian man and a white English girl were opposite and made love quite audibly. More disturbing was the fact that when I met them on the stairs one evening, he was assisting her upwards as if she was rather drunk, but she was under the influence of some drugs. Our landlord was aware of this and said 'that she came from a good home', and they moved on to who knows what.

Their room was then occupied by about three or four, I assumed, descendants of West Indians, who had music playing very late into the night and into next day. They did not appear to have any work to go to and so had no structure to their days. In the bedroom adjacent to me were a couple that I never saw and only knew of by their conversation and actions which I could hear in my room as I tried to relax on the bed following a morning training run on my Mondays and Tuesdays off. They appeared to spend all day in bed having repetition sessions of lovemaking. My eyes had certainly been opened there to another side of life and I wanted to move to a place of my own.

On my Sunday run on the 13th of January, on the Grand Union Canal towpath, on the return journey I was tired and I fell very heavily and bashed my right knee very hard, cutting it, so that it became rather painful. This was a nuisance because I had been selected to represent Warwickshire in the Inter-Counties cross-country the following Saturday the 19th of January at Derby. The course was very tough, with a steep long hill to be climbed on each of the three laps. I fell over in a ditch, banged my painful knee and cut my elbow; so one side of me was muddy from head to toe. I finished a disgusted and very grubby 154th.

By the end of January, we were back to the normal working week, which pleased everyone, except perhaps the miners. On the 9th of February in the Midlands Cross-country championships I finished 45th and 5th counter for our team, which finished 4th.

The following Saturday, the 16th of February, I ran for AAAC in the Scottish National cross-country championships at Coatbridge and had a very poor run indeed. I felt tired as soon as I started, so all I could do was battle round trying my best and eventually I finished 42nd, the only consolation being that I contributed to Aberdeen AAC gaining 3rd team medals.

On the 4th of February I left my bed-sit in Cadbury Road and moved to a two-bedroom terraced house at 82 Booths Lane, Great Barr, Birmingham. I had purchased this house for £6700 and E. G. Seagroat and Co, dealt with the legal transaction. Mr Seagroat was an ex-active Birchfield Harrier. This change of residence necessitated altering my running routes to and from work. I had access to the canal, 'The Cut' near the top of Perry Park, which I joined and followed to under 'Spaghetti Junction', where I changed canal towpaths and followed this next canal to near my work at Shaftmoor lane. This route was 'traffic free' apart from joining and leaving and, once the evenings became lighter, I was able to do 'effort sessions' on the towpaths on my evening run home. My old pal Les Macallan came to stay with me while he was on a violin-making course in Birmingham, so it was good to have his company. This was quite a change for Les, who had previously been a welder. An itinerant houseguest was Harry Rocks, an Irishman, who ran for Birchfield harriers, but was working away most weeks. He did not have a key but I left a kitchen window unlocked so that he could get in as necessary.

John Graham also came down on a few weekends to stay a couple of nights and run in Birmingham cross-country League races, initially as a guest and then as a counter for Birchfield Harriers. This elicited a letter of disapproval in 'Athletics Weekly' (AW) from Coventry Godiva Harriers about Birchfield's practice of signing up Scots to enhance their team scores. This prompted Ian Stewart to counter with a letter, which was published in the following week's AW and attributed to Ian Stewart and Dan Ritchie, which amused me.

On Saturday the 2nd of March, although my waking pulse was still high at 54 I decided to go with the Birchfield team, to Sheffield to compete in the English National Cross-country championships in Graves Park, which would be my debut in this famous event. I felt okay at the start, but on the 2nd of the three laps my intestines began to give me trouble which added considerably to my difficulties on this muddy, gruelling course. I was very glad to reach the finish in 410th position and head for the showers, despite the fact that they were cold.

I think that my poor performance was due to running too many miles in training rather than concentrating on fartlek and effort sessions with fewer miles covered.

On Sunday, 10th of March, in the Cannock Chase 21 miles trail race, organized by Stafford AC and sponsored by Ansells Brewery, I finished 9th of 118 finishers, in very bad weather as sleet and snow fell throughout the race. Jeff Norman won in 1-59-25, ahead of J Wigley, 1-59-58 and my teammate Mick Phillips, 2-01-21-18. Road relays were underway by the following week and I was selected for the 'A' teams at: Leicester, Harborne and the eight-man Midland road relay championships in Sutton Park, where we finished third team.

On the 31st of March, the day after running in the Midland road relay championship, I drove up to Edale in the 'Peak District', accompanied by club mate Joe Patton, to run in a 22 miles fell race called the 'Don Morrison Edale Skyline'. I did not take this race very seriously and so I was quite pleased with my run, finishing sixth in 2-53-26, out of a field of 100 starters. I was quite strong on the uphills, which was gratifying, but I lost a great deal on the downhill sections and on the very rough stony patches. In addition, I made three navigational errors and lost a lot of ground to Denis Weir who finished 4th. I had been running with him or ahead of him for most of the race. My prize was a pair of mountaineering socks. The course started in Edale and climbed to 'the Nab and onto the top of Jaggers Clough and then down and up to 'Win Hill, followed by a down and up to 'Lose Hill', followed by: Mam Tor, Lord's seat, Brown Knoll and Grindslow Knoll, before returning to Edale. The total ascent was calculated as 4700 feet and the distance as 22.1 miles (33.8Km). Harry Walker was first in 2-40-10 ahead of Martin Weeks, 2-45-24 and Joss Naylor 2-48-26. It was an enjoyable day out in a new part of the country for me and Joe enjoyed it also.

On Friday the 12th of April after my run back from work I drove to Laugharne in South Wales with Roy Tilling, Mal Pickering, Nigel and Colin Jackson to a site, where we had hired a caravan for a long weekend. Over the next three days we did a mixture of sessions on roads, paths and Pendine Beach. In a fartlek session with the lads on this beach I had to stop after 6 miles because a muscle in my groin seized up, like a cramp.

After three more days of my groin muscle cramping during runs, I went to the Edgbaston health clinic, seeking treatment for the problem. The physiotherapist, Mr. Price thought that it was a strained muscle and gave me some infrared treatment and suggested some exercises. This did not cure the problem, but gradually the occurrence of cramps reduced. On a morning run to work I tripped and fell going down a bank by a lock on the canal. I cut my knee and hand badly, so I had to return home as my cuts were full of dirt requiring cleaning and disinfecting to prevent them becoming infected. Thankfully I was able to resume training the following day.

My next race was the Rugby marathon on Saturday the 4th of May, which was also the Midland Counties Championships. I passed 10 miles in 53-32 with the leading bunch, but at about 12 miles my legs suddenly became very heavy and stiff, so I had to let the leading group go. As soon as I slowed I felt worse and slowed even more. I felt like dropping out, but I decided to continue for a bit longer. I did not get any better, but I managed to pull back 4 runners, which encouraged me and I passed 20 miles in 1-51-55. My legs were very painful and stiff, but I do not think that I had run out of glycogen. Jeff Norman was first in a course record of 2-19-37 ahead of Ray Donkin 2-20-19 and Tom O'Reilly, 2-22-03, while I finished 6th in 2-28-27 and Jacko (Colin Jackson) was 9th in 2-30-23.

Four weeks later on the 1st of June, Jacko and I travelled up to Hull for a 20 miles road race. I had introduced more interval sessions since the Rugby marathon with sessions of 8 X 800 metres; with a 400 metres jog recovery, averaging 2-17. In the 'East Hull 20', Jacko set the pace to about 4 miles, where he slowed and urged me to go on, which I did, passing 5 miles in 26-02 and 10 miles in 52-56, but after this I found it hard work because of the strong wind and by then hot weather conditions. I passed 15 miles in 1-21-00 and I began to feel glycogen depleted with around 2 miles remaining. I was pleased to win, but I was not content with my time of 1-50-28. P Wright was 2nd in 1-54-17 and Pete Flatman was next in 1-55-37 and Jacko was 5th in 1-56-57. My prize was a 25-piece dinner service.

Two weeks after this on my Monday morning run to work I felt dreadful and I felt really ill after I finished. I noticed that my urine was very dark with blood, which was rather alarming. This appeared to clear up over the next few days, but I still felt dreadfully weak, which was alarming, as I had entered the Scottish Marathon on the coming Saturday, the 22nd of June.

Although I started in the Scottish Marathon Championships from Meadowbank, I failed to finish. I set out purposefully and went through 5 miles in 26 minutes with the leaders, but soon after this I began to feel very tired and I began to drop back as my stride got shorter and shorter. I reached 10 miles in 55-30 and by the turn I was ready to drop out, but I persisted in the hope that I might recover, but at 15 miles, I felt like I was jogging. I stopped at 16 miles feeling that there was no point in going on to record a time of about of 2-36 to 2-40. I was very despondent about my poor performance. Perhaps I had some infection, which was causing me to feel ill in the preceding week. I was left in a state of confusion trying to analyse what might be the cause of my failure and how I might do things differently in the future.

After two weeks of greatly reduced training, and by then on my summer holidays, I tackled the Mamore hill race at the Kinlochleven Highland Games on 6th July. I started well and the pace felt easy as Alan Partridge, Brian Finlayson and I broke away, but when we began climbing I began to flag and just felt very weak. Towards the top of the initial climb, Peter Duffy and the eventual winner, Phil Dolan, came past. I finished a tired 7th.

Following this Colin Youngson and I went hill walking/scrambling around Glen Coe and Kinlochleven, using our two-man tent as accommodation and also self-catering and when possible continuing Colin's Campaign for Real Ale (CAMRA) pub search. On Monday we climbed 2 Munros (mountains over 3000 feet) in 5.5 hours, 4 on Tuesday in 6.5 hours, 2 on Wednesday in 6 hours and 2 on Thursday in 5 hours. We were rather pleased with our 'bag' of big hills. Two days later, the 13th of July, at the Inverness Highland games in Bught Park I ran in the 5000 metres and finished a tired 3rd behind Sandy Keith and Ian Mackenzie.

In the Elgin Highland Games 15.5 miles road race on Saturday the 20th of July, I started cautiously but felt tired at the initial pace and a pain developed at the back of the knee joint on my left leg. This became very painful indeed. I thought that I would have to stop, but I decided to carry on and thankfully the pain diminished. After the race my left leg was very painful. Alastair Wood won in 1-19-35 ahead of Sandy Keith, 1-22-16 and I was 3rd in 1-25-42.

On the 9th of August 1974, a group of us went to the south coast for a camping adventure. Apart from Ian Stewart we all ran in the 'Swanage 12' road race the following day and won the team race with Roy Tilling 6th, Colin Jackson 7th, me 12th and Mal Pickering 17th. We each received a pewter tankard, which we christened that evening.

AT LAST, ANOTHER ULTRA

I seemed to lack the motivation to run during the following week and only covered 42 miles and this persisted into a second week. However, I decided to run in the Two Bridges race the following Saturday (24th August) and I was very pleasantly surprised at how well I ran. My training had been very patchy since the Scottish marathon debacle so I decided to start cautiously and passed 5 miles in 30-31. After this I started to move through, so it was a good feeling picking up places one by one and passed 10 miles in 60-17 in 16th place. I realized that I had gone off at too easy a pace and I should have gone with the leading bunch, as I reckon that I was running at the same pace as the leaders apart from Jim Wight from 15 miles, which I passed in 1-30-39. I passed 20 miles in 1-59-44 in 14th, 25 miles in 2-30-08 in 11th, marathon in 2-37-04 in 10th, 30 miles in 2-59-47 in 7th and 35 miles in 3-29-56 in 5th and held this place to finish. The 'carbohydrate loading diet' obviously worked well for me on this occasion. Aberdeen AAC won the team prize with Bob Heron 2nd in 3-32-04, Alastair Wood 3rd in 3-32-43 and me 5th in 3-36-58. Jim Wight won by a large margin in 3-26-31.

Three weeks later, the 14th of September, I travelled to Blackpool with the club to run in the Illumination Trophy meeting. I ran in the 3000 metres and was rather apprehensive and I found the initial pace fast, but this eased off and I settled into the 2nd group. This broke up with 4 laps remaining and I finished 6th about 50 yards behind the 2nd placer, who recorded 9-02, so I estimate that my time was about 9-11.

MY LONDON TO BRIGHTON DEBUT

I wanted to experience running in the famous 'London to Brighton' road race, which at the time was 52 miles 1172 yards long, so on Saturday the 28th of September 1974, I drove to London with Colin Jackson, who was to be my second. We settled into our accommodation, ready for the race on Sunday and then Colin went out for the evening while I went to bed early.

Early next morning, after getting changed in some grand building fairly close to the start, I made my way with other runners to the start by 'Big Ben'. On the first stroke of 7am we set off across Westminster Bridge. I started fairly easily and was running with Ian Burgess and Dave Bagshaw, but by 5 miles I felt that we were going a little too fast, so I let them go and tried to maintain an even pace and passed 10 miles in 57-10. Shortly after 20 miles (1-57-06), Tom O'Reilly came past as I struggled up a hill. By about 28 miles I began to run better again and pulled back Bagshaw and Burgess and went ahead of them. Then I was out on my own and the miles seemed to take longer and longer to pass. The muscles in my legs were twitching and everything ached; even the muscles in my cheeks. My groin muscle also gave 4 twinges, but thankfully it did not go into spasm. I found this run hard on my mind – the continual banging of my feet on the road seemed maddening. I had to concentrate as much as possible over the last 16 miles. With about 1.75 miles remaining I could see Tom O'Reilly and I started to put in a little more effort and caught and passed him with about 600yds remaining. I was delighted to have finished the course and even more delighted to have finished in 3rd place. It was an exhausting run and I had to be helped downstairs to the dressing rooms, where I sagged into a deckchair and relaxed, while every muscle in my body ached and my head swam. Colin had been very helpful, giving me drinks every 3 miles from 10 miles. It also helped to have someone to give me information about the course and my race position. I wrote in my diary: *I do not think that I will tackle this race again, because the traffic was dreadful and highly dangerous. Because of the crosswind blowing, exhaust fumes came our way and I suspect that we were suffering from carbon monoxide and lead poisoning by the end. However, it is indeed a classic race and I am pleased to have taken part.*

On finishing I had been introduced to the Mayor of Brighton and his wife and then to the actress Dame Flora Robson. In my tired state I thought that she was Dame Flora McLeod of McLeod from Dunvegan castle in Skye, so I told her that I had relations at Carbost, which is near Dunvagen. She probably thought that I was suffering from some brain problem after running all that way and kindly took me by the arm onto the pavement. At the post-race tea in the 'Old Ship Hotel', The Mayor of Brighton, Alderman Danny Sheldon presented the awards. John Newsome was first home in 5-16-07 ahead of Cavin Woodward in 5-16-13 and I was third in 5-24-54, just 30 seconds ahead of Tom O'Reilly. Colin was very pleased for me.

The following Saturday I made the mistake of running in the Wimbledon '10' with some Birchfield pals and had an absolutely abysmal run. My legs were as stiff as boards after about three-quarters of a mile and I could scarcely move. Then to add to my discomfort I had to stop for a number two and had to walk about a hundred yards to find a suitable place. I decided to finish rather than drop out, so I completed the course in 62 minutes, which must be a personal worst.

Around this time, I began considering my future and decided that I should return to Aberdeen and seek work in the oil industry, which was then developing quickly. Although I enjoyed my work at Lucas Aerospace, which was challenging and interesting, my life was a repeating cycle of running, working, running, sometimes three times a day, Monday to Friday. Weekends were taken up racing or training on Saturdays and two sessions on Sundays. Also I began to think more about the environment in and around Aberdeen and realised that I missed this. I was also aware that my cross-country running was not progressing and that my goal of a few years ago to get selected for the Scottish team for the International cross-country championships was not going to be realised. I was thinking of taking my running less seriously and becoming a recreational runner when I moved north.

I therefore began applying for employment opportunities in Aberdeen and some time later I attended interviews at BP and then a service company, Under Water Diving Inspection (UDI).

My next race was on Saturday the 2nd of November in the R.R.C 30 miles track race at Walton-on-Thames. I was running well passing 10 miles in 53-35, 20 seconds behind Mick Molloy from Eire, and 20 miles in 1-50-24, but then I began to tire and my pace dropped, but I was 4 seconds inside record schedule at 25 miles and passed the marathon distance in 2-26-09, which was my fastest marathon that year. I faded to finish in 2-49-33 and I was very disappointed at not being able to break the world record after being so close for most of the way. The winner, Mick Molloy, broke the record with 2-44-47 after leading from the start. I never caught up with him. Subsequently he won a marathon in Belgium in 2-18-45 after going half a mile off course, when leading. My legs were very painful by the finish and this may have been the limiting factor, as the 'carbo loading diet' seemed to have worked well. Bob Heron was 3rd in 2-52-59. Fred Howe retained the UK national record with 2-48-08 achieved in 1962.

Two weeks later, the 16th of November, I ran the 4th stage of the Edinburgh to Glasgow relay for Aberdeen AAC. I did not run very well and I was only 11th fastest. Our team in running order was: Bob Heron, 8th fastest, Sandy Keith 12th, Danny Buchan, 10th, me, Pete Duffy 15th, Alastair Wood 10th fastest, Andy Law 4th and Graham Laing, who was 6th fastest and brought us home in 7th place.

On Sunday the 1st of December I started in the Barnsley marathon, but abandoned it after the first lap of 16 miles. The course was very hilly and I had nothing in my legs after about 2 miles and began to drop back after this. I passed 5 miles in 27-00, 10 miles in 58 minutes and 15 miles in 1-27. The carbohydrate loading diet did not appear to help on this occasion and in fact it seems to have had an adverse effect. I was pleased to watch Alastair Wood winning this race.

I returned to Aberdeen for Christmas with my parents and had some good runs over familiar territory with Alastair Wood and Colin Youngson. I finished 1974 with a total of 4988 miles training and racing.

REVIEW

At 30 years of age, Donald Ritchie seemed to have reached a crossroads. He wanted to leave Birmingham, return to North-East Scotland and maybe become merely a recreational runner! There was no doubt that his cross-country running had not improved from university days, when he won the Scottish Universities title and was a decent 13th in the very competitive Scottish National. Certainly he had won some road and hill races but his times had not improved since a 1971 marathon in 2.23.31.

Frequent problems had flared up e.g. diet, digestion, blisters, accidents, injuries and illnesses. Although Donald was addicted to training miles (over 140 in many weeks) they had not aided progress in events up to the marathon. In fact, he seemed to have difficulty in resting before important events and often over-raced, or ran in events he should have side-stepped.

Yet his determination, ability to persevere through suffering and basic stamina remained unquestioned. Surely he could recognise that his best races had been ultra-marathons, such as the Two Bridges and the London to Brighton. With sensible preparation and better luck, could he achieve his undoubted potential at similar events? Yet further difficulties were to come………

1975

Again the first race of 1975 was the Warwickshire Cross-country championships at the same venue as last year, but there was less mud. I felt OK on the hills, but I had trouble running on the mud and ploughed fields and finished 13th. Birchfield Harriers were 2nd team. Three weeks later in the third Birmingham cross-country league race at Perry Barr Park I finished 29th.

Around this time a typical week's training would be as follows.

Monday, 10.5 miles on roads in 64 minutes, alternating two minutes hard pace, two minutes easy pace with one minute hard pace, one minute easy pace.

Tuesday, the 'Hardwick' route with Mal Pickering in 60 minutes. This included 9 efforts alternating two minutes hard and one-minute easy. (10.5 miles)

Wednesday, morning run to work at an easy pace in 75-30, at night ran back in 68-30 incorporating efforts, alternating 2 minutes hard pace, 2 minutes easy pace with one minute hard pace, one minute easy pace doing 9 of each (23.2 miles)

Thursday, the Erdington route at a hard pace in 53 minutes with Mal and John. (10 miles)

Friday, morning run to work in 73-00 and at night I ran back in 72-00 incorporating efforts, alternating two minutes hard pace, two minutes easy pace with one minute hard pace, one minute easy pace and did 9 of each (23.2 miles)

Saturday, 12 X 400 metres with Mal in 70s to 73s with a 200 metres recovery jog. (4.6 miles)

Sunday, morning run for 79 minutes with Mal: 10 miles fartlek around the parks in afternoon. (22.5 miles)

Weekly total: 104.5 miles

In the Midlands cross-country championships at Reddich on the 8th of February, I had a very poor run. I finished 48th and 6th man for the Birchfield team. We were 3rd team, thanks to Ray Smedley. Mick Phillips, Mike Peak, Roy Tilling and Mal Pickering and I was very pleased to get a medal because it was my last chance.

The following Saturday in the Scottish National cross-country championships I had a very disappointing run and finished about 50th.

On Saturday the 1st of March, I ran in the English National cross-country championships at Stopsley, Luton, in the Birchfield Harriers team, and finished 328th. I saw Steve Ovett win the junior race. Tony Simmons won the senior race in 46-24, 8 seconds ahead of Bernie Ford, who was 36 seconds ahead of Grenville Tuck.

I accepted an employment offer from 'Under Water Diving Inspection' (UDI) as a Satellite Navigation Engineer, served my notice with Lucas Aerospace and after a 'farewell do' with some of my fellow test engineers I finished on Friday the 28th of February 1975.

NORTH SEA OILWORKER

I drove up to Aberdeen to stay with my parents at 89 Willowbank Road and started at UDI on Monday the 3rd of March. By Friday I was on a semi-submersible oilrig, the 'SEDCO 700' about 100 miles North of Shetland, accompanying another engineer to learn how to set up our equipment in preparation for the 'rig' being towed to a new exploration location. Our equipment allowed us to receive signals from six United States Navy satellites in polar orbits, spaced at intervals like a birdcage around the earth. They were developed for US submarines to get updates on their location when they surfaced in an ocean anywhere. These satellites were tracked by three 'Earth Stations' and their orbital coordinates for the next 24 hours calculated and this data was transmitted to and stored by the satellites. They then transmitted their data to receivers on Earth, which with suitable processing allowed the receiving equipment to give its position with an accuracy of about thirty metres. This was the forerunner of the Global positioning system now commonly available from pocket-sized equipment.

The reason for oil companies using our equipment was that the geological survey of the ocean floor had been done using the same equipment, and they wanted to drill exploratory wells at specific locations based on inspection of the geological survey results. Once the 8 anchors, in a radial configuration, had been lifted by two workboats, they would begin towing the rig to the new location. Our equipment received an input, through an interface from the rig's gyrocompass and the course displayed on a plotter. Every time a satellite passed over, the plot would be updated, and any necessary course alterations noted by the 'rig Boss' (sort of Captain) and passed to the tugs by radio communication. Once the equipment was installed and running satisfactorily there was little for us to do apart from the check after a satellite pass. As the rig was being towed, there was plenty of time for reading and sampling the four meals provided daily for the two-shift crew. On approaching the desired location, the rig slowed to a stop and the anchors were laid in the same pattern as before, which allowed the rig to be pulled this way and that as necessary to get as close as possible to the required location. Satellite updates when the rig was stationary were accurate within 10 metres, which satisfied all concerned. At this stage we could dismantle our system, pack it up for transportation by helicopter back to Sumburgh and onto Aberdeen. This move of SEDCO 700 was quite lengthy and we were on there for twelve days. I did try jogging around the helicopter landing deck, but found this impractical because of the wind possibly blowing me over the edge!

The UDI base was in the Bridge of Don Industrial estate, which was very convenient for Balgownie track or Murcar golf course, both of which I used for lunchtime training sessions.

It was to be another 5 weeks before my next offshore trips: SEDCO 704, for 5 days, 4 days ashore, SEDCO 135F for 9days, 11 days on-shore, before returning to the same rig for just 2 days, then after two days on-shore, to the 'Ocean Rover' rig for 3 days.

Following a week on-shore, I ran in the Ben Lomond (3129 feet) hill race on the 8th of June; my first race since the English 'National' on 1st March. I started well, but I soon developed an enormous oxygen debt and walked hands on knees most of the way up and finished 13th of the 62 starters in 1-29-00. After a further week on-shore I was sent to the 'Zapata Ugland' rig for nine-days work. On finishing that I had only one-day on-shore before five days work on the 'Aqua Star' rig. A few days after this, my next work was for 'Elf' in the Norwegian sector of the North Sea. My equipment was loaded into the back of a twin engined Cessna at Aberdeen airport and I climbed aboard only to be told that the other front seat was for the co-pilot and so I had to go in the back with my gear. The pilot flew us to an airport near Stavanger, arriving in darkness, where my equipment and I were taken along the side of a fjord to the helicopter base, where I met the Norwegian surveyor, Egil Tveit Msc, who would be working with me and in charge of the job. We were transported by helicopter to the McDermott barge DB22 in the 'Frigg' oil and gas field. This was my base, but I had to visit the Brown and Root barge 'LB Meaders' and the semi submersible rigs: 'Neptune 7' and 'Deep sea driller'. During this time my 31st birthday was passed quietly on the 6th of July.

The task for the DB22 was to move a production platform 'jacket' from the seabed, where it had been wrongly placed, to a hill on the seabed so that more of the structure would be above the sea surface and less of a danger to shipping. This was a major, complicated engineering task and a new jacket (QP1) had been built and towed to DB22, ready to be placed in the correct location.

On the 19th of July a McDermott 'Brass Hat' (Boss) arrived on DB22 and gave the Indian catering staff a dressing down, having seen and sampled the food on offer to his workers. The following evening, when the replacement 'jacket' was close to the required location he gave the order 'put the son-of-a-bitch down here' and it was done.

On Monday, 21st July, we were required to take our equipment onto QP1 to establish accurately the location. The sea swell was too much for the barge DB22 to get close enough to put a gangway across to QP1 so we would have to be transferred by 'personnel basket'. This is a solid circular base for equipment with a rope network on the outside, which up to four people hold on to, with their feet on the base, and the arrangement is attached by a cable to a large crane jib about 400 feet in length. While being transferred from the DB22 barge by the personnel basket (along with Egil Tveit and two Spanish welders) onto the QP1 jacket, as the crane operator was raising the basket it swung in the wind and I was struck by the basket. This knocked me over the side of QP1 into the North Sea 33 feet below. I did not have much time to think while I fell, waiting for the splash and knowing that I had never learned to swim. When impact came I entered 'head and shoulders' first and could see all these bubbles above me, so I must have forgotten to close my eyes, but thankfully I had closed my mouth and remembered to hold my breath. As I was wearing a water-skiing, buoyancy jacket I surfaced, and stuck my legs, arms and head back, so that my mouth and nose were out of the water level and 'floated very nicely', according to Egil. I had difficulty breathing as I had liquid in my throat, which I assumed was seawater, but this cleared somewhat after a few splutters. The crane operator lowered the basket into the sea as near as he could to me and I tried to move towards it, but the swell caused it to keep moving away. Eventually I managed to catch hold of the basket and to drag myself in, still spluttering and I was disturbed to see that I was coughing up bright red frothy arterial blood. Having escaped death by drowning, I feared that I might die from internal bleeding. I was hoisted onto DB22 deck and aided by the 'Medic'. I was warmed up in the warm showers and because of my coughing blood, a helicopter was arranged to take me to Stavanger hospital. I arrived there five and a half hours after the accident and was given a thorough examination, including a chest X-ray, by a doctor, who said that the blow from the personnel basket must have burst a blood vessel in my lungs, but that this had now sealed. Another surprise was having my rectal temperature measured along with my height and weight, which had increased to 70.5Kg because of my inactivity and eating while on DB22. I was discharged and made my way to the 'SAS Royal Atlantic Hotel', where UDI had reserved a room for me once they had been informed of my accident.

I spent the night there reflecting on my 'close shave' with potential death, felt that I had been given a second chance at life and resolved to make the most of it.

On the 22nd of July I went to work on the 'Deep Sea Driller' rig, which was in the dock in Stavanger and this rig lasted for 7 days. While I waited on the 'Deep Sea Driller' to be towed out from the docks I had time to think about my future and came to the decision that my current employment was not what I wanted to continue.

I had previously considered teaching as a possibility, as I felt that I had experience and knowledge that I could pass on to pupils to their benefit. I decided to 'take the plunge', so to speak, and would submit an application to Northern College in Aberdeen for the secondary education teacher-training course when I got back on-shore. I had found out previously that my degree would allow me to teach Physics or mathematics, so I opted for Physics. I also knew that one could combine the teacher-training course with the Diploma in Education (Dip Ed) at Aberdeen University, by attending the Northern College in the mornings and the University in the afternoons. The Dip Ed would give me another year running for the University Hare and Hounds club, so I was very keen to apply for a place on this course too. I would have to resign from UDI, where I was receiving a generous salary plus offshore allowance, but pursuit of money was never a high priority for me.

On Tuesday the 29th of July I was back to the UDI base and was teased good-naturedly by my colleagues over my 'North Sea diving'. Later I had my first run for 26 days when I ran for 55 minutes in Counteswells forest with Mal Pickering and Roy Tilling, my Birchfield Harriers training pals, who had come up from Birmingham for a holiday with me. Next day Mal, Roy and I ran from the Linn of Dee, where we were camping, up to Derry lodge and up the path towards the Lairig Ghru and back. On the following day we hill-walked for 12 hours 15 minutes, covering about 30 miles and climbing approximately 7000 feet. We moved next morning and hiked about 6.5 miles with packs up Glen Ey to Altanour Lodge, where we camped. From there we hill-walked for 9 hours, covering about 17 miles including three 'Munros' on the following day and the day after we hill-walked for 4 hours, covering about 7 miles and climbing another two 'Munros'. After that it was back down Glen Ey to my waiting car, where we loaded up our gear and I drove to Glen Coe and found a suitable campsite there. On succeeding days, we climbed the Aonach Eagach ridge and then scared ourselves on a route mistake, trying to climb Bidean nam Bian, which meant that we had to keep going up, because we felt that it was too dangerous to try descending, so we were committed to our choice of a difficult route. We were all relieved when we emerged onto a much gentler ridge leading to the summit.

The following day on the 7th of August, I drove us to the Glen Nevis campsite and next afternoon, climbed Carn Mor Dearg and Ben Nevis in 7.5 hours, covering about 12 miles and climbing about 5000 feet. The following afternoon I drove us back to Aberdeen, our adventure holiday over and Mal and Roy headed back to Birmingham.

The following Tuesday, 12th August, I was back on the 'Ocean Rover' drilling rig on a job that lasted for 11 days. I returned from this job on the 21st of August and finished my employment with UDI the following day, having worked my agreed notice.

I had arranged to join a Birchfield Harriers trip to Holland for the Enschede marathon; so on Wednesday the 27th of August, I drove to Peter and Rita's in Wishaw and continued on Thursday morning to Birmingham. During this drive I realised that I had forgotten to take my passport with me, which was a worry. I joined the Birchfield Harriers group and drove to Harwich to catch the ferry over to Holland. On arrival I had to explain that I had left my passport at home so I was given a temporary visa, much to my relief. On arrival in Enschede we found very warm (80.6F) conditions and with high relative humidity.

In the marathon on Saturday the 30th of August, I felt OK early on as I was running easily, passing 10 miles in 64 minutes and halfway in 1-22-42. After this I began to increase my pace and pulled back some places. I began to feel weak around 18 miles and slowed up rather badly over the last 3 miles, in the very warm weather, finishing 73rd in 2-54-38.8. My ex-club mates from Birchfield placings and times were: Roy Tilling 29th in 2-32-37.8, Mick Phillips 44th in 2-39-57.8, Mal Pickering 62nd in 2-51-03.6 and Kent Kirby 101st in 3-03-10.8. My adversary in many Scottish races, Sandy Keith from Caithness, but now running for Edinburgh AC, ran very well to finish 2nd in 2-18-43, to Ron Hill who won in 2-15-59.2.

At Zandvoort the following day, we relaxed, mucking about in the outdoor pool and beach before travelling on to catch the overnight Ferry to Harwich. I arrived back in Aberdeen the following Tuesday, the 2nd of September and on the 3rd, I did a VO_2 max uptake test on the treadmill and my value of 56.2 was very poor and confirmed that, not surprisingly, I was quite unfit.

In the Knockfarrel Hill race on the 27th of September, I felt unable to go with the leaders and finished 4th to help AAAC win the team race. Mel Edwards won in 36-16, ahead of Ian Johnstone, Inverness Harriers and Donnie McLean of Forres Harriers. In the Alves to Forres road race, the following Saturday, I was 7th behind Graham Milne, Alastair Wood and Ian Johnstone. AAAC were first team.

TEACHING PRACTICE, AUH&HC AGAIN AND REGAINING FITNESS

On Monday the 6th of October I began my first teaching practice, in Aberdeen Grammar School in integrated science class and a Physics class. This seemed to go quite well and my 'crit' (observed) lesson was successful although I received some constructive criticism.

At lunchtimes I ran from the School up round Hazlehead and back, and once school had finished I would go to Kings for my second session, usually of intervals on the grass there.

In the Dunfermline '15', on 19th October, over three five-mile laps I went through 5 miles in 26-40 and 10 miles in 54-54. I had pains in my intestines on the last lap, but apart from that I felt reasonable and finished 5th. Nigel Bailey (ESH) won in 1-16-51 from Doug Gunstone (EAC) and Bill Yates of Maryhill. Aberdeen AAC was 1st team with Alastair Wood 4th and Bill Ewing 13th in addition to my 5th place.

Our Hare and Hounds produced an encouraging result in the East District Cross-Country Relay champs near Edinburgh on the 1st of November. I ran the first leg and could not cope with the early pace, but moved through to hand over in eighth place and our team eventually finished seventh, which was rather pleasing.

On the 15th of November I ran the 5th stage of the Edinburgh to Glasgow road relay for A.A.A.C and was 6th fastest on this stage with 27-48 and moved up one place to 8th. Our team finished in 9th place.

We were back near Edinburgh for the National C-C relay championships, on the 22 of November, on the same course as was used for the East District relay. I ran the 1st leg for the Hare and Hounds and handed over in 16th place. Ron Maughan from our 'B' team shocked me by running 15 seconds faster than I did.

In the Cross-Country match, on the 6th of December, at Stirling University between the Scottish Universities (SU) and the Scottish Cross Country Union (SCCU), Northern Ireland (NI) and the British Civil Service (CS), I finished 19th and was 4th counter for the SU team. Lawrie Spence was first ahead of Paul Kenney and John Graham. Our team finished 2nd to the SCCU team and ahead of NI and the CS.

In the week beginning on Monday 8th December, my mileage peaked at 196.5 miles, which was the most I had run in one week and must have contributed to my rather low weight of 9 stone 3 pounds. **This mileage was certainly not necessary for cross-country racing and I was conscious that training must not become an end in itself but must be a means to an end.**

On Sunday afternoon the 14th of December I was driving an Aberdeen University minibus with a 'Harriers' team to Stranraer on our way to Belfast and our 'Irish Tour'. In Belfast the following afternoon, we ran a Cross Country race against Queens University (QU) and the new University of Ulster (NU). I was pleasantly surprised to win, as I felt tired and weak at the start. Pat McGourin (QU) was 2nd and A Harrison (NU) was 3rd, Steve Taylor 4th and Gerry Hannon (QU), later to become an impressive marathon runner, was 5th.

On Tuesday the 16th of December, I drove the minibus with our team to Galway on the west coast, ready for a race against Galway University on Wednesday. In the race I felt extremely tired and could not raise my pace to keep up with the leading 2 Galway runners and finished third. Later I ran 10 miles on the roads with John Potts, who used to run for Birchfield Harriers, but he married an Irish nurse and was now living and working in Galway. I stayed overnight with John and his family after a night out in Galway.

On Thursday I drove to Dublin, where we had a free day before our race against University College Dublin (UCD) on Saturday, 20th December. I should have won this race as I felt good, but I had to hang back with the leading UCD runner, as I did not know the course in Phoenix Park. Once we were out of the Park and on the road back to the finish at the boathouse, I made an effort, with about a mile remaining and got away by about 10 yards. However, Kingston Mills regained contact and outsprinted me. Steve Taylor was 3rd and Ron Maughan 5th.

In the week beginning Monday the 22nd of December I decided to run a very large mileage as an experiment to evaluate the effect on my body and performance. That day I covered 44 miles in two sessions and **by Sunday afternoon I had accumulated 251 miles.** I did not know if this sort of mileage was beneficial or harmful. My resting pulse was consistently higher and I put on weight during the week. Strangely, at that time I had no intention of trying to run in long distance races!

I finished 1975 with a total mileage of 4235 miles.

1976

By the beginning of 1976 I was halfway through my teacher-training course and the Dip Ed. I particularly enjoyed the Psychology content in the Dip Ed and realised that I could have enjoyed taking a degree in this subject.

On the 9th of February I began my second teaching practice, this time at 'Albyn School', a girls-only school and quite different from my last placement at Aberdeen Grammar School. The girls were very polite and extremely well behaved and so were not representative of what I might be faced with in a 'normal' State school.

My running was disappointing in the first 3 months of the year, due to tiredness, illness and taking part in races when I wasn't fit. It seemed that I had become 'trapped', for several weeks, in a cycle of running high mileages followed by excessive eating of carbohydrates to satisfy my resulting hunger/cravings – often for the wrong foods – and poor performances.

I started my interval sessions again on April the 8th, with 15 X 600 metres on Kings field in 116s to 117s with a 300 metres recovery jog and I felt these hard. On Friday of that week I travelled to Belfast with the rest of the Scottish Universities team invited to participate in the Guinness-sponsored 'Portadown to Mary Peters Track Road Relay'. We were accommodated in the plush Country Club Hotel, near Craigavon in Ulster. Unfortunately, on an evening 2.5 miles jog on the adjacent golf course, I felt quite rough with pains in my stomach and a headache. In the race I was given the third stage, which was only 3.1 miles, so I was not looking forward to it, as I doubted my ability to run fast enough, especially as I was still feeling quite unwell. A morning toilet visit had indicated that all was not well with my intestines. Thankfully I ran reasonably well and was 5th fastest on this stage, the fastest being by Paul Lawther. Fraser Clyne had handed over to me in 4th place and I lost one place before handing over to Willie Sheridan, who brought us back to 4th. Our team finished 4th of the 18 teams participating, so everyone was happy and the organisers were pleased that our team had agreed to participate despite the political 'Troubles'.

On the 2nd of May, having increased the number of weekly interval sessions and effort sessions since my last race in Ulster, I tackled my first track race of the year. I represented Aberdeen AAC in the 'Pye Cup' preliminary match at Grangemouth Stadium. I ran in the 10,000 metres and made a break after 8 slow laps in windy conditions, and went on to win in 32-18 ahead of Colin Martin in 33-05. I was pleased with my performance and felt that I was at last making some progress.

The following Friday, the 7th of May, I drove from Aberdeen to Rotherham, where I arrived at my host family's home about 11 hours later having covered 362.2 miles. On Saturday the AAA Marathon Championship got underway in very warm and humid conditions, with the temperature well over 70°F. I started well but began to feel rather rough and my intestines started complaining and I had indigestion. This may have been due to excessive eating earlier in the day when I had a 1514-calorie breakfast. I had to ease back and had thoughts of dropping out, but after a while I began to feel better. I passed 10 miles in 54 plus, 15 miles in 1-23. My feet were very painful by then from the hot road and perhaps because I was not wearing socks. 20 miles was passed in 1-52 and I was then hoping that I could survive to the end. Cavin Woodward, with whom I had been running for a long time, began to draw away and despite the last 2.75 miles being slightly downhill, I could not take advantage of this because of my painful feet. I finished in 45th place in 2-29-30 and I could see Willie Day finishing a lap ahead in 2-27-59. Colin Youngson, who had started very fast despite sciatica, slowed down a lot to end up 40th in 2-27-56. I had a blister under the hard skin of the heel on my left foot and two blisters under the hard skin on the ball of the same foot. Barry Watson won in 2-15-08 from Jeff Norman, 2-15-17 and Keith Angus, 2-15-55.

Before the 1976 AAA marathon. Colin gets his excuses in early; Donald listens patiently, while Cavin just laughs. Photograph by Arthur Walsham.

In the evening the son of my host family took me to his 'working man's club' and I enjoyed this one and only experience. On Sunday, after breakfast and thanking my host family for their kind hospitality, I set off driving home. The total cost of petrol for the journey was £8.17 and my trusty 'Hillman Imp' averaged 51 miles per gallon, being driven at 50 miles per hour.

My final teacher-training placement was at Harlaw Academy; where I met a former first year University pal teaching technical subjects and a former AAAC club mate teaching Biology. I quite enjoyed my time there, which also coincided with their annual 'School Sports' day. Soon it was time for end-of-course examinations, followed by my usual 'post exam blues'. I duly qualified to teach and registered with the 'General Teaching Council' for Scotland. Prior to this I was offered a post teaching Physics in 'Our Lady's High School' in Wishaw, which I accepted, knowing that Peter and Rita Duffy lived there and I had a good knowledge of the area around there. However, one of my fellow graduates on the teacher-training course was reported to have failed the final exams, which I find hard to believe. He was scheduled to start teaching in Lossiemouth High School, so now there was a vacancy there, which I applied for and was accepted. This was obviously part of some 'plan' over which I had no control and I would just have to go along with the flow and play my part in it.

On Saturday the 19th of June 1976, I participated in the road and trail race from Braemar to Aviemore through the mountain pass called the Lairig Ghru. I found the early pace very leisurely, but I was content to stay with the pack until past Derry Lodge, where I made a break on beginning the ascent on the path, but only dropped Steve Taylor. The path became very rough and I had difficulty running on it and lost the lead. By the top of the pass, however, I had got back to 20 metres behind the leading 4 runners.

The descent proved rather difficult for me and I lost more and more ground on the leaders. As I entered the forest section I stopped to spend a penny and on the 2nd stride upon re-starting I stood on a tree root, went over the side of my left foot, heard something crack and felt a severe pain. I tried to continue, but my foot was extremely painful and I realized that I had done something serious. I hobbled 4 miles down to the road, where I got a lift to the finish at the police station in Aviemore from Graham Milne, who tried to reassure me by suggesting that it was a sprain. My foot became more and more painful and by the time we reached Aberdeen I could barely walk. I went to the accident and emergency facility at Woolmanhill hospital, where an X-ray revealed that I had a fractured 5th metatarsal. The treatment consisted of some bandages and strapping and time to heal, so I would be out of action for some time. Colin Youngson had planned that he and I would walk the Pennine Way that summer, so reluctantly I had to withdraw from that promising adventure.

To keep myself gainfully employed I returned to UDI for some temporary work and by the 19th of July I was working on the Bredford Dolphin semi-submersible rig and the 'Piper A' production jacket for 15 days. I was operating and maintaining underwater video surveillance and recording systems, using Sub Sea equipment. My only problem encountered was water ingress, because of the pressure at the operating depth, into the cable connector at the camera interface. Each time that this happened, the equipment had to be hoisted to the deck and I would have to cut off the old connector and fit a new one and 'seal' it to prevent seawater ingress. This was my last work for UDI

On the 3rd of August 1976, after 44 days of no running, I jogged 6 miles in about 40 minutes with Ronnie Maughan and Clyde Williams. Because of my lay off and boredom eating offshore, my weight was up to 11 stones 3 pounds.

Graham Milne had given up his teaching post in Robert Gordon's School and taken a post at Milne's Institute in Fochabers and was living in Elgin with his wife Wilma. When he learned that I was to teach at Lossiemouth High School he invited me to stay with them in their flat at 14 Institution Road, until I got a place of my own, which was very generous. I gladly accepted his offer and moved in with them on the 16th of August. I began morning runs of 5 miles, mainly on grass, with Graham on the 17th. On Saturday, 21st August, I ran in the 10 miles road race at the Nethy Bridge Highland Games and was pleased to finish 2nd.

Two days later in the morning run with Graham something in my left groin was painful. At night I set out on an 8 miles road run, but I had to stop at 6 miles because a muscle or nerve in my groin was hurting very badly and I had to get a lift back. After four non-running days I tried to resume jogging, but the problem was still there and after a further week I consulted a GP in the doctor's surgery below Graham and Wilma's flat. I was seen by Dr Dawson, who had studied at Aberdeen University, an athletics 'Full Blue' who was wearing his blues tie. He prescribed some pills and advised rest. A week later, with no improvement, after a further consultation with Dr Dawson, he diagnosed a muscle insertion that had been pulled away from the attachment to the bone; he would refer me for physiotherapy treatment at Dr Gray's Hospital.

TEACHING AT LOSSIEMOUTH HIGH SCHOOL

I had started my teaching career at Lossiemouth High School on the 17th of August 1976, along with five other 'probationers', all younger than me. My head of Physics was Jeff Patterson, who was, friendly, helpful, and jolly and periodically organised excellent parties at his home the 'Cheddars' on Quarry Road, Lossiemouth. The deputy head teacher, Ken Jackson, was also a Physics graduate, with a degree from Cambridge. Our headmaster was Mr. Archie Boag, who was a Math's graduate. My classes were 1st and 2nd years for integrated science, 3rd and 4th years for 'Ordinary Grade' Physics, 5th year for Higher Physics and a 'non- certificate' class. In the latter class were children trapped in school for an extra year, for no good reason, apart from the fact that the School leaving age had been raised fron 15 to 16. They were known as 'Raising of the School Leaving Age' (ROSLA) kids, which reminded me of a song by the band 'Orchestral Manoeuvres in the Dark'. There was no syllabus to follow for these children to work towards, so it was up to each teacher to come up with ideas and make the best of this unfortunate situation. Most of the class had jobs lined up, such as joining a father's plumbing business, joining a fishing boat, etc and were not motivated to do much in class time. I first tried some practical electronics once I got some components and soldering irons sourced, but enthusiasm for this soon declined. Later I did some polymer science, which involved practical exercises to make some simple plastics, again with limited interest. I encountered surnames in my classes that I had never heard of before with a high proportion of Mains and Mores.

Graham's wife, Wilma learned that one of her fellow teachers at East-End Primary School was moving home, so her current home was available for purchase. I viewed the flat and decided that it would suit my needs and started the buying process and soon moved in following my six-week stay with Graham and Wilma. My flat was the downstairs conversion of an old semi-detached house, so I now lived at 'Flat 1, Craggan, Maisondieu Road, Elgin. The property had a back garden with a lawn, a vegetable garden and also a garage. The flat conversion had been poorly done as I later found that one electrical socket was still connected to an upstairs circuit, and the back boiler in my open fire heated upstairs' water, which I did not mind as I rarely had time to put a fire on. I decided to have a house warming party, assisted by Wilma, who did the catering. The event was quite successful, I think, with twenty-two guests attending.

I began making 'Home brew' stout, placing the fermentation barrel above the hot water tank, which was in the bathroom. This proved satisfactory, with each batch slightly different because of variations in the basic recipe. It came to be known to consumers by various aliases such as electric soup, truth drug and grievous bodily harm (GBH for short).

Two of my fellow teachers, Ron Grant and Ian McColl, and I decided to start a cross-country club and began to recruit members for our twice a week training sessions after school. Graham Milne and Peter Chalmers had a similar club going at Milne's High School and Mr. Arbuckle at

Keith Grammar School had also organised a club, plus there was a cross-country club at nearby Gordonstoun School, so we could arrange inter-School competitions.

On Saturday the 9th of October I drove a minibus with the Lossiemouth High School cross-country team to Thurso for a North district cross-country league race. This was quite an adventure for the youngsters, whose enthusiasm faded as travel sickness hit several as we progressed north on windy roads.

On 19th of October, in the evening I received physiotherapy treatment on my left groin and right Achilles tendon from Malcolm Morgan, the head of the Physiotherapy department at Dr Gray's Hospital. This proved effective and the following Monday I was able to resume a gentle 2.5 miles of running.

Because Graham Milne had joined Forres Harriers (F.H), and since there appeared to be no cross-country club in Elgin, I decided to join them also. My first race with them was the North District cross-country relay champs at Inverness on the 7th of November. I ran the first leg and went over my right ankle about 150 metres after the start. This gave some trouble on this run because of the resulting pain, but I was able to complete the lap and handed over in 3rd place. Forres went on to win the event. However, I ran with little distinction in North District cross-country league races.

Since I resumed training in late October, after my injuries were cleared, I had averaged 50 miles per week with a mixture of morning and evening runs. On Tuesday evenings Graham and I would travel to Forres to train with Ian Mackenzie 'The Boss' and the rest of the Forres Harriers. On Thursday evenings Ian and some Harriers would travel through to Elgin, meeting at Morriston playing fields where, despite the darkness, we usually ran repetition 200 metres on the decaying cinder track.

By the end of December, I had run a total of 3034 miles in 1976, which was quite a lot less than in previous years. Surely things could only improve?

1977

Our first race of 1977 was the North District cross-country league race at Lossiemouth on the 8th of January. I was quite pleased finishing 4th behind Ian Mackenzie, Terry McBrien (RAF) and Donnie McLean (F.H) That weekend I completed my second week of 100 miles, having gradually increased my training runs over the preceding weeks. Two weeks later the North District cross-country championships were at Fort William, hosted by Lochaber AC. The course was over a dreadfully dangerous hilly route and I eventually finished 9th.

By February once I had sorted out the logistics of having clothes to change into etc I began running 8 miles to work on Tuesdays to Friday mornings and running back 7 miles on Monday and Wednesday evenings, but I varied this to suit any changes in my circumstances. With Club sessions on Tuesday and Thursday nights and two long runs at weekends if not racing this gave me weekly mileages of around 115 miles.

My next race on the 5th of March was a cross-country race from Balgownie Track in Aberdeen, where I was very pleased to finish 3rd behind Paul Kenney and only 2 seconds behind Graham Milne, with Mel Edwards 4th.

The following week, as the evenings became lighter, I introduced an effort session, alternating one minute hard, one minute easy with two minutes hard, two minutes easy on my Wednesday night run back from School. On Thursday evenings I started sessions of 10 X 400 metres with 200 metres recovery jog at Morriston track in Elgin.

During the first 3 days of my Easter holiday from school I went camping and hill walking with some Aberdeen University Hare and Hounds pals from earlier years. We drove to the Linn of Dee then walked 7 miles with packs to the ruins of Bynack Lodge where we set up camp. We then walked 6 miles and climbed Carn Bhac (3014ft). Next day I walked 19 miles and climbed another distant

Munro, Carn an Righ (3377ft), with John Lamont and on the following day I walked 7 miles with a pack back from Bynack Lodge to the Linn of Dee.

Two days later, the 7th of April, in the Lossiemouth 10 miles road race, which started and finished inside RAF Lossiemouth, I finished 4th having experienced trouble from my insides, which hampered me somewhat. Terry McBrien won in 50-23 ahead of Alastair Wood AAAC, 50-26 and Ian Mackenzie, 51-30, and I finished in 51-45.

A REAL BREAKTHROUGH

On Friday the 29th of April 1977, having been granted a day off school, I was travelling by train to London and then to Epsom to stay with Don Turner and his Mum prior to the 50Km track race next day. At 07:15 next morning I had breakfast of: a small plate of cornflakes with milk and sugar, one boiled egg, two slices of toast and marmalade and one cup of tea. The Epsom and Ewell 50Km track race started at 09:30. Cavin Woodward and I set a good pace and passed 10Km in 34-36 together, but soon after this I was on my own, feeling good and running well. I passed the marathon distance in 2-23-58 and 30 miles in 2-45-38, which placed me 3rd on the world 'all time' list. I finished in 2-51-38, which improved New Zealander, Jeff Julian's world best by 5 minutes 18 seconds. I was delighted with my performance, which came as a surprise. My 10Km splits were: 34-18, 34-36, 33-30, 34-05 and 35-09. I wore my Reebok 'World Ten' shoes and got only one blister on my left big toe. Kevin Gill was 2nd in 3-04-11, Mike Newton 3rd in 3-05-06 and Cavin Woodward 4th in 3-14-20.

I was now in possession of a 'World Best Performance', which most people consider to be a world record, especially as the criteria to be satisfied for both are the same. I believe that the difference in the names is something to do with the International Amateur Athletics Federation (IAAF) wording.

After the race I travelled back by overnight train and arrived in Elgin on Sunday morning.

At school and among my club mates, my performance was met with approval.

In the Spean Bridge to Fort William 10 miles road race on Saturday the 4th of June, there was a head wind and I could not break away from Ian Mackenzie, who sprinted past me at the end in 53-44 to my 53-45.

On Saturday the 11th of June, I attended an invitation to Maud for a 'superstars' competition, which was part of their gala and finished last in the competition. The following afternoon I ran in the Scolty hill race from Banchory. I felt very tired, but I managed to reach the top in 3rd, behind Mel Edwards and Innis Mitchell. On the descent Ian Mackenzie came past rather quickly and also caught and passed Innis and Mel to win by 12 seconds, so I finished 4th.

On Thursday evening the 23rd of June at night I ran a 5000 metres track race at the Queen's Jubilee meeting at the dilapidated track in Morriston Park. I was pleased to win in 15-8.9, finishing 20 seconds ahead of Ian Mackenzie. This run was very pleasing as it was my fastest 5000 metres for five years! The children at the event were very enthusiastic in their support for the runners in the 5000 metres. Next morning, having been granted another day's leave of absence from school, I left Elgin at 07:15 by train to travel to London and onto Uxbridge to run in a 50 Km track race on the 25th of June. I arrived in Uxbridge at 21:30 and was met there by Roger Cressy, who took me to his home where he and his wife Norma fed me. After sampling some of Roger's fine 'home brew' I headed for bed.

In the Hillingdon 50 Km track race, I started strongly, going with Cavin Woodward's fast early pace. He began to slow and Jim Mouat caught up and went into the lead so I went with him, passing 5 miles in 26-51, 10 miles in 54-04 and 15 miles in 1-21-32. I took the lead after 15 miles, but Jim passed me again, so I was content to follow him especially as there was a stiff breeze on the home straight. We passed 20 miles in 1-49-20 and we were inside the record schedule for the 30 miles and

50Km. At about 21 miles I felt the pace slackening, so I took over the lead and Jim dropped quickly. I passed 25 miles in 2-17-07 and the marathon in 2-23-59, but by 27 miles I was beginning to struggle, yet the other runners and the crowd gave me great encouragement.

With 9 laps to go I lapped Joe Keating for the 2nd time. He then caught me and came past, which was a surprise, and he was running well, so I let him lead me for about 5 laps. As I lapped Jim Mouat again he increased his pace and led me through the last 4 laps and I reached 30 miles in 2-45-50. Despite these assists I was 4s outside my record time with 2-51-42. Conditions were not as good as at Epsom, since the weather was much warmer, with a hazy sun shining after early rain and the breeze was a hindrance. The cinder track surface became rather loose and I found that I was slipping when running fast in my flat racing shoes (Reebok 'World Ten'). I was disappointed at not improving the 30 miles and 50 Km times, but I was pleased to beat a classy field of runners. My 5Km splits were: 16-27, 16-56, 16-57, 17-01, 17-02, 17-20, 17-22, 17-12, 17-46 and 17-39. Joe Keating finished 2nd in 2-54-54 ahead of Jim Mouat 2-56-06, Fred Howell 2-59-13, Tom Roden 2-59-32, and Cavin Woodward 3-00-39. Again I travelled back overnight from London.

The following Saturday, 2nd July, at the Forres Highland Games in the 11.25 miles road race, I broke away from Ian Mackenzie at about 3.5 miles and passed 5 miles in 25-00, which was pleasing. I found it hard work on the hill section and on the run into the wind from about 7.5 miles on. I was pleased to win in 58-27, which was a course record, especially as I had been out celebrating the end of School term on Friday evening.

I had completed/survived my first year of teaching and after a 'shaky' start, felt that my 'skill' at managing classes was improving. My non-certificate class settled, once we agreed that I should not expect too much effort from them. The last topic that I presented to them was 'brewing science', which with some history of brewing I managed to spin out for some weeks. The practical part was making some 'home brew' beer from a kit that I had purchased from 'Boots'. I asked each class member to bring in two empty screw-top lemonade bottles ready for filling once the fermentation was finished. These bottles were duly filled and stored in the bottom of a cupboard in my room. On the last day that I saw this class before the end of term they retrieved their bottles and were told that as they were 'under age' the beer should be taken home for some adults to sample. Some of these pupils were bussed to and from school from along the coast at Hopeman and Burghead and predictably some yielded to temptation and opened their bottles and began consuming the contents on the upper deck of the bus, which led to 'unsatisfactory behaviour' and resulted in a complaint to our school from the bus company. I was made aware of this the following morning when I was summoned to the headmaster's office to explain myself and receive a severe reprimand and an order not to repeat making home brew beer in class!

I had acquired a nickname of 'Noah' from the school pupils, which seemed to be related to the children's cartoon series on television with characters Noah and Nelly, who looked after the animals on their Ark called the Skylark. Perhaps my substantial bushy red beard, where I would occasionally park a pen or pencil, led to my pseudonym. Later this developed to 'Nutty Noah' for reasons unknown to me. This caught on with some staff and would raise a laugh in the staff room by addressing me as 'N-N'. Some pupils used another nickname of 'Carrot' because of my red hair and others as 'Beady', I assume from beady eyes. Some other staff had interesting nicknames: Jimmy Stephen, who taught technical subjects was 'Joe Soap', Dr Jim Anderson, who taught Biology was 'Ally Bongo', the gym teacher Malcolm Murray, was 'Sosh' and another was 'Compo'.

My colleagues were supportive and the banter was good in the small crowded male staff room at break times. Lady teachers had a separate staff room, because of the limited capacity of the one used by the men. The staff wanted to mark my 50Km record in some way and decided to purchase a cup to be called 'The Don Ritchie Cup' to be competed for at the annual School sports. It was to be awarded to the first boy and the first girl in the 1500 metres race, sharing it for six months each.

I was asked by Mr. Boag, our headmaster to present the cup to the winners on the first occasion and on subsequent sports days for several years.

When I began my teaching I was advised to purchase a strap from Lochgelly, so that I could administer punishment as necessary, without going to borrow someone else's belt. Being a moderate pacifist I did not want to have to indulge in corporal punishment, having experienced it while I was a pupil. However, some pupils got me sufficiently enraged by their actions that I had to resort to using it occasionally but as I gained experience I was able to reduce its use. On one occasion I used it on a boy who was passing wind loudly, I assumed on purpose, egged on by his classmates, and persisted doing so despite my warning, so he called my bluff. His mother wrote a polite note objecting to her son being strapped for an 'act of nature', noisy or otherwise and that a 'telling off' should have sufficed. With hindsight I realise that I should have dealt with this situation differently, and with more experience I might have defused the situation by saying that he had a talent that could be exploited on the stage and jokingly offering to be his manager.

On Saturday the 9th of July as part of the Queen's Jubilee year a Highland Games was organized in the grounds in front of Innes House in warm sunny weather. I ran in the 11.5 miles road race, which consisted of three laps. On the first lap Alastair Wood and Bill Tonner were with me, but Alistair dropped out and Bill slowed on a small hill during the 2nd lap. I went on to win in 58-20, which was 1-30 ahead of Tonner, with Innis Mitchell 3rd. I developed a very painful blood blister on the ball of my right foot, because the Reebok 'World Ten' shoes were not suitable for road racing, but apart from that I felt strong and comfortable. I was given an award for the most meritorious performance of the Games.

Following the completion of the games, I travelled to Braemar with Peter Chalmers, a Mathematics teacher from Milne's High School in Fochabers, so that we could participate in the Grampian Region Mountain Leadership course run by 'Chizzer' Childs. After settling into our hostel accommodation we joined two of our roommates on a walk to the nearest pub for a relaxing few pints. This course would allow me to take school pupils on hill-walking trips, as an aid to our Chemistry teacher Les Davidson, who was organizing the hill-walking club, and trips to the Cairngorm Mountains. For the next 4 days we completed practical exercises, including rock climbing, abseiling, navigation and equipment use and a scramble up the 'Red Spout' gully on Lochnagar. From Thursday to Saturday we were on our expedition in the Cairngorms, walking and climbing 42 miles in boots and with packs. We slept in mountain 'Bothies' and had one-night exercise on Ben Macdui when we slept under the stars at around 3600 feet. Because there was no light pollution and the sky was clear, the stars and planets looked wonderful and it was a real privilege to see this. I really enjoyed the course as a whole, which was completed on Saturday evening the 16th of July in Braemar.

On the 31st of July Colin Youngson and I drove to Kinlochewe for a camping and hill-walking mini-holiday. Over the next three days we did some short runs, some long walks and climbed two Munros, (Beinn Eighe and Liathach) to add to our gradually increasing tally. Two days after returning from our camping trip at the Newtonmore Highland games in the 5000 metres I finished 2nd behind Graham Milne, but ahead of Ian Mackenzie. I then ran for 67 minutes along the road towards Elgin before Graham picked me up and drove me home as we had arranged.

Graham and I had decided to start a little business venture during our summer holidays from school, by placing an advert in the 'Northern Scot' local newspaper, offering domestic electrical appliance repair and electrical wiring installation. We received some calls to repair vacuum cleaners and washing machines, but we found this to be unprofitable due to our combined incompetence. We did much better when Alan Brown, a fellow teacher at Lossiemouth, required extra electrical sockets and lights in his home in Fochabers. With Graham as my 'apprentice' we completed the installation and testing in 3 days and made a modest profit, so all concerned were happy. Graham and I decided that this was a good time to cease our business experiment and we agreed that teaching was a much more secure source of income.

A TOUGH, COMPETITIVE RACE

On Friday evening the 26th of August of that week I eventually arrived at HMS Rosyth accommodation at 01:30am on Saturday after a tiring three-train journey. Later in the 'Two Bridges' race I started well and went with Cavin Woodward and Mick Orton and we passed 5 miles in 27-19, 10 miles in 54-44, 15 miles in 1-23-20 and 20 miles in 1-51-39. I began to feel tired at about 22 miles and on the steep hill leaving Bo'ness, at around 24 miles, I was unable to keep pace with Mick and he pulled away. I felt dreadfully tired and could not pull back any of the lead that he had gained. I passed the marathon point in 2-28-06, 59 seconds behind Mick and 28 seconds ahead of Cavin. Before 30 miles Mick had started to slow, but I was also not going well and being pulled back by Alex Wight and Cavin. Alex and I passed 30 miles together in 2-51-15, 17 seconds behind Mick and 12 seconds ahead of Cavin. Alex pulled away from me before the Forth Road Bridge and Cavin passed me while we were crossing it.

I felt like dropping out as I felt that I was going so slowly. However, I was still gaining on Mick Orton and Alex was also slowing down. I passed Mick on the down-slope of the bridge towards Inverkeithing and passed Alex on the hill going up to Inverkeithing. I could make no impression on Cavin's lead and he was actually going away as we passed 35 miles in 3-21-02 and 3-22-04 respectively. I was extremely glad to finish this race, which was my hardest for years. My time was 8 minutes faster than when I last ran this race in 1974. I wore my Karhu road racing shoes and found them excellent. I relied on the drinks stations and this was fine except at one later in the race, when I had to stop to find my drink, so a Second to help would be an advantage in such races. Sixty of the 74 starters finished. Chief timekeeper, Raymond Hutcheson, again produced an excellent statistics-packed 'Results Booklet'.

Results: 1) Cavin Woodward 3-27-10, 2) Don Ritchie 2-28-34, 3) Alex Wight 3-29-08, 4) Fred Howell 3-29-51, 5) Joe Keating 3-30-51, 6) Mick Orton 3-32-18.

On the 29th of August school resumed and I got back into my routine, but altered my Wednesday sessions. In the morning I ran to school by my 8 miles route. At night I ran back by my 12 miles course and incorporated a pyramid session of: 2 X 1, 2, 3, 4, 5, 6, 6, 5, 4, minutes efforts with equal time easy running recoveries.

I planned for the London to Brighton race and built my training up with weeks of 107, 138, 150 and 145 miles, while maintaining my effort sessions. I was a little lax in applying for an entry for the race, so the RRC Hon entries secretary, Mile Tomlins wrote: 'I fear you may have missed the boat', but he would accept my entry if it arrived by first post on Tuesday the 6th of September. This was 19 days before the race date, but I suppose this was for organisational reasons. I received confirmation that my entry had been accepted, much to my relief. On the week of the 'Brighton' I did a glycogen depletion run of 22 miles on Tuesday after school and maintained a low carbohydrate diet for the next 2 days. I ran to and from school by my 12 miles route on Wednesday, 12 miles route to work on Thursday morning and I felt remarkably well despite being on the 'diet' and 8 miles at night with Donnie McLean and Graham. On Friday morning I ran my 10 miles course at an easy pace and then began eating carbohydrates at breakfast before going to School. On Saturday I traveled by train all day down to London.

LONDON TO BRIGHTON TRIUMPH

On race day morning, the 25th of September, I was up early as the accommodation that I got was 3 miles from the changing rooms for the London to Brighton race and I had underestimated the time that it would take for me to walk there. Consequently, I arrived in an agitated state, having had to jog part of the way, and quickly got changed, declared, and off to Westminster Bridge just in time for the 7am start. Fortunately, a fellow with a Ford van volunteered to be my second and dispense my drinks along the route, an offer I gladly accepted. I started quite quickly because of my pre-race tension, but

I soon eased off. I let Bob (or Rab) Heron go on and later let Norman Wilson go past as well, since I gambled that they were running at too fast a pace to maintain and that I could catch them later. I continued running at an easy pace with Cavin Woodward, Mick Orton and Mike Kearns and passed 5 miles in 28-31 in joint 3rd. By 10 miles reached in 56-58 I was 5th, 54 seconds behind Bob and at 20 miles I was 4th, 63 seconds behind Bob as I passed this point in 1-58-13.

Bob was over 7 minutes ahead of me at one point, but when I decided to start a push for home at 30 miles I began to pull him back. Only Mike Kearns tried to come with me and he held a gap pretty constant for a while, but gradually he dropped back and I moved into 3rd. At about 37 miles I saw Norman Wilson and gradually caught him and moved to 2nd place and at Bonley (39 miles 179 yards) I was just over 3 minutes behind Bob. Soon after I caught sight of Bob Heron, who seemed a long way off and I had doubts about catching him. However, I was encouraged by the fact that I was pulling him back, and I caught and passed him on Dale Hill at about 46 miles and pushed on. After the top of Dale Hill, I began to get cramp in my quads and calf muscles, which occurred every 20 metres or so. I had to try to run with straight legs and the finish seemed to take an eternity to come. I felt fine in my upper body, but my legs were in a bad way.

I was absolutely delighted to win this 'classic' race, especially on my Mother's birthday. My condition was fairly good after finishing, which was encouraging. I had no serious blisters from my Karhu racer shoes. **I realised that I had finally found an event, long distance running, that suited me.** I went for a walk along the Prom and had a couple of pints of beer courtesy of a newspaper reporter who had requested an interview with me.

Weather conditions in the race were not great with a headwind part of the way and some very heavy rain showers. My time of 5-16-05 was 4th fastest of all time. Bob Heron was 2nd in 5-19-47, with Cavin Woodward 3rd in 5-23-36. Later at the tea and presentations I was delighted to receive the 'Arthur Newton Cup' and the 'Ernest Neville gold medal'

I arrived back in Elgin at 09:22 on Monday after travelling on an overnight train from London to Inverness and then on to Elgin. I had very little sleep as I had the 'Arthur Newton Cup' with me concealed in a black bin bag, which was quite a responsibility, so I was very tired at school. After school I ran for 2.5 miles and found that my scrotum was very painful as a result of the previous day's race.

By the following Saturday my cold, which, had started 4 days earlier, was very bad and I felt rough. Fortunately, I got a consultation with my GP who diagnosed bronchitis and he advised against running with the fever I had, as it could cause inflammation of the heart muscle, which could be rather serious. With this warning in mind I ran a 21 miles course, with half in the forest with Graham Milne, at an easy pace. Four days later after work I had a follow-up consultation with my GP, who gave me the 'all clear' as my lungs were clear, despite the fact that I was still coughing up mucous and phlegm.

Three days later in the North District cross-country league race at Thurso I finished 3rd after a rather lazy race. I had slept on the back seat of the hired bus for most of the way up from Elgin, having boarded the bus first at the depot.

TWO MORE WORLD BEST PERFORMANCES

On Friday, the 24th of September, I had been granted another day's leave of absence, again with no deduction of salary and travelled down to London by train. Flying, although much quicker, was prohibitively expensive at this time. On Saturday, 25th September, I started in the 24 hours track race at Crystal Palace, organized by the RRC. I ran for 100.5 miles before stopping to have a massage and to look at my feet, which were hurting badly. I had 2 blisters on my left foot and my right had 3 blisters plus a cut. I changed my shoes and tried walking, but I could not make myself run again. The outside of my right foot was also painful from favouring the inside where the blisters were. I

Lapping Joss Naylor in the 24-hour race at Crystal Palace.

had been wearing my Karhu racing shoes without socks and I began to feel my feet, which I thought were adequately taped, painful at about 40 miles when the track got hot from the strong sunshine, although the air temperature was only about 65°F. My legs also began to feel painful, which they had not been in the London to Brighton. I expect that it was something to do with running on the 'Tartan' surface, which was a new experience.

During the run I took about 200ml of long chain glucose polymer in solution at 10% concentration with vitamin C and a potassium tablet and 'Accolade' alternately at 15-minute-intervals and a bottle of 'Dynamo' every 2.5 hours. In addition, I took salt tablets, about six in all and one quinine tablet for cramp prevention. I got twinges of cramp after 90 miles and I also took a couple of aspirins to try and subdue the pains from my feet. Tom O'Reilly informed me at about 80 miles that I was on record schedule for 150Km and 100 miles, which surprised me, so, although my feet were hurting a lot, I decided to press on rather than stop and tend to my feet.

I had to make a pee stop after 1.5 hours, but not again until after 100 miles. I passed 150Km in 10-36-42, which reduced Cavin's record by 8-13 and I passed 100 miles in 11-30-51, which improved Cavin's record by 8-33. I was very pleased to break these two records, but I regretted having had to drop out. I retired to the changing rooms where I met Chris Brasher, who said that he knew my mentor, Alastair Wood. I then tried to sleep using Tom Roden's jacket as a cover. Tom won the race with 251.459Km, from: Derek Funnell, who covered 234.557Km; Fred Howell with 219.929Km; and Joss Naylor 4th with 212.976Km. The distance achieved when I decided to withdraw was 166.4Km. My ten-mile splits were: 62-24, 63-05, 62-48, 62-40, 65-01, 68-39, 73-30, 76-38, 77-19 and 78-47. My 50Km time was 3-15-02 and I passed 100Km in 6-39-59.

Once the race was over I travelled to Birmingham to see some of my Birchfield Harriers pals and stay over there as I was on the 'tattie holidays' from school. My feet were too painful to allow running for the next 4 days. By the next weekend my feet had recovered and on Sunday morning I ran for 23 miles around Monaughty Forest in beautiful weather and I realized that I was very lucky to be able to run in such a fine environment.

By the following week I had a bad cold again, which worsened, so I consulted my GP again. He gave me antibiotics to fight the infection and a mixture to help soothe my cough. A few days later my pulse was up to around 88 and my shoulders and legs began to ache, so I assumed that I had succumbed to flu. Five days later after another consultation with my GP, he gave me a different course of antibiotics and an inhaler.

On Saturday the 5th of November, the F.H team went to Fort William for the North District cross-country relay championships. After jogging over the course, part of which was on the Ben Nevis path, we decided that it was too dangerous to race over and, following some discussion, Forres Harriers withdrew from the event, as did Inverness Harriers. Mike Scott from Forres insisted on running the first leg along with men from Lochaber AC and RAF Moray. The runner for RAF Moray fell badly and could not finish, so the race was declared null and void and would be held at another venue later in the season.

On Sunday, 20th of November our F.H team set out in the early morning for Edinburgh to take part in the Edinburgh to Glasgow road relay for the club's first time. The rain in Forres became sleet on the Grantown road and snow soon after. We got stuck in the snow on the Dava moor and had to turn back. Conditions were very bad and at one point we had to have someone running in front of the car so that the driver could see where the road was. On returning to Forres we did a hard 7 miles run in 40 minutes to get rid of our frustration.

In the North District cross-country league race at Elgin, on the 3rd of December, I finished 5th behind Graham Milne, Terry McBrien, Innis Mitchell and Brian Turnbull. The following Saturday I ran the 3rd leg of the North District cross-country relays, which had been abandoned at Fort William, and were now being held at Lossiemouth. I moved our team, F.H through to 1st place, which was maintained to the finish. In the annual F.H cross-country Christmas handicap a week later I finished a tired 4th on my least favourite course around 'Cluny Hill'.

On Wednesday the 28th of December I went bothying to Corndavon Lodge with Ronnie Maughan, Robin Thomas and John Lamont. We walked about 7 miles to the Lodge, taking turns to pull a sledge, with a barrel of beer on it, through the snow. Next day I ran for 76 minutes from Corndavon Lodge down the track and some road and back, for some reason feeling very tired!

Once I returned to Aberdeen, Mal Pickering and Roy Tilling arrived from Birmingham to experience a Scottish New Year. I finished 1977 with a total of 5168 miles, which was an average of 99 miles per week. **It had been my most successful year, not only in training but especially in racing.**

1978

On New Year's Day 1978, Ron Maughan, Mal, Roy and I ran a 'weary' 23 miles round Monaughty forest.

The first race of 1978 was the North District cross-country league race at R.A.F Kinloss on the 14th of January, which Bill Tonner, RAF, won by 2 seconds from Ian Mackenzie and Graham Milne, while I finished 4th. The following Saturday, in the North district cross-country championships at Inverness I finished 5th after a dour struggle with Terry McBrien. Ian Mackenzie won from Bill Tonner and Brian Turnbull of Inverness Harriers.

At the end of January, I was invited to Grampian TV Studios in Aberdeen as a contender for the Press and Journal 'Sports personality 77', which was rather unexpected. I attended the programme, which was recorded and enjoyed the experience. Overnight accommodation was provided in the 'Quaint Ways Hotel', near Queen's Cross, for rugby player Nairn McEwan and me. Nairn was displeased at the attitude of the owner and said that he would write a letter complaining about this to Erica Nicoll at Grampian Television. The programme was transmitted on the 2nd of February and, as I anticipated, a footballer was chosen by the public vote. I was pleasantly surprised to receive a £15 fee for taking part in the programme, plus £10 expenses.

By early March I was running various routes to and from School; sometimes 20 miles back on a Monday, 14 miles on a few mornings and 7 miles back. In addition, I ran with the club on Tuesday and Wednesday evenings and this added to long runs at the weekends gave me around 160 miles a week and I felt good on it.

Unfortunately, on a morning run to school my left knee became painful on the left side, and later in the day it became stiff and swollen with fluid so I did not attempt to run home. Three days later my left knee, sore when I began to run home after school and after about 2 miles gave a crack, followed by severe pain. I was forced to walk, but fortunately I got a lift back to Elgin from my colleague Ron Black, who happened to be passing. I went directly to my GP, Dr Dawson, who gave me a hydrocortisone injection into my knee, but this did not appear to help. My knee was no better next day and could not support my bodyweight when bent at the knee joint. Dr Dawson sent me to Dr Gray's hospital for an X-ray, which showed that there was no structural damage. Ten days later I consulted a doctor again about my knee and this time I saw Dr Brown. He examined my knee and suggested that a piece of cartilage had broken off and become trapped between some parts of the knee. I then went to get an opinion from Malcolm Morgan, the head Physiotherapist at Dr Gray's. He disagreed with the piece of cartilage theory and diagnosed one of the small ligaments down the side of my knee being pulled. There was a little knot or nodule on it and he gave me some ultrasonic treatment on it. Eleven days later I went back to consult Malcolm, who diagnosed 'periosteumy', which is the covering of the bone being pulled off by a tendon. He fitted a supportive bandage, which appeared to help and next day gave me another treatment session on the knee using microwave and then ultrasonic treatments. Following several physiotherapy treatments from Malcolm I was able to resume running and by the end of April I reached 55 miles for the week and assumed that my enforced rest would be beneficial. On Monday the 1st of May in the evening I ran my 22 miles Monaughty Forest course in 2-15-00 and I was pleased that my left knee gave no trouble, so I was confident that I must be healed.

For some time, I had been thinking of attempting a 100Km race, but there were none in the U.K. and I had mentioned this in one of my letters to Charlie Greenlees, an Aberdeen AAC club mate, who was now married to Marja in Finland. He suggested running in the well- established 100Km at Hartola in late June, near midsummer. This appealed to me, so I asked him to arrange an entry for me and see about a flight through the 'Finnish Church Guild', which could arrange reduced fares on flights for members, which thanks to Charlie, included me. I began organizing my training from 'May Day' with this race as my goal.

At the end of the month in the 'Lochaber 10' up Glen Nevis and back at Fort William I finished 2nd in 54-53 to Ian Mackenzie winning in 53-49. I felt listless from the start and got dropped early, but after the turn I pulled some ground back.

As the summer term at School ended, my 2nd year as a probationary teacher was now complete and I was pleased to have achieved full qualification as a teacher, and to know that I would continue teaching at Lossiemouth High School after the holidays in late August

By Sunday the 25th of June I had completed my buildup with weeks of: 99, 127, 157,137, 173, 189, 179 and 171 miles. On Monday evening I ran my 23 miles Kellas-Dallas route in 2-25-40 and I felt good, despite being on the low carbohydrate phase of the 'Saltin diet', having run my glycogen depletion run on Saturday. On Tuesday the 27th of June at 04:20 I ran my 20 miles course in 2-11-50 and still felt okay. Then at 07:15 I began my train journey to London. On arriving there I made my way to John and Anne Dixon's home where I stayed overnight. John had been a club mate at Aberdeen AAC many years before and his wife Anne was Malcolm Murray's (Sosh's) daughter.

On Wednesday, I went to Gatwick Airport where I caught the flight to Helsinki. Charlie Greenlees and Tapio Pekola met me at Helsinki Airport and we went for an excellent meal, which included plenty of carbohydrates. This meal was 56 hours before the 100Km race I had come for. Later I ran for 62-40 from Helsinki stadium before watching some events at the 'World Games' with Charlie and Tapio. On Thursday I rested and in the evening we went to view the Games again and saw Craig Virgin of the USA win the 10,000 metres. The first 5 were under 28 minutes.

FINLAND: A WORLD ROAD BEST FOR 100 KM

The following day, Friday the 29th of June, Charlie and I travelled by train up to Hartola for the 'Suomi-Juoksu 100 Km' and marathon. Charlie was to run in the marathon and I was making my debut at 100 Km. Our race started at 20:00 with the firing of a shotgun. Weather conditions were good and I felt superb, so I increased my pace after 10Km, as I felt that the pace was too slow. I knew that Cavin Woodward had run 6-19 something for 100Km in France and I wanted if possible to run faster than this. No one came with me and I passed the marathon in 2-31-30 and 50Km in 3-01-00 and finished in 6-18-00, a world best. I lost about one and a half minutes due to going off course by following a cyclist past a turning, so I had to retrace my steps and covered about 600 metres extra. I was very pleased with my run, as I never became glycogen depleted. The course was a mixture of tarred and dirt roads with slight undulations. I wore my Karhu 'marathon' shoes with socks, in an attempt to prevent small stones from getting into the shoes. I had two blisters: on the little toe of my left foot; and under the hard skin to the left of the ball of that foot.

On finishing, I was picked up and thrown into the air several times by a group of men. This was rather alarming, but it appears to be some tradition. Italian brothers, Louis and Elvino Gennari, were second in 6-53-something. Because of the northern latitude of Hartola I could see perfectly well at night, because there was twilight between the sun setting and rising again. I became rather tired towards the end and was longing for the finish over the last 10Km, so I was furious when the cyclist near the end guided me the wrong way.

The modified 'diet' seemed to have worked well. On the low carbohydrate stage, I included salted peanuts, cabbage, diabetic chocolate, plain chocolate, orange juice and apples in addition to the protein. My drinking pattern every 10km was: 200ml of Dynamo; alternated with 200ml of 10% long chain glucose polymer with vitamin C, potassium and salt. I had no stomach problems. My ankles became swollen following the run and one armpit was rubbed raw by my vest strap. My prize was a wooden rocking chair and I received 20,000 Finnish Marks in expenses.

Charlie wrote the following piece about a meeting in the dormitory, the evening after the race, which with his permission I include here.

In June 1978, Donald was having a couple of weeks in Finland, where I was living at the time. The highlight of his visit was to be his participation in an international 100Km race at Hartola, a small town in central Finland. Combined with this event was a comparatively short race – a Marathon, and I was to run this. Both races were to start at 10pm since twilight was as dark as it ever got at midsummer so far north.

I ran a mediocre Marathon then, on the remaining adrenalin, drove around the 100Km course to see how Donald was doing. It was 1am – the darkest hour but still only dusk and silent, totally still, on the undulating country road that wound through the tall, endless forest. Not even a bird cheeped. They were grabbing a one-hour nap between sunset and sunrise. Presently I was aware of a faint thump, thump, thump in the distance, but getting nearer. Then I saw him, maybe two hundred metres away; a silhouette, but unmistakably Donald, that relentless, rolling drive yet, on a night like this, eerily, heard before seen. I shouted some encouragement and he replied with a synopsis of performance and ambience. He looked impressively unstoppable as he pounded past and on into the sleeping, unsuspecting forest.

Donald was still only halfway through his race. I headed for base. No other runner came in sight before I turned off the course two miles back. Maybe now I could sleep a few hours. I slept promptly enough and deeply, yet I had this dream – I don't usually dream. I was in this dungeon of a tall, square tower that had open, internal balconies. These were lined on all floors with people leaning over them and shouting across at each other in unrecognisable languages – the tower of Babel no doubt. But occasionally, through the racket, I could hear a syllable that was vaguely familiar. The chatter went on and on. Then after what seemed a long time, I realised the noise was getting closer and closer until it was in the room with me. It was about this point that I knew I was no longer dreaming — yet the chatter continued. I couldn't work out where I was and I couldn't gather my thoughts but there seemed to be only two voices now, both gabbling in a foreign language that wasn't Scandinavian. At times they were shouting and often together. Then, in the rare gaps, this familiar plaintive squawk.

I prised my eyelids open and what I had to accept as reality was stranger than the dream. Two little men who looked exactly the same were shouting and gesticulating violently at a tall character across a small table. All three were standing and the tall character occasionally got in with, 'Aye, oh aye'. It was then I realised he was Donald. Noting that I was awake, he enquired through the clatter; 'Charlie, can you understand what these two are saying?' I couldn't, but whatever it was it was repeated frequently in what I took to be Italian, with vehemence and by each, one echoing the other. Eventually the tirade stopped. They threw up their hands in despair and left the room gesturing to each other.

From clues along the way, we concluded that the gist of what they were trying to convey was that, though Donald had won the race (by a street) they, the Gennari brothers, who had been second and third, were, nevertheless, much better runners than Donald as they — one or the other — had won here, there and everywhere. Everywhere that is except where Donald had been running. It seemed important to them that Donald should understand his inferior status but he just scratched the back of his head in that thoughtful way of his.

They had the last laugh though; second and third prizes were Finnish Design glass pieces that would pack nicely into a holdall surrounded by sweaty running gear to ward off damage — and customs officers. Donald's first prize was a Finnish country rocking chair! 'Hand luggage' quipped an onlooker. I did a deal with Donald that left the cumbersome chair in Finland. When we moved back to Scotland it had to have a crate specially made for it. I'm sitting on it now and, if I rock hard enough, it pounds — like Donald down a Finnish forest road.

I wrote the following report on the race for the RRC 'Newsletter' No 98:

The 100Km race at Hartola was held on 30th June and 1st July 1978. The course consisted of a single lap, with more than half being dirt roads. The first half of the route was gently undulating.

In January 1978, I began building up my training with the object of running a decent marathon at the AAA event in May. My plans were foiled by a serious knee injury in mid-March. The invitation to run at Hartola came via Charlie Greenlees in April, when I was still out of running due to the knee problem. I accepted the invitation on the assumption that I would be fairly fit by the end of June, when the race was to be run.

After daily ultrasonic and infra-red treatments from Malcolm Morgan, head of the physiotherapy department of the local hospital, I was able to resume running (one mile jog) on the 1st of May. My knee ached a lot, but always recovered after thirty minutes on finishing a run. Gradually I increased the mileage and by June had reached 100 miles per week. In addition, two races were included, my first since January: a 6 miler, where I was 7th; and a 10 miler, in which I was second.

A week before departing for Finland, I ran a 31-mile course to get the feel of the marathon plus. This proved to be a good confidence booster as I ran it comfortably in 2-58-10. It also served as my glycogen depletion run and was followed on successive bays by 23 miles and 20 miles.

Two days before the race, Wednesday, I arrived in Finland, where Charlie met me. We, together with Tapio Pekola, went for a massive meal and then a 10-mile run a few hours later. The evening was spent watching the first day of the World Games. Thursday was spent eating and relaxing with another visit to the World Games at night. On Friday we travelled to Hartola, where Charlie was running in the marathon held in conjunction with the 100Km. I was anxious to get started, even more so, when the Italian Gennari brothers spoke to me via their manager. They informed me that one had run 6-16 and the other 6-21. It seemed that I would have a hard race with these two.

At 20:00 we were off when the starter fired what appeared to be a shotgun. A Finn set off at a respectable pace, so I tagged along as did the Italians and Tanninen, a previous winner. The pace slackened and it felt uncomfortably slow. I seemed to me that I should run this 100Km as hard as possible and get a good time, as I did not want to make a habit of running 100Km races. At 10Km the time was 36 minutes plus, so I decided to press on. Nobody hung on, so I was now committed and Tanninen gave chase. Weather conditions were good and I enjoyed running in the cool of the evening and through the light night.

The marathon distance was passed in 2-31-30, twenty seconds ahead of Tanninen, who retired shortly afterwards. Fifty Kilometres was reached in 3-01-00 and although I felt fine, the thought of the remaining 50Km was rather daunting. Also worrying me were the dirt roads, whose surfaces were often loose with lots of small stones, which I did not want in my shoes.

By 70Km, reached in 4-17, I was 20 minutes ahead of the Italian pair. By this stage I was having to concentrate hard and was beginning to long for the finish and questioning my sanity. However, the Kilometres passed and with 10Km remaining, I knew that I should finish OK. With about 3Km remaining, I was directed off course by the cyclist accompanying me. I felt that it was the wrong way, but assumed the cyclist knew the course. We were recalled by shouts from other cyclists after covering about 300 metres past a junction where I should have turned right. I was upset by the thought of the time loss, which probably amounted to around two minutes.

The finish was reached in 6-18-00 and, after crossing the line; I was picked up by three burly Finns and thrown three times up in the air. Apparently this is the Finnish custom. Next home were the Gennaris in 6-53-00, but by this time I had gone to bed, knackered but satisfied.

The following morning Charlie and I indulged in a two-hour eating session in the refectory of the school, where the race started and where competitors stayed. There was a continuous supply of food for the competitors, many of whom were still arriving in the heat of the day (90°F at noon). With this race over I set out to have a relaxing holiday in Finland.

I rested on the following day and then Charlie, with his charming Finnish wife Marja and I, travelled to Marja's family's lakeside country cottage, which was reached by a rowboat. I ran for 62 minutes on dirt roads through the forest from there and back. My legs felt fine, but my blisters were painful. I did some work on the blisters, but one on my right foot became infected a few days later, causing a swelling in the lymph gland in my right groin. I went to a Sports Clinic in Helsinki to get some treatment for my right foot. The Doctor I saw said that the infection was clearing and made a pad for the blister. This consultation cost 50 marks, about £6.

I stayed with Charlie and Marja in their traditional Finnish wooden home in the country outside Helsinki and assisted in rigging up a bathing area. The toilet was traditional dry, lift the wooden lid from the wooden bench type, in a small shed outside.

While I was there a baptizing for their son, Sami was organised, so a lot of Marja's family arrived for this and I was honoured to be Sami's godfather.

A week after my visit to the Sports clinic my right foot blister, which had gone down to four layers of skin was sufficiently improved to allow me to resume running. On my early morning runs I would see elk and once a mother elk and calf.

I found the headquarters of Karhu shoes in Helsinki and arranged a meeting at which I explained that I had been using Karhu racing shoes for some time, obtaining them from Alastair Wood, who was importing them. I told them that I found these shoes excellent and that I had recently won the Hartola 100Km in 6-18-00 wearing a pair and, in view of this, would they consider sponsoring me. They agreed to this and would supply me with shoes and kit, so I was very pleased.

On the 16th of July, 2 weeks after the 100Km, in a 22.5Km race at Putaja over a rather hilly course, I ran with the leader, but with only about 3Km remaining I felt the need to make a stop for a number two. I decide to slow down to avoid having to stop and made it to the end safely in 2nd place in 1-14-06, with the winner finishing in 1-13-36 and the 3rd in 1-15-21.

After my morning run on 17th July, Charlie took me to Tapio's flat in Helsinki, where I was to stay for the rest of my time in Finland. Charlie needed space in their home for Dave Clark and his family, who were arriving for a few weeks visit. Later in the day I became ill and my pulse rose to 86. My head was painful, I ached all over and I experienced severe pain when I moved my eyes, and daylight hurt them, so I had to keep the blinds down. Three days later I felt a good deal better, my headache was less severe and I was able to run for 40 minutes and included 2 one-minute efforts, which felt difficult. On the 21st of July, I travelled for 5 hours on the train to Jakobstad at 63° 45[1]

North with Charlie, Marja, Dave Clark and family. The weather was excellent and the evening was superb.

On the 22nd July I ran in the Jakobstad marathon along with Dave Clark, a Scot who lived in England. He had been an Aberdeen University Harrier before me. After about one mile someone stepped on my right shoe and caused it to come off partly, so I had an annoying stop to refit it. The pace of the leaders was too quick for me, so I could not get back in contact. I passed 10Km in 33-11and reached the turn of the out and back route in 1-11-50. I could not maintain my pace on the way back and decided to run at an easier pace and finished 9th in 2-29-39.3. My feet were all right in my Karhu shoes with no socks. Strangely I did not feel this event very hard. This race was to serve as my glycogen depletion run for the Woodford to Southend race the following Saturday, but I did eat some carbohydrates at the post-race banquet. Jorma Sippola won in 2-20-57 from Danny Flynn, 2-22-44.5 and Peter Klemets 2-22-47.8 and Dave Clark was 4th in 2-22-57.

The following morning, I ran easily for 1-26-00 around Jakobstad and then went to a barbecue with the 'Lenkki Boys', the local running club, which was most enjoyable.

Back in Helsinki, I stayed another 3 nights in Tapio's flat and then caught a flight to Luton on the 26th of July. I made my way from there back to John and Anne Dixon's home. The following morning, I ran in Wanstead Park for an hour and began serious eating of carbohydrates at 09:20, but the low carbohydrate phase of my diet had not been very strict. The weather was warm with the temperature reaching 81°F. I walked around London, sightseeing for about eight hours the following day.

On the following morning, the 29 of July I ran in the Woodford to Southend 40 miles race, (measured by time trial cyclists), which was started at 09:30 by the Mayor of Redbridge, after he had given us a short address. I felt good for 3 miles, but then my legs began to feel stiff. I was struggling and Tom Roden and Cavin Woodward dropped me. I lacked energy and I wanted to drop out, but decided to keep going in the hope of an improvement. I felt a little better between 18 miles and 30 miles when I caught and passed Tom. The last 10 miles were a real struggle as my legs were so painful that I felt like crying. This was my hardest and worst race for quite a while. The temperature was 79°F and the relative humidity was 91%, but thankfully I had no foot problems from my Karhu shoes with no socks.

After the race there was a reception and tea, with the Mayor and Mayoress of Southend-on-Sea in attendance. The mayor presented the awards after short speeches. Cavin was congratulated on 'His most magnificent run today, under the most humid conditions he turned out an incredible time for this lengthened course'. Cavin's time was 3-50-14, I arrived in 3-59-35 and Tom Roden was 3rd in 4-06-06.

My old Birchfield Harriers club mate, Joe Patton, followed the race and afterwards we (along with Tom Roden, Mick Baggs and some others) went to 'The Sun' in Lamb's Conduit Street in London for some beer and to meet Mike McLeod's coach, Alan Storey. After several weeks virtually alcohol free, except through Finnish government shops, I was more sensitive to the effects of the beer on my exhausted body. Therefore, rather than have me heading back to the Dixons' home, Mick Baggs got me a spare bedroom in London University Halls of Residence, for which I was very grateful. I returned to John and Anne's next morning and ran an easy 5 miles on extremely painful legs and then went across the common with John for a lunchtime pint or two. By the following evening, the 31st of July, I was back in Elgin, safe and sound after my 'adventures'

After my 12 miles run the following morning, I drove to Ullapool and located the 'unofficial' campsite of Ron Maughan and Robin Thomas, with whom I had agreed to go camping. On the 2nd of August after my morning run we boarded the ferry for Stornoway on the Isle of Lewis and, once we had set up our tent on a site on the outskirts of Stornoway, we set out on an exploratory run.

For the next 2 days we could not motivate ourselves to run in the very bad weather conditions, probably because we had no way of drying our kit. On the 4th day we returned to Ullapool and I drove us all back to Elgin, where Ron and Robin camped in my living room for a few days and greatly assisted in exhausting my 'home brew' stock.

Four days later, the 9th of August, we enjoyed a six-hour jog in the mountains from Loch Muick, which covered 6 Munros, including Lochnagar.

On the 12th August in the Nethy Bridge Highland Games road race, in continuous rain, I was pleased with my run and won in 49-44, from Ross McDonald, 53-40 and R. Hopkins, 53-44.

On the following Sunday I ran my 31 miles course feeling tired early in the run and struggled. This served as my glycogen depletion run for the Two Bridges race the following Saturday. My total for that week was 164 miles, which was probably too large an increase from preceding weeks of 86 and 110 miles. By Wednesday evening I was feeling quite rough and my legs appeared puffed up.

On Saturday the 26th of August, after a breakfast at 07:30 of two cups of tea and two spoons of honey I ran in the 'Two Bridges' race and finished a tired 5th. I felt comfortable early in the race and six of us passed 10 miles together in 55-07, but I could not go with Bob Heron when he made a break at the Kincardine Bridge. He and Ian Leonard, a 2-21 marathon man from Rhodesia, passed 15 miles in 1-22-57, while Cavin, Mick Orton and I passed in 1-23-31. I felt very tired and I was an isolated 5th by 20 miles, which I reached in 1-53-00, almost a minute and a half behind Cavin and Mick. After Bo'ness I had difficulty going up the steep hill and Joe Keating passed me soon after this. I passed the marathon point in 2-31-48, 62 seconds after Joe. I reached 30 miles in 2-55-31, almost six minutes behind Bob Heron and Cavin, who had gone through in 2-49-24 and 2-49-28 respectively. Later I passed Leonard on the Forth Road Bridge as he slowed a lot. My finishing time of 3-32-49 was 4-15 slower than the previous year. I began to try to analyse the reason for my poor run, considering the various influencing factors, but came to no specific conclusion. I ran in Reebok 'World Ten' shoes and found them unsuitable for such road races because of the minimal cushioning, so I suffered from painful feet. Cavin had run brilliantly and his time of 3-24-45, was the 2nd best ever behind Alex Wight's 3-24-07 in 1972. Bob Heron was 2nd in 3-26-22 followed by Mick Orton, 3-28-09 and Joe Keating in 3-28-37. This year a record 72 runners finished this classic race.

THE BRIGHTON AGAIN: SETTING A NEW COURSE RECORD

An infected blister that required medical intervention and a course of antibiotics interrupted my build up for the London to Brighton, by missing 2 days. On Sunday the 24th of September, in the late afternoon I ran my 31 miles course in 3-00-48 as my glycogen depletion run for the carbohydrate loading diet, in preparation for the London to Brighton the following Sunday. This gave me 138 miles for the week, with the previous one at 132 miles. I continued my normal training the following week up to Thursday, when after my evening session with the club lads, I began eating carbohydrates at 20:30, which was 58 and a half hours before the event. On Friday I rested and on Saturday the 30th of September, I travelled by train to London where I stayed overnight with John and Anne Dixon.

For breakfast on Sunday morning, 1st of October, I had two digestive biscuits with honey, and then the taxi that I had ordered on Saturday night arrived and the driver took me to the changing accommodation for the race. After registering, changing etc about half an hour before the start of the London to Brighton race I consumed 200ml of 'Dynamo' and, full of nervous tension and excitement, made my way to Big Ben. I started steadily with Bob Heron and then we began to chase Cavin Woodward and Mick Orton. We caught them at about 5 miles and passed 10 miles together in 55-31. Mick dropped back at about 12 miles, so then there were 3 of us and as I felt quite good I led for stretches. Bob dropped next and stopped for a call of nature. He never regained contact with us and later dropped out. I passed 20 miles in 1-54-34, 18 seconds behind Cavin.

Cavin made a break at about 24 miles, which I did not feel capable of following, so he pulled away and was 58 seconds ahead at Horley. He was always in sight and at about Gatwick Airport he made a pit stop, so I was close to him again. Cavin was slowing, and I gained in confidence after having resigned myself to finishing 2nd. Gradually I pulled him back and caught him shortly after 30 miles. He came with me as I passed him but, little by little, I drew away from him and extended my lead. I felt that if I could hold my lead to the top of Pyecombe Hill, I could win. My legs and feet felt rather painful, but I managed to keep pushing myself to the finish. My time of 5-13-02 on that year's course, which was 1048 yards longer because of a diversion, was worth at least 5-09-02 on the previous year's course. This meant that it was one mile longer than the 1972 course on which Alastair Wood set the record of 5-11-08, so I felt that I could now claim to be the record-holder.

Don Ritchie (104) and Cavin Woodward (28) battling along the Brighton Road.

Naturally, I was delighted to win for a second time and in such a good time. At the tea afterwards in the 'Old Ship Hotel, the Mayor of Brighton, Councilor Alfred Feld, presented the awards, so I was proud to receive the 'Arthur Newton Cup' and the 'Ernest Neville gold medal'. Cavin finished 2nd in 5-18-30; Tom O'Reilly was 3rd in 5-28-57; and then came Mike Newton 5-31-19, Tom Roden 5-37-53 and Bob Holt in 5-38-57.

Afterwards I caught the overnight train to Inverness, again guarding the 'Arthur Newton Cup' in a black bin liner, and duly arrived back in Elgin at around 09:30 on Monday morning and not exactly ready to face classes soon after this.

The start of a road race in Cooper Park, Elgin, with several friends prominent.

By Friday I had obviously recovered, since on Saturday in the Alves to Forres road race I was pleasantly surprised to be able to run quite well. I ran with Alastair Wood to just inside Forres, where I had to let him go because my calf muscles were tightening up. Graham Milne won in 28-07 from Ian Mackenzie, 28-16 and Colin Donnelly, 28-46 followed by Alastair Wood, 28-55 and I finished 5th in 29-01.

A North District cross-country league race and the first leg for Forres 'A' team in the North District cross-country relay championships followed in the next 2 weeks. The day after the cross-country relay, Sunday the 21st of October I ran a 26 miles 'glycogen depletion' course in forest and road for a weekly total of 161.5 miles.

I maintained my normal training on the following week with 20.5 miles on Monday in two sessions, 28 miles on Tuesday in two sessions and 28 miles in two sessions on Wednesday. On Thursday I began eating carbohydrates again at 06:30 and then ran to work by my 14 miles route. On Friday, with another day's paid leave from school, I travelled to London by train for most of the day and made my way to John Lamont's home near Hendon, where I was to stay overnight.

100KM TRACK TRIUMPH: A RECORD LASTING 36 YEARS SO FAR.

On Saturday morning, the 28th of October 1978, I had two cups of tea and three rich tea biscuits for breakfast and then John drove me to Crystal Palace stadium for the 100Km track race organised by the R.R.C. John was to be my handler, so I gave him my drinks and a schedule of when I would require them. My first was half an hour before the race start, when I drank a bottle (200ml) of 'dynamo'. Martin Thompson, an Australian physiologist, asked me if I would participate in a study he was conducting into Cortisol metabolism and I agreed. To do this accurately a small amount of marked Cortisol, flavoured with cordial and required to be taken prior to the start. The race pace felt good for a start and Cavin Woodward, Mick Molloy and I passed 10 Km in 34-06, 20Km in 1-09-21. My insides began to give me trouble and at about 16 miles I had to stop to go into the changing rooms to use the toilet, (due to the Cortisol, possibly). On rejoining the race, I was a lap and a half behind Mick and Cavin. I gradually caught up and was then a lap behind and the leaders' time at 30Km was 1-46-55. At 40Km the time was 2-23-12, 1-22 behind Molloy and Cavin and at 50Km it was 2-59-59, 7 seconds behind Cavin, but I was now 1-37 behind Mick.

I started to unlap myself and, as I did, Mick Molloy came with me and then passed me and got a lead of about 150 metres, plus the lap. He then 'blew up', so I caught and passed him. From then on I felt strong and pulled further and further ahead of the field. I passed 40 miles in 3-52-55 and I was pleased to break the 50 miles record with a time of 4-53-28, 11-26 ahead of Cavin. However, I found the last 12 miles very hard, but I never became depleted of glycogen. I passed 60 miles in 5-56-57 and **completed the last of the 250 laps in 88 seconds to finish in 6-10-20, which was a World Best – even in 2015, this mark has never been beaten!** My legs and feet were not too bad. Mick Molloy had to leave the track for quite some time after he faded and on rejoining continued in his socks. Cavin also had to leave the track, but for a much shorter time. Several years later, when the I.A.U recognized 6 hours as an event, my distance of 97.2Km at 6 hours in this race was also accepted as a World Best Performance.

Some other intermediate times were: 60Km 3-36-29, 70 Km 4-13-59, 80 Km 4-51-48 and 90 Km 5-30-45. My 10-mile splits were: 55-28, 59-26, 58-51, 59-30, 60-33 and 63-29

Results: 1) D Ritchie 6-10-20, 2) C Woodward 6-38-48, 3) Mike Newton 6-48-08, 4) Jan Knippenberg (Holland) 7-07-50, 5) Mick Molloy (Eire) 7-26-11.

John was an excellent handler and promised to take me to a 'Real Ale' pub in the evening to celebrate the occasion. Later on, he fulfilled his promise and we walked to the pub, where we sampled some of the extensive range of real ales on offer. On the walk back we picked up carry out meals to round off a memorable day.

Overtaking Malcolm Campbell during my 100km Track World Record.

On Sunday evening I travelled back to Inverness by the familiar overnight train and on to Elgin. I could not run for the next 3 days because I lacked motivation and had a feeling of anti-climax.

On Sunday the 19th of November I ran in the Edinburgh to Glasgow Relay for Forres Harriers on Stage 6 into a strong headwind. I was 14th fastest, 3-18 behind the fastest, Nat Muir of Shettleston Harriers. I did manage to improve our position by one place to 15th, which was maintained to the finish.

I attended an interview for a lecturing position at Robert Gordon's Institute of Technology (RGIT), on the 21st of November, which did not go well once one of the interviewing panel became annoyed with the photocopy of my application that he had, inferring that I had disregarded the instruction about what colour of ink should be used!

In subsequent North District cross-country league races, I was 6th at Thurso and 7th in the third and then 8th in the AAAC cross-country race at Balgownie on 17th December.

Before the Forres Harriers Christmas handicap race on the 16th of December I received a telegram at 'Craggan' inviting me to the 'Runners World Running Week' at Palo Alto in California, between Christmas and New Year and requesting me to 'call collect'. Joan Frazer, who was with me, then told me that this was like a reverse charge call, so I telephoned accepting this opportunity. My outbound flight tickets arrived towards the end of the following week. I had to go to the USA embassy in Edinburgh as soon as I could to get a visa, once my Christmas holidays started.

On Wednesday the 27th of December I caught the 10:10 flight from Glasgow to London, Heathrow. I made my way to Terminal Three for the Pan-Am flight to San Francisco and checked in and went to the departure gate, where I recognized Brendan Foster among the waiting passengers. I resisted the temptation to go and ask him if he was also going to attend the 'Runners World Running Week'. The flight took off in the early afternoon and followed a route north-west, passing fairly close to Glasgow, where I had started from earlier that morning, as the pilot headed towards Greenland.

Darkness followed for a while then twilight and full daylight, which was a surprise for me, as we flew over a frozen northern Canada. We were following the sun, but by the time we reached San Francisco we were in darkness again.

Brendan Foster and I were met at Arrivals by a representative of 'Runners World', who drove us to our Motel accommodation at 'Rickeys Hyatt House' in Palo Alto, the base of 'Runners World' magazine and other running publications. Brendan wanted to go for a run, so once we had checked in and had been given our accommodation units, we went for an estimated six and a half miles run in pleasantly warm weather.

The following morning, after a run with Brendan in and around Palo Alto, he introduced me, at breakfast, to John Walker, who had won gold in the 1500 metres at the 1976 Montreal Olympics. Later that day I met with Bob Anderson the editor and owner of 'Runners World', who gave me my 'timetable' and a programme of the events taking place during the week. In the evening I was delighted to join Bob for dinner in a nearby restaurant, with Ron Clarke and his wife and Australian marathon runner, Derek Clayton. I had never expected to meet these marvellous runners.

On Friday the 29th of December I ran fifteen miles at a hard pace with Frank Bozanich, an ex Marine. This was when I first encountered the terms: **ultra distance and ultra marathon**, which were used for races, longer than the marathon. Frank specialized in such races, so he and I were classed as **'ultra runners'**.

I met 'Runners World' editors: Joe Henderson, Amby Burfoot and Rick Benyo, all of whom were very friendly and welcoming. Later I was part of a panel at 2 seminars and tried to answer any questions directed at me sensibly, but I lacked practice in using the radio link hand-held microphone. I also met Fred Lebow, the director of the New York marathon and he invited me to participate in the 'New York 100 miles', which was scheduled for late June. I accepted his invitation because it would be an opportunity to visit this well-known city.

On Sunday the 31st of December at midnight in the 'Runners World' five miles race I finished 57th in 25-33 after covering the first mile in 4-55. Alberto Salazar won in a very fast time of 22-13. I got a shock when Greta Waitz eased past me, so I had to increase my effort to pass her and to stay ahead of her to the finish. **I counted this race as part of my 1978 total, which amounted to 5736 miles, the highest yearly total I had achieved. It had been a second year of success at what I now knew to be ultra-marathons.**

1979

On New Year's Day I participated in the 5 miles fun run and later I ran for 6 miles with Ilona Andersen. In the afternoon Amby Burfoot drove us over the hills to the Pacific coast where we ran for about one and a half hours along the beach and back, with our pace building towards the end.

As the 'Running Week' was drawing to a close, Ilona Andersen, who I had met and run with some days earlier invited me to stay for a few days at her sister's home in Oakland. I accepted her offer and made arrangements for my return flight date to be put back. Ilona was from Michigan, with an Italian father and Finnish mother and her late husband was an agricultural engineer. Her sister, husband and family made me welcome and during my stay with them they drove us to see Napa Valley and sample some wines. Another trip was to the Giant Redwood trees in 'Muir Woods'. Ilona showed me all the sights of San Francisco, which I greatly appreciated.

On Saturday the 6th of January I said goodbye to Ilona, her sister and family and boarded an overnight flight bound for London Heathrow, with a stop at Los Angeles. On Sunday I caught my flight to Glasgow where Joan Fraser met me. My mini-van was snowed in and, as there was a petrol shortage, I decided to postpone travelling North until daylight next day. This meant that I missed the first day of our new school term, which greatly annoyed, rightly so, Mr. Boag our headmaster.

I settled back into work and a familiar training routine and then after a week I caught flu, an occupational hazard in teaching, which laid me low for a few days. By the end of January, I had got back to 100 miles plus a week and maintained this until my first race on Saturday the 3rd of March. This was the North District cross-country league race at Lossiemouth where I felt that I ran quite strongly, finishing 4th behind Brian Turnbull of Inverness Harriers, Ian Mackenzie and Ross Arbuckle, both of Forres Harriers. On Sunday I ran around my 32 miles course to complete 144 miles for the week. I did not regard this as a glycogen depletion run for the 50Km track race scheduled for the following Saturday, as I decided to try running that race without using the carbohydrate loading diet.

TRAVEL DIFFICULTIES BUT ANOTHER WORLD TRACK BEST

On Friday morning the 9th of March I ran to work by my 8.5 miles course. My headmaster, Mr. Boag, refused my request for leave of absence for part of the day, so that I could travel to Altrincham for the race on Saturday and suggested that I make alternative travel arrangements. Dave Atwell the race organiser had booked me into the 'Unicorn' Hotel for Friday night, but I was not going to be able to use this facility. I telephoned Ron Maughan to arrange a pick up and accommodation and after work I drove to Inverness where I caught the 19:28 London train and got off at Wigan. Ron Maughan and Mary met me there at 03:30am on Saturday and drove me to Crosby, near Liverpool, where they were living. At 04:30am I crawled into a sleeping bag on a couch and tried to sleep.

Later that day I rose at 9am and had two cups of tea before Ron, Mary and John Lamont drove me to Altrincham for the 50Km track race at Timperley in Altrincham, near Manchester, sponsored by Instrumentation Laboratory (UK) Ltd. I felt O.K. and convinced myself that the journey and lack of sleep would not affect me. The track was a clay material with a loose top surface. The weather was cold and windy, so conditions for a fast time did not look promising. I wore my old Reebok 'World Ten' shoes, Finnish shorts and a teeshirt.

We started at 12:00 and Cavin went straight to the front and I followed him through the first lap in 72 seconds and the first mile in 5-11. I felt good, so I went into the lead after six laps and broke away from Cavin. It was just a question of keeping a good pace going from then on. Ron, Mary and John had gone shopping in Manchester and they did not return with my drinks until I had covered 15 miles, so I was becoming worried that I would become glycogen depleted. Then I had 250 ml of glucose polymer, which was: a quarter of a pound of long chain polymer in a pint of water plus some vitamin C and some crushed potassium tablets. I seemed to feel stronger after this and I was able to keep my pace up and I had repeat drinks every 5 Km after this. My time at the marathon was 2-22-48, which was my fastest-ever and very encouraging. My feet became quite painful, but if I kept pushing on they did not feel too bad. I passed 30 miles in 2-44-36 and finished with a 77 seconds last lap for a final time of 2-50-30. I was very pleased that I had succeeded in improving my existing World Best by 68 seconds. The wind was quite annoying, as was the fact that I often had to run quite wide, when lapping the 26 runners in the field. My 10Km splits were: 32-25, 33-21, 34-08, 35-07 and 35-29.

Results: 1) Donald Ritchie, Forres H, 2-50-30, 2) Cavin Woodward Leamington AC, 2-55-24, 3) Tom O'Reilly, Small Heath H, 2-56-34, 4) Dave Atwell, Altrincham & Dist AC, 2-59-58, 5) Mike Newton, South London H 3-06-34, 6) George Kay, Stafford AC, 3-07-31.

Ron and Mary drove me to Liverpool Rail station on Sunday morning, where I caught a train to Glasgow and from there to Inverness. In Glasgow Joan Fraser met me and treated me to an Indian meal to celebrate my new 50 Km World Best.

The following Saturday, 17th of March, in the final North District cross-country league race at Inverness I felt surprisingly good and finished 3rd.

On Saturday the 24th of March, I was very pleased to win again the Knockfarrel hill race at Strathpeffer. On the climb I felt remarkably good and Mel Edwards, Innis Mitchell and I were then leading. Although I felt good and strong I decided to delay my effort until later. With about one and a half miles remaining I went to the lead and pressed on. I found it very hard to break away and had to push myself to the utmost to achieve a very satisfactory win in 39-10. Innis was 2nd in 39-15, followed by Mel, also in 39-15.

On the 29th of March I received a letter from John Softley, Secretary of the Scottish Marathon club, informing me that: *'at our AGM held last night, you were elected an Honorary Life Member of the Scottish Marathon Club'*. I was very honoured to receive this totally unexpected tribute.

On Thursday the 12th of April, during my Easter holidays from school, I agreed to go to the Isle of Man for the 'Athletics Festival' with a group of Aberdeen University Hare and Hounds runners. They had obtained an Athletics Association mini-bus and we drove to Crosby near Liverpool where Ron Maughan and Robin Thomas joined us. On Friday morning we caught the ferry from Liverpool to Douglas where I shared a room in a guesthouse with John Lamont. In the evening I finished 48th in the 5.5 miles road race in Douglas. On Saturday I ran the first leg of the road relay for our Aberdeen University 'B' team and finished in 15th. On Sunday in the hill race at Peel I finished 36th and then, after two pints of beer, I ran back to our guesthouse in Douglas in 1-21-30, for a total of 105 miles for the week.

On Saturday 28th of April I ran in the Epsom & Ewell 40 miles track race and had a hard time. We heard at 07:10, that the track was flooded and when we arrived at 08:30 it was only partly flooded but the race was cancelled. However, after some discussion, it was decided to hold the race despite the state of the track. Helpers used sponge mats from the pole vault pit to soak up water from the track puddles, and then removed the sodden sponge mats to wring them out, before repeating the process. This was effective in removing the majority of the water. We started one and a half hours late at 11:00 and I ran quickly with Cavin and passed the first mile in 5-07. Underfoot conditions were bad and soon I was getting covered in mud as the track became 'cut up' and the cold wind blowing down the back straight was very taxing. My 10 miles time was 53-57, but I felt tired and passed 20 miles in 1-50-53, the marathon in 2-26-34 and 30 miles in 2-50-0. A record time was out of the question and I found it increasingly hard to run 92 seconds laps, so my last 10 miles took over 64 minutes and I finished with 3-54-07. It also rained during the race and six competitors dropped out. My ten-mile splits were: 53-55, 56-11, 59-54 and 64-07.

Results: 1) D Ritchie, Forres H, 3-54-07, 2) A Smith, Burton AC 4-08-27, 3) C Woodward, Leamington AC, 4-12-54, 4) G Kay, Stafford AC 4-13-32

On Sunday I ran for 2-58-00 with John Lamont from Queensbury and I felt quite strong, which was encouraging.

Just over a week later my left ankle became very painful and swollen, so I had to stop running and seek help from 'Magic' Malcolm Morgan. He gave me physiotherapy treatment, which he repeated on the following three days, while I rested it. On Friday of that week I ran my 12 miles course at an easy pace to see how my ankle felt. As it was not too bad I decided that I would go to the AAA marathon at Coventry on Sunday.

In the AAA marathon at Coventry, on the 13 of May, unsurprisingly, I had a tough time. The weather was very hot with the temperature at 75°F and although I felt quite good for the first few miles, I began to struggle. I passed 5 miles in 26-21 in 28th place and passed 10 miles in 54-18, but I was slowing. At 15 miles I was 36th in 1-24-16. Tom O'Reilly passed me before 20 miles, which I reached in 1-54-51 in 34th. I was very tired by then and felt like giving up and abandoning the run. I managed to avoid this and finished a disappointed 31st in a poor 2-35-10. I felt rather ill afterwards and was on the point of vomiting a few times. Stupidly I had not run in my Karhu shoes and someone noted this, and this resulted in a letter from Ian Stewart, who was then associated with the managing director, G. W. James, of Karhu-Titan UK, indicating his displeasure. I responded with a letter of apology for my poor judgment.

ITALIAN SAGA

Next Sunday morning, the 20th of May, I ran my 32 miles course as the glycogen depletion run in preparation for a 100Km race in Italy the following Saturday. My right ankle was very painful, but the intensity of the discomfort varied. On Thursday at 07:00, I ran my 20 miles course from Willowbank road in 2-02-00 and began eating carbohydrates again at 09:30. At 11:30 I got a flight from Aberdeen to London and from there to Milan. From there I caught a bus into the city centre and found the railway station and the train times to Florence and caught the first available one. I finally arrived in Florence at 02:30 on Friday and had to spend the night in the train station waiting room, because there was no place for me in the hotel I was due to stay at. Later I walked in the city for quite a long way, sightseeing.

The following day, the 26th of May, Giors Oneto of Spiridon Italy, who had invited me, registered me for the race and brought my race number to the hotel, where I was trying to stay cool and relax. He also organised a cyclist to carry my personal drinks as I had requested. In the afternoon I ran in the **Florence to Faenza 101.5 Km race known as 'Del Passatorie' and managed to win despite losing around 14 minutes, because of a 'mix up' at the start. As a result, my 5Km time was a ridiculous 33-10! The temperature was 88°F and the relative humidity 60% at the start of the race and the course was a difficult one with 900 feet of climbing out of Florence, then later a 3000-foot climb over the mountain pass.** My cyclist was surprised to see me so far down the field, but was encouraged to see me making progress. He kept calling me Daniel, which for some reason kept reminding me of the bible story, Daniel going into the lion's den.

I ran hard to catch the leader, which I did at about 36 miles, but with about 25 miles remaining my legs were very painful. I felt like dropping out to stop the pain, but I am glad that I was able to keep going to the finish. The atmosphere was tremendous, with people turning out in the towns along the route to cheer the runners. The finish in Faenza was in a floodlit square packed with cheering people and we had to run up a ramp to a stage to finish. It was a marvellous race and I was delighted to have won. My feet (in Karhu racing shoes) were in a very bad condition.

Results: 1) D Ritchie 100Km 6-48-18, finish 6-52-33, 2) V Mileto (Italy) 100Km 7-03-14, finish 7-07-05, 3) R Chovinard (Canada) 100Km 7-05-50, finish 7-10-41, 4) L Gennari (Italy) 100Km 7-06-43, finish 7-13-02, 5) M Docezal (Czech) 100Km 7-25-06, finish 7-29-36, 6) C Pappa (Italy) 100Km 7-42-27, finish 7-46-16, 7) K Baumgartmer (Germany) 100Km 7-48-41, finish 7-52-33.

Some time later I wrote a detailed account of my trip, which I called **'The Italian Job'**, which is included here:

In March 1979 I received an invitation from Giors Oneto, of Spiridon Italy, to participate in a 101.5 km race from Firenze (Florence) to Faenza. As I had not visited Italy before, I readily accepted the invitation to this race to be held on a Saturday near the end of May. To reach Faenza from Firenze the Apennines have to be crossed, and the race was named "Del Passatorie" after a bandit who operated in these mountains. Passatorie from what I can gather was a Robin Hood sort of character. The arrangement for this race was that I should organise my own travel and would be reimbursed in Faenza. Following some correspondence with Giors I established that there was no airport in Firenze so I would have to fly to Milan and then take the train. Arrangements were made for travel and soon departure date arrived. From Elgin I caught a train to Aberdeen, a bus to the airport and then the flight to London.

This part of the journey had already occupied some six hours. Next there was the flight to Linate airport in Milan. From there I got a bus into the city and managed to locate the Central Station. By now it was 8:00 pm and I found that the next train to Firenze was at 9:30 pm.

My next priority was to get some food, so I headed off to see what I could find. A restaurant provided spaghetti something de Mar, which I deduced should be some seafood. It turned out to be spaghetti mixed with a sauce containing a sort of shellfish hotchpotch including the shells. There were quite a variety of shells, some of which including the razor and mussel I recognised. Some had edible bits inside or at least remains, but mostly they were empty. I also found bits of chopped up octopus' tentacles in there. It was quite a change from Luigi's fish and chips at home. Once I had reduced this course to shells only, I finished off with some excellent ice cream and fresh strawberries.

Suitably refuelled, I returned to the station, purchased my ticket and carefully located the correct train. Although it was half an hour before departure time the train was packed and there were people in every corner. Train travel was inexpensive here so I expect that this accounted for the popularity. I resigned myself to a long stand in the stifling heat. We got underway exactly on time, and the draught through the open windows caused by the train's motion, reduced the discomfort caused by the heat. Eventually after a tedious journey Firenze was reached. It was now half past midnight and I had to find my hotel. Clutching the letter from Giors with the name of the hotel on it, I sallied forth. There were several police in and around the station, but they did not seem the type you ask directions from: they were wearing bullet-proof waistcoats and carrying sub-machine guns. Later I found one with only a pistol so I asked him. He could not speak English and I could not speak Italian but despite this he was able to indicate the general direction to go in. Further directions were sought from one of the several painted ladies I passed and I found the hotel, or at least a door with the sign "Melegano" above it. What a relief; I had been travelling since 6:30 am and it was now 1:00 am.

After repeated bell ringing the door was unlocked and opened by a sad looking man with a very pale complexion who was wearing a striped nightshirt and spectacles with very thick lenses. I showed him the letter, he looked at it and then said "No English", which I took to mean that he could not understand or speak English. He did have a few words of English, such as "Hotel Full" and "you tomorrow". It was clear that he was not going to invite me in or suggest any alternatives. As he closed and locked the door, I thought, "This is another fine mess I have got into". I decided the best thing to do was to return to the Railway Station and make use of the Waiting Room. The station was a very grand building with marble floors and many marble pillars supporting marble arches and the roof. Even the benches in the Waiting Room were made of marble. It was fairly crowded in there but I got a bit of a bench. Some people were stretched out on the benches sleeping soundly and snoring profusely; others were in sleeping bags on the floor; while some played cards, smoked and drank wine.

During the remainder of the night I managed to doze off a couple of times. At about 7:00 am there was a stir as the cafeteria at one side of the room began to open up. It took me some time to establish the system for obtaining some food. You had to go to the cash desk and pay for the items you wished to have. You then got a receipt, which you present, to the assistant behind the service counter. She then hands over the required item without having to touch the unhygienic money. I managed to get the equivalent of a buttery roll and a cup of coffee. Once this was dispatched I made my way back to the Melegano, now open. Behind the reception desk was the sad man I had met earlier. He indicated that a room would be available at 10:00 am. I asked for breakfast, but eventually found out that the hotel did not provide meals and he indicated that I should go to a cafe. This I did and somehow got mixed up with a party of American tourists from a similar non-breakfast-providing hotel. As no one asked me to pay or anyone to pay, I left with them, the beneficiary of some package arrangement.

After an exploratory walk, I discovered that Firenze had great character with lots of interesting looking streets, buildings and lots of smells - some appealing and some rather unappealing. On returning to the Hotel Melegano a room was available so I checked in, deposited my kit in the room and set off to see something of Firenze. I was fascinated by the city: the Ponte Vecchio bridge over the Arno river, the magnificent buildings around the Piazza del Duomo, and the art, which was everywhere. In the couple of galleries, I managed to visit was work by Leonardo da Vinci, Michelangelo, Botticelli and many other renowned artists.

Several hours later on my way back to the hotel, some pizza in a cafe tempted me. I bought a piece and sat down on a stone bench to eat it. This was a mistake; at least sitting down was, as after a few mouthfuls, I became drowsy and then fell asleep in mid-chew. Some time later I was awakened by flapping wings and loud cooing as my pizza was being eaten eagerly from my hand by numerous pigeons.

Back at the Hotel, Giors Oneto greeted me, welcomed me to Firenze and invited me to join him, his wife and other invited runners for dinner at 8:00 pm. This was a lengthy and enjoyable event, finishing about midnight. Little thought was given to the race we had come to run next afternoon.

Next morning after an extra-long lie, I began preparing for the race, which was due to start at 4:00 pm. With bottled water I made up my 10% solution glucose polymer drinks, about three litres. Next I taped vulnerable parts of my feet, and made sure my shoes and kit were comfortable. Finally, I trimmed the number bib to a manageable size, being careful to leave the sponsor's name intact. Giors then arrived with the owner of 'Atala' Sports: they manufactured kit and shoes. He offered me £1000 if I would run in Atala shoes. I explained that I could not run in new shoes and also as an amateur, a rather naive one, I could not accept the money. As he was rather disappointed, I agreed to wear the Atala vest in exchange for a selection of Atala kit and shoes.

Soon it was time to make my way to the start in Piazza della Signoria. As it was only 3 km from the hotel, I decided to walk there, so I headed off with my bulging kit bag in one hand and a couple of carrier bags of drinks in the other. These encumbrances impaired my progress through the crowds of people, mainly tourists milling around. It seemed incongruous that, amongst these relaxed people, there was me weaving my way, with tension and apprehension mounting inside me, towards a testing time. On reaching the Piazza, I was amazed to see how many runners there were jostling around; later I found out that there were almost 3000 starters. What a contrast to the UK where 20 runners in an ultra distance race is considered normal. I located the bus, which would transport kit to the finish in Faenza, and deposited my labelled kit bag in it. Next I had to find the cyclist who was going to be my second during the race. Just as I was getting ever more anxious, not quite panicking, Oneto arrived with my cyclist and introduced him. He was a large, burly, cheery man with a big walrus moustache. I gave him my drinks and arranged to meet him at 10 km. I could now relax a little knowing my kit was on the bus and my support was organised, so I went off to find some shade from the blazing sun. The temperature was about 32 degrees centigrade. There was quite a carnival atmosphere with a band playing traditional music, and a group performing with huge whips, which they cracked loudly. I found some shady steps and sat down and began sipping from my pre-race bottle. While packing for the trip at home, I found that I was short of a few drinks bottles so I took whatever was available, including an empty half-bottle labelled Smirnoff Vodka. This served as my pre-race container. A reporter from one of the Italian athletics magazines recognised me and began to ask for some information such as: How would I run in the race? How had I prepared? What did I think about Firenze? What did I think about Vito Mileto? etc. As I had never heard of Mileto, he explained that this was the winner of the race last year and the year before that. Finally, he asked what I was drinking on such a warm day. Being in a rather flippant mood by now, I just pointed to the label on the half-bottle containing the colourless glucose polymer solution. He noted it down in his pad with a rather puzzled look on his face. Perhaps he thought that it was a refinement of the carbohydrate loading diet. Once he had exhausted his questions and gone, I made my way to find a toilet for a final pre-race check. These were hard to come by but I managed to use the facilities in a cafe off the Piazza.

On emerging from the cafe, a reporter with a camera crew from a local TV station recognised me and wanted to interview me. I was reluctant as it was now only fifteen minutes before departure time but I agreed when it was pointed out that it would take only a few minutes. About five minutes later, the interview completed I made my way to the start line, and observed that there appeared to be considerably fewer runners in the Piazza now. I reached the front row with a couple of minutes to spare. Ahead was the lead car containing the starter, who was standing so that his torso was protruding through the sunroof of the car. He was holding a stopwatch in one hand and a raised flag in the other. On either side of the car were police motorcyclists who kept revving their engines of their Moto Guzzis impatiently. As the 4:00 pm start time grew closer and closer, the tension heightened as a sixty-second countdown was started and the revving became more vigorous and more frequent. Suddenly the tension was released as the flag dropped and we surged forward, after the speeding car and the motorcyclists.

After about 2 km I was joint leader with a tall thin Italian and we continued to pull away from the rest. Just before the climb out of the city began at around 5 km, I was surprised to overtake some runners wearing race numbers. They were jogging and as we continued the 900 feet climb on the zigzags up to Fiesole we passed increasing numbers of these joggers, I could not understand how this had occurred. At first I thought that somehow we had gone off course and ended up doing a loop, and were now passing through the field. I abandoned this notion and decided that the less serious runners who had just wanted to complete the course before the cut off time — midday tomorrow — had set off a little early. By the time I reached Fiesole at 10 km, I must have passed about

1500 runners struggling on the stiff climb. My cyclist met me there and he gave me my first drink with an anxious look."Prima fifteen minutes", he said,"No, I am Prima"I said. He repeated his information, and I suddenly realised that it was not only the joggers who had got underway prematurely. I was furious and immediately increased my pace. In my early days I used to run handicap races: quarter, half and mile races at Highland Games, but I never dreamt that I would do a 101.5 km handicap race. The course now undulated and on sections I could see runners, not so many now, various distances ahead. As I caught these up one by one, it was obvious that these were not joggers. I began to think that my pace might be suicidal in the warm conditions, but these thoughts were ignored in my anger-driven charge. After Vetta le Creci at 23 km and at a height of 1560 feet, the route descends into the next valley and there was some shade. At about 30 km I caught and passed one of the French runners."You have a problem?"he asked as I swept past. I did not attempt to explain and simply grunted yes. In Borgo San Lorenzo at 35 km it seemed that the entire population had turned out to cheer the runners on. The main street appeared to be completely full of people but as one approached they moved apart, providing a metre-wide path to run along through their cheering midst. What an inspiring atmosphere they created. I had never experienced anything like it before.

On leaving Borgo the climbing began again, a short sharp incline then a gradual rise into the Apennine Mountains, where the real hill climbing started. Ahead I could see the road snake up the mountainside, terrace upon terrace. Now the sun was much lower in the sky and often blocked by the surrounding hills. I caught the Gennari brothers running together, and they shouted some encouragement as I passed. My cycling second was pleased with my progress and kept calling me Daniel. He pointed up to the road a couple of terraces above, and indicated that there was the 'Prima'. Next I caught and passed the Canadian, Richard Chouvinard, as we neared the top of the pass, at Colla di Casaglia, which was at 3000 feet. The top of the pass is at 52 km, and then the remaining 49.5 km to the finish is almost entirely downhill, steep at first then gradual until the flat plain is reached 5 km before Faenza. I let rip on the first downhill and soon caught the second, a Czechoslovakian, and gained on the leader who was accompanied by a posse of cyclists, motor scooterists and others on mopeds. I caught the leader, Vito Mileto, and swept past into the lead with about 45 km to run. I was running strongly although my feet were very sore from the hot road and my quads were becoming very painful. Every 2 km there were marker boards indicating the distance to the finish, which I found quite comforting. As darkness fell at about 8:00 pm the entourage of bicycles, motorcycles, mopeds, scooters and cars, which I had acquired on assuming the lead, provided plenty of light but too much company. The continual blowing of horns, general noise and exhaust fumes, especially from the two-stroke engines became increasingly annoying as I became more tired.

We came to a level crossing with the barriers down but some of the cyclists rushed ahead and opened them bodily. I had enough sense to check that the train was not too close before running across the rails. I passed through more towns and it seemed that all the inhabitants had turned out to cheer the brave runners. There were bonfires and bands playing which all contributed towards producing a really stimulating atmosphere. A car with a film crew would draw alongside me every now and again to make some recordings with the aid of some powerful spotlights. I was longing to be finished but I had to be patient and just keep working away. At last I reached the final five kilometres of the race with the lights of Faenza clearly visible. Crowds of people lined the route over the last couple of kilometres all cheering loudly. I actually had to jog the last 100 metres as the TV crew had difficulty making its way through the crowds. At the finish one had to run up a ramp on to a stage so that one could be presented to the huge crowd gathered in the floodlit square. These were a marvellous few moments, which I will always treasure.

My feet were very painful; my quads were not much better, so I requested some medical assistance. I was helped to the room where the medics had set up their centre. After some foot repair work, I requested some aspirin to dull the discomfort I was experiencing. A couple of minutes later a doctor appeared bearing a fairly large syringe. This did not look like any aspirin I had ever seen, so I informed him that I wanted aspirin, not an anaesthetic. He assured me that it was indeed aspirin. I decided that I wasn't feeling that bad after all and declined the medicine.

After a shower I was taken to the Hotel Vittoria and, on passing through the square I could see a whole ox had been roasted on a spit. People were queuing to purchase roast beef rolls with salad, along with cups of red *wine. At the hotel I consumed a large quantity of strawberries and ice cream, plus a few beers before trying to sleep. The prize presentation was scheduled for midday on Sunday. Before this I got a note of the results: my time was 6:52:23; Mileto was next in 7:7:05; and Chouvinard third in 7:10:41. The times were good despite the heat; even the Italians said it was warm. I bought some newspapers to see if there were any race reports. One paper had a full-page report on the race and had the headline: "Ad Uno Scozzese Amante della Vodka la Centro Chilomeiri del Passatorie". This and a further mention in the report referred to my pre race bottle. I wondered how many Italian ultra runners would try this 'method' before their next 100 km.*

Prize presentation took place in the square on the finishing stage in front of a large crowd, which had gathered to show their appreciation of the runners' efforts. My award was a ceramic plaque about one metre by about three quarters of a metre portraying Passatorie in three dimensions. The other prize from the main sponsors, the wine company of the region, was one hundred bottles of wine: fifty each of Trebbiano and Sangiovese. This was rather unexpected and I began to ponder how these might be transported back, or alternatively disposed of. With Giors Oneto's help the latter option was more feasible. The method of disposal was not novel but was satisfactorily accomplished.

Del Passatorie had been an unforgettable experience and a 'good adventure'. All I had to do now was get back to Lossiemouth for work at 9:00 am on Tuesday.

AND SOON IT WAS OFF TO NEW YORK AND ANOTHER RECORD RUN

Two weeks after the 'Passatorie' I ran my 32 miles course in 3-05-55, which was close to my fastest. The weather conditions were very pleasant and I finished this glycogen depletion run at 20:15. On Tuesday the 12th of June after work I drove to Wishaw to stay with Peter and Rita Duffy prior to my departure to New York for the 100-mile road race. Next morning, I drove to Prestwick airport and caught the BOAC flight, a VC10 to New York. In the early evening after meeting Fred Lebow, I ran 8.5 miles in Central Park with a runner from the New York Road Runners Club. This was quite an experience as there were thousands of other runners of all shapes and sizes doing the same thing. I began eating carbohydrates on completing this run. I rested most of the following day, but did do some walking in Manhattan.

On Friday the 15th of June, the race was to take place, so I rested most of the day, before starting the 100 miles race in Flushing Meadows at 19:00. Weather conditions were warm and humid with the temperature at 85°F, but I started at around 6 minutes per mile pace. I went through the marathon in 2-40-50, but found this hard because of the heat. The 44-lap course, each measuring 2.273 miles, around Meadow Lake was flat apart from two hump-backed bridges. My feet became very painful, but they lost feeling at about 50 miles, which was a blessing. I had passed this point in 5-23-4. I stopped to put some tape over a blister that had formed on my right foot, but this painful foot made me limp noticeably from then on. The temperature fell slightly and averaged 78°F throughout the run. I passed 100Km in 6-49-38 and 150Km in 10-47-16. I was very glad to finish and to get the **World 100 Miles Road Record** too. If the temperature had been 20°F less I estimate that I could have run about 40 minutes faster. Before the start Dr Michael Sacks asked me if I would participate in a study that he had concocted, concerning mental ability during this 100 miles event. This would involve him or one of his three colleagues cycling along with me for a short period every twenty miles and asking questions. I agreed to participate and at 20 miles I was bombarded with questions requiring: recall, repetition and changing sequences of words. My mental ability was still fairly OK at 40 and 60 miles, but by 80 miles I was concentrating hard on trying to maintain a good pace and had little mental capacity for responding sensibly to questioning. I do not know what the analysis of the data they accumulated indicated, but in my experience I found that mental ability decreases proportionally with the pace and distance run.

Results: 1) Don Ritchie 11-51-11, 2) Lion Caldwell 13-33-45, 3) Park Barner 14-14-09, 4) Stuart Mittleman 14-34-40. 5) Dave Obelkevich 15-15-56, 6) Jack Bristol 16-24-03

I wrote the following report for the RRC Newsletter, No. 99:

I arrived in New York at around 15:00 hours on Wednesday the 13th of June, after a seven-hour flight from Prestwick. I had been invited to compete in the annual 100-miles road race, organised by the New York RRC.

After customs formalities, I was met by a representative of the RRC and driven to the city in a 'yellow cab'. It was quite a thrill to see the New York skyline for the first time and the cab driver gave a commentary as he drove along.

At the New York RRC headquarters on the fifth floor of the West Side Y.M.C.A., I met Fred Lebow and his team, plus Frank Bozanich, with whom I was to share a hotel room. After some more formalities we went for a run around Central Park. The thousands of runners there — all shapes and sizes — astounded me. It was great to see so many happy, healthy people.

Thursday and most of Friday was occupied with interviews, sight-seeing and eating. At about 13:00 hours on Friday I lay down on the bed and tried to gather myself for the coming test of fortitude. A few hours later I was being driven through choking rush-hour traffic to the race venue in Flushing Meadow Park. The race was scheduled to start at 19:00 hours and the route was 44 laps around a lake in the park. The road was flat, with the only 'climb' being over two hump-backed bridges each lap of 2.273 miles.

The weather was hot, so I made sure that I was well hydrated before the start, by which time the temperature was 85°F. I set off at six —minute mile pace and was soon sweating profusely. I drank twice per lap in the hope of preventing dehydration.

Frank Bozanich came with me, but dropped behind after about three laps. I kept the pace at 6 minutes per mile for about 26 miles and then began slowing. My marathon time was 2-40-46. My feet became painful from the hot road after only 20 miles and I began to have doubts about finishing. However, I pressed on and, although my feet became progressively more painful, I reached a point where I lost all feeling in them. This happened around 50 miles and was a great relief. I felt much better then and my legs felt fine.

Although it was now dark the temperature never dropped below 70°F. An unexpected problem was hordes of flies, which appeared in black clouds as the sun went down. I was getting protein instead of carbohydrates.

There were people in the Park all night doing various things, having parties, entertaining each other, etc.

As dawn broke, I had about 20 miles remaining and the sun gave me a fillip. Eventually, after 11 hours 51 minutes 11 seconds, the exercise could cease. It was a great relief and satisfaction to have finished. Frank Bozanich had stopped at about 50 miles, although he rejoined the race later and ran some laps with me before 'calling it a day', or should I say night.

I soaked my feet for half an hour in a bucket of cold water, to extract some of the heat from them. They were not as bad as I had expected: the worst blister being a blood blister, under the hard skin on the ball of my left foot.

Ted Corbitt presented me with the 'Ted Corbitt Cup', about an hour after finishing. It was a pleasure for me to meet Ted.

I was taken back to the hotel, where I lay on the bed and relaxed for five hours or so. I felt sorry for the runners still out on the course as the temperature rose to 87°F during the day and the last to finish took some nineteen hours.

There were twenty-seven starters, but only eleven finished. I think that if it had been a lot cooler, say 50°F, I could have run about 40 minutes faster. The New York RRC were very pleased with the result and it was a pleasure to experience the ensuing 'star' treatment over the next three days. Lion Caldwell was second in 13-33-45, followed by Park Barner in 14-14-09.

The following afternoon, one of Sri Chinmoy's disciples, Chanakya, took Frank Bozanich and me to meet Sri Chinmoy and his disciples. He had composed a song about me, which the female choir sang, which was rather touching. Sri Chinmoy then presented me with a huge trophy, which was eventually delivered to the UK and to me by two of his disciples.

On Monday the 18th of June I did some walking in New York before the overnight flight back to Prestwick. I was very uncomfortable during this VC10 flight because my legs hurt so much and there were no spare seats to lie across.

Bozanich, Ritchie and Sri Chinmoy discuss training.

I tried some running on reaching home but I had to abandon this, as there appeared to be a deep blood blister or bruising under the hard skin on the ball of my left foot. Following another attempt at running I decided to rest to allow my foot to recover. By the following week I was able to resume training, but by Friday I lacked the motivation and stopped for some days. I seemed to have sickened myself of running, but then I got going again and did some days of good training before faltering again.

On the 27th of June I received a surprise letter from 'Time & Life' informing me that I had appeared in the July 2nd issue of 'Sports Illustrated Faces in the Crowd' and included a copy of the article on my participation in the 100 miles race in Flushing Meadows. The letter continued: 'Each person featured in this section of the magazine receives an Award of Merit Trophy'. A fine inscribed silver cup duly arrived.

Another spin off from the 100-mile race was a letter from Dean Reinke of Brooks Shoe Manufacturing Co., Inc, asking if I was interested in receiving Brooks equipment for racing and training needs. I would also be a prospect 'to receive expenses for racing needs'. Because I was receiving shoes and kit from 'Karhu' and as I was very pleased with their shoes I decided to decline his tempting offer.

The week after my 35th birthday I did a lot of running, usually in two sessions a day, and finished with a total of 190 miles, which was probably asking for trouble, but I continued this high mileage into the following week. By Thursday, I had a painful right Achilles tendon and did not run, but next day it felt much better, so in the afternoon I ran my 32 miles course at a strong pace in 3-03-28, which must have been my fastest ever. The following day, Saturday the 21st of July, in the Elgin Highland games 10 miles road race I finished 2nd to Alastair Wood in 55-26, which was embarrassing for the organizers, who had expected me to win. I did not treat the event with sufficient respect by continuing my hard training the previous afternoon and this prevented me from racing at my best. On Sunday morning I ran my twenty-three miles Kellas-Dallas route in 2-34-00 for a weekly total of 157 miles. **I was conscious that I was in danger of becoming obsessed with mileage. The following week I ran only on three days because I was lacking motivation again.**

SWISS MOUNTAIN CHALLENGE

I had received an invitation from J.C. Pont, to run in the Sierre to Zinal mountain race in Switzerland, which I had accepted. I contacted some of my running pals to find if they would be interested in participating in this race and combine it with a holiday in France/Switzerland. Everyone agreed so on Tuesday the 31st of July, with Graham Laing as my passenger, I drove to Birmingham via Kirkcudbright over 2 days. In Birmingham Mal Pickering joined us and I drove on to John Lamont's home in Epsom. John Lamont had arranged for Graham to meet someone from Shaftsbury Harriers, with a view to Graham joining this club as a second claim member and he would not be going further with us. Ron Maughan joined us at John's and we were soon on our way to Dover, with John driving his well-laden Vauxhall Viva. Rather than search for a campsite near Dover we slept in the car, fairly close to the seafront, after sampling some Fremlings 'Tusker Ales'. We caught the ferry to Calais next morning and in the evening we ran for about 9 miles in Amiens. I had trouble with my left knee, which became swollen and stiff. For the next 3 days we drove down through France in stages: Vittry-Le-Francois, St Laurent, camping and running until we reached Chamonix. There we stayed for a few days enjoying the good weather and magnificent scenery and some challenging runs, one up to a glacier.

On our way over to Switzerland Ron and I ran for 73 minutes up to 6500 feet from Col de Montets, enjoying the scenery, cool air and sunshine. John discovered that he had lost his passport somewhere in Switzerland, probably at our last campsite. A telephone call to the site office informed us that it had not been handed in, so we were advised to go to the British Embassy in Geneva to get temporary documentation for John. We drove there, located the Embassy and after hearing John's story an official did the needful. She also invited us to have our passports stamped with the Embassy logo, for its rarity value. Later that day we arrived in Sierre where I registered for the race and was given my agreed 'expenses' and the address of my host family, who would provide 4 days 'board and lodging'. John, Mal and Ron entered the event too. We then had a day to relax before the race on Sunday the 12th of August.

The 6th edition of the 31Km Sierre-Zinal Mountain Race started at 08:00 and required 2000 metres of ascent. I had to walk most of the early part, as did others because of the steepness of the ascent through the trees. Many passed me on this section, but later when I was able to run I pulled back a lot of places. When the path became narrow and stony I slowed a lot as I picked my way along. The views across to the mountains were spectacular when I got a chance to look. Also I became very tired and despite slowing I did not recover, which might have been due to the altitude of up to 2387 metres on that section. On the 745m descent to the finish in Zinal I lost many places finishing 129th in 3-20-47. John was the best of us three, finishing 107th in 3-16-43 followed by Mal, 118th in 3-18-42 and Ron, 300th in 3-48-58. There were 1051 participants listed in the race results booklet, which reflects the popularity of this race. There were 1117 'tourists', who set off at 04:30 to walk the course.

The following day we went to Zermatt and used the cable car to get well up the mountain. As we were wearing only running shoes and shorts one of the Germans, as we left the cable car, shouted 'the shwmming pool is that way'. We then jogged further up on trails. The scenery was breathtaking. We felt a little concerned about having a problem with the heat and the altitude, so we did not venture too far. By evening we ran about five miles of fartlek from our campsite in Aigle after a fairly liquid meal. Over the next 3 days we made our way to Brussels with overnight stops at: Hirschorn and near Heidelberg.

Ron Maughan had been at some meeting at Brussels University earlier in the year and was familiar with the campus. He suggested a track session, so we agreed and ran 8 X 400 metres with

400 metres recovery jog; at Brussels University track and I was quite surprised to average 68 seconds for these. Ron's next idea was that we should sleep in a park near the diplomatic quarter, rather than find a campsite, which he assured us would be perfectly fine and that this was convenient for sampling some of Brussels nightlife. He managed to navigate us to the bar, which he had found earlier in the year, which sold bottles of McEwans 'Scotch Ale'. This was new to us apart from Ron and was a bit like dark barley wine. Following this sample of the nightlife we all slept well under the trees in the park. Next morning, the 17th of August, we ran a 'diplomatic fartlek' session in the park and woods where we had spent the night.

John then drove us to the ferry port where we caught the ferry back to Dover and then continued back to John's home in North London. There we transferred kit from John's car to mine and I drove to Birmingham, where Ron, John and I said goodbye to Mal in a pub called the 'Harrier', which had many old photos of Birchfield Harriers. I continued driving to Crosby with Ron and John as my passengers. Following our morning run next day John and I continued our journey north, stopping overnight at Kirkcudbright and reaching Aberdeen on Monday the 20th of August. Later that day I was back in Elgin, not exactly refreshed from my 'adventure' summer holiday.

On Tuesday morning I went to consult Magic Malcolm Morgan about my left knee problem, which had been troublesome since early August. He found that there were three muscles in my thigh, which were strained and in spasm, like being cramped or contracted permanently. They were not functioning and as 2 of them were stabilizing muscles, the bone below the knee was not in-line with the thighbone and this was causing my knee pain. The treatment he gave me was: infra-red, ultrasonic and massage. Malcolm advised me to avoid running for about 6 days. When I resumed running on the 1st of September I felt very weak and my left knee did not feel right yet, but by two days later it appeared to be okay.

During the summer term, I saw an advert for a lecturing job in Control and Electronics at Moray College of Further Education in Elgin, which appealed to me, as I was keen to pass on my knowledge of these topics. I sent in my application in May and on returning from my 'summer holiday' I found, amongst the accumulated letters, one inviting me for interview in early July. Because I had not responded to this letter, I assumed that another candidate had filled the position, so I was surprised when Gordon Robbins, the Head of Engineering came to see me, as I had no telephone line then, and asked if I was still interested in the position. I assured him that I was interested; so a few weeks later I was interviewed for the position and was successful. On the 5th of September 1979 I received confirmation of my appointment, as 'lecturer B' in Instrumentation, Control and Electronics at scale point 10, with a salary of £5703 per annum, commencing on Monday the 15th of October.

A few weeks after resuming training, although my left leg felt fairly good, I had a 'touch for health' session at Cluny Hill College, from an 'alternative therapist' recommended by Ian Mackenzie. It was a remarkable experience and involved balancing muscles by rubbing some 'key areas'. The idea is to squeeze toxins from the lymphatic gland system and assist the removal of waste products from the muscles. The therapist, 'Ed', also found that I had a vitamin A deficiency and that my gall bladder was being overworked, so he suggested that I avoid fried and fatty foods. He also warned against using white sugar. His system for coming to these conclusions involved a series of tests to find out from the 'body intelligence' what the problems are. He asserted that 'one's body is integrated and the awareness noted and this awareness tells the therapist which key area to work on'. I was rather sceptical at first, but I was astounded by the results he achieved. With my confidence in my leg restored I was eager to regain my fitness quickly for the 'Brighton', but made the mistake of more than doubling my mileage in a week to 177 miles. In the following week something got pulled in my right quads and I had to consult Malcolm again. He gave me physiotherapy treatments on the following two days.

PROBLEM RACES

Two days after my last physiotherapy treatment I started on Sunday the 30th of September, in the 29th London to Brighton race, which was now over a 54 miles, 460 yards course. I felt fine, passing 10 miles in 58-18 along with Allan Kirik, from New York, Bob Heron and Tom O'Reilly. Tom, Bob and I passed 20 miles in 1-56-41 and I was leading at Horley, 24 miles, 891 yards in 2-22-07, nine seconds ahead of Bob. However, I began to get very stiff thighs, especially in both groin regions, so that I was barely able to move my legs forward. I began to slow drastically as my stride length became very short. Bob Heron caught and passed me, and then the American Allan Kirik, who I had met at Flushing Meadows, passed me. By Crawley, 31 miles and 416 yards I was third in 3-03-33, 26 seconds behind Alan and 1-17 behind Bob. I abandoned the race and dropped out at 33 miles. My previous injuries did not bother me and I was convinced that the problem was my very scanty preparation because of injury problems. Allan Kirik went on to win in 5-32-37, becoming the first and only American to win this famous race. Martin Daykin was second in 5-45-06 ahead of Bob Heron, 3rd in 5-47-05, with Dave Francis (Fife AC), 4th in 5-50-10. There were a record 168 entries, 141 of who started and 106 finishers.

In the week following my Brighton failure my legs were too painful to allow running for two days, but two sessions of physiotherapy from Malcolm restored them to almost normal and I finished with 83 miles for the week. In the following week I overdid my training again and ended with 201 miles and felt quite good on Saturday but rough on Sunday, the last day of my training week.

Following my 100 miles run in New York, Fred Lebow invited me to the New York Marathon, therefore on Thursday 18th of October, after my mega mileage week I caught a flight from Prestwick to New York. On Friday morning I ran about 7 miles in Central Park and felt rather unfit. I shared a room in the Sheraton City Square Hotel with Tom Anzack from La Crosse in Wisconsin. We ran for about eight and a half miles together in the morning the day before the marathon.

On the 21st of October, in the **New York City Marathon** I performed very poorly. I ran the first 2 miles as hard as I could and experienced heart fibrillations at about two and a half miles. I felt quite rough, but I tried to push on. As I tried harder the more fatigued I became. It was a very embarrassing and upsetting experience for me. I never expected to run so badly or to beaten by a woman. Anyway I completed the course. Apart from the race I enjoyed my few days in New York, where I was treated as a semi-elite runner and got invited to a few receptions along with Ron Hill. At the 'Brooks' reception, Dean Reinke arranged to send me some models of Brooks shoes for evaluation, with a view to supplying me with Brooks shoes and kit. Grete Waitz broke the Women's World Record in 2.27.33; I managed 2.36.43 in 154th place. Bill Rodgers won in 2.11.42, from Kirk Pfeffer (2.13.09) and Steve Kenyon (2.13.30).

On Tuesday the 23rd of October, after saying goodbye to New York RRC runner Michelle Adams, I caught the same overnight flight to London Heathrow as Ron Hill. There I got a flight to Glasgow, where I caught a train to Prestwick so that I could get my car and drive to Elgin.

On Friday evening, the 26th of October I travelled to London by train overnight and I was fortunate to be able to sleep in a first class carriage. I started in the 24-hour race at Crystal palace track the following day and I ran too quickly early in the event, passing 10 miles in 57-17, 20 miles in 1-56-30 and 40Km in 2-26-01. My marathon time was faster than the previous week's New York at around 2-35. By 30 miles, passed in 2-58-32, my left foot began to bother me, so I stopped to change shoes. This helped for a while, but it began to hurt again and I stopped 5 more times to put plaster over the sore areas. This did not cure the problem, so I decided to abandon the event and dropped out at 54 miles and 1197 yards. None of my previous injuries bothered me, so this was encouraging. Dave Jones from Blackburn Harriers won with 153 miles and 1143 yards, from Joe Record from Australia with 142 miles and 1674 yards and Graeme Peddie, Epsom and Ewell Harriers third with 140 miles and 1219 yards. My 10-mile splits were: 57-17, 59-13, 61-53, 70-25 and 77-12.

I did not run for the following three days and wrote in my diary: *I am mentally tired of running.* During the following week I had influenza and was off work for 4 days. It was a virulent infection.

By then I had started work at Moray College, where the environment was much more relaxed than Lossiemouth High School. I had to reorganize my training, running courses from Craggan and back before work and after, instead of running to and from work in Lossiemouth.

After recovering from flu I ran in two North District cross-country league races, finishing 11th and 10th. For most of November I had trouble motivating myself to train, so I suppose it could be classed as a month of 'active rest'. In early December my left calf muscle and my left quads were very tight and painful. I received physiotherapy treatment from Magic Malcolm every second day until the problems were cleared.

During my Christmas holiday from College I agreed to go on a hill-walking trip between Christmas and New Year with some running pals. On Thursday the 27th of December I drove Ron Maughan, Brian Gordon, Robin Thomas (Y.P) and John Lamont to Glen Feshie and then walked with a large pack for 5.5 miles to the Bothy in Glen Feshie, which was to be our base for a few days. The barrel of beer that Ron had asked me to get, we had to leave in the boot of my car, as we had not improvised a trolley and rolling it to the Bothy was not practical.

On the following day John, Brian and I walked for 9 hours in the hills, through difficult conditions because of the snow and climbed four 'Munros'. On returning to the Bothy, John and I had a meal of skirlie, beans and mash washed down with beer that Ron and YP had fetched from the car earlier.

John and I were persuaded to go to collect more beer and set off with a rucksack full of empty containers to walk the 5.5 miles back to the car. On arriving at the car we sampled some of the extremely cold beer, filled our containers and set off back to the Bothy. We arrived back at the Bothy having walked a total of 30 miles that day. Although it was rather late, Ron and YP were not in bed and eagerly consumed some of our load before crawling into their sleeping bags. John and I continued chatting in front of the fire and managed to incur the wrath of a woman 'Bothier' trying to sleep a few feet away, so we shut-up and went to our sleeping bags. I cut wood for the fire the following morning, before walking to the car with John to collect more beer, but found that the remaining beer had frozen, so we had to return 'empty handed'.

We vacated our temporary home on the 30th of December and walked with my heavy pack from the Bothy to the car. My car was a Ford Escort (GSO 460G) automatic at that time and because of the very cold conditions, and after lying for 4 cold nights, it would not start. We got a 'Primus' stove going under the engine sump to warm up the oil and engine and this strategy proved successful, as, after some time, the engine started.

I drove back to Elgin, where Ron and YP decided to stay at my home, 'Craggan' to see in the New Year. Later, in a bizarre accident, I cracked a rib and a consultation with Malcolm next day confirmed that one of the floating ribs on my left side was fractured, so he applied strapping to minimize movement.

On checking my total mileage for 1979 I found it to be 5721.5 miles. It had been a year of two halves: marvellously successful for six months; then rather frustrating, with injury, illness, and either too much or too little training leading to disappointing races. Perhaps I should be more cautious.

THE EIGHTIES

1980

I did not run for the first two weeks of 1980 to allow my rib to heal, but after that I resumed running, increasing my weekly mileage week by week and was back at 103 miles for the week at the end of January.

From mid February I had a recurring problem with my left calf muscle, which Malcolm Morgan unknotted by physiotherapy treatment every second day, until the problem was sorted. Malcolm said that the lump of tissue in my left calf must have been limiting my efficiency. This scar tissue was from an old injury, which had never been treated properly. Later that day I became ill with pains in my chest, so I consulted my Doctor about this, and he suggested that I had some virus, and warned me about the dangers of running with a virus infection, but could offer no appropriate medication. All in all, I was a little depressed. Once I had recovered I got going again, but by mid March I had a recurrence of the left calf muscle trouble, which needed more treatment from Malcolm.

My first race of 1980 was a week later on Sunday the 30th of March in the Lochaber Glen Nevis 10 miles road race, where I finished in 54-59 and I felt O.K. Monday was the beginning of my two-week Easter holiday from College, therefore as I had been invited to a 50Km race in Niort in France on the following Saturday, I accepted, as I would not require time off work. On Tuesday I drove to Crosby and stayed overnight with Ron Maughan. On Wednesday after my morning run with Ron, I drove to Epsom to stay with John Lamont.

On Friday the 4th of April, I left my car at John's and travelled to Dover, where I was to catch an overnight ferry to Calais, which I thought I did. I do not know how it happened, but I was on the wrong ferry and on Saturday morning found myself in Zeebrugge rather than in Calais. Another fine mess!

I caught a train to Brussels Central and from there, joined a train to Paris, took the Metro to another station and from there, a train to Niort, where I arrived several hours behind schedule. Michael Rouelle the race organiser was relieved to see me and I was given accommodation with Michael and his wife Michelle.

NIORT 50KM

On Sunday the 6th of April, in the Niort 50Km race I started well with 3 of us: Martin Daykin, Bernard Gaudin and myself leading at 5Km. However, I began to feel weak and had stomach ache from the strong French coffee, which I had taken liberally before the start. I had read somewhere that coffee promoted the release of free fatty acids into one's bloodstream and that this was a beneficial effect. I began dropping back and feeling sorry for myself. By 20 Km I was joint 3rd, but after the turn I began to run a little better and I managed to finish a safe 3rd. Martin Daykin won in 2-58-47 from Bernard Gaudin, 3-00-50 and I finished in 3-05-44 with Yves Seigneuric 4th in 3-14-20. Michael Rouelle treated us to a fine meal in the evening.

On Monday I ran easily for about 13 miles with Michael Rouelle. My legs were quite painful, but I was happy that my left leg was much better. Michael showed me around La Rochelle on Tuesday and I spent 2 more days being very well looked after by Michael and Michelle and visited the Gymnasium that they operated.

By Friday I was back at John's in Epsom and ran a hard four and a half miles with him on Epsom Downs. On Saturday I drove to Crosby, stayed at Ron's and continued to Elgin the following day.

TWO VERY GOOD ITALIAN RACES

My aim then was to get well prepared for the Turin to St Vincent 100Km on the 5th of May, which I had been invited to and had accepted. My build-up went well and I peaked at 179.5 miles in the week before the race.

On Thursday the 1st of May, after work, I caught a train to Dyce, got a taxi to the airport and caught the flight from Aberdeen to London. I could not proceed to Turin as planned because of a baggage handler's dispute, so British Airways arranged for me to stay overnight in a nearby hotel. On Friday I was able to complete my journey to Turin, where I was met by Julianne and taken to my accommodation in a sort of boarding house. Arrangements were made to have meals in a nearby restaurant, which I enjoyed with a 'Bier Grande'.

The **Torino to St Vincent 100Km** race was started at 07:00 on the 4th of May, in a square in Torino. I was delighted by the conditions – a light drizzle of rain. The start was quite brisk, with five local runners pushing ahead, but I gathered that they were not intending running the whole way. By 10Km I was 2nd behind someone who was not intending running more than 20Km. I felt fine, but I had occasional stomach pains and I thought that I might have to make a pit stop. However this passed and I began to feel comfortable again.

At about 60Km the course followed a valley and climbed gradually, following a river, and passed through several quaint old villages with cobbled streets. I later found out that this was the route followed by Hannibal and his elephants after crossing the Alps. After five hours I was very tired, but averaging around 17Km an hour according to my support crew car's speedometer, which I could glance at as they delivered my drinks every 20 minutes. The last 6Km after leaving the river was a series of uphill hairpin bends with a gradient of 8% climbing to about 2000 feet, which I found very hard – causing my heart to fibrillate occasionally. I was very pleased to finish and to win in a good time of 6-35-00 ahead of Loris Gennari, 6-50-35

I sent the following report on the race to the RRC newsletter:

The race started at 7am from Via Garibaldi, near the centre of Turin on 4th May 1980. There were about three hundred starters, including about fifteen women. There was a heavy 'Scotch mist' and it was raining lightly as we got underway, splashing along the paved roadway.

We ran a loop of about thee-quarters of a mile and returned to the starting line, where several runners joined the race. There were 4 moving quite quickly out in front, so I gradually pulled them in, taking 3 others with me.

On reaching these 4, one of them became rather agitated and upped his pace considerably, while the others managed to explain to me, that they were only running about 15Km and that 'Better runners' do not normally go with them. I kept a steady brisk pace and the pack dwindled, until only Loris Gennari was left. I was about 60 metres ahead of Loris by 10Km and committed to leading.

Time and the Kilometres passed slowly, but I was pleased with the cool damp conditions. As far as 60Km the course meandered along flat, quiet roads, but a gradual climb followed up a valley.

We passed through a number of interesting villages with cobbled streets and the scenery became more spectacular. The rain had stopped and the rugged mountains with snowy upper slopes could be seen more clearly on either side of the valley.

After about four and a half hours running I was beginning to get very tired and I felt I had run out of Glycogen. However, my pace did not slow too much and I tried to relax. I was worried by reports about the last 6Km, which I had been told, had an 8% gradient. Periodically I would look at my watch and try to estimate my finishing time, which I calculated as around six and a half hours. After about six hours, I rounded a sweeping bend and saw the road snake up the mountainside. It looked fearsome and so it proved to be. I felt as though I was walking up in places and it required much effort not to do so.

After about 4Km of climbing, the gradient eased off and on turning another corner I was in St Vincent. The road levelled out and there was a slight downhill through the village.

I wondered where the finish was and I got a nasty shock when I was directed to run up a steep zig-zag, making about 1800 feet of climbing in all, to a large Hotel, which was the finish. It was a great relief to win and I was able to enjoy a few beers, until the prize giving in the evening. My time of 6-35-00 was a new course record, but I was unable to find out exactly what the previous record was.

This was a well-organised race and pre-race publicity ensured good spectator support along the route, particularly in the villages. I was provided with a support crew of two in a car, who gave me drinks as required.

Result: 1) D Ritchie 6-35-00, 2) L Gennari 6-50-35, 3) J L Bode

On Wednesday the 14th of May a camera crew and an interviewer from Grampian Television followed me around my 15 miles morning run, which I completed in my fastest time of 1-25-00. Cheryl Paul interviewed me before and after this run. At night in windy conditions I ran my 32 miles course in 3hrs 21 minutes and I felt rather tired over the last four miles. I got rather inspired that week and ended up with a total of 204 miles and felt ready to defend my title in the 'Del Passatorie' the following Saturday. I did not plan to use the glycogen depletion/carbohydrate loading diet for this race.

On Friday the 23rd of May, I travelled to Aberdeen to catch a flight to London and from there to Milan. There I got a bus to the rail station, where I caught a train to Florence and on arrival walked to the same hotel as last year and was allowed entrance this year.

On Saturday, in the **Florence to Faenza 'Del Passatorie' 101.5 Km road race**, there was lightning and a thunderstorm before the start and there was heavy rain for the first 6 Km. I got a good start with Vito Mileto when the race got underway at 15:50, 10 minutes early.

On the climb out of Florence, Carlo Papa pushed the pace and I let him go and he was soon out of sight. By about 22 miles he was 5 minutes ahead of me but, on the climb through hairpin bends up to the 3000-foot pass, I caught and passed him and by the summit of the pass I was one minute ahead. On the descent I extended my lead, but my quads were very painful. With about 28 miles remaining, I thought that I would be unable to finish because my legs and neck ached so much. I kept taking the long chain glucose polymer of 10% solution every 20 minutes and this seemed to help. Gradually the Kilometers passed and I reached Faenza. It was a wonderful relief to finish and to savour my victory – over myself as well as the other runners. My time was 2 minutes slower than the previous year and was not as good because I lost about 15 minutes at the start last year. Results: 1) D Ritchie 6-54-14, 2) Carlo Papa 7-15-31, 3) Loris Gennari 7-25-06, 4) Elvino Gennari 7-30-35.

I wrote the following more detailed account of the race for the RRC newsletter.

Three weeks after the Torino-St Vincent 100Km race I was back in Italy for the annual Del Passatorie 101.5Km race from Florence to Faenza on 24th May 1980.

The weather was quite different from last year's scorching 32°C, being humid and overcast. About half an hour before the 4pm start, a thunderstorm began, but we seemed to be on the edge of it, as the rain was not too heavy.

I made sure of getting a proper start this year by sticking close to Vito Mileto, a three times winner of the event. We jogged around the side streets so that we ended up in front of the 3200 plus competitors, jamming a street and square.

As start time approached tension mounted, the blowing of horns became more frequent and the general hubbub increased by the minute, until the impatient mob of runners could be contained no longer and we were off.

I checked my watch and found we were ten minutes early, but there was no way anybody was going to stop this running torrent. I ran a hard 200 metres and was the joint leader with Mileto. This lasted briefly, as while we were running around the perimeter of a square, outside the barriers, many cut diagonally across so we found ourselves back in the forties. We worked our way through these runners and were then surprised to see more in front, who had appeared from somewhere.

By about 3Km there were about five of us together: Carlo Papa, Mileto, the Gennari brothers and myself. The rain was now extremely heavy, causing streams to form in the gutters.

On the climb out of the valley in which Florence lies, Papa was running strongly and I let him go, estimating his pace to be excessive. By the top of the climb I had been rejoined by Mileto and Loris Gennari, both of whom appeared to be going easily.

As the road levelled out I increased my pace slightly and got away from these two, but Papa was still pulling away from me. By 10Km the rain had ceased, the road becoming dry.

At 20 miles, where we passed through a village and began climbing again, I was informed that Papa was five minutes ahead. I did not feel comfortable and I was sure that was not running as well as I could.

As I drew closer to the start of the steep zigzag climb to the top of the 3000ft pass, someone told me that I was catching the leader. The climb seemed steeper than last year and my cycling second, the same man as I had the previous year, got a tow from a motor cyclist. It became cooler and fresher as altitude was gained.

About halfway up I could see the leader on the terrace above. He was moving very slowly; mind you I wasn't exactly bounding up myself. I caught him soon after and by the top of the pass at 50Km I had a lead of one and a half minutes.

Going down the other side I relaxed, but both thighs were sore and the distance markers every 2Km seemed to take longer and longer to come up. Gradually my thighs eased and I settled into a steady survival pace.

The course passed through several villages with narrow streets and it appeared that most of the population had turned out, lining the streets to yell encouragement, some offering vino to the competitors. The atmosphere was very festive in these villages and this helped me. A public address system, mounted on a car, kept the spectators informed on the race situation and they could also hear a race commentary on the radio. A T.V. camera car filmed the race.

It became dark at about 9pm and by this time I had a deep ache in my legs and I could feel a blister bursting on the sole of my foot, near the heel. I longed for the finish and vowed never to run another 100Km race. With about seven miles remaining I could see the lights of Faenza; the end was in sight. Finally, I reached the town and ran through the streets lined with cheering people, to the haven of the finish.

The race finishes in the central square, which is floodlit. One has to run up a ramp onto a bandstand to be presented to the crowd.

It was a very satisfying victory, as I had to work very hard for it. My time was one minute 41 seconds slower than last year, so I did not have such a good run this year. Mileto had to withdraw from the race as he had breathing troubles, following a recent bronchitis attack.

At about 11pm that evening, I watched the one-hour programme of the race on TV; quite a difference from U.K. coverage!

Results: 1) D Ritchie 6-54-14, 2) Carlo Papa 7-15-31, 3) Loris Gennari 7-25-16, 4) Elvino Gennari 7-30-35.

My legs were too painful to allow running for 5 days after the 'Passatorie' and I was concerned, because I had agreed to run in a 50 miles race in Oulu in Finland two weeks after the 'Passatorie'. Matti Hannus, an Editor for Tapio Pekola's 'Joukija' magazine, had arranged this for me and he was also one of the organisers.

On Sunday the 1st of June I ran my 34 miles course in 3hr 17 minutes in beautiful weather, which allowed me to run without a vest. This run was my glycogen depletion run in preparation for next Saturday's race in Finland.

On Thursday, 5th of June, I travelled to Helsinki via Aberdeen, London and Luton. Charlie Greenlees met me at Helsinki Airport and took me to his home in Louma. On Friday morning Charlie and I ran 5 miles from Louma in very warm conditions of 27°C and then went to Helsinki and caught the train North to Oulu.

TOO SOON FOR A GOOD RUN IN FINLAND

At 6pm on Saturday, 7th of June, I started in the **Kesayon Unelma 50 miles road race from Oulu**. The weather was warm at 25°C, I found the mosquitoes quite a nuisance and my right ankle began to swell after their voracious attack. I decided to set the pace, but found it difficult and I passed 10 miles in 57 minutes and the marathon in 2-34-30. Three Finns kept pace with me and I began to feel rather fatigued and, shortly after we passed 50Km in 3-05-30, both my quads became very stiff and painful near the tops and I had a pain in the ball of my right foot. I could not respond when two of the Finns stepped up the pace and I lost heart as my quads became worse and I abandoned the race at 33 miles.

I was disappointed, but I am sure that I did the right thing in stopping. It appears that I had not recovered from the 'Del Passatorie' two weeks before. The organizers were sympathetic and invited me back for next year's race. I accepted the 2000 Finnish marks towards my travelling expenses, but felt that I had not given the LSD-Oulu club value for money.

Results: 1) Risto Laitinen 5-03-16, 2) Arto Tanninen 5-14-38, 3) Pentti Kaijala 5-22-17, 4) Pekka Termonen 5-56-32, 6) Alan Smith (UK) 5-56-49 {26 finishers}

I sent the following report to the RRC newsletter:

I arrived in Helsinki on 5th June 1980 and went out to Louma to visit Charlie and Marja Greenlees and their family, spending the night there. We had a good gossip and did a couple of therapeutic runs, enjoying the scenery and the 28°C (72°F) summer weather.

On Friday evening Charlie and I took an overnight sleeper train to Oulu, the venue of the race, which is on the Gulf of Bothnia, a hundred miles south of the Artic circle. We arrived in Oulu early next morning and were met by Matti Hannus.

After breakfast we went to pick up Alan Smith of Leamington C & A C, from the campsite. He had arrived the previous day, via a long devious route. The rest of the day was spent relaxing in Matti's home, fighting off the persistent mosquitoes and scratching some of the many previous bites. They seem to sense strangers and are keen to sample a new brew.

The firing of a rifle set the sixty or so runners off at exactly 6pm, in brilliant sunshine, with the temperature at 25°C. Apart from one desperado, who blasted off, nobody wanted to set a decent pace, so I decided to take on this task.

I led through 10 miles in 57 minutes, through the marathon in 2-34-30 and 50Km in 3-5-25. Although it was not a very fast pace, I was not feeling good and I still had three Finns on my tail. By 50Km both thighs were giving problems and becoming increasingly difficult to move. I was also having bad pain from my right foot. One of the Finns sensed that I was in trouble and moved past, taking another with him. I continued in the hope of improvement, but none came and the third member of the Finnish trio passed me as I slowed.

About this time I got some information on how Alan Smith was doing; I was told that 'Alan Smith is completely spent and is swearing all the time'. I hoped he would be all right and I wondered why we embark on such difficult 'adventures'.

After a few more miles my foot was worse and my thighs were also deteriorating so I decided to stop, as I was no longer running properly.

Being so far north it did not become dark, but the sun dipped under the horizon and the temperature dropped to 15°C.

The leader, I learned was Laitinen and he kept up a good pace and was on schedule for sub-five-hours. He slowed, however, over the last seven miles to end up three minutes over, but some twenty minutes inside the previous course record. Second was Arto Tanninen, a 2-21 marathoner, the nineteen-year-old son of Ensio Tanninen, who won the Vets class with 5-35-45. Alan Smith recovered remarkably well to dip under six hours in seventh place.

The course was mainly flat, but there were some longish straight sections, with a slight gradient. Near the start and finish cycle paths were used. Generally, the surface was good, except a few stretches of dirt road. Most of the route is flanked by trees, and is attractive if you can spare the time to appreciate the surroundings. The race was well organised and officiated, with no traffic problems.

Next morning, free food was provided in a restaurant beside a lake, prior to the awards ceremony at 10am.
Results: 1) R Laitinen 5-03-16, 2) A Tanninen 5-14-38, 3) P Kaijala 5-22-17, 4) E Tanninen (V1) 5-35-45, 5) M Moilanen 5-44-16, 6) P Termonen 5-56-32, 7) Alan Smith 5-56-49, 1st Woman: H Vesteri 7-00-35

On my return home I had too much College work to catch up on so I could not fit in running and then a few days later I became ill, which left me very tired for several days. On resuming training, I pulled a muscle in my left calf during a 15-mile run, which was rather a nuisance.

Malcolm Morgan again provided physiotherapy treatment over the next 2 days.

Ron Hindley had planned for many months to organise the first 100Km road race in Britain, from his hometown of Grantham to Lincoln Cathedral and back. He wanted to choose a route that passed through villages and that each village should be involved in the race, by providing a drinks station, helpers and marshals. He achieved this very well and also got the RRC involved. I was invited to the inaugural race scheduled for Sunday the 22nd of June. I had agreed to participate, but because of my calf injury I informed Ron that I could not run, but he wanted me to come to the race as a guest.

On Saturday I travelled by train to Grantham, where I stayed with Dr Davis and his wife Philomena and their family in the village of Barrowby. Next morning, I tried a run around Barrowby and found my left calf muscle was a little tight and stiff, but not too bad, so I was encouraged. I attended the 'Lincolnshire 100Km race', which started and finished at Harlaxton Manor, near Grantham. This race was regarded as the first British 100Km championship. The sponsors were 3M, UK, the manufacturer of all-weather 'Tartan' tracks. I then watched the race develop over the next several hours along with Cavin Woodward, also present as a guest along with his wife Carol.

Mike O'Brien won in 6-59-13, closely followed by Mike Newton in 7-00-39 and Dave Dowdle in 7-06-09. Ron Hindley had designed unique oval medals, the shape of the earth and because 100 Kilometers is a sub-multiple of the circumference of the earth through the poles. They are inscribed with: 'Veneri vires cedant' ('Let Strength give way to Grace') on the gold for the first lady, 'Vir inter Viros' ('Man among Men') gold for the first man and 'Virumque Cano' ('and I sing of a man'), for silver and bronze. The mint in Birmingham produced the medals, from specially crafted dies.

Ron Hindley founded the 100Km Association shortly after this to promote 100Km running throughout the United Kingdom, *'for the common man'*, to encourage first timers to try the 100Km run and to organise a regular 100Km race. Ron assumed the role of president of the Association in addition to his other roles and continued until 1987, by which time the 100Km Association was firmly established. He proposed that I should become President and at the next AGM of the 100Km association on the 6th of March 1987, I was elected to this role, which I was honoured to accept. I continued as President for twelve years before nominating the 100Km Association Chairman, Geoff Oliver be elected as president and this was accepted at the next AGM of the Association

AN AMERICAN ADVENTURE – BUT INJURIES PERSIST

At the end of summer term at College I caught a flight from Aberdeen to London and made my way to stay with John Lamont, who was now living in his famous Shaftsbury Harriers club-mate Dave Bedford's home in Finchley, while Dave and his wife ran their club in Luton. Next day I ran in a six miles road race, not very well, with John Lamont at Chalfont St Peters. That evening John drove us up to Dave Bedford's club in Luton and we went out for some drinks with Dave. Somehow John got 'lost' and I had to sleep on a couch at Dave's. Next day I caught a train back to London and made my way to John's to find that he had found his car but not the club and after some shut-eye had driven back to Finchley.

On the 3rd of July I got a standby flight on a 'Laker Airways' DC10 to New York. At immigration the officer asked me how long I wanted on my visa, so I guessed at 4 weeks and he stamped the appropriate date for departure in my passport. This later proved to be a poor guess. As I had made no accommodation arrangements I telephoned Allan Kirik, who came to meet me and then took me to Queens to stay with some of the Sri Chinmoy group.

I spent about 5 weeks in the USA, mainly in New York, but also via Greyhound buses travelled to Washington, Virginia, Michigan and as far as the exhilarating Niagara Falls. Often I stayed with running acquaintances but sometimes used my one-man tent. It was a great trip, but spoiled by my grumbling left Achilles, which did not heal.

Once back in Elgin my chronic injury appeared to be OK again, following a run, but I was very tired. I decided to rest for the following 2 days and sampled some of the home brew that I had bottled at the end of June, which was in excellent condition.

I resumed work and was glad to get back into my routine and familiar training routes. Early on Saturday morning the 23rd of August, I drove down to Rosyth to support John Lamont in the 'Two Bridges' race. He ran well, passing the marathon in 2-37-38 and finished 7th in 3-44.13. John and I stayed overnight in the accommodation provided in the Royal Navy base at Rosyth after attending the social at the civil service club.

On Sunday we ran 8 miles in Glasgow, while watching the World Veterans Marathon championships and we were pleased to see Don Macgregor win.

The following Saturday in the Inverness to Drumnadrochit road race, I ran with Ron Maughan at a comfortable pace and we finished 7th equal in 1-31-16. On Sunday I ran 22 miles with John Lamont, from Elgin around Monaughty Forest, in 2hr 19 minutes. John coped well with this course, but was becoming concerned at the three-stage climb to the turn at the top of the ridge. I felt good on the return road section and this run gave me 108 miles for the week. My training appeared to be progressing well in the next two weeks of 100 and 131 miles but mid-way through the week after that, my right heel became very painful. The pain was concentrated on the lump I have on my right heel around the region where my Achilles tendon attaches to the heel bone. My heel was red and hot to touch and I could feel it throbbing, so I was rather depressed.

I consulted 'Magic' Malcolm, who gave me some ultrasonic treatment on my heel, but he was not sure what the problem was. He repeated this treatment 2 days later and this seemed to help.

In the Aberdeen Milk Marathon on the 28th of September, incorporating the Home Countries International, from Balgownie pavilion, I had a hard time. I set off cautiously but my heel hurt and I reached 10 miles in 59-27. Soon after this I became very tired and began running very slowly, passing 20 miles in 2-01-56. The last 6.25 miles were very difficult and I felt dreadful. I finished 20th in 2-42-53, I could not remember when I last felt so bad after a marathon. I obviously lacked a lot of consistent training. There were 87 finishers and the Aberdeen AAC team of Graham Milne, Peter Wilson and I were 2nd team behind Fife AC. Local runner Graham Laing, representing Scotland, won in 2-19-33 from Don Fairclough (Eng) 2-21-46 and Mike Critchley (Eng) 2-23-18.

My heel problem persisted for week after week, despite periodic physiotherapy treatments from Malcolm. Nevertheless, I continued to turn out for Forres Harriers in North District cross-country league races and cross-country relay races. On the 27th of October my waking pulse was elevated to 62, so after work I went to see my G.P, who diagnosed flu and signed me off work for 2 days.

On the 28th of November in the North District cross-country league race at Lossiemouth I ran surprisingly well, despite my lack of training, and finished 4th, behind Drew Smith, Innis Mitchell and Ian Mackenzie.

Between Christmas and New-Year Ron Maughan and I went to Corndavon Bothy for a few days.

I finished 1980 with a total of 3782.75 miles, quite a lot less than previous years, mainly because of my restricted training in October through to December, because of the heel problem.

REVIEW

With hindsight, I might have managed better the stresses and strains of ultra-distance running, particularly at the world class level to which I aspired, and might have avoided several months of physical pain. After the triumphs and disappointments of 1977 -1979, it seemed that, although I had the necessary underlying talent and stamina, at least a couple of months of high mileage seemed necessary to prepare me for successful racing. I had a tendency to run too many miles and to ignore warning signs like niggling injury or extreme tiredness leading to infections. In addition, because I often tried to pack several successive ultra races into my holidays, I did not give myself time to recover, which led to further problems. Yet to cope a great deal of training was essential; and races almost inevitably involved considerable suffering and strength of mind in very difficult circumstances. My two Italian races in May 1980 had been real highlights but the rest of the year had been frustrating. Could I manage my body better in future? Or was it a matter of trial, error and waiting for eventual good fortune?

1981

My first race of 1981 was the North District cross-country league race in Inverness on 10th January, where I was quite pleased to finish 5th behind Brian Turnbull, Ronnie Campbell, Ian Mackenzie and Roger Boswell.

Four weeks later, following a month of trouble free training, I ran in the North District cross-country championships at Forres. I had a good run and finished 3rd, which was pleasing. Dave Lang won from Ian Mackenzie and I finished six seconds behind Ian.

Then I developed a stomach ulcer type complaint as I kept rifting a bloody taste and my stool was black, indicating internal bleeding somewhere. After work I consulted my doctor about this and she prescribed some appropriate tablets, which cleared the problem in 2 days.

In the final North district cross-country league race in Thurso on the 7th of March, I finished 2nd after miscounting the laps while leading and going the wrong way. This mistake ruined my concentration and I lost to Ian Mackenzie again.

Throughout March I got good training in, averaging over a hundred miles per week, with Sunday runs of 26 miles and one of 34 miles.

A DECENT PERFORMANCE IN FRANCE

On the evening of Wednesday, the 1st of April I drove John Spencer to Mike McCulloch's home in Grantown-on-Spey, where we were to stay overnight in preparation for travelling to Niort for the 50Km race. On Thursday morning we set off with Mike driving his Austin Maxi all through the day and then overnight to Southampton, where we caught the ferry to Cherbourg on Friday morning. From there he drove down to Niort where we arrived very late that night and reported to Michael Rouelle, who sorted out our accommodation. Next morning, we ran an easy six miles and on Saturday we ran in the seventh edition of the **50Km Baratange race** organised by Le Sculptural-club of Niort, which was a different course from last year and now 50.5 Km, but still out and back. On the way out, Martin Daykin, myself, and another runner with long hair, established a good lead. Martin and I were surprised that our fellow runner was English and called Patrick Macke. Patrick was unknown to us, so when he made a break at about 8 miles, we let him go, assuming that he would slow later. This did not happen however so at the turn I ran as hard as I could in an attempt to catch him, but was unable to. Yet I was pleased to finish 2nd in a fast time. I had no problems in the race apart from not being able to run quickly enough. John finished 20th in 3-43-15 and Mike was 22nd in 3-43-30, so we were second team with a summative time of 10-22-14, less than ten minutes behind the winning team. Results:

1) Patrick Macke 2-53-05 (2-49-37 at 50Km, 2-23-00 marathon),
2) Don Ritchie 2-55-29 (2-52-25 at 50Km, 2-24-30 marathon),
3) Martin Daykin 2-57-55 (2-54-27 at 50Km),
4) Bernard Gaudin 3-00-32 (2-57-40 50Km)

These times would indicate that the course measurement was suspect.

The post-race dinner was held in a rustic farmhouse restaurant out in the country, where one had to avoid the loosely-chained guard dog on visits to the outside toilet. The meal was excellent as was the wine and entertainment.

John Spencer had to get back to the UK before Mike and I, so he made his own way back, while Mike and I took time to see more of France. On Monday the 6th of April we set off and in Coulon, a region near Niort in pleasant countryside, we ran for an hour in warm weather. That night we discovered that the tent I had borrowed turned out to be a toilet tent so we had to sleep the night in a lightning storm in Mike's car and this would be the case for the remainder of our journey back through France. Next evening, we camped near a small town called Pontlevoy, where there was a huge Abbey, which was very impressive. The following evening, we ran in the forest near Fontainebleau, which was very pleasant and the huge boulders in the forest awed us. At night on the 9th of April we ran a hard six miles in Calais while waiting to board the ferry for Dover. From Dover Mike drove to the Epsom Downs where we ran and then continued to John Lamont's at Finchley, where we ran again, before an evening meal, home brew sampling and an overnight stay. Mike drove home to Grantown-on-Spey on Saturday with a stop at Keswick.

On Sunday, 12th of April, we ran in the Glen Nevis 10 miles road race, where I was quite pleased to finish 3rd. I made the mistake of having a cooked breakfast at Mike's parents' home, so during the race I experienced very bad intestinal problems. As I was fairly close to the finish, rather than stop, I pressed on, had an accident, and ran straight into the changing room. Along with Mike and Ian Johnstone, Forres Harriers won the team prize. Dave Cooney was hit by a motorbike while lying seventh at 8 miles and was taken to hospital but later discharged. Dave Lang won in 50-41, which was a new course record by 4 seconds. Eddie Stewart finished 2nd in 50-55, my time was 53-43 and Mike was 11th in 56-56.

Two weeks later on Tuesday 28th of April, having completed 2 weeks of my build-up for the 'Passatorie' I had to cut my evening run short because I had an annoying pain in the left groin, which was worse going downhill, but was present every time my left leg landed. On Wednesday I consulted Malcolm about this and he gave me appropriate physiotherapy and said not to try running until this problem was fixed. I received physiotherapy treatment from Malcolm every 2nd day apart from weekends. Twenty days after the injury occurring I was very pleased to be able to run my 15 miles course and felt only a little pain in my groin. I was able to run 81 miles that week, but this was only a week before the 'Passatorie', so I was not well prepared, but as I had made arrangements I decided to go and hope for the best.

OUT OF ENERGY IN ITALY

On Wednesday evening the 27th of May, I drove to Inverness Railway Station, parked my car there and caught the 19:30 train to London. Next morning, I made my way to Luton Airport to catch a flight to Milan and then to Florence by train. I arrived there at 14:30 and made my way to the Hotel Melegano, where I was to stay. On Friday I walked for about six hours sight-seeing in Florence in rather warm weather with the temperature reaching 80°F, which would not be good if it were the same next day during the race.

On Saturday the 30th of May, I started in the **Firenze to Faenza 'Del Passatorie' 101.5Km** road race. As appeared to be normal, the race started with a mass false start ahead of the scheduled start time of 16:00. On this occasion we got underway approximately 15 minutes early, but I had made sure that I was part of this mob in order to get a 'fair' start with the rest. After the leading group of about six of us had run about 1.8Km the police and an official car from the race organization blocked the road. Apparently this was to be the 'official' start this year. I had not seen Vito Mileto earlier, but now he was there, so I thought that was strange. I was confused, but I suspected that he might have been 'caught out' by the start and managed to get a lift in the official car to the front and stopped the race for his convenience. I do hope that this was not the case, but his 'turning up' seemed rather suspicious to me, although I may have completely misunderstood what was going on.

Anyway after this second start a group of about eight of us set a fair pace in the 80°F temperature. Mileto did quite a lot of corner cutting and pavement running, so most followed his example, but I tried to stick to the course and was continually having to try to make up lost ground. I ran a little harder and found myself in the lead so I decided to set a steady fairly hard pace. I found climbing the hill out of Florence difficult and I was caught by a group of five runners, who then passed me and started to pull away and I was soon in 'oxygen debt'. When the course levelled out after Fiesole I recovered and caught them again but I was not feeling strong. Downhill, I pulled ahead only to be caught by the pack on the next uphill. On the next long downhill I got away again and established a lead of one minute by 25Km, where I realized that I had been running at too hard a pace and that I had little energy left. I had a pain in my left quads and left calf muscle and my feet hurt already. I also felt quite sunburned and very hot. Deciding that I could not face the remaining 46.5 miles, including the climb up to the pass, I abandoned my race.

I observed the rest of the course by car and was able to appreciate the human nature of this race, and also see the scenery. Melito won in 6hr 54 minutes, which I think might be incorrect because I saw him finish at 22:56 and we started before 16:00. Loris Gennari was second. I was invited back for next year's race, so I would like to try again and possibly show Melito a clean pair of heels. At least my groin injury was not troubling me.

On returning to Elgin I got three weeks of inconsistent running with weeks of 71, 32 and 102 miles. In the weekend of the middle week I had gone hill walking/climbing in Glen Feshie with John Lamont. I also had to take two days off running to mark exam papers that week.

At the Forres Highland Games on the 4th of July, in the 11.25 miles road race, despite my apprehension, I went with the leaders; Graham Milne and Willie Day. Their pace was quite hard for me and I soon dropped back, but maintained third place until about eight miles when Ian Moncur came past. My erratic training for the past months told and I could not keep up and finished fourth in 1-02-49, some 5 minutes outside my 1977 course record. Forres Harriers won the team race, with Mike McCulloch 5th and Ian Johnstone 6th.

By Monday, 6th July, my 37th birthday, my right groin became rather painful and prevented any useful training for the next three weeks. Physiotherapy from Malcolm began to ease the problem but then my groin injury returned after only about 400 metres into a trial run and was so bad that I had to walk back. It was like some muscle suddenly going into spasm and not releasing its grip on something in my groin. A few weeks later my groin eased off so I gradually resumed running.

I decided to purchase the ground floor of 'Lossiebank' in Hill Street, which was a two bedroom flat overlooking the river Lossie and Morriston playing fields. It had a large garden, a lot of it on a steep slope and overgrown, and another building, probably an old stable, by the riverbank. There was also a Victoria plum tree in the garden, which yielded a bumper crop of fruit each September. I purchased this from Andrew Veitch for £21,500 and moved in on the 3rd of August 1981.

On the 19th of September, in the Thurso 4 X 2 miles road relay, I was pleased with my run recording the 2nd fastest time for the lap and also pleased that Forres Harriers won ahead of Inverness Harriers. The following Saturday in the Inverness Harriers 4 X 3.8 miles road relay, I ran the first leg, felt good and I was pleased to come in first. Our Forres team won, with Ian Mackenzie running the fastest lap time, while I was 2nd fastest and teammate Ian Moncur was 3rd fastest.

On Sunday the 27th of September, in the Aberdeen 'Milk Marathon', which incorporated a Home Countries International match, I was quite satisfied to finish 15th in 2-30-33. The weather was rather poor with a strong wind blowing, so I decided to go with the leading group for some protection. Between seven and eight miles, while running along the Prom with the wind behind us, I got dropped and was about 20 metres adrift coming onto King Street. I was exposed to the strong wind all along this street and lost about 400 metres by the end. I pressed on chasing Stuart Easton, but by about 12 miles I was caught by the 2nd group while going up Holburn Street. I was too tired to go with them and take advantage of the wind cover they could provide. I began to recover along the North Deeside road, passing halfway in 1-13-19. On the South Deeside road, I caught and passed a further three. I am sure that I could have run under 2-30 if I had been able to stay with the lead group longer and benefitted from the wind cover. I was running for my old club Aberdeen AAC and we won the club team prize with Fraser Clyne, Peter Wilson and me. My intermediate times were: 5 miles in 27-20, 10 miles in 54-40 and 15 miles in 1-24-42. Max Coleby (Eng) won in 2-21-29 from Martin Knapp (Eng) 2-21-30, and Don Macgregor (Sco) 2-21-52.

On Saturday the 3rd of October, in the Alves to Forres race I finished 4th. I did not feel too good because I had a couple of disturbed nights because of toothache, which I had tried to alleviate with Disprins and whisky. George Reynolds won in 31-02 from Ian Moncur, 31-11 and Peter Wilson 31-23, while my time was 31-44.

On the following Monday my right hamstring was tight and painful and I received two physiotherapy treatments from Malcolm, which helped a lot. In view of this I decided to go ahead with my planned 24 hours race at Copthall Stadium at the weekend. On Saturday the 6th of October, I started in the 24 hours race, running with Martin Daykin up to around 30 miles. I passed 50Km in 3-25-55, by then three minutes behind Martin. My right hamstring became very tight and I became very tired rather suddenly. I could not see the point of carrying on, feeling like that, so I stopped after 5 hours and I had covered 42.75 miles. My 10-mile splits were: 66-29, 64-56, 65-06 and 81-48. Mark Pickard won in a new UK national record with 263.466Km, ahead of Mike Newton with 255.760Km and Dave Goodwin with 249.06Km.

In the Black Isle marathon on 24th of October I finished 2nd in 2-33-38, which was pleasing as I had a head cold. Dave Geddes won in 2-29-58, with Innis Mitchell 3rd in 2-43-18.

My right hamstring problem recurred the following week, which restricted me to 38 miles.

Once this had eased, I returned to 100 miles a week and I was able to maintain this for several weeks before my motivation started to lessen. Starting a morning run of 5.5 miles with Dave Lang helped to keep me more committed, and it was good to have company, as most of my running apart from some weekends was done alone. Dave, who was now the manager of the Bradford and Bingley building society in Elgin, always had a very positive attitude and was an enthusiastic, talented runner. On Sunday mornings my longish run at that time was often along with Dave, George Wallace, Ian Moncur and sometimes John Spencer. George and John were both serving in the RAF, while Ian taught biology at Forres Academy.

Over the years, I had become friends with Philip Cruickshank and Raymond Cameron, who became involved in running and helping the Elgin Athletics Club by coaching, along with Ken Davis and Marion White. I helped to a certain extent, but I was not prepared to give a commitment to coach youngsters. Philip (Phil) lived with his parents not very far along Maisondieu Road, so he was a frequent visitor to my flat in Craggan, to chat and sample some 'home brew'. Phil agreed to buy Flat 1, Craggan from me for £11,000.00, took possession on the 30th of November and set about redecorating it to his taste.

On Saturday the 12th of December I helped Phil Cruickshank drive a hired 'Sherpa' minibus, with young athletes from Elgin AC, to compete in an inter-area cross-country match in Stirling. It was a harrowing drive down in poor weather conditions. The windscreen washer would not function, so I investigated and found that the pump motor was operating, but rotating in the wrong direction, so I reversed the wiring connections to rectify the problem. Conditions were improved on the return journey.

On Christmas day I drove down to Kinellar, outside Aberdeen, for Christmas dinner at Annie and Bob's along with their family and Mum and Dad. On Boxing Day, I ran my 18.5 miles Monaughty Forest course and found underfoot conditions difficult because there was a lot of ice. Later in the evening I felt severe pain in both groins and had difficulty walking. The following day my groins were very bad and I could barely walk. I had, however, arranged to go up to Alltna-giubhsaich at Loch Muick with Ronnie Maughan and Kate, John Lamont and Leigh. I drove to Aberdeen to meet Ron and Kate and then drove up to Glen Muick as far as the bridge after the cattle grid. From there we had to walk one and a half miles through deep snow to the Bothy. I was in considerable pain at the start and I told Ron and Kate to go ahead to get the fire going. The pain eased a little as I went on, but it took me two and a half hours, a nightmare journey, to cover the distance in the dark and deep snow. Later in the evening John Lamont and Leigh arrived.

Two days later we walked 1.5 miles back to the cars, which we had to dig out of the snow. My groins felt much better. My car would not start, so we had to push it about a mile through snow until we reached a suitable downhill to push-start the car.

On the last day of 1981 I ran my 12.5 miles course and was very pleased that both groins were trouble-free. I finished this frustrating year of injuries, bouts of illness and fluctuating levels of motivation, with a total of 3935.5 miles.

1982

Following three weeks of good training, my first race of 1982 was the North District cross-country championships held in Elgin from Morriston playing fields on the 23rd of January. I had a good run and even took the lead at the end of the first lap, which might have been foolish, but it kept the pace going. Ian Moncur, Dave Lang and I broke away, but I lost contact with them on the hill on the 2nd lap. From then on I was about 8 yards behind, which they extended on the finishing stretch. I was very pleased with my run. Ian Moncur won in 31-04, one second ahead of Dave Lang, who was 15 seconds ahead of me. North District cross-country league races at Inverness and Alness in February yielded 3rd and 4th placings behind Ian Moncur and George Reynolds and in the second behind George Reynolds, Ian Mackenzie and Roger Boswell. In the final North District cross-country league race at Thurso on the 3rd of March, I felt good and pushed the pace in places and eventually finished first in 33-05. I was delighted with this run and it was very satisfying finally to win a North District league race. Gorge Reynolds was second in 33-13 and Ian Moncur was third in 33-39.

In the following week, Ian Moncur and I began training together, on Wednesdays in the early evening after finishing our work. We would run fifteen or eighteen miles at a good pace and intended continuing this until July.

On a visit to Charlie and Marja Greenlees's home in Glen Elg on Saturday the 13th of March, I ran 15.5 miles up the valley then cross-country/hill over a saddle in the hills and down the valley on the other side. During the rough section, while running through a stream, I badly twisted my right foot, which caused rather a lot of pain. I was depressed and distressed by this, but I was able to continue. On Sunday my right foot was extremely painful and I was unable to run. My throat was also very painful; I was coughing up yellow mucus and also my gum hurt following a tooth extraction earlier in the week. On Monday, 15th March I received physiotherapy treatment on my right foot from Malcolm and after the microwave treatment it felt a little better. I also visited my Doctor to get antibiotics for my throat and the tooth socket and 'Brufin' anti- inflammatory tablets to see if they would help my foot. Luckily, by the end of the following week my right foot injury appeared to have cleared up, as had my throat/lungs infection.

On Saturday the 3rd of April the JOGLE, ten-man relay, sponsored by 'Access' credit cards, started at 12:00 from John o' Groats. Colin Youngson and I were in Van Four and our first session was at 18:00 from Golspie to Bonar Bridge. We alternated five-minute efforts, as all pairs were to do. On taking a minor road over the hills to Bonar Bridge, we cut this to two-minute efforts because the road was rather hilly. We handed over to George Reynolds and John Robertson about half a mile up the Struie Hill.

Our second session was on Sunday from 04:00 to 06:00 and started about halfway between Spean Bridge and Fort William. It was a pleasant morning and I enjoyed my sessions, before we handed over just before the entrance to Glencoe.

At 14:00 our third session began near Glasgow Cross and involved taking the 'best line' as I followed 'local' man, Gordon Casley, on his bike. We encountered many difficult hills going through Cambuslang to Hamilton and Lesmahagow, where our stint finished.

Our fourth session was from midnight to 02:00, starting before Penrith and we managed to get within 200 metres of the top of Shap Fell. Shortly before this we had passed the halfway point of the relay, where Gordon Casley was playing celebratory bagpipes.

At 10:00 we were again on the road between Warrington and Weaverham and we finished our fifth session at Whitchurch. Colin found a real ale pub in Wem, so we sampled some Wem ales. We ran again at 18:30 from between Hereford and Monmouth to after Tiverton. A visit to a pub in Chepstow made a welcome break.

Our sixth effort was at 02:00 on Tuesday, taking over somewhere between Churchill and Highbridge at about Sidcot. This stretch became flat and was very good for fast running. We handed over beyond Bridgwater.

Van Three runners had been combined with Van One runners because Alastair Wood and Mike Murray appeared to be tiring. Van Two failed to arrive to take over from Van One, so Colin and I had to run again at about 06:50 around Stockleigh, just as the road became very hilly. After about 30 minutes Graham Milne and Alastair arrived and we then alternated 5-minute efforts for a further 1hour 30 minutes.

Later the runners from Vans One and Two joined us in Van Four and there were also six runners in Van Five. We each ran two-minute efforts for one hour per van. I did a further 48 minutes of hard running by this method. This gobbled up the remaining miles and we soon reached Land's End.

Our time for the relay was 77 hours 26 minutes and 18 seconds, taking almost one and three-quarters of an hour off the record of 79 hours 8 minutes and 8 seconds already held by Aberdeen AAC since 1973. Our team members were: Fraser Clyne and Peter Wilson, Graham Milne and Graham Laing, Alastair Wood and Mike Murray, Donald Ritchie and Colin Youngson, George Reynolds and John Robertson.

Colin Youngson wrote a descriptive piece about our stint over the undulations up towards Shap summit, and some excerpts should give a flavour of the experience.

"The night is mild, the atmosphere invigorating. Pity about the headwind, but they ought to be used to it after four hundred miles. Traffic is sparse, so it is easy to spot the travelling fairground moving steadily through the darkness towards them. Green, white and orange, radiating light in all directions, Van Three trundles by, they cheer, and then clamber into their own Van Four which follows close behind.

With ten minutes to go they synchronise watches over the radio, then drive ahead for the final warm-up 'sprints' before this, the fourth two-hour session. Sure enough, Alastair, the elder statesman, insists abruptly that they take over three minutes early (and who are they and Greenwich Mean Time to argue?) The Van Four Show is back on the road again. Two miles before Kendal in the cool midnight Colin soon eases into a stride pattern rather faster (he hopes) than the eleven miles per hour target. The first five minutes in the glare of the headlights seem less effort than usual. Right on schedule Van Four overtakes and he strives to accelerate to his partner and the haven of the dormobile.

Donald's familiar figure chugs along like a souped-up traction engine, puffing and blowing rhythmically but generating a lot of power. All too soon for Colin, it's his turn again and this time the strengthening breeze dictates treadmill formation. Traffic-permitting the van slips past the runner as soon as possible after changeover, and then tackles the awkward task of providing shelter without hindering progress. Hugh is on the stopwatch, lolling indolently against the kitchen sink beside the open rear door 'talking' driver Andrew into the appropriate spot, where he can see Colin in the mirror and he can avoid asphyxiation from the exhaust fumes. Too close to the back-step and you bruise your shinbone and lose pace; too far away and you lose the windshield and the incentive of 'chasing' this mechanical rival. There is only a ten-yard gap between these extremes and to keep the van in the correct position, a delicate touch on brake and accelerator is essential.

As Andrew gentles the pedals, Colin forces adjustments to the speed by means of hand-signals and urgent gasps; Hugh muses and occasionally checks the watch; while Donald sweats into Colin's towel on the bed, relaxing as completely as possible in a mere five minutes and sometimes glancing without interest at his friend's straining figure."

"*Last half hour, past Shap village and the* **real** *hills have appeared — long relentless drags winding over the fells. The temperature has dropped with the gain in altitude and a cutting Arctic wind whistles into us, piercing the runners' sweat-stained teeshirts. A grey cheerless place and an insane time to be running. There is an air of unreality about it all — the pool of light sliding along the tarmac behind the floodlit vehicle, the lone figure struggling to keep up, pursued by the shadows of night. Tiredness eats insidiously into your whole body, but can be ignored if the incentive is sufficient — and they really want to reach 'half-way' before handing over. Every five minutes is a flat-out effort — thirty seconds to loosen up and get into full stride behind the van, then fighting on uphill at maximum tempo, fists pumping rhythmically, oxygen sucked hard from the icy air until 'Three minutes gone' is called; then an attempt to maintain pace until 'thirty seconds', when the comfort of the windbreak is brusquely removed as the van accelerates, leaving the runner alone to stride out of the darkness to his team-mate before bouncing up the step and crashing heavily onto the bed. Purr of engine, reek of exhaust fumes, gasping for breath, throbbing in head, dryness of throat, sour smell of perspiration — these are the sensations of a leaden-legged Jogle runner nearing the end of the session.*"

Donald and Colin in 'The Bull and Dog'.

"At five minutes to 2 a.m., a weird sound, blown down the wind from a distant lay-by, tortures their ears. As Donald grinds up the inevitable slope, the unlikely figure of Gordon can be picked out through the windscreen, as he paces back and forth in the gloom, piping a piercing pibroch. Without thinking, Colin bullies Andrew into a quick acceleration and jumps out to join a puzzled Don, and the two of them run the last fifty yards to the so-called 'mid-point' of Jogle 1982. Then Colin completes the final half mile to Van Five. Exhilarated, they collapse into J4."

*"Ten hours later, near Whitchurch in 'The Bull and Dog', real ale pub of the trip, they interrupt the hilarity to rush out and cheer on George and Jogle 5 as they roll on inexorably to the new End-to-End record. While the J4 men sip their third pints of Wem Ale, the Jogle seems highly enjoyable and they wouldn't have missed the experience for anything. **Resilience – and a poor memory for suffering – is all you need!"***

The following day we travelled for most of the day to London, so that we could return the campervans and I went on to stay with John Lamont in Epsom.

On Friday the 9th of April I flew out to visit Jana Vackova, a Czech 100Km runner whom I had met at the 'Passatorie', who lived in Houlobkov, Czechoslovakia. On Sunday I ran one lap of the Houlobkov 100Km course in 2-19-43 in very cold conditions with snow and wind. On Monday, 13th of April, I ran in a 20Km road race on an out and back course from Horazdovice, which is south of Pilzen. The temperature was chilly at 5°C, but there was no wind. Three of us led past 10Km in 36-03, but I got away just after the turn and I was pleased to finish first in 68-43 ahead of K Duchek, 70-07 and J Jedicka 70-54.

By Thursday, 16th of April, I was back in Epsom with John Lamont and preparing to get back to Elgin. I picked up my parents on Saturday to attend the wedding of Alan Ferguson, my cousin and Kate at Bankfoot church. I was an usher at the church and also provided a taxi service for guests from there to the reception.

On Saturday afternoon the 22nd of May, I ran my 34 miles 'Oakwood' course in 3-11-26, which was pleasing, especially as I was not consciously trying to run at a hard pace. This was my fastest time for the course and boosted my expectations for a good performance in the 'Passatorie' in a week's time. I decided to have a rest day on Sunday, which gave a total of 143 miles for my six-day week.

TROUBLE AT DEL PASSATORIE

On Friday the 28th of May I travelled to Florence and stayed in the usual Hotel Melegano. Next afternoon in the **Florence to Faenza 'Del Passatorie'101.5 Km** race the start was much better organized this year, and our race numbers were stamped about five minutes before the start. However, the field got away before the official start time of 16:00 hours. I ran at an easy pace, because of the high temperature of 31°C. Thomas Rusek of Czechoslovakia and I ran together and we gradually pulled the leading group back. On the long climb out of Florence I began to feel in some trouble and I could not understand why I felt so bad, so I had to ease my pace and drop back. I regained contact with the group later and began to feel a little better. I started edging ahead and pulled 2 others away from the group and we caught the 2 early leaders. I kept my pace going and one Italian came with me as the others dropped.

A strong headwind developed and I had to face this coming down the valley as the Italian refused to take a turn in the lead, despite my running quite slowly into the wind. Passing through Borgo San Lorenz the Italian dropped back, so I was a clear but tired leader. I found the climb out of Borgo exhausting and realized that something was wrong. I began to feel very weak and slowed right down. The Italian who had stopped at Borgo had started again and, when he caught me, we battled on together as he was also very weak. He stopped again and I pressed on for a couple of miles more before grinding to a halt at the start of the climb over the mountains. I could not do any more, although I tried a few more jogs. I could have cried with frustration. There was a buzzing noise in my ears and I knew that I was quite badly dehydrated. I thought that I had been drinking enough, but perhaps my body was not accepting it or perhaps the concentration of my drinks was not appropriate for the higher temperature. I think that I may have been partially dehydrated before the start, because I had a mild fever in the week before this race; had painful glands on either side of my neck that week; and was not sleeping properly.

After I had stopped I began vomiting, and continued to do so periodically in the ambulance until I reached Faenza, where I was given an intravenous saline drip in the medical facility to restore my blood electrolyte balance and to re-hydrate me. I began to feel better after about half an hour. Vito Mileto came to see me as I was lying on the bed receiving my drip and shook his head and said something about running too fast in such weather, or that was what I thought he was communicating.

Apart from the problem with this run I enjoyed my stay, the hospitality in Faenza and meeting Jana again. **On reflection I should have arrived on Thursday instead of Friday, so that I would have had longer to assess conditions and perhaps modify my race strategy to better suit the hot weather. Also I should not have tackled such a race after the symptoms I had experienced in the previous week. However, I was committed and I had to go reclaim my airfare. I am convinced that I was fit enough, as indicated by my 34 miles run the previous Saturday. By next afternoon I felt quite depressed, but had to accept my failure and try to learn from it.**

I had hoped to win this race again to receive the unique ceramic plaque presented to winners in addition to the one hundred bottles of wine from the race sponsors. A Canadian exchange Primary schoolteacher broke one of my two plaques from previous wins. A group of us were sampling 'Linkwood' 12 years old malt whisky in my house and the whisky caused the Canadian to lurch against my plaque, which I had foolishly placed on the mantelpiece, and knocked it onto the stone hearth with inevitable consequences. There was nothing I could do except say that I would just have to win another next year – but unfortunately I never did. I picked up the broken parts and found a picture framer in Elgin, who was able to wire and cement it together very well, so you would have to look very closely to see the breakage lines.

On the 1st of June I travelled back from Italy and met John Lamont, Lee and John Kelly for some beers at Euston Station, before catching the overnight train to Inverness.

SO FAR, 24 HOURS IS TOO FAR

On Friday the 18th of June, at mid day I set off driving to Altrincham with Mick Francis and arrived there at 21:10. We pitched our two-man tent at the edge of Timperley track. After finding some food we returned to our tent and settled down for the night.

On Saturday I started in the Altrincham 24 Hours track race on Timperley track at 13:00. Mick Francis, who was to be my second, had helped me prepare drinks and food for the race. I started gingerly with laps of 1-47 to 1-50, but then settled down to laps of 1-45 to 1-44. After 3 hours things were fine and I ran 12 laps at exactly 1-41 and passed 50Km in 3-39-46. However around 6 hours I began to get a very bad ache in my quads and the small of my back. I persisted and passed 100Km in 7-17-22. Shortly after this I gave in to the pain and decided to abandon the race after 257 laps (102.8Km).

On analyzing my failure, I concluded that I lacked mileage in my legs and lacked sufficient long runs to accustom my legs to accepting the demands of 24 hours runs. Also if one can push hard enough in such races, one's body produces its own pain-killing chemicals, which allow one to continue running. Anyway I resolved that, if I tried 24 Hours again, I would try to run around 200 miles a week for about three months prior to the race and include one 34 miles run each week. At least I had not run out of energy. Results: 1) D Cooper 234.564Km, 2) K Thomson 214.914Km, 3) K Jordan 209.768Km,

In the week following this 24-hour attempt I ran only 13 miles, because I lacked the motivation to run.

On the following Saturday in the Forres Highland games 11.25 miles road race I felt tired from the start and could not handle the pace being set by Ian Moncur. He dropped me after about half a mile and just went further away until the finish. I ran as hard as I could, but there was nothing in my legs. Ian's winning time was 58-30 and I finished 2nd in 61-23 ahead of Mike McCulloch in 62-40.

TRICKED AT THE START AGAIN IN ITALY

I had been invited to the Pistoia to Abetone race in Italy so, 3 days before race day, I travelled to Florence, where the temperature was 31°C.

On Sunday the 11th of July I ran in the 7th edition of the **53Km race from Pistoia at 65 metres elevation to Abetone, a ski resort in the Apennines at 1388 metres**. The race was scheduled to start at 07:30, but the gun went at 07:28. I was somewhat concerned that I could not see the Gennari brothers or Possi. Since I had gone to find a last minute toilet about ten minutes before the start; they seemed to have 'disappeared'. The other invited runner, a German 2-19 marathon man, and I quickly got to the front and he commented that we had made a good start. I said nothing as I suspected that we had not made such a good start. My suspicions were justified as a kilometer later we began to catch up lots of runners and the line of runners stretched as far as one could see. At 5Km the climbing started and we could see runners on the double bends and terraces well above. I felt quite good and was running well although the weather was warm. At 10Km we were told that the leader ('Prima') was 10 minutes ahead! This brought forth some curses from my German running companion. I presumed that 'prima' had set off about 10 minutes early with the joggers.

At 15km the course levelled out and it was a pleasant change to run on the flat through Le Piastre at 761 metres and then slightly downhill. I caught the Gennari brothers at about 20Km and passed them easily as I was running at a much faster pace. By San Marchello at 30Km I was 4th and close to the 2nd and 3rd runners. Many people turned out to watch the race as we passed through the villages. The temperature was now around 32°C and I was drenched in sweat – even my shoes were soggy.

With about 18km remaining I was joint 2nd, with two others, but I was now feeling rather weak and I had to let the two go. I recognized the symptoms of dehydration, so I drank at every opportunity and my motorcycling second provided me with 200ml of my glucose polymer drink every 5Km. As the course started to climb again and became steeper I eventually had to walk. I walked and jogged over the next 10Km and fell back to 14th place. However, I was determined to finish the race and, after many drinks of water and glucose polymer, I began to revive and could run again. I passed 3 and almost caught 2 more before finishing 11th in front of St Zeno Cathedral. The air was much fresher at the finish at this altitude.

My German running companion from earlier came past me during my walk/jog section but later I saw him stop about one Kilometer before the finish and he told me as I passed him that he did not want to finish in 'such a race', so that was his form of protest.

I was quite pleased with my run and I think that I learned more about running in the heat, in that I need to drink more frequently than I think is necessary and that one can recover by walk/jogging.

Perhaps I was lucky to finish 11th because the first 10, in addition to plaques and cups, received cash prizes, which I as a naïve British amateur could not have accepted.

I enjoyed the trip and my stay afterwards in the Hotel Albergo Giordini in San Marcello was good. That evening I watched on a communal television in the hotel, the final of the football 'World Cup' and experienced the huge celebrations when Italy beat Germany.

On returning home, I learned sadly that my Grandfather, John Ferguson, had died on Sunday, possibly when I was running. He was 93 when he passed on, so he had a good span.

On Saturday, the 17th of July, I drove up to Thurso to stay overnight with Sandy Gunn and his wife before the marathon that Sandy had organised.

On Sunday morning I received a shock when I realized that I had forgotten to pack my Karhu racing shoes, so I had to run the Thurso marathon in an old pair of Brooks Vantage trainers. Brian Turnbull and Sandy Keith went into the lead and I and several others followed closely. The pace felt easy and I was worried that we were going to run slowly all the way. By 6 miles some had dropped off and there were 4 of us left and shortly after this we were three. Sandy Keith and an Englishman from Weymouth and I passed half way in 1-14-25 and I decided that it was time to increase the pace to see what I could do. Sandy dropped back but the Englishman came with me – thankfully he began to drop after 15 miles. From then on it was just a case of trying to keep a decent pace going.

My feet were quite badly cut up by the old shoes, but I was pleased to win and although my time of 2-30-53 was not very good it was 4-30 inside the course record. I found the race easy and had no problem with lack of energy, only lack of speed. John Bolton was second in 2-33-35 and R. Allemano 3rd in 2-48-11. First woman was Priscilla Welch from Shetland (in 11th place in 3-04-05) who at that time was stationed at Saxa Vord with her army husband. She would eventually go on to represent Great Britain in the marathon at the 1996 Atlanta Olympics, finishing 6th, a few months before her 40th birthday.

The following Saturday I travelled to Inverness Highland Games at Bught Park to run in the 5000 metres track race, but I missed it because it was the first event at 14:00. I went for a run down the Caledonian Canal bank to Loch Ness and back on the other side. While I was out on this run someone had been through the kit bags in the changing rooms and had taken the money I had concealed in mine, so I got 'done' again by the sneaky thief, which was disappointing.

The following Sunday on my 34 miles course I was going well, until at about 23 miles I experienced a stab of pain on the inside back of my right buttock. It was very painful and debilitating and I assumed that I had pulled a muscle or part of one, located between groin and hamstring. I could not run so I walked about 4 miles before getting a lift home and arrived there in quite a disappointed frame of mind.

On Monday I went up to the Physiotherapy Department of Dr Gray's Hospital to consult Magic Malcolm Morgan. He was on holiday for another 2 weeks, so Janis had a poke around and found a tender spot, which she diagnosed as some torn muscle fibers on my hamstring. She administered short wave treatment, then 25 minutes of infrared followed by ultrasonic treatment. I received the same physiotherapy from Janis for the next two days and this helped greatly in the healing process so by Sunday it was 'back to normal'.

Mid-way through the next week, 11th August, as I bent down to pick something up, I felt a sharp pain in my back and I was almost stuck in that position. Because my back was not easing I went to the Physiotherapy Department, where Hazel the 'back specialist' made a few movements with my legs, which made my back feel a bit easier, which was a welcome relief.

Four days later on Sunday the 15th of August, I ran in the first 'Moray Marathon' in warm and windy conditions. I went into the lead at about 6 miles and pulled away from Ian Moncur and John Robertson, passing 10 miles in 54-30 and 15 miles in 1-21-04. I was running well and I felt good. In Lossiemouth I began to feel tired and I had difficulty with the strong wind along by the harbour. I passed 20 miles in 1-49-58. Over the last four miles I found the conditions difficult and I was getting dehydrated, so my pace dropped considerably and I was glad to reach the finish in 2-29-36. Alastair Wood came through for 2nd in 2-35-02, well ahead of Ian Moncur, who finished in 2-43-48.

There was a feeling among the runners that the course was over-distance, so I would have to try to get it measured by a Jones counter, on a bicycle calibrated over a measured mile. Adrian Stott from Edinburgh, an accredited course measurer, agreed to assess the course so he, Elgin marathon runner Duncan Davidson, who also had a Jones counter and a calibrated bicycle, and I cycled around the course on a summer evening. The measurement indicated that the present course was 315 yards beyond the standard marathon distance, so the route would be modified for the next edition of the race.

On Saturday the 21st of August, in the 10 miles road race at the Nethy Bridge Highland Games I had a very bad run. I felt tired early in the race, my stomach felt tight and my intestines hurt. Ian Moncur was first in 52-59.6 ahead of A. Rioch, 53-18 and I finished 3rd in 53-58, with Mike McCulloch just 2 seconds behind me. Two days earlier I had been feeling weak and suspect that I was bleeding into my stomach because I had stomach pains and had been passing black stools.

The following Saturday in the Drumnadrochit Highland Games 15.5 miles road race from Inverness to the Games field in Drumnadrochit I finished 10th out of 68 starters in the slow time of 1-28-14. I felt bad from the start and things did not improve, as my strength was drained away and I felt breathless at the least extra exertion. Whatever I had wrong with me, beginning on the 18th of August, had still not cleared. I began to worry that I had some blood or liver disorder. Graham Laing won in 1-17-43 from Colin Youngson, 1-19-42 and Ian Moncur, 1-22-48.

By the end of August, I felt much better and put in 2 weeks of good training with 164 and 137 miles, with the Knockfarrel hill race at Strathpeffer on the 11th of September, at the end of the 2nd week, in which I finished 5th.

On Sunday the 19th of September in the Aberdeen Milk Marathon, which incorporated the 'Home Countries' International competition, I was pleased to finish 7th in 2-24-00. I started very steadily and, since I had agreed to take part in a drinks survey for Ron Maughan, I had to drink 100ml of electrolyte replacement drink, Dioralite, at each refreshment point. This must have delayed me a little as I had to slow down while drinking. I felt fine throughout the run and the time passed quickly. Wales won the international team race from Scotland, with England third followed by Northern Ireland. Aberdeen AAC won the men's team prize with me, John Robertson 17th in 2-30-45 and Brian Maher 21st in 2-33-05. Aberdeen AAC were also second in the men's team race with the 'B' team of: Kevin Martin 22nd in 2-34-57, Alastair Wood 25th in 2-36-59 and Alistair Neaves 27th in 2-38-49. Fife AC was 3rd team. Aberdeen AAC was also first (and second) team in the women's team race. Gerry Helme (Eng) won in 2-15-16 ahead of Ieuan Ellis (Wal), 2-16-47, Fraser Clyne (Sco) in 2-19-58 and Colin Youngson (Sco) in 2.21.03.

AFTER A GOOD TRAINING PERIOD, 100KM TRIUMPH IN SPAIN

I had accepted an invitation from Soto Rojas to run in the **Santander 100Km road race**, on Saturday the 25th of September, so on Thursday, 4 days after the 'Milk Marathon'; I caught an overnight train from Inverness to London. On Friday morning I walked for about 3 hours from Victoria Station to Hyde Park. Later I caught a train to Gatwick, where I got my flight to Bilbao. I was met there by Michael and William, who was to be my interpreter, and then driven by Michael to Santander. This journey was very tedious and frustrating because there were traffic jams going into Bilbao and after that there were many trucks to try to pass on the windy undulating road to Santander and the 105 Km journey took us about 3 hours. We stopped in Castro Urdiales for a meal, which was good, and I had a bottle of beer, which was very strong at 16%! I finally got to bed in the Hotel at 23:30.

My wake-up call at 05:15 (04:15 UK time!) got me up by 05:30 to prepare drinks. We left the hotel at 06:10 in darkness and rain and arrived at the start at 06:30. The race got underway at 07:06 and I started cautiously. Martin Daykin, two Spaniards and I broke away from the rest quite early and I was leading at the first checkpoint, before going the wrong way, but I did not lose much on being called back. I did not like the recording method of having the cards we had around our necks having to be punched at checkpoints because this lost time and interrupted our run. By 30Km we were still together, but by 35Km I was going away without any increase in effort. After this the course started

a long climb but I felt strong. I passed 42.195Km in 2-31-24, which was satisfactory. At 60Km I was back at the start/finish and had to repeat the 40Km loop just completed, which was a prospect I did not relish because of the testing hills. However, I pressed on, trying to relax, and achieved a good steady pace. The Kilometers seemed to pass slowly, but once 90Km was reached I felt much happier and the last 6Km through Santander was good with plenty public support. I was glad to finish and pleased with my time of 6-28-11, which was about 30 minutes inside the previous course record. Martin Daykin finished in 6-44-50 ahead of Vito Mileto, 6-56-20 and Domingo Catalan, 7-01-09. Chris O'Carroll, Martin Daykin's club-mate, finished 6th in 7-27-16. The banquet in the evening was very enjoyable – it was held in the castle on the promontory where the race had started. Next day I was travelling back to the UK and on to Elgin with my prize of a leg of cured ham.

On succeeding weekends, in the Alves to Forres road race I finished 4th behind Fraser Clyne, Ian Moncur and Neil Martin, but in the first North District cross-country league race at Thurso I was never in contention and finished a tired 4th behind Neil Martin, Ian Moncur and Brian Turnbull.

On Friday the 15th of October, I travelled to London to stay with John Lamont, prior to the 100Km on the following day.

40 MILES TRACK WORLD BEST PERFORMANCE

I started in the RRC 100Km track race at Barnet Copthall Stadium, Hendon, with the intention of attempting to break the 40 miles record. Joe Keating held the current record with a time of 3-49-32, set at Ewell Court, Epsom on 28/04/1973. Tim Johnson (who had been 8th in the 1968 Olympics marathon and subsequently world record holder for 30k track) heard of my intention and offered to help, so we alternated two laps of pace-making each. We passed 10 miles in 54-43, 15 miles in 1-22-35 and 20 miles in 1-50-42. At about 24 miles I could not take my turn at pace-making, so Tim pulled away and gained about one second per lap, until at 40Km I was 12 seconds behind. I passed the marathon in 2-26-29 and soon after this I noticed that Tim was no longer increasing his lead on me. From then on I gradually pulled him back and by 50Km I was 2 seconds behind, so I passed him soon after this. After that, it was just a question of pushing on, and John Lamont was a great help, providing my drinks and information regarding my pace. It was touch and go, whether or not I could get the record. I started counting down the laps from 24 to go, trying to concentrate on reducing their number as quickly as possible. I managed to keep the pace fast enough to pass 40 miles in 3-48 34.7, which was a great relief. After this I eased off and found that my leg muscles, hips groins and buttocks ached very badly. I could not force myself to run hard enough to overcome this pain so I decided to call it a day at 40.5 miles. My Intermediate times were: 10Km 33-52, 20Km 68-08, 30Km 1-42-59, 40Km 2-18-27, 50Km 2-55-11 and 60Km 3-32-32. My 10-mile splits were: 54-41, 56-02, 58-09 and 59-43.

I was pleased to break the 40 miles record, which had been held by my early mentor Alastair Wood before Joe, in spite of the poor conditions of rain and a strong wind straight down the home straight. I was grateful to Tim Johnson for assisting me with pace-making – it was a generous gesture. Peter Sugden won in 7-07-21.4 from Charlie Hunn, 7-12-18.9 and Alan Fairbrother 7-58-34.7.

In the Black Isle marathon, on the 23rd of October, in good weather, I set the pace from early in the race and had Craig Ross for company. I led until Cromarty, but on the long hill out of Cromarty I let Craig lead for about four miles while I gathered myself for an effort to win. At about 21 miles I increased my pace and got away from Craig. I felt quite tired over the last one and a half miles. My time of 2-24-28 was a new course record by exactly 5 minutes, and 30 seconds and I had run 7-10 faster than last year. During the race I had only one glucose drink at 10 miles. Craig Ross finished in 2-25-18 ahead of Ian Graves, 2-27-44. Alastair Wood was 5th in 2-36-07.

Two weeks later I ran, or rather participated, in the 2nd North District cross-country league race at Fort William. The tough and dangerous course on the Ben Nevis side of the River Nevis was waterlogged and the streams flooded. I lost interest in the race after having to ford the first stream and finished well down the field.

On Sunday the 14th of November, I ran the fifth leg of the Edinburgh to Glasgow Road Relay for AAAC. Jake 'The Snake' McPhee of Victoria Park AC tripped me from behind, with about 1.5 miles remaining. I fell heavily and cut my knees, my hands, right elbow and chest. I picked myself up and ran on as best I could, having lost about 10 seconds due to the fall.

In the 3rd North district cross-country league race over my disliked Cluny Hill course in Forres two weeks later, having missed some training while my 'fall injuries' almost cleared, I felt weak and lacked strength. My cut knee was infected and I had a swollen painful lymph gland in my groin so I finished 6th. I caught flu the following week, which laid me low and I should not have run in the Forres Harriers Christmas cross-country handicap two days after the flu had cleared. I finished last, feeling weak.

I finished 1982 with a total mileage of 5003 miles. No wonder I was tired, after a year which had been much better than 1981. I had learned a lot from difficulties between May and July; and August to October had been particularly successful.

Gelindo Bordin, the great Italian runner who later won the 1988 Olympic Marathon, has written "Champions have to climb to the top through defeats and setbacks. You cannot have success without setbacks. What you should do, after a bad performance, is to have a positive look to the future. I am deeply convinced of the fact that, if an athlete has a high degree of determination, he will become mentally even stronger during the years. With patience, you will eventually succeed." **With such a philosophy, surely he would have been very good at ultra-distance racing!**

1983

1983 began with the North District cross-country league race at Culloden Academy on the 7th of January, followed by the North District cross-country championships at the same venue. I was 5th in the former and 6th in the latter, which was won by Paul Kenney ahead of Neil Martin and Ian Moncur. In the North District cross-country league race in Elgin on the 5th of February, I was pleased to finish 3rd behind Ian Moncur and Dave Lang.

On Thursday evening the 10th of March, I caught an overnight train from Inverness to London to participate in the RRC 50 miles track race, to which I had been invited. Friday was spent resting in John and Lee's flat in Epsom.

IMPROVING MY OWN WORLD TRACK RECORD FOR FIFTY MILES

The 50 miles track race was held at Barnett Copthall Stadium on the 12th of March and sponsored by 'London Runner' and Pharmaton. John and Leigh were to be my seconds. My aim was to take this opportunity to improve my record of 4-53-28. My run went quite well and I passed the marathon in 2-27-23, 50Km in 2-55-36 and 40 miles in 3-49-40. Then I began to fade quite badly, had to work as hard as possible for the last 10 miles, and began counting down the laps from 24 to the finish, concentrating on maintaining the required pace. I finished in 4-51-49, which improved my 'World Best' by 99 seconds. It appeared that I had insufficient mileage background for long races at present. Also I finished quite dehydrated and experienced cramp in my calf muscles during the last 2 miles. I wore well-worn and comfortable, 'Walsh' flat racing shoes, with some holes in the uppers, which brought some comments from Doug Gillon, the Glasgow Herald sports reporter, who was watching the event. I had a very painful blister in front of the ball of my left foot, probably due to running anti-clockwise round the track for so long.

Leslie Watson, also a Scot, was first lady and set a women's world record with 6-20-42, so it was a 'double Scotch' as Doug Gillon wrote in his report in the Glasgow Herald on Monday. Dave Dowdle of Gloucester AC was second in 5-20-40, ahead of Robert Broad, Havering AC, in 5-22-50 and Richard Dalby, Gloucester AC, 5-24-51.

I was presented with the RRC 'Balfe Cup' and later, after ratification, an RRC plaque indicating that I had set a 'World, UK All-comers and UK National Record for 50 miles'. My 10Km splits were: 34-20, 34-29, 35-02, 35-35, 36-00, 37-16, 38-32 and 38-47.

Unknown to me, Doug Gillon contacted Nike on my behalf and told Charlie Spedding about the poor state of my racing shoes. A few days later I received a telephone call at work from Charlie Spedding, who said, 'I hear that you could use some shoes' and offered to supply me with Nike shoes and clothing. I readily accepted his offer and was amazed to receive a potato-sack-sized bag of shoes, vests, shorts and tracksuits. This sponsorship was unofficial, as I was not required to sign any contract, but I continued to receive 'Bags' of kit periodically for many years. Max Coleby was my contact person at Nike after Charlie Spedding.

A week after the 50 miles race, I went for a previously planned adventure run. Izzy drove me to Ian Moncur's home, where his wife, Margo drove Norman Miblock, Ian and me to Grantown-on-Spey. We then ran back to Ian's home in New Elgin, by the road north of the Spey, then across to Dallas and down to Elgin. It was an interesting run with quite a variation of scenery and altitude. I was rather tired towards the end of the 36 miles course.

The following Saturday, the 26th of March, Forres Harriers had a team in the Scottish national six-stage road relay in Strathclyde Park, near Hamilton. The format was one shorter lap then a longer lap alternated. I ran stage 4 and felt I ran quite well, picking up 3 places and losing one. Our team finished in 11th place, which pleased us all.

In the Glen Nevis 10 miles road race on the 3rd of April, I was rather disappointed with my performance. Just after the start someone fell and my left shoe got pulled off. I was annoyed, as I had to hobble to the verge and fix it back on with some difficulty before rejoining the race in last place. I did not feel strong and I could not get back to the leaders. I was wearing my new Nike Terra TC shoes, which were very bouncy, so I thought that they might take some getting used to. I finished 10th in a slow 52-53. Paul Kenney won in a course record time of 49-30 ahead of George Reynolds, 50-24 and Graham Crawford, 51-22.

In the Dingwall to Evanton and return 10 miles road race the following Saturday, on a very hilly course, my first half was quite good, but I faded on the return journey. Ian Moncur was first in 52-27 and I finished runner up in 54-07 ahead of Brian Turnbull, 54-14. I had not eased my training for these races, with weeks of 97, 130, 139 and 145 miles, in preparation for my first attempt at the London Marathon the following Sunday.

On Friday evening, the 15th of April, I travelled with Ian Moncur to Aberdeen, where we caught the 'Night Rider' train to London. After an uncomfortable overnight journey, we duly arrived in London. Following registration for the marathon, Ian and I went our separate ways. I went to Epsom to stay with John Lamont and Leigh. We all went for a 4 miles run on the Downs in beautiful weather and afterwards we sun-bathed.

THE LONDON MARATHON: SUB TWO-TWENTY AT LAST

In the London Marathon on Sunday the 17th of April, I managed to set a new personal best and finally break 2-20. I got rather carried away at the start and ran the first mile in under five minutes, then 5 miles in 25-07, 10 miles in 51-13. Half way was reached in 1-07-42 and although I felt fairly comfortable I knew that I would slow. I passed 20 miles in 1-45-17, which was my fastest, but I was slipping back through the field by this stage. However, I managed to keep up a reasonable pace over the last 6.25 miles although I was very tired. My finish time of 2-19-35 was very pleasing. My finishing place of 90th gives an indication of the good standard of the runners. I think that my lower-than-usual body weight, resulting from consistent training leading up to this race, had helped. I wore the Nike Terra T C shoes and had no problems. I was running for Aberdeen AAC and with Graham Laing (2-14-20) and Fraser Clyne (2-14-29), we were second team, behind Invicta A.C, in the AAA championships and my share of the prize money, which amounted to £100, was put into a trust fund for future appropriate use.

John Lamont finished in 2-23-05 a personal best, while Leigh completed in 3-14-39 and her brother recorded 2-41-10. Ian Moncur also set a personal best of 2-21 and we shared our day's experiences on the return 'Night Rider' to Aberdeen. We noticed that quite a few of the passengers were runners, all wearing their finishers' medals.

Two weeks later I ran for four hours eight minutes on an 'adventure' course from Charlie and Marja Greenlees' home in Glen Elg. I ran cross-country over a mountain pass at 1800 feet and then descended into Glen Sheil. From there I ran back to Glen Elg by the road. The 'one in four' hill section was very stiff, but I felt comfortable.

Since September 1982, I had taught an evening class at Moray College, preparing students for the Radio Amateurs Examination (RAE) and the course culminated with the examination on Monday evening the 16th of May. Because I did not have the RAE certificate I sat the examination along with my students and a few weeks later I received my certificate along with my scores, a distinction in the technical paper and a merit in the regulations paper.

BAD LUCK IN THE PASSATORIE

On Wednesday evening, the 25th of May, Izzy drove me to Inverness to catch the 19:30 overnight train to London. From there, next morning I caught a coach to Luton airport for a flight at 12:00 with Orion to Milan Malpenza airport. On arrival there, a bus into Milan got me to the railway station in time to get the 19:50 train to Florence, which arrived there at 00:48. I walked to the hotel where there was supposed to be a reservation for me, only to find that no reservation had been made and no room was available. Fortunately, I got a double room in a nearby hotel for the equivalent of £22 a night. Next day I walked in Florence for some time and then relaxed.

On race day, Saturday the 28th of May, I woke with a headache, feeling nauseous and with severe diarrhoea, so I had to visit the toilet frequently. I began to feel better but found the wait in the hotel lobby, before it was time to go for the race, rather long and tiresome. Giors Oneto had registered me and collected my race numbers. I had made up my drinks for the race to be given to the personal cyclist, who had seconded me in previous races and whom I had requested again. For some reason he did not show up, so one of the race officials arranged another cyclist instead, so I gave him my 1.5 litres of 10% concentration Maxijoul solution. The other drink I had was one litre of electrolyte replacement with glucose, (ERG), again at 10% concentration, which I was to alternate with the Maxijoul. He took this bottle, but in his excitement dropped it and the plastic bottle burst open, so that was the end of my ERG. I was annoyed but tried not to get upset. Meanwhile the cyclist informed the official that he would have to give my drink to someone else when the hills started, because he could not cycle up the steep hills and this message was conveyed to me.

The start was very well organized that year and fair, so we got underway exactly on time to much noise, mainly blaring horns. I ran easily and felt comfortable and the weather did not feel too oppressive. A group of three broke away, but I held back and a 2nd group of about 10 runners developed. As we moved along at a sensible pace the group I was in thinned out and on the first downhill Mileto and three others gradually pulled away to about 20 metres, a gap which I later closed. We caught the leader soon after and he joined our group. Without increasing pace, I was surprised that some of our group, including Mileto dropped back. By Borgo San Lorenz there were 3 of us in the group and I felt quite good. On the climb out of Borgo I had no trouble maintaining my pace and soon after this we lost one more. Things seemed to be going well and I was pleased when my companion dropped back. He caught me again as we began the serious climb up to the pass. He came past me and opened a gap of 15 metres, which then stayed the same. However, I became very weak and could not maintain my pace and, within the space of 2 minutes, I was shuffling along and a minute later I had to walk. I felt completely drained, so I walked and jogged for some time before deciding to stop. I could see no point in trying to continue in that condition, but I was very disappointed and annoyed. Perhaps I was dehydrated, although I was trying to keep to a drinking schedule of two gulps every ten minutes. My lost ERG may have prevented this. Perhaps the bug I had picked up the day before had weakened me. The lower back muscles around my kidneys were painful soon after the start and got progressively worse, so this might have had some significance. I am sure that I did sufficient, but not too much training, leading up to this event.

I got a lift to Faenza with Vito Mileto who had also dropped out. My strained Soleus muscle, which Malcolm had treated in the previous week was OK. I experienced intestinal discomfort during and after the run. Mauro Cillia of Italy won in 6-57-08, from fellow Italian Fausto Colletti, 7-18-33, with Fred Muller of Germany 3rd in 7-19-15.

My failure in the Passatorie made me quite depressed and the tedious journey back home seemed more irksome on this occasion. However, I felt able to resume running to work on the following Wednesday morning.

Two weeks after the Italian race, in the Forres Harriers 8 miles, two-lap road race for the 'Don Ritchie Cup' I felt tired from the start and eventually finished 7th. Fraser Clyne won from Paul Kenney, Craig Ross and Charlie Haskett.

In the Loch Rannoch marathon, on the 16th of June, I was quite pleased to finish 5th of the 427 runners. The antibiotics course that I had begun on Monday, prescribed to clear my bronchitis, did not seem to have any adverse effect. I went with the leaders and I felt quite comfortable as we ran out into a headwind. Our group of eight reduced to four on a steep hill at the top of the loch. Soon after this I began to struggle when George Reynolds increased the pace. I dropped back and Ian Graves caught me. I felt very weak but continued as best as I could. Later Dave Wyper caught me, but I managed to recover and pull away again. George Reynolds ran very well to win his 'Local' marathon in 2-24-09 ahead of Rod Stone, 2-25-23, Don Macgregor, 2-26-51 and Ian Graves, 2-27-18. My finishing time was 2-28-something.

Wednesday the 6th of July 1983 was a great day: on my 39th birthday, Isobel (Izzy) Stewart (an ex-colleague at Lossiemouth High School) and I were married at Elgin Registry Office. My best man, Robert Fordyce, had organised an excellent 'stag do' the previous weekend, by hiring a bus for a mystery tour, which delivered us to Aviemore for the 'adventure'. Dorothy Wright, an ex-colleague of Isobel was 'Maid of honour'. We had the wedding reception in our home, where David Dowie from Moray College Catering Department, along with some pals, attended to the catering. Drinks provided by the 'Still' Lossiemouth, were available at the 'open' bar in our hall. The evening party for family and friends went very well.

In the Caithness marathon from Thurso, on the 17th of July, Dave Clark and Paul Kenney set a brisk pace and once I had joined them I began to feel uncomfortable, so after 1.5 miles I decided to drop back. I joined the second group of: Sandy Keith, Brian Turnbull, Willie Miller and Steve Cassells. Sandy dropped back by 7miles, as did Steve, so Willie, Brian and I passed 10 miles in a slow 56-42, and soon after this I began to drop and reached halfway in 1-14-28. John Boulton, who had been second to me the previous year, passed me soon after halfway. Willie dropped out at about 16 miles and I passed Brian at about 18.5 miles, despite running quite slowly. I finished 4th in a slow 2-37-04. Dave Clark ran very well setting a course record of 2-20-34, ahead of Paul Kenney, 2-23-48 and John Boulton 2-34-55.

On the following Saturday, the 23rd of July, I had the honour of being 'best man' at the wedding of John Lamont and Leigh in Epsom. Izzy and I stayed at John and Leigh's house in Epsom for 4 days while they were off on their honeymoon.

Five days later on the 28th of July, I was again 'best man' at my running pal, John Spencer's wedding to Anita in Buckie.

I began to resume serious training in August with long Sunday runs. A typical example was: an early morning run from Lossiemouth, where Izzy and I were living, to Elgin, where I would meet Ian Moncur and run the Kellas-Dallas route in 2hr 9 minutes. I then ran back to Lossiemouth for a total time of 3-29-00 for the 35 miles covered. My weekly mileage was up to 150 miles by then as I prepared for important races ahead.

On Sunday the 14th of August, in the second Moray Marathon from Cooper Park in Elgin, there was a very encouraging entry of 202 runners. Brian Turnbull and I set a fair pace and got clear of the field right away. We passed 5 miles in 27-50, which seemed surprisingly slow, but the weather was very warm with the temperature at 70°F in the shade at 10:00 and there was a strong warm wind and this might have hindered us. We passed 10 miles in 56-31 and Brian began to drop back at Burghead with calf muscle problems. I pushed on through Cummingston and Hopeman, feeling strong, passed 15 miles in 1-27-29 and then ran through Lossiemouth. Coming out of Lossiemouth the wind was very troublesome and I felt tired as I passed 20 miles in 1-56-00, which seemed rather slow. Over the last 6.25 miles I began to have problems with cramp in my calf muscles and I had quite a struggle over the last 3 miles, so I was glad to finish in 2-36-11. Times were slower that year because of the heat and wind. The shade temperature had risen to 81°F during the race and there was brilliant sunshine. Alastair Wood was 2nd in 2-39-33 ahead of Jim Ash, 2-42-28.

At the Nethy Bridge Highland Games on the 23rd of August, where the shade temperature reached 82°F, I was pleased to finish second to Ian Moncur in the 10 miles road race.

On Friday evening the 26th of August, Mick Francis and I set off for Rosyth and the Two Bridges Road Race, in Mick's Mini Cooper. We had some excitement on the way down when a hose on the cooling system of the engine ruptured, producing rather a lot of steam under the bonnet. Fortunately, we got a replacement hose fitted in a garage in Kingussie and we were able to complete our journey without further incident.

DUEL WITH CAVIN IN THE TWO BRIDGES

In the Two Bridges race Cavin Woodward and I started quickly, but Cavin then slowed the pace quite a lot, allowing Dave Francis and Ian Graves to join us and we ran through 5 miles together in 28-38. The pace quickened and Ian let us go, so Cavin, Dave and I passed 10 miles in 58-11. We kept a steady pace until 15 miles, reached in 1-27-54, at which point they pulled away as I rummaged for my drinks at the refreshment station. I had to work quite hard to get back to them and by now Cavin had upped the pace and was 10 metres ahead of Dave. Cavin and I pushed on through Grangemouth, and I increased the pace to try and get away, but Cavin hung on and we ran through 20 miles together in 1-56-30. On the long hill at about 21.5 miles I sensed that I was stronger than Cavin and so increased my effort near the top and opened a gap of about 10 metres, but within 1.5 miles he had caught me. We passed 25 miles in 2-26-37 and the marathon in 2-32-55. I felt unable to break away so we ran together past 30 miles in 2-57-55. I made an effort as we started to cross the Forth Road Bridge and gradually prised open a gap that, by halfway across, two cyclists following the race, said was 30 metres. Coming off the Bridge someone said that my lead was 70 metres, but people's judgments on these things are often wildly optimistic. I sneaked a look across as I went around the roundabout and started going under the motorway, but could not see Cavin on the slip road, which pleased me. I pushed on up the hill through Inverkeithing, after which I was told that Cavin was 200 metres behind. I relaxed and ran easily but strongly towards the finish. The last mile is slightly uphill and I found it quite hard, so I was relieved to reach the finish in 3-34-39. I was delighted to win this race after so many attempts. Cavin and Carol were very gracious in defeat.

The weather was warm at times and windy, which probably accounted for the slower times that year. Cavin finished in 3-35-10 and Allan Hardy (Burnham Joggers) was 3rd of the 109 finishers in 3-44-04.

MY FIRST SCOTTISH MARATHON VEST

On the 18th of September 1983, I received my first Scottish vest, a near veteran at 39 years old, when I represented Scotland in the Home Countries International, incorporated in the Aberdeen Milk Marathon. I made a promising start, passing 5 miles in 26-07 with the leading group and maintained contact, but after going past the Beach Ballroom I had to ease back and let the group go. I had Ian Moncur, Charlie Haskett and Craig Ross for company and we ran together behind the leading group. At the first drinks station I had difficulty drinking and running so I slowed to consume my drink and had to make a big effort to regain contact with my group, so I could relax again. We passed 10 miles in 53-13 and, along the North Deeside road I felt comfortable, but could not increase my pace. I almost got run over by a Mini on this road. At Maryculter Bridge I had my last drink, where I tried de-fizzed coke, but I only had one mouthful because I found it too sweet. I tired quite a lot towards the end, which was annoying, and could not stay with Charlie Haskett, so I was a little disappointed with my run because I was hoping to finish with a faster time than my 2-25-20 in 9th place. Kevin Johnson of England won in 2-19-01 from Trevor Hawes of Wales, 2-19-41 and Calum Bark of England, 2-19-57. Peter Wilson was the first Scot in 6th place in 2-21-53.

I had agreed to run in the London to Brighton race after receiving a request from the RRC to participate, so the following Friday evening I travelled to London and on to Epsom to stay with John Lamont and Leigh.

POST-MARATHON LEG TROUBLE IN THE BRIGHTON

On Sunday morning the 25th of September morning, as the 'Brighton' got underway, I went with Cavin on his usual fast start, but after about 2 miles the bunch caught us and there were then 10 in the lead pack: 5 South Africans, 2 Americans and 3 Brits. We passed 10 miles in about 58 minutes and 20 miles in 1-57 something. Soon after this I found myself in the lead as Bruce Fordyce stopped for a pee. I pushed on a bit and got about 40 metres clear. Fordyce and 2 of his countrymen caught me about 2 miles later, so I ran along with them. By 25 miles I was having problems with my legs as my muscles, especially the quads, became tight and painful. I slowed down a lot and shuffled along. Another South African passed me, but at 40 miles I was still under 4 hours and my leg pains were easing, so I got going again and moved back to 4th and then 3rd. I was pulling back the second runner and passed 50 miles in 5-01-something, but I could not catch him. I was disappointed with my performance, but **perhaps last Sunday's marathon had taken more out of me than I thought**. Bruce Fordyce won in 5-12-32 ahead of Graham Fraser also of South Africa in 5-23-29 and I finished in 5-24-23 in 3rd place.

I had received an invitation from Mike Callaghan in Athens, who was the coordinator of the first Spartathlon, the original ultra-distance race of 250Km, from Athens to Sparta and scheduled for the 30th of September and 1st of October 1983. This race was to be over the route taken by Pheidippides in 490BC to solicit help from the Spartans, asking them to fight against the Persians, who were about to invade Athenian territory at Marathon. A team from the RAF led by 56-year-old wing commander John Foden, who was also a student of Greek history, completed a trial run over the route with John Scholtens and John McCarthy, to prove its feasibility in October 1982. I decided that I could not justify asking time off work for this, so close to the start of a new session, and suggested that Dave Francis from Fife take my place. The race was won by a 27-year-old unknown Greek runner called Yiannis Kouros in a very fast time, which led to some unkind suggestions that he was sponsored by Yamaha motor scooters. He silenced his critics by winning the 320Km Danube race the following April and in July broke the six-day record (by a clear 12 miles) that George Littlewood had set in 1888. Kouros completed 623 miles 1023 yards.

A week after the 'Brighton' I was late for the start of the Fraserburgh half marathon, which was scheduled for a 1-30 pm start. We arrived in Fraserburgh at 1:27 and I almost got to the start in time. I saw the runners coming towards me and passing me as I ran down to the start. I was then last and on reaching the start line I set off in pursuit of the 150 plus runners. I moved through the field, but I could not get higher than 4th, where I finished in 72-26 on my watch. Peter Wilson was first in 67-54 ahead of Jim Ash, 71-08 and Mike Murray, 71-38 and I was given a race time of 73-06.

In the 4th edition of the Black Isle marathon on the 22nd of October, only Ian Graves came with me and we passed 5 miles in 26-54, 10 miles in 53-46 and halfway in 1-10-16. At about a mile before Cromarty I established a lead of 50 metres, but on the steep hill out of Cromarty I slowed and Ian closed on me. I let him pass and ran behind him, up the long hill to the top of the ridge, to recover. We passed 20 miles in 1-52-09 and I got away from Ian after that and I was pleased to win in 2-26-07. Ian finished in 2-27-19, with Frank Harper next in 2-32-30.

On the following Friday night, I travelled down to Coatbridge with Ian Moncur and Mick Francis, who were to be my seconds in the Sri Chinmoy 24 Hours race at Coatbridge track next day. Ian, Mick and I stayed overnight at Ian's mother's house in Motherwell.

A WORLD TRACK BEST FOR 200 KM

On Saturday morning, the 19th of October, we got set up for the Sri Chinmoy 24 hours race, which was organized by Adrian Stott and the Sri Chinmoy team. Our race started at 12:00 and we were soon circling the track monotonously. I had company for some time, which I appreciated. Ian went off to watch his football team, Motherwell, play a match. Izzy arrived to support me and had booked into a nearby hotel. My time at the marathon was 3 hours exactly and I felt OK but the wind was troublesome, with some very strong gusts.

At about 4 hours I began to get aches in the tops of my quads and my back, which surprised me, because I thought that the easy pace would prevent problems. I took two painkiller tablets, which helped and I felt much more relaxed and even slightly euphoric. I passed 50 miles in 5-52-52 and 100Km in 7-25-47. I kept plugging away, reached 150Km in 11-41-41 and passed 100 miles in 12-44-14. I felt quite comfortable, but the wind was wearing me down a lot and the wind probably accounted for the slower times at the earlier distances.

At about 14 hours rain began and, with the wind already stronger, conditions became rather arduous and I had to concentrate hard from then on trying to maintain my pace. The wind became so strong that it blew over the gantry holding the large timing clock display. Izzy, Ian and Mick gave me plenty of encouragement and information regarding a possible record for 200km. From 37 laps before 200Km we began counting down and I tried to push harder. I began to feel nauseous and had to stop to vomit, and then continued feeling better, but I had to stop again to vomit. Eventually I reached 200Km in 16-32-30, a mere 10 minutes inside Mike Newton's record (World Best). I ran another lap because I was aware that the lap counters might have made a mistake, as had happened to Martin Daykin, who had stopped after he thought that he had set a 200Km record. I then walked a lap before going into the changing rooms to put on dry clothes and a wet suit. While inside I began vomiting again, so I decided to lie down in the warmth of the changing rooms. I vomited twice more after taking some water and squash and then again, after taking the yogurt suggested by Adrian. Izzy and I walked a couple of laps after that, but I felt miserable and made the mistake of feeling sorry for myself and wanted to go back inside again to rest. I had a roll and jam, which tasted fine and stayed down, so it seemed that I was requiring solids rather than liquids. I had some grapes and another roll with jam, which also stayed down, so I began to perk up. I went back to the hotel with Izzy and went to bed for an hour. We then returned to the track where I walked for much of the remaining time with Dave Francis. There was a great camaraderie amongst the runners, especially towards the end of the shared ordeal nearing completion. If the weather had been better I think that I should have run between 40 minutes and one hour faster for the 200Km. Dave Cooper won with 151 miles 1098yds, ahead of Richard Dalby with 147 miles 470yds and I finished 3rd with 131 miles 419yds.

On resuming running on Tuesday, 1st November, my right groin became painful and my right knee became very sore – this seemed to build in intensity until it became unbearable. Malcolm worked his magic on my groin and knee, so on Sunday the 13th of November I was able to run the 5th stage of the Edinburgh to Glasgow Road Relay for the North District team. I ran 28-22, which was 34 seconds faster than the previous year, when I got tripped. I picked up 3 places, but I was short of pace. Our team eventually finished 14th. Aberdeen AAC, including several of my Jogle friends, finally won this classic relay race, after a close tussle with Bellahouston Harriers.

Soon after this I caught flu, which is probably an occupational hazard of teaching (and being tired from racing and training) and this laid me low for several days. My 1983 running year ended with the Forres Harriers 'Christmas Handicap' cross-country race in Grant Park and Cluny Hill.

On checking my training diary, I found that I had accumulated 6011 miles in 1983. This was my highest-ever total in one year.

1984

My first race was the 3rd North District cross-country league race in Elgin on the 14th of January. I was pleased to finish 5th. Paul Kenney won ahead of Willie Miller and Neil Martin.

My right groin became very painful during a run the following week and after about three miles it went completely and I had to walk back home, very annoyed and frustrated. Malcolm Morgan diagnosed a nerve problem and gave me ultrasonic treatment, which produced a big improvement.

ISLE OF MAN 40: CAVIN VERSUS DON YET AGAIN

I had been invited to a 40 miles road race in the Isle of Man, so on Friday the 25th of February I drove to Glasgow Airport and caught a flight with Manx Airways to Ronaldsway in the Isle of Man. Dougie Corkill met me there and drove me to Onchan to meet Phil and Ann Cain, who were to be my hosts for the weekend. They were both runners in 'Boundary Harriers', so we had a lot in common.

On Saturday morning runners assembled in the 'Bowl' (King George V Park) in Douglas for the race, organized by Boundary Harriers and were sent on our way at 10:00. Cavin Woodward set a brisk pace and we passed 5 miles in 27-36, 10 miles in 55-26, 15 miles in 1-23-45 and 20 miles in 1-52-23 and the marathon in 2-28-29. The weather conditions were cold with a slight wind, which became troublesome as we tired. Cavin said that he felt cold, but I did not think that it was too bad. We passed 30 miles in 2-51-19 and at 35 miles in 3-21-50 I was 23 seconds ahead of Cavin. I finished in 3-53-14, with Cavin fairly close behind in 3-54-14 and Gareth Hawkes 3rd in 4-21-47. My arms, legs and hands were all very red due to the cold. I had a few blisters and my right heel was very painful. I was pleased with the run because I had no real problems despite a lack of long runs over the winter.

All runners in the 40 miles race and walkers in the 30Km race were invited as guests to the Boundary Harriers Annual Dinner, Awards Ceremony and Dance' in the evening. This proved to be an enjoyable occasion in one of the hotels in Douglas. Bob Meadowcroft from Bolton Harriers became increasingly impressed by the quality of the local 'Okell Ales' as the evening progressed, an opinion I agreed with!

A week later in the final North district cross-country league race I finished 5th, which I thought was quite satisfactory, as the course did not suit me too well. The following morning, I reintroduced my 35-mile run, by running from Lossiemouth to Elgin, where I met Mick Francis and Donald Gunn and we ran around the Kellas/Dallas course in windy weather. I ran back to Lossiemouth, feeling very tired and with pains in the top insides of my quads and my buttocks. My overall time was a slow 4-05-15. I intended to make this my 'Sunday run' for the foreseeable future if circumstance would allow it.

The North District cross-country championships at Thurso on Saturday the 17th of March was on a new course, out past the Technical College, with the changing facilities in the College. We started quite quickly and I was with Mike McCulloch and Ian Moncur, chasing Willie Miller. I was pleased to finish 3rd behind Willie and Mike on this tough course.

Three weeks later, on the 7th of April, in the 'Tom Scott', I started quite quickly and passed the first mile in 4-45, by which time the race was beginning to settle down and I found myself running with Martin Craven, Murray McNaught and Colin Martin. Our group passed 6 miles in 29-42. For the remainder of the race I began to tire and I finished 18th in 50-55. John Graham won in 47-09 from Douglas Frame, 47-42 and Terry Mitchell, 48-12.

I had been asked to carry a message in a baton from the Lord Provost of Aberdeen to the President of 'Marathon Oil', who was to be at Castle Fraser, Monymusk, to host a celebration there for the success of the 'Brae Field' and start the Marathon Oil 16 miles road race from there to the Beacon Sports Centre Bucksburn. Because I was on the College Easter holiday I could accept this task so, on Wednesday morning the 11th of April, I duly departed from the Town House in Union Street, Aberdeen, with the message in a baton given to me by Ballie Law. Once getting clear of Aberdeen I ran out the Alford road accompanied by Colin Martin on his bike. We went off course at Kirkton of Skene. Shortly after this, having run for one hour thirty-five minutes, I accepted a lift in a police car, which took me to within half a mile of Castle Fraser so that I could arrive there in time. I ran the remaining half-mile, then entered the castle grounds and went past the runners ready to start their race. I was directed into a large marquee, where I handed over my baton. The message was read aloud by the toastmaster while the President of Marathon Oil paid no heed to me. He then proceeded to start the race before I had got changed into my racing kit, despite my declared intention to run in the race. By the time I had changed I started about 200 metres behind the last runner leaving the grounds. I was rather annoyed, but gradually worked my way through the field as I increased my pace for some time. I became tired, could not run fast and I eventually finished 20th.

On the 22nd of April, in the Glen Nevis 10 miles road race up and back the glen, I made a promising start, passing one mile in 4-47 with Mike McCulloch. I began to feel distressed by the pace around 4 miles, but we passed 5 miles together in 26-00. Mike pulled away between six and seven miles as I felt a little weak on the short sharp hills. Mike won in 51-53 and finished 2nd in 52-46, with Roger Boswell 3rd in 54-56. Because the weather was very warm most ran slower times that year. I decided that I needed an easy week to be fresh for the Dundee Marathon the following Sunday.

DUNDEE MARATHON: DIPPING UNDER 2.20 AGAIN

Izzy and I travelled down to Dundee the day before the City of Dundee marathon on the 29th of April, and stayed overnight in a hotel, so that I would be well rested for the race. The start was quite fast with the first mile under five minutes, but we soon settled down and passed 5 miles in 26-24. There were 9 of us in the leading group and we passed 10 miles in 53-11 and half way in 1-09 something. The pace was gradually increasing, and between 15 and 16 miles Terry Mitchell pulled away with Don Macgregor and Charlie Haskett chasing. Alastair Macfarlane and Murray McNaught then began to get away. I was finding the pace difficult to maintain and had to ease back before 20 miles in 1-46-53 while chasing McNaught. He caught Macfarlane and I also caught him but could not drop him or catch McNaught. We did catch Terry Mitchell, who was struggling. I felt good on the downhill finish but could not run any faster and although I was 4th with 200 metres remaining, Alastair Macfarlane sprinted past. I finished in 2-19-58, which was quite pleasing as it was my second time under 2-20. I was disappointed that I could not go with the leaders at about 15.5 miles. However, I felt quite comfortable after the race and my legs were not painful. Don Macgregor was first in 2-18-16 ahead of Charlie Haskett, 2-18-41, Murray McNaught 2-19-44 and Alastair Macfarlane 2-19-56.

Two weeks later I travelled to London by an overnight train and made my way to John and Leigh Lamont's home in Epsom, to get ready for the 4th edition of the London Marathon the following day, the 13th of May.

LONDON MARATHON: ANOTHER DECENT RUN

In the race things seemed OK, but my first mile in 5-05 felt harder than it should. There was quite a blustery wind and the sun was breaking through the clouds. I passed 5 miles in 25-54 and 10 miles in

52-32, which was slower than last year, but did not feel that I should run any harder. I was surprised to see Ian Thompson at about 15 miles. I pushed on, but a big group caught me and we passed 20 miles in 1-47-something. Soon after this I felt quite perky and pushed on, catching people all the way, including George Reynolds and Graham Laing. Someone passed me in the Mall, but I finished quite strongly. I think that the wind and sun may have adversely affected times, so my 2-21-33 might have been worth sub 2-20 the previous year. I did not think that running the Dundee marathon two weeks previously had any adverse effect, but I cannot be sure. My position was 73rd, while the previous year I was 92nd in 2-19-35.

On the following Saturday I ran in the North District 5000 metres championships, and finished 4th behind Willie Miller, Calum Murray and Neil Martin, who just outsprinted me by point five of a second for the bronze medal.

I fitted in a 138 miles week before my next race from Edinburgh to Glasgow, on the 3rd of June. Izzy was to be my second, so we thoroughly studied the map of the route before setting off for Edinburgh on Saturday afternoon, the 2nd of June. The day before I felt tired, my back ached and, during the day, I developed a painful throat so I took a 2.5 grams dose vitamin C. This seemed to help, as my throat was no worse on Saturday. We stayed with Rachel Hollas and after a night on Rachel's floor on an airbed, we rose at 04:50 to start preparing for the 07:00 start of the 50 miles Edinburgh to Glasgow Road Race. Adrian Stott of the Sri Chinmoy AC group based in Edinburgh organized this race. He used his course measurer's experience to set up the course to be 50 miles, as measured by the calibrated bicycle with the 'Jones counter' and with the short course correction factor included.

EDINBURGH TO GLASGOW 50 MILES ROAD RACE

I had not slept very well and felt a bit rough. The vegetable Biryani of the previous evening seemed to be passing through satisfactorily, so I was happy with that. After a few cups of tea, we made our way to Meadowbank Stadium. The start was delayed to 07:15 for some logistical reason. I ran two laps of the track at a very slow pace with Colin Youngson, while Dave Francis and Richard Dalby raced off. Out on the road, after about half a mile I decided to increase my pace and chase Dave and Richard. I ran at a comfortable pace, but was fearful of going too fast. I caught them and ran with Dave through 5 miles in 30-03 as Richard had dropped back. I gradually increased my pace and passed 10 miles in 58-53, which was slower than I expected, but there was quite a lot of climbing in the first section. I reached 15 miles in 1-27-28 and 20 miles in 1-57-28. Since getting clear of Edinburgh there was a following wind, which was unusual because the prevailing wind is from the West. I passed 25 miles in 2-26-25 and the marathon in 2-33-something and 30 miles in 2-56-17. About this point I felt a blister burst on my right heel and this was quite painful for a few miles, but then it eased off, but I had my usual heel pain. I passed 35 miles in 3-26-50 and 40 miles in 3-57-53. The weather conditions had become quite bad around 35 miles with heavy rain and turned much colder on this higher section of the route. I found the last 10 miles quite hard, but did not become glycogen depleted, but just fatigued and could not get under 5 hours. I do not think that this was one of my best runs; it was competent but uninspired. Perhaps I had been racing too frequently to be in top condition. However, it was special to run over nearly all eight stages of the prestigious 'Edinburgh to Glasgow' route, counting them down.

Izzy gave my drinks every two miles after 5 miles alternating XL1 and glucose polymer with 2 grams of 'vitamin C' per litre, which worked well. Having Izzy along made the race more enjoyable – it was good to see her every two miles – and her support was a big help.

I finished in 5-03-44 ahead of Dave Taylor in 5-24-37 and Colin Youngson, 5-28-15. Colin had struggled during the last 5 miles but was delighted that Aberdeen AAC (i.e. the two of us) had won first team trophies. "At least I selected the right teammate!" he said.

My left groin became painful again and, on my run to work, I had a worrying confrontation with a snarling aggressive dog and its owner. By that evening I had a sore throat and I had been sneezing during the day. As my groin problem and the cold I developed were easing during the week, I decided to go ahead with the trip to Dusseldorf. On the 15th of June, I travelled from Aberdeen Airport, to London and on to Dusseldorf by BA Trident aircraft. Keith McSkelly, a Sunday training partner from several years ago, met me at the airport and drove me the two and a half hours to his home in Bochun in Halle. He had somehow got me an invitation to a prestigious 10 miles road race, which was not by any means my forte.

On Saturday evening the 10 miles road races at Borgholzhausen started at 21:30. This was a Volkslauf or People's run, which had previously been won in about 53 minutes, which should have suited me well. I did not feel great because of my streaming cold and associated phlegm, but I duly started in the elite 10 miles race. I got a good start, but the pace was fierce and I had to ease off, and from then on I dropped back through the field, passing 5Km in 16-08 and 10Km in 33-24. The race was over 5 laps in the town and on lap 2 Carla Beurskens passed me and I could not keep up with her. I plugged along, being passed every so often by one or two. It was quite a relief to finish and in a reasonable time. After the race I could not recover my grey Nike tracksuit and sweatshirt, so I presume someone made off with these. Andreas Weniger won in 47-15, ahead of J. Daecher 47-19, and English runner M. Longthorn, 48-08. Fifth was a 62-year-old, G Miecke, who finished in a remarkable 48-10. First lady, Carla Beurskens finished 40th in 52-36 and I was 52nd in 53-32.

On the following Friday, the 22nd of June, the boil which had developed in my right armpit was larger and more painful, and my elevated resting pulse rate indicated that I had an infection to fight off. 'Magnapen' 500mg tablets to be taken four times daily were prescribed by my GP. Optimistically, I assumed that they would have no adverse effect on my performance in the 100Km race in two days time.

The following morning, the 23rd of June, Izzy drove me to Elgin train Station where I caught the 05:55 train to Aberdeen and from there changed trains for Kirkcaldy, Doncaster and Grantham, where I arrived at 16:50. Ron Hindley, the Lincolnshire 100Km road race organiser, and his daughter met me there and drove me to the home of David and Philomena Davies, where I was again to stay the weekend. In the evening there was an enjoyable pre-race meal at the George Hotel in Grantham, followed by after-dinner speeches.

'BRITISH 100KM CHAMPION' DESPITE MEDICAL PROBLEMS

On race day, Sunday the 24th of June, I rose at 06:30 and started preparing for the 2nd edition of the Lincolnshire 100Km race from Grantham to Lincoln Cathedral and back. We started at exactly 08:00 and a couple of runners went off at an extravagant pace. Richard Dalby and I ran steadily at 6 minutes a mile pace, but I found this quite difficult. I got rid of a lot of mucus during the first 10 miles and my boil/abscess had burst.

The weather conditions were not promising because the sun was shining from a cloudless sky and there was a wind, which aided cooling, but it would speed dehydration. I tried to run easily, so I was quite happy to let the pace drop slightly. We passed the marathon in 2-40-34 and fairly soon after we entered Lincoln, where we followed a circuitous route and climbed up to the Cathedral, which was quite magnificent. The descent was by a steep cobbled narrow lane, which was difficult for me. At 50Km, reached in 3-12-00, I decided to make a move to try and win the race. On the hill back out of Lincoln I got away from Richard and then it was a question of trying to relax and maintain a decent pace. My feet were becoming quite painful. Clouds had formed so we were shielded from the sun for periods.

David Davis, my host and second, gave my drinks every 2 miles after 10 miles.

I ran on, slowing gradually but feeling quite comfortable, yet eager to be finished so the last 30Km seemed to take a long time to pass. It was a great relief to reach the finish in 6-48-15. I was very pleased indeed to win the 'de facto' British championships at 100Km. The course was not easy and the weather was unhelpful – I had sunburned shoulders and arms. I wore my Nike 'Mariah' shoes but once again they caused my right heel to blister and bleed. Larry Pratt was 2nd in 6-56-00 and Richard Dalby 3rd in 7-03-00.

On the 6th of July 1984 I reached 40 years and entered the Veteran ranks, well before they were labelled 'Masters'. My first race in this new category was the Elgin Highland Games 10 miles road race on the 7th of July, where I finished 4th behind Simon Axon, Peter Wilson and Mike McCulloch. The following afternoon in the Macduff half marathon, after a gentle start I worked through to finish 3rd of the 96 finishers. The weather was again very hot, with the temperature reaching 82°F. Calum Murray won in 1-10-26 from Mike McCulloch 1-14-07 and I finished in 1-16-09. It was a new experience to be offered 'Vet prizes' in these 2 events.

The following weekend I resisted the temptation to run the Forres Highland Games 11.25 miles road race and instead, with Izzy, I drove up to Thurso for the Caithness Marathon, scheduled for Sunday the 15th of July and checked into the same hotel as last year.

I started the marathon cautiously, and the pace felt fine, but perhaps on the slow side. I passed 5 miles in 28-24 with Dave Taylor and then started to increase the pace. At Halkirk we had to face quite a strong headwind, so I was glad when Dave took the lead from about 9 miles to 10 miles, which we passed in 57-41. At about 11 miles Robin Thomas caught us and took the lead, but on the run down to Thurso, towards the end of the first lap, I increased the pace and Robin dropped back. Dave and I passed halfway in 1-14-28. Dave was starting to struggle on a hill so I increased my pace and pulled away at about 14 miles. I passed 15 miles in 1-26-16 and 20 miles in 1-54-28. The next section into the wind with a few stiff climbs was difficult but the miles rolled by quite quickly. I tried to stride out over the last mile, but could not increase my pace much. It was good to win this race again, although my time of 2-31-25 was rather poor. Izzy gave me my drinks: 'Mineral plus six' by Wander at 5 miles and every 2 miles after that and she was very encouraging. Robin Thomas was 2nd in 2-34-07, with Dave Taylor 3rd in 2-35-45.

On the following Friday evening in the White Ash hill race, which was part of the Fochabers Gala, I was pleased to find a very good course for running and was able to finish first.

On Sunday, the 5th of August, Izzy and I ran in the Grantown on Spey half marathon, which was organized by Mike McCulloch, who lived there. I set off at a steady strong pace, passing one mile in 5-05, but after this I began to feel oxygen debt starting, as I was hanging on to Mike McCulloch and Martin Dean. I managed to stay with them until just before 7 miles, with the highest point on the course being reached soon after. Martin had opened up a gap on Mike and he was pulling away from me. I passed 10 miles in 54-46 and shortly after this I met Izzy on the way out. I was annoyed that I could not run any faster and I realised that an easy week would be necessary the following week in preparation for the Moray Marathon. After I finished I jogged back along the course with Mick Francis to meet Izzy and we met her just before 10 miles on this tough course, which she reached in 1hr 59 minutes. She finished her debut half marathon in good style for such a testing route. Martin Dean won in 1-10-47, ahead of Mike McCulloch 1-11-14 and I was 3rd in 1-12-44.

The following Saturday, at about 9 p.m., we managed to excuse ourselves from the wedding reception of Ewan and Pauline – one of the daughters of a colleague. The idea of leaving early was so I would not be too tired for the race next day.

GOOD MORAY MARATHON WIN BUT THE TWO BRIDGES PROVED HARDER

On the 12th of August, in the 3rd Moray Marathon from Cooper Park in Elgin, I started quite strongly and only had Ian Moncur for company. We passed 10 miles in 54-06 and, going into Burghead I relaxed, and let Ian take the lead to Hopeman. We alternated the lead until 16 miles when I sensed that that Ian was tiring, so I increased my pace. The gap opened quickly and I pushed on to the finish feeling quite good. I wore my Nike 'Mariah' shoes. Izzy gave me 'Mineral plus six' drinks at: 5 miles, 8 miles, 10 miles and every 2 miles after this to 24 miles. As the weather was warm and sunny these drinks helped a lot. It was also good psychologically to get encouragement from Izzy every 2 miles. I was pleased with my run because I felt good and finished fresh and my time of 2-29-17 was a new course record by 19 seconds. Ian Moncur was 2nd in 2-38-38, just ahead of Alastair Wood in 2-39-00. There were an encouraging 225 finishers.

A fortnight later in the Two Bridges Road Race from Dunfermline Glen, a group of about 10 of us passed 5 miles in 28-08 and shortly after this a tall American upped the pace and this reduced the pack to 4. He increased his pace again so I went with him, hoping to benefit from his pace-making, and we passed 10 miles in 55-06, which was about 3 minutes faster than the previous year. I realized that I was running too fast as we charged across Kincardine Bridge. Then I dropped him by about 50 metres, but decided to slow, as there was a long way to run. He caught up and introduced himself as O'Connelly, a 2-16 marathon runner. We ran together through 15 miles in 1-24-04 and soon after this another runner, who I later found out was Barry Heath a Royal Marine officer, joined us. The wind was quite troublesome going through Grangemouth and we all tried to shelter behind each other. O'Connelly dropped, which surprised me, while I continued through the marathon in 2-32-04, with Heath just behind. Charlie Trayer the other American joined us as the pace slowed into the wind. By 30 miles Heath and I had got away from Charlie, but I was finding it difficult to hang on to Heath. I gave way going over the Forth Bridge and lost ground more quickly going through Inverkeithing.

Eventually I finished 3 minutes behind Heath and only 6 seconds ahead of Trayer, who said that he had too much respect for me to come past, although he could have. I was annoyed that I felt weak over the last 5 miles. **Perhaps I did not ease off enough during the last week. Or perhaps I am missing my 35 miles training runs around the Dallas route, because I have been racing so frequently. Perhaps I should have used the carbohydrate loading 'diet' again.** Barry Heath intended to run the London to Brighton, so I would try to be in my best condition by then.

Izzy handed up my drinks, alternating 'Mineral plus 6' with 'XL1', which must have helped in the warm and sunny weather conditions. Heath's winning time was 3-31-46 and I finished in 3-34-47 just ahead of Charlie Trayer, 3-34-53, with Cavin Woodward 4th in 3-43-03.

In the North District 10,000 metres track championships, on the 8th of September, on the new all-weather track in Inverness, Calum Murray and Willie Miller set off at a good pace, but I decided against going with them. There was quite a strong breeze on the home straight, so Neil Martin, Scott McMillan and I took turns at leading and sheltering. I made a break by hanging on to Calum, who was lapping us. This tactic worked beautifully as after about two and a half laps later I was clear of the next runner by about 100 metres. I relaxed a bit as I was feeling the effort rather hard. My 3rd place in 32-42 pleased me. Calum won in 30-34, from Willie in 31-45.

By Monday 12th September, I had a boil on the right side of my right knee, which started to cause pain in the lymph gland in my right groin. During Tuesday my leg became worse so I consulted Dr White, who examined the boil and said that I had caught the infection just in time and prescribed 'Ceporex' 500mg capsules (Cephalexin). Because of the swelling I could not bend my knee, and felt quite ill at night and all I could do was sit in a chair with a straight right leg. I increased the dose of antibiotics to 4 a day and by Friday my leg felt easier and a good deal of the redness had gone so I thought that I should be able to run in the Aberdeen Milk Marathon on Sunday. I did not know how much this infection would have affected me, but 4 days without running should mean that I was well rested.

ABERDEEN MARATHON: NOT BAD BUT AFFECTED BY INFECTION

In the Aberdeen Marathon on the 16th of September (which incorporated the Home Countries International) it was pleasing to be able to run after my troubles during the week. The pace was good from the start at 5-20 per mile and I felt very comfortable in the drizzle and a light breeze. I passed 10 miles in 55-04, with an Irishman leading from Colin Youngson, Charlie Haskett and an Englishman, followed by George Reynolds, the other two English runners and myself. By Cults I had lost about 50 yards and was not recovering from a bad patch, so from then on it was just a case of survival. An Irishman came whizzing past as we turned down at Milltimber to cross the Dee. I passed 20 miles in 1-50-43 and at 23 miles an English runner caught me and we battled it out until 25 miles, when I had to let him go. I was pleased to finish 9th in 2-26-35.

My poor showing over the second half of the race might have been linked to the antibiotics or to the effects of the poison from the boil/abscess. Anyway I felt very frustrated at not being able to continue running with the leaders for longer. I wore my 'Eagle' racing shoes without socks but found them on the thin side for marathons. I had contemplated wearing them in the London to Brighton, but this would not be practical.

The new course for the marathon was more challenging because of extra hills. Our Aberdeen AAC team of Pat McErlean, 16th, Roddy MacFarquhar, 17th, and I were first club team and Aberdeen AAC 'B' and 'C' teams finished 2nd and 3rd teams respectively. Mark Burnhope, (England), won in 2-19-36 from George Reynolds, (Scotland), who ran brilliantly, finishing 2nd in 2-21-04, with Alan Catley (England) 3rd in 2-21-09. England won the home countries international match with: 1st, 3rd and 5th; from Scotland, with Charlie Haskett, 4th in 2-21-37 and Colin Youngson 6th in 2-23-36. Northern Ireland finished 3rd.

THE BRIGHTON: HARDER AS A VETERAN?

Three weeks later on the 7th of October I ran in the London to Brighton over the new 53.5 miles course, which I found to be more difficult than the old version. We started at an easy pace and progressed in this fashion, passing 10 miles in 59-58, up to about 14 miles, where we began a 500-foot climb. Most of the group stayed in contact, but during the 5 miles or so on this higher ground on narrow roads, Peter Sugden started to move away, leaving Barry Heath and me to pass 20 miles in 2-02-31. Just before rejoining the A23 there was a very steep descent, so no benefit was gained by our climb. At about 26 miles I decided to push on after Peter, who was now 2 minutes ahead. Barry Heath and Mike Critchley came with me. I found the course, with many climbs and descents, quite tiring. Critchley dropped back, but Heath stuck with me and we passed 30 miles together in 3-03-20. Just before 40 miles I got a small stone in my left shoe and it lodged on the left side, but I did not want to stop and lose time, so we passed 40 miles in 2-04-11, still together. The stone subsequently caused a blister.

John Lamont was looking after me and handing up drinks every 2 miles or 3 miles. I was alternating 'Mineral plus 6' with the long chain glucose polymer. Most of my earlier drinks had been ERG.

At about 47 miles I began having cramps in my left calf muscle and in both forearms in front of my elbows. I began to struggle as we began the last climb at Pyecombe hill, which was much steeper than the old course hill. I lost contact with Heath and slowed quite considerably, but I could see Sugden, with Heath closing quickly on him. I passed 50 miles in 5-07-08, 2-44 behind Barry. Although I relaxed on the following downhill and flat, I could not make any impression on Heath, who was now out of sight. Some time later I started catching Peter and I passed him with about a mile remaining. Barry Heath finished in 5-24-15, while I struggled in with 5-28-27, just ahead of long-time leader Peter Sugden 5-29-21 and a below form Cavin Woodward 5-42-55. I was awarded the 'Wilf Richards Cup' as first Veteran over 40.

Another cold and another boil followed soon after the 'Brighton' so I decided to stop racing and try to concentrate on building up for a 24-hour race so, following weeks of: 153, 161, 174 and 162

London-Brighton 1984, Barry Heath, Cavin Woodward, Don Ritchie.

miles I hoped that I could produce a good performance.

BAD WEATHER AGAIN AT COATBRIDGE 24 HOURS

On Saturday the 24th of November 1984, I started in the Sri Chinmoy 24-hour race at Coatbridge track at 12:00. The weather was bright and breezy to start with, but after a couple of hours the wind grew stronger and lashing rain started.

My pace had been slightly ahead of my planned 8 miles an hour, but the wind and rain were beginning to take their toll and both Martin Daykin and I were having problems. At about 10 and a half hours I was down to a shuffle and then a walk and I could hardly get my legs to move forward. I went into the pavilion where I put on dry clothes and ate bread with jam and bananas. After about 20 minutes I was back on the track and after walking a couple of laps I was able to start jogging and then I was pleasantly surprised to begin feeling reasonable once more. However, after about 17 hours, I began to have difficulty and had to walk. I felt dizzy and, on going into the pavilion, began to vomit. I went to the hotel with Izzy where I got an hour in bed before my helper, Ian Moncur collected me at 08:00.

By then I felt a good deal better, got back on the track at 08:15 and walked a few laps before beginning a slow jog, which I was able to maintain until the end. I was pleased to be able to complete the event but disappointed that I could not put up a better performance. The weather had been atrocious with the wind so strong that it almost stopped runners in their tracks on the bottom bend.

Ian Moncur and Mick Francis were good seconds to me and it helped to have Izzy there, giving me encouragement. Dave Cooper ran a steady race and kept going while most of us fell to pieces. Stuart Bennett was the revelation of the race and kept running very strongly even in the final hours. I was quite ill after the event – probably some form of motion sickness, like seasickness.

Results: 1) Dave Cooper 148 miles, 2) Stuart Bennett 142 miles 1140 yards, 3) Donald Ritchie 136 miles 1390 yards. On weighing myself the following morning I was surprised that I was still 11 pounds below my normal weight.

I finished 1984 with 6046 miles (a new record total) of training and racing accumulated over the year.

1985

The Scottish National Veterans cross-country championships were held in Callendar Park, Falkirk, on 10th of February. The roads were clear of snow except for a stretch of about two miles near the summit of Drumochter pass. We arrived in Falkirk at about 13:00 and after some time located the changing accommodation. The race was scheduled to start at 14:30, but this was delayed fifteen minutes. I had only had one cup of coffee for breakfast and I forgot to take anything to eat or drink prior to the start. The weather was bitterly cold, but this was soon forgotten as the race got underway.

I went into the leading group and found the pace quite comfortable. The first of the two hills on each lap, I found quite a test, but I could keep in contact. Gradually three of us pulled away from the rest, with Allan Adams forcing the pace ahead of Dick Hodelet, with me hanging on. On lap two Alan stormed up the hill, but momentarily went off course, allowing Hodelet to take the lead from myself in second. Allan regained contact very quickly and we were all together again. Going into the final lap I was feeling tired and my insides were knotted up, although I was able to hold on, but on the hill I lost about 5 yards and Bill Scally was closing on me. I managed to keep the gap the same until the last hill where I really began to struggle. Bill passed me at the top of this rise and I tucked in behind him, in the hope of picking up my pace over the last 300 yards to the finish. Unfortunately, I had nothing left and he pulled away in the finishing stretch. I was disappointed that I could not cope with the pace. Dick Hodelet won from Allan Adams. If I were to try this event again, I would have to train specifically for it, doing hill sessions and effort sessions. However, I was pleased to finish ahead of old adversaries: Donald Macgregor, Martin Craven and Hugh Barrow.

Two weeks later Mike McCulloch drove us down, from his home in Grantown-on--Spey, to Glasgow Airport, where we caught the 11:45 flight to the Isle of Man. My ticket was provided by Manx Airlines as part of their sponsorship of the Boundary Harriers 50Km run and walking races. Mike had to pay his own fare of £82 return. Again Phil and Ann Cain were to be my hosts.

ISLE OF MAN 50KM

On Saturday morning the 23rd of February 1985, the 50Km race in the 'Bowl' (King George V Park) in Douglas got underway at 10:00 with Jeff Norman, Mike Critchley and I pushing on, but I did not find the pace too easy although we were not running that quickly. Just before 20Km, as I had a drink, Mike increased the pace and I lost contact and could not get back to him and Jeff. From then on the gap gradually increased, but Mike had to make a pit stop and then began to slow. Jeff passed the marathon in 2-24-41, Mike in 2-25-46 and I recorded 2-27-37, which was 52 seconds faster than in the 40 miles race there the previous year. Jeff lapped me with about 11 laps of the 819 metres circuit remaining. He was running fractionally faster than me and the gap between us did not appear to be increasing. I was pulling back Mike, but realized that there were not enough laps left to catch him. Yet I was quite pleased with my run because nothing had gone wrong – I just could not run any faster. I wore my Nike 'Terra' shoes, which caused blisters on both big toes. Jeff's winning time of 2-53-21 was a new World Veteran Best for a forty-year-old. Mike Critchley finished in 2-56-21 and my time of 3-56-39 was also inside the previous World Vet's best. Mike McCulloch finished 5th in 3-23-01. In the evening we again enjoyed the hospitality of the Boundary Harriers at their annual dinner, awards ceremony, and dance.

A few days following this 50Km race I experienced an irregular heartbeat, which persisted for a few hours. I learned that this was known as atrial fibrillation and could become quite debilitating.

The following Saturday I attended the sad funeral service for Ian and Heather Mackenzie's oldest son who had died from Leukaemia after a long struggle.

On Saturday the 23rd of March, in the Highland News Half Marathon in Inverness, I got a good start and the early pace seemed quite easy. The one-mile point was part way up the first climb and our leading group passed in 5-05. Graham Laing began to pull away soon after this and I got detached from the group on the hill. I passed 10 miles in 52-50, but lost time on the next short sharp hill. I was quite satisfied to finish 9th in 69-24. Graham Laing won in 64-37 from Simon Axon 66-14 and Peter Wilson 67-29.

On Sunday, the 31st of March, in the Grantown on Spey 10Km race, organized by Mike McCulloch, I got a good start with Graham Milne and Mike McCulloch and passed the 2 miles point in 10-01. I began to lose contact soon after and began having intestinal problems, as I must have eaten too much for breakfast. I managed to avoid a toilet stop by slowing slightly, finishing 3rd in 32-45. Mike McCulloch won in 31-23 ahead of Graham Milne in 32-27.

On Sunday the 14th of April Banff 7 miles road race, (actually 7 miles 600 yards), was a good course on quiet country roads around various farms and quite undulating. Because there was a strong wind blowing, nobody wanted to take the lead, so Mick Wright ended up in front with Graham Milne, Alan Reid, Charlie McIntyre and myself trying to shelter behind each other. At about half way Charlie increased his pace and I hung on for a while as Graham dropped back. Charlie won in 38-03, while I finished 2nd in 38-32 ahead of Graham 38-52.

On the following Friday evening I caught a train from Elgin to Inverness and then the overnight train to London Euston. The journey was not too stressful and I was able to sleep quite well and arrived in Euston at 07:25 on Saturday morning.

I ran from Euston down to the Royal Festival Hall and registered for the marathon and then had a look around the exhibition before catching a train from Waterloo to Epsom. At about 15:00 John Lamont and I went for a jog around the common for 27 minutes. Dave Lang's brother, John Lang, called with the sample bottles for the study I had agreed to take part in. We ate our spaghetti bolognaise at 18:50.

LONDON MARATHON

We were up at 05:40 next morning the 21st of April, to get to the marathon start. There had been quite a frost and the car was iced up. I telephoned Izzy to confirm that that she was still okay as regards our expected baby. We caught the 07:21 train to Blackheath and then had to pass the time as best we could until the start. I did not feel excited enough and my brain felt fuzzy. At the start I was in the 5th row behind the women's start, as I did not know that they had the left hand side of the road and that invited runners had the right side. Because of this when the cannon went off I was delayed and could not begin running at the pace I wanted. I had to dodge around women, slow and then accelerate to get through and at the same time try to avoid being tripped up. My first mile was about 5-12, but then I speeded up and ran the next one in 5-03. I arrived in a group containing Dave Clark and Mark Burnhope so I settled in with this group. Pete Sugden joined us and we passed 10Km in 31-47. At about 9 miles I began to feel the start of fatigue before passing 10 miles in 51-51. At about 12 miles I felt a sudden weakness and had to drop my pace considerably. George Reynolds passed me at this point. I passed the half way in 68-37 and began to recover. I tagged onto a group, which came past, but I lost ground at about 20 miles, which I reached in 1-46-03. From then on I slowed. The first woman, Ingrid Kristiansen, caught me at about 24 miles, on her way to a new Women's World Record of 2.21.06. I was able to hold on to her and her accompanying press/film milk float for some time, but then had to relax and let her go. I passed George Reynolds at around 24.5 miles, but about 5 passed me between there and the finish, which I reached in 2-21-26 in 77th place.

This was my third-fastest marathon, but I was disappointed that I faded over the last seven miles. Perhaps I had not done enough long runs, because I think that my speed was quite adequate and it was my endurance that let me down. I was not dehydrated and I felt okay afterwards, apart from a desire to vomit and go to the toilet. At each appropriate drinks station I took the XL1 available. One of my reflections was that perhaps I should try reducing my bodyweight. The weather conditions were good and this course is definitely suitable for attempting to achieve a fast time.

On the following Thursday Izzy and I went to Aberdeen to see my Dad, who was very ill. It was heartbreaking to see him so sick and lacking even the energy to speak. We were told that he had cancer of his spine and would not live. On Friday evening we visited again; and once more on Saturday. We were pleased that he seemed a little better as he was able to recognize us and understand what was being said, although he was too weak to speak and could only nod. He did, however, indicate that he would like milk and I gave him this through a spouted cup. As we left he waved goodbye and I felt very sad that he was terminally ill.

On Sunday the 28th of April, Izzy drove me down to Dundee from Aberdeen for the Dundee Marathon on a cold and windy day. The early pace was slow and at about 4 miles the leading group began to break up as someone increased the pace. The group of 8 was running at around 5 minutes per mile by 8 miles and we passed 10 miles in 52-58, which was quite pleasing. By about 11 miles I began to struggle and could not force myself to hold on any longer. I eased back and was caught by Peter Wilson, Stuart Easton and someone else that I did not know. I felt better having some company and ran with them. Peter and I shared the work into the wind and we completed the rest of the distance together. Approaching the finish, I tried to out-sprint him, which annoyed him and he accelerated away. I was quite satisfied with my run.

WITHIN THREE DAYS, GRIEF FOLLOWED BY JOY

Later I learned that my Father had died at 11:00am during my run. I am sure that he would have wished me to take part, because he was always proud of my running achievements. Murray McNaught was first in 2-20-25, ahead of Craig Ross 2-23-10, Doug Hunter 2-24-25, Ian Graves 2-25-44, Charlie Haskett 2-26-06, Peter Wilson 2-26-31 and myself 2-26-35.

On Tuesday the 30th of April 1985, at about 06:45, Izzy had the first signs that her next baby was ready to arrive so I contacted our Medical centre and an ambulance was dispatched from Elgin. I accompanied Izzy and arrived at Aberdeen Maternity Hospital at about 10:30. Izzy's second daughter, Anna was born at 16:25, which delighted us both. Mum's sisters, up for Dad's funeral service, were able to visit Izzy and Anna that evening.

The following day, 'May Day', I visited Izzy and Anna in the morning and both were well. In the afternoon our family had Dad's funeral at the crematorium at Hazlehead, Aberdeen.

Izzy and Anna got home on Saturday afternoon, so I was invited out with the lads in Elgin to 'wet the baby's head'.

At Inverness Airport on the 18th of May, I turned up for my booked return flight to Glasgow, which was a prize from the Dyce half marathon. However, because of bad weather, the flight was cancelled, a coach took us down and I arrived there at 20:10. Then I caught a bus from Anderson Bus Station to Newton Mearns Cross and walked to Dave Lang's home, where I arrived at 23:15. After some spaghetti bolognaise and a beer I got to bed at 00:40.

Later that morning my alarm went at 06:15 and I had arranged with Adrian Stott to pick me up from Dave's and we got to Wishaw Sports Centre for the 'Motherwell Marathon' at about 08:20. After registering I got organized and, 15 minutes before the start, I had 4 teaspoons of powdered coffee washed down with 250ml of Maxijoul solution. The weather was pretty unpleasant with slight rain and a wind. I started, carrying 250ml of my Maxijoul solution plus ascorbic acid, {1g per litre}, and drank this in stages up to 3 miles. I felt fine and the pace was easy, but began to pick up at around seven miles and our group thinned to 5 as Mike McCulloch and Dave Taylor dropped off.

After Newhouse roundabout we started running quite fast on the downhill stretch through Bellshill and Holytown. At about 18.5 miles Charlie MacDougall surged away and our group began to split up. Ian Moncur and Dave Fairweather went after Charlie, but I began to feel weak and had to ease back. I managed to get back to them on the long downhill past Ravenscraig into Motherwell, but I was dropped soon after. From then on it was just a question of plugging away and hoping that I might feel stronger again. I was reasonably pleased with my run, as it was not a do-or-die effort. The Maxijoul and Vitamin C did not appear to help. I had to visit the toilet on finishing, which indicates that I did not get my previous evening's eating properly timed. I was not distressed after finishing; I just could not run fast enough. I did not know how I could improve matters as I felt that I was training correctly. **Probably I was running marathons too close together to get sufficient physical and emotional recovery.** Charlie MacDougall finished 1st in 2-26-52, ahead of my training buddy Ian Moncur, 2-27-26 and Dave Fairweather, 2-27- something and I was 4th in 2-28-04.

Three weeks later on the 9th of June, in the 'Marathon Oil' 16 miles road race from Castle Fraser to Bucksburn Community Centre I was tired from the start, due to heavy training, and could not keep up with Don Macgregor. However, I did not feel any worse as the race progressed and was pleased to catch and pass Graham Milne, Peter Wilson and Ian Graves. My stamina seemed quite satisfactory, after a few weeks at higher mileage. My former Hare and Hounds club-mate Colin Youngson ran particularly well to win in 1-20-59, ahead of former marathon great Ian Thompson, 1-21-00 and Graham Laing 1-21-08. I finished 10th in 1-26-26. Linda Bain was first lady – 21st place in 1-30-27.

On Saturday the 22nd of June I caught the 05:47 train from Elgin to Aberdeen and onward to Grantham, where I arrived at 14:56. I made my way to the home of David and Philomena Davis, where I was staying again.

ANOTHER VICTORY IN THE LINCOLNSHIRE 100KM

On Sunday the Lincolnshire 100Km got underway at 08:00 at an easy pace in good weather with light rain and a warm wind. I ran with Paul Taylor until 6 miles when he decided to drop back. I increased my effort and passed the marathon in a quite slow 2-46-02. The wind became quite troublesome as most of the route headed into it. Also the sun had broken through and conditions had become rather warm.

I pushed on, taking my drinks from David Davis every 3 miles, alternating 'XL1' and 'Maxijoul'. I had no problems with my legs or muscles, but was conscious of my stomach becoming painful. The 'XL1' and Glucose polymer were not being absorbed any more and were just accumulating in my stomach. I felt quite nauseous, but did not actually throw up and I am sure that this hindered me over the last 10 miles. I was very glad to reach the finish and I soon vomited three times in fairly quick succession and was surprised at how much liquid came out. I lay down for 20 minutes, after which I felt much better. Apart from being sick, I was pleased with how well I felt after the race and how quickly I recovered. Paul finished in good condition and he had a couple of cans of beer to relax. My finishing time of 6-47-40 {6-47-27 on my watch} was quite satisfactory. Paul Taylor finished 2nd in 7-35-58 and Tom Glare was 3rd in 8-08-33.

On Sunday, 30th of June, in the Buckie half marathon, I got off to a leisurely start and after being briefly misdirected; the field began to sort itself out. Charlie McIntyre and Alan Reid set the pace and continued to pull away, with Charlie finishing in 67-27. I was quite pleased to finish 2nd in 69-44 and Jim Farquhar was 3rd in 70-32. I thought that the course might be under-distance.

Next weekend in the Elgin Highland Games 10 miles road race, on Saturday the 6th of July – my 41st birthday – I found the early pace difficult, perhaps due to an effort session on the previous Thursday. Simon Axon went off course near the end, so Calum Murray won in 52-24, from Ian Moncur, 52-43 and I finished 3rd in 53-37.

On Sunday the 7th of July, the Banff half marathon was a Veteran's only race that year. I gradually pulled away on the difficult course, with a climb in a series of switchbacks out to the turn. I could not run faster than six-minute miles on the way out and turned in 40-20. On the return journey I managed to extend my lead, finishing first in 78-31, ahead of Jim McDowell 89-59 and R Robertson 90-00.

On Wednesday morning the 10th of July 1985, we set out on our summer holiday and reached our first stop, a camping and caravan site called Ashes Lane, between Kendal and Windermere at about 6pm, where we pitched our large family tent. On Thursday we explored Kendal and Windermere, walking for several hours in the continuous rain. The following morning, we packed up the tent in the rain and set off for Birmingham and, once past the Manchester to Liverpool Ship Canal, we experienced improved weather. We located North Solihull Sports centre and pitched our tent in sunny blustery conditions on the inside of the track as the weather became quite warm. I felt exhausted by 8pm, when we were at last able to eat.

Winning the 1985 Lincolnshire 100km.

SICK IN THE 24 HOUR RACE

On Saturday morning, the 13th of July, we woke to bright sunshine and, as race time approached, the weather became quite warm and windy. At 10:37 the 3rd 'Nike' 24-hour track race got underway with 38 starters, which meant that there was plenty of action on the opening laps. The temperature gradually rose, but thankfully some clouds started to form, so periodically the bright sun was obscured. I set off at a slow pace in order to conserve energy, working on the assumption that I might run with more effort in the cool conditions of the evening. I covered just over 8 miles in the first hour and kept this pace for 3 hours. However, I began to find difficulty in maintaining this speed and found myself slowing, which was quite alarming.

I had been drinking electrolyte {dioralite} every 15 minutes and Maxijoul on the hour, but I began to develop stomach pains and did not feel like drinking more. Martin Daykin gave me 'settlers' which seemed to help a little. He also gave me a cap and I put wet muslin around my neck and pressed on, hoping that I would improve. At 12 hours I had only covered 80.2 miles and although I was in 3rd place, I was rapidly losing interest in the event. I started to vomit periodically and tried some more settlers and even a glass of red wine from Bruce Slade. I also tried a 'Codeine' tablet, and 'Solpadine' tablets, but none of these produced a permanent cure.

After about 14 hours I decided to take a rest and, after an unsuccessful attempt at a bowel movement, went to our tent. I rested and slept for 4 hours and then went back out and ran, jogged and walked for the rest of the time to the finish. I was 18th when I restarted and moved to 12th by the finish.

The highest temperature during the day had been 77°F and this dropped to 55°F at night, although during the heavy rainstorm it must have dropped a further 15 degrees.

I was disappointed that I had suffered this sickness problem. Perhaps I was unable to absorb my drinks or maybe the concentration was incorrect for the temperature conditions. Martin Daykin ran well to finish with 152 miles 713 yards ahead of 'Mr. Consistent' Dave Cooper with 145 miles 72 yards and Kevin Dwyer with 141 miles 401 yards. My distance was 116 miles 528 yards. I had passed 100km in 8-15-31, so I was not running excessively fast during the early stages of this race.

From Birmingham we drove to Letchworth, where we were to stay with Izzy's brother, Bill Tait, and his wife Carol. From there we headed home via Tamworth to visit friends there. On the following day we returned to Lossiemouth in about 11 hours.

In the Inverness Junior Chamber of Commerce/Turnbull Sports 10Km road race in Inverness on the 17th of July, I made the tactical error of not going with Graham Milne when he started to move away. Charlie McIntyre, Charlie MacDougall and another runner were mis-directed at the turn and finished behind us. Simon Axon was first home in 30-11, ahead of Alan Wilson 30-29 and Mike Turner 32-00, while I was 7th in 33-05 and Lynda Bain was first Lady in 33-27.

INJURED FOR THREE WEEKS – AND AGAIN IN THE ABERDEEN MARATHON

On the 29th of July my right heel became quite painful, under where there had been a blister from the 24-hour race. This had become infected with the telltale evidence of discomfort and swelling in the lymph gland in my groin. I consulted a Doctor to try to get some antibiotics for my heel to prevent it from becoming worse, but she thought that my body was dealing with the infection satisfactorily and refused my request.

Four days later I made the mistake of trying to resume running and hobbled along the beach to the cliffs and back. Because my heel was still rather painful, and I was landing on the ball of my right foot only and letting my heel come down gingerly, as a consequence of this I soon began to get a pain in my right calf muscle near the top of my Achilles tendon. Next day my heel was discharging pus. My heel felt a little better by the following day, but my right Achilles tendon and calf muscle were painful.

Foolishly, a few days later, Sunday the 4th of August, I decided to attempt the Grantown half marathon. I had the intention of running easily, but fast enough to be First

Veteran. After about one mile I began to have increasing pain at the top end of my right Achilles tendon and this pain became very intense and it felt as though a muscle in my right calf was in spasm. I had to slow down and shortly after 3 miles I had to stop to massage the muscle in the hope that this would clear the problem. I started again, but soon had to stop and then decided to abandon the run. Once I had stopped, I could barely use my right leg, being unable to push off from it. I got a lift back to Grantown from the police in their Landrover vehicle.

On Monday afternoon Malcolm Morgan inspected my right Achilles tendon and lower calf muscle. He found a couple of nodules on the tendon and some muscle damage on a stabilizing muscle and not the main calf muscle. He administered Infra-red heat treatment followed by Radio Frequency for about 15 minutes and then ultrasound. It was terrific to get such attention, which was in stark contrast to that offered by the lady Doctor I first consulted.

Following two optimistic jogs of two and a half miles during the week, my calf and Achilles felt a little easier. On Sunday I started in the Moray Marathon and was able to run reasonably well for the first couple of miles, but I still had to favor my right leg. The pace was not fast – about six minute miles – and I was running with Brian Turnbull and Graham Flatters. I was hopeful of catching the leaders and by 7 miles the gap was down to 70 yards and I would normally have gone on to take the lead, but my leg was becoming worse. By 9 miles I was in trouble and could not maintain my pace, slow as it was. Ian Moncur saw me at 7 miles and at 10 miles and told me later that I was favouring my right leg by then. I struggled on, but there was no way I could pull back any ground on Brian and Graham. My right heel was hurting and the second skin I had put over the sensitive right region had not done its job, because when I stopped to investigate at about 13.5 miles and removed the second skin I saw a blister had formed. I hobbled on until Malcolm Morgan drove up and I stopped to let him have a look at my leg. He advised me to drop out before I did more damage. My right calf muscle was very tight and I could not use my leg at all well. I was glad to stop, as the exercise was now pointless. Then I could hardly walk. Graham Flatters went on to win in 2-41-something.

For the following 3 weeks 'Magic' Malcolm Morgan gave me physiotherapy treatment on my right Achilles tendon and right calf muscle on Mondays, Wednesdays and Fridays. I had been selected to represent Scotland in the Home Countries International match incorporated in the Aberdeen Milk Marathon on the 15th of September, so I was desperate to become injury-free. Once I got the 'all clear' from Malcolm I completed weeks of: 104, 128 and 129 miles in preparation for this race.

In the Aberdeen Milk marathon, running for the Scottish team, I was disturbed that I found the initial pace a little difficult to handle. When Colin Youngson moved away with 2 Englishmen and an Irish runner I could not keep up. By about 4 miles I began to have a pain in my right Achilles tendon, which caused me to struggle to run properly. I decided to try to finish rather than drop out while wearing a Scottish vest. My run developed into a nightmare and I was very relieved to finish eventually. My Achilles tendon was extremely painful, as was the blister on my right heel, which had enlarged and burst and was oozing blood. Dave Catlow of (England) won in 2-22-54 from Colin Youngson (Scotland), 2-23-58. I learned that I had finished 38th in 2-57-43.

Malcolm reassured me that the Achilles tendon injury was not a major problem, when I consulted him after work the following day. A week and a half of no running, with ultrasonic treatment from Malcolm every 2nd day, allowed the tendon to heal.

I was able to resume training around the beginning of October and my first race, after this latest injury, was the Buckie 10Km road race on the 20th of October. I started cautiously and was conscious of my right heel and right Achilles tendon, but they did not bother me too much. I wore my Nike 'Eagle' racing shoes and found them too thin-soled for me, so I decided not to use them again. Colin Farquharson won in 30-30, ahead of Charlie McIntyre 31-20 and Pat McErlean 31-44 and I was 8th in 32-50.

KNACKERED IN SWITZERLAND

Two weeks later on Saturday the 2nd of November, I travelled to Geneva and was met at the airport by Luc Kronener. He then took Duzan and I to the 'International Hotel', where invited runners were to stay and got checked in. My room on the 7th floor provided an excellent view of the city and the lake. At about 8pm we were taken to a restaurant for a meal, but the choice was rather limited to steaks or omelettes. I asked for fish, but ended up with a mushroom omelette with rice, with tinned fruit to follow.

On Sunday I rose at 05:30 to start preparing for the 100Km, which was due to begin at 07:00. I had some fruit juice and two cups of black coffee and then made up my Maxijoul solution at 10% concentration and ERG solution. We left the hotel in darkness and in frosty conditions to go to the start. Unusually, I did not feel properly psyched up for the race and, sure enough, as we got underway I felt lethargic and did not go with the leaders. I found the pace alarmingly hard, but later I began gradually to close on the leaders and caught up at about 14Km. We passed 20Km in 1-13-23, but shortly after this I had to let them go because I was feeling uncomfortable. I fell further and further back and more and more runners passed me. The marathon took 2-46-11 and I staggered on to 50Km. There was nothing left in my legs and I felt completely drained, so I finally decided to abandon the race at 60Km and try to analyse what had gone wrong.

I deduced that I had some infection, perhaps a mild flu, as I had been feeling 'off colour' since the previous Saturday. My pulse had been elevated all week and I had been sneezing and had a raw throat.

Vaclav Kamenik from Czechoslovakia ran very well, wearing Nike Mariah shoes, winning in the excellent time of 6-23-00. At night we were treated to a plush reception and an excellent meal in the Intercontinental Hotel. This proved to be a very pleasant social occasion and I enjoyed the company of Mary and Peter Sugden, Frank Dietzel and many others.

Four weeks later and, after more physiotherapy on my right Achilles tendon and a course of antibiotics to clear my throat infection, I ran in the North District cross-country championships at Kinloss on 30th November. The course through the woods was very twisty with rock-hard ruts in places. I did not run well on this course and I am sure that I could have performed much better on a more traditional course. Our Forres Harriers team: Mike McCulloch, Ian Moncur, Ian Mackenzie, Mick Francis, Ron Cowie and I were first team. I was the first veteran in 15th place. My right Achilles tendon started hurting on the last of the 3 long laps and the snowy frozen rock-hard rutted field section was probably the cause of this.

This Achilles tendon problem had persisted for several months, by the end of 1985 and I was anxious that it might develop into a chronic injury.

On checking my training diary, I found that I had accumulated 5222 miles in 1985, less than the previous year due to my injury problems.

1986

I decided to limit my racing in 1986 and my first race was on Sunday the 9th of February at Bisopbriggs for the Scottish Veterans cross-country championships. In the race I did not run as well as I had hoped, and by the end of the first of the 5 laps I was on the back of the lead group in 4th place. The snow on the course made running very difficult and I faded to finish a tired 12th, 2 seconds behind Roddy MacFarquhar in 11th and 4 seconds ahead of Mel Edwards in 14th, so at least we packed well to secure 2nd team place, 11 points behind Pitreavie. Brian Scobie won in 44-18.

ISLE OF MAN 50KM

Three weeks later on the 1st of March I was back on the Isle Man for the 'Manx Airlines' 50Km race at the Bowl in Douglas. Once again I stayed with Phil and Anne Cain. In the race I began to feel bad during the 2nd lap and had to drop my pace and let the leaders go. At around halfway I began to feel a little easier and began to catch the 5th placed runner. I caught and passed him some time later and began to unlap Steve Kelly. He stopped at the marathon, so I moved into 3rd. I was pleased to finish, but was annoyed at how weak I was. Jeff Norman won in 2-53-26, passing the marathon in 2-25-27; Peter Sugden finished 2nd, in 2-57-41, (marathon 2-28-34); and I finished 3rd in 3-06-48, (marathon 2-35-43). Mick Francis, my weekend training pal and club mate, was pleased to finish in 3-19-09, (marathon 2-41-00).

In the evening we were again guests of the Boundary Harriers at their annual Dinner, presentations and disco at the 'Palace' Hotel, which we all enjoyed. Later I received £30 from Boundary Harriers towards the travelling expenses for Mick and I between home and Glasgow airport. The flight to Ronaldsway with 'Manx Airlines' was complimentary as part of their sponsorship.

In the Dyce Half Marathon on the 23rd of March, I found the initial pace comfortable, but after about 1.5 miles I began to struggle and dropped away to finish 7th in 73-03. I was first vet but did not get the advertised 'Dan Air' return ticket to London as only 2 were sent. Colin Youngson won in 67-52, ahead of Kevin Best 68-41 and Steve Edmunds in 70-31.

On the 28th of April I received a letter from the British Amateur Athletic Board informing me that 'in view of the modest balance remaining in my trust fund' it was being closed and a cheque for the balance of the fund (£29) was included. This represented my share of the prize money won by the AAAC team in the London Marathon of 1983. What alluring prizes can be won by amateur athletes!

On Saturday the 19th of April. I drove to Aberdeen train station, via Kinellar to visit Mum, who was ill and staying with my sister Annie. I caught the train to London and then made my way to the Royal Festival Hall to register for the London marathon. There was a tremendous crush at the exhibition, but I met Phil and Ann Cain from the Isle of Man. I then caught a train to Epsom where John Lamont met me and took me to his home where I was to stay the night. When I telephoned home, Izzy informed me that Claire had broken her leg in a skiing accident, which was quite a shock.

Early next morning John and Leigh drove me to Waterloo station, where I caught a train to Greenwich and made my way to the 'red start', which was for veterans and everyone else that year. Rain was falling heavily and the park was quite muddy. At the start I was on the 2nd row, when the gun went, so I got a good start. However, I soon began to feel a pain in my lower front chest and stomach and could not go with the leaders, although the pace was reasonable. My time for the first mile was 5-20 and I was slowing down by then. I got the same taste in my mouth as I would after having eaten Ox liver, like a blood taste coming from my stomach. It made me wonder if I had an ulcer, but perhaps it was connected with the kidney beans in the spaghetti bolognaise I had eaten late the previous night or the cup of strong black coffee I had drunk at 06:40.

I kept going although I felt like retiring from the race by about 5 miles. The red start includes a hill, which is not encountered from the 'blue start', so we were at a slight disadvantage. When the routes merged, I found myself running near Mary O'Connor, from New Zealand, who I assumed was probably the second woman.

My intermediate times were slow, with 54-30 for 10 miles and 1-51 something at 20 miles. I began to run a little more comfortably by 23 miles and passed about 20, including Dave Clark and Tim Johnson, before the finish. My finish time was 2-30-43, which was very disappointing. Perhaps I had picked up Izzy's cold, which she had had since the previous weekend. My running had been going quite well, so I had been reasonably hopeful of having a good run in this race.

Two weeks after my London Marathon disappointment, I walked around the Science Museum in London for about 4 hours, before catching a flight to Turin at 8 pm. I was met there by a representative from the **Turin to St Vincent 100 Km race** and taken to the hotel where I was to stay, arriving at midnight.

ITALIAN 100KM TRIUMPH

On Saturday the 4th of May 1986, I was called at 05:40 and, after rising and preparing, I had some bread and jam and weak tea, hoping that this would prevent the intestinal pains that I experienced in the London Marathon. A mini-bus arrived at 06:30 to pick up last year's winner, Boris Backmaz and I and took us to Torino for the start of the 100Km race to St Vincent. Runners were gathering in a large square, doing the usual pre-race things. There appeared to be about over a 100 runners. The start was well ordered and the initial pace was sedate and after a small lap we re-entered the square and then we were off heading out of Torino.

There appeared to be no cheating in this race, which was good to see. The weather was fine, being overcast and quite cool. At 5Km I was given my first drink and I had to stop, drink its contents and return the bottle to my second in his car for refilling. At later 5Km drinks intervals, my second said to give my bottle to his wife, who would be 50 metres ahead and this arrangement worked well. There were seven of us in the leading group at 5Km and nothing much happened until about 15Km when 2 drifted off the back to leave 5.

After 2 hours of running, there were 2 of us left: Boris Backmaz and I. At about this time I felt a spit of rain and I thought that it would be great if we had rain. A drizzle developed some time later into quite heavy rain. I was feeling fit and conditions for me were excellent. The course went over some undulations and, on one of the down slopes I let my pace increase and then kept this higher tempo for some time. Boris came with me, but he gradually lost ground, so I was pleased and then eased into a steady comfortable pace.

My helper second shouted what I thought to be the 50Km point, so I checked my watch and I was very encouraged to see 3-06-and a few seconds. However, I was confused shortly after as I passed through a town where there was a large banner across the road, proclaiming something and crowds of people. I wondered if this was actually 50Km and on checking my watch saw that my time was 3-23-something, so if this was 50Km I might be heading for a seven hours time at the finish. I pushed on, hoping for the best, and wondering what the coming Kilometers would bring. Time seemed to pass quickly and the rain had eased off, but there was still quite a lot of water on the road in places. On some uphill sections there were small rivers flowing on each side of the road. The course wound up the valley, with steep slopes running up to snow-covered tops. There was a short tunnel at one point and a few overhanging cliffs to negotiate, before I passed a marker indicating 20Km to the finish. At the next marker for 10Km to the finish my time was 5-50, which was a good boost, but I knew that the last 10Km included a 3Km climb up the mountainside. This climb of double bends was at a very stiff gradient and I felt like I was making slow progress, but eventually it levelled out and there was a gradual descent into St Vincent. However, the route continued through the centre, before the turn and the final climb through a couple of double bends to the finish. I found this last climb very tiring and could not go any harder, although I knew that I must be close to my course record. Eventually I reached the hotel car park and the finish. I was delighted to have won, especially after my various problems since July 1985. My confidence was boosted and it was a wonderful feeling to be in good form again. I was pleased also to have won for my ill Mother, Izzy, and family. The next few hours before the presentations were spent having a shower and sitting in the hotel lounge overlooking the valley below and sipping wine from my 'Soda stream' drinks bottle.

I wore Nike 'Air Edge' shoes and I had no trouble with my legs or feet and my legs felt a lot better than usual after a 100Km. My time of 6-36-02 was pleasingly close to my course record of 6-35-00. Boris Backmaz was second in 7-15-27 and G Rivietto 3rd in 7-37-02. Later in the evening, Boris and I were returned to our 'Hotel' on the mountainside and discovered that it was a monastery, but we never saw any monks, only leftover wine and bread from their supper. Boris indicated that we should take some of this bread and wine, to sustain us until morning.

A week later, on the 10th of May, Izzy and I went to Roxburgh house on Deeside near Aberdeen to visit my Mum, who had been taken there on Thursday. She was very ill and unconscious and it was very sad to see her like that. Later Mum tried to talk to us and it was pitiful to hear her sort of whimpering. The nurse came in and asked us to leave while she gave Mum another morphine injection. Mum died later that evening at about 22-40, with my sister Annie at her side. The last morphine injection was probably sufficiently potent to end her life. Mum would be sadly missed, but she had a very strong religious faith and had come to terms with her impending death from lung cancer some months earlier, as no treatment would be effective.

In the Aberdeen Milk Marathon on the 25th of May, incorporating the Home Countries International I ran with little distinction, but finished in much better condition than the year before. I was indecisive at the start, but opted to go with the 2nd group and tried to shelter from the wind. Going up Union Street and down Holburn, I felt quite comfortable for a while, but began to lose contact by the harbour. Along the Prom, I started to feel better and regained contact with some runners and by the Bridge of Don I could see a white vest of England and two Scots runners ahead. I reached the half distance in a slow 1-15-10. The next section involved climbing into a headwind, which knocked the stuffing out of me, as I had no company, which I had tried to arrange for this section. Murray McNaught dropped out just before I caught him after the climb. I struggled on into the wind and made little impression on Doug Cowie, who I could see ahead. In fact, I lost ground to him towards the end and was relieved to be finished. The ball of my left foot was particularly painful and I am not sure if it was bruising or a hot spot in my shoe. Ray Maule of England won in 2-22-56 from Neil Featherby (England, 2-23-53), Kevin Best (England 2-24-58), and Colin Youngson (Scotland) 2.27.55. I was 9th in 2-36-53.

Two weeks later on the 8th of June, I had agreed to run all the way from Inverness to Lossiemouth via Elgin along with the Rotary Club of Elgin, who would run the distance in a series of relays. The idea was to raise awareness of the event and maximize the amount that could be raised for their specified charity. At 06:30 I was picked up and taken to Inverness in a minibus along with the members of Elgin Rotary club. We began the run at the Moray Firth Radio Station in Inverness and I had a new set of running companions every 2 miles as a new group of Rotarians took over. There were 4 groups who ran in rotation. The run went quite smoothly and the weather conditions were fine. We arrived at the finish at 'Duthies' at Lossiemouth harbour, after about 5 hours and 40-odd minutes. It was a long run, but I was pleased at how I felt and my feet and legs were fine. During the run I had 'Mineral plus six' drinks every three miles or near enough.

On Tuesday evening, the 17th of June, I became ill and had a painful stomach, vomited and had a headache. Next day I still felt quite ill and decided not to run. My back muscles were painful and my skin was sensitive. Waves of nausea swept over me and I had noises in my ears. I was also dizzy and I thought that this was some form of flu. At night I went to bed at 21:00. My waking weight was down to 9 stones 4.5 pounds. During the next two days I began to recover and estimated that I should be able to run in the Lincolnshire 100Km on Sunday. There was a rumour that water for some of the competitors' drinks for the previous Sunday's Forres Harriers 8 miles road race had been mistakenly sourced from the Mosset burn, so this would be a possible cause of my ailment, if the rumour was true.

On Saturday, after a disturbed night I realized that I had not continued to improve, but had become worse. My stomach felt bloated and I kept rifting 'rotten egg' gas. However, I decided to set out for Grantham, to return the winner's cup, drove to Elgin Station and left the car there for Izzy to pick up later. I caught the 06:51 train as it was pulling out, having had great difficulty climbing over the bridge to the appropriate platform. I had eaten no breakfast and I did not feel like eating on the train journey to Aberdeen and on to York. At York I had to change trains and had a couple of pints of beer to settle my stomach. At Grantham Station Philomena Davis met me and drove to her home where I was to stay with her and David again. I went to bed for 2 hours and had violent dreams. At 18:30 we had the eve-of-race dinner at Grantham College, at which I ate sparingly and I was in bed by 22:10.

On Sunday, the 22nd of June, I woke feeling quite a bit better, so at 06:00 I had a slice of 'whole meal' bread with jam. My insides did not feel so bloated as before and I made the decision to take part in the 100Km run.

A MIRACLE VICTORY IN THE LINCOLNSHIRE 100KM

The Lincolnshire 100Km started at 08:00 and I felt OK in the early stages as the pace was quite relaxed and the weather was excellent with a slight drizzle falling. One chap in our group looked rather frisky and he set off after the runner ahead, who was going to the marathon only, and by 15 miles he was out of sight. I was beginning to get annoyed with the person I was running with as he kept changing pace and at about 22 miles he increased his pace again, but did not slow this time, so I let him go. I reached the marathon distance in 3rd place in a slow 2-52-10 and shortly after this Paul Taylor and Terry Tullett caught me. I stopped to spend a penny on the descent into Lincoln. By the Cathedral I passed a tired runner and moved into 4th place. At 50Km my time was 3-26-00 and I felt that I wanted to drop out, but I decided to press on for a bit longer. I caught Paul and decided to have a go at catching Terry. At about 65Km I caught him and pressed on. From being on the point of dropping out, I was now leading the race and in a position to win it, if my strength held out. By 80Km I was very tired, but I got a report that I was 3 minutes ahead of Terry, which was not enough to allow me to relax. At 90Km my lead was down to 2 minutes and I dared not look behind. I became very tired and felt like I could hardly move my legs, so I felt sure that I would be caught. However, I managed to get up the last climb without walking, before the run down into Grantham. The last 2 miles seemed endless and I was extremely happy to reach the finish. I was very relieved to have won despite my poor time of 7-02-46. It was one of my hardest efforts. Ron Hindley noted in his race report: '*Don Ritchie was received by the Red Cross in a very reduced state, needing half an hour's rest before his bath*'. I wore my Nike 'Air Edge' shoes. Terry Tullet was second in 7-09-02, followed by Paul Taylor in 7-22-45.

On the following Sunday, the 29th of June at the Buckie half marathon, the weather was very warm (86°F) and sunny, which probably adversely affected most runners. Izzy also ran, but covered 1.2 miles extra because the direction signs near the end had been removed. Simon Axon was first home in 68-37, ahead of Keith Best 71-28 and Charlie McIntyre 74-40, while I finished 4th in 76-06.

The following Saturday, in the Elgin Highland Games 10 miles road race Simon Axon won and I finished 5th.

The day after, on my 42nd birthday, Izzy and I went to Stonehaven to run in the half marathon. The course was a difficult one with several stiff climbs to overcome. Graham Crawford won in 71-16 from Rod Bell, 73-35 and Richard Hanlon, 74-39. I felt very tired and finished 12th in 78-36 but first vet. Izzy did very well to finish this tough route.

On Sunday the 3rd of August, Izzy and I ran in the Grantown-on-Spey, 'Speyside Sports' half marathon. There was a good entry of about 150 runners and, after a cautious start; I gradually worked through to joint 3rd with Mick Francis. I suspected that he was not in top condition, so I pressed on, but had no hope of catching the leaders. I held onto 3rd place in 75-53. Izzy finished in 3-01, suffering from strawberry picker's back! Alan Reid won in 71-12, ahead of Danny Bow 71-54.

In the 5th edition of The Macallan Moray Marathon, on the 10th of August, the initial pace was quite steady, with 2 runners along with Mick Francis and I setting the pace. We ran up the hill to Bishopmill at quite a hard tempo and then, going up Spynie brae, Mick and I broke away. Mick began to drop back at about 8 miles, so I passed 10 miles alone in 58-08, which was rather disappointing. I increased my pace on the hill out of Burghead and then I had to face the wind to Lossiemouth, which I found quite a struggle. I passed 20 miles in a slow 1-59-42, and from there managed to maintain

6 minutes per mile to the end. My time of 2-36-45 was rather poor, but it was good to win and to be faster than in the Aberdeen marathon. George Stewart gave me 200ml drinks at: 5, 9, 13, 16, 20 and 23 miles, where I alternated Mineral + 6 and Maxijoul with vitamin C. Izzy started in the half marathon, but she stopped at about 5 miles because of painful leg muscles. Mick Francis was 2nd in 2-44-43, with D Murray 3rd in 2-46-37.

The following Saturday in the Nairn Highland Games half marathon, there was a large entry of around 150 runners and, after a steady start, I began to work through the field. I felt quite strong and I was pleased with my run. Danny Bow won in 71-22 and I finished 2nd in 73-04, just ahead of Ian Gollan in 73-23.

HANGING ONTO THE LEAD IN THE TWO BRIDGES

A week later, on the 23rd of August, I rose at 05:25, left the house at 05:50 and drove to Rosyth, arriving there after 164 miles of driving at 08:23. I registered for the Two Bridges race and submitted my drinks of 200ml of 'XL1' and 'Maxijoul' in plastic bottles for the following drinks stations: 7, 12, 18, 21, 24, 26, 29 and 32.5 miles. We set off from Dunfermline at 10:00 and the initial pace was quite comfortable as Cavin was more restrained than usual. We passed 5 miles in 28-18, 10 miles in 57-28, 15 miles in 1-26-49 and 20 miles in 1-55-30. However, I was annoyed at having to make slight detours and stop to find my drinks bottles and lost ground. As we started the climb after Bo'ness I tried to relax and consume my drink, while a young Tipton lad ran up strongly and was 90 metres ahead by the top. I started to pull him back again as we approached 25 miles, which I reached in 2-25-48, and at the marathon my time was 2-32-51 and I was 10 metres behind. I was quite pleased with my time there as it indicated that I could run a faster time in a standard marathon, because I was not running at full effort in this case. I got the lead at around 26.5 miles and pulled away on the long drag up to Newton. At the drinks station there, again I had to stop to find my drink.

I began to get pains in my left hamstring, which I thought was cramp and this became quite severe, so I thought that I would have to stop to massage it or worse still drop out. I could not use my left leg properly and my rhythm went, so I felt that I was hobbling from then on. At 30 miles my time was 2-56-09, so I was on schedule for a reasonable finish time if I could continue. However, my left leg problem prevented me from running well, so I passed 35 miles in 3-28-28 and was extremely pleased and relieved to reach the finish first. The lower left part of my left hamstring was extremely tender when I stopped running and I was practically immobilized. It was good to have won, but I feared that my hamstring might be seriously injured. My finish time was 3-36-37, with Richard Dalby 2nd in 3-39-00 and Mick McHale 3rd in 3-40-38. Later I found out that the brave Tipton lad was 20-year-old Billy Evans, who eventually finished 7th in 3-47-39, but was soon to prove a serious contender in this event and other ultras.

Malcolm fixed my hamstring, and a month later I travelled down to Glasgow for the Glasgow Marathon in my colleague Jim McDowell's car, along with his wife Irene and their son David. After registering for the race at the Anderson Centre and looking around the stands, I caught a bus to Newton Mearns Cross, and walked from there to Dave Lang's home, where I was to stay the night.

The following morning, the 21st of September, I had breakfast of one slice of toast with jam and a mug of coffee. Then Jenny Lipsi, a friend of Dave's, who was running in the marathon, gave me a lift in to the start area. There was not too long to wait and after a 2nd toilet visit I made my way to the front with Jim McDowell. I was in the 3rd row, but I got off to a good start and went with the leading group of about 20 runners. Then I lost contact with the pack and ran out Great Western Road with Colin Martin, as the pack, with Allan Adams on the back of it, pulled away.

I passed 10 miles in 54-17, but on crossing the river Clyde there was then an exposed section and I had to lead into the wind, which I did not like, and Bellahouston Park was also difficult because of the wind. At 20 miles my time was 1-51-51 and then we entered Pollok Park.

A Spanish runner passed me in the last mile but I overtook a Turkish runner in the last half-mile. I was quite pleased with my time of 2-26-50, 25th place and 2nd Vet, as it was a lot better than previous marathons that year. I was particularly happy that my left hamstring and my right heel were no problem. Kenny Stewart won in 2-14-04, ahead of Dic Evans, 2-17-57, and J Konieczny in 2-18-30.

On the following Saturday, the 27 of September, in the 'Ness Motors' 10 miles road race in Inverness there were over 200 runners. Simon Axon was first home in 50-19, ahead of Bruce Chinnick, 50-29 and Neil Martin, 53-06. I finished 10th and first Vet in 55-14, quite satisfied.

STEADY IN THE SANTANDER 100KM

On Friday the 3rd of October, Izzy, Claire, Anna and I drove to Aberdeen airport where we caught a flight to Heathrow, which went well until Anna vomited over Izzy, the seat belt and the seat. This caused some confusion, but with the help of the stewardess we got pretty well cleaned up. At Heathrow we had a wait until the 'Iberia' flight to Bilbao, which allowed Izzy to buy a blouse so that she could change out of the sickly jersey.

At Bilbao we were met by friends of Soto Rojas and two cars were used to transport us along with two Belgians, (the organizers of the Torhout 100Km race), to Santander. The roads were, narrow very undulating, very busy and the weather was hot (27°C earlier in the day). After a brief stop at Castro Urdallies, we finally arrived at Santander and the race registration at about 21:15. I was rather tired and had a headache. We were taken to our hotel and had a meal at 22:00. I got to bed at 23:00, but it took some time to get the children organized and settled, so I think that I finally drifted to sleep at around midnight, having set my alarm for 04:00.

My waking pulse next morning was 45, so I knew that my threatening cold had not developed. I rose at just after 4am and had a slice of brown bread, got my kit on and then went back to bed for some time before going down to reception at 05:30. Reception was deserted, but outside in the misty darkness I could see a couple in tracksuits loading the boot of a Volvo. I got a lift with them to the registration/finish, where I used the toilets a few times, before finding a quiet bench, which I lay out on for about half an hour. At 06:40 I put my tracksuit in the numbered bag, deposited it at registration and then made my way to the start. I signed in and met Jana, Thomas Rusek and Kamenik, who looked rather fit. The weather was very misty, so visibility was down to about 15 metres, but it was quite mild.

At 07:00 we were off and I got near the front, where a large group had developed. I began sweating profusely. Thinking that Kamenik and Catalan would be the men to watch, I kept close to them. The early pace was comfortable, so I let the race develop and by 5Km three had broken away. At about 7Km I decided to give chase, but I found that I was making little or no impression on the 2, who were visible ahead. I was rather upset by my 10Km time of 40-something, so I tried to increase my pace, but I found this difficult.

Approaching the end of the small loop I was surprised at how far ahead one runner in a red vest and cap was. I thought that he was a Spaniard, but found out later that he was Celeo Da Silva from Brazil. The other 2 in front of me, I later found out, were Bruno Scelsi from France and Roos Hanspeter from Switzerland. I was making no impression on these 2 and felt that I lacked energy. However, at about 30Km I sensed that the gap was reducing slightly and sure enough, little by little they got nearer, until on the run down to Boo I was almost in contact with them. Shortly after this, on the climb out of Boo we reached the marathon, with Scelsi passing in 2-41-42, Hanspeter in 2-41-47 and me in 2-41-56, while Da Silva had passed this distance in 2-33-08. I was disappointed by the slow marathon time, as I had hoped to run through in about 2-35, feeling fresh. Instead I was far from fresh, but had to make the best of the situation. Soon after the marathon I caught and passed Hanspeter and then Scelsi, who ran with me back to Santander. In the crowded streets of Santander, we caught up with Da Silva and on the descent to the turn for the last lap I edged ahead.

The mist had cleared some time ago but the sun did not break through. I kept drinking every 15 minutes, my drinks being carried by an accompanying cyclist, arranged by Soto at my request. On starting the last 40Km loop I had a lead of about 250 metres over Scelsi, but Catalan and Kamenik were only about 500 metres behind. At about 64Km Catalan swept by me on a hill and he was running much more strongly than I was. I could not respond and had to watch him rapidly increase his lead until he disappeared from view.

By about 70Km I finished the 780ml of my prepared 'XL1' drinks, so then I started taking 200ml of 'Dioralite'. It may be coincidence, but I began to perk up after my 'Dioralite', so I felt a bit happier. From then on I drank 'Maxijoul' at 10% concentration, still at 15-minute intervals, but I only had a couple of gulps each time. I supplemented this with the occasional cup of water at refreshment stations. 80Km was on the downhill section to Boo, but I was too weary to take advantage of the down gradient. My right heel was blistering in the usual place and the small toe on the same foot was very painful. Nevertheless, I pressed on and eventually reached 90Km, surprised that no one had caught me; I was not distressed, just tired, and I knew that I could finish if nothing went wrong. I quite enjoyed the last 5Km through Santander and the run down to the finish. I was quite content to finish 2nd. Izzy and the girls were at the finish, which had its usual inspiring atmosphere. Domingo Catalan of Spain was first in 6-32-09 and I was 2nd in 6-47-49, with Bruno Scelsi 3rd in 6-57-08. After the finish we enjoyed relaxing until the awards ceremony. Claire had 2 camel rides, which were provided free. I was presented with a very elegant cup. We could now enjoy our week's 'Tattie holidays' in Santander.

On the following Thursday morning, the day before we were due to leave, we went to the beach in the morning and then had a Civic Reception in the Town Hall at 13:00, which was very enjoyable. Before the 'Prime Minister' of the region of Cantabria arrived, we sat in an anteroom and Isobel posed under a portrait of Queen Isabella of Spain! The Prime Minister was very pleasant and he presented me with three beautiful inscribed books on the region of Cantabria. He gave Izzy a brooch with the crest of the region on it and he handed felt pens and stickers to Claire, Anna and also Jose, Soto's son. Then we had drinks and some beautifully prepared delicious snacks. Hemma acted as interpreter. This was the first Civic Reception that I had attended and it was a delight.

We returned to the beach after lunch for a few hours, and then we went into Santander again, for me to purchase pearls for Izzy. Soto, his wife, Luth-Mari and Jose came to our hotel in the evening to say goodbye and we had some drinks at the bar before dinner and more wine at dinner.

On Wednesday evening the 22nd of October, I picked up Ron Maughan from Elgin Station as arranged and, after dinner, I drove him through to Dingwall for the running forum, with Ron Hill, Ron Maughan and me on the panel. Ron Hill was there to present some national award to the Minolta Black Isle Athletic Club, with thanks mainly due to the efforts of Ray Cameron. Ron Hill was very entertaining.

TWO TROPHIES AT THE BLACK ISLE MARATHON

On Saturday the 1st of November, although I had a head cold, I decided to run in the Black Isle Marathon. I picked up Jim McDowell in Elgin and drove to Fortrose where, after registering and changing, we boarded the buses to take us to the start in Culbokie. There were 116 starters on this cold morning with a north wind blowing. We were sent on our way by a phone call from a lady in Wick, via Moray Firth Radio transmission.

The initial pace was comfortable and quite adequate as 2 runners from Cumbernauld AC set the pace, which tended to fluctuate quite a lot. One of the Cumbernauld runners, John Duffy, increased the pace a little and pulled away and Charlie Noble chased after him, but both slowed and dropped back. I started to set the pace at about 4 miles, kept it steady and had John Duffy for company. He asked me if I had run in the Glasgow marathon, and on hearing that I had, he informed me that he had also run there and finished with 2-29-00. He seemed quite strong and at about 9 miles I began to feel a little tired and my chest was hurting a little. I thought that he would probably win this race, but I was going to hang on for as long as I could. We passed half way in 1-12-48, which was quite satisfactory and I appeared to be running more comfortably by then. My confidence increased and as we approached Cromarty, John made a short stop to tie a loose shoelace. He caught up soon afterwards and we ran through Cromarty together and also up the long hill after Cromarty. With about 7 miles remaining I increased the pace and gradually pulled away from him as the course levelled off and then the gradual downhill began. I checked my mile time between six miles and five miles to go and was pleased to see 5-24. I maintained this pace most of the way to the finish. I was very pleased to win this marathon again and my time of 2-28-38 was satisfactory in view of my cold. John Duffy was 2nd with 2-32-58 and Mick Francis 3rd in 2-33-41.

Brian Grasson of Sri Chinmoy A C was running and it was good to see him again, but unfortunately he was unable to finish. Being a member of the **Scottish Marathon Club**, he had brought with him the '**J. F. Walker Memorial Trophy**', which had been awarded to me this year, for my lengthy contribution to the sport of marathon and ultra-running in Scotland. This was presented at the beginning of the awards ceremony. The whole day went very well and was a credit to Ray Cameron and his team of helpers

On the 29th of November, in the North District cross-country championships at Elgin, around the usual course at Morriston playing fields, Borough Briggs and Elgin Academy, I started quite well, but faded and finished 17th but first Vet. Bruce Chinnick of Forres Harriers won in 37-30, 8 seconds ahead of Chris Armstrong. Forres Harriers Christmas handicap, and the Elgin AAC Christmas handicap were my last cross-country races of 1986

On the 13th of December we went skiing at the Lecht ski centre. The weather conditions at the Lecht became rather bad and, on leaving, I skidded our fully loaded car on the downhill, while trying to avoid a car in the middle of the road. Three people were pushing this car up the hill. I managed to avoid crashing into them but we ended up crunching into the snow bank on the hillside of the road, which was very fortunate, since there was quite a drop on the other side of the road, and a snowplough was also coming up the hill towards us as we slid down. The snowplough driver helped me push the car out onto the road again and we were relieved that, luckily, there was no injury to anyone or damage to our car.

On checking my training diary, I found that I had accumulated 5407 miles of training and racing in 1986.

1987

On the 8th of February 1987, I drove through to Mel Edwards' home in Bridge of Don and got a lift with him down to Mussleburgh Race course for that year's Veterans cross-country championships. Our Aberdeen AAC team was at a disadvantage in that we were called to line up next to the rails on the left side of the racecourse and there was a right hand turn very shortly after the start. I ran at a hard pace from the start and after about three-quarters of a mile, I got onto the back of the leading group of about 9. This group began to break up and I was at the back running with Ken Duncan with Allan Adams ahead. After the lap of the lagoons, I began to experience massive oxygen debt and had to reduce my pace, allowing Roddy MacFarquhar to catch and pass me and then John Linaker and some other runner that I did not know. I managed to hang on to this fellow and recovered as we started the second lap. I pulled back Linaker, but made little impression on Adams, so I finished an exhausted 9th. My chest was painful and I had occasional coughing fits, bringing up phlegm. We were second team, with Roddy 6th, Mel 16th and me 9th. The winning Pitreavie team members were: Ken Duncan 4th, John Linaker 10th and Bill Ewing 15th. Brian Scobie won in 32-32 from Brian Carty, 33-00 and Dave Fairweather 33-10.

The following Saturday morning I set out on my Monaughty course, but got involved in the 'Snowman' car rally, which was using the forest roads. I had to keep stopping and jumping up the banking to avoid the cars, which were hurtling along, going in more or less a straight line. I eventually decided to leave my course to the rally and as I did I heard a crash. I jogged back and saw a Ford Escort upside down with bits hanging off it. I presumed that the occupants were okay, as spectators were assisting in trying to turn the car back the right way up. I took a different route out of the forest and reached tarmac near the top of the road coming from Pluscarden to Rafford. I ran back through Elgin and arrived home in 3-25-22 for my estimated 31 miles route.

On the 27th of February, I drove to Glasgow airport for my flight to the Isle of Man, which was delayed for an hour because of bad weather at Ronaldsway airfield. Dougie Corkill met me and we drove to Phil and Anne Cain's, with whom I was to stay again. After a meal we went to see the 'Laxey Wheel', a huge waterwheel originally used to pump water from an adjacent mine and then went to Douglas and the Foresters bar for two pints of Castletown bitter. We met some of the runners there including 4 Irish runners who were all attempting 50Km for the first time next morning.

A DECENT RACE IN THE DOUGLAS 50KM

The Boundary Harriers, Manx Airlines 50Km race in the Bowl Park in Douglas got underway at 10am and a few local runners set a brisk pace. I ran at a comfortable but good pace and was surprised that Jeff Norman did not come with me, being content to run about 25 metres behind. I passed 10Km in 33-42 and 20Km in 68- something, with Jeff still waiting behind. As the race progressed I felt my strength diminishing, so at 25 miles Jeff joined me and we ran through the marathon in 2-27-21. Soon after this I dropped behind Jeff to get some shelter from the slight wind on the home straight and this provoked Jeff to increase his pace. I tried to respond, but my legs were in constant velocity mode and so I lost contact with him. From then to the finish I was struggling to keep a reasonable pace going and was glad to finish. I felt rather nauseous by then, but was quite pleased with my run, which was 9-48 faster than I had managed in 1986, but 21 seconds slower than my time in 1985 when I had finished 3rd in 2-56-39, after passing the marathon in 2-27-37. So that year my time from the marathon to the finish was 29-02, while this year it was 29-39. I wondered if my Dioralite drinks strategy was successful or whether I should have combined it with Maxijoul. Jeff Norman finished in 2-55-15, while I recorded 2-57-00 ahead of Paul Bream, 3-09-40.

Again the 50Km runners were guests at the Boundary Harriers annual dinner, dance and presentations evening in the usual hotel in Douglas, which was enjoyed by all present.

Three weeks after the 50Km, on the 22nd of March in the Inverness Half Marathon, I ran quite well to finish 13th in 70-18. Simon Axon won in 65-44 from Colin Youngson, 66-29 and Frank Harper 66-37.

Two days later I was forced to consult a doctor about a boil on my back, which had been giving me a lot of discomfort for the past week. I could feel more effects of the infection – from the boil becoming progressively worse – in the lymph gland in my groin. At the surgery I saw Dr White, who cut open the boil and squeezed out the pus and wrote a prescription for antibiotics to clear the infection.

SOLO LAND'S END TO JOHN O' GROATS, 1987

I finally decided to go ahead with this project (LEJOG) for 1987 during our Easter holiday. Planning had started about a year earlier, after I had talked to several friends about the possibility. My route would be the reverse of that used by the ten-man relay team from Aberdeen Athletic Club run in 1972, a total distance of 844.17 miles. A schedule was planned, which assumed that I could cover at least 84 miles a day for ten days, which would establish a new record for this journey on foot. The Guinness Book of Records people were contacted to find what criteria were required to authenticate such a record. The record authenticated by the Guinness book of records was that established by Ken Craig of South Africa, who had completed the journey from north to south in 12 days one hour and 15 seconds in 1984. Fred Hicks had claimed that he completed the journey over an 876 miles route in 10 days three and a half hours in May 1977, but without documentary evidence.

I decided to use this run as a vehicle to raise funds for the 'Cancer Research Campaign'. John Diffey of 'Riverdale Products' volunteered to be the charity coordinator and also produced promotional materials and 'Ritchie's Run' commemorative tee shirts for sale to add to my charity income.

My team of helpers were running pals: Graham Milne, Peter Chalmers, Mick Francis and Malcolm Morgan the head of Physiotherapy at Dr Gray's Hospital.

Local sponsors were sought and Macallan-Glenlivet Whisky became a major sponsor and others were: the Arthur Duthie Organisation, Lossiemouth, McRae and Dick.

Glen Elliot and fellow Rotarians, Doug Winchester, Alex Scott and Raymond Wood, arranged that Rotary clubs near our route could arrange overnight accommodation near to the end of each day's session, as their contribution to charity.

We departed on our adventure on Saturday the 4th of April and after an overnight stop in Bridgwater arrived in Penzance on the 5th.

On Monday the 6th of April I began my run at Lands End at 07:00 with quite a lot of media interest – there being two press photographers and a TV video team.

I ran very cautiously and was soon faced with some fierce hills, but things seemed to be going OK. I finished my first day in Lifton after 12 hours and 44 minutes of running covering 83 miles.

On 'Day Two' I started running at 07:00 in heavy rain accompanied by Mick Francis. In Tiverton we lost our way, which cost us valuable time before regaining the route to Taunton and Bridgwater. I decided to stop in Bridgwater having covered 80 miles.

On 'Day Three' we set off at 06:55 and I was running comfortably, which gave me encouragement and confidence that I was adapting to this regime and that I could cope with the schedule that I had set myself.

In Bristol I observed that there was evidence of intestinal blood loss in my stool. From Monmouth I followed the A466 for Hereford and on the descent of a 1 in 8 hill I felt a sharp stab of pain in my left shin on the left side of the bone. I had to stop immediately and sat on the verge, rather stunned. I tried to jog but could not because the resulting pain was too debilitating. I was taken to our overnight stop, the Moat House in Hereford. I had completed 73 miles, about 10 miles short of my target. Malcolm did acupuncture on my left leg, which by this time was swollen with a red region around it.

On 'Day Four' I walked with Malcolm for company, to Hereford. With my left leg feeling worse, Malcolm having wrapped an elastic bandage around it to keep the swelling down. Later he strapped it to restrict movement, but I could not run. I stopped at Hope under Dinmore, having walked 23 miles since starting that morning. we decided that I should stop there for the day and go to our accommodation in the 'Lion Hotel', Shrewsbury. Malcolm suspected that I might have a stress fracture in my tibia, so after some discussion with him, I decided to abandon my attempt, which was a relief to everyone.

We went through to the 'Raffles' restaurant, which was very classy and had an excellent dinner, after which we retired to the bar for debrief and definitely put LEJOG 1987 to rest.

The following morning, we all headed home after taking the stickers off our vehicles, so this was the 'official' disbanding of the project. **Our adventure finished in failure, which must have disappointed all involved, my sponsors and my supporters, but it strengthened my resolve to try again and to succeed.**

Over a week later Malcolm examined my left leg with his fingers and came to the conclusion that I had a stress fracture over a one-centimetre length of my tibia bone. He said there was no treatment apart from rest and he advised me not to try running for 2 weeks.

On reflection, I realised that the stress fracture was probably due to my choice of running shoes. I had been using light training shoes, which would probably be classed as 'Racer-Trainers' and some well-tried comfortable racing shoes. I vowed that, on my next attempt, I would wear the most supportive and cushioned training shoes that I could source; and also run down hills very cautiously.

Despite my failure, people honoured their sponsorship pledges so that, once all the sponsorship and donations had been collected, I was able to hand over a cheque for £2400 to Mrs. Watson, of the Elgin and District branch of the Cancer Research Campaign.

I resumed running on the 27th of April and was delighted to feel no pain from my left shin.

On Saturday the 16th of May I decided to test my leg over an extra long and quite hilly road course. I started the hardest climb about two and a half hours into the run and was pleased at how I handled it. I reached home after 4-32-01, happy how I managed this run. Later I measured this route, using our car, as 36.75 miles.

A week later, on Sunday the 24th of May, I ran in the Aberdeen Milk Marathon for the Scottish team in the incorporated Home Countries International. I started cautiously and because of the wind the pace was quite restrained. A group of 4 broke away: Colin Youngson, Mick McGeoch (Wales) and two Englishmen. A lone Welshman followed, with our group of eight behind him. We reached 10 miles in a shade under 59 minutes and halfway in 1-18-06. Soon after this the course climbed at right angles to the wind and the race began in earnest. One member of our group dropped back, then it was me who could not handle the increased pace and I dropped off. From then I gradually lost ground to the group, which eventually broke up. I felt tired and weak, but it was good to see Izzy and the family at various points around the course. I finished 11th in 2-34-27, which was 2-26 better than last year. I was a little disappointed that I was not as strong as usual over the closing stages. Scotland finished 2nd team behind England. Ian Corrin of England won in 2-27-42, from Colin Youngson of Scotland, 2-29-21 and Rob Hall, also of Scotland in 2-29-54.

In the days following the marathon I had a particularly painful left calf muscle. Malcolm examined it, diagnosed a strain in the Soleus and gave me RF treatment through four electrodes. Because of that strain, I was apprehensive about the 'Passatorie' 100Km race I had agreed to participate in on Saturday the 30th of May.

DEL PASSATORIE 100KM

On Thursday the 28th of May, I travelled by train from Elgin to Inverness and from there by overnight train to Glasgow with a sleeping berth. I slept well and walked from Queen Street Rail station to Anderson Bus station, where I caught a bus to Glasgow airport. There I caught the flight to Milan via Manchester. I caught a bus into Milan and made my way to the railway station and took a train to Faenza and arrived at 19:00. At the Station I met Boris Backmaz and we walked to the town centre together. This was a change from previous years when I had gone to Firenze where the race began. I thought that I would try this option and make use of the transport provided from Faenza to the start on the morning of the race. I went to the Vittoria Hotel but they had no reservation for me but, once Walter Del Borgo arrived, he sorted things out and I got a room. Then I went for a meal with Walter, his wife Sylvie and their family.

On Saturday morning the 30th of May, I boarded the transport to Florence (Firenze), which was due to depart at 09:00. This was a lot earlier than I had anticipated and planned for, but I decided to go on the bus as many others were doing so. I met Joseph from Portugal and Boris Backmaz along with Norman Roos and his Scottish wife Irene.

The bus got underway at about 09:30 and went up to Bologna before going across and down towards Firenze, stopping for coffee at a cafe at around 10:45 on the way. We arrived in Firenze at about 12:00 and I spent about an hour watching Joseph, Boris and another Italian tuck into a hearty meal. Joseph had a couple of beers and was in good form. After this we made our way to the start area although there were still three hours before the gun and conditions were warm at 84°F. I met Walter, got my race number and then tried to get a cyclist to take my drinks and a race official arranged this for me, which was a relief. I also met Goris Oneto, who was as gregarious as ever. Time passed slowly, but eventually it was time to have my number stamped and assemble at the start. I was pleased to see that the start was strictly controlled, with marshals preventing runners sneaking down side streets and cheating by getting away earlier.

We got off at 16:00 exactly and I tried to run as easily as possible while still keeping the front of the field in sight. I felt fine on the climb out of Firenze, which lasted for about 40 minutes. Duzan had established an early lead, but I reckoned that we would catch him later. My drinking pattern was to be: Dioralite, Dioralite, Polymer in that sequence at 20 minutes intervals, plus water when available. I felt relaxed, but a pain started to develop in the sole of my left foot and a sharp cutting pain in my left Achilles, like a stone had lodged between my shoe and ankle. I stopped to investigate, but found nothing. My left calf muscle appeared to be all right, which pleased me. After about one and a half hours we began to drop down into the next valley and I held back to minimize the damage to my right heel.

A group of about 6 gradually moved away as I fiddled around in the second group of four, trying to conserve energy until the mountains. By about 32Km I decided to increase my pace and go after the group, who were now several minutes ahead. On leaving Borgo San Lorenz I was catching Duzan and passed them soon after. I was surprised at not being able to see anyone else going up the mountain to the pass. I moved into 3rd place just over the top of the pass. I could not see the first two ahead, but then I caught sight of the second on a road below. However, I was not running strongly and I never caught sight of him again. I pushed on, but my strength was on the wane and by 70Km I was desperately tired and had to walk for some time. I had some hot lemon tea and a wafer biscuit at a feeding station, which helped me to feel a bit better. From there to the finish I ran as best I could, but could not respond as several runners came past in ones and twos. Eventually I reached the sign for 1.5Km to the end and **was very relieved to finish this race. I was rather disappointed with the way that I faded, but this could be due to several factors: the Aberdeen marathon the previous Sunday or the results of my efforts in the LEJOG, plus 3 weeks off due to the stress fracture. Anyway I would have to take it easy until the Belgium 100Km race.** I wore my Nike 'Spiridon Gold' shoes. Jean Marc Bellocq of France won in 6-52-44, from Rossetti also from France, 7-04-00 and Mocnik from Yugoslavia in 7-20-08, while I was 8th in 7-47-00.

I did the reverse journey back to Elgin and arrived there at 05:45 on Tuesday the 2nd of June, having travelled by overnight train from Glasgow to Inverness.

Two weeks after the Passatorie, in the Forres Harriers 8 miles road race, Donald Gunn won in 40-10 from Tim Jones. I lacked strength and faded to finish 10th. After the race I ran 16 miles home so this, along with the race, was to be my glycogen depletion run. I would then start the low carbohydrate phase of the 'diet' as a prelude to carbohydrate loading, to see if this would help improve my stamina in the coming Friday evening's 100Km in Torhout in Belgium.

Next Thursday the 18th of June, I travelled to Brussels and on to Torhout where, after registering for the race, I was taken to stay with my host family, Wilfried and Rita Vierstraete and their children Jurgen and Nathalie.

In the morning, I had a light breakfast of bread and jam at my hosts' and then at mid-day had a few potatoes and sliced tomatoes. So after a restful day I assembled for the 20:00 start of the 'Night of Flanders' 100Km in Torhout. Prospects looked grim, since rain was pouring down as I left my clothes for after the race in the place for baggage, walked down to the start with Frank Thomas, and then we worked our way near the front of the start line. The start was in a narrow street with a small grandstand on the right side and throngs of people on each side. A TV film crew was there and there was a commentary, with various well-known runners being introduced to the public.

WORLD CHALLENGE 'SILVER' IN THE TORHOUT 100KM

Eventually the waiting was over and we were off on **the first edition of the International Association of Ultrarunners (IAU) 'World Challenge' under the patronage of the IAAF**. The front rank moved through the narrow streets of Torhout at a brisk pace, so I hung back rather than go with the leaders as I felt that I was running fast enough. Domingo Catalan was not in this leading group of about 8, so I was quite content being 80 metres adrift. 10Km was passed and after this there was a slight climb before heading back into Torhout and passing the 15Km marker near the starting point. Domingo Catalan came up to me shortly after this, and we ran together, gradually pulling back the leading group. We came to a dirt road with many large puddles, so I was very cautious on this stretch, weaving to avoid the puddles incase I got grit into my shoes from splashing through them. As a consequence of this I lost ground and passed 20Km in 9th place in 1-10-27, but when we reached the tarred road again I began to close on the leaders once more. I caught Charlie Trayer and Barney Klecker of the USA, who were running with Stefan Feckner of Canada. I decided to run with them rather than go after Catalan, who was about 20 metres ahead with Jean Paul Praet and someone else about another 15 metres ahead of them.

The checkpoints and refreshment stations were inside sports halls, which we had to run through, and this was quite an experience with all the lights, TV cameras, food, music and lots of cheering people. At one of these at 28Km our personal cyclists were to join us, so I was looking forward to getting my drinks. A posse of cyclists joined me as I had pulled away from my group, but I was dismayed to find that none had my drinks. The cyclist who identified himself to me could not speak English and could not understand very well my requests and did not appear to have my drinks. I let the others catch up as I was feeling a bit dispirited although I was running OK and I had been taking the occasional drink of water or 'Ergovise'. Charlie and I were moving away from Klecker and Feckner as we approached Middelkerke. There I saw Dirk Strummane and bawled at him 'Where are my special drinks, Dirk?' Shortly after this we reached the seafront, where I could hear the sound of bagpipes, which gave me a boost and soon passed two pipers.

I passed 50Km in 3-04-16, which was pleasing, as was the fact that my special drinks turned up in the possession of my grinning cyclist. I pulled away from Charlie, but he caught me again before 60Km, which we passed together in 3-44-42. I moved away from Charlie again and reached 70Km in 4-25-17 to Charlie's 4-27-08. We were now 2nd and 3rd behind Catalan as Praet had retired. The rain had never stopped, but it became torrential and now it was just a question of holding on to the finish, which I eventually managed. My time of 6-40-51 was a disappointment for me, but I was pleased to be 2nd. Later I found out that 760 metres had been added to make sure the course, measured by a surveyor's wheel was at least 100Km. I wondered how long last year's 'super fast' course had been. I had to go for dope testing on finishing and had to sit around in wet kit for some time. After I found that my post race bag was not where it should have been. I discovered that it had been taken around the course with the bags of those likely to stop at 50Km, so it was some time before I could get changed into more appropriate clothes. Domingo Catalan of Spain won in an excellent 6-19-35 and Roland Vuillemenot of France was 3rd in 6-43-22, while the winner of the Passatorie two weeks earlier, Jean Marc Bellocq, was 4th in 6-47-13.

I made my way back to Wilfried and Rita's home, went to bed and slept well for a few hours. Later that day at 16:00 the awards ceremony was held in the sports hall and was very well organised with live music and live trumpeters to do the fanfares. The first ten in the men's race received prizes and we were all on the stage together. Although I was also **First Veteran** there was no mention of this.

After travelling back home on Sunday I was pleased to be able to resume running to work on Monday morning with no problems from the 100Km race. On Sunday I ran in the Buckie half marathon on a warm day (73°F) and after a cautious start at three miles I was in joint 6th place and running with George Sim. I increased my pace to drop him, but made only a small impression on the lads in front, yet I was quite pleased to finish 7th in 73-38. Simon Axon won in 69-39, from Charlie McIntyre, 70-25, with Alan Reid 3rd in 71-53.

The following Saturday, the 4th of July, I drove Izzy and our family up to Dornoch for the half marathon and 2 miles fun run. I ran at a steady comfortable pace in the 2nd group. Then I moved through the field with Ian Gollan and by 4 miles we came to a steep climb on the course, followed by undulations. These, combined with a brisk headwind, made it an interesting and a particularly enjoyable race for me. I began to lose ground to Ian Gollan after 11 miles and I had to work hard, to finish 5th in 76-24 and stay ahead of Mick Francis by 4 seconds. Simon Axon won again in 75-17, with Willie Miller second in 75-42 and John Mackay third in 76-05.

On Friday 11th of July, I developed a rather painful index finger on the right hand, which had become swollen as had the back of the hand. Fortunately, I got a consultation with Dr White, who diagnosed some form of infection and prescribed the antibiotic flucloxacillin. He also wanted me to keep my hand in an elevated position for forty-eight hours; otherwise, he said, 'the consequent pus formation could destroy your hand'. I thought that this was a bit of an over-reaction, but decided to follow his advice, which also included no running so I missed the Forres Highland Games road race. I was able to resume running on Monday as my 48-hour curfew had expired.

By the following Friday I felt quite a wreck and my condition deteriorated, with my temperature reaching 101.8°F. I had developed some sort of flu and felt unwell all next day, with hot and cold in cycles, which persisted through Sunday. By the middle of the following week I was more or less back to normal and running again. On Friday the 31st of July, Izzy and I drove to Dornoch and checked into the 'Dornoch Hotel' for a night to use my prize from the Dornoch half-marathon.

On Sunday, the 2nd of August, in the Grantown-On-Spey half marathon, I was surprised to finish 2nd to Alan Reid, who recorded 73-something. My time of 76-31 was 38 seconds slower than the previous year, probably due to the wind.

Next Sunday the 9th of August, in the Macallan Moray Marathon, my start was very cautious and the first mile was a shade under six minutes. I increased my pace and ran up Spynie Brae quite strongly and opened a gap. Mick Francis and a chap from Fife AC caught me after this hill and I slowed to run with them to try to get some shelter from the wind. However, the pace was too slow, so I pushed on and felt that I was running well and the slight headwind on the stretch to Burghead was not too troublesome. The 10 miles timing point appeared to be at the incorrect place as I was given 58-something. I passed 20 miles in 1-55-17, feeling OK, but I could feel the usual blister developing on my right heel. I was satisfied with my run, but my winning time was a little poor at 2-31-50. Mick Francis, also of Forres Harriers, was 2nd in 2-39-27 and Jim Carruth, Kilbarchan, was 3rd in 2-39-30. Forres Harriers won the team race. Izzy gave me drinks at: 5, 9, 13, 16, 20 and 23 miles and my niece Sarah McKenzie collected the empty bottles. I alternated 200ml of 'Dioralite' with 200m of 'XL1'.

The following day we drove to the Normandy Hotel at Glasgow Airport, where we stayed overnight, prior to catching our 07:00 flight to Reus in Spain for our two-week summer holiday. On arrival there we found out that we were destined for the Hotel Calypso in Salou. Each morning I would run between 4 and 6 miles, sometimes to Pineda and back.

When it was time to return to Glasgow the Spanish Air Traffic Controllers were on strike, so we had to be transported by coach to an airport in France to get a flight back. We duly arrived back home at 04:00 on Sunday. Later that morning I was pleasantly surprised to complete my 22 miles 'Boar's Head' route in 2-19-22, which was a 6 second improvement on my previous best, which encouraged me. On Monday I returned to work and resumed my running to and from College.

HARD WORK IN THE TWO BRIDGES

On Saturday the 29th of August I drove to Rosyth and arrived there at about 9am. After registering and handing in my drinks I met Mick Francis and Jim McDowell, my Forres Harriers teammates. This was the first time that the Harriers had managed to raise a team for the 'Two Bridges'.

I got off to a good start, accompanied by American, Charlie Trayer and Mick McHale. We passed 5 miles in 27-43, 10 miles in 56-10 and 15 miles in 1-25 18. I felt fine and, on leaving Grangemouth, Charlie and I were on our own. However, soon after this I became aware of losing my strength, but was able to keep up with Charlie and we passed 20 miles in 1-55-03. I found it increasingly difficult to stay with him, so I had to ease back in Bo'ness and, on the steep hill at about 21 miles, I lost a great deal of ground as I shuffled up. The marathon point was reached in 2-34-33, which was about 2 minutes slower than last year. I had no strength, both legs hurt and I had the occasional twinge of cramp in my calves and quads. It was a question of survival then and I tottered on, passing 30 miles in 2-59-55, before going over the Forth Road Bridge. Soon after 35 miles a young Tipton runner, who I later learned was Billy Evans, breezed past. I tried to increase my pace, which I managed to a certain extent, but not enough to prevent him pulling away. I was extremely pleased to get to the finish; racing is so much harder when you are running poorly.

I was quite disappointed with my sub-par performance, as I was rather optimistic about having a good run, but I expect my 11 days of easy jogging, when on holiday for 2 weeks, were not great preparation for this race. My time was 4-42 slower than last year and 12-45 slower than my best in 1977. Driving down on the morning of the race was probably also detrimental to my performance. I had drinks at: 7, 12, 18, 21, 26, 29 and 32.5 miles, alternating 200ml of XL1 and 200ml of Maxijoul. Charlie won in 3-36-27 from Billy Evans, 3-40-53 and I was 3rd in 3-41-19. There were 95 finishers.

SANTANDER 100KM: DIFFICULT BUT SATISFACTORY

On Thursday the 1st of October, the day after beginning my carbohydrate loading, I woke with a painful throat, which was a worry. Friday was taken up with travelling to Santander. Izzy gave me a lift to Elgin train station, where I caught the 06:50 train to Aberdeen and got off at Dyce station and took a taxi from there to the airport. I took the 11:05 flight to London and then the 15:30 flight to Bilbao, where I arrived at 17:10. I was rather disturbed to find that there was no one there to meet me and take me to Santander as arranged. I waited until 18:30 before deciding that I had been forgotten and caught a taxi to the rail station in Bilbao, but the traffic was very heavy, so by the time that we got there my driver was dubious about there being a train, and he thoughtfully pointed out the auto bus station. I paid my fare and entered the train station and consulted the timetable board, to find that there was a train to Santander at 19:00. I glanced at my watch; it was 19:02, I raced up the steps to see if the train was still there. A small train, with its door still open, was at a platform, I rushed along asking a guard on the way if this was the train for Santander and he confirmed that it was and I jumped aboard. No seats were available so I had to stand for the greater part of the 3-hour journey to Santander. I had a headache and my cold was no better. On arrival I got a taxi to the 'Rseidencia Tempe Leibra', arriving there at about 22:00, too late to get a meal. Mick Francis and Donald Gunn met me there and I had some of their bread before phoning Soto Rojas to inform him of my arrival, and also telephoned Izzy to let her know that I had arrived in one piece. Hemma, who was supposed to meet me at Bilbao, phoned me to tell me that she had mistaken 17:10 for ten past seven and had been at the airport at that time. I got to bed, rather tired, at 23:20.

I had set my watch alarm for 05:30, but woke before this after a rather restless night, punctuated with a couple of bad dreams. Heavy rain was falling outside with the occasional crack of thunder. I got my kit on and went next door to see Mick and Donald and then we went down to reception to meet our transport to the start at 06:00.

After 2 minutes silence for a woman who had died during the year, and who had some strong association with the race, we got underway at 07:00 in less heavy rain. I found the start surprisingly slow, so I found myself in the lead after 200 metres, but a big group came up and we ran together for a while. I then went ahead with 2 others following me and after the small loop I was joint 2nd but only about 100 metres ahead of Domingo Catalan and a group of about 6. They caught me at about 22Km and we ran together for a while before Domingo and I began to pull away and passed the marathon together in 2-46-00, 4-04 slower than last year. By then the weather had changed to strong sunshine, a brisk wind and low humidity. We ran on together and on the climb into Santander I lost ground and also collided with a careless pedestrian, which brought me to a halt. Catalan was then 25 metres ahead and I thought that the race was over, but I was surprised that I was able to catch him and we ran through the finish area to begin the last 40Km lap together.

I began to gain confidence and went ahead, but soon tired and drifted back to him. Yet at about 65Km I went ahead and opened a gap of about 100 metres and maintained this for some time. Domingo came back up to me at around 75Km and then got away from me on a hill, as I could not move any faster. This occurred at a bad point on the course as we were climbing around the mountain and it was exposed to the winds. I pushed on through 80Km, then around 84Km my right small toe became exceedingly painful and I almost stopped to investigate it. However, I pushed on and the pain faded and I was able to concentrate on the race again. My cyclist, the same chap as last year, was very attentive so I had no trouble with obtaining my drinks or sponges. I drank 1.5 litres of 10% 'Maxijoul' solution and 1.5 litres of 'Dioralite', alternating 200ml of every 20 minutes. I was in good condition apart from my lack of strength and I was not hurting.

The remainder of the race passed quite quickly and I finished in 6-43-58, which was 3-51 faster than last year. I was 7-22 behind Catalan, compared to 15-40 behind him the previous year and 21-16 behind at Torhout, so I was fairly pleased with my run. Domingo Catalan, who would be a Vet next year, recorded 6-36-32 in winning and Ramon Alvarez Saniz was 3rd in 7-12-36. Mick finished in good condition finishing 28th in his first 100Km with 8-53-56 and Donald, also in his first 100Km finished 44th in 9-47-14, in good condition as well. Eleanor Adams was first lady in 14th with 8-04-48, which was a new British record. Following this race my 'Europa Cup' points total was now 572 points.

On Sunday I travelled back from Santander, to Bilbao, London and Aberdeen and, as I had met Ronnie Maughan at Heathrow, we were able to have a chat on the way up. He gave me a lift to the rail station in Aberdeen in his new car. Izzy met me at Elgin Station at 21:35 and drove me home. It was good to be back.

THE LONGEST RACE OF MY LIFE

Twelve days after the Santander 100Km on Thursday the 14th of October I began fuelling up for the race on Saturday: the 4th edition of the **'Super Maratona dei Nuraghi' a 254Km race from Cagliari to Sassari.** There was a threatened strike by Italian Air Traffic Controllers starting on Friday, but I had to take the chance that I would get to Cagliari. Izzy and I drove through to Inverness and had dinner at Izzy's Mum's. Claire was to stay 3 nights at Grandma's, so after Izzy and family had departed and arrived home safely, I walked across to the rail station and caught the 11:40 sleeper train to Glasgow.

From Glasgow Queen Street Station on Friday morning, I walked over to Anderson bus station and caught a bus to Glasgow airport. I caught the 'Poundstretcher' flight at 08:50 to Milan via Manchester. The flight from Milan to Cagliari was delayed, but on arrival there a representative of the race met me, and he took 'Ojeyé (the architect from Switzerland, who was on the same flight) and me to the 'Hotel Mediterraneo'. After checking in I had to go for a medical examination and then attended a meeting with other participants to learn how the race would be conducted. Race numbers and 'goodie bags' were given out and after this we had dinner. I managed to telephone Izzy before going to bed at around 22:00 and as the bedroom was air-conditioned this helped me sleep.

I woke at my normal time of 06:30 after a fitful sleep and, after preparing myself, went down to reception area around 2 hours later and had some self-service breakfast. I had a plate of muesli, two portions of fresh fruit salad and some bread. My driver came to collect me from the hotel at 09:15 and drove me to the start in quite warm weather. Apart from the 30 runners in the 'Supermarathon' there were quite a lot of runners preparing for a 14Km race, including about 10 from the RAF on detachment to the NATO force in Sardinia.

We got underway at 10:00 and I tried to run as gently as possible. I had decided to wear my Nike 'Air Sock' racers, hoping that they would afford my legs maximum protection. The weather was hot as I ran along with Maximilian Klemencic from Yugoslavia. However, after about one and a half hours my right foot, small toe and the bones around that area were becoming rather painful, so I decided to stop and put on my 'Spiridon Gold' shoes. Initially these seemed fine, but soon the pain returned and became almost unbearable and extended into my calf muscle. I decided to increase my pace a little to see if this would help dull the pain. Eventually the pain diminished; I expect the endorphins were doing their job.

I began moving through the field and some time later I found out that I was 3rd. Later I passed the 2nd placer, who was walking and I thought it odd that he should be doing this after only 6 hours, but perhaps it was part of his plan. By then I was feeling fine and I decided to push on and try to enjoy the 'adventure'. I was alternating drinks of Dioralite and Maxijoul at 10% concentration every 20 minutes, provided by my accompanying team of 2 in the car. I could see one runner in the straight ahead and I recognized Duzan Mravlje, who was also walking stretches. I sailed past him into the lead, for better or worse. A local runner joined me so that his wife could take a couple of photos, but he got carried away and ran with me for over an hour, during which time I passed 100Km.

At around 18:00 the sun began to go down, the temperature began to fall from the 26°C it had been earlier in the day, and soon it was dark and quite pleasant with a clear starry sky. The hours were slipping by and at around 11 hours I began a long climb up to Cuglieri at an altitude of 479 metres. There was a large crowd assembled there and I felt good as I passed 151Km with a lead, I was informed, of 35 minutes. I estimated that if I could cover the next 100Km in 10 hours, I should finish in 22 hours, but I had no idea how I would cope with the remaining distance. I had previously managed 136 miles in 24 hours, but with a few hours off. This time I planned to continue for the full 24 hours and longer if necessary.

After passing through Cuglieri the course wound down towards sea level at Bosa at 174Km and this was followed by another climb of 400 metres to Monte Mannu at 190Km On the next section I was caught, after leading for 12 hours, and was surprised that it was not Duzan who passed, but someone wearing a Kosice vest, who I later found was Milan Furin. He was going a bit faster than me and, although we were running downhill, I could not increase my pace, as I was very weary. As I approached Alghero dawn was breaking and soon it was daylight again. I needed a bowel movement and the resulting black mucus indicated that I had been bleeding into my intestines. I became a bit dispirited in Alghero when I saw a sign indicating 34Km to Sassari. Duzan came past me as I walked for a stretch – he was also walking, faster than me – but soon began running again once he had finished eating a croissant. I jogged, but my stride length was rather short and I felt completely drained. My supply of 'Maxijoul' had been finished some hours ago and I was taking Dioralite, so perhaps this was part of the reason for my low energy state. However, it might have been due to the waste products in my muscles. I did eat 3 pears and some biscuits earlier, which should have helped provide energy.

By then the sun was shining brightly as I continued my walking and jogging and another Yugoslavian runner passed me as I was having another bowel movement and he gradually disappeared into the distance. Then I suffered a nosebleed, which was a nuisance, and the race doctor drove alongside to enquire if I wanted to retire. He also asked if I had provoked my nosebleed, which I took to mean was I picking it, rather than provoking it by running 200 plus Km, so I just said no and kept shuffling along. With 24 hours elapsed I had 9Km to the finish, so I estimate that I covered 152 miles in this period. Boris Backmaz passed me also using a style of running about 20 strides and then walking five. This seemed quite effective, as I could not keep pace with him when I was jogging.

The last Kilometers passed slowly and I had difficulty keeping a straight course, but eventually I reached Sassari, where I had to follow course markers to the finish, which was in a stadium. I longed to be finished and, on turning one corner, I could see the entrance to the stadium. I ran with all the eagerness that I could muster to it and shambled around the track to finish the longest race of my life. I wanted to lie down there and then, the doctor organised a stretcher and I was transported into a cool building where I was l given a medical check. I lay on a bench in the changing room for some time feeling quite good mentally and with not too many physical pains but exhausted. The wife of one of the Yugoslavian runners started my recovery by getting me to drink a couple of bottles of Peroin beer before eating some of the food provided.

Because of this rest and food, I felt a good deal better, and after receiving prize money and saying goodbye to Giors Oneto and Maria Pia I was driven to Olbia, where my Hotel was paid for in advance, as was the taxi to take me to the airport next day. I was pleased to have completed this race and the prize of 1,600,000 Lira (£723.63), was a good bonus.

Results: 1) Milan Furin (Czech) 23-59-11, 2) Dusan Mravlje (Youg) 24-44-31,
    3) Franc Kaucic (Youg) 24-46-56, 4) Boris Backmaz (Italy) 25-19-56,
    5) Donald Ritchie (Sco) 25-28-51, 6) M Klemencic (Youg) 27-39-16,
    7) S Lazlo (Hun) 2-02-09, 8) I Sipos (Hun) 28-05-18,
    9) E Do Loi (Italy) 29-37-35. 10) P Mocnik (Youg) 29-51-35,
    11) C Sterpin (Italy) 30-05-10, 12) S Satta (Italy) 30-29-52,
    13) G F Toschi 30-44-06, 14) F Vanacore (Italy) 32-11-07,
    15) M Krivda (Czech)

This long race bumped my mileage up to 200 miles for the week.

The following day, Monday, 19th of October, I was travelling back from Albia to Milan, to Manchester, to Glasgow and on to Aberdeen, where Izzy met me at 22:10. It was good to see her and be back home.

After 2 easy weeks I decided to run in the Black Isle Marathon on the 31st of October. Although I got excited in the normal way for this race, as soon as we got underway I was conscious of feeling it difficult to run at the modest pace of the leaders. Charlie Noble increased the pace and a Shettleston runner and then Mick Francis followed him. This left a group of 6 of us and one of the group commented that I must have had a 'long one' last week, to which I replied '2 weeks ago' but did not elaborate.

I was determined to do my best and tried to run a bit faster. On any uphill gradient I found the group surging past me and had to make more effort to keep in touch as the group pulled back Mick and John Duffy of Shettleston. On a long straight I managed to increase my tempo and reduced the group to Charlie McIntyre, John Duffy and me, with Charlie Noble about 40 yards ahead. Approaching 9 miles, Duffy made a move and said later that he got fed up waiting for someone to pick up the pace. I was soon struggling and passed 10 miles with Charlie McIntyre in 57 minutes and tried to shelter behind Charlie as the course turned into the wind, but he slowed to a walk and beckoned me to lead. I thought that I might as well try to keep the pace respectable as Charlie Noble and Duffy were pulling away.

Approaching Jemimaville two runners caught us and McIntyre fell behind as I tried to go with them. They pulled away easily and I observed that one was from Dundee Hawkhill Harriers (DHH) but did not recognize the other vest. As we neared Cromarty I could still see Duffy, the DHH man and his companion and Charlie Noble about 40 metres ahead of me. On the hill out of Cromarty I gradually pulled Charlie back and then had a rest behind him, before pushing on again with 7 miles remaining.

I had pain in my left quads, but it was not too bad – my problem was lack of strength. Obviously I had not recovered from the race in Sardinia, as I had struggled with training in the 2 weeks since then. The remaining miles passed quite quickly and the one-mile to go marker was soon reached and I finished 4th and 1st Vet in 2-42-31, which was my slowest marathon for many years, but I was pleased to have finished. Rod Bell (DHH) won in 2-35-18, from John Duffy (Shet) 2-36-07, with David Murray (Falkirk) 3rd in 2-36-28.

On Monday on the 16th of November I felt a lot stronger than in recent weeks, so it looked like **it had taken me 5 weeks to recover from the Cagliari to Sassari race**. Because of this I felt able to reintroduce my Saturday 'Hills' session. My hill effort session was surprisingly hard but satisfactory with my long hill times of: 2-14, 2-13, 2-15, 2-13, 2-14 and 2-15. On the School Brae sessions my times were: 1-34, 1-33, 1-35, 1-33, 1-35 and 1-37. The idea behind these was to prepare me for some cross-country races.

The first of these was on Saturday, 28th of November, at Fairbairn House near Muir of Ord for the North District Cross-Country championships. The course, a Ray Williby special, was horrendous and totally unsuitable for a championship event, becoming very narrow after only 100 metres, followed by a twisty up and down path, before opening out into a boggy track. After crossing the river there was a hands and knees climb, then a stretch of forest track, followed by another hands and knees climb over the ridge onto another track, which we ran down almost to the bottom of the hill, before cutting across and climbing back over the ridge. Another track was picked up and this took us back towards the House, but led to a one in two descent by the side of a barbed wire fence to the flat again. I lost a lot of ground on this section. From the short section of flattish ground, we encountered another 'walking' hill before dropping down to the start/finish by another dangerous descent.

On the 2nd of the required 2 laps I ran into some concealed wire while overtaking Peter Scott on a stony section and crashed down, cutting both knees, left thigh and my hands. I lay there spread-eagled, debating whether or not to continue. As nothing was broken I decided to jog on, but with little enthusiasm. John Diffey came past me near the end and I did not know my finish position, but I think that I was 5th Vet. My time for this 7 miles course was over an hour!

Having recovered from my cuts and bruises I finished racing for the year on the 12th of December, with the traditional end-of-year Forres Harriers Christmas cross-country handicap. I ran rather poorly, being very weak on the hills, and lost ground on each climb, but on the flat I was running satisfactorily. I finished the end of the College term with flu, which laid me low for several days. I learned from Frank-N Dietzel that I had won the 1987 '100Km Europa-Cup Competition', but he did not know how the points were worked out for the 'Cup'.

On checking my total training and racing miles in 1987 I found that they amounted to 5650 miles, which was an average of 108.65 miles per week.

1988

My racing in 1988 began with the North District cross-country league races in Elgin on the 9th of January and at Aden Country Park near Mintlaw. I finished 17th and 13th respectively in these events. I resumed the 'Hills' effort sessions on the 23rd of January, with a view to improving my cross-country performances.

On Sunday the 7th of February, I drove to Aberdeen and found the A96 was not good between Fochabers and near Pitcaple because of snow and ice. However, I arrived in Aberdeen at 9am and met the rest of the Aberdeen AAC Veterans team at Marischal College quadrangle. We had an uneventful drive to Clydebank, where the Scottish Veterans Cross-Country Championship was to be held at

Dalmuir golf course. I jogged around the course with Colin Youngson and found it to be quite testing, with several stiff hills, some 360 degrees turns and side slopes.

Five minutes before the start the rain became sleet and then wet snow. We got underway and I positioned myself behind Roddy MacFarquhar, but after about half a lap I was being too cautious and sheltering behind another runner so we lost contact. I was not generating enough heat and, being under-dressed for the conditions, felt very cold and began to seize up and drift back through the field. The course became very slippery and I lost time picking my way around. Eventually I finished a shivering and disgusted 34th. Colin Youngson won and Graham Milne was 3rd, while Mel Edwards had an outstanding run to finish 7th and first over 45. Roddy was 10th (2nd M45), John Gallon 26th, I was 34th, Jim Morrison 46th (but 2nd M50) – and we won the team race!

Two weeks after my Scottish Vets debacle I ran in the final North district cross-country league race at Inverness and had a good run finishing 5th. This was somewhat surprising, as I did not ease off training for it, so it was a good confidence booster.

On Friday, the 26 of February, I drove to Glasgow airport and arrived safely after a journey of 198 miles. From there I caught the flight to the Isle of Man, where Tony Varley met me at Ronaldsway. We waited for Dave Kelly, who arrived on the flight from Blackpool, and then Tony drove me to Phil and Ann Cain's home where I had a relaxing afternoon and evening.

ISLE OF MAN 50KM

In the 'Manx Airlines' Boundary Harrier's 50Km race, next morning in the 'Bowl' (King George V Park) in Douglas, the starting pace was cautious. As soon as Jeff Norman began to increase the pace I felt it hard and had to let him go. It was not an excessively fast pace, but I felt breathless and uncomfortable. I ran with Dave Kelly but he dropped me after some time. However, the 25 metres gap was not increased so I caught him again and we passed half way in 1-29-50. I pulled away from him as he began to experience problems. Jeff lapped me with 18 laps remaining, but I could not pick up my pace to go with him. I did not have a particularly good run, passing the marathon in 2-32-54, 30 miles in 2-56-57 and finishing in 3-02-47, which was 5-47 slower than last year. I was a little disappointed with my performance; I lacked vigour and strength. Jeff finished in 2-58-27 and Graham Youngson was 3rd in 3-18-10. Once again, in the evening we were guests at the Boundary Harriers Annual Dinner and Awards event, which was enjoyed by all present. The following morning, I caught the 09:45 flight to Glasgow and drove home through strong winds and snow showers.

On Sunday the 13th of March I ran for AAAC in the British Veterans cross-country championships at Irvine. I got off to a good start and felt OK, but after about a mile I began to develop oxygen debt and had to let Roddy MacFarquhar go – we were in the mid-20s at that time. Soon after this I began to feel quite drained and my heartbeat became irregular, a sort of fluttering, as I tried to keep my pace going. Many runners passed me and on the first climb up from the beach, Mel Edwards overtook me. I managed to hang on to him and then gradually got away again as I recovered. Eventually, after the prescribed laps, I reached the run-in to the finish and passed 2, who then re-passed me. I was quite exhausted and felt nauseous and it was quite some time since I had felt that bad after a cross-country race. I was 42nd in 34-47 and Mel was 46th. Our teammate Colin Youngson ran extremely well to finish 2nd, 24 seconds behind the winner, Alun Roper (Wales), while Graham Milne was 11th and Roddy in 21st also ran well. AAAC received team bronze medals.

In the Inverness half marathon on the 20th of March, the field of 796 starters was not as strong as in previous years and I settled onto the back of the 2nd group. I moved through as the group split up and by 2 miles there were 6 in our group in joint 6th place. Steve Cassells caught me at 9 miles and I ran with him through 10 miles in 54-25 and we gradually pulled back Graham Milne, but not quickly enough. We caught and passed Charlie McIntyre and I tried to drop Steve over the last mile, but I could not shake him off and he out-sprinted me. My time was 1-11 slower than last year. Chris

Hall won in 66-10 from Alastair Walker, 66-31 and Graham Laing, 68-54. Graham Mine was 6th and first Vet in 71-20, while Steve Cassells was 7th in 71-26 and I was 8th in 71-29 and 2nd Vet. Izzy and Claire ran in the 4 miles fun run. My stomach was upset after the event.

SILVER AGAIN IN THE SCOTTISH MARATHON AT LOCHABER

My next race was on Sunday the 24th of April, when Jim McDowell picked me up at 07:50 and drove to Fort William for the Lochaber marathon, which that year also incorporated the Scottish championships and the Scottish Veterans championships. Colin Youngson, the previous year's winner, was not participating as he had run in the Boston Marathon. Allan Adams was injured, as was Brian Carty, so this left Colin Martin as my main threat. We set off quite slowly and a group of 6 had formed by the time that we left Fort William and this reduced to 5 by Banavie. I decided to wait rather than push the pace and when I did increase the pace at 9 miles no one dropped. I had to stop at the next drinks station to retrieve my personal drink, which was a nuisance as I lost about 25 yards. However, I made this up and used my increased pace to reduce our group to 3 by the turn. There was a slight breeze against us on the return journey, so I sat in with our group, but on reflection I should have increased my pace in an effort to break Colin.

At around 18 miles I managed to drop Bill McNeill of Pitreavie but Colin was still there. I tried again at Corpach to get away, but did not succeed, so we ran together to Fort William. With about 700 yards remaining, just after crossing the River Lochy, Colin increased his pace and I tried to respond, but could not and the race was over. I felt quite strong, but lacked speed and so received another SAAA 'silver' medal. Colin Martin's winning time was 2-30-09, while I finished in 2-30-26 and Bill McNeill recorded 2-36-39 in 3rd. Apparently in Scottish Marathon Championships only Donald Macgregor (1965-1986) and I (1967-1988) had won medals 21 years apart!

About two weeks later I had haemoglobin in my urine during and after runs to and from work, and next day I experienced a burning sensation when urinating. Dr Pleasant tested my sample and she confirmed that it contained haemoglobin and protein. She diagnosed a urinary infection and prescribed the antibiotic, 'Septrin' to clear this.

On Sunday the 22nd of May in the Aberdeen Milk Marathon, which incorporated the Home Countries International event, Frank Harper shot off and I tucked in at the back of the chasing group. I found the pace a bit ambitious, so I drifted back, was joined by a Welsh team member and we ran up King Street together. My Welsh companion and I ran through the start/finish area and then I decided to push on, as there was a tailwind along the Prom. I could see two of the English team ahead and by 18 miles I had passed one and the other by about 19.5 miles, but I was now slowing down, while the Welsh runner was powering away. I passed 20 miles in 1-52, and caught sight of Colin Youngson as he was crossing Persley Bridge. The climb up from this was stiff and we then faced a headwind from there to the finish. I could not make any impression on the group ahead, the Welsh runner having caught one of his teammates and Colin. I battled on and finished 11th in 2-29-50, which was quite satisfying, not far behind Colin (2.28.38), who was first Vet in 10th. Forres Harriers were 3rd team as, in addition to my 11th place, Mick Francis was 15th and Jim McDowell 58th. I wore my Nike 'Spiridon Gold' shoes, which were fine apart from pain in my left foot at the front of the sole. This was my glycogen depletion run, so I would be on a low carbohydrate diet until next Wednesday at midday. Hammy Cox of the Scottish team won in 2-21-15, from teammate, Frank Harper, 2-22-20 and Alan Robson of Edinburgh Southern Harriers (ESH) in 2-25-03. With Doug Cowie, 5th in 2-26-21 and Colin Youngson 10th, Scotland won the International Team award, from Wales and England.

DEL PASSATORIE AGAIN: FIRST VETERAN

On the following Thursday night, the 26th of May, I caught a train from Elgin to Inverness and from there, an overnight sleeper to London. I spent next morning in Kensington visiting the Science

Museum before travelling to Gatwick to catch a flight to Linate airport in Milan. As the flight had been delayed an hour I was anxious to catch the first available train to Firenze, so I took a taxi to the Railway station. This proved to be rather expensive at 24,000 liras. The first available train to Firenze was at 19:33, which got me there at 22:30. Giors Oneto met me at the station and took me to his home where Mira Pia cooked me some spaghetti. He then escorted me to the 'Prima Via Hotel', where he had booked me in.

I slept well and actually fell asleep again until 11:00 next morning the 28th of May. Following this I bought 4 litres of water and made up my Leppin 'Enduro Boost' mixture. Oneto picked up my race numbers and I went around to his house for a few hours. Ojey, from Switzerland, was there and they had lunch, but I abstained. We got ready and made our way to the start at about 15:00 and I managed to locate Mr. Calderoni and to make contact with the cyclist, who was rather perturbed when I presented him with my 4 litres of drinks. However, after some mutterings and assistance from me he succeeded in fitting them onto his bike. This done, I thanked him, and got into the starting area to drink 200ml of Enduro Boost. I wanted to 'spend a penny' (urinate), but there was nowhere that I could decently go, so I managed a little in the huddle of runners.

The 'Del Passatorie' 101.5Km race got underway at 16:00 and the initial pace was quite swift. Weather conditions were good with rain earlier in the day and only hazy sunshine, with the temperature about 23°C. The climb out of Firenze went well and I ran with Jean Marc Bellocq up to Fiesole, where the first refreshment station was. Soon after this the course levelled out and I caught sight of my cyclist, which was quite a relief, as I intended to drink 200ml every 20 minutes. Approaching Borgo San Lorenz a runner came past and the group began to split up. I pushed on in pursuit of this runner, who I later found to be Di Gennaro, and caught him on the climb out of Borgo. I felt quite strong and ran on alone but, soon after beginning the climb to the Passo Della Colla, Di Gennaro came past with his running companion and I objected to this non-official runner. They were going a bit too hard for me on this climb so I relaxed, as I had to run my own race. Jean Marc came up next and encouraged me to go with him, 'come wiz me'. I tried for a little while, but I decided that the effort was too great and I let him go. He soon caught Di Gennaro and they ran together catching and passing those ahead.

I caught and passed Duzan and then Kovacs and later Roig. By the time I reached the top of the pass at 913 metres, the leaders were out of sight, but I could see the 3rd placed runner. I had a new cyclist, a young woman, who spoke excellent English and was very attractive. I could see the leaders quite a long way ahead as the road zigzagged down the hillside. I caught and passed the 3rd runner and received a report that I was 4 minutes behind the leaders, but gradually this extended to 5 minutes and then 6 minutes. I realised that there was little chance of me closing this gap so I relaxed and concentrated on finishing in the best possible condition. **I appeared to have lost the ability to push myself to the limit, as in the old days, but if I had got the lead it might have been quite different!**

The Kilometers rolled past and I felt quite comfortable apart from my painful quads. With about 6 Km remaining Kovacs came past, going quite a lot faster than me and, despite encouragement from my youthful cyclist, I let him go after a token attempt to increase my pace. I wondered if I had drunk enough, as I had only used two litres of my 10% 'Enduro Boost' instead of my planned 4 litres, although I had no dehydration problems. I think that my problem was just general fatigue, rather than lack of fuel.

Soon I was into the last 2.5Km in the outskirts of Faenza and large crowds of enthusiastic people lined the route. I managed to pick up my pace over the last 500 meters and enjoyed the finish. My time was pleasing as it was only 1-49 slower than my winning time of 1980. The winner's time was outstanding and Bellocq also ran better than ever – he had run 6-31-00 for 100Km a month earlier in France. He told me later that Di Gennaro was too strong for him over the last 7Km, reeling off Kms at 3-30 each, while he could not increase his pace and maintained 4 minutes per Km. Di Gennaro of Italy, had passed the 100Km point in 6-31-55 and finished in 6-37-10, which was a course record, while Jean Marc Bellocq of France passed 100Km in 6-34-52 and finished in 6-41-09. Attila Kovacs from Hungary was 3rd with 100Km 6-48-00, to finish in 6-53-29 and I was 4th and first Vet with, 100Km 6-50-00 and a finish in 6-56-03.

Later I found out some information on Di Gennaro: he was 38 years old, a relative newcomer to running and had a marathon best of 2-22-00. He was unemployed at that time and had prepared thoroughly for this, his first 100Km race. Apparently, one of his training sessions was: 30Km easy, then 70Km at race pace on the Passatorie course, followed by 20km easy!

Two weeks later in the Forres Harriers 8 miles road race, after a cautious start, I finished 7th on a very warm afternoon. Then I ran sixteen miles home into a stiff headwind. This and the race served as my glycogen depletion run and I began low carbohydrates meals at 19:00. On Wednesday I began carbohydrate loading at 18:00 and followed this by a day of cycling to and from work and then a rest day.

CRIPPLING INJURY AT THE LINCOLNSHIRE 100 KM.

On Saturday the 18th of June, I travelled to Grantham by train via Aberdeen and arrived there at 17:30. David Davies, my host again, met me at the station and, after taking me to his home, he kindly drove me up to Lincoln where I attended the eve-of-race dinner. As I was President of the 100Km association, Ron Hindley asked me to do the formal part. The meal, in the refectory of North Lincolnshire College, was prepared and served by tutors and students of the catering section of the College and was a very good standard. As always my return rail fare was reimbursed, along with a dinner invitation.

On Sunday, the 19th of June, David drove me to Lincoln for the 8am start of the Lincolnshire 100Km road race, which that year was to start in Lincoln, go to Grantham and return to finish in Lincoln. David was to be my second again and he had all my prepared drinks. At the changing accommodation I met Geoff Russell, Mick Francis and many more competitors that I recognized, including Patrick Macke. This was Geoff's first attempt at 100Km and it looked like being a severe initiation as the temperature was already high and the sun was shining from a cloudless sky.

I got myself organised, including last minute toilet calls and then made my way to the start. We got underway at 08:00 in the Pedestrian Precinct. As we ran along this I was flanked on either side at the head of the pack. At the end of this pedestrian section there was a road at right angles to it and a policewoman there to control the traffic. As we approached she held up her right arm to stop traffic coming from our left. There was some confusion as to which way to go and the runner on my right, Colton Reid, veered to the left as I think he may have mistaken the policewoman's signal to the traffic as a direction indicator for the runners. Anyway I tripped over his legs and fell very heavily onto the pavement with my left knee taking the full impact of my fall. I was stunned and lay sprawled on the pavement, as some runners stopped to help and others ran by. Colton asked if I was OK, but I could not speak, so he lifted me to my feet, but I just fell down again. Mick Francis helped me up and I tried to run, but my left knee was exceedingly painful. I expected the pain to ease as it does when you scrape your shinbone, so I hobbled along using my left leg as a crutch only and even began to pass some runners. My situation did not improve, since I could see a swelling like a pigeon's egg growing out of my left kneecap and I could not use my left leg properly. Halfway up the hill out of Lincoln I met David, took two painkillers and then carried on.

Soon after this I realised that it would be impossible to get back into the race, so I stopped at an ambulance and the medics put on a tight bandage and advised me to retire. I agreed to do this and got into David's car. He drove me back to his home in Barrowby where I telephoned Izzy to let her know of my condition.

I got a train at 12:30 from Grantham to Doncaster and had great difficulty walking to the correct platform. As I had some time before my next train from Doncaster, I decided to make my way painfully over the connecting bridge, to the adjacent platform where the bar was. However my effort was in vain, as the bartender was closing down, since it was then 2pm on Sunday. I caught the train to Inverness and, during the journey, managed to make a few painful shuffles to the Buffet car for 'anaesthetic' drinks. On arriving at Inverness at 21:15 I could not bend my left leg and so could not walk off the carriage, so a wheelchair was summoned by Izzy. It was comforting to have the family with me.

I was manoeuvred into the back of our Ford Cortina estate and Izzy drove me to Dr Gray's Hospital in Elgin, where a sympathetic doctor had a look at my knee but said that I would have to return next day for an X-ray. A nurse wrapped my knee in cotton wool, bandaged it up and gave me some painkillers prescribed by the doctor. Now I could only fit in the boot of the car and thus was transported home, with the odd groan, in 'Carry on Doctor' style.

Next day, Monday the 20th of June, Maggie Cooke drove me to Dr Gray's hospital, where an X-ray indicated that I had a fractured left patella. It was decided to send me to Foresterhill Hospital in Aberdeen for more specialized advice and treatment. I was taken through in an ambulance and on arrival after another x-ray taken to a treatment room on a trolley. A doctor with a pleasant sympathetic manner, who did some running, said that he would have to aspirate my damaged knee. This meant removing the blood from around the knee joint, so first a local anaesthetic was given, then a much thicker and larger needle and syringe was used to probe and suck. I could feel the needle going through various layers of ligaments as he probed from both sides and at different angles. This was a painfully disturbing experience and was not one I wanted to experience again. As I was moaning somewhat the doctor asked the nurse if she would like to 'hold Mr. Ritchie's hand'. On completion of this I was shown the contents of my swollen knee joint – some 150ml of blood had been extracted. I was then taken to the plaster room, where Mark Wislenski, from Buckie, referred to as 'Pluke', by his classmates, put on a plaster under the supervision of the journeyman. He had been one of my 'work skills' students at Moray College, about 5 years ago. This plaster extended from my groin to my ankle. I was then taken up to a ward just in time for dinner. Painkillers were provided every 4 hours, so my knee felt comfortable. I was pleased to see Izzy later when she came to visit. Russell Smith from the P & J came to interview me and also a girl from BBC Radio Scotland with a tape recorder interviewed me. **My planned LEJOG for July was definitely off.** After that I relaxed and drifted into sleep.

My second attempt at the LEJOG had been planned for the 11th of July 1988, with my support team of: Malcolm Morgan, Graham Milne, Peter Chalmers, John Diffey plus Glen Elliot and Noel McPartlin as committee members. In May I had modified my morning training route to work, to include a testing three-stage hill climb and following descent into Elgin. This was to prepare me for the hills and descents that I would encounter, mainly on the first section of the LEJOG. I had decided that I would run at night to avoid the high volume of daytime traffic and also enjoy cooler weather conditions. To make this safe I would require a well-lit cyclist to accompany me in the twilight and darkness hours. A major drawback of this plan was that there would be the absence of people around to witness my run as required by the Guinness Book of Records.

Dr Scotland did his rounds next morning, accompanied by the doctor who had aspirated my knee. I was to be allowed home, so I telephoned Izzy and arranged for her to pick me up in the evening after her work. In the afternoon Ron Maughan came to visit and we had a good chat – he returned later with three cans of McEwans Export! Izzy arrived at about 20:00 and, after collecting some notes from the Ward Sister for Dr Gormley, I was wheeled out to the exit by a Porter. I had been practicing walking with crutches and could have walked, but this was much quicker. It was good to be going home and we arrived there safely to a warm welcome. However, the leg plaster acted as an anchor in bed and this restricted sleeping posture options.

My colleague, Maggie Cooke, picked me up next morning and drove me to work. Ray Murray was surprised to see me back as was Murray Dunin, who had arranged cover for my classes. Len Hall carried my books to 'T Block' and I got underway sitting with my plastered leg elevated by putting my heel on another chair. My leg ached by the end of the day, so I sat on the couch with my leg up most of the evening. By next day Calum McCallum had stopped making special arrangements for me as he could see that I was coping OK. I was getting used to my plaster and crutches, but the palms of my hands were becoming sensitive and threatening to blister and again my leg ached after the day's work.

Ron Hindley wrote in his race report: *'The race was overshadowed by an accident to one of its beloved favourites, Don Ritchie, who fell in the starting surge in a tangle alleged by a witness to have been caused in the first instance by an interfering photographer, who signalled the stream to turn left, surprising the attendant police. Don sustained a broken patella, but he bravely carried for some 2000 metres before retiring. We were all very shocked, not least Isobel waiting in Lossiemouth. The later news is that he expects to be out of plaster by mid-July, but how soon he can start training again is uncertain. His fitness and vast experience must be powerful factors'.*

By Friday the 1st of July I observed that my left quads were wasting away as the plaster was loose and I could now reach quite a long way down inside from the top of it. A week later I managed to walk without crutches. My left quads had wasted so much that the plaster was slipping down and chafing my Achilles tendon and causing a hack to form, which became infected. I decided to make a support arrangement for the plaster, so I put a piece of wood down inside, between plaster and thigh, and used an electric drill to cut a quarter inch hole through the plaster. I passed a string through this hole and made a supportive harness for the plaster, which passed over my left shoulder and this worked quite well preventing further chafing.

On Thursday the 14th of July Izzy drove me to Aberdeen Royal Infirmary (ARI), Foresterhill to have my progress assessed. The plaster was cut open lengthwise on both sides, leaving a case around my leg when they removed the top half, 'the lid'. I was disappointed to see how swollen my knee still was and how much my quads had atrophied. There was dried blood around my knee and bruised blood down the calf. I was taken for an x-ray, during which my leg was momentarily removed from its casing. It felt very peculiar and when I had to bend my knee for one x-ray shot, I was disturbed at how stiff the knee joint was. My leg was then popped back into the comforting and supportive casing.

A doctor examined the X-ray photographs and said that the fracture had healed up well and then asked me to tighten my left quads. Then I had to raise my leg to the straight position. He was satisfied with this and said that I should get physiotherapy treatment in Elgin and return to this clinic in 3 weeks. So that was it. After 23 days in plaster, my patella was all right but my knee joint was swollen and very stiff. The muscles in my left leg were so weak that I definitely required crutches to walk now. So my intentions of going for a jog in the evening after having my plaster removed were very naïve!

LENGTHY REHABILITATION

At home I measured the circumferences of my right and left knees, and right and left thighs, to establish the differences. The results were: right leg, knee 38 cm, thigh 52 cm; left knee 40 cm, thigh 48 cm. Over the next two days I became more confident in using my left leg and the following day I could walk gingerly without crutches. I began attending the physiotherapy department at Dr Gray's Hospital where my knee joint was bent painfully, a little at a time; feeling like it was going to burst. A programme of exercises to strengthen my left quads and to increase knee joint mobility was undertaken. I had physiotherapy each morning following the same sequence for the rest of the week, with the result that my knee joint could bend a good deal more and with less discomfort and my leg looked a little less like a stork's.

On Saturday the 23rd of July, we began our summer holidays with Izzy and I sharing the driving, down to the home of her brother Bill and his wife Yvonne in South Shields. My knee ached after driving for a few hours.

We watched the Great North Run with Yvonne's parents, Jean and Doug, at the bottom of 'The Bank' at the 12 miles point. It was good to see some top roadrunners, including John Treacy and Steve Jones, in action. There was terrific support for the 27000 runners taking part.

On Monday the 1st of August I tried a jog/hobble and managed 3 minutes before the top of my left quads became very tight and painful. I walked, stretched and jogged for about 10 minutes. I repeated this on the following 5 mornings. On the morning after arriving home I jogged for 15 minutes on the golf course and beach. My knee felt a little easier and my left quads were also not too bad.

I had been asked to act as starter for the half-marathon at Gordonstoun, which is run in conjunction with the Macallan Moray Marathon. Having done my starter duties, I drove around the marathon course to see how the marathon runners were progressing. As the weather was hot at 75°F, I asked Mick Francis if he required any drinks, to which he said yes, so I gave him 200ml of 'Leppin' FRN alternated with 200ml of 'Dioralite' every 2 miles from 10 miles. Mick pulled through from 4th at 10 miles to win, which made me very pleased.

By 8th August physiotherapy was reduced to every 2nd day. The following day I drove to A.R.I. for my appointment with Dr Scotland, who was very pleased with the movement in my knee joint and the absence of pain when he pressed the patella. I did not have to return to his clinic unless I had further problems with it, which was encouraging to know.

By the end of that week I tried to relax and run normally and had jogged 13 miles and I was pleased that my left quads were a lot less troublesome.

That weekend we purchased a second-hand caravan for use on family holidays and during my **planned JOGLE for April 1989**.

I began using the treadmill after my physiotherapy sessions, covering the equivalent of 4Km and my times dropped from 18-25 to 16-40 to 16-08.

I gradually increased the duration of my Jog/runs and within a couple of weeks had reached 50 miles for the week. My physiotherapy treatments were completed as I returned to work after our 'summer holidays'. I decided to try cycling to work; and running home by my 8 or 8.5 miles course one day; and run in and cycle back on the next. This proved quite a successful reintroduction to training, but my left knee began protesting so I had to ease back, accepting some lifts in to work from Maggie Cooke.

Over the next weeks I gradually decreased cycling and increased running as my left knee function improved and left leg muscles strengthened. **By the week ending the 18th of September I was back to 100 miles.**

MORE THAN THREE MONTHS ON, A RETURN TO RACING

My first competition was on Sunday the 2nd of October, in the 13th edition of the Alves to Forres road race along the A96. I found the starting pace hard, but settled down and tucked in behind Mick Wright and we moved through from small group to small group, until we finally stuck with a group including Mick Francis and Donald Gunn. Lynda Bain came past but I could not match her pace. I finished 28th out of 110 starters in 35-16 for the 6 miles 312 yards course. I enjoyed racing again and my knee gave me no problems. Jim Doig won in 30-35 from Bruce Chinnick, 30-42 and Ross Arbuckle 31-12.

Our caravanning holiday during the 'Tattie Holidays' from School and College began on the 8th of October as we towed our caravan to Torvean Caravan Park in Inverness. Rain poured all next day and I did not get around to running. However, the morning after, at the Bught Park track I ran 8 X 800 metres with a 400 metres recovery jog. My times were rather slow and ranged from 2-48 to 2-56, so I was dismayed at how badly I was running. Next day I had a much more stimulating run down the road towards Lochend, and then took a side road off to the right, which climbed up the hillside through a forest. I was climbing for over 12 minutes, with some gradients of 17%. On my way back I went to Lochend and tried to run back on the left bank of the Caledonian Canal, but this proved rather difficult so I cut across to the main road.

Our next location was the Stakis Caravan Park in Aviemore and from there we visited various places of interest. My runs from there took me to Loch Morlich and a bit beyond, part of the Lairig Ghru, but it was so rough that I cut back. On the last three days I ran a very pleasant circular route to Kincraig, Loch Insch and Inshriach along the B970, Feshiebridge and back to Aviemore. We all enjoyed our 'Local Holiday' and returned, refreshed, to work on Monday.

Two weeks later on the 29th of October in the Black Isle Marathon. I was very keyed up and started quickly, but not as fast as Charlie Noble, who shot off into a good lead. After some time, I was joined by someone I did not recognize. He was running strongly and ominously chatty.

Izzy, George, Claire and Anna were driving around the course supporting me. After Izzy gave me a drink, I threw the empty bottle for Claire to catch! This worked well and I consumed planned drinks of 200ml of 'Dioralite' at 7, 10, 13, 16, 19 and 22 miles.

We caught Charlie at about 8 miles and then ran as a group of 3 until about 11 miles, when he faded. The 2 of us passed the halfway point in 1-13-26 but, going into Cromarty, I began to feel the strain of the pace and by the waterfront I was struggling, but positioned myself behind him as we left Cromarty and headed up the initially steep climb. My strength had gone and I lumbered up the hill as my companion pulled away. I steadily lost ground to him and by the top of the hill I was down to 3rd place, having been caught and passed by a small chap from Fife AC, who I later found out was Tom McCredie. I tried to increase my stride length when I reached the level ground, but seemed to be making no impression on the two ahead. Yet gradually I began to close, and then caught McCredie soon after Rosemarkie and the leader was not far ahead by then. However, there was not enough distance left in which to catch him so I had to settle for 2nd place. My knee had not bothered me, thankfully, but a lack of training background showed in my weakness on the hills. The Forres Harriers team won the team race with 2nd, 5th and 16th. I learned that the winner was Mike Ryan of Dundee Hawkhill Harriers (DHH), who finished in 2-34-30, ahead of me in 2-34-56 and Tom McCredie (Fife AC) 2-45-10. I had no ill effect from my knee, except increased discomfort and an ache for a few hours after the race.

I was planning a charity John o'Groats to Land's End solo run for the next Easter holidays and I wanted to test my left knee out with a long run. To do this I entered for the Sri Chinmoy indoor 24-hour race to be held in the Kelvin Hall, Glasgow on 19th November. I fitted in weeks of 135 and 140 miles after the Black Isle marathon, before easing down on the week of the event.

On Friday the 18th of November after work and a meal at home, Mick Francis, Donald Gunn and I set off for Glasgow at 18:30 and arrived there at about 22:30. We soon found our hotel, the 'Lorne' and got settled in. I got to bed by 23:15.

SUCCESS IN THE KELVIN HALL INDOOR 24 HOURS

After breakfast next morning we set off for the Kelvin Hall and on arriving there it was good to see Izzy, Claire and Anna together with George, who had made rapid progress and arrived soon after 11:00. Mick and Donald, my seconds, set up their station with all my requirements and schedule for drinks and food.

The race got underway at 12:00 around the 225.6 metres lap, carefully measured by Raymond Hutcheson. I ran cautiously around the outside and behind the banked indoor track, while others set off rather quickly. I continued at a comfortable pace, drinking 200ml of 'Dioralite' at 20-minute intervals except, on the hour, I drank 200ml of 10% 'Maxijoul'. I also had jam sandwiches arranged for 5 hours and then 4-hour intervals, plus a banana on the other hours. Donald and Mick looked after me very well. Izzy and family went for a snack and her friend from schooldays, Irene, and her husband arrived back with them. They all went off soon after to visit Irene's home and then returned at about 21:00. Once Izzy had got the girls to bed in the hotel, she came back at around 23:00, remained for a few hours and was of course good at offering moral support.

Things were going quite well and I had no problem with my knee but, after about 17 hours, I began to slow drastically and started taking painkillers to relieve the discomfort. Izzy arrived at about 05:00 and remained for a couple of hours before returning to the hotel to get the girls ready. By then my leg muscles were very fatigued, and in particular the quads were very tired, so I found it difficult to lift my feet. This meant that I was scuffing my feet on the floor as I moved forward, but I was determined to finish the race running/jogging if possible. Perhaps I should have taken a break for a massage to try to revitalize my legs, but I decided against this option and kept up my slow progress.

By 09:00 Izzy and the family had arrived for the finishing stages and the last few hours passed quite quickly, which was a relief. I could not increase my pace despite the highly motivating atmosphere in the last 20 minutes. Yet I was satisfied with my performance and the fact that my left knee had not caused any problems. I was very pleased to complete the event, the first time that I had been able to do so. Izzy and Adrian Stott were delighted for me and everyone offered their congratulations. During the run I set the following Scottish Indoor records: 40 miles in 5-00-46, 50 miles in 6-41-21, 100Km in 8-07-01, 12 hours 87 miles and 62 yards, 100 miles in 14-16-17, 200Km in 19-08-49. I sat down in a chair on finishing and could not motivate myself to move, so I was carried in it to the showers. My distance covered was 144 miles 1009 yards and Bob Meadowcroft was 2nd with 132 miles 602 yards and Dave Wallace 3rd with 126 miles 126 yards. Ray Hubbard was next with 120 miles 1005 yards, followed by Mike Briggs with 112 miles 874 yards.

After the awards ceremony we left for home at about 2pm - once I had been carried to the car – and we duly arrived home at about 19:30. My left knee was no problem during the run, but it did swell with fluid for a few days after this strenuous effort.

I resumed shuffling to and from work (on still rather painful legs) the following Thursday.

Two weeks later, I went on a therapeutic meandering run with Mick Francis and Donald Gunn over the golf course, then West Beach, round Lossiemouth, East Beach, into the forest and then picked up my 'Ponds' route. From there we went up the 'Boars Head' route, along to the shooting range and then left onto the beach path. Dusk was approaching, but the path was well defined. With about 2.5 miles remaining we moved onto the sand, where Mick had difficulties and had to walk, with Donald and I taking an arm each, to keep him moving. He managed to jog from the footbridge off East Beach to Stotfield Road, but he had to be escorted the last 300 metres to our home. Mick had an ear infection and had been taking antibiotics for 9 days to clear the infection, so I expect that this was the cause of his problems. We were out for two and a half hours.

In early December I ran home after work via Dr Gray's Hospital to gave Malcolm his Christmas present, a bottle of 10 years old Macallan Whisky. I told him of my plans for the JOGLE run next Easter. He did not volunteer, which was understandable, as he had already given up two weeks holiday for my previous unsuccessful attempt. He agreed to show my helpers, in particular Donald Gunn, how I should be massaged.

In the Forres Harriers Christmas cross-country handicap race, over the usual horrible course in mid December I finished last again. Ross Arbuckle was fastest. A week later, in the Elgin AAC

Christmas cross-country handicap, my time was 2nd fastest for the flattish grass course but there were only 12 participants.

This completed my races for 1988 and, on summing up my racing and training miles, I found that, despite my injury lay-off, they amounted to 5054.5 miles, which was an average of 97 miles per week.

1989

My first race of 1989 was on the 13th of January in the North District cross-country league race in Elgin where I was quite pleased to finish 10th after a good battle with Andy Pratt.

On the 5th of February in the Scottish Veterans Cross-Country Championships at Balgownie in Aberdeen I made a good start and was tucked in behind Mel Edwards with about one 3rd of the race gone. However, I began to tire, ended up in severe oxygen debt and 6 passed me before the relief of the finish. Colin Youngson won in 31-36, Graham Milne was 7th, Roddy MacFarquhar 8th and Ben Preece 9th, but he had not been entered in the Aberdeen AAC team. Mel was 13th, Ken Hogg 15th and I was 18th. AAAC retained the team title. I realised that my mileage had been too high recently to run well in such races. I had felt stronger in the League race in Elgin two weeks previously.

After this race I trained for 7 weeks, concentrating on building up mileage, peaking with 164 miles, in preparation for the JOGLE. A vomiting bug laid me low for 2 days during this time. At the end of this period I ran in the Inverness Half Marathon and, after a cautious start, I worked through with George Sim and Roddy MacFarquhar. I had to ease back on the steep downhill near the finish, to the River Ness, to avoid excessive stress on my muscles. I managed to out-sprint George for 14th place in 72-31 and was second Vet, behind Colin Youngson, who ran 70-06.

THE SECOND SOLO J.O.G.L.E

Saturday April 1st, I began my attempt at 12:02 and reached Land's End at 03:27 on Wednesday the 12th of April.

Later I wrote the following account of my JOGLE:

JOHN O'GROATS TO LAND'S END SOLO RUN, APRIL 1989.

The seed of the ambition to run from the most Northerly point on the island of Great Britain, John o'Groats, to the Southern extremity, Land's End, was sown in my mind many years ago. On long Sunday runs in the late 60's with Alastair Wood and Steve Taylor, we used to discuss occasionally the possibility of an "End to End" Relay Run. Enthusiasm for the relay grew, and in April 1972 I was part of the eight-man Aberdeen A.A.C. team which completed the John o'Groats to Land's End (J.O.G.L.E.), estimated at 867 miles, in 80 hours, 25 minutes, some 45 minutes outside the record set by Reading A.C. in1967. Using the experience gained, Aberdeen A.A.C. improved on Reading's record, by 23 minutes, the following April, but I was not able to participate in this "adventure". The idea lived on, and in April 1982 I was a member of a very strong Aberdeen A.A.C. team, which reduced the record to: 77 hours, 26 minutes and 18 seconds.

Since then, the idea of a solo run grew steadily stronger, until in June 1986, I decided to plan an attempt during our two-week Easter Holidays from School and College in 1987. Both of my parents had died of cancer – my father in 1985, and my mother in 1986 – so the time seemed right to attempt the run, and raise funds for Cancer Research, through sponsorship. After months of planning, my attempt began at 7.00am on the 5th April at Land's End. I had decided to start there, to make use of the prevailing wind, which in April is from the West, and the "homing pigeon" effect. My support team consisted of: Graham Milne, co-ordinator for the run, Peter Chalmers, in charge of navigation, Mick Francis, who looked after my requirements on the road, and Malcolm Morgan, (Magic Malcolm), the head physiotherapist from Dr Gray's Hospital in Elgin.

I set a schedule for ten days, and my strategy was to run for one hour, and then walk for five minutes, before running another hour, continuing in this fashion until 1.00pm, when I would take a break of one hour. The afternoon and early evening would be similar. On the first day I finished in the town of Lifton, having covered 83 miles in 12 hours, 44 minutes of running and walking.

Next morning, I set off in pouring rain which was miserable. Mick and I got lost in Taunton, which wasted time and energy. I ended the day in Bridgwater, having covered 80 miles, plus 1 mile in the wrong direction. Day Three started well: the sun was shining, the road was flat for about 16 miles, and I felt quite good. However, many miles later in the early evening between Monmouth and Hereford my attempt floundered. I was running down a steep hill before St. Weonards when suddenly a severe pain developed in my lower left leg, making further running impossible. Treatment from Malcolm that evening proved ineffective. Next day was a miserable experience; walking, or rather, limping along at less than 4 miles per hour. At Hope under Dinmore, which I reached in the late afternoon, I abandoned the attempt, after consultation with Malcolm, who could see no chance of the injury improving. Later the injury was diagnosed as a stress fracture in the tibia.

I made a complete recovery from this, and wanted to try the J.O.G.L.E. run again. However, before committing myself, I wanted to give my leg a good test, so I accepted the invitation to run in the Cagliari to Sassari race of 254Km in Sardinia, on 17th October. I completed the run in 25hr 28min 51s, with no leg problems, apart from the normal one of not being able to move them quickly enough.

Having passed this test, I decided to make a second attempt, starting on the 11th of July 1987 from Land's End. Everything was set up for the attempt, so it was a bitter blow to all involved, when the attempt had to be postponed on the of 19th June. On this day, soon after the start of a 100Km race in Lincoln, I collided with another runner and fell very badly, onto the pavement. I fractured my left patella, and had to endure the next three and a half weeks with my left leg in plaster, from groin to ankle. Following the plaster removal, after daily physiotherapy and muscle strengthening exercises, I regained full bending movement in my knee, but my leg looked rather like a stork's. I was able to start jogging on 7th August, and progressed to full training by 12th September. I wanted to test the knee to see if I could contemplate another J.O.G.L.E. run the following Easter. I ran the Black Isle marathon on 29th September in 2-34-56 with no ill effects, except increased discomfort and ache in my knee for a few hours after the race. Then on 19/20th November I ran in the indoor (200m track) 24hr race in the Kelvin Hall, Glasgow, and managed 144miles 1009yds. My knee was no problem during the run, but did swell with fluid for a few days after.

I decided that I was sound enough to plan another attempt for 1989, again in our two-week Easter Holidays from School and College; this time I planned to go from John o'Groats. My reasoning was; it is much easier to get to John o'Groats from Lossiemouth, my home, and in the event of my knee giving out, which I thought might happen after three days if at all, it would not be so far to get home. There was, however, more likelihood of head winds going this way. I set up the attempt to begin on 1st of April at 12noon (no longer an April fool, hopefully), which was the first day of our two weeks Easter holiday from School and College. My support team consisted of: Isobel, my wife, Donald Gunn and Mick Francis, both team-mates from Forres Harriers, George Stewart, plus Claire and Anna, our family. Isobel, assisted by George, was to tow our caravan, provide meals, wash kit, and make a video record of parts of the run when she got a chance. Mick took responsibility for route finding and keeping the logbook, while Donald was to administer massage after each running session. They would also both collect names and addresses for the witness book, as required by the Guinness Book of Records, should I break the record, as planned.

As on my previous attempt I decided to use the run to raise funds for the Cancer Research Campaign. Sponsor forms were distributed to Lossiemouth High School by Isobel, to Moray College by me and others were given to family and running pals to elicit donations.

On my first attempt two years earlier the 'confirmed' record for the End-to-End was 12 days 1 hour and 59 minutes, by Ken Craig, a Scot living in South Africa, who ran between 29th August and 10th September 1984. Fred Hicks had claimed to complete the run of 876 miles between the 20th and 30th of May, 1977 in 10 days 3 hours and 30 minutes. The Guinness Book of records included his claim before introducing requirements for documentary evidence: log book and record of 'sightings'. Since then the record for the run had been improved on two occasions. On the 28th of June 1988, Al Howie from Saltcoats in Ayrshire, but who lived in Victoria, Canada, completed his run from John o'Groats to Land's End in 11 days, 3 hours and 18 minutes. This improved the existing record by 22 hours and 41 minutes. In a letter to Albert Middleton, the manager of the Co-op in Buckie, who had given Al food for his run, he said 'Beside the running the main problems were the traffic and the ever-changing weather'. Richard Brown, although primarily a race walker, had used a combination of race walking and running to reduce the record time to; 10 days 18 hours and 23 minutes, finishing on the fourth of October 1988, so this was the time that I had to attempt to beat.

One of Isobel's pupils, Julie Walker, was eager to help with fund-raising, and through her enthusiasm, her father, Stuart Walker, who operated a taxi service in Lossiemouth, agreed to be the 'link' person. I arranged that at the end of each day's run, either Mick or Donald would telephone Stuart, from the nearest public telephone box, with information on my current progress. Stuart would then pass this information to appropriate contacts when they telephoned for 'latest news'.

On Friday the 31st of March, after work, we set off for Golspie, where we were to stay at Donald's parents' holiday cottage. Mick and Donald drove the minibus, supplied by our main sponsor, "The Macallan" whisky distillers, who would also pay for the fuel for their van. I had all the seating removed except that for the driver and passenger, so that it could easily carry all our provisions, kit and a bicycle, and also so that I could lie out in it for massage.

Overnight Mick developed severe toothache, so he and Donald set out early to try to find a dentist in Wick, while we made our way to John o'Groats some time later. My plan was to ease into the run by starting with a half day and intended to run to Brora. At John o'Groats it was bitterly cold, and a strong South-East wind blowing, so a wet suit, hat and gloves were necessary. Mick and Donald arrived about 30 minutes before noon, having found a dentist in Wick, who fixed Mick's tooth for free as his contribution to our run, which by now was known as *"Ritchie's Run 89"*.

Nine friends and supporters turned up before the start, to wish me luck and see me off, which I greatly appreciated. I planned to start exactly on the 12 noon time signal from a B.B.C. radio station, but I selected the wrong station on the car radio in the excitement, and there was no time signal, so my actual departure time was 12.02.

I set off to cheers and was soon alone, tackling the first of many hills, running into a strong headwind in this very exposed region, and I wondered what the next ten days would bring. To try to minimise stress, and hopefully avoid injury I had decided that I would not run for more than three hours in a session, and that I would have at least 30 minutes break between sessions. I intended to run 3 times 3-hour sessions, followed by 2 times 2 hour sessions, plus whatever else was necessary to complete the target mileage if it was practical. During the 30minute rest I would change kit, and shoes if necessary, take food and drink, and receive a massage and stretching routine from Donald. Malcolm Morgan had demonstrated the techniques on me a few weeks before, while Donald and Mick observed, and Isobel made a video recording for reference. To gain skill, we think that Donald practised massaging his girlfriend's legs!

After I had covered about three miles, Donald and Mick began running alternate miles with me, to try giving me some protection from the wind on the exposed road to Reiss. Soon Wick was reached, and we passed through with some encouragement from local people. I stopped at Thrumster for my first rest period, which passed quite slowly, but I was sure that this would not be the case later in the run. I continued down the undulating A9 road, which afforded some spectacular views of cliffs, sea and mountains. At the Berriedale Braes I was very cautious of the steep descent, fearful that excessive jarring might provoke another stress fracture, so I walked down the steepest part, a practice I would continue on all future steep downhills. The climb from Berriedale was O.K., and there were several other stiff climbs, before the descent to Helmsdale at sea level again. From there the road is almost flat, and I could see the lights of Brora, eleven miles away. This section appeared to take a long time to complete; it was quite annoying seeing the lights, which did not appear to be getting any closer. I finished in Brora at 10.45pm, having covered 65 miles.

I had difficulty sleeping that night, and was feverish, so I had a 'medicinal' miniature of The Macallan. Peter Nicol, the commercial manager of Macallan, had given us a box of miniatures, for offering to witnesses who signed my witness book as a thank you and as a possible product promotion. In the morning I was choked up with a cold; the cold, which had been threatening over the past week, had developed into a Class One cold. After breakfast we returned to Brora, and I began running from last night's stop at 6.10a.m. The wind was not a problem until the high exposed ground from the south end of Loch Buidhe to Bonar Bridge. Going over The Struie hill was very hard as the wind was so strong at times that I had difficulty staying on my feet. I was glad when the descent to the Cromarty Firth began, as there were trees either side of the road, offering some protection.

Shortly before crossing the bridge over the river Averon, a sharp pain on the front of my left patella developed, and I worried that this might signal the start of problems with this knee. However, applying some freeze spray eased it considerably, and eventually it faded away and I forgot about it.

Raymond Cameron and members of the Minolta Black Isle A.C. joined me a couple of miles before I rejoined the A9, and ran with me in relays from there to the Kessock Bridge at Inverness. It cheered me up to have this enthusiastic support, and they also helped to shield me from the wind. At Kessock Bridge, Colin Bailey had arranged a group of veteran Inverness Harriers, to run with me from the bridge to within a few miles of Slochd Summit. Again they were a big help against the wind, and in lifting my morale. It became colder, and by Slochd Summit there were flurries of sleet. I was tired and anxious to see the turn off for Carrbridge, where I was to stop. I reached there at 10.05 pm, having covered 84.7 miles and feeling very tired. It had been a hard day with the wind and hills.

Donald drove us to the Caravan Park in Aviemore, where we were to spend the night and we all appreciated the hot showers. Next morning was frosty as I set off from Carrbridge at 6.05 a.m. I felt comfortable, and it was peaceful running along the B9125 road rather than the A9; I would have plenty of it and its traffic later in the day. The day developed into a pleasant morning, with no wind, and the sun was out, which was quite encouraging. My first three hours took me to Kingussie, only 19.5 miles, but I had come to accept this as the norm if I was to avoid injury, and complete the task. After Newtonmore I rejoined the A9, and after about 4 miles, I had company from Graham Milne, who had driven up from his parents' home in Pitlochry. It was good to have his company to my next stop at Drumochter pass. By now Isobel had arrived, and the hot soup she offered was very welcome. Peter Scott, a club mate of Graham's, who was involved in the planning of the previous attempt, also arrived. He and Graham became my support team until Pitlochry, while Donald and Mick went ahead to Graham's parents for a meal and some much needed sleep. Peter ran with me on my next three-hour session, and then Graham took over again until we reached Pitlochry, where a refreshed Mick and Donald resumed their task.

About one mile after rejoining the A9, after the Pitlochry section, I could see a figure running towards me, and on getting closer I recognised that unmistakable running style: it was Ian Moncur. I knew he was pleased to see me, as he began jumping up and down, waving his arms in the air and shouting at the top of his voice, "Where the hell have you been?". I had asked Ian prior to the run if he would like to run a section, and he readily agreed, so earlier in the day I had asked Graham to telephone him to let him know my location, so that he could plan a meeting. Unfortunately, Graham had given him a very optimistic estimate of my arrival time at Ballinluig, so he had expected to meet us some three hours earlier. Ian ran with me for two hours, down to Dunkeld turn-off, by which time it was quite late. I left the A9 soon after to go to Bankfoot, where we finished at 11 pm, with a total of 81.8 miles for the day. In view of this late finish, Mick suggested what I had also been considering – that I start one hour earlier in the mornings.

There were no hot showers at our night stop, at Scone Palace Caravan Park near Perth, so we did without. Next morning, I began running at 5.12am, and only covered 17.5 miles in the first session to Glenfarg. I was coping with the run, but getting weaker daily, and certainly not adapting to it, as some people suggested would happen. My cold had progressed into bronchitis, which was rather worrying.

Adrian Stott from Edinburgh joined me about five miles before my next stop at Hill of Beath. It cheered me up a lot to have his company. I developed a nose-bleed, the first of many, so I had to run along spattered in blood, and with a wad of toilet tissue in my nostril to stop the flow – just another nuisance. As we approached the Forth Road Bridge, snow began to fall, and there was a very strong East wind. Isobel passed us on the bridge, and so was able to video us coming off the other side. Adrian ran with me around the Edinburgh Bypass, which was very busy, and extremely nerve-racking to run on, due to the fast and heavy traffic. We were both very relieved to get off and head for Penicuik. I observed at my next toilet stop, in some roadside cover, that as on the day before, there was evidence of intestinal blood loss; something else to try and remedy. Adrian left us at Leadburn Inn, with best wishes for our "history in the making" event, and a flask of fresh tea plus a £5 donation from the Inn staff.

More snow fell on my next session down to and through Peebles, where I missed the most direct route onto the B7062 road. With the drop in altitude the snow turned to sleet. Somewhere on the narrow road, as Mick and I ran along in the light from the van behind us, the lights suddenly veered to the right. Mick and I turned to see what had happened and saw that the van was off the road on the right hand side. Donald had fallen asleep while driving at such a slow speed. Thankfully there was no ditch and we were able to get the van back onto the road. I finished by Traquair House at 10.26pm, having covered 80.6 miles. It was quite a long drive to the Caravan Park at Tushielaw Inn, made difficult due to the snow on the B709 road, as we followed it over the hills. Again there were no hot showers, and it was after midnight by the time we had finished our 'evening' meal.

Later that morning, at 4.00am, we had to push the Macallan Van off the site, as the tyres were slipping on the slushy and muddy grass. I began running from last night's stopping place at 5.16am, and soon faced a long climb over to the A708 junction, and then another climb, over to Tushielaw. The roads had a covering of snow, and it was quite therapeutic running through this quiet countryside, apart from sheep noises, as dawn broke.

Mick and Donald took turns at driving and sleeping, so that they would be fresher later in the day. I followed the meandering B709 on to Eskdalemuir, then down into Langholm, and we left the hills behind us, as the flat country around the Solway Firth spread out before us. I crossed the English border in the late afternoon, which gave me a morale boost.

Apart from my bronchitis, and intestinal blood loss, I was now beginning to get stomach pains, despite regular eating. I worried that I might be developing an ulcer. Also the inside of my mouth was very sensitive, almost raw, so it was an effort to eat; especially anything hot or with salt in it. I pondered possible courses of action to combat this problem. I had already given up quite dilute orange squash in favour of water, or tea or electrolyte drink after the second day. I noticed that my sore mouth was aggravated by eating bread and jam, so I decided to eliminate sugar from my diet to see if this would help. I ate dry wholemeal bread along with an electrolyte drink, and a banana every hour. Within a day of this regime my stomach pains vanished, and there was no longer evidence of intestinal bleeding. The inside of my mouth, however remained raw.

I passed through Longtown and approached Carlisle along a very busy A7; it was the rush hour. I was very tired and flopped into the van at my next stop at the North side of Carlisle. Following this rest stop, Donald guided me through Carlisle and onto the A6 road, which I followed as darkness fell. Mick accompanied me, with a torch, to our finishing point at the Northern outskirts of Penrith, reached at 11.11 p.m. This gave me 81 miles for the day.

Next morning, I started at 5.11am, and felt comfortable on the run up to Shap Fell. I did not like the steep descent after Shap summit, and had to go very cautiously to avoid putting too much stress on my legs. Mick joined me as I approached Kendal to guide me through, before dashing off to buy another pair of shoes from Pete Bland's shop. I was extremely tired by this time, and covered only 16.9 miles in this, my second session, which finished about two miles South of Kendal. During my massage in the rest period, I kept falling asleep and going straight into a dream. Donald did very well in his massaging sessions, but we soon used up all the massage oil, so Johnson's Baby Oil was used, but this caused some hairs to get pulled out on the insides of both thighs, causing boils to occur there. These were another source of irritation. Next we tried "crisp-n-dry" cooking oil, which worked well, but it left a pungent sickly smell on any kit contaminated with it, and on the air bed used for massage, which was also Donald's night bed!

I put on lighter shoes to see if this would help matters, as I pushed on to Carnforth and Lancaster. I felt very weak, and wondered how much longer I could keep going. My concern grew so I decided that I would run less than was planned, so that I could finish earlier and get to bed earlier. I finished at 9.27pm in Preston town centre, having covered 72.4 miles.

Next morning, I got underway at 5.20am, and followed the A49 to Wigan and onto Warrington. I felt a bit fresher, but still managed only 17.3 miles in my first session. After Stretton I ran through some attractive countryside and just after mid-day logged 500 miles. During the afternoon I had another nosebleed, and this became a regular occurrence until the end. Rather than stop I stuffed a piece of toilet paper up my nostrils to stem the flow of blood. I finished the day at Wem at 9.25pm, with another 73.1 miles added to the total. My plan now was to run at least 70 miles a day to the finish, instead of my planned 80 miles, as the latter was proving too stressful and might promote a breakdown.

My 5.02am start the following morning was my earliest, but I felt tired, and covered just 16.7 miles in my first three hours session. It was frustrating to be going so slowly, but at least I was still running, and had no injuries. The owners of Lower Lacon Caravan Park at Wem, Shropshire, where we had stayed the previous night, waived their charge as their contribution to our charity.

Going through Shrewsbury I passed by the Lion Hotel, where we had stayed in 1987 following the abandonment of my first attempt. I passed through some attractive countryside as I followed the A49 to Church Stretton and Ludlow.

The weather became quite warm in the afternoon sunshine, and I was tempted to put on shorts, but I discovered that it was not quite warm enough on stopping. It was rather pleasant, running from Ludlow through Richard's Castle and Luston to Leominster along the quiet B4361. Passing through Leominster I felt some twinges in my right calf, and began to worry that this might be the start of an injury. After a few more occurrences, they did not reoccur, which was a relief. I passed Hope under Dinmore, where my previous attempt finished, and my thoughts returned to that miserable day two years ago, when I was very downcast. Hereford was reached at dusk, and then I ran on and up the long climb to the A466 turn off. I finished at 11.07pm, north of St. Weonards, with a total of 73.6 miles, for the day.

Donald Gunn wrote about a communications problem that we had that morning: There were lighter moments during the run, such as one sunny morning during the latter stages, when I ran over to the side of the road Don was running on, to ask which drink or kind of food he wanted for one of his regular snacks, which were always done on the run. Due to a combination of the cold he had caught at the start of the venture and sheer fatigue, his voice had all but disappeared, so Don whispered something, which was barely audible. Another few yards on I repeated the question.

Ah! A butty! It sounded like. Off I trotted back to the van, avoiding the traffic. I spread a nice big homemade jam butty, sprinted down the road to catch him up again. No, he waved - he didn't want my offering and hoarsely whispered something. Sorry, Don, can't quite catch what you're saying. Again he shouted - which can only be described as a whisper. Yes! I caught it this time. So off I went again and returned with a peeled banana. Wrong again - he waved his arm. This time I was going to get it right. So running alongside as close as possible without tripping him, I heard the whisper above the noise of the traffic: IT'S A LOVELY DAY.

At 05.08 am next morning, I started quite aggressively, and gave thanks that I was still running, as I passed the spot where my stress fracture had happened two years previously. Monmouth was passed through, and my run down the Wye valley, early on this Sunday morning was pleasant. I reached the Severn Bridge at about 11am, and weather conditions were quite warm again. In Bristol, Mick and I navigated to the Clifton Suspension Bridge; only to discover that the road we were to have taken down to the riverside was closed. I decided to go over the bridge and go down on the other side, assuming that we could find a bridge at river level, and cross back to rejoin our route. This was a mistake, because, despite our city map, we got disorientated, in fact thoroughly lost, and wasted time going in the wrong direction. However, we asked directions from local people and after clambering over a couple of fences and a railway line we regained our route.

By my next stop, on the climb out of Bristol, on the A38, I had only covered 12.2 miles in the last three hours session. During the next section, the road was very busy; I assumed that it was people returning to Bristol, after a Sunday afternoon outing. Mick's sister, Hilary, joined us after Bristol, and assisted Izzy to locate our night's Caravan Park, and get set up ready to receive us later. Once over the Mendip Hills, the road became flat, just like the batteries of our torch. Rain began to fall, so I splashed along holding this torch, which was almost useless. Mike fetched the batteries from the rear light of the bicycle, but they soon faded also. Despite this, I managed to avoid damaging myself in any potholes near the roadside. I was aiming for Bridgwater, and eventually reached the outskirts, where I stopped for the day. It was 11.25pm, and I had covered 71.8 miles.

Next morning I got going at 05.01 am and made my way through Bridgwater and on to Taunton. In my first session I covered 17.4 miles, which was quite encouraging considering my poor condition. Tiverton was next, then a very hilly section across to Crediton. As I was still concerned about excessive leg stress, I chose to walk on steep downhill sections. I decided to try four three-hour sessions, rather than switch to two-hour sessions. On the next session I had a sharp pain on the left front side of my chest, which was aggravated by swinging my left arm, in my normal running action. I had to run along with my left arm folded against my chest to ease the pain. I thought that I must have pulled a muscle; due to all the coughing I had been doing over the past few days, because of my bronchitis. Then I wondered what a collapsed lung felt like. When I mentioned my new problem to Donald, who had arrived to accompany me over the remaining few miles to Okehampton, he suggested that it was probably indigestion. I took this to mean, "Stop feeling sorry for yourself and get on with the run". I reached Okehampton at 8pm, in a very tired condition, with only 14.7 miles covered in the last three hours. I had a 66-minute rest before continuing with Mick (and a rejuvenated torch) towards Lewdown where I finished at 11.18pm, with 74.2 miles added to the total. I was now 88 miles from the finish, so the next day should be the final one.

Izzy told me about the problem she had while towing the caravan between Tiverton and Crediton, when she met a truck on a narrow hump-backed bridge, with a sharp corner on the road on the other side. The truck driver asked her to reverse the caravan from the bridge and he was rather taken aback when Izzy said that she could not reverse the caravan over the bridge successfully. After a few choice words the truck driver got into the car and reversed the caravan clear of the bridge for her and returned to the truck to continue his journey. Izzy then drove on to the caravan park near Launceston for our night's stop.

Donald Gunn later wrote this about my stop and massage at 8 pm in Okehampton: Another amusing incident occurred during one of our massage and stretching sessions which I gave Don (at the end of each running session) in the back of our van. He was particularly tired and kept on falling asleep, which presented a problem. Some of the stretches required him to indicate precisely at which moment to stop the stretch so as to avoid injury. So I started to repeat the words "more, more", listening for the 'grunt', at which point I would hold his leg for around thirty seconds. Unknown to us, there was small bunch of local teenagers outside the van, which was parked in a corner of the village square. We then realised what the youngsters found so funny. Because Don was lying on his back, all they could see was his naked legs sticking up above window level and me stripped to the waist because of the heat in the van. The only conversation that could be heard was "more, more"!

I began my last day at 05.18am, with a sense of excitement and apprehension. My chest pain of the previous day had gone, but I was concerned that something might go wrong even at this late stage of the run. About an hour into the run a headwind began to blow, and rain followed. Amazingly quickly, the wind became a gale and the rain became torrential. I battled on against the elements, the gale increasing in ferocity, as I climbed onto Bodmin moor. The regional newspaper reported: 'Gales bring havoc to South West, winds gusting to 80 mph raged through Devon and Cornwall in a seven-hour gale'. In my first three-hour session I only covered 15.4 miles. On my next session I was concerned that some of the gusts of wind would blow me into the path of a truck, or some other vehicle, so I asked Donald to drive the van ahead of me, so that I could get some protection, and so maintain a straight course. By the Bodmin Bypass the rain had ceased, but the wind was still strong. This second session yielded only 15.3 miles, and an even poorer 15.00 miles was achieved on the next. I changed into lighter shoes for my fourth session, and felt that I was running better, and covered 16.6 miles. However, on the next, a two-hour session, I only managed 9.7 miles, finishing at the entrance to St. Ivel factory, Hayle at 11.08pm. I began my final session at 11.47pm, knowing that I had to complete the remaining 16.2 miles in 6hr 38min, to break Richard Brown's record. By now the wind had died, and it was a peaceful night with a clear sky, and a near full moon. On reaching Penzance, not thinking clearly, I took the Bypass road rather than going through the town, which turned out to be a mistake, as I appeared to complete a large semicircle, involving some nasty climbs. As I left the Bypass, a signpost indicated 9.5 miles to Lands End; at least I was almost there, but I was very tired and it seemed to take ages to reach Sennan, where I could smell the sea. As I ran towards the finish a floodlight came on, to allow the B.B.C. South-West camera team to record the finish. I stumbled and almost fell on a speed control ramp in the road, and was confused as Land's End was completely different from what it had been like two years earlier. There were new buildings, but I eventually found the hotel on the cliff top, and the "official" signpost, where I finished at 3.27am.

At last it was over! I had finished the journey of 846.4 miles, on foot, in 10 days 15 hours and 27 minutes, a mere 2 hours, 56 minutes faster than Richard had achieved. I was very relieved that we had got through it, without any mishap to myself or my support crew and my family. After hugs all round, we opened the bottle of Champagne, given by Albert Middleton, and drank to our successful project. I was very grateful to Mick and Donald for their dedicated and uncomplaining attention throughout each long day and to Izzy for her unfailing support. They each contributed a great deal to the success of the run.

Once the camera crew had signed our witness book we made our way to Lower Treave Caravan Park at Crows-An-Wra. It was about 4.30 am before we got to bed; normally we would be preparing to start another day's run at this time. I found it difficult to sleep, as had been the case throughout the run, and got up at 9.00am. It was wonderful, not to have to go out and run!

Later, after making various telephone calls, we returned to Land's End, to see in daylight the new developments, and to sign the "End to End" book. Mick and Donald set off for home in the afternoon, as Mick had to get a flight to Boston for the marathon, surely having had a unique preparation for it!

Izzy and I and the girls stayed another night at Crows-An-Wra, the girls enjoyed watching the tortoise in the site owners' garden. While there, a stream of yellow liquid suddenly poured from my nose, as though someone had turned on a tap. Izzy on seeing this commented that it was my brains running out, which we both found appropriately funny, and we ended up with a 'fit of the giggles'.

It took us four days to get back to Lossiemouth, and we arrived home on Sunday the 16th of April in the early evening. I had then to prepare for my return to work next day. We were certainly not refreshed after our Easter Vacation! My weight on Monday the 17th of April was 9 stone, 7 pounds, which was around 7 pounds below normal; so since I had been snacking almost continuously, during waking hours, since I finished, I estimate that my weight must have been down to 9 stones.

The aftermath of the run was not what I expected. I was not injured, just very weak, and my health/immune system had broken down. Apart from the continuing bronchitis, I had swollen glands either side of my neck, and my pulse was always ten beats above normal. My G.P. prescribed antibiotics, and they worked sufficiently well for me to resume running on the first of May. I had difficulty sleeping, for about five weeks after finishing the run. I would be very restless, and keep thinking it was time to get up and get ready to run, or I would dream that I was running and getting lost.

Being an optimist, prior to my JOGLE, I had entered for the Lochaber Marathon on 23rd April, and the first British Athletics Federation (B.A.F) and Road Runners Club 100Km championship, on the 7th of May, but I had to withdraw from both events. My poor health continued throughout the summer: each time I began to train hard, I picked up another infection. I had 7 courses of antibiotics, plus two decongestant mixtures, before I began to get back to normal in early September. I felt stronger each week, from then, and I knew I had recovered when I ran 6-51-14 in the Santander 100Km, in Spain, in October.

In association with the run, my many helpers and I raised £5666.85, for Cancer Research, of which £2900 went to the Moray Branch of the Cancer Research Campaign and £2766.85 was donated to the Breast Scanner Appeal for Elgin. This made the run all the more satisfying. I have great respect for anyone who completes the 'End to End' journey on foot, as I know how difficult it is.

Postscript.

There were several record attempts after 1989 but most petered out after three or four days. Richard Brown, whose record I had broken, sent me a card, saying 'congratulations on your record, enjoy it until I get it back'. I thought that he was joking, but six years later I realised that he was not.

Although not fully fit, I could not resist the call of Aberdeen Marathon, so on Saturday the 27th of May, I towed our caravan to Hazlehead Caravan Park and set it up there. Izzy and I were pleased to attend the reception for the Aberdeen Milk Marathon, Home International runners and officials at the Beach Ballroom in the evening, thanks to Graham Milne.

In the race next morning I found the pace of the leading group too hard so I had to ease back. Our group worked together along the Prom, each taking one-minute lead into the wind. Izzy got caught in traffic and did not make contact until I was on the Scotstoun road. By then our group was down to 3 as Steve Cassells had slipped off the back. When we turned out of the wind I pushed on and passed 3 before the finish. My time was quite slow, at 2-41-42 in 11th place, but I was pleased with my running over the last 7 miles. Ian Bloomfield of England won in 2-22-30, from Terry Mitchell of Scotland 2-24-53 and Mick McGeoch Wales 2-25-57.

My next 100km race was looming so I ran weeks of 127 miles and 152 miles before the taper week with the carbohydrate loading. On Wednesday, the 21st of June, I began stoking up on carbohydrates at the evening meal and decided not to run on Thursday and Friday. On Saturday I caught the 08:30 flight to London and then caught the 11:30 flight to Paris, where Monique and Marc Fornari met me as arranged and drove me to their home.

After a rest Monique took me to visit Versailles, which was very impressive. The weather was rather warm at 30°C so I was apprehensive about conditions for next day's race. Following this I went to bed for a couple of hours. We dined outside at 19:30 with their twin children and two other 100Km runners plus Patrice Bellocq, Marc Bellocq's brother, who was to be my cycling second in the race.

PARIS 100KM

I rose at 02:00, (01:00 UK time) on race morning, the 25th of June and started preparing for the **'100Km et Relais de la Division Leclerc' race from Paris to Rambouillet.** Some friends of Monique picked us up and drove us to the start in Paris at Porte d'Orleans. This was the IAU International Championships and the French Championship race. Weather conditions were very warm as we started at 04:00; I did not feel fresh and found the initial pace hard, which was disturbing. I began to get going after a while and moved through and ran with Patrick Macke for some time in, I guess, joint 4th. Later a large group, mainly Germans, joined us and we became part of it. As we reached the country the atmosphere became cooler, but there were some stiff climbs followed by steep descents, which I did not like. Our group began to break up on this undulating section and I was on the back of it.

Gradually I began to feel easier and moved better and by 50km, reached in 3-16, I was 3rd and quite confident, even thinking that it might be possible to win the race. However, my quads became very painful and it was not possible to stride out, so I had to reduce speed and shuffle along. I struggled on and got passed by 10 runners before the finish including the eventual winner, Bruno Scelsi. Yet I was pleased to complete the course, even though my time was not very good at 7-21-34 in 13th of the 329 finishers. I drank one litre of Leppin 'Enduro Booster', one litre of 'Dioralite' and one litre of 10% Maxijoul solution during the race and I felt fine apart from my leg muscles. Patrice was a good help and particularly encouraging when I began to struggle with my quads pains and the increasing air temperature, which became very hot by the end. Bruno Scelsi of France won in 6-47-08 from Bruno Joppen of Holland, 6-49-54 and Herbert Cuntz of Germany with 6-51-18. After receiving my expenses of 1200 French Francs, I got a lift back to Paris and made my way to the airport. There was a bomb scare and a controlled explosion carried out on the suspect abandoned luggage, which added even more excitement to my day. Painful leg muscles prevented me from running for two days following this race.

The weekend, the 1st of July, we towed our caravan to Dornoch, which allowed me to run in the Dornoch half marathon. I felt tired from the start and finished 13th and 2nd Vet. In the Forres Highland Games 11.25 miles road race the following weekend I was rather tired and finished 12th.

On the 9th of July, we began the summer holidays using our caravan and towing it to Bught Caravan Park in Inverness. The following day we headed for Hereford in stages, with stops at: Blair Drummond Caravan Park, Gatebeck Caravan Park near Kirkby Lonsdale, Drayton Manor Park Caravan Site. On the 14th of July, we reached Hereford and set up our caravan at the Hereford racecourse site.

The John Tarrant Memorial 50 miles road race was organised by Mick Wildig, a running partner, friend and later mentor of John Tarrant. Mick Wildig wrote in race information pack: *'John was banned by the pompous, arrogant, antiquated International Athletics Association, the British A.A.A. and local Hereford A.A.A for receiving £17 in a boxing hall'*. John became an excellent runner and, despite being banned, he used to jump into the start of races at the last minute and became known as the 'Ghost Runner'. He produced many excellent performances including a World Best for 40 miles of 4-03-28; and had a marathon best of 2-22-35.

HARD WORK AT THE JOHN TARRANT MEMORIAL 50 MILES

On Sunday the 16th of July, in Hereford, the John Tarrant Memorial race started at 09:00 in brilliant sunshine and I went immediately into the lead. At the first junction I began turning in the wrong direction before being summoned back by those behind. I settled down and ran with Martin Daykin at a fair pace. We pulled away from the rest and at the end of the first of the 5 ten-miles laps, passed in 62 minutes, we were well clear. I had put out drinks for stations up to 20 miles and this caused me to slow or sometimes stop at refreshment stations to get my drink. Consequently, I had to speed up after these stations to regain contact with Martin. There were a couple of challenging hills on each lap, which would take their toll later.

By the end of the 2nd lap, Izzy, George, Claire and Anna had arrived and they gave me drinks from then to the finish. At 20 miles Anna offered me my drink, but I failed to collect it properly. George grabbed the bottle of drink and charged after us, but I could hear that he was not able to catch me so I slowed and looked around. George shouted, 'Here, catch!' and threw my drinks bottle, which hit me around my neck and fell to the ground, so I stopped to retrieve it and consume its contents. Martin was now some 40 metres up the road and it took me about a mile to close that gap.

We passed the marathon in 2-42-something, which was OK for the testing course and the high temperature. By about 28 miles I was feeling weak and began to slow and I had to let Martin go. I felt drained, my legs would not work any faster and I felt that I was practically jogging on lap 4. At the start of lap 5, I jogged along eating an ice-lolly (given to me by Izzy), which was much appreciated in the hot conditions. On this final lap at around halfway through, Tony Lenagan came past and I could not respond. I was pleased to reach the finish and was quite exhausted by then. I was quite disturbed at my poor condition: my stamina was poor and I could not run fast either. **Obviously I was not fully recovered from my JOGLE run at Easter.** Martin finished in 5-27-55, ahead of Tony Lenagan, who recorded 5-38-29 and I finished 3rd and 1st V45, in 5-43-14. Eleanor Adams was 4th in 6-04-00.

After a further 5 days at Hereford, sightseeing around the area, we moved down to Chepstow racecourse Caravan Park. Two days later we found a Caravan Club site at Ash called Willow Park. This was a small interesting site, by old gravel pits stocked with fish, and there was a resident flock of Canada Geese, plus other birds. Claire and Anna enjoyed watching the anglers and were allowed to 'help' some. On a very pleasant run along the bank of the Basingstoke canal, I was pleased to see a kingfisher, a jay and various other birds. While at this site we visited our friends, Roy and Edith Richards and their daughter Fiona. After three pleasant days spent in and around Willow Park we began moving north to a Caravan Club site in a farm field off the Icknield Way, about 4 miles west of Dunstable. Izzy remembers, one morning there, chasing Claire around the field in an attempt to brush her hair.

We continued north with stops at Drayton Manor Park, Rawcliffe Manor Caravan Park, Gosforth Caravan Park and then drove home in stages.

STILL STRUGGLING

In the Macallan Moray Marathon on the 6th of August, I was lacking some confidence because of my previous week's illness. The initial pace was modest, but Mick Francis started to push on up to the Bishop's hotel and on the climb up to Spynie I began to fall back. I felt that there was no way that I could complete the race at that pace. The pace was still modest and at about 5 miles Charlie McIntyre took off and no one had the courage to go with him. If I had been well I would have relished the challenge and gone with him. However, I had to be content with retaining contact with my group. Bill Adams lost contact approaching Burghead, so I thought I would be at least first Vet.

Bill Adams came storming past followed by Ray Hubbard, but none of our group was prepared to pick up the pace and I could not as I was already at full stretch. On the climb into Lossiemouth past our house, I was floundering as our group broke up, but I managed to run with Mick, who was feeling rough. I managed to run well enough to move up to 3rd place, a position that I maintained until crossing the river Lossie with only about 700 meters remaining, when Colin Hunter charged past. I was rather happy to finish this race. Charlie McIntyre won in 2-31-58, from Bill Adams 2-40-31 and Colin Hunter 2-44-20, while I finished 4th in 2-44-54.

The legacy of my JOGLE ill health persisted, and I had another two courses of antibiotics to clear a painful throat and swollen painful glands in my neck. I felt too ill to run, but resumed running with a gentle 6 miles on golf course and beach on Monday the 21st of August. **Although I felt apprehensive because of my poor health, I decided to participate in the Two Bridges race next Saturday.**

Izzy and I left home at 06:10 on Saturday the 26th of August, for Rosyth, and after some sustained fast driving, we reached there at 09:20. Rain had been falling since Aviemore and was still falling quite heavily as the 22nd edition of the 'Two Bridges' race got underway.

I made a cautious start, passing 5 miles in 29-42 and 10 miles in 59-25. By Kincardine Bridge I was running with Andy Stirling and Mick McHale in joint 6th place. Izzy was giving me drinks every 3 miles alternating 250ml of 'Isostar' and 250ml of 10% Leppin FRN, and each time I took a drink, I lost some ground on my companions, which I had to make up. By 15 miles, reached in 1-29-35, I had lost contact and faced the increasing wind alone, before reaching 20 miles in 2-00-52, which was acceptable. Dave Kelly caught me on the climb out of Bo'ness and I ran with him for some time before having to let him go at about 25 miles. I passed the marathon point in 2-42-57, which was an improvement on my Moray time. The headwind and driving rain made conditions quite arduous. I passed 30 miles in 3-08-38 and coming onto the Forth Bridge I could see McHale, but I made little impression on the gap between us. Coming off the Bridge, Andy Battye came storming past and he was soon out of sight up the hill in Inverkeithing, which I staggered up. I was pleased to reach the finish, even though 3-55-07 in 9th place was my slowest time for the course. Mick McGeoch won in 3-36-02 from Gwyn Williams 3-39-44 and Geoff Large 3-43-40.

Following two more infections, my health improved and I got back into a proper training routine. In the Dufftown Seven Stills 10km race on Sunday the 23rd of September I finished 7th and Bill Adams from Lerwick was first vet in 4th place. In the Dallas to Forres 10Km road race the following Saturday, I had to hold myself back on the initial downhill section to prevent damaging my quads. Graham Laing won in 30-43 from Colin Youngson, 31-12 and George Reynolds 31-15. I was 13th and began the low carbohydrate phase of the 'diet' after this run.

On the following Wednesday morning the 4th of October, I ran my six and a half miles beach course to the cliffs and back by the golf club house, before I began eating carbohydrates again at breakfast. I then cycled to and from work.

Thursday was a rest day for Saturday's Santander 100K, as was Friday. I felt quite tight after my carbohydrate loading as Izzy and I left for Aberdeen Airport that morning to catch our 11:35 flight to London. As we had plenty of time there before our flight to Bilbao we went into London – Piccadilly Circus and Knightsbridge – to visit Harrods, which was very interesting. We met Malcolm Campbell as we went for our flight to Bilbao and he told us of the proposed stage race on the Great Wall of China in August 1990. We arrived at Bilbao at about 20:33, where we were met by Christina and her driver and driven to Santander and to race registration at Magdalenian Park. Soto, Luth-Mary, Jose and Hemma were there along with other helpers. I got my number package and then we were taken to our hotel where we got to bed at about 01:00, so not long before my 04:30 rise!

SANTANDER 100KM: FITTER ONCE MORE!

On Saturday the 7th of October, the 10th edition of the **City of Santander 100Km road race**, got underway at 07:00. The initial pace was quite slow, but gradually began to perk up and a group of 6 of us passed the first control point at 10Km in 40-32. Shortly after this the Russian Kovel joined us, but I lost contact again on the next hill. The pace became quite erratic, so I tried to maintain a steady pace, which meant that I kept losing and regaining contact with the group of 4, who were doing fartlek. By 20Km there were 5 of us together, which became 4 quite quickly as the pace gradually increased.

Saraiva from Portugal and someone else began to open a gap on Costa from Brazil and myself and, as I thought that I was running fast enough, I did not try to go with them. About a 3rd of the way around the first 40Km loop one of the leaders dropped out, leaving Saraiva alone about 2 or 3 minutes ahead. Halfway round this lap I got away from the Brazilian and started to chase the leader. I passed the marathon in 2-45-58, 1-48 behind Saraiva and 1-36 ahead of Kovel. I passed 50Km in 3-16, which I thought was fine.

At the beginning of the last 40.278Km loop I was 3-41 behind Saraiva and 4-06 ahead of Kovel. I worked hard to close down the gap to the leader, but could only reduce it to 2-12 at 80Km. After this the gap began to widen again, and did so dramatically when I was forced to stop, because of an exceedingly painful second smallest toe on my right foot. I thought that something must have jammed between it and the front of my shoe, but on removing my shoe and sock I could see nothing that I could remedy. I put my sock back on inside out so that the rib would not cause problems, tied up my shoe and set off again. My toe pain subsided after some time, which was a relief. I was pleased to finish 2nd and my time was quite satisfactory. Apart from two painful toes I was in good condition. I had to go for doping control by the 'Real Federacion Espanola de Atletismo' and produced the required urine sample to be put in sample bottles 'A' and 'B' for analysis. Luis Saraiva's winning time was 6-46-10; I recorded 6-51-14 for first V45; and Miguel Nava was 3rd in 7-05-24. Eleanor Adams was the first lady in 17th place in 7-48-33. There were 88 participants and 46 finishers.

The following day, Sunday, 8th of October, we were travelling back to Bilbao, London and Aberdeen and on to Lossiemouth. I was pleased to be able to run my usual routes to and from work on Monday.

A week later, Saturday the 14th of October was quite a contrast as I ran in the first North District cross-country league race at Thurso.

We decided to have another caravan outing and went to a site by the A9 near where the Dornoch Bridge was to be built. I did not sleep well because I was feverish because of another infection. In the late afternoon on the following day we climbed Fireish hill and I had to carry Anna quite a lot.

On Friday the 24th of November, Izzy and I were guests of honour at the Minolta Black Isle dinner and dance in the Royal Hotel in Dingwall. It was an enjoyable evening and we stayed overnight in this hotel.

The following morning, after breakfast, we went to Invergordon to visit Isa and give her some paintings from Anna for her and Tommy (Isobel's Uncle, ex Squadron Leader Thomas Tait). Back at Dingwall I got a lift from Ray Cameron and John to Dornoch for the North of Scotland cross-country championships. I had to ask John to stop before Bonar Bridge so that I could vomit. I felt quite unwell and on arrival at Dornoch I lay out in John's car for about an hour to try to recuperate. After a jog I felt a bit better but in the race my stomach or something in my intestines became quite painful and I had to ease my pace. I finished 20th, helping Forres Harriers to be first team, with counting members finishing: 3rd, 4th, 5th, 14th, 20th and 21st. Alan Reid won comfortably.

On Saturday the 16th of December, I drove to Glasgow to attend the SAAA AGM in the Kelvin Hall. I was honoured to receive an engraved Caithness Glass Bowl in recognition of my ultra-distance running.

I finished 1989 with a total of 6472.miles, training and racing, a new personal record, which was an average of 124 miles per week.

THE NINETIES

1990

In mid October 1989, I decided that I would **attempt the RRC indoor 24-hour race, scheduled for the 3rd and 4th of February 1990 in Milton Keynes shopping centre**. This race incorporated the first International, I.A.U. Championships, the first B.A.A.A Championships and the first English A.A.A 24-hour Championships. I began training for this on the week beginning the 6th of November and **over the next 6 weeks I ran 1653 miles including 10 Monaughty 50Km Sunday runs. I knew that I had prepared as well as I thought possible.** On the 13th week I began to ease off by only cycling to and from work on Thursday.

After teaching at RAF Lossiemouth on Friday morning, I cycled up to college as usual at 12:20. Izzy picked me up from work at 15:50 and drove me to Inverness Airport, to get the 17:30 Dan Air flight to London. The flight was delayed until 20:00, so it was quite late by the time I arrived in Heathrow. John Lamont had waited patiently and was there to meet me and drove us to his home in Guildford. After a meal and some chat, I went to bed at around 23:30.

The following morning, I watched the Commonwealth Games on TV for a couple of hours and then went back to bed for an hour or so. Around midday I went down into Guildford with John to buy a bed, plus some bananas and bread for my race. We had rice and mince Dansak in mid-afternoon and a medium packet of 'Sun Maid' raisins. Heavy rain fell all day.

ONLY JUST MAKING THE START

We departed for Milton Keynes at 17:20, but soon found ourselves trapped in a huge traffic jam on the M25. It was incredibly frustrating waiting to move forward a little, while the time to get to the race was running out. Eventually after one and a half hours, in which we covered about 7 miles, the traffic began flowing. The heavy rain during the past few days and that morning had caused a landslip in the embankment, so mud and water were streaming onto the carriageways.

John then had to drive very quickly on the M1, up to 95 miles per hour, in an effort to reach Milton Keynes before the start. I managed to extricate myself from the passenger seat, get into the back seats where my kit bag was, and change into running kit, as John drove at 80 mph past the Luton turn-off. Thankfully he had been to Milton Keynes for the English National cross-country and knew where the shopping centre was, so we found it easily, arriving at 19:55. I rushed out of the car and into the shopping centre and soon found the start. Adrian Stott quickly got my number, but I fumbled nervously when I tried to pin it on, so Adrian did the necessary and completed this task for me. He could see my agitated state and urged me not to start too quickly, which advice I readily agreed with. Fortunately, the race over the 969 yards course did not start until 20:04.

WORLD BESTS IN THE ROAD RUNNERS CLUB 24 HOURS INDOOR RACE

I was so relieved to be underway after that nerve-racking and emotionally draining journey. I did not have time to make a toilet visit before the start, so I had to stop for this purpose once I had settled into the race. Andy Milroy wrote: '*on the 3rd of February 1990, the greatest 24-hour field ever assembled lined up to contest the inaugural championships. Thirteen different countries were represented*'

After a cautious start, at one hour I was lying 8th. Gradually I improved my position, until at around midnight I was the leader. I ate every hour, alternating one slice of white bread with a ripe banana. I drank every 20 minutes, rotating Maxijoul, Isostar and Leppin Enduro Booster.

On Sunday I continued running steadily at what I thought was a suitable pace and maintained my lead. Each hour the information board was updated and I could see how I was progressing. Usually I had extended my lead by 1Km each hour. **I passed 100Km in a decent time, which was encouraging.** As I approached 100 miles, Adrian informed me that I would be inside 13 hours and I passed that distance in 12-56-13, a new World Indoor Best, which was pleasing. The next major mark was 200Km, which I reached in 16-31-08, again another indoor world best. I was delighted with this as it was also an improvement on my own record of 16-32-30, set at Coatbridge some years ago.

With about 5 hours remaining I began to get twinges and pains in my lower right quads. However, these did not become any worse so I was able to continue jogging. I was very tired and found the last 3 hours rather hard so I was very relieved when the finish came.

I had improved my own 24 hours best by 22 miles and set a new World Indoors Best of 166 miles 425 yards, which was also a World Best for the over 45-age class. I was delighted with my distance and also winning the race, the first International 24-hour Championships. So I was the **AAA champion, the British (BAAB) champion and the International champion**. My training for the event worked very well and I was extremely pleased for everyone involved that it all went so well (once I finally got there). I was not sure if I ate sufficiently throughout the run. Later I found that Bryan Smith of Australia was 2nd with 156miles 276 yards and Roy Pirrung (USA) was 3rd with 154 miles 313 yards. John Lamont looked after me very well.

Once the awards ceremony was over, John drove me, a very dozy passenger, to his home in Guildford, where I could indulge in the luxury of sleep. On Monday, 5th February, John drove me to Heathrow to catch the 09:00 flight to Inverness airport and there I got a bus to Inverness and a train to Elgin. After an afternoon at work I cycled home. On Tuesday after cycling to and from work I went to the sports injury clinic at Dr Gray's Hospital in the evening and received treatment on my right quads. I cycled to and from work for the remainder of the week.

On Monday the 12th of February I was feeling able to resume running, so that was 'Day One' yet again! During the day I received physiotherapy treatment on my right quads from Malcolm. On Friday it was ultrasound on my right quads and laser treatment on my left hamstring, which had begun to bother me. The laser treatment had an effect very quickly, which was quite amazing.

In the Inverness half marathon on Sunday the 18th of March, I got off to a good start, being tucked in with the leading group for the first couple of miles to get protection from the wind. I started to enjoy my race after a bad patch as Andrew Newlands and a chap from Dundee Hawkhill caught me at about 8 miles and we had a good tussle between us to the end. A runner charged past me on the line and into the finish chute. I reckon it was a dead heat for 11th place in 74-07. Charlie Haskett won in 67-48, from Jim Doig 68-48 and Graham Laing 69-26.

On Saturday the 31st of March Izzy and I drove to Aberdeen airport where we caught the BA flight to London Heathrow. From there we caught the Iberia flight to Madrid where a person from the Madrid 100Km organization met us and drove us to the 'Hotel Tryp Asturias'. Rafael Garcia-Navas, the President of the organizing committee, had invited me and also agreed to pay for Izzy to accompany me, which was very kind of him. There we met Domingo Catalan and Luis Saraiva, who were both looking forward to the race next day. After checking in we went for a walk before going to register for the race at 18:00. Following this we had dinner at the Hotel at 20:00 and then got to bed at around 22:00.

PROBLEMS IN MADRID 100KM

At 06:00 on Sunday morning the 1st of April, we boarded a coach from the Hotel, which took us to the start of the 4th edition of the **'Pedestres Villa de Madrid'** 100k. The race got underway in the rain and dark at a couple of minutes past 07:00, as the starting pistol failed to fire on 2 occasions.

The first of the ten 10Km laps was completed in 38 minutes and a few seconds by our leading group of 6, 20Km was reached in 1-17-56, with the leading pack still 6, while Roig passed in 1-20-27 and Gonzales in 1-24-26. Shortly after this Catalan made a break and Saraiva quickly went after him. I decided to refrain from chasing them up the long climb and to give chase once the course levelled out again. This I did and regained contact at about 24Km.

Rain was still falling and conditions were becoming slightly uncomfortable. The laps were quite undulating, with a stiff climb just after the start of the lap. By 30Km, reached in 1-56-49, the rest of the original leading group had caught up. Catalan made another effort but I could not match his or Saraiva's pace and they passed 40Km in 2-34-59, while I passed in 2-37-18, Roig in 2-41-28 and Gonzales in 2-48-51. I passed the marathon point in 2-46-25.

At around 47Km I had to make a pit stop for a bowel movement, as I had been feeling uncomfortable for some time. I was annoyed, since in recent years I had not normally had this problem, but perhaps I ate too late previous night and had taken too much protein. I passed 50Km in 3-19-03, with Catalan leading Saraiva by some 6 minutes at this point. At 60Km Catalan led in 3-49-38, with Saraiva passing in 3-55-00 and I passed in 4-04-41 only 14 seconds ahead of Roig. I was feeling very tired and had tightness in my diaphragm region, which prevented me from taking full breaths. Roig passed me on the 7th lap and I was interested to see that he ran on the pavements, which I expect saved some distance at corners. I had to make another pit stop for a bowel movement at around 64Km, between two parked cars on a quiet part of the course. I reached 80Km in 5-37-01, with Catalan still leading in 5-21-09 to Saraiva's 5-22-30 and Roig passing in 5-30-12. As I entered the small loop at about 84Km I saw Catalan approaching walking, which was a surprise. I splashed on through the rain and began my final lap. With about 3Km remaining, Gonzales came past but I was too spent to fight him and was very glad to finish this race.

What caused this poor performance? I had a slight cold earlier in the week. Perhaps I trained too hard with insufficient rest, or perhaps my food intake the previous evening was unsuitable. It could be that I had not recovered from the 24-hour race on 3/4th of February. Luis Saraiva (Portugal) won in 6-48-34, from Domingo Catalan (Barcelona), 1st Vet, 6-52-16 and Christian Roig (France) in 6-57-28. Victor Gonzales (Oviedo) in 4th was 2nd Vet in 7-09-46 and I finished 5th and 3rd Vet in 7-11-49.

On the following day Izzy and I walked for about 9 hours, sightseeing in Madrid and using our Panasonic video camera, which we had purchased to make recordings on my JOGLE the previous April. We travelled back from Madrid on Tuesday the 3rd of March, departing at 09:20 on the Iberia flight to Heathrow and from there on the B.A flight to Aberdeen, where we were greeted with snow. We arrived home safely at about 5pm.

As Izzy and I were on our Easter holidays from work we decided to use our caravan for another mini-adventure. Before we could do so I had to deal with the first batch of Tutor Marked Assignments (TMAS), which required marking and sending to the Open University (OU) in Milton Keynes. I had accepted a Tutor's post for T281 after a recommendation from Rob Tyson and an interview by David Crabbe. I found the OU course material excellent and I enjoyed meeting the students at Tutorials.

Once I had completed marking TMA 01 and sorting out the caravan-to-car lighting connections we finally got away at about 5pm and drove to Aviemore, where we stayed for a day. Our next site was down the A9 at the Caravan Park at Blair Castle. We stayed there for 2 days and I thoroughly enjoyed a run up into the hills south of Glen Tilt and on subsequent mornings, runs up Glen Tilt and back on a 'Land Rover' road.

We moved on to Argyll Caravan Park near Inveraray, where we had an overnight stop, before we continued on to Lochgilphead Caravan Park. While there we were pleased to visit our friends Charlie and Marja Greenlees and their family, Helena and Sami.

Next overnight stop was a site near Oban, on the Loch shore and next day we made it home safely. This allowed us 2 days in which to prepare for returning to School and College work. I was pleasantly surprised on the Saturday when I ran my 22 miles 'Boar's Head' route in my Nike

'Duellist' racing shoes in 2-15-19, which was my best for this course by almost 3 minutes. I was very encouraged by this run

Unfortunately, by Tuesday I had a raw throat and congestion in my upper respiratory system, which was a worry because I was due to run in the Lochaber Marathon on Sunday. My throat was still rather painful by Saturday, so I got a throat swab taken at the health centre.

TWO DECENT MARATHON PERFORMANCES

On Sunday morning the 22nd of April, I set off for Fort William and picked up Mick Francis and Dennis Murphy in Forres to complete our Harriers team for the Lochaber Marathon.

I started cautiously and then moved through with Mick to join the lead group of 6 as we chased a runner from Edinburgh AC. This continued until about 10.5 miles when I increased the pace, which broke up the group. A runner from Alnwick Harriers, David Henderson, and I pulled away from the rest, passing 13 miles in 1-16-34. At the turn we began to close on the leader, but I could not maintain my pace, Henderson moved away and a runner from Falkirk Victoria Harriers caught and passed me.

By then the sun was shining and conditions became quite warm. The early leader was caught and passed by each of us in turn, and then the Falkirk runner began to fade, so I passed him at about 19 miles. I gradually pulled back the leader and by Lochy Bridge I had reduced the gap to 20 metres. I caught him soon after this and ran on for a particularly sweet win. I was extremely pleased to win a marathon again, even though my time of 2-34-01 was not outstanding.

I wore my Duellist shoes and, although I had some discomfort from the ball of my left foot, they were fine. Fifteen minutes before the start I drank 200ml of Leppin Enduro Booster, and during the race I drank 330ml of the same at 10.5 miles and again at 16.5 miles. I had no problems with lack of energy. David Henderson from Alnwick was 2nd in 2-36-14 and Colin McLennan 3rd in 2-39-05. Forres Harriers won the team race!

Subsequently I enjoyed a good period of training before my next race on Sunday the 27th of May. I had been selected to be part of the Scottish team in the 'Home Countries' competition, incorporated in the very last Aberdeen Milk Marathon.

As the race got underway I went with the leading group, which by King Street was about 14 strong. I began to feel the pace on one of the climbs on King Street and eased back as did fellow team members, Colin Youngson and Doug Cowie. A Welsh runner drifted back too. We did regain contact with the leading group briefly, before dropping back going up Union Street. We gradually lost ground on the leaders along the North Deeside road. Charlie Noble caught us and we ran past 10 miles in 56-06. As we approached the beach again we caught sight of Dic Evans, who had had to make a pit stop, so we thought that we might catch him. Charlie Noble lost contact with us as we passed halfway in 1-13-55, which was faster than my Inverness half marathon time.

Weather conditions were good, with sunshine and only a slight southeast breeze. I felt quite comfortable so I started to push on as we left the Ellon road. Colin was in trouble, but Doug Cowie came with me as I chased after Dic Evans, although he got away again. By 18 miles Doug had dropped and I pressed on passing 20 miles in 1-54-34, feeling fine. As I ran up the hill from Persley Bridge I caught sight of a runner at the top, which encouraged me to chase him. In the last 3 miles I passed a runner from Shettleston, Jim Evans, and a member of the English team.

I was very pleased indeed with my run and my position, which was the best I had achieved in several attempts at this marathon. As I was the first Aberdeen AAC member to finish I received the 'Freddy Edwards Memorial Cup'. Brian Goodwin was our team manager and he looked after us well. All members got a full set of Scottish team kit.

The English team filled the first 3 places, with Chris Tall first in 2-23-32, followed by Stan Markley in 2-24-53 and Brian McEvoy in 2-25-46. Charlie McIntyre was our first team counter in

(4th in 2-26-50), while I was 7th in 2-31-00, with Doug Cowie 10th in 2-32-55. Afterwards we had a meal with Annie and Bob (my sister and brother-in-law), but I restricted my carbohydrate intake to a very low level, as the marathon was my glycogen depletion run.

Having endured 3 days on the low carbohydrate phase of the carbohydrate loading diet it was a relief to begin carbohydrate loading at suppertime on Wednesday, 30th of May. I was preparing to race in the 2nd edition of the B.A.A.B 100Km championship in Nottingham. I had to decline participating last year because of my poor condition resulting from poor health following my JOGLE. This time I would be well prepared.

On Saturday the 2nd of June, I caught the train from Elgin to Aberdeen and eventually to Nottingham, where photo-journalist, Rob Howard met me as arranged and drove me to the National Watersports Centre at Holme Pierrepont. After checking in and obtaining a room, we went to a reception given by the sponsors, 'Pork Farms' at 19:00. I had eaten sufficiently during the day: a high carbohydrate breakfast, then bananas, bread and jam sandwiches, raisins and a litre of 10% Leppin 'Carbo Booster' on the train journey. At the reception I only ate a couple of apples, some grapes and a banana. On returning to the Sports Centre I gave an interview to Rob before retiring to bed.

NO DIFFICULTY IN BECOMING NATIONAL 100KM CHAMPION

I woke at 06:00 next morning the 3rd of June 1990 and prepared for **the 2nd National 100Km championships** at Holme Pierrepont. John Foden, the race organiser, had arranged for me an attendant/second, who was one of his teammates, and had introduced us at the reception. I gave him my drinks along with my schedule of requirements.

The course was 21 laps, in a clockwise direction, of the 4.762 Km long lakeside perimeter road. We got underway at 08:00 in overcast windy conditions. The wind was on our backs on the back straight and almost directly into our faces on the home straight. A group of 7 quickly formed and our pace seemed satisfactory. There were 2 Russians, a German, the Swiss runner Hans Peter Roos, Charles Khudube from Botswana, Erik Seedhouse and myself in the group. I enjoyed the lap course, which was flat and there were geese and ducks with youngsters on the grass and by the water's edge. There was also a heron by the artificial lakeside and later, individuals and teams rowing events, training on the lake.

We continued at a fair pace but, on each run down the home straight, slowed drastically. Gradually our group diminished; first the Russians lost contact, then Hans Peter. We passed the marathon in 2-49, which was rather a shock, so soon after this I increased the pace slightly so that the German lost contact then, surprisingly, Erik dropped. This left Charles and me to pass 30 miles together in 3-14-17 and 50Km in 3-20-something. We alternated leading into the wind on the home straight and on Charles's turn there was a shower of rain, which with the wind made conditions rather unpleasant. On the following back straight I got away from him and a gap quickly opened. Erik was falling further back all the time, which was comforting for me. I then had 8 laps to complete on my own, which became increasingly difficult on the home straight as the wind intensity increased.

I was happy with how I felt, as I had plenty of strength and was running strongly. As the race progressed I was closing on Erik, but he stopped running, and was being assisted to walk as I passed him. I lapped the German, who was 3rd and reached 50 miles in 5-23-16. After passing Charles, I had lapped the entire field, something I never anticipated. I finished in very good condition in one of my least stressful 100Km races.

I drank 300ml of Leppin Enduro Booster at 10% concentration, 10 minutes before the start and 150ml of the same at the end of the 2nd lap and then every subsequent lap. My modified carbohydrate loading programme must have been successful also. I wore my 'Duellist' shoes, which were excellent. Izzy sent light to my feet and heart, which I am sure also helped. I was delighted with this performance. There were 57 finishers from 88 starters.

My prize, apart from the **AAA gold medal**, was 'one week's safari holiday in Botswana to compete in the Kalahari 100Km race on the 5th of August', worth about £1200, but as this would clash with our family holiday I had to decline this excellent prize, so it went to Rolf Henneman. My winning time of 6-46-29 was a World Best for an over 45 years. Rolf Henneman finished 2nd in 7-30-54 and Charles Khudube from Botswana was 3rd in 7-36-44. Hilary Walker won the ladies race in 8-38-45, from Valentine Enachi (USSR) 8-48-39 and Susan Ashley 8-58-14.

Mick Francis had driven down for the race, so I accepted a lift with him as he drove home overnight, arriving in Lossiemouth at 03:30. I had some sleep before going to work. I got a lift up from Maggie and a lift back from George Marshall; and did not run although **my legs felt fine. My weight that morning was 9 stones 7 pounds and my waking pulse was 47 beats per minute, so I was in good condition. Apart from being tired in the Madrid 100km, I had been fortunate to have an almost perfect build-up to the 24 Hours in Milton Keynes and this Nottingham 100km.**

I had agreed with Adrian Stott of Sri Chinmoy AC to run in the track 100Km that he was organizing in Livingston. On Saturday the 23rd of June, three weeks after the National 100Km Izzy and I drove down to Edinburgh to stay with Rachel Hollas in preparation for the race.

WORLD AGE-GROUP BESTS AT THE FIRST SCOTTISH TRACK 100KM

On Sunday morning the 24th of June, we made our way to Livingston, West Lothian, and after a few circles we managed to find the Craigswood Sports Centre and the track. The first 100Km track race in Scotland got underway at around 07:08, due to the late arrival of Jimmy Shaw.

The pace I set was aimed at a finishing time of around 6-35-00, passing 10Km in 40 minutes and 20Km in 1-19-something. There was quite a strong wind blowing, which slowed us on the back straight. Rain began falling at around 09:30 and there were some nasty heavy showers of rain. I passed the marathon distance in 2-46 and 50Km in 3-17. At 40 miles I recorded 4-15-15 a new World Track Best for over 45s. This was previously held by Bernd Heinrich (USA) with 4-24-54. At 50 miles my time was 5-23-02, another over 45 best, improving on Bernd Heinrich's 5-34-24.

I felt fine, apart from a desire to visit the toilets for a sit down, but I did not want to stop and lose time. With about 6 miles remaining, Izzy told me that if I could speed up by 1.5 seconds a lap, I would get the over-40 World Track Best. I was able to pick up my pace and finished strongly and completely composed in 6-46-10. This was 32 seconds faster than the time Gerd Boldhaus had set in 1984. Naturally, this time was also a World Best for the over 45-age category.

I was extremely pleased with this run, which confirmed my current good condition; and was sure that I could have improved by at least 10 minutes if there had been closer competition. Izzy gave me drinks of 150ml of 10% concentration Leppin Enduro Booster, every 15 minutes, and of course encouraged me. There were 18 entries, 2 of which were ladies. The pre-race modified carbohydrate loading diet I used proved effective again. Andy Stirling finished 2nd in 7-37-53 and Alan Young was 3rd in 8-23-00. Kay Dobson was first lady in 10th place in 9-51-28.

Eight days later I had to visit the medical centre to receive a typhoid vaccination in my left arm. This was one of the requirements for the Great Wall of China race. Next day my arm had become quite painful. After work I had to get a lift back from Maggie, as I felt rather unwell. Two days later I had to take the car to work so that I could drive back to Lossiemouth for a medical examination at 10:30, which was also a requirement for China. Unfortunately, on Saturday of that week, I received notice that the Great Wall of China race had been postponed, which I interpreted as meaning cancelled.

At the Forres Highland Games I ran in the 11.25 miles road race and found the early pace was brisk, but was able to hold onto Andy Newlands and Alistair Neaves. Andy began to drop by 3 miles and Ally began to slow at about 4 miles, so I pressed on up the stiff climbs. I felt tired, but was running well and pushed on to win, improving on last year's time by 4 minutes and 19 seconds with 62-09. It was super to win this race again after 12 years. Ally Neaves was 2nd in 63-22 and Andy Newlands 3rd in 64-26.

On Monday the 9th of July, we set off on our summer caravan holiday, making our first stop at Blair Atholl Caravan Park. This allowed me another opportunity to run up Glen Tilt and back, about 8 minutes faster than my time for this course in Easter. I experienced a nosebleed after about 3 miles on my run, so I arrived back at the caravan spattered in blood.

Next stop was at Thack-A-Lee Park in Penrith and I did an exploratory run from there before moving on to Drayton Manor Caravan Park, for canal towpath runs. After 2 days, we moved to Hereford Racecourse Caravan site to get ready for the 50-mile race on Sunday.

HOT WORK IN THE 'TARRANT 50'

On Sunday, the 15th of July, in the **John Tarrant Memorial 50 miles race** my hopes of a relaxed race vanished when I spotted Erik Seedhouse stretching. After a minute's silence in memory of John Tarrant, we were off. The initial pace was sedate, as the temperature was already rather high. Erik, Tony Lenagan and I passed the one-mile marker together but, on the climb soon after, Erik and I went away and completed the first 10 miles lap in 63-51, which was sensible in the warm weather conditions.

I got away from Erik as he slowed to take his 'Leppin' Enduro Booster at the start of lap 2, but he soon caught up. At about 3 miles into this lap Erik began to increase the pace and I decided to let him get away. He got about 20 metres ahead but did not extend this, so I gradually pulled him back and we were together again by 19 miles. We had completed the second lap in 60-59. Again I got a gap on Erik at the start of lap 3 as he consumed his drink and he caught me at about 4 miles into this lap, but as soon as he reached me I increased my pace, as I suspected that he would have had to work quite hard to close the gap and would now be looking for a recovery period. Much to my delight, my strategy worked and he could not hang on. I passed the marathon in 2-43-05, which was pleasing and completed this 3rd lap in 62-25 to Erik's 62-50. I started lap 4 with a lead of 35 seconds.

By then the high temperature was taking its toll and I began to tire. Every 3 miles I was drinking 150ml of 'Enduro Booster', provided by Izzy, and I would give my empty bottle to Claire, who would position herself some 100 metres down the road. This arrangement worked well and I supplemented the 'Leppin' with water from the feed stations. My 4th lap took 68-05 and I was concerned that Erik would be catching me, but his lap was 72-42, so my lead going into the last lap was 5-12. This last lap was quite a struggle and I had to concentrate hard to keep running. Consequently, I was very pleased and relieved to finish this race and to win. My last lap took me 74-30, while Erik took 76-57.

When I crossed the finish line and relaxed my concentration, my head began to feel quite light and I said to Izzy that I wanted to lie down urgently. My voice had all but gone and I had to keep repeating my request until I was assisted into Hereford F.C. and to lie out on a wooden bench, where the first aid lady, Izzy and Anna, attended to me. I had bad cramps in both legs, which came on when I tried to move. Gradually I recovered and was able to take a bath with assistance. I had a burst blister under the ball of my left foot, which stung in the bath. Erik collapsed on crossing the finish line and had to be carried in, apparently out for the count. This was the closest that I had come to fainting.

Later, at the presentation of prizes, the Lady Mayor informed us that this had been the hottest July day in Hereford for 17 years and that the temperature, according to local radio, was over 90°F. Of the 58 starters only 19 finished the course. I had finished in 5-29-50 and Eric completed the course in 5-37-29, with J. Rowland 3rd in 6-17-22, Norrie Williamson 4th in 6-24-38 and James Zarie 5th in 6-33-54.

On Monday I felt very drained and could not run, but we all enjoyed the warm weather as the temperature reached 88°F. Once we had moved onto Wish-hanger Lane Farm caravan site, the weather continued to be warm. I had entered the 50 miles and Lincolnshire 100Km races as preparation for the Great Wall of China stage race. Despite this race being abandoned I decided to go ahead with my plans. In the week between these 2 races, all I could do was some recovery jogging on pleasant woodland tracks and roads.

ONLY ONE WEEK LATER, THE LINCOLNSHIRE 100KM

On Sunday the 22nd of July, I ran in the Lincolnshire 100Km, for the first time since I fractured my left patella in a fall soon after the start of the 1988 edition. The weather conditions were much kinder, with a stiff easterly wind and overcast. I would not have relished having to run another ultra-marathon in hot conditions. I was given 'Number One', a nice gesture, but this was sent to our home after we had departed on our summer holidays, so I could not use it. There was no starting gun and we were sent on our way by an informal 'off you go then' from Anne Devlin. Erik Seedhouse was there, but he was entered for the 50Km race, which was finishing in Lincoln, so I let him go along with another runner who looked like he was going for the 50Km. I settled in to my run and was in joint 3rd as we passed 10Km in 40 minutes, which was just fine. My intention was to have as easy and relaxed race as I could and still win. I reached the turn around in the Stonebow in Lincoln after 3-30 and I noted the time from the turn until I met the 2nd runner. He was Paul Taylor and over 7 minutes back, so I had a lead of about 14 minutes. Then I had the lead car to guide me, and Izzy was giving me drinks in the same sequence as the previous Sunday. The run became a bore over the last 30Km so I was pleased to see the finish. This was the 4th time that I had won this race and the time was probably my slowest at 7-12-17. Paul Taylor was 2nd in 7-33-3, with Kevin Marshall 3rd in 8-18-17 and Sue Ashley (in 9th place with 9-16-59) was first lady.

We began making our way home, with stops at Sudbrook Caravan Site, a site near Skegness, and the temporary location of 'Middle Engine Lane' in North Shields. This latter site, where we stayed for 3 days, allowed us to visit the gardening exhibition at Gateshead and also the Metro Centre there. Our next halt was not far up the coast at Proctors Stead Caravan Park, which allowed us to explore the region there. We stopped in a Caravan Park in Melrose for a day and then drove home in time for the Moray Marathon the following day.

Although I was tired and not properly recovered from my 2 recent ultra marathons I decided to run in the 9th edition of the Macallan Moray marathon on Sunday the 5th of August. Erik Seedhouse, our houseguest for the weekend, set a brisk pace, so George Sim and I went with him and, after about half a mile, Colin Hunter and Robert Wood from Dundee Road Runners joined us. I began to feel the pace as we got to the top of the hill by Spynie Hospital and lost contact at the first refreshment station and, although I tried to regain contact on the downhill, I made no impression on the group. In Lossiemouth, Mick Francis caught me on Shore Street and I ran with him for about a mile. Between 23 and 24 miles I caught and passed two to become 5th, a position I maintained to the finish. Erik won convincingly in 2-28-29 ahead of George Sim in 2-34-28 and Colin Hunter with 2-34-16. I was pleased that Mick ran so well to finish 4th in 2-35-21, while I recorded 2-35-47. Izzy gave me my drinks again.

Monday, 6th of August was 'Day One' again and I resumed my structured training programme, so that by the end of the week I had accumulated 120 miles despite receiving my 2nd typhoid vaccination for my non-trip to China.

In the Nairn Highland Games half marathon on Saturday, 18th August, I felt lethargic before the start. Once underway I began to run quite well and moved through the field, passing 10 miles in 56-25 and got to within 3 metres of Danny Bow, before he began to move away again. I finished 10th of the 147 starters in 74-18, 2nd Vet, 12 seconds behind 1st Vet Danny Bow with 3rd Vet, Innis Mitchell, close behind in 74-26. I was quite pleased with that run.

ANOTHER TWO BRIDGES VICTORY

On the following Friday evening, the 24th of August, Mick Francis and I drove down to Rosyth for the 'Two Bridges' road race next day. Mick and I stayed at HMS Cochrane in room 55A along with two others. I had a relaxed morning, which was much better than driving down on the day of the race, as I had done in previous years.

Once the race got underway, I led out of the Park and then Erik Seedhouse set off at a fast pace, so I went with him, but after about 600 metres decided to let him go. He pulled away by about 30 metres and I followed at a fast but comfortable pace and regained contact with him at about 2.5 miles. We ran together through 5 miles in 27-57 and then on to 10 miles in 57-07. After 15 miles, which we passed in 1-27-16, I took the lead, as I felt good and Erik appeared to be slowing, and I opened a gap of about 8 metres, but he closed it and we were together again. At around 18 miles I led again and this time broke away, passing 20 miles in 1-57-25 to Erik's 1-57-33. I pushed on through Bo'ness and managed the stiff hill after that quite well. At the junction where the route turned left I could see Erik about 80 metres behind. By 25 miles Don Turner said that I had a lead of about 400 metres. I passed the marathon point in 2-35-42. By now the weather was quite warm and humid and I found the hill after the marathon quite stressful, but I maintained a fair pace, passing 30 miles in 2-59-30, which was satisfactory.

The last section, with the climb up through Inverkeithing, was quite tough, but I was able to maintain a fairly strong pace. I was very glad to win this classic race again, but my 3-37-59 (on my watch) was a bit slower than I expected, based on earlier intermediate times, but the finishing times were affected by warm conditions. There were 75 finishers, from an entry of 110, which included 20 from Tipton Harriers. My time was given as 3-38-00 and Alan Smith of Tipton was second in 3-42-47, while Erik Seedhouse was 3rd in 3-48-05 and Mick Francis had his best race over this course finishing 4th in 3-59-17. Hilary Walker was first lady in 15th overall in 4-15-23.

On the following Friday in the evening Andy Milroy telephoned me to tell me that I was invited to the 100Km in Duluth, USA, on the 27th of October.

During a run home from work a week or so later, I was delayed because one of my front tooth crowns fell out, bounced off my wrist, went onto the road and then the verge. After about 20 minutes of searching I was pleased to find the detached crown.

On Tuesday the 18th of September I received a letter from John Legge informing me that I had been **selected to represent Great Britain in the IAU 100Km World Cup (Championships) in Duluth, USA; and that I would get a 'British Vest' (my first at 46 years old!) for this race.**

My glycogen depletion for the Santander 100Km was accomplished on Sunday, 30th September, when I ran my Monaughty course with a sprightly Mick Francis in 3-18-31. This gave me 156 miles for the week. I began eating my high carbohydrate diet on Wednesday, 3rd, October, at 05:20. Then I ran on the golf course and beach to the cliffs and back by the golf clubhouse before I cycled to and from work.

A SECOND VICTORY AT LAST IN THE SANTANDER 100KM

On Friday the 5th of October, I travelled from Elgin to Dyce and then flew to London and continued to Bilbao airport. From there, Walter and Vittoria drove Malcolm Campbell, Mark Smith from the USA, Peter Mann and another German and I to Santander. We stopped for a meal at Castro Urdallies, a beautiful coastal town. We arrived in Santander at midnight and after registration, where I managed to get some drinks bottles, we got to our hotel, the RHIN, at about 00:40. Not much time for sleep before the race start!

My alarm call was at 05:30. Filling my drinks bottles and labelling them were tasks that occupied 30 minutes. William took us to the Palace shortly after 6:00 and I made my way down to the finish area to use the toilet facility there.

Following a minute's silence, we were off at 07:00 and by the time we reached the main road I was part of a leading group. I got my first drink at 10Km, which we passed in 39-something. By the end of the first lap of 19.444Km I was 5th in 1-15-19, part of a group of 7, including two Kenyans, with marathon bests of 2-15 and 2-17, who were attempting 100Km for the first time. Luis Saraiva, last year's winner was 13th in 1-17-38, while Domingo Catalan was 17th in 1-17-42, both part of a group of 10 runners. Our group began to break up at about 25Km as the two Kenyans ran a bit erratically. Wilfred, the taller of the Kenyans, asked me if the pace was too fast and each time I reassured him that the pace was perfect at 40 minutes per 10Km.

By 35Km I had taken the lead on the long hill up to the extreme point on the big lap. On the downhill section the small Kenyan, Andrew Tumo, caught up and we passed the marathon point in 2-43-50. Wilfred was next in 2-44-32 and Saraiva was now 4th in 2-45-30, with Catalan 6th in 2-47-12. Tumo had a very distinctive running action with his arms held high in front of his chest and with a galloping action. He pulled ahead by about 10 metres then slowed, I caught and passed him, but then he repeated the manoeuvre twice more in the next couple of Km. He then began to fall back and by 45Km, Tumo was about 30 metres behind me.

As I approached 50Km, someone shouted that the Portuguese, Saraiva, was catching up. I passed 50Km in 3-14-48 and decided to maintain my pace, then to go with Saraiva if he caught me. He caught me at about 52Km along with Wilfred Kiplagat, so I began running with them, glad of the company. We completed the first large lap at 59.722Km, with Saraiva leading in 3-52-33, from Kiplagat in 3-52-34 and me in 3-52-35. Catalan was next in 3-55-07 along with Valmir Nunes from Brazil.

I began to increase my effort on a hill at 63Km and on the next climb at 65Km I got away from Saraiva and Kiplagat. If they were to beat me they were going to have to work hard to do it. By this time the sun was shining from a cloudless sky and the temperature quite high as I pressed on past 70Km. At 80Km the course has a climb back out of the valley and I was able to look across to the road I had just run down; there was no one in sight, so I estimated that I must have a lead of some 900 metres or more.

By 90Km a motorcyclist shouted that Saraiva was 6 minutes behind, so I could afford to relax and enjoy the last 10Km. As I approached the finish I began to feel quite emotional: I was going to win this classic race again, 8 years after my previous victory. In my 4 other attempts I had finished 2nd. I finished relaxed and in good condition and my time of 6-40-23 was a pleasant surprise as I had expected 6-45 or 6-46.

Later I heard that Kiplagat had collapsed and had to be taken to hospital for intravenous re-hydration. Luis Saraiva was 2nd in 6-52-29 and Valmir Nunes 3rd in 7-01-27, Tomas Rusek 4th in 7-13-46 and Jose Costa (Brazil) 5th in 7-14-00. There were 100 participants and 54 finishers.

A week later I felt lethargic and had a wheeze, which developed into a cold. Because we were on our 'tattie holidays' (now the October break, but when I was at school children were given the week off to pick potatoes 'tatties' at surrounding farms), we took the opportunity to take our caravan to Scone Palace Caravan Park for a week. On one of my morning runs from there I saw two albino pheasants, which I presume are rather rare.

On Thursday the 25th of October I started my long journey to Duluth, USA. My route involved train to Glasgow, a flight to Chicago and then on to Minneapolis. Leo Kniebel, along with Roland Vuillemenot of France and Tarak Kauff, met me there. It was a pleasant surprise to meet Tarak again. Leo drove us with two Australian girls to the National Sports centre, where we were to spend the night. I shared a room with Roland. There were 2 sets of bunk beds per room and we had to make the beds up before use. I think that it was about 22:00 local time before I got to bed.

On Friday, following a high carbohydrate breakfast, we were driven 180 miles, through flat farmland until we neared Duluth, when some hills became visible. As we passed over the shoulder of Spirit Mountain we got a spectacular view of Lake Superior and Duluth.

By 2pm we reached our accommodation, the 'Park Inn' on the lakeshore, where I shared room 214 with Erik Seedhouse. He was already there and resting in the room. He said that he had recovered from the pleurisy that had forced him out of the London to Brighton. I rested while he went into Duluth with Stephen Moore. At 16:30 we all went over to the Duluth convention centre to pick up our numbers and sweat shirts.

PROBLEMS IN THE WORLD CUP 100KM

I wrote the following report for the RRC newsletter:

The IAU 100Km World Cup, Duluth, 27 October 1990.

This race, under the patronage of the I.A.A.F., was incorporated in the 'Edmund Fitzgerald' 100Km at Duluth, Minnesota. A 50Km race using the second half of the 100Km course and a relay race over the 100Km route, were also arranged, providing an ultra-distance running festival. These events were organised by a large team of volunteers from the American Lung Association Running Club, under the directorship of Bill Wenmark. This club is based in Minneapolis, some 180 miles south of Duluth.

The race was named after the 'Edmund Fitzgerald', the largest ore-hauling ship on the Great Lakes, when she was launched in 1958. On the 10th of November 1975 she left Duluth loaded with Taconite, which is partly processed iron ore and got caught in one of the worst storms on Lake Superior, really an inland sea, with 100 mile an hour winds and snow. She broke up in the storm and sank; there were no survivors from the 29 crewmen.

I arrived in Minneapolis at about 8 p.m. on the 25th of October and Leo Kniebel, from the race organization met me along with Roland Vuillemenot of France, who had arrived a little earlier. Leo drove two Australian girls and us to the National Sports centre, where we were to spend the night. I shared a room with Roland. There were two sets of bunk beds per room and one had to make the beds up before use.

At breakfast next morning we met the Australians and Yiannis Kouros, who was being looked after by Tarak Kauff of the Sri Chinmoy athletic club of New York. Following our high carbohydrate breakfast, we were driven in luxurious mini-buses the 180 miles up to Duluth. The land was flat until we neared Duluth when some hills became visible and the road climbed. As we passed over the shoulder of Spirit Mountain we got a spectacular view of Lake Superior and Duluth. Soon we reached our accommodation, the 'Park Inn' on the shore of Lake Superior. I shared a room with Erik Seedhouse, who had arrived the day before.

In the late afternoon we all went over to the Duluth convention centre to pick up our numbers, sweat shirts and attend a press conference. I was surprised to see that the entry fee for the race was $75.00, before 1st September and $150 after that! Leo introduced me to Darryn Kozak, who was to act as my handler during the race. I went to the spaghetti dinner and I had a small portion. I returned to the Motel and was in bed by 8 p.m. local time, but I found it difficult to sleep and I was conscious that my heart was thumping and at quite a rate. I put this down to pre-race tension. I woke at midnight and could not induce sleep again.

Erik and I rose at 04:30 and began our final preparations for the race. Erik left at 05:00 with Steven and his wife Kath. Isobel, my wife telephoned soon after to wish me luck. I left with Darryn at 05:15 for the 70 miles drive to the start in the cold and darkness. We arrived at 06:30 and it was even colder at this altitude of 1400 feet and with a wind blowing. I decided to use olive oil on my arms and legs to give me some more thermal insulation. The finish would be at 600 feet on the shore of Lake Superior.

The start was just outside a village called Finland and we got underway at 07:00 under a clear starry sky and I settled into the pack of 50 or so. I had to agree with Bill Wenmark, the race organizer, who stated that 'this is absolutely the greatest field you'll ever see assembled'.

As dawn came in I could see about 3 runners some way ahead of our group. We passed 10Km in 38-10, which surprised me as I thought that we were working harder than that pace. This was probably an early indication that I was not functioning properly.

We pulled in Charlie Trayer of the USA as the group began to split up and 7 of us began to move away. In the group were: Charlie Trayer, Heinz Huglin of Germany, Roland Vuillemenot of France, Yiannis Kouros of Greece, Stefan Feckner of Canada, Hanspeter Roos of Switzerland and me. We caught Tom Zimmerman of the USA and Ray Krolewicz also of the USA. Ray announced that we were joint 2nd, as Russell Prince of New Zealand was ahead and out of sight.

Domingo Catalan moved through to join us and the group began to reduce soon after this. Ray Krolewicz was first to drop, then Hanspeter, followed by Tom Zimmerman and Stefan Feckner, then Charlie Trayer. Our group consisted of: Domingo, Roland, Heinz, Yiannis and me, with Yiannis in the lead.

By now we were running on unpaved roads, which was a mixture of compacted earth and gravel. By the next section of paved road, I had begun to struggle; I had tightness across my middle and I could not breathe fully. I felt weak and slowed dramatically. Tom Zimmerman and Stefan Feckner came past and then Charlie Trayer caught me. I began to feel a little better and I was able to run with Charlie for a while. We passed the marathon in 2-47-something and then Charlie began to drop behind. I had lost sight of those ahead and I knew that my race was over some time ago, so my priority was now to complete the course. I passed 50Km in 3-18-something and I could see Tom Zimmerman ahead. Now we were passing runners, who had started their 100Km at 6 a.m.

I got a pleasant surprise when Erik came charging past at about 55Km, but I was too tired to say anything coherent. Soon after this I caught and passed Tom Zimmerman, but I was in a poor condition and I could not stride out on the long downhill section to Lake Superior at two Harbours. My quads were also giving quite a lot of discomfort, which puzzled me, as I had not had problems of this nature for years.

My pace continued to decline and around 73Km Herbert Cuntz of Germany came pattering alongside. He beckoned me to run with him, but as I was locked into survival pace, I had to decline his offer, so he moved ahead. Some time later Christian Roig of France passed then Bruno Joppen of Holland passed me. I felt frustrated as I wanted to run with them, but my body refused to comply.

At last I reached the finish at Brighton Park, very pleased to be finished this distressing experience. It was luxury to just lie down on a camp bed, with a couple of blankets over me, in the medical tent for some 40 minutes. A Doctor checked my blood pressure a couple of times and as it proved satisfactory, I vacated my bed a little reluctantly, for more needy cases.

Initially I thought that my poor performance was due to incomplete recovery from my race at Santander 3 weeks previously. However, in June I had carried out a simulation of this situation to investigate if 3 weeks was sufficient recovery time. Three weeks after running 6-46-29 in the National 100Km championships at Holme Pierrepont I ran 6-46-10 in a 100Km track race at Livingston and felt good. This proved to me that 3 weeks was sufficient recovery time for me.

When I got up from my rest I began to cough up unpleasant looking yellow phlegm and later I was aware of a rasping sensation low in my left lung. This infection problem probably caused my poor performance.

I was pleased to learn that Erik had finished 6th in a personal best time and that Eleanor had won the ladies race. Steven was forced to retire at 75Km in 13th place, due to bouts of violent sickness, which caused dehydration, which was a big disappointment for him and Kath, but I am sure that he will have learned from this experience. I was disappointed with my 10th place in 7-11-14, but it was the best I could manage in the circumstances. I was proud to run in Great Britain kit and to be part of the G.B. team.

On returning home I went to our medical centre and I was not surprised to find that I had an infection in my left lung and that a course of antibiotics was prescribed to sort it out. I was not aware of this infection prior to the race and although I had a wheeze over a week before the race it seemed to clear up, but my pulse was above normal in the days before the race. This I put down to apprehension and excitement. It seems that I must have had this infection in the week before the race and my immune system had been using up energy fighting the infection, leaving me weakened for the run.

Results: 1) Roland Vuillemenot (France) 6-34-02, 2) Russell Prince (New Zealand) 6-38-00, 3) Stefan Feckner (Canada) 6-42-12, 4) Yiannis Kouros (Greece) 6-43-34, 5) Heinz Huglin (Germany) 6-50-51, 6) Erik Seedhouse (Great Britain) 6-55-14, 7) Herbert Cuntz (Germany) 7-05-30, 8) Christian Roig (France) 7-06-50, 9) Bruno Joppen (Netherlands) 7-07-49, 10) Don Ritchie (Great Britain) 7-11-14

The following morning after breakfast we attended a meeting on 'the State of Ultra Distance running', which was well worthwhile. I was pleased to meet Doris Brown, formerly a five times winner of the International Cross-Country Champion, who was the IAAF representative at the meeting.

We left at 1pm with John Foden driving the mini-bus. He was very angry with Malcolm Campbell and Andy Milroy, who at the I.A.U meeting earlier that morning had agreed to hold the I.A.U, world 100Km challenge in Barcelona in 1992, rather than at Holme Pierrepont as was informally agreed. This influenced his driving, as he was at times well over 80 mph although the speed limit was 65 mph.

Back home, I discussed with Dr Faulkner the possibility of medical monitoring prior to an important race. **He agreed it would be desirable to have a respiratory system check and a throat swab done, say two weeks before the race and possibly two weeks ahead of that also.**

On Saturday the 3rd of November, early in the morning, Izzy and I drove to Grandma Tait's in Inverness, where we had a cup of tea and watched 'Trans World Sports' for the feature on me, which pleased both Izzy and myself. Following this we drove to Fortrose on the Black Isle for the festival of running. Izzy was to run in the 10Km, her first race for some years. She was using this run to raise funds for Leukaemia research.

I ran in the marathon, making a cautious start, as my legs were still painful. Mick Francis gave me my drinks at: 7, 12, 17 and 21 miles. The initial pace was fine, but John Duffy of Shettleston Harriers began to pick up the pace and opened up a 50 metres gap. Mitchell McCredie then began to pull away, while I hesitated. At about 5 miles I began to chase McCredie and I caught him after some time. This effort, however, weakened me and soon I began to struggle and lose contact with him. I then maintained a comfortable steady pace and at around 15 miles I could just see McCredie in the distance. By 20 miles I was closing in on him and approaching 23 miles he was slowing dramatically and actually stopped to spend a penny. He was reduced to a walk soon after this and he retired once I passed him. He was having trouble with his calf muscle again. I finished a distant 2nd, but I was pleased to feel so much better than the previous Saturday. Izzy completed the 10Km without difficulty and was keen to participate in more and longer races. John Duffy won in 2-31-16 and I finished in 2-37-55.

On Thursday the 6th of December my right knee was painful and stiff following my morning run to work. On my run home after work I was conscious of right knee tightness and, after about 20 minutes, something gave a crack on the outside of this knee and the accompanying pain brought me to an abrupt halt. I walked about 6 miles home on a wet windy night. On Friday Malcolm Morgan examined my knee, gave me treatment and suggested I try a short run on Sunday, but to cycle until then. By the 17th of December my right knee pain became worse. Malcolm, found two spots of damage on the medial ligament on the inside of my right knee, where the ligament fans out. He gave me treatment from a combined ultrasonic and pulsed high frequency currents machine.

A week later I was still unable to run, as my right knee was extremely painful, even when not walking, so I cycled to and from work and received physiotherapy treatment from Malcolm and he recommended that I did not try running again until Boxing Day. My knee was no better a few days later, which was quite disappointing, but Malcolm had said that I should be able to run the injury out soon, so I forced myself to go to the Lighthouse and back. I experienced considerable discomfort from my knee towards the end. The pain appeared to be coming from the covering of my tibia, the periosteum. By the last few days of December my right knee was improving.

I learned that I had finished second, five points behind Roland Vuillemenot, in the IAU 100Km 'inter-continental cup'. This was based on our two best performances and on our positions in the rankings for the year, 1990. Despite recent injury, it had been a very good year for me.

On checking my total training and racing mileage for 1990 amounted to 6121 miles, an average of 117 miles per week.

1991

By the first weekend of January 1991 my right knee was much improved, allowing me to run a 21 miles course. Throughout the remainder of the month my training went well, but was not geared to cross-country running. My first race in 1991 was on Sunday the 3rd of February, when I ran for Aberdeen AAC in the Scottish Veterans Cross-Country Championships at Linlithgow. I was surprised and annoyed, when I arrived at the finish after the second lap of the fields, as I thought that there was another lap to run and. Ian Elliot won in 31-56 from Colin Youngson 32-44 and John Kennedy in 32-48 and I finished 38th.

In the Inverness half marathon on Sunday the 17th of March, I felt quite good for about a mile after which I began to feel the pace too stressful. My left quads were protesting at the pace and becoming tight and painful with a burning sensation, which restricted my speed. Also I had some irregular heartbeats, fibrillations, which were a little alarming. I passed 10 miles in 56-53 and 2 runners passed me from then to the finish. My time of 74-36 was poor, but could have been worse. I finished 21st and first over 45 Vet from the 536 finishers. Rain fell throughout the race and I wore a thermal long sleeve vest under my Forres Harriers vest and a hat and these, plus the sodden shoes, added weight. James Hill, Dundee Hawk Hill Harriers (DHHH) won in 67-23 from Simon Axon, Hunters Bogtrotters (HB), 67-23 and Chris Hall (DHHH) 67-24.

I then concentrated on preparing for the Madrid 100Km in early April. On Friday the 5th of April I drove Izzy and the family to Aberdeen Airport for my flight to London. Izzy and the girls were to go into Aberdeen to do some shopping. At Heathrow I caught a flight to Madrid. On arrival there, 2 members from the race organization and also Nigel Robinson met me and presently Eleanor Adams joined us. We were driven towards Madrid, but were halted at one point on the motorway to allow the King of Spain to pass. Our hotel was the same one as last year, the 'Hotel Tryp Asturias'. Once I had checked in and seen my room I went for a stroll around the local area. I drank a litre of 10% concentration Carbo Booster during the day.

GRABBING A THIEF

On Saturday morning I went for a walk, with the aid of a city map, and bought bread and mineral water on my way back to the hotel, where I had lunch. Following this, I dozed off in my room for 3 hours. Then I caught the Metro at Sol to Portazago, which was close to the start of the 100Km race, where we had to register at the stadium and pick up our numbers and 'goodie bags'. Apart from a Tee shirt these included a vest, shorts and a very comprehensive guide to 'The Best of Spain'. Having completed registration I returned by Metro to Sol. On my way back to the hotel I bought a lemon sorbet ice and, shortly after this, I was aware that someone had spat on my right sleeve and was rubbing it off. As I glanced to my right I felt him extracting my wallet from the left shell suit pocket with his left hand. I swung around instinctively and grabbed him by the collar with my right hand, losing my ice and shouted at him. He passed my wallet to his accomplice, but I managed to grab it as he tried to place it under the arm of his mate. Two well-dressed Spanish men, one with an E.E.C badge in his jacket lapel, helped me and held the pickpocket. A shopkeeper telephoned for the police and we waited until they arrived, while my sorbet was melting in the gutter. In due course a police van arrived and I was ushered into the back with the pickpocket, as I was required to go to the police station to make a complaint against this man. There was some delay, so we sat there and the policeman offered us a cigarette, which the pickpocket accepted and began smoking as did the policemen. Eventually he drove to the police station where I described the incident and then, as I was not offered a lift back, I walked to the hotel and arrived at about 21:00. The whole episode had occupied about 2 hours. Instead of taking dinner so late, I took two oranges and went to bed at 21:45, reflecting on my encounter with the thief.

FIRST VETERAN IN THE MADRID 100KM

At 05:00, which was 04:00 UK time, on Sunday the 7th of April, I received my alarm call and, once I had put on my racing kit, began filling my drinks bottles. I had made up Enduro Booster solution by putting the appropriate quantity of powder into two litre and one litre plastic bottles and then adding water. Even after 24 hours some of the powder had not dissolved, so this process was not altogether satisfactory. I planned to take 150ml every 5Km after 10Km, with the usual 250ml pre race drink.

At 05:30 the coach arrived to take us to the start, calling at another hotel on the way and we arrived at the start at 06:10. I finished filling my drinks bottles and gave them to two helpers that Rafael had organised for me; one could deal with the even Km drinks, while the other took charge of the 5Km drinks.

At 07:00 the runners in the **100Km 'Pedestres Villa De Madrid' race** got underway in the dark. The initial pace felt fine and the first 10Km lap was completed in 38-11, with Saraiva, Nunes, Rusek, Vuillemenot and I in the leading group. Vuillemenot ran erratically and would take a lead of 40 metres and then drift back to the pack. At 20Km Vuillemenot was leading in 1-16-39 with the rest of our group passing this point in 1-16-46. Our group caught Roland and we ran together in the bright sunshine. We reached 40Km in 2-32-59, which was quite pleasing, but I forgot to check the marathon time a little over 2Km later.

By 50Km Tomas Rusek had dropped off as we passed in 3-11-something. I began to lose contact with Saraiva and Nunes on the next lap so that by 60Km they passed in 3-50-50, while I passed in 3-52-34, Vuillemenot in 3-53-53 and Rusek in 3-54-00.

I continued to fall behind although I was not in difficulty, just tired, but later I began experiencing stiffness and pain in my left quads. This was most noticeable on the downhill sections. This problem caused me to slow more as the race progressed.

By 80Km, Saraiva was through in 5-11-58, with Nunes 8 seconds later, while I passed with Ramon Alvarez in 5-20-20. Vuillemenot abandoned the race at 60Km so in 5th place was Konstantin Santalov of the USSR, who passed this distance in 5-21-56. I could not match the pace of Ramon, who was accompanied by his second running alongside him and they pulled away. By then the temperature was up to 25°C. I managed to hold onto 4th place to the end and was quite pleased with my run. Anyway, it was the best I could manage. I received 50,000ptas for 4th place.

Nunes, from Brazil, ran very well indeed, improving his best by 16 minutes and setting a new course record of 6-35-41. He was 26 years old, so he could have a big impact in 100Km races in the future. Domingo Catalan and Christian Roig dropped out.

Santalov from the USSR was only 25 and has a marathon best of 2-14. This was his first 100Km race, so I was sure that he had the potential to improve dramatically in this event. I wore my Asics LD racers, which served me well, but I would have benefited from wearing socks.

Results: 1) Valmir Nunes (Brazil) 6-35-41, 2) Luis Saraiva (Port) 6-45-28. 3) Ramon Alvarez Saez (Spain) 6-46-18, 4) Don Ritchie (Ecosse) 6-54-10 {1st Vet}, 5) Victor Gonzalez (Spain) 6-57-

59, 6) Konstantin Santalov (USSR) 7-02-32, 7) Vaclav Kamenik (CZ) 7-18-04, 8) Jose Alves Costa (Brazil) 7-18-50, 9) Elias Barroso 7-26-04,10) Francisco Lopez (Spain) 7-41-03, 11) Juan Martinez Segado (Spain) 7-44-01, 12) Tomas Rusek (CZ) 7-47-58, 13) Eleanor Adams (GB) 7-57-03 (1st Lady). (80 starters but only 13 finishers.)

Having travelled home on Monday, I soon consulted Malcolm Morgan about my left quads. Malcolm found 3 locations of injuries and he eased the resulting tightness by massage and this was followed by ultra sound treatment, which much improved my leg function.

On the 22nd of April, I picked up Mick Francis and Donald Gunn and drove to Fort William, to run in the Lochaber Marathon. After registering I arranged for my drinks to be sent to the 10.5 miles and 16.5 miles first aid stations. There was a good entry of 167 starters and the initial pace felt fine, but after a couple of miles I had to speed up to maintain contact with the leaders. We passed 10 miles in 57-06 and at the turn there were 11 in the group as the pace began to quicken. Three fell behind leaving 8 of us to fight it out. I began to struggle at around 14.5 miles and had to let the group go but, as it began to break up, I began to catch some. I was 7th and at 20 miles reached in 1-54-45. I passed Neil Martin and then Henderson from Alnwick Harriers, who had been 2nd the previous year. By Banavie I caught and passed the 4th runner and was now concentrating on pulling in the 3rd, caught him at about 25 miles and got past quite easily. The 2nd runner was in sight and I was gaining on him, but the finish intervened before I could catch him. I was very pleased at how well I ran over the last 7 miles. My drinks of 330ml of Enduro Booster did not show up at 10.5 miles or at 16.5 miles as required, but both were offered at 18 miles, so I took one. I think that this helped me run well in the finishing stages. My time was an improvement of 3-21 on my winning time in 1990. Forres Harriers won the team race again. Jim Cooper (Springburn) won in 2-28-34 from Les Atkinson (Alnwick H), 2-29-47, while I finished 3rd in 2-30-40.

A few days later I had an infection in my gum, associated with my upper left incisor tooth. My dentist, Tim Griffiths gave me an appointment and after an X-ray, he drilled a hole in the tooth and extracted the root and some pus. He left the hole so that the remaining pus could drain out and prescribed 'Penicillin V', 250mg tablets. However, my infected tooth became very bothersome, so I had it extracted, which was a great relief.

On Saturday the 4th of May I caught the 08:40 bus to Inverness, where I jogged to Bught Park to meet Adrian Stott and other members of the Sri Chinmoy centres, who were to begin the British leg of the **'Peace Run'** there. Once the 2-mile fun run was completed I gave an interview to Charlie Bannerman for BBC Scotland and then at 10.18 set off on the run to Findhorn by a convoluted route. I ran down onto Riverside Drive and across the footbridge then up to near the castle to pick up the old Edinburgh road. I followed this road, now accompanied by a second in a car. I must have missed a turn, although I am sure that the road signs still indicated the old Edinburgh road, as the road got narrower and after about 1.5 miles of climbing it ended.

By now I was on Drumossie Moor, so I turned left and picked up roads in a new housing development, and these took me under the A9, after which I had to follow the old A9, back down past the Drumossie Hotel until I picked up the B9006 road. On this road I climbed back up onto Culloden Moor and now had company and, as I had not run here before, I found it interesting. We began to follow the side of a valley passing through Cantraybruich, then Croy, with the River Nairn in the bottom of the valley. We were now on the B9001 and followed this to Nairn. There the group gave a presentation to the town dignitaries.

We followed the reverse route of the Nairn half marathon route, which eventually took us past the entrance to Brodie Castle. Soon after this we joined the A96 and followed this to Forres and from there we completed the last section to the Findhorn Foundation at the 'Park', where we arrived at 15:20. My total running time was 5 hours and I estimate that I ran 35 miles. It had been an interesting and enjoyable day. Adrian and his family gave me a lift back to Lossiemouth.

On Sunday, the 12th of May, in the 9th and final edition of the City of Dundee Marathon, my start was fine and I tucked in with the leading bunch, but I drifted off the back as I began to find the pace too hard to maintain. I was pleasantly surprised to regain contact with the group by the time we got to Riverside Drive at around 6 miles. I got my first drink at 9 miles, but had to stop to retrieve it from the table. This, plus trying to drink it, caused me to lose contact with the group, but not with John Duffy of Shettleston. We ran past 10 miles in 55-24 and the halfway point in 1-13-06, which was pleasing. Now, however, we were exposed to winds and our pace slowed.

I got my 2nd drink, again 330ml of 10% solution of Enduro Booster, at 17.5 miles. At 18.5 miles we were joint 10th and I decided to try to push on, passed 20 miles in 1-55-50 and was pulling in the runner ahead. There were some stiff climbs after this and I managed to catch and pass 3 runners in the last 2 miles, including George Sim, which was pleasing. My time was a little disappointing, but if I could have held onto the main group until the start of the return journey, I am sure that I could have produced a better time. I was, however, quite pleased with my run. Hugh McKay (fife AC) won in 2-26-03, from Rod Bell (DHH), 2-26-10 and Ewan Wilkinson, 2-29-22; David Hamilton (DHH) was 4th in 2-30-39, with Dave Fairweather (Cambuslang) 5th and 1st Vet in 2-31-00, while I was 6th in 2-32-03. There were 959 finishers, which I thought was excellent.

I was delighted to be selected for the Great Britain team to compete in the IAU 100Km World Cup to be held over the 'Del Passatorie' course. On Sunday the 19th of May, Mick and I ran the Monaughty course in 3-09-35, which was our best for this 50Km course. This was my glycogen depletion run and I would then be on a low carbohydrate diet until Wednesday morning.

On Thursday the 23rd of May, Izzy drove me to Elgin Station where I caught the 06:48 train to Aberdeen, where I went for a walk before catching a bus to Aberdeen airport to board the 11:35 flight, to London. At Heathrow I made my way to Terminal Two to meet the rest of the G.B. team for the IAU world cup, incorporated in the 100Km Del Passatorie. There were 17 in our party: Erik Seedhouse, Stephen Moore, Mick McGeoch, Gwyn Williams and me in the men's team, Eleanor Adams/Robinson, Hilary Walker, Hilary Johnson, Marianne Savage and Sue Ashley in the women's team. Dave Walsh was our team manager, and also travelling with us was: Andy Milroy, Malcolm Campbell, Dave Beattie, John Foden and Sue Ashley's husband or boyfriend.

I wrote the following report for the RRC newsletter:

100Km Del Passatorie 1991

The 19th edition of this classic race was held on the 25th of May 1991 and incorporated the I.A.U. World Cup under the patronage of the I.A.A.F. Unlike many 100Km races the Passatorie is a mass participation event with more than 3000 participants each year. It is also particularly demanding as it entails a climb over the Appennine and temperatures of 27°C plus is often encountered, during the first three hours of the race.

Until 1990 the course was accepted as being 101.5Km and there was a 100Km check point 1.5Km from the finish. However, Harry Arndt undertook the dangerous task of measuring the course using a 'Jones Counter' on a calibrated bicycle and the course was modified to be 100Km.

The British contingent, apart from Erik Seedhouse, who had gone out a day earlier and Patrick Macke, who was making his way by train from Germany, arrived in Bologna at around 5:20 pm on Thursday the 23rd of May. We were driven in a mini coach from there down to Faenza and delivered to the appropriate Hotels. The 'Al Moro' was to be our base for the next four days. I shared a room with Gwyn Williams, Patrick Macke and Mick McGeoch.

We discovered next morning that our Hotel did not provide breakfast, so we made our way to the Hotel Vittoria, where John Foden, Andy Milroy, Malcolm Campbell and Dave Beattie were staying and managed to get breakfast. This became our breakfast arrangement for the rest of our stay in Faenza.

Our personal drinks for the race had to be handed over to race officials' care at 6 pm on Friday. A box was provided for each aid station every 5Km. With the aid of a code sheet we deposited our bottles in the appropriate boxes, despite the confusion introduced by the two extra boxes for extra aid stations on the climb.

On 'Race' day two coaches were arranged by the organisers to take the runners to Firenze, where the race was due to start at 4 pm. They were scheduled to depart at 9 am, but we actually got underway at 9:30, heading towards Bologna before heading for Firenze. A stop was made at a service station on the motorway in the mountains. I recognized many of the runners milling around when the coaches emptied. The Germans were not among them. I assumed that they had made arrangements to stay in Firenze prior to the race, as I had recommended to John Legge that the GB team should do.

We arrived in Firenze and some time was spent negotiating the narrow streets before the driver decided to let us off at 12:00. Dave Walsh navigated us to the 'Savoy Hotel', where resting facilities had been arranged in a function room and the floor soon became covered with prostrate 'resting' runners. Dave went off to find the University of Firenze 'Boat House', where arrangements for us to rest prior to the race had been made thanks to Lynn Fitzgerald.

Once Dave had located the 'Boat House', we moved there accompanied by Elias Marope and Charles Khudube of Botswana.

Slowly the hours passed until it was finally time for us to make our way to the start in Pizza della Signoria. Thousands of runners were milling around in the square in the bright sunshine. The elite runners were arranged in a roped section some 20 metres ahead of the mass of runners about 10 metres ahead of the official start line. Andy Milroy, using his sternest teacher's voice and assisted by Dan Brannen of the IAU, managed to persuade us to shuffle back the required distance.

Tension mounted as the start time approached and then released as the gun sounded at 4 pm. I was surrounded and found it impossible to run at the pace I wanted. Once we reached the next square I was able to start moving through and soon reached the loose group at the head of the field. Erik was some 80 metres ahead of this group with someone else, 20 metres behind him. This was the eighth time that I had participated in this race, the first being in 1979, and I knew that there was a lot of hard running ahead, so I tried to relax.

The first aid station came surprisingly quickly and I missed my drink. The weather was quite warm, at about 24°C, but this was not a problem. I settled into a comfortable pace just behind Bellocq as we began the climb out of Florence, which lies in the valley of the Arno River.

Soon I began to struggle and feel quite rough as the climb continued. My legs felt very heavy and many passed me on this section up to Fiesole, at 10Km. Italian, Vito Mileto, one of my rivals from the past, came pattering past. He had won this race on four occasions and as the spectators along the route recognized him, they shouted his name. Some also recognized me and shouted encouragement.

As the climbing eased I began to recover and was able to run a little better. I started to move through again, so by Vetta Le Croci at around 23Km, I was with Gwyn and Steven Moore. At a height of 518 metres, this was the finish of the first climb, which was followed by the first downhill into the next valley. By Borgo San Lorenzo at 25Km I had caught several more, but I had no idea of my position in the race. At about 36Km I passed Patrick, who then came past me a few Km later, running strongly.

As the next climb developed I was just behind Rosetti of France and this continued as we made our way up the mountain. A Russian came past, but then stopped at the next aid station. I passed Rosetti and was surprised to see Erik ahead. He was struggling and I soon passed him; the continual climb had caused some sort of back problem for him. It was a relief to reach the top of the pass at Colla di Casaglia, at an altitude of 913 metres, all downhill to the finish from there.

There was no one in sight ahead, but it was never far to the next bend, so there may have been someone within catching range. On one of the zig-zags soon after I could see a runner below; a German, I thought, so I pressed on. For some time, I had been aware of a burning sensation in my right heel, so I stopped to check if my sock was wrinkling, but I found nothing out of place. The downhill *running was obviously causing the problem. I tried to run normally and forget about the discomfort. On this downhill section, groups of cyclists would come shooting past, sometimes on both sides of one, which was rather disturbing. I also had a close encounter with a car. Later in the darkness, there were sections when one was completely alone and it was quite peaceful.*

At about 10Km from the finish I felt the blister, which had developed under my right heel, burst and the warm liquid gushed into my sock. Soon after this I was aware of someone catching me. Gradually he drew alongside me and began to pass and I was able to see he was a very lanky German, wearing tights and listening to his personal stereo. I could not increase my pace to go with him and he began to disappear into the darkness. Next, along came Herbert Cuntz, of Germany, running strongly. My condition was quite poor by then and I longed for the finish. The straight tree-lined road, once I reached Faenza, seemed very long. At last I reached the sanctuary of the finish, and found out that I was eighth.

I had to report to the anti-doping control, having been randomly selected. I was concerned about my blister, but decided to leave dealing with it until later.

The winner, Valmir Nunes of Brazil, ran extremely well, achieving an excellent time on this difficult course. Roland Vuillemenot of France also ran very well, recording a personal best on this course. Eleanor Robinson retained her women's title with another excellent run.

Our GB men's team (Patrick, me, and Steven Moore 13th in 7-23-21) finished third team, which was satisfactory.

1) Valmir Nunes (Brazil) 6-35-36, 2) Roland Vuillemenot (France) 6-39-14,

3) Jean-Marc Bellocq (France) 6-52-55, 4) Heinz Huglin (Germany) 7-02-49,

5) Jurgen Mennel (Germany) 7-10-08, 6) Herbert Cuntz (Germany) 7-10-21,

7) Patrick Macke (G.B.) 7-10-53, 8) Donald Ritchie (GB) 7-13-26,

9) Sergei Kopylov (USSR) 7-19-55, 10) Dietmar Kimes Germany) 7-20-04 {1161 finishers}

On Sunday morning I did some slow walking, with a plaster over the burst blister on my heel. There were trophies for 3rd team place and I received 12 bottles of the sponsor's wine for 8th.

On Monday we were taken by mini coach up to Bologna Airport where we had to wait a few hours for our flight at 15:05 to Heathrow. Then I caught the 17:45 flight to Aberdeen and from there took a taxi to Dyce Station to catch the 20:05 train to Elgin. Izzy met me at Elgin station and drove me home. As ever, it was good to be back again.

My legs seemed in surprisingly good condition so, on Thursday, 30th May, I decided to attempt the National 100Km championships in Nottingham. Therefore, on Saturday I took the train to Inverness, York, Sheffield and Nottingham. Then a bus took me to the National Watersports Centre. I checked in to the accommodation, a single room for £16.65, telephoned Izzy and then began making up my race drinks. Mick Francis arrived and I went for a coke with him and his handler before continuing making up my drinks. I got to bed at 22:00.

Mick gave me a call at 06:00 on Sunday as requested and I joined him for some breakfast. I had a couple of slices of white bread toast, some cornflakes and a cup of coffee. I noticed that some of the runners were tucking into fried egg, sausage and bacon, plus fried bread, which I thought would be rather unsuitable for me. After this I got organised for the race and met my handler, Viv, who had looked after me the previous year, and passed on my kit and drinks with my drinking schedule. After 250ml of 'Leppin', ten minutes before the start, I planned to take 150ml of 'Leppin' every lap from the end of the 2nd onwards.

NATIONAL 100KM CHAMPIONSHIPS: TIRED LEGS BUT A DECENT RUN

At 08:00 the race for the **AAA/RRC National 100Km Championships** got underway with no one prepared to set the pace, so soon Erik Seedhouse and I settled down in front with 2 Russians for company. Our first lap took 18-36, but the next was faster. My legs felt fatigued from the 'Del Passatorie' race a week earlier, and I was not sure how I would be able to finish satisfactorily. Soon our leading group was down to 3, but then I began to lose contact and a gap of about 60 metres developed. As this gap remained the same for some time, I decided to try to close this to get some assistance and shelter from the strengthening wind. I was able to catch up and then to press on with Erik as the remaining Russian dropped behind.

I began to weaken and had to let Erik go on, and some time later one of the Russians came past, running very well. He caught Erik and began to pull away from him. My aim then was to maintain 3rd place and I could see that, across the lake, Patrick Macke was not gaining on me. I reached 50Km in 3-15-49 and by 40 miles I lapped my weekend training partner, Mick Francis, who was starting to have problems, and the next time I lapped him he was walking. I passed 50 miles in 5-27-21 and, with just over 2 laps remaining, lapped Patrick Macke and we ran together for about a lap, before I got away, going into my last lap.

I was very pleased to finish 3rd and delighted to get under 7 hours as I had estimated that I could expect a time of about 7-20. My blistered heel was OK; the strapping and Vaseline worked well. My prizes, apart from the AAA bronze medal, were a P&O ferry ticket and a £50 'Ron Hill Sports' voucher for the best combined World Cup and National championships time.

Erik Seedhouse won in 6-42-03, a course record, ahead of Farid Zapirov (USSR), 6-47-5, with me 3rd in 6-56-55. Sylvia Watson was first lady in 8-22-56, which was a ladies' course record. 60 of the 88 starters finished.

My journey back from Nottingham was rather tedious, with changes at Crewe, Preston where I had a 2.5 hours wait and Edinburgh, where my wait was 3.5 hours from 03:30. I eventually got back to Elgin at 10:40 on Monday, rather late for my first class at College. As it was a Lossiemouth Holiday, Izzy and I had an Indian meal at lunchtime in Elgin.

Almost two weeks later, as I ran home, I suffered considerable discomfort and had a terrific desire to urinate, so I stopped and as I expected there was haemoglobin present in my urine. I went straight to the Laich Medical Centre. Dr Sabiston kindly saw me at short notice about my urinary tract infection and he readily prescribed Septrin.

Two days later I participated in the Norco Rotary 'Marafun', relay marathon in Elgin city centre. Prior to this I did a 'lap of honour' with as many runners as wished to do so. Our team of: Graham Burgess, Stan Thompson, George Reynolds, Jim McDowell and me, finished 3rd, which was very pleasing. It was an excellent event and was enjoyed by one and all.

A few days later, on Thursday the 20th of June, Izzy drove me to Elgin Rail Station to catch the 05:45 train to Inverness and onto Edinburgh. I caught a bus to the airport, which got me to the airport in plenty of time for my flight to Brussels, via Glasgow, where we had to disembark while the aircraft was refuelled.

Heidi, representing the race organization, met me, but we then had to wait for Malcolm Campbell and for John Burgess from South Africa. Eventually, Heidi drove us to Torhout, where I was taken to stay with the same family as on the last occasion I ran here in 1987. Wilfried and Rita looked the same, but Urgen and Nathalie had grown a lot. After eating some spaghetti, I went to bed at about 22:30; it had been a long day.

On Friday I slept through to 15:00! Tomas Rusek and a friend arrived soon after this and they went for a sleep following their long drive from Bruno in the Czech Republic. I had a little to eat, some potatoes and tomatoes, and then made up my drinks for the race. A cyclist had been arranged for me and I had met him the previous evening. After my pre-race drink I planned to have drinks at 5Km intervals from 10Km to 90Km.

Rain was falling, just as in 1987, as we made our way to the sports hall and, once I had organised my kit for after the race, I made my way to the start. There an announcer asked invited runners to come up onto a stage, where we were presented with a small bouquet of roses and each introduced to the crowd. By then the rain had stopped and conditions for running were good; and soon it was time to clamber over the barriers and line up for the start. I recognized many of the participants but some, like Andy Jones from Canada, were new to me.

TORHOUT 100KM: ANOTHER SATISFACTORY RUN

At 20:00, after a 10 seconds countdown, we were off racing through the narrow streets of Torhout in the 12th edition of the **'Nacht Van Vlaanderen' 100Km**, which incorporated the Belgian championships. As there was a wind I decided to go with the leading pack to ensure that I got some shelter. A leading pack of 14 formed, including Praet, but Andy Jones had already gone ahead, despite our brisk pace. I was not surprised when we passed 10Km in 36-25 and heard that Jones was 2 minutes ahead. We maintained this pace through 20Km, but by then the group was a little smaller and consisted of: Praet, Vuillemenot, Saraiva, Schnyder, Bosten, Seedhouse, Santalov, Gack, Van Huylenbroeck and me plus another Russian.

We passed 30Km in 1-51-00 but, some time after this, I began to feel the pace and had to let the pack go. Heavy rain began to fall again as I passed 40Km in 2-29-35 and I was surprised to be pulling in Santalov and his teammate. Erik had fallen behind me, but was quite close. I passed these 2 at about 46Km as Santalov had to make a pit stop in some bushes, while his pal sat behind me sheltering from the headwind. He dropped off as we reached Middelkerke, where Erik caught me. I managed to go with him and it was a great help having him to run with and we passed 50Km in 3-10-00.

Soon we were heading back into the darkness, leaving the west end of Middelkerke behind, and I began to feel a little livelier and was able to push on and leave Erik. I could see flashing lights of the lead vehicle in the distance ahead, indicating the position of the leaders, but there were various other groups of vehicle lights nearer. I passed 60Km in 3-52-00 and 70Km in 4-35-00 and then caught a runner, who turned out to be Hans Schnyder. I had a long section on my own after this and reached 80Km in 5-21-38.

At about 88Km Erik came past, running quite strongly so, as I passed 90Km in 6-07-00, I could see Saraiva, with Erik pulling him in quickly and passing him. I also caught him and gave him a salute as I passed. At around 94Km Santalov came charging past, running strongly and he closed rapidly on Erik, but they were soon out of sight, so I could not witness the race unfolding between them. The last few Km seemed to take ages, as I was very tired, but at last I reached the streets near the centre and the crowds there lifted my spirits to strive for the finish. Around the next corner was the welcome sight of the banner and I ran up the ramp onto the stage to complete the race. I was relieved to be finished and pleased with my run. At my request, I was driven back to the sports hall to collect my kit, but again, as in 1987, my kit had been uplifted and taken to Middelkerke for some reason. My cyclist drove me back to Wilfried's house, where I had a bath before going to bed in an attempt to sleep.

Wilfried was also running in the 'Night of Flanders 100Km', accompanied by Rita on her bike, and he finished in 8-43-36, which pleased him. When they arrived home with Rusek and his pal I got up to congratulate them. John Paul Praet of Belgium won in 6-33-51, from Roland Vuillemenot 6-41-11 and Konstantin Santalov, 6-48-42. Erik Seedhouse was 4th in 6-50-15, while I was 5th in 6-52-09, with Luis Saraiva next in 6-55-16. Terry Tullett fell during the night and dislocated his shoulder. Eleanor Robinson, previously Adams won the ladies race in 8-12-41, from Hilary Johnson 8-49-38 and Hilary Walker 8-52-51. There were 191 finishers.

My legs felt quite good and in the afternoon I attended the prize presentation ceremony in the sports hall, which was well organised. The prize money extended from 50,000 Belgian francs for first to 10,000 for 5th and the same for anyone under 7 hours. My 10,000 for 5th converted to £166.00. The evening was spent relaxing.

On Sunday morning Wilfried took me to the post-race Ultra Run clinic, which was held in a hotel about 5Km away. This was a very interesting event and each person present was given a booklet containing the contributions from every member of the panel. Lunch was provided but Wilfried and I went home for ours.

After lunch I watched the Belgian triathlon championships, which were covered completely on television. At 4pm Wilfried returned me to the hotel where we were picked up by a bus, which took us to Middelkerke for a reception at the casino. Here the prize money for the race placing was distributed, along with nibbles and drinks. Following this we were taken back to the same hotel where there was a meal with complimentary drinks followed by a disco and more free refreshment. There was a very pleasant atmosphere as runners from many nations enjoyed each other's company. Host families were also invited to participate. Afterwards Roland Vuillemenot surprisingly drove me back to Wilfried and Rita's.

TRAVEL RUSH

After breakfast on Monday 24th of June, Rita drove me to the swimming pool to meet the bus, which was provided to take runners to Brussels Airport. However, when we arrived at 08:05, there was no bus so Rita drove me to Wilfried's parents, but there was no one in, so she drove home and telephoned Dirk Strummane. It was decided that I should take the train, so Rita drove me to the rail station, via Wilfried's work place. At the station I attempted to purchase a ticket but was told that they would accept Sterling but not my Royal Bank of Scotland bank notes. This meant that I had to go to a bank, which opened at 09:00, to cash my prize check. Having done this, we returned to the rail station, where my ticket was duly issued, along with a list of place names and times for this route. The first available train was going to Bruges at 09:30, so I caught this and changed there for a train for Brussels Central. At the stop before Brussels Central I asked some guard if I had to change there for the airport stop, but they indicated that I should remain on the train. The train left Brussels at 10:55 and was going to the Airport, but to my consternation it did not stop there, so I had to get off at the next station, which was Leuven. By now I was in a panic as it was then 11:15 and my flight was due to depart at 12:00. My only hope was to take a taxi, so I approached a driver and asked him if it was possible to get to the Airport by 12:00. As he thought that this was feasible we set off. Some determined driving by the driver got us there by 11:45 and relieved me of 2700 Belgian Francs. Next I had to persuade someone to check me in, which I managed to do at the 2nd attempt and then I had to jump the queue at passport control and get through security. This done I began running towards gate 52. My trophy, which was in my backpack, fell out and clattered on the floor, so I had to delay and stuff it back in. I reached Gate 52 but there were several: 52F, 52G, 52H and 52I, though I quickly found the appropriate one by consulting a departures monitor. I arrived at 11:55 for my 12:00 flight and was relieved to see that the passengers had not boarded the coach to take them to the aircraft yet, so I could now calm down and relax. After this hectic comedy routine, at least the rest of the journey home was uneventful!

On Sunday, the 30th of June, I had promised John Diffey, the organiser of **the Lairig Ghru Race** to participate in this run from Braemar to Aviemore. Izzy, who was to be my second, and I had a relaxed drive over from Lossiemouth. Ben Preece and I set off at a brisk pace at 11:00 and we had a good lead as we crossed the River Dee at Mar Lodge. We were directed up a Landrover track, well before the turning on the old route that I had run many years before. I shouted to Jeff Cummings to contact Izzy, whom I had asked to give me a drink at the turning just after the bridge over the River Lui. I was annoyed at my error and felt sorry for Izzy, who would be left waiting for me.

Ben was much stronger than me over the rough track, but I managed to maintain contact. On reaching the River Lui on the much-improved road, I was able to increase my pace again and had 10 metres of a lead as we reached Derry Lodge. Here we had to wade through the river and by the Luibeg Burn we were together again, but once we forded this and climbed over a deer fence, Ben started to pull away on the climb. The path became rough and I had difficulty running on it, so I was soon caught and passed by another runner and then another. I stumbled on and decided that I must concentrate on getting through without injury and to forget about racing. More runners came past me as we approached the Pools of Dee and the Boulder Field. Most of my energy was spent going up and down and sideways and only some usefully used in going forwards. At least the weather was good with sunshine and showers.

Once over the top of the pass I had to pick my way down and another 3 passed me, but eventually the going became easier and I stopped to remove a stone, which had lodged in my right shoe. On reaching the forest I was careful to avoid the sharp tree roots, one of which had caused a broken metatarsal in my last attempt in 1976. Having safely negotiated the descent I reached the flat ground, but by then I was quite tired and was glad when I reached the road. I was relieved to see Izzy opposite the Stakis Hotel with a welcome drink. I finished 10th in 4-06-32, just pleased to have got through without injury or a fall. There were 29 finishers. Ben Preece won in 3-27-45, from Jim Carruth 3-33-10 and Charlie Love 3-33-37.

Friday, the 5th of July, was the start of our summer holidays, so I drove to and from work as we were preparing to depart in the caravan. I had entered the West Highland Way race scheduled for early next morning.

I wrote the following report for the RRC newsletter:

The West Highland Way Race 1991
I have no difficulty in remembering our wedding anniversary; it is on my birthday, the 6th of July. This year Isobel and I celebrated this dual event in a novel way: I ran the West Highland Way race and Isobel was my support team.

The West Highland Way is a long distance footpath from Milngavie on the outskirts of Scotland's largest city, Glasgow, along the shores of Loch Lomand, Scotland's largest Loch and on to Fort William at the bottom of Britain's highest mountain, Ben Nevis. Since it opened in 1980, this 95 miles route has become a very popular walk, passing through some of Scotland's most beautiful and varied scenery. This route was the natural choice for a challenging ultra-distance race.

At 3 a.m. on Saturday the 6th of July our adventure was underway and 44 of us left Milngavie Station, cheering like children on a Sunday school picnic. Soon we were into the darkness, running along a path by Allander Water, with the aid of torches, then through Mugdock Wood. The air was warm and there was no wind, which was pleasant.

After about two and a half miles on a section close to the river, we had to run over a series of duckboards and I managed to fall at the start of one of these, banging my right knee. It ached a bit, but there was no serious damage. As it started to become light, I increased my pace and caught the leading group of six by four miles.

Being an optimist, since the race began at 3 a.m., I planned an anniversary dinner for Isobel and I in Fort William that evening. My optimism was rather askew, as I had overlooked the 9,200 feet of climbing and worse, the descents and the non-runable sections involved.

By the first checkpoint, 12 miles into the route, just to the east of Drymen, Mick Francis and I had pulled ahead. I received my banana and Leppin drink from Isobel there. The next section involved a climb through Garadhban Forest, followed by a section of open country, before we began the climb of Conic Hill. By then it was a beautiful warm morning with a cloudless sky and from the summit of Conic Hill we got a superb view over Loch Lomond and the mountains around. The descent to Balmaha at 18.5 miles was quite steep in places, Mick had fallen there during the previous year's race, but we arrived safely in the car-park at 5:45 a.m.

From there we followed the West Highland Way path around by the Lochside, over small hills, through woods and so on. Occasionally we would pass groups of people sleeping near the Lochside, others camping and some cooking breakfast over open fires. At Rowardennan the road ends, so Isobel gave me my first bum-bag of provisions for the next section of 14.5 miles to the Inverarnan check point.

Mick began to drop back as we passed 26 miles on the forestry track, which was a good surface to run on. At about 30 miles the track finished and the path became very rough and twisty, slowing progress drastically. At Inversnaid I got a little lost and wasted time and energy locating the correct onward path.

The trail was very rough, and I had to scramble over boulders on occasions, but improved as I approached Ardleish. Mick's second, John, had rowed across the Loch and was waiting there with drinks for Mick. At Beinglas Farm, Isobel gave me a replacement bum-bag of provisions and I headed up Glen Falloch, now exposed to the brilliant sunshine and the temperature began to soar. By my next feed point at 44 miles I was rather tired and feeling very warm. I later found out that the temperature reached 96°F during that day.

More climbing was encountered as I skirted around Crianlarich then descended, crossing then re-crossing the A82, before reaching Tyndrum at just over 52 miles, the next check point. The following section to Bridge of Orchy was good to run on. From there a hilly section was covered to reach Inveroran Hotel, the next checkpoint at 61.7 miles. Isobel was alarmed to see me staggering towards her to receive my new supplies. I assured her that I was just tired and that I would stop if I got too bad. There was buzzing in my ears and I was light-headed so, despite regular drinks, I was dehydrating.

On the next section, over Black Mount and Rannoch Moor, I was unable to run up even the slightest incline, so I began walking and jogging alternately until I began to recover slightly. Kinghouse Hotel was the next checkpoint at 72 miles and I reached there in a depleted state at 3:35 p.m. Continuing, I reached Altnafeadh at 75 miles; it was then 4:15 p.m. From there the Devil's Staircase had to be climbed and I managed this with great difficulty. My head felt like it was going to burst, I was giddy and my legs had no strength. I was wrecked!

On going over the top I followed the well-defined path, some parts of which were extremely rough with large and small sharp stones. Progress was slow due to the surface and my weak condition, plus the fact that I also experienced periodic cramps in both quads.

In Kinlochleven I felt completely exhausted and had to rest on a wall for some time. I reached the next checkpoint by the School at just after 6 p.m. Isobel was very encouraging, and I set off up the next hill, with only 14 miles remaining. Once I reached the Old Military Road I was able to jog and walk on the inclines, until I tripped and fell headlong onto the stony path. I could not lift my feet high enough to clear stones on the path, so running became impossible. I expected to be overtaken at any time. The noise in my ears became more pronounced: at one time I thought that I heard galloping horses approaching, and actually looked around to see where they were coming from.

At the end of this road I was delighted to see Isobel, who had found the difficult access to this point. It was 8:40 p.m. and cooler as I set out on the last section There were some short stiff climbs, which I had great difficulty coping with. In addition, in the twilight, my eyes began playing tricks on me as I imagined that I saw a boy and a dog. At last I reached the top of the ridge, began the zigzags down onto the forestry road into Glen Nevis and was able to jog again. Later on this road I was delighted to meet Izzy, who had walked up from the Glen Nevis road and we jogged down to the Glen road together. She had done a magnificent seconding job. Soon we reached the Glen Nevis road, but I was unable to jog for more than 100 metres at a time. At last I reached the finish at the Nevis Bank Hotel.

John Aimes had arrived about ten minutes before me, much to the annoyance of Mick, who had dropped out and had been 're-hydrating' at the hotel awaiting my finish. John Aimes had taken the road from Blar a Chaorainn to Fort William, instead of following the official West Highland Way path.

It was lovely to be finished, after such an adventure. As it was then 10:44 p.m., the anniversary dinner would have to wait!

The 'first-aid' nurse was very caring and took Izzy and me to the hotel room allocated for distressed finishers, where I lay on the bed with a damp towel on my head for 15 minutes. I had some dioralite, which caused me to *start vomiting. The 'squeezy' I had taken earlier was still recognizable, and I was surprised at how much liquid I brought up. It appeared that I had not been absorbing what I had been drinking over the last 3 hours. What a way to spend my 47th birthday and our 8th wedding anniversary!*

In the shower I had bad cramp and had to get Izzy to assist me out of the confined shower cubicle as I had become rather stuck.

Results: 1) D Ritchie 19-44-11, 2) J Aimes* 19-34-53, 3) W Dodds* (lady) 20-23-19,
4) N Rose 21-25-00, 5) A Stott* 23-03-30, 6) A Nicholson 25-41-56,
7) J Templeton & M Williams 26-56-53, 9) S La Porte & T Wilson 28-52-12, {22 finishers, 50%}
* *These finishers did not follow the correct route from the last checkpoint.*

I was too ill to get to the start of the awards ceremony later that day, but did eventually get along to receive the trophy for a year. I felt very rough, but was pleased that, by the afternoon, I could drink and eat without vomiting again.

The following day, Monday, my legs were painful and I still had buzzing in my ears, but on Tuesday we continued our caravan holiday by moving on to North Ledingham Caravan Site near Connel. On Wednesday we caught the ferry from Oban to Mull and visited there and also Iona and had a very pleasant time.

We moved to South Shields the following day and set up at Lizard Lane Caravan Park. Following this we moved to Rawcliffe Caravan Park at York and then onto Drayton Manor Park, in heavy rain. We made the most of a stop at the Caravan Park at Stratford upon Avon, before moving on to Hereford racecourse Caravan Park.

On the 21st of July, after 2 weeks of minimal running since the West Highland Way race, I participated in the **John Tarrant Memorial 50 miles road race at Hereford** organised by Mick Wildig. There were fewer participants that year, probably due to the fact that the Lincolnshire 100Km and 50Km races were also being held on that day. I started at a moderate pace and an unknown runner accompanied me. He looked strong and, at about 4 miles, asked if I did many of these long races, to which I replied 'quite a few'. He informed me that he was Geoffrey Backhouse and that this was his first ultra and that he had not run further than a marathon. We completed the first 10-mile lap in 65-something. Izzy, Claire, Anna and George were my support team, supplying me with drinks at 3, 6, and 10 miles on each lap as well as encouragement. The weather was warm and humid and I did not feel very frisky. At about 17 miles my companion, Geoffrey had to make a stop for a call of nature, so I increased my pace a little to create a gap. I passed 20 miles in 2-09 and felt OK, so from then on it was just a question of keeping going. My 4th and 5th laps were rather slow at 70 and 75 minutes respectively as the warm conditions were taking their toll. Also my right heel hurt and a blister was developing under my left big toe.

I was relieved to finish and pleased to have won this race again. I found this a hard one, reflecting my reduced fitness due to an extended racing programme and limited recovery time. I wore my Asics 'Bordin racer' shoes. My winning time was 5-40-15, with Tony Lenagan 2nd in 5-53-35, Dave Russell 3rd in 6-42-95 and Geoffrey Backhouse finished 4th in 6-45-42.

Following the presentation of trophies in the Berni Inn, Imperial Hotel, Hereford, which sponsored the race, there was a meal followed by an excellent evening disco, which Claire and Anna thoroughly enjoyed, as did Izzy, George and I. We left at 01:30 to return to our caravan on Hereford Racecourse.

Two days later we moved onto a Caravan Park near Coomberton, where we left our caravan. From there I had arranged to use my P & O voucher by taking a ferry from Felixstowe to Zeebrugge. We arrived in Zeebrugge at 08:00 next morning and set off to drive to Brugge.

We were camping: our first site was near Leuven and then we moved to a Debinnenvart. We stayed a few more days there, during which time Claire was able to meet her friend Alana, whose father was ex-RAF Lossiemouth, but now on detachment at some NATO base. Three days later, I drove back to Zeebrugge and caught the overnight ferry back to Felixstowe. We arrived back at 07:00 on Wednesday the 31st of July and picked up our caravan and I drove to Lizard Lane Caravan Park in South Shields. On Thursday we were up at 05:30 preparing to leave Lizard Lane for home. I drove to Inverness and then home, a distance of 329 miles.

Friday the 2nd of August was 'Day One' again! I felt quite unfit and flabby and my left groin was giving me trouble on my 4 miles jog.

On the 4th of August, in the Macallan Moray Marathon, the initial pace was brisk, thanks to a chap from Liverpool accompanied by Mick Francis and me, but this eased and, on the climb up to Spynie Hospital, Ron Kirkton caught us. Mick began to fall back by 5 miles, so I was left to do battle with Ron. I had raced against him on several occasions and always beaten him. However, he was running confidently and I was lacking preparation, so on the climb up to the 'Red Craig' I began to lose ground and gradually the gap widened through Cummingston and I began to struggle badly.

At halfway I was on schedule for 2-40, but I was slowing and Mick caught me at 20 miles and I ran with him for a couple of miles before I was able to pull away and managed to hold onto 2nd in a rather slow time. It was the best that I could manage after my hard racing schedule and lack of training over the previous month. Ron Kirkton won in 2-38-18, ahead of me in 2-46-13 and Mick Francis 2-50-29.

In the Nairn Highland Games half marathon on the 18th of August, I felt rather listless and finished 15th in 77-01, probably a personal worst. Graham Milne won in 70-38 from R. Watt, 70-51 and George Sim 70-54.

On Friday evening, the 23rd of August, Izzy and I drove with the girls to Edinburgh to stay with Rachel Hollas. We arrived there at 01:00 on Saturday and all slept on airbeds on her floor. We rose at 06:30 and prepared for my run in the **Two Bridges Race** again, from Dunfermline. It was good to see Cavin Woodward there, back in the ultra running scene. Cavin set off at a good pace as usual and led the race. I chased and caught him and then Gwyn Williams joined us. We passed 5 miles in 29-05 and 10 miles in 59-20 as a stiff west wind was hindering our progress. I felt all right, but not totally comfortable as we reached 15 miles in 1-30-41. On turning left soon after this, Cavin began to increase the pace and I was pleased to be able to go with him, as did Gwyn. Going through Grangemouth I assumed the pace-making role and Cavin dropped off, but Gwyn came with me and I got a shock when Andy Stirling and Mick McHale caught us. We passed 20 miles together in 2-00-45.

Andy took the lead and pushed on and I went with him, but going through Bo'ness I had to let him go and, on the long hill after this, he moved well ahead as I struggled up. Mick McHale passed me on this hill, but once I recovered I caught him and we set off in pursuit of Andy, passing the marathon in 2-38-49, which was quite an improvement on my Moray marathon performance. I was catching Andy on the flat and downhill sections, but he was stronger on the uphill sections. Gradually I got closer to Andy as I passed 30 miles in 3-02-10, 42 seconds behind and headed onto the Forth Bridge. Coming off the bridge I got frustratingly close as we began to tackle the hill through Inverkeithing. Although I was very tired and lost ground on this climb, I made this up again on the next downhill section. I passed 35 miles in 3-33-15, 25 seconds behind, as I continued my chase, but I could not catch Andy and had to settle for 2nd.

I was pleased for Andy and I was satisfied with my run. Izzy, Claire and Anna gave me my drinks: 200ml of Enduro Booster, every 3 miles from 7 miles onwards. Andy Stirling recorded 3-41-04 to my 3-41-28, with Mick McHale next in 3-44-36 and there were 71 finishers.

Over several weeks I continued high mileage in preparation for my next 100Km in Santander. On Friday the 4th of October, after Izzy and I ran our usual course around Lossie, I got a lift to work from Maggie Cooke, who also very kindly drove me down to Elgin Station to catch the 10:42 train to Aberdeen. There I caught a bus to the airport in good time for my flight to London. My next flight to Bilbao was several hours later.

That year there was no delay at passport control at Bilbao, so I was through quickly and met by an official from the Santander 100Km race. He drove me to Santander and, after meeting Soto and his son Jose, I was taken to the Hotel RHIN, the same one as last year. I had some fruit there before going to bed at 15 minutes before midnight.

FIRST VETERAN IN THE SANTANDER 100KM

I wrote the following account for the Road Runners Club magazine.

100Km Cuidad De Santander 1991

The X11 edition of this 100Km race was held on the 5th of October and also incorporated the 7th edition of the Spanish championships.

I arrived about 11 p.m. on the 4th of October and by the time I settled into the Hotel Rhin it was almost midnight. At 5 a.m. I began preparing my drinks for the race and got myself ready. This took longer than I anticipated and it was 6:25, before I was ready, which meant that I had to jog the 1.5Km to the start carrying my three litres of drinks. Once I had located the appropriate official to receive my drinks, I got to the start with at least five minutes to spare and suitably psyched up.

At 7 a.m. we got underway in a slight drizzle and joined a large loose group at the head of the field. Nunes, the current World Champion from Brazil, had gone off strongly and was already 200 metres ahead after about 3.5Km, with two Moroccans also some 50 metres ahead of our group. At the top of a stiff climb at around 4Km Luis Saraiva of Portugal, the winner of this race in 1989 ran ahead and to the left to spend a penny or more behind a large refuse bin. Unfortunately, he tripped on some rubbish there and we saw him go down. He never recovered from this and eventually abandoned the race due to the chest injury that he suffered from that fall.

The first lap of the course had been changed from last years; it was an out and back leg with the turn at 10Km. At this point I was with the group of about six, including Santalov as we chased the Moroccans and Nunes. By 20Km our group of six were some 100 metres behind the Moroccans and Nunes was out of sight. He passed the control point at 24.382Km in 1-29-10, followed by the Moroccans, Brahnin and Zenati in 1-30-15. Our group of Santalov, Lev Gitterman and Alexey Cononov, all of the Soviet Union, along with Alfredo Blanco of Spain and myself passed this point in 1-30-44.

We caught and passed the Moroccans and then our group began to break up as the pace started to take its toll. Santalov and 2 other Russians began to pull away from me, so I became a detached 5th. At around 35Km Sergey Kopylov joined me, so it was more like a Russian 100Km championship than the Spanish championship. Kopylov then pushed on past, but I was able to regain contact and we ran through the marathon together in 2-40-47. Nunes had gone through this point in 2-36-30, followed by Santalov in 2-37-33. Third was Gitterman in 2-38-42, then Cononov in 2-39-27.

Kopylov got away again on the next climb at Boo, but I caught up once again and managed to get away from him. I passed 50Km in 3-12-18, which was quite pleasing and I felt that I was now running well and I began to close on Cononov. At the start of the final lap the gap between us was just 80 metres, as he passed this control point in 4-00-17 to my 4-01-05. Nunes had passed this point in 3-54-10, Santalov in 3-55-11 and Gitterman 3-57-27.

I could not close the gap to Cononov and after some time the gap began to widen. Over the last 20Km I struggled as, I was weak, having glycogen depletion symptoms (no carbo loading diet this time). Thankfully no one caught me during this section.

Nunes ran bravely under pressure from Santalov and managed to fend him off, no mean feat.

I did not receive all of the drinks of Leppin 'enduro booster' that I had prepared, but I got enough and supplemented these with Isostar, which was available at the feed stations. There were some very heavy rain showers during the race. My prize was 70000 Pts, which converted to £364.74.

Results: 1) Valmir Nunes 6-36-53, 2) Konstantin Santalov 6-37-20,
   3) Lev Gitterman 6-44-03, 4) Alexey Cononov 6-47-27,

5) Don Ritchie 6-49-13 {1stV45}, 6) Miguel Blanco Nava 6-57-22,
7) Farid Zaripov 6-58-53, 8) Sergey Kopylov 7-00-31,
9) Erik Seedhouse 7-00-34,
10) Ramon Alvarez Sainz 7-07-24, 1st Lady: Eniko Feher (Hun) 8-37-49

On Sunday, 6th October, I caught flights from Bilbao to London and then London to Aberdeen, followed by train from Dyce to Elgin, where Izzy and family met me and I was home by 5pm.

A week later I towed our caravan to Glen Nevis, by Fort William to be ready for the Lochaber half marathon, which Izzy and I were to run in next day, the 13th of October. I started at a fairly strong pace and joined two Shettleston Harriers, who appeared to be running at the speed I wanted. I was quite satisfied to finish 8th in 75-06. Then I jogged back on the course to meet Izzy and met her at about 9.5 miles. She ran well to finish in 2-25-39, which was an improvement of 10 minutes on her previous best. Mark Gormley won in 68-00 (course record), from Graham Wight 69-38 and John Stewart 70-48. I was 1st veteran and received a 40oz bottle of whisky, given by the Highland Hotel. There were 81 finishers.

During the following week I developed a cold, which became a worry as I had entered the National 24-hour championships, which were scheduled for 26/27 October. Fortunately, my cold was much improved by Friday the 25th, but it felt like it might go into my chest. After work I caught the train to Dyce and then the flight from Aberdeen to London Heathrow. John Lamont, who was to be my second in the 24-hour race, met me there and drove me to his home in Guildford.

VICTORY IN A PERSONAL BEST AT THE NATIONAL 24 HOURS CHAMPIONSHIP

I rose at 07:00 on Saturday and finished mixing drinks for the race. I had breakfast of six slices of toast with honey at about 09:00. John and I set off for Copthall stadium, Barnett, at 10:00 and arrived there in plenty of time at 11:05. Final adjustments were made to my kit and equipment in conjunction with John, who had my eating/drinking schedule.

We got underway at 12:00 in good weather conditions, no wind, dry and a temperature of about 55°F. I led, running at what I thought was an appropriate pace, and after a few laps Erik Seedhouse joined me, so we were able to run and chat together for some time. Paul Bream caught up and then went ahead, to establish a lead of about three-quarters of a lap. I increased my pace slightly to maintain this gap and Erik eased off, preferring to run at a more cautious pace.

I planned to eat every hour after 3 hours, alternating a ripe banana, a 'Power bar' and cooked white rice, so I began this sequence at 3pm. After one hour, I started drinking 200mls of lemon and lime flavour 'Enduro Booster' every 20 minutes, and later would alternate this with 'Isostar'. I found that I had to urinate at least once an hour over the first 3rd of the race. Things seemed to be going fine and I regained the lead after about 6 hours and, as the temperature dropped in the evening, I put on my thermal top. I passed **100 miles in 12-44-28, which was 2 minutes inside the previous over 45 World best**, which was an unexpected bonus. I felt fine and I thought that I was judging my effort correctly.

My training partner and club-mate, Mick Francis, had moved through to 3rd place and was running well. My next target was **200Km and I passed this in 16-19-16 to set a new World Best Performance.** This was satisfying and I knew that I had set myself up to run over 170 miles. Another 46 miles would do and I had 7.5 hours to do it in! However, I began to slow dramatically, until I could only achieve 5 or 6 miles an hour, which was disappointing, but I had to make the best of it and at least I was still able to run. My stomach was painful and I felt nauseous and it became an effort to eat. I suspected that I was bleeding from my stomach and wondered if it was due to the lemon and lime 'Enduro Booster' being too harsh on my stomach lining. Perhaps plain Leppin would have been a better choice. I pressed on, but had to make three visits to the toilets during the last quarter of the race, and received confirmation that I had been bleeding, from the colour of my stool.

Mick had moved to 2nd and I was delighted for him. Gradually the last 2 hours passed and then excitement rose as the last few minutes were reached. I managed to raise an 'emotional spurt' over the last 40 seconds and it was great to be finished and to have exceeded my previous best. John had been an excellent second throughout the race and also afterwards. My distance was 166 miles 1203 yards; Mick Francis achieved 155 miles 1107 yards; and Dennis Weir finished 3rd with 148 miles 1003 yards. Paul Bream achieved 144 miles 464 yards and Richard Brown covered 141 miles 1373 yards for 5th place. Doina Nugent was first lady with 110 miles 1063 yards.

Following the presentations, John drove me back to his home in Guildford, where I had an hour's sleep. He and Vera then drove me to Heathrow where I caught the 17:25 flight to Aberdeen. I got a taxi from the airport to Dyce Station in time to catch the 20:04 train to Elgin. Izzy met me there and drove me home. It was, of course, good to be back.

On Saturday the 2nd of November, Izzy and I travelled to Fortrose for the Black Isle 'festival of running' half marathon and marathon respectively. Izzy completed the half marathon in 2-28-53, which was probably a superior performance to her Lochaber run, because of the more demanding course at the Black Isle.

Not surprisingly, I felt tired in the marathon, and the chasing group, trailing Fraser Clyne, dropped me after about 3 miles. Then I regained contact and gradually this group broke up, but on the hill out of Cromarty I could not keep up and began drifting further behind. Mick Francis caught me and I was able to get some help running into the wind as he pushed on. I took over near the top of the climb and was surprised to see John Duffy in trouble, so we caught and passed him. I then set off in pursuit of the 2 runners ahead and gradually caught one, but the other was safe. My legs were rather tired and I was pleased to reach the finish. I was quite satisfied with my 4th place in 2-45-45. Forres Harriers were 2nd team.

Fraser Clyne won in 2-27-18, which meant that my course record of 2-24-28 in 1982, survived. Mick McHale was 2nd in 2-37-21, with R Milton 3rd in 2-45-07.

Two weeks later, on the 16th of November, Izzy and I ran in the Glen Clova half marathon. I got off to a comfortable start, but as soon as I came to the hills I began to struggle. The hills were generally short but sharp, which seemed to knock the energy out of my legs. I began to move a little better, and between 6 and 7 miles picked up 4 places, and had visions of catching more, but I tired and passed 10 miles in a slow 59-24. Eventually I finished 21st in 78-26 and Izzy finished in 2-22-04, which was her best and surprising on this tough course. Fraser Clyne won in 67-20, a course record. It was a well-organised race with a good atmosphere. There were 209 finishers.

There were no suitable races in December, so I just maintained my training throughout this month. On summing my training and racing miles for 1991 I found that I had accumulated a considerable total of 6592 miles, which was an average of 126 miles per week. It had been another successful year, with several highlights.

1992

My 1992 racing began on Saturday the 4th of January when I participated in the North District cross-country league race at Elgin. I was pleased with my run, as I was able to move through on laps 2 and 3 to finish 13th and 4th counter for Forres Harriers.

Following this I received the **Donald McNab Robertson Memorial Trophy for Road Running**, via Colin Bailey, who had collected it on my behalf at the AGM of the **Scottish Amateur Athletic Association** on the 21st of December. He passed it to the Inverness Harriers team, who in turn gave it to Hamish Cameron of Forres Harriers.

Throughout January I maintained around 160 miles a week including one effort session. This would have been fine as preparation for an ultra, but was not suitable for cross-country racing. Despite this on Saturday the 1st of February I ran in the North District cross-country league race at Aden Park at Mintlaw. I felt quite strong, but once I came to the slippery field, followed by the twisting paths through the woods, crossed by tree roots, I had problems. My right knee gave some twinges on laps one and two, but on lap three it really started to hurt on this section, so I was virtually running with one leg. It appeared to recover once I got onto reasonable paths again and I finished 20th. Later I was coughing up yellow phlegm again.

It was a few days before I could consult Malcolm Morgan about my right knee problem. Initially he thought that I had somehow damaged the edge of my cartilage and gave me ultrasound on the area and arranged to treat me again in 2 days time. On Wednesday the 5th of February I tried running to and from work and on both runs my knee was painful, which was quite depressing. I had to abandon the following morning's run after a minute because my right knee was too painful. Later Malcolm investigated my back to see if there was a neurological cause for my knee pain. He found a muscle in spasm in the top of my right buttock, which he loosened off with deep massage, which was rather uncomfortable at times. I cycled to and from work for a week and then introduced 3-mile morning jogs and received physiotherapy treatment from Malcolm every 2nd day. **Time was running out for me as I had been selected for the Great Britain team to run in the IAU 100Km World Cup in Palamos, Spain, on the 16th of February.**

On Monday, 10th February, I ran the usual 3-mile course around Lossie with Izzy and thankfully my right knee discomfort was diminishing. I cycled to and from work as usual and received treatment from Malcolm at 08:30. The following day I developed a pain in the front of my right knee while I was standing in my Lab. I was upset by that latest adverse development. On Wednesday the 12th of February, my right knee felt much improved and was almost back to normal. I cycled to Elgin and received treatment from Malcolm again at 08:30. He and I were both confident that my leg would be all right in the 100Km on Sunday. I would have to run the 100Km off the December-January training and forget about the two and a half weeks of minimal activity.

On Friday, 14th February, I caught the early flight from Aberdeen to London Heathrow, and went to Terminal 2 and picked up my ticket from the Iberia desk for the journey to Barcelona. Hilary Walker and Doina Nugent were also on this flight. On arrival at Barcelona we met some other lady members of the British team and many other national team runners who had arrived earlier. A bus, hired by the race organizers, picked us up and departed for Palamos, on the Costa Brava, where the IAU 100Km 'World Cup' was scheduled for Sunday. We arrived there at 7pm, registered for the race and received our hotel vouchers and information packs. The British team members and some others were transported by mini bus to the 'Hotel Ancoro', which had been completed only recently. I was sharing a room with Patrick Macke and team manager Dave Walsh. We had dinner at 8pm and I got to bed at about 10pm.

After Sunday's race, I wrote the following report for the RRC Newsletter:

100Km IAU World Cup, Palamos 1992.

A 100Km road race was organised in Palamos on the Costa Brava in 1988, in memory of Margarita Frigola. She was an ultra-distance runner from Palamos, much admired for her spirit and dedication, which led to yearly improvement until she became Champion of Spain at 100Km. Tragically, 'in the flower of her life' and at the peak of her sporting career, she lost her life in an accident during a training session.

On the 16th of February the fifth edition of this memorial race was held and incorporated the IAU World Cup event. Support for the event was excellent, with entries from thirty-one countries, from Finland and Sweden in the north to Argentina, Australia and New Zealand in the south, Japan in the east and Canada and USA in the west.

As an introduction to the race a parade of national teams was scheduled for 4:30 pm on Saturday afternoon. Each team in their National colours was given their national flag and marched behind a local schoolgirl holding a sign indicating in Spanish, the team she was leading. I was pleased to be asked to carry the Union Jack flag. There was a large appreciative crowd at the start/finish area on the promenade to witness this spectacle. This ceremony was another important development of the 100Km World Cup. It was surprising that there was no Italian team present.

On Sunday morning we were up at 4 am preparing for the 6 am start. Breakfast was available for those who wished it. In the lobby we sorted our drinks into carrier bags, one for each of the 25 aid stations. Patrick and I got a lift to the start from Kath and Steven Moore.

At about 5:50 I gave my shell suit to Dave Walsh our team manager and entered the starting area behind the barriers. The Russians arrived at the start with about 5 minutes to spare. Konstantin Santalov was his usual cheery self.

At 6 am we were sent on our way by a pistol shot. I started cautiously and then increased my pace and worked through to a big group near the front of the field. This group contained: Santalov, Nunes, Vuillemenot, Steven Moore and Patrick along with many others that I did not know. Ahead was a smaller group of about five, chasing the lead vehicle. I felt fine and the pace was comfortable. When Nunes saw Santalov he ran over to him, then took his arm and raised it, which I thought indicated that Nunes was expecting Santalov to be the winner today. I also thought that Santalov was the race favourite, but at this stage he was taking things quite casually.

At about 12Km Nunes began moving away, so we thought that was the last we would see of him, but he did not maintain his increased pace and within a couple of Km he had drifted back to us. Heinz Huglin then began to move ahead and I decided to go with him, but after some time I eased my pace and Huglin pulled ahead of me. Luis Saraiva of Portugal joined me and as daylight came I could see a group ahead and I recognized Erik in there. We were gradually gaining on them and duly joined them on leaving the town of La Bisbal. There were six of us in the group: Heinz Huglin, Stefan Feckner of Canada, Erik Seedhouse, Ulf Anderson of Sweden, Louis Saraiva and me passing the half marathon point in 81-01. There was a single runner and the lead vehicle some way ahead of us.

We ran together until the feed station at 30.8Km in Madremanya, where I began to struggle with the pace on the climb away from this village. Several runners passed soon afterwards, including Santalov and then Nunes some time later. I began to get twinges in my left hamstring, which was disconcerting.

At about 39Km Domingo Catalan came past, running his usual controlled race. My twinges were becoming more frequent and this caused me more worry. I passed the marathon distance in 2-43-33 in the company of a Frenchman, Hans Schnyder of Austria and a Moroccan. A few Km later my left hamstring went into spasm and I came to an abrupt stop. The French runner also stopped to support me until a medic came over to treat me. He laid me on my back on the road so that he could stretch my hamstring and free the spasm. While on my back I saw Patrick and Steven pass by, running together.

When the medic had done his work and cleared the spasm I resumed my run, rather shaken and with my confidence eroded. In Gerona the sole Japanese runner came scampering past. I developed an urgent need to make a 'pit stop'; with a scarcity of bushes I had to nip behind a rubbish skip. Soon after this I passed the 50Km point in 3-17-59, so I realised that I could still achieve a good performance if nothing else went wrong.

Unfortunately, both quads started to tighten and become painful. My stride shortened and by 60Km I was down to survival pace. I shuffled on, passing 50 miles in 5-45-14, hoping for an improvement, but there was no revival. My quads became even more painful, with downhill sections really difficult to cope with.

Eventually I reached the coast and after a few more undulations, Palamos itself was reached. The last Kilometer was along the promenade and the latter part had been lined with barriers to keep the enthusiastic crowds off the course. Each finisher got a rousing reception from this crowd. I was extremely relieved to reach the finish. Dave Walsh and Patrick assisted me to the massage area, where I noticed that my right knee was swollen. The massage restored some more mobility, but I was still in a sorry state.

However, I was glad to learn how well some of the other team members had performed. Erik had improved his best to 6-33-03 in finishing 3rd, while Steven also made a breakthrough to finish 7th in a fine 6-43-52. Patrick *had some quads problems, which slowed him to 28th in 7-16-28. I was 39th in 7-34-21, almost a personal worst.*

Carolyn Hunter Rowe ran very well to finish 3rd in the ladies race in an excellent 7-56-50 and the other ladies' results were: Sylvia Watson 6th in 8-19-16, Hilary Walker 8-24–58, Sue Ashley 9-03 and Marianne Savage 9-26. Hilary Johnston had to drop out due to the after-effects of flu.

Domingo Catalan, who had failed to finish a 100Km race during the previous two years made a remarkable comeback to finish 2nd. His time of 6-30-37 was a new Veteran record. Konstantin Santalov continued his relentless progress towards establishing himself as the current World's best 100Km runner.

The Great Britain ladies team was 2nd behind Germany and the men were 3rd team behind Germany and Spain.

Men: 1) Konstantin Santalov (Kazakhstan) 6-23-35,

2) Domingo Catalan (Spain) 6-30-37, 3) Erik Seedhouse (Great Britain) 6-33-03, 4) Bernard Curton (France) 6-33-47

Ladies: 1) Bagmanova (Russia) 7-44-51, 2) Marta Vass (Hungary) 7-53-3260,

3) Carolyn Hunter Rowe (G.B) 7-56-50

{289 finishers, 595 entries}

On Monday, my quads were extremely painful when I rose at 05:00 to get ready for the bus from our hotel at 06:00, which took us to Barcelona airport. My flight was not departing until 10:30, so I waited with Hilary Johnson, Marianne, Sylvia, Jeff (Sylvia's partner), Andy Milroy and Harry Arndt.

At Heathrow I met with Hilary Walker, who had been on the same flight, and John Legge, who treated us to lunch. Then I had a long wait until my flight to Aberdeen at 17:25. Annie met me at Aberdeen and drove me back to Blackburn for a cup of tea and a short visit. She then drove me to Dyce railway station to catch the 20:05 train to Elgin. Izzy met me at Elgin station and drove me home by 21:45. Claire had put up a welcome home poster and made a medal for me, very nice. It was good to be home.

My right knee was still swollen on Tuesday, so I cycled to and from work. Malcolm managed to give me physiotherapy treatment at 1pm. Eventually my knee recovered thanks to Malcolm's every other day physiotherapy and on Monday the 24th of February I was able to resume running to and from work using my old railway line route.

On Sunday the 1st of March Izzy and I ran in the Nairn 10Km road race. I started off fairly well, but after 2.5 miles my legs began to seize up and they would not move freely or quickly enough. Runner after runner came past me over the last 2 miles and I finished 35th in 36-34. Izzy ran strongly to set a personal best of 61-46. John Bowman won in 31-46, from Graham Fairley 31-52 and Graham Milne 32-36. There were 234 finishers.

Two weeks later, on the 15th of March, Izzy and I ran in the Inverness Half marathon, but Izzy had to abandon the run after about 6 miles because her right ankle was giving her excessive pain. I started cautiously and got into a group going at the pace I wanted. By 7 miles I was running flat out with Mick Francis and 2 others, but around 9 miles I began to fade a little and lost contact with Mick. I was pleased with my 10 miles time of 55-58, but lost 5 places from there to the finish. My time of 74-24 was quite satisfactory, being 12 seconds faster than the previous year, but 17 seconds slower than 1990. Forres Harriers were 3rd team, so we each got a voucher for £8. I finished 29th and 2nd Veteran in the over 45 years category.

A week and a half later, I travelled to Aberdeen Royal Infirmary to have the root removed of the canine tooth, which I had broken on a power bar during the 24-hour race the previous October. It proved a rather stubborn root to extract and kept breaking up, so eventually part of my jawbone had to be drilled away to get better access, which enabled the remaining root to be extracted. Dr McLeod, the surgeon remarked that there was some infection there, but that it should clear up without antibiotics, now that the source was removed. This infection may have been causing some adverse effect on my training. Afterwards I called in to see Ron Maughan, now Professor Maughan, who had a lab on the ARI site.

On the following Sunday I ran the Monaughty 50Km course as my glycogen depletion run and began the low carbohydrate diet at 12:00. This was in preparation for the next weekend's Madrid 100Km.

I developed a cold during the week and by Friday the 3rd of April, it was quite a lot worse, but it was not affecting my pulse rate, which was reassuring. Izzy and I travelled to Aberdeen airport for the flight to London and there caught the flight to Madrid. On arrival Heinz Huglin, Rafael's wife and another two from the race organization met us. The 6 of us managed to squeeze into a smallish Renault and headed for Madrid City.

As we drove rain started, then an electric storm began and hailstones clattered down, so the gutters were soon full of rushing water and some sections of road were flooded. Our accommodation was the '4 star' 'Hotel Breton'. Our airfares and our hotel stay from the 3rd to the 7th of April were paid for by the race organization, for which we were very grateful.

The hotel staff laid out breakfast for those runners that wanted it on Sunday morning and the Russians took full advantage of this facility, but I only had a cup of coffee. The bus arrived at 06:00 and transported us to the race start.

The V1 edition of the **100Km Pedestres Villa de Madrid**, which incorporated the V111 edition of the Spanish championships, got underway at 07:00. Ahead of us lay ten undulating 10Km laps. I started cautiously, aiming for 40 minutes for the first few 10Km laps. I completed the first in 40-39, but as there was a fairly strong wind on certain parts of the lap, I decided to increase my pace to join the leaders in order to get some shielding from this wind. At the end of the 2nd lap Louis Saraiva of Portugal and Roland Vuillemenot of France were leading in 1-19-37. I was in the 2nd group containing: Domingo Catalan of Spain, Konstantin Santalov of Russia, Heinz Huglin of Germany, Jean Paul Praet of Belgium, Ulf Andersson of Sweden, Thomas Rusek of Czechoslovakia, Miguel Blanco Nava of Spain, Vaclav Kamenik of Czechoslovakia, Luciano Pardo Dos Santos of Brazil, Andrei Gondas of Czechoslovakia, Lajos Fazekas of Hungary, Ramon Alvarez of Spain, Alexander Massarygin of Russia, Amado Hernandez Lopez of Spain and Enrique Carmona Herrerias of Spain, all passing in 1-20-19. Erik Seedhouse, who had complained before the start that he was unwell, was already in difficulty, passing in 1-23-41.

I remained in this group through 30Km, but soon after this I began to struggle on the hill at the start of the 4th lap and lost contact with the group. At 40Km Saraiva led in 2-37-24 from the group, who passed in 2-38-50, followed by Vuillemenot in 2-39-50, while I passed this point in 2-40-47. At 60Km Heinz Huglin and Miguel Blanco Nava were leading in 3-58-24, followed by Catalan, Santalov, Saraiva, Praet, Fazekas and Massarygin in 3-59-00, while I passed in 4-09-28. My condition deteriorated further as time went on and I had no strength and appeared to be approaching exhaustion. I was perplexed as my training had been going well leading up to this race. I had, however developed a cold 4 days prior to the race.

At 80Km the leading pack of Santalov, Catalan, Praet, Blanco Nava and Massarygin passed in 5-19-27. Saraiva was next in 5-25-47, then Gondas in 5-28-58. I shuffled on as best I could, passing this point in 5-47-38, but I was finding it increasingly difficult to move my legs and to make progress in a straight line.

As I neared the end of my 9th lap, I was surprised as Santalov and Massarygin came past, running easily and intent on staging a dead heat finish. On my last lap I heard voices of runners approaching behind and one voice was a woman's, so I thought that I was about to be beaten by a woman in a 100Km for the first time. I was expecting the leading lady to come past, but was relieved to find that it was Doina Nugent of Ireland, who was a lap behind me. Eventually I reached the finish completely exhausted; my last 10Km lap had taken 62-12! I had drunk 4 litres of 10% solution Leppin 'Enduro

Booster', but I did not appear to derive any benefit from it.

Konstantin Santalov was given first place over Alexander Massarygin, although they dead heated in 6-42-22 and Jean Paul Praet was 3rd in 6-43-33. I found that I had finished 14th in 7-44-49, which was a little embarrassing.

Nurzia Bagmanova (Russia) won the ladies race in 8-04-33, from Doina Nugent 8-42-53. There were only 24 finishers from the 90 starters.

On Monday, Izzy and I did some walking in the 'Parque Retiro' and later in the Botanic Gardens. On Tuesday the 7th of April, we caught our flight to Heathrow, followed by one for Aberdeen, where we picked up our car and drove home.

On Thursday the 9th of April, I cycled the Speyside Way with John Diffey, Graham Milne and Noel McPartlin, to survey it and decide if it was suitable for a 50Km road and trail race. Izzy and the girls joined us at suitable accessible points, including a pub lunch in Aberlour.

During my 'Ponds' course a couple of weekends later I came across a large salmon lying on the beach near the 'Boar's Head'. I wrapped it in my T-shirt and continued with my run, with some difficulty, as I had to keep my left arm in a fixed position to support the salmon.

On Sunday the 26th of April I ran in the Lochaber (and Scottish Veterans Championship) Marathon from Fort William. Because of the wind the initial pace was rather slow as I ran in the leading group of 6 including Colin Youngson, George Reynolds, Peter Faulds and Derek Cruickshank. Davie Fairweather had already moved ahead. We passed 10 miles in 59-08 and our group began to break up as Faulds began to chase Fairweather, then George and Colin went after Faulds. I could not handle the increased pace and had to let them go. At the turn I was in joint 6th position, but I gradually pulled away from my companion and began closing on Fairweather, who had been overtaken by Colin and George.

I reached 20 miles in 1-59-54, almost catching Fairweather. He stopped to walk just after 21 miles, but he was running again when I passed him. I caught Faulds, shortly before the Canal Bridge at Banavie.

Lochaber Marathon 1992. Left to right: Donald, Colin and George.

The last mile and a half into the wind was rather difficult but I was pleased to feel strong over the last 6 miles. Colin Youngson won in 2-36-23, from George Reynolds, 2-37-06 and I was 3rd and first V45 in 2-38-42. Forres Harriers won the team race with 2nd, 3rd and 6th finishers. There were 122 finishers.

While in Madrid, I had accepted an invitation to another 100Km race near Barcelona in early May.

On Friday, 1st May, I caught the flight to London Heathrow and then continued to Barcelona. Elena, her usual bubbly self, met me, along with Malcolm Campbell, and drove us to Sabodell where we were to stay in the 'Hotel Urpi'. Elena became lost on the way there so we had a tour of the countryside before reaching our destination at around 9pm. We had dinner and then I went to bed at 23:00.

I slept well and managed to stay in bed until 9am, listening to the rain on the roof window. The breakfast, available from 05:00 until 12:00, was excellent as one could select what one wanted from an extensive display of attractive foods. I had lunch with Erik Seedhouse at 13:30, both choosing spaghetti. In the late afternoon after further resting I went for a walk to find a supermarket to get bottled water to make up my drinks for the race. The Spanish Grand Prix was also scheduled for Sunday and the distinctive sound of racing cars on practice runs could be clearly heard from the racing circuit somewhere in the distance.

I had 2 oranges and a banana at 19:30 instead of dinner. Elena had arranged a meeting for 20:30 and there informed us of the arrangements for the race. Rain had fallen continuously throughout the day.

On race day, Sunday the 3rd of May, I was awake before my alarm call at 04:00 and as the bus to take us to the start was due to leave at 04:30, I quickly got dressed in my race kit. Breakfast was laid on an hour earlier, for those runners who required food. I did not take any, but the Russians as usual ate heartily.

IMPROVEMENT IN BARCELONA

Our trip in the mini coach to the start of the 1st edition of the **'Trofeu Domingo Catalan' 100Km** in Palau de Plegamans on the outskirts of Barcelona took some 30 minutes, so we arrived at the sports hall near the start at about 05:15. A few minutes past 6 o'clock the race got underway in light rain. We had eight 12.5Km laps to complete, with approximately 2Km of dirt roads on each lap. Because of the rain the first section of the non-tarred road of about 400 metres was muddy and rutted, which posed quite a handicap in the dark on the first lap. On subsequent laps it was easier to select a suitable route on this section.

Roland Vuillemenot took the lead and by the 2nd lap was 80 metres ahead of Erik and Kamenik, who was followed by Santalov and Praet. I was in a group of four in joint 6th place, but gradually our group broke up and I ended up running alone. I passed 50Km in 3-16-02, which was quite satisfactory.

There were 3 feed stations on the lap and I used the one at the start/finish and the one at about 8Km, having 200mls of 'Enduro booster' at each of these on each lap. I began to close on the tall Russian ahead, but had to make a pit stop for a 'number two' with about one and a half laps remaining. I began to struggle and was surprised when another Russian, running strongly, came past near the end of lap 7. He went on to finish 5th. On the last lap Ramon Alverez Saniz came scampering past. I could not increase my pace, so I suppose that my glycogen stores were empty. I was pleased that nobody else passed before the finish. I was satisfied with my run and encouraged that my condition was improving again.

Konstantin Santalov (Russia) won in the excellent time of 6-22-28, ahead of Roland Vuillemenot (France) 6-37-54 and John Paul Praet (Belgium) 6-41-28. Erik Seedhouse (GB) was 4th in 6-48-38 and I had finished 9th in 6-57-31. It was good to get under 7 hours again.

Generous prize money was on offer and Santalov received 500,000 Pesetas, while I received 40,000 (£207.35) and the prizes extended down to 15th place at 5.000 Pesetas. The 1st lady was Marta Vass (Hungary) in 18th place in 7-56-45 and she received 300,000 Pesetas

The following day I rose at 05:00, packed, went down for breakfast and was able to do the excellent self-service breakfast justice. Elena had agreed to drive us to the airport at 07:30. There was a problem getting out of the hotel car park, which was in the basement. A card was put into a reader, which initiated the opening of a large metal gate at the top of the ramp on to the street. Because of the 5 people plus luggage in the car, Elena could not drive up the ramp in the 30 seconds before the gate began to close again. When reversing down the ramp she scraped onto the ticket box, making a scratch and an indentation on the metalwork of the car, which was rather unfortunate. I got out and jogged up the ramp to lighten the load. This time Elena succeeded in driving up the ramp in the time allowed.

The remainder of the journey to the airport was uneventful and I caught the flight to London along with Doina Nugent. There I caught a flight to Aberdeen and train to Elgin, where Izzy picked me up.

Malcolm Morgan sorted out my post race right hamstring a few days later. I realised again how very fortunate I was to have Malcolm to help me. I had 3 weeks to prepare and be healthy before my next 100Km championship race.

On Saturday the 30th of May, Izzy drove Mick and me to Elgin train station where we caught the 06:50 train to Inverness, and then the 07:50 train to London as far as York. We continued to Sheffield and Nottingham, arriving at 16:23. Adrian Stott had joined us at Edinburgh and he was also staying in the 'Swan' Hotel so, by bus and foot, we made our way there. Mick and I were allocated room 203 at a cost of £24.50.

Tony Jones had several items of G.B. kit (old Nike stock), for me, which was much appreciated. We went for a light meal at a Chinese restaurant near Trent Bridge. I had curried vegetables with rice for £3.50. When it was time to pay, Mick discovered that he had lost his wallet. Back at the hotel, the receptionist telephoned the taxi firm we had used earlier and as a result Mick's wallet was located and retrieved. I went to bed at 21:00.

BRITISH CHAMPION AGAIN

On Sunday, 31st of May the first **British Athletics Federation (BAF) 100Km championships** got underway at 08:00 in warm, humid and sunny weather. Stephen Moore set the pace and I followed, with Erik Seedhouse just behind me. Steve's pace was rather fast, so on the 3rd lap I decided to ease back and let him and Erik fight it out.

I was glad to see that the gap between them and me did not get excessive. Erik began to drop back, and gradually I caught up and went past at about 25 miles. The gap to Stephen was reducing each lap and I caught him on the 10th lap and moved into the lead. I was running comfortably, but wondered if I could maintain my effort. I passed 50Km in 3-12-30, 37 seconds ahead of Stephen. By this time the weather was rather warm, but the southeast wind kept one cool. At 50 miles (5-21-24) I was working hard and keeping an eye on Erik, who was now 2nd. My left calf muscle was cramping over the last 4 laps, which was a worry, but I managed to keep pushing myself although I was slowing, and eventually I was on the last lap and trying to raise my pace a little, but to no avail. I was delighted to win this race again.

Once more, Vivian was an excellent and most attentive 'second', seeing to my needs at the completion of each lap. I drank 200mls of 10% solution plain 'Leppin' on each lap after lap 2. I had no foot trouble, so I was delighted with the Reebok 'Racer X' shoes. Because of the warm windy conditions, more than half the 97 starters dropped out, including Mick, so there were just 37 finishers. My time was 6-51-54, with Erik Seedhouse 2nd in 6-58-10 and V Tivikov (Russia) 3rd in 7-18-27. Carolyn Hunter-Rowe was first lady in 6th place in 7-39-59.

Because I had difficulty in producing a urine sample for the anti-doping check after the race, Mick and I missed the train we had planned to catch. We caught a train to Crewe at 20:20 and, once there, Mick managed to obtain a sleeping berth on a sleeper train to Inverness, which was passing through Crewe at 01:20. This was a good move and I got back to Elgin by

10:40. I had not worn socks in the race and noticed that my ankles were swollen because of sunburn. Later I discovered that I had painful sunburn on my upper arms, shoulders and the back of my neck.

I cycled to and from work for a few days and then resumed running to and from work. My next 100km, in Belgium, was in 3 weeks, so I had time to be fairly well recovered.

On Thursday the 18th of June I caught a train from Elgin to Aberdeen and then a bus to the airport to catch a flight to London Heathrow and from there a flight to Brussels. On arrival a representative of the Night of Flanders 100Km race met me. He fetched the car, a new Renault 16 valve sporty type, which was part of the sponsorship arrangements, and drove me to Torhout. I was staying with Wilfred and Rita again and met my cyclist, Mario, who would give me my drinks during the race.

FIBRILLATIONS IN FLANDERS

On Friday, I was surprised that I had slept on and off until 5pm. I rose and started preparing for the 23rd edition of the **Nacht Van Vlaanderen 100Km**. At 20:00 we got underway and my main concern was to avoid being tripped as we were starting simultaneously with the marathon and 10Km runners. I did not feel very lively, but worked my way through to join Erik Seedhouse and Ulf Andresson. We passed 5Km in 18 something and at this early stage I was in trouble, as I began to have periods of heart fibrillations and a pain developed in my upper right arm. This was rather alarming and debilitating as well as depressing, but I decided to press on as best I could, hoping that my condition would improve. On the slight incline back into Torhout I could not maintain the pace and became detached from the group. Although I regained contact and we passed 10Km in 39 something, I was not comfortable.

By 12Km I was losing contact again, although the pace was moderate, and at 15Km I felt that I was running as hard as I could, but it became impossible to sustain this effort. I drifted back and Erik came past and then Valeri Mikhailovski. At around 20Km I managed to regain contact with Valeri as I began to feel better and then ran ahead of him. This did not last long and I soon began to drop back despite Valeri's offer to shelter behind him from the headwind. Hans Peter Roos came past, but I caught and passed him about 5Km later. My marathon time was a slow 2-49-34 and in Middelkerke I passed 50Km in 3-20-12 and then Bruno Scelsi and Denis Thierry passed me and then someone else a short time later.

Sand had been blown off the beach, so the road along the seafront was almost blocked in some parts. Another runner passed and I passed someone as I settled down for the return journey to Torhout through the dark countryside. I got a surprise when Niall Bairamgalin from Russia, came past. He seemed to be quite comfortable and I was frustrated at not being able to increase my pace to match his. As time went on I caught and passed a few runners and I was pleased to eventually catch and pass Niall, by then in rainy weather.

I was glad to see the 95Km marker, which signalled the start of the finishing section, with each Km to the finish marked. Soon I reached the brightly lit streets near the centre of Torhout and then around the next corner was the haven of the finish. It was over, after a rather difficult run. My pulse rate was 76 beats per minute (bpm) at 04:00 and 62 bpm at 08:00 so I was recovering, thankfully without a permanent heart problem.

John Paul. Praet won in 6-24-46, from Konstantin Santalov, 6-34-55 and Alexander Massarygin, 6-34-56, Farid Zaripov 6-38-33 and Roland Vuillemenot 6-44-38. Erik had finished 8th in 6-54-42 and I found that I had finished 15th in 7-12-33. There were 187 finishers.

On Sunday, I travelled back from Brussels to London and on to Aberdeen. Izzy met me at Aberdeen airport and drove me home.

On Friday the 3rd of July Izzy picked me up from College after our end of term. We set off in our caravan for our summer holidays in the early evening and drove to Blair Atholl Caravan Park and set up there. I was able to enjoy another run up Glen Tilt from there on Saturday morning, before moving to Little France Caravan Park in Edinburgh. Our next site was Lizard Lane in South Shields. From there we moved to Wetherby racecourse site.

On Wednesday the 9th of July, over the last ten minutes of a run, I developed heart fibrillations, which was disturbing. We moved to the caravan site in St Neots and from there to Hereford racecourse site, with a brief stop in Evesham, where the traffic exhaust pollution was rather bad.

On Sunday the 12th of July I ran in the **John Tarrant Memorial 50 miles Road Race** from Hereford football ground. About 400 metres after the start I began to stride out to close the gap to the leader, Jeff, who had taken the initiative from the start. Suddenly I felt a burning pain in the top of my left quads, which seemed to have a paralyzing effect on my left quads in general. I eased back in the hope that I would recover. However, on the first small incline on the bridge over the railway line I was really struggling and could barely keep in contact with Gwyn Williams and another fellow.

Nevertheless, I decided to carry on and try to make the best of the situation and hope that my problem would clear. By 3 miles I had lost contact, but regained it by 5 miles when Gwyn and his companion turned the wrong way at a junction and had to retrace their steps. We were together at the end of the first of 5 10-mile laps in 63-45, while Jeff had gone through in 61-40. On lap 2 my left leg had stabilized a bit, but I was tired, could not hold my pace and took 65-45 for that lap, while Gwyn and his partner recorded 64-25 and 64-27 respectively. Gwyn's running companion, a tall fit-looking fellow, retired from the race shortly after this.

On lap 3, I passed Izzy, who had completed 11 miles and was looking quite comfortable. I informed her that I was doubtful of finishing because I had a leg problem and also a pain in my left kidney region. However, I decided I might as well finish by jogging to the end. Apart from my left leg problem I was feeling depleted of glycogen, which may have been related to a suspected liver problem earlier in the week. I stopped at 23 miles to try to stretch my left quads, but this proved ineffective. At 24 miles Tony Lenagan caught and passed me and I completed lap 3 in a pathetic 75-05. Gwyn was now leading from Jeff and Tony, but on lap four I surprisingly caught Jeff at about 34 miles and later at 37 miles Claire told me that Gwyn had retired, so I was suddenly now in 2nd place. I completed lap 4 in 74-55 to Tony's 71-40.

I passed Izzy on lap 5 at about her 21.5 miles and she was still quite happy. I completed lap 5 in 76-55 to Tony's 72-11 and I was extremely pleased to have finished this run, one of my worst; I was completely depleted. After a quick shower I drove around the course with George and the girls to meet Izzy, who was the only woman in the race. She carried on to complete 34 miles within the 8.5 hours time limit. Well-done Izzy! This was a sentiment shared by the enthusiastic race organizer, Mick Wildig.

Tony Lenagan (Wigan Phoenix – V 45) won in 5-45-26, while I recorded 5-56-15 in 2nd, with Andrew Radgick of the 100Km Assoc 3rd in 6-03-29. There were 29 finishers from 42 starters. Later we all enjoyed the now traditional evening disco at the Berni Inn, Hereford.

We moved to Dan-Yr-Ogof caravan site in south Wales to visit the caves there and also Brecon. We were rather annoyed at having to pay a fine for taking up two parking places in a car park, while only purchasing a parking ticket for one. So this incident hastened our departure from Wales. We moved to a caravan park at Christleton near Chester, where we stayed a few days to explore Chester. We moved on to a site near Ramshorn in Staffordshire, where I resumed running. From there we moved to Edisford Bridge and the following day we had a long drive to the site at Scone Palace. The following morning, I followed my usual route from there and felt encouraged by this run. In the afternoon we drove home.

Malcolm Morgan treated my left quads problem a few days after our return. He gave me 2 more treatments before Sunday the 2nd of August, when I attempted the Moray Marathon (and Scottish

Championship). My left quads problem began again after about one mile and on the climb up to Spynie Hospital I slowed to almost a walk. I lacked strength and felt tired as I lost contact with the 2nd group and Bill Adams came past. I struggled on, wondering what was wrong with me, causing lack of strength and tiredness. The thought came to me that perhaps I had M.E. In the last 5 miles I managed to pick up a couple of places to finish 15th in a personal worst for the Moray Marathon of 2-54-45. Fraser Clyne (Metro Aberdeen Running Club) won in 2-25-38, from John Duffy (Spango Valley), 2-28-25 and Stuart Mills (New Zealand) 2-30-16.

On Monday I had a consultation with Dr Kirk regarding my lack of energy. He took samples of my blood to send to Aberdeen for analysis.

Malcolm gave me physiotherapy treatment on my left quads on Tuesday and Thursday and pronounced me fit to run in the UK 24-hour championships in Birmingham at the weekend.

On Friday the 7th of August, I picked up Mick Francis at 07:30 and we drove to Glasgow, arriving there around 4 hours later. Once I had located the Buchanan Bus station I parked the car in the nearest multi-storey car park and we carried our gear to the bus station. Our bus departed for Birmingham at 12:30 and duly arrived there, after several stops, around 18:30. As we had a lot of luggage, (nine litres of 10% solution 'Leppin', a box of bananas, my kit and Mick's kit) we hired a taxi to take us to Mason Hall of residence at Birmingham University. Once we had booked in and located our room, we sallied forth in search of a suitable meal. An Indian restaurant was found on the Bristol Road and two vegetable curries with rice were obtained to take away. Another taxi was used to get us back in time to see Liz McColgan win a silver medal in the 10,000 metres in the Barcelona Olympics Games, as we ate our curries. I went to bed at 22:10 leaving Mick in the Students' Bar with Dave Cooper and Andy Milroy.

On Saturday I woke at 07:30 and noticed that it was raining heavily. For breakfast I had a large bowl of 'Alpen' muesli moistened with orange juice and two slices of toast with honey. As the rain was still pouring down, Dave Cooper offered us a lift to the track in his 'Fiesta' car, which we accepted, along with Andy Milroy and Marie Caldwell. It was quite a tight squeeze to get Mick, Andy, Marie and our kit, plus me into his car, but we did and got to the Birmingham University track safely. I then got changed in the old gym.

A wooden hut had been allocated for the runners' handlers/seconds to use, which we investigated and found a strong smell of human excrement and, in the dim light, Mick unfortunately put his kit bag down on the source! Later they transferred to a tent on the inside of the track. Peter Shirley, a doctor who had been based in Dr Gray's Hospital in Elgin for a few years and ran for Moray Road Runners, but was now based in Birmingham, arrived to assist Mick with seconding me during the race.

24 HOURS HAT-TRICK

The **AAA of England 24-hour Championships** race organised by John Walker and sponsored by Brendan Fleming, a local solicitor, who was also running in the race, got underway at 10:30 in heavy rain blown by a westerly wind. Carolyn Hunter Rowe, advised by Tony Jones, was racing for a good 50Km time and set off at good pace, while I settled into what I thought was a suitable tempo.

Time passed slowly to begin with, but Carolyn's run, as she picked up World Best Performances at 25 miles, 30 miles and 50Km, added interest. The rain eased and the wind dropped, so that conditions became quite pleasant, but perhaps a little too humid. I ran comfortably and my quads problem was not bothering me at this easy pace. Every 20 minutes I drank 200mls of 10% concentration 'Leppin' and on the hour a banana. After about 4 hours I had to stop to trim a toenail, which was cutting into an adjacent toe on my right foot. I continued to extend my lead over Ian Gunn as the hours passed.

At about 13 hours there was a violent electric storm with spectacular lightning and thunder, followed by very heavy rain, so I put on my thermal top and track pants. The electricity supply was cut to the pumps supplying air to the inflatable tent. This straddled the first five lanes of the track. We ran under this canvas on each lap, since it housed the recorders – but the tent began to deflate! Quickly the recorders, with their sheets and tables, were evacuated so that the race could continue. This was a major problem, which was dealt with admirably by John Walker and his team of helpers. However, two recorders were trapped inside the collapsed tent and needed rescuing. Peter was called upon to use his professional training to treat one of the trapped women.

During the period that the tent was down we had to run outside the back of the tent in lane seven or eight, which must have added some considerable distance over successive laps. In due course a maintenance electrician managed to restore the electricity supply to one pump, which was sufficient to inflate the major part of the tent. This allowed the recorders to move back in and runners to pass through again. Later the electricity supply to the other pump was restored and normality was restored. Another electric storm occurred with ensuing heavy rain.

At about 15 hours I changed from my Reebok 'Racer X' shoes to my Reebok 'Inferno' training shoes because my left foot was becoming rather painful. I was feeling rather tired, but I was pleased that my left quads were giving no problems. At about 18 hours I had a slice of white bread plus a cup of tea with milk and two spoons of sugar, which caused me to begin to feel better and I began to pick up my pace. I assume that my system appreciated the sugar rather than the 'Leppin' that I had been using until then. From then to the finish I replaced my 'Leppin' by similar cups of tea, but had them only every 30 minutes.

I was pleased that I was able to keep up a reasonable pace until the end, and delighted to **win my 3rd consecutive 24-hour UK championship**. Mick and Peter were very competent and attentive seconds. My intermediate times were: 50 miles 6-12-29, 100Km 7-47-08, 100 miles 13-21-21 and 200Km 17-35-44. My distance was 161 miles 1521 yards; Ian Gunn was second with 141 miles 1135 yards; and fellow Scot, John Softley, 3rd with 127 miles 889 yards.

After the awards presentation, which was held immediately after finishing, and brought forward to suit me, Peter drove Mick and me to the bus station. We caught the 11:35 bus to Glasgow, but soon after the start of our journey I started to feel nauseous and had to ask for sick bags. On 3 occasions I had to stagger to the coach toilet like a drunken man. It was a difficult journey and I would not recommend a long bus trip soon after a 24-hour race. At last we arrived in Glasgow at 17:30 and picked up the car from the multi-storey car park and after paying the £27 fee, I drove to Perth. Following a brief stop there for toilet and chips, Mick drove the rest of the way home, arriving at 22:00. Izzy was not there to greet me as she had gone to India to see Sai Baba and stay for a few weeks in his ashram. I had been wondering how she was getting on as I ran round and round the track at Birmingham University.

On Wednesday the 12th of August I got the results of my blood test, with no abnormal levels indicated.

Three week after the 24-hour run I attempted the 25th edition of the **Two Bridges Road Race** on Saturday the 29th of August. There was a larger entry of 120 for this silver anniversary event. At the start Charlie Trayer took the lead and was joined by Alan Smith of Tipton. I moved up to join them, but found their pace too hard to sustain so I eased back. The Barnes brothers from Tipton came past and then Mark Guichard. I ran with Mark and we caught Fitzroy Barnes, but I felt quite uncomfortable, with tightness in my diaphragm and my left quads also giving trouble. I began to struggle by 3 miles! Robin Thomas came past and a group of 6 including George Reynolds and Mick Francis. I was able to join them, but I got detached at the 7 miles feed station, where I had to stop to find my drink. I regained contact with Mick when he stopped for a pee. Someone from Pitreavie passed and then a group of 3 joined us and we passed 10 miles in 62-55. I felt very tired, but I had to make the best of it, and I managed to stay with this group until we turned left onto the road towards Grangemouth. Another 2 passed on this section and, on approaching Grangemouth Docks, I was surprised to see Archie (or Ken) Duncan of Pitreavie AAC running strongly as he passed by.

I began to settle a bit and caught Fitzroy Barnes again at about 20 miles and then Charlie Trayer, who was suffering from foot problems. Approaching the marathon, I realised that I might be less slow than my awful Moray marathon performance. I passed the marathon in 2-51-48, 13-03 slower than last year! Before 30 miles I caught sight of another runner ahead, who I identified as George Reynolds and I caught him going over the Forth Bridge and then overtook Mark Guichard and then Delaney Barnes going through Inverkeithing. I could see someone else, but they were too far ahead to catch. I finished 11th in 4-00-52, a personal worst for this course. This was quite worrying, as I had to represent Great Britain in a 100Km race in 2 weeks time.

Peter Baxter (Pitreavie AAC) won in 3-47-48, from Ken Duncan (1st Vet – Pitreavie AAC) 3-48-58 and Paul Rogers (Tipton Harriers) 3-49-32. Mick Francis, now Moray Road runners, was pleased with his 5th place in 3-53-03. Pitreavie won the team race, from frequent victors Tipton. There were 98 finishers.

Thankfully, over the next 2 weeks my form improved and I became more optimistic about running in the IAU European 100Km championship in Holland.

However, on Tuesday, 8th September, 6 days before the race, when I began to run back after work, I found my left knee too painful to be able to run normally and it had become swollen and stiff. I jogged and walked home by the old railway line route. I expected that my quads caused this knee problem or stabilizing muscles in my thighs. The swelling in my left knee had gone down considerably by Wednesday morning. Malcolm saw me at 12:15 and as I suspected, he said that there was no problem in my knee joint. My left quads and a little section at the top of my calf muscle were causing the problem. He massaged my quads to loosen them off and then applied ultrasound to them and the top of my calf muscle and repeated this treatment on Thursday.

On Friday the 11th of September, I caught a train to Aberdeen and then a bus to the airport, where I caught the Air UK flight to Amsterdam. In Schiphol Airport I caught the 16:05 train to Groningen using a 3-day pass, which cost 79 guilders. At Groningen I caught a local train to Winschoten, where I arrived at 20:00. Hilary Walker was there to meet me and showed me to the 'York Hotel', where the G.B. team were beginning dinner.

A round of applause greeted my arrival, which was rather touching. Following the meal, Tony Jones took me to De Klinker Centre, where I met my host family, De Boer, who took me to their home at Dennenweg 14.

On race day, Saturday, 12th September I woke quite early and had a light breakfast of bread and jam. At 12:00 the G.B. team met at De Klinker to collect our numbers and have a pre-race briefing from John Legge. Following this I had a little lunch of risotto with my host family at 13:00.

At 17:00 my hosts took me to De Klinker and I joined the rest of the G.B. team. After a photo call and some relaxing we were introduced to the crowd assembled inside the part of the building we were to run through, where seating was installed either side of the passageway. As the start time approached I realised that I had not even tried a jog yet, so I gingerly pattered out onto the road. I still felt a pain behind my left knee and I was favouring my left leg but I decided that I would ignore this once the race got going.

FIRST VETERAN AT THE EUROPEANS

At 18:30 the **IAU European 100Km Championships** got underway and I ran cautiously, aiming for 40 minutes for the first 10Km lap and managed to stick to this schedule quite well. I passed 10Km in 39 something and 20Km in 1-18 something. Mike Hartley had joined me at about 7Km and we were running at a similar pace. My knee did not bother me, which was a great relief. Malcolm Morgan had done a good job on me, once again. We passed the marathon in 2-46 something as we moved through the field. We caught Stephen Moore and ran with him for a while before he began to drop back due to stomach problems. We passed a group of about 5 containing Valerie Mikhailovski, and later Ulf Andresson and then Roland Vuillemenot. I was delighted at how I was running and hoped that nothing would go wrong. With about 2 laps remaining I caught Thierry Blot, but he rallied and I could not hang on to him. I got away from Mike on the last lap. I was very pleased with my run, especially after problems earlier in the week. Mike ran very well to take over 30 minutes from his personal best. Jean Paul Praet ran an excellent race in a superb time. G.B. men's team secured bronze medals, with Stephen Moore our 3rd counter in 23rd with 7-33-01.

Jean Paul Praet (Belgium) won in 6-16-41, which was a World Best, from Konstantin Santalov (Russia), 6-28-45 and Bruno Scelsi (France), 6-42-40. I finished 7th and first Vet in 6-52-20 and Mike Hartley finished 8th and second Vet in 6-54-59.

Hilary Walker won the ladies race in 7-55-12, ahead of V Vanderhaeghan 7-59-19 and Eleanor Robinson 8-06-18. The G.B Ladies: Hilary, Eleanor and Sylvia Watson were first team, ahead of Belgium. There were 212 starters and 210 finishers, a very good ratio.

My host and his youngest son met me at the finish and took me to their home, where I had a hot bath. I went to bed at 03:30, but slept little before rising at 07:30. The awards ceremony was at 12:30 in De Klinker, but we had to be there for 12:00. I was very pleased to learn from Niall Bairamgalin, that I was the **European Veterans' 100Km Champion**. I enjoyed the presentation ceremony, which was very well managed.

After lunch, my host family drove me out to see some of the surrounding country, including a sluice on the German border and then a small fishing village. There were many dykes to prevent flooding. In the evening the G.B. team had a meal together.

On Monday I travelled back from Winschoten, via Amsterdam, where I had a couple of hours to have a look around. I arrived back in Elgin at 18:40, where Izzy met me and drove me home.

I then had only two weeks to get ready for the first Scottish Athletics Federation (SAF) 100Km championship. I had to recover from Winschoten and rely on Malcolm to sort out a troublesome left quads problem.

On Saturday the 26th of September I drove to Kings College, Aberdeen to give my Open University (O.U.) T292 'Instrumentation' tutorial from 11:00 to 13:00. Following this I drove down to Heriot Watt University on the outskirts of Edinburgh. Once I had paid £13.25 and been allocated my accommodation, which turned out to be an excellent room, A217, in the conference centre, I had a meal of chili con carne and rice in the student refectory. I marked a few O.U. students' assessments before going to bed at 21:30.

SCOTTISH CHAMPION, 25 YEARS AFTER MY FIRST MEDAL

On Sunday morning my alarm woke me at 05:00 and I rose to get ready for the first **Scottish 100Km Championships**, which was due to start at 07:00. I prepared myself, and went to the car to leave my clothes, and then to the reception building to deposit the room key, before going to the sports hall to collect numbers.

Following a briefing from Adrian Stott (Sri Chinmoy AC), the race organiser, we all walked across to the start. Andy Stirling was looking fit but, as we shook hands, he told me that his father had died and that he had been buried just 2 days ago.

From the start I ran cautiously to see what the lap was like, and was surprised to find a section of stony path, which was potentially slippery. This section required an acute turn at the entrance and the exit also required caution to negotiate safely. 'The loop had been measured by Raymond Hutcheson, Scotland's senior course measurer and was exactly 2 miles 141 yards, (3347Km), so runners had to complete 29.87 loops. I had calculated a pace for 7 hours, so I checked my watch as we completed the first lap and again after the 2nd lap, which was slower than my target. Going into lap 3, I increased my pace a little and found that by the end of that lap I had got back on schedule, so I knew the required pace. After 2 more laps, Andy began to speed up, each time that we came to

In the Scottish 100Km championship.

the muddy 20 metres section at the end of the path through the trees and on the climb up to the lap scorers. I would then spend the remainder of the lap catching him up. This continued until about 26 miles, when Andy began to slip behind and I was able to get away from him. I pressed on lap after lap and then I was surprised, as I approached the lap counters, to see Andy in a car being driven off home. I found out that he had abandoned the race a few laps earlier because of stiffness. I could relax now, but decided to maintain my pace as long as possible rather than slow down.

I kept working away, counting off the laps and hoping that nothing would go wrong. On the last lap I realised that I was going to win my **first Scottish championship gold medal at 48 years old, 25 years after gaining the silver one in the 1967 Scottish Marathon**. I was delighted to win this inaugural Scottish 100Km championship. I finally had a 'gold' medal to add to my three silvers from the marathon championships and two silvers from the track 10 miles championships.

The lap used for the race had a flat section followed by a gradual winding downhill and then a short flat section, a slight incline and then an up and down before the long drag back up to the start. Norrie Williamson calculated that the total climbing amounted to over 3000 feet – the equivalent of a 'Munro'! My time of 7-01-27 was close to the target and surprisingly it is still the course record. Ian Mitchell was 2nd in 8-48-03 and Dave Wallace 3rd in 9-27-29. There were 9 finishers from the 24 starters.

I had a 6-day recovery of no running before my next adventure, a stage race from Barcelona to Madrid.

On Friday the 2nd of October, after work, I got a flight from Aberdeen to Heathrow, where John and Vera Lamont met me and took me to their home in Guildford, where I slept that night. On Saturday morning John drove me back to Heathrow where I caught the 07:50 Iberia flight to Barcelona. On arrival there I got a bus in to the city and bought a map, which enabled me to navigate to the hotel reserved for the runners. I was pleased to meet Saraiva again there. The receptionist informed us that there had been a change of plan, since there were now insufficient rooms in this hotel to accommodate all the runners and helpers. A taxi was called and we were taken to the

'Barcelona Sants' a 4-star Hotel. Before lunch, Ramon Alvarez Saniz, Alfonso Meza, Saraiva and I walked down to Domingo Catalan's running equipment shop. He was pleased to see us, and there was a good atmosphere but he was busy with customers. Following lunch, I went for a short walk and did some shopping in a nearby supermarket.

At 20:00 there was a meeting of the runners and the President of the 'Canal de Isabel 11, Club Deportiva', who introduced each runner in turn and issued their numbers, a process that was continued after dinner was announced. We were all assembled for the **640Km stage race from Barcelona to Madrid.** The overall winner would receive $12,000, 2nd, $7,000, 3rd, $4,000, 4th, $2,000 and 5th, $1000. The winner of a stage would receive $500 and 2nd $250. Medical assistance would be provided as necessary throughout the race and participants would be covered by all-risk insurance.

THE RAIN IN SPAIN: ORDEAL BY ELECTRIC STORM

On Saturday morning, 3rd of October, all runners were taken to the Olympic stadium and at 09:00 we ran one lap of the track and exited out through the marathon gate and on down into Barcelona to the statue of Columbus on the seafront. Santalov and I laid a wreath at the bottom of the column on behalf of runners and the organizers. The weather was a warm 27°C.

We were taken by bus to the start of the first stage at Ingualada in the town square and, at about 11:30, 26 of us set off for Madrid. I started cautiously, running with Patrick Macke (GB), while others went out at a much faster pace. We soon began climbing and by 20Km had reached the top of the ridge at 800 metres and to the North we could see the Pyrenees. The remainder of the run was downhill, apart from one small climb. I had lost contact with Patrick, but caught him again and we moved through, passing Don Mitchell of New Zealand and closing on Kojima of Japan. Patrick went away from me on a hill to catch Kojima and they ran together to the finish in Reuss. I passed Jose Costa of Brazil before the end. Most runners thought that this stage was longer than the stated 79Km and more likely 87Km. Pascal Didellon from France and Alfonso Meza from Mexico did not finish. We were taken to the Hotel Gaudi in Reuss for that night's food and accommodation. Konstantin Santalov (Russia), Jose Corredor (Spain) and Luis Saraiva (Portugal) finished together in 5-55-01, while I finished 8th in 6-16-34.

We set off on stage 2 from Reuss at 09:00 on Sunday and I was pleased that my legs felt quite good. Patrick led saying, 'Yesterday was a holiday but today is work'. I ran in the 2nd group of about 8, which stayed together until we began a climb that continued for 20Km to reach an altitude of 625 metres. Corredor and Saraiva had gone ahead and I stayed with Rusek (Czech). Santalov and Desksen (Russia) and Kojima were also ahead of us. We caught and passed Kojima and then Patrick, but he pulled away on the next climb and I lost contact with the group. By Mora La Nova, where we crossed the Rio Ebro I was about 300 metres behind. Rusek began to tire as Patrick and the two Russians sped on up the next long climb. A strong wind was blowing and this was becoming tiresome for me. Gradually I caught Rusek and pulled away from him. We finished in Gandesa at an altitude of 325 metres. I was tired, but pleased with my run. My roommate Don Mitchell had to abandon the race on this stage. We found out later that Kojima had been struck by a car and taken to hospital. Thankfully he was not badly injured, but was kept in hospital for 24 hours for observation. Don Mitchell gave me the remainder of his 'Carboplex' powder, which provided complex carbohydrates, vitamins and appropriate minerals. J Corredor was 1st in 5-12-02, followed by Andrei Desksen, 5-21-43 and Patrick Macke in 5-21-59, while I had finished 6th in 5-42-18.

On Monday we departed on the 62Km stage 3 at 09:00, from Gandesa and again Patrick took the lead. I ran with Rusek, Corredor and Saraiva, but Saraiva set off to pursue Patrick. At 20Km the Russians and Costa caught us and then pulled away on the next climb. Rusek and I ran together and caught Costa, but no one else. We finished this stage together in Alcaniz. So far so good! A Desksen and Santalov were joint winners in 4-20-00, with Corredor next in 4-27-40. Rusek and I finished in joint 6th in 4-41-22.

Fraser Clyne had requested daily progress reports of the race, so each evening, with a purse of appropriate coins, I would locate a public telephone, (no cell phones then) and call Izzy and give her the information, which she could pass on to Fraser when he telephoned.

Again at 09:00 on Tuesday, we departed on stage 4 from Montalban, an 81Km run and as usual Patrick pulled away. I felt good and headed the chasing group of Saraiva, Rusek and Costa. We climbed up to 1430 metres over a pass and then dropped down before climbing back to 1375 metres. I was surprised by how hilly this region of Spain was. At about 40Km Saraiva began to pull away and none of us could hold his pace. I got away from Costa and Rusek at about 50Km. By then we were running in brilliant sunshine with no shade, so conditions became rather warm. At about 65Km the Russians came past and I could not increase my pace to go with them. The last climb to the finish in Teruel was quite tough, but I was pleased with my run. Corredor had to abandon the race because of an injury. Patrick Macke was first in 5-45-30, followed by Saraiva in 5-48-13 and Santalov and Andrei Desksen in 5-56-43, while I had finished in 5th in 6-02-22.

Stage 5 on Wednesday, from Teruel to Albarracin was only 38Km long and each runner was set off at 3-minute intervals, with the lowest in the classification going first. As I was 5th in the rankings I departed 3 minutes after Rusek and 3 minutes ahead of Saraiva. I set what I thought was a suitable pace, but Saraiva caught me after about 7Km. I could not go with him, which would have helped me, as there was a slight headwind. I became conscious of my left quads problem as I tried to push on and was beginning to feel restricted. In the distance I could see Rusek, but I was making no impression on the gap between us. On the downhill approaching Gea De Albarracin the Russians came past and they were soon out of sight and then Patrick passed. I pushed on to the spectacular town of Albarracin at an altitude of 1150 metres. Rusek had managed to go with Saraiva when he caught him and had run 9-35 faster than me, taking back the 9-06 I had gained on him on stage 4. He was naturally very pleased about this turn around, but I was shocked. Santalov finished first in 2-26-32, ahead of Desksen, 2-29-32 and Saraiva 2-33-14, while I was 7th in 2-48-46.

I had a particularly poor sleep on the night before stage 6 on Thursday. Over the previous few nights I had fallen asleep after a couple of restless hours, but on this occasion it must have been about 04:00 before I finally fell asleep. I suspected that this was a symptom of overtiredness. Jacques De Reguefeuil, my roommate since Don Mitchell departed, had asked for an alarm call at 05:30, but for some reason this call was made at 04:30 and this ended the possibility of further sleep. We had to have an early breakfast because this 6th stage of 112Km was due to start at 07:00 at Los Santos and there was to be a 40 minutes bus journey to reach the starting place.

Patrick and the Russians took the lead, while I joined Rusek and Saraiva as we climbed to 1350 metres in the first 15Km. I did not feel very good, but I managed to stay with them. At 40Km I had to make a toilet stop, but managed to regain contact with them. Because of a headwind, Rusek and I took it in turns to lead, but Saraiva would not share in this work. When Rusek had enough of leading he would slow and move to the side and I would take over. On a climb near 50Km, he did this again, but I did not respond, as I felt weak. He immediately put in an effort as he deduced the reason for my reluctance, and was soon moving away and I was left with Saraiva for company.

Between 60 and 70Km I began to struggle badly as my left quads problem worsened and in addition I began to feel completely drained and probably depleted of glycogen. Saraiva moved away and I was left to struggle on. I stopped again for another Number two and then found that I could not get going again because of the discomfort from my left quads. Following some self-massaging of my quads I was able to start running again, but at a very poor pace. I had also developed a pain in my diaphragm region, which restricted my breathing to shallow breaths. Due to the altitude and the wind, plus my low work rate I began to feel cold. When the support bus came along, the support team responded by giving me tights and a long sleeved top. I struggled on jogging and walking, with 4 runners passing me at different times, until I reached the finish in Cuenca. It had been a disaster of a run, but I had completed it. I was too shocked to copy down the complete results in the Hotel that evening. I just went to bed until dinner was ready. For the first time I had wine with dinner as many others had been having on previous evenings.

There were now 11 left in the race from the 26 starters and quite a number had been eliminated on this stage, by failing to meet the cut-off time of 3.5 hours after the first runner completed the stage. The finishing order was: K Santalov, A Desksen, P Macke, T Rusek, L Saraiva, S Leinonen (Finland), P Medina (Argentina), R Alvarez (Spain), P Mann (Germany), and I was 10th.

The following morning, I received a massage on my left quads and calf muscle from the masseuse in the race support team. This 7th stage of 78Km began at Alcocer at 08:00 and I began cautiously, aiming just to get through it. Initially I ran with Ramon, Primitivo, Costa and Seppo, but then Seppo, Costa and I moved away from the Spaniards. By 30Km the Spaniards had caught us again and Costa began to drop behind, but this group split up as everyone was running at different efforts. Black clouds rolled in and an electric storm began as I was on a plateau at 1000 metres when the resulting heavy rain started and I became rather cold in my teeshirt and shorts. Someone from a support vehicle gave me a long sleeved top, which protected me, although it soon became heavily sodden. I splashed on, passing Ramon, who had stopped for some massage, and gradually the rain eased and became steady light rain. Later the sun broke through and conditions became pleasant again and I gave my soaking top to the next support vehicle that came along.

My left quads were giving some problems, but mainly I was just exhausted and on the next climb at about 53Km I struggled and began to walk on the steepest gradients. As I reached the summit of the climb I noticed that the sky ahead was becoming very black again and I feared that another electric storm was brewing. Sure enough, lightning started flashing overhead with impressive thunder followed by torrential rain. My spirits sank as I began to get colder and I asked the police motorcyclist who had drawn alongside if he could use his radiotelephone to request some assistance for me. He tried, but indicated that he could not raise anyone. Shortly after this, as I was becoming increasingly concerned about falling victim to hypothermia, I saw a van from the race organization approaching and I waved it down. The driver could see me eyeing his tracksuit top, so he indicated that he needed this himself. Instead I accepted a blanket, which I wrapped around me and began walking along the road in the rain, followed by the van and the police motorcyclist, quite a bizarre sight.

A short time later the van drew alongside me and the driver offered to take me into the vehicle. I accepted and my race was effectively over as we sat there for a few minutes as the rain turned to sleet and then he drove me to the finish in Guadalajara only 9Km away. Had there not been that 2nd electric storm or if I had suitable clothing I could have completed that stage, as I found out that the rest was flat or downhill. However, I made the decision to stop to protect my health. Costa also abandoned the race, so now there were just 9 left.

Santalov and Desksen finished together in 5-46-17, ahead of Patrick Macke 5-52-38, Saraiva 6-18-38, Medina, 6-24-49, Rusek and Leinonen, 6-33-46, Alverez 6-49-08 and Peter Mann, 7-18-06.

Rain was falling as the remaining 9 runners set off on the 8th and final stage on Friday, from Alcala to Madrid, which had been reduced to 38Km because of police objections to runners completing the race in the centre of Madrid at Colon Square. I travelled in the coach, which followed the last runners, who were Rusek and Mann, in the continuous rain. We all got out of the coach to run the last 3Km with these last runners and I found it quite difficult to keep up. I could not take deep breaths due to the pains in my diaphragm region when I attempted to do so. My intestines or something in my lower abdomen hurt when I ran.

There was much jubilation and celebration in a local bar at the finish. Following this a coach took us to the Hotel 'Breton' near Madrid centre. After lunch, Seppo, Jacques and I went for a walk in the rain to Colon Square. Jacques continued to the Park, while Seppo and I returned to the hotel using part of our now disintegrating city map. At 19:00 we attended a ceremony at the statue of Columbus in Colon's Plaza, where Santalov and Eiko Endo from Japan, the only lady participating in the stage race, placed a wreath at the foot of the column.

At 21:00 we had a formal dinner at 'Restaurante Daniel', where the food was excellent. After the speeches and the presentation of prize money, there was a 'Typical Spanish (southern region) Folklore' performance by Spanish Flamenco dancers. We returned to the hotel at about 01:00.

The overall results were:

1) K Santalov 40-39-29, 2) A Desksen 41-13-35, 3) P Macke 42-12-00,

4) L Saraiva 43-30-56, 5) T Rusek 45-25-55, 6) P Medina 48-35-12,

7) R Alverez 48-44-46, 8) S Leinonen 50-09-54, 9) P Mann 50-17-26

Later that day I travelled from Madrid to London to Aberdeen and then got a taxi to Dyce rail station where I caught a train to Elgin. Izzy met me at the railway station there and it was good to see her again and it was a great relief to be back home.

In November I received a cheque for $1000 for participating in the Barcelona to Madrid race.

Cycling to and from work for a week aided my recovery and I was able to resume gentle running by the weekend.

On Saturday the 31st of October, 2 weeks after the 'Spanish adventure' stage race, rather optimistically, I decided to run in the Black Isle marathon. The initial pace was modest so I decided to tag onto the leaders, Andy Stirling and two Carnegie lads. By 5 miles Andy and I were clear, but then he increased his effort and moved away, and my left leg problem at the top of the quads began to play up, so I eased back and let him go. After Cromarty on the long hill there was an increasingly strong headwind blowing. I managed to cope with this and with about 4 miles remaining I was able to increase my pace again. I was pleased with this run.

Andy Stirling won in 2-36-15 and I finished 2nd in 2-42-08, with J. Douglas 3rd in 2-45-58.

In November I maintained a base load of running, with no efforts or hill sessions and a maximum long run of 21 miles. In view of this I was not prepared for cross-country racing, but I agreed to turn out for my club in the North District cross-country championships at Fraserburgh at the end of November. The course was a 3-lap course that included a section on the sand dunes, which I found very hard on my legs and in particular it aggravated my left quads problem. I ran as hard as I could and had a fairly satisfactory run to finish 30th and 6th counter for Forres Harriers, who were second team.

On Saturday the 5th of December Izzy, Claire, Mick Francis and I departed at 06:30 for Glasgow and the Copthorne Hotel in George Square. There, in the very pleasant George and Burns room, I was presented with the **SAAA George Dallas Memorial Trust Trophy** and plaque for 1992. Tea and sandwiches for the invited guests followed this presentation. After this we went shopping and it was 18:00 before we departed from Glasgow. In Perth we had an enjoyable meal at an Indian restaurant and arrived home just before midnight.

I finished 1992 with an accumulated training and racing mileage of 6114 miles, which was an average of 117 miles per week.

1993

On the 23rd of January 1993, Mick gave Colin Hunter and I a lift to Dingwall for the North District cross-country league race there, organised by Minolta Black Isle A.C, but really by Ray Williby, a hill runner. Weather conditions were rather bad with snow falling and the course was 3 laps of a small hill, with underfoot conditions very wet, muddy, snowy and slippery, due to the falling snow. After one lap I was last, mainly because of my very cautious descent from the hill and I decided to abandon the run because I considered the course far too dangerous.

In the evening we celebrated Izzy's birthday with a party.

The following Sunday, 31st January, I participated in the Scottish Veterans National cross-country championships in St Andrews for the Aberdeen AAC team. The course was good, as was the weather, and I was quite pleased to finish 47th out of 349 and 4th counter for AAAC, which ended up 4th team by only 9 points. Brian Kirkwood won in 30-55, with my teammate Colin Youngson 5th and 1st M45.

I had accepted an invitation to run in the USA 100Km championships to be held in Central Park New York at the end of February. This gave me a fillip and I increased my weekly training mileage to prepare for this challenge.

On Wednesday the 24th of February, after running to and from work, I caught the train from Elgin to Dyce, arriving at 22:58, when Annie met me and drove us to her and Bob's home in Blackburn, where I stayed the night. Bob drove me to Aberdeen Airport at 05:30 on Thursday morning, where I caught the BA flight at 06:50 to London Heathrow and went to Terminal 3 to check-in for American Airlines flight AA101 to New York. This departed at 10:00 and arrived in New York at 13:05, local time.

At JFK airport I was met by Peggy, who drove me into Manhattan, along streets with snow piled on each side, to the YMCA on 92nd Street and Lexington Avenue, which was called 'De Hirsch Residence', where I was allocated room 1008. After settling in I went out to try to change some money and, after standing for some time in a line in a branch of 'Chemical Bank', I was told by the cashier that it was closed and only payrolls were being processed. Following this I was passing the Metropolitan Museum of Art, so I entered the building and offered pounds as entry payment to the museum, hoping to get some dollars in my change. This strategy did not work as I was granted free admission. Once I had walked through this very large museum I returned to the YMCA and by now the weather was even colder at 20°F, which was 12 degrees below freezing. I went to bed at 19:00, which was 24:00 back home.

Chanakya from the Sri Chinmoy group met me at 10:00 the following day and drove me to the Sri Chinmoy 'Smile' restaurant in Queens. Sri Chinmoy was there in the enclosed area out behind the restaurant and he was honouring 2 representatives from a cinema company, who had allowed his devotees to train in their building. Sri Chinmoy did this by physically lifting them overhead on a specially designed frame and also similarly honoured me, which was also symbolizing a spiritual uplifting. Following this we re-entered the restaurant, where I had a double vegetable curry. On the way back to Manhattan, Chanakya helped me exchange some pounds sterling into dollars.

Back in the YMCA I went to Malcolm Campbell's room and we walked to the New York RRC headquarters for the race briefing. Once this was completed, race numbers were issued as well as $100 to the invited runners to purchase food. After telephoning Izzy, via the operator, from a call box where I became very cold, I went to bed at 19:00 local time.

TOUGH TIME IN FREEZING NEW YORK

I rose at 04:30 on Saturday, the 27th of February and completed my preparations for the race, incorporating the **USA 100Km championships and the IAU North American championships**, which was scheduled to start at 07:00. At about 06:10 I walked in bitterly cold weather, to the Church of Heavenly Rest, where the pre-race changing was located. Chanakya, who was to be my second, arrived and I gave him my drinks and my schedule of 300mls of 10% solution 'Leppin' at the start of each lap, from lap 2 onwards.

Our band of 136 runners got underway from the start/finish at East Ninetieth St and Fifth Avenue, at just after 07:00, running one mile out and back before beginning the 15-lap course in Central Park. I started gently, but began to increase my pace and moved up to join a group in about joint 5th place. Andy Jones was pulling away and Erik Seedhouse, Valmir Nunes and Stefan Feckner were in joint 2nd about 200 meters ahead. By lap 3 I had moved to 3rd, but began to tire badly and by the end of lap 4, about 18 miles, I was struggling in 5th place. I passed the marathon distance in

2-53 and 50Km in 3-27, having already had to stop at one of the portable toilets for a sit down job. From then on I had to keep going as best I could as I became completely drained and the 'Leppin' seemed to have no beneficial effect. Perhaps the head cold that had started on Friday was affecting me, or the conditions as the weather was still extremely cold at 27°F and the water in the cups at the feed stations was freezing over.

Another sit-down toilet visit was necessary as the laps passed slowly, but eventually I was on my last lap. I was extremely relieved to finish this race and 9th place was not too bad, but my time of 7-53-23 was a personal worst. I was randomly selected for a doping test, so an official from NYRRC escorted me to their headquarters, accompanied by Chanakya. There I produced the required urine sample after consuming 3 cans of fruit punch Gatorade.

We returned to the Church of Heavenly Rest for some food and the awards ceremony. I was pleased to meet Alan Kirik there, as I had last met him in 1980. He introduced me to his new wife and we caught up on our news. Also there was Jim Shapiro, who had visited me in Elgin several years ago, during his research before writing his book on ultra-running. In addition, I had met Fritz Muller as I ran round in Central Park.

During this time, I gave a lengthy interview to a lady from the Sri Chinmoy team for their magazine. Following my return to the YMCA, I rested for a while before going for a short walk. I bought some halva from a grocer's shop at 23:15. At about 23:30 I telephoned Izzy and went to bed.

Valmir Nunes (Brazil) had won in 6-45-35, from Stefan Feckner (Canada) 6-51-51 and Brian Hacker (USA) 7-11-49. First lady was Marta Vass (Hungary) in 8-13-54, with K Clark-Setnes (USA) second in 8-21-19 and E McCurtain (USA) third in 8-29-28.

On Sunday morning I went round to Jim Shapiro's for brunch and to meet Valmir Nunes, who was staying with Jim. Jim had spent two years in Brazil and could speak Portuguese and it was interesting and informative to be able to communicate with Valmir through Jim. Valmir was now a full time runner and he trained 50Km a day in two sessions, running on the beach. His best marathon time was 2-18.

Jim had given up running and now participated in ultra-distance swimming and kayaking. He also showed his reclining bicycle, which looked very comfortable and which was capable of high speeds. It was designed and built by an aircraft engineer in California.

Around midday I said goodbye to Jim and Valmir and returned to the YMCA, where I telephoned Chanakya, who came to pick me up and drove me to Queens. Sri Chinmoy was at the tennis courts and we arrived in time for prasad. It was one of the disciple's daughter's birthdays, so she received a cake and 'Happy birthday' was sung to her. Following this we went to the 'Smile' restaurant, where I ate a vegetable curry, while some bajans were sung. I bought some T shirts and bags for Claire and Anna.

Chanakya then drove me to JFK airport, where I checked in and waited for the others to arrive. Malcolm Campbell joined us at a café and time flew by, until we had to say goodbye to Chanakya and boarded the American Airlines flight at 18:15. We were soon airborne and heading for the UK. Erik, who had had to drop out because of hamstring problems, came to chat until the meal was served. Malcolm and I enjoyed some complimentary drinks before drifting off to sleep.

I arrived back in London at 06:50 on Monday and transferred to Terminal One to catch the BA flight to Aberdeen and it was quite a shock to see snow on the ground from just outside London. I got a taxi round to Dyce rail station, where I caught a train to Elgin and arrived there at 13:05, in good time to take my afternoon classes. After work I got a lift home from Chris McLeod. It was good to be home again. Anna was particularly excited to see me back.

During our Easter holidays we set up our caravan at Haughton House Caravan Park at Alford for a week. I decided to experiment with daily single early morning runs ranging from 23 miles to 34.5 miles over undulating back roads, using Ordnance Survey maps to plan my routes and estimate the distances. After a week of these runs I had logged 183 miles. During the 2nd week of our holiday I was back to 'normal' training from home.

I began to feel tired in training, which was worrying, as I had been selected to represent Great Britain in the IAU 24-hour European Championships in Basel on the 1st of May.

Four days before the race I felt extremely tired and had discomfort in my left Achilles tendon, which was quite alarming and, after work, I had 3 problem teeth extracted. Malcolm gave me some laser treatment on my Achilles the following day. He was sure that the problem was not my Achilles, but something in front of it near the heel bone.

On Friday, 30th April, my GB teammate, Mick Francis, picked me up in his new (to him) Toyota MR2 sports car and drove to Aberdeen airport. We caught the flight to Amsterdam, where we met Eleanor and Nigel Robinson and their son Miles, who had flown from Newcastle and they joined us on the flight to Basel.

On arrival there we joined the wrong channel at passport control and entered France instead of Switzerland and there was nobody to meet us there. After some time, Mick spotted Mike Aris on the Swiss side of the border fence, so we had to retrace our steps and go through passport control for the Swiss border. We then went by taxi to the 'Hotel Garni', where a few teams were staying.

On Saturday the 1st of May, we went by taxi to St Jakob Park, where the race was to take place, so that we could participate in the opening ceremony at 10:30, where I got the honour of carrying the British flag. The Mayor of Basel gave a speech of welcome followed by a speech by a representative of the Swiss Athletics Federation and then Malcolm Campbell, the president of the IAU, gave a short address. A group of Sri Chinmoy disciples then sang a song of welcome, which was very nice.

BAD ONE IN BASEL

After some final preparations the **IAU European 24-hour championships** got underway at 12:00 with 143 runners in the competition. When the start was called there were several ranks of runners ahead of me, so I started rather slowly along with the others around me. I was very crowded and I began to get agitated at not getting a clear run, but I held back to get an idea of the correct pace. The first lap of 1.675Km was completed in 8 minutes something. I gradually worked through, until after 5 laps I was in joint 4th place with 2 Latvian runners. Gradually we worked up to the leaders and then Nikolay Safin and I moved into a lead. We ran on together for lap after lap as the sun broke through the clouds and conditions became quite warm and rather humid.

After about 5 hours I got a surprise when James Zarei came past, going quite quickly. I decided to let him go because his pace seemed rather rapid. Some time later I began to get away from Safin and then I caught James, who was in trouble and running rather slowly. I was then in the lead and as I approached 100Km I was closing on Safin and about to lap him. I passed 100Km in 7-52-08 and felt comfortable as I pushed on. However, at about 10 hours I began to slow badly and Safin began to pull me back until he was only one lap behind. When he caught me he was able to pass easily as I was unable to respond. I struggled on and Safin soon un-lapped himself and took the lead.

I was completely drained and began to question what I had done wrong. Perhaps I had trained too hard and not recovered sufficiently or perhaps the local anaesthetic for my teeth extraction was having some adverse effect. Perhaps I was dehydrated, although I had been drinking 200mls of 10% solution of 'Enduro Booster' every 20-25 minutes. However, this may not have been enough, especially since I had difficulty getting the drinks at the required time.

At about 13 hours I went in for a massage, but instead the homeopathic practitioner in charge used kinesiology techniques to decide what was wrong with my body, by placing vials of different substances on my chest and moving my right arm to test its strength. He decided that I lacked magnesium and gave me some to swallow and he then gave me a rather ineffective massage. I had asked for effleurage, but he concentrated on certain points and then he told me that my left leg was longer than my right one due to a misalignment of my pelvis and spine. This problem he treated by working on pressure points on my thumbs! After this bizarre session I returned to the lap and achieved a reasonable pace, but after about an hour I was back to walking again. With about 9 hours remaining I went to have another massage, this time by the other 2 people in the medical tent, but again it was not a proper massage.

Tony Jones persuaded me to take a rest, so I crawled onto the airbed alongside James Zarei. I asked for a banana, but fell asleep before I could eat it. James and Norrie Williamson, who were also in the tent, were asked to resume the race as I slept. Sandra Brown was my next bedmate, but I was only semi-conscious of this. I woke a couple of hour later and offered to go back out, but Tony and John Legge said that there was no point.

Mick was running very well, while James, Norrie and Ian Gunn were all bravely plugging away. In our ladies' team, Marianne was in trouble early in the race and walked most of the time and Hilary Walker was also in trouble as was Sandra, but they kept going. Eleanor became sick and had to abandon the race.

Safin continued to run strongly to the end, but I later found that he failed the doping test by testing positive for some steroid, so his win was nullified and he received a four-year ban.

The awards ceremony held in the Park was followed by a meal in the nuclear bombproof bunker in the centre of the park and continued until 16:00.

Nikolia Safin (Rus) had achieved 264.7718Km ahead of, H Dreyer (Ger) with 259.265Km and M Tuhovcak (Czech) with 257.965Km, Mick Francis (GB) ran very well to finish 5th with 244.743Km.

On Monday, 3rd May, Mick and I got a taxi to the airport and caught the KLM flight to Amsterdam and from there we caught a flight to Aberdeen. It was good to be back home.

There was nothing obvious wrong with me, so I resumed training that week and began my twice-weekly effort sessions. However, I received a shock when, following my morning run, I appeared to be urinating blood. I suspected a urinary tract infection and Dr Sabiston confirmed this and prescribed an appropriate course of antibiotics.

On Friday the 20th of May, after work I travelled to Aberdeen airport and from there caught a flight to East-Midlands by 'Business Air' via Dundee. From there I got a bus to Nottingham and then walked to the 'Rufford Hotel' where I was booked in for two nights for the G.B Ultra Distance Squad weekend, courtesy of the British Athletics Federation (BAF), who also paid for my flight from Aberdeen.

On Saturday I attended a 100Km squad meeting at Holme Pierrepont Water Sports Centre and participated in the seminar that afternoon, which was a thoroughly enjoyable event.

SILVER IN THE NATIONAL 100KM

On Sunday the 22nd of May, the **UK National 100Km championships** got underway at Holme Pierrepont, at 08:00 in overcast mild weather, but with an easterly wind blowing down the course back straight. A group of 6 formed: Neil Featherby, 2 Russians, Greg Dell, me and someone else that I did not know. We completed the first lap in just over 20 minutes. Neil, who was intending to run only 60Km, took the lead and sheltered us from the wind as the group adopted a single file arrangement. At this stage I had no idea who Greg was, since all I had picked up was him telling Neil that he had run 2-28 in that year's London marathon and that this was his first 100Km. He was slim, wore a ponytail, earrings and had a goatee beard. His running was smooth and he seemed comfortable.

The pace increased on the next lap, which was completed in 17-50, but decreased slightly on the next to 18-00, which was fine. Our group became 5 as the potentially better Russian fell back because of a leg problem. Neil was highly amused when one of the Russians asked for tea at the drinks table at the far end of the lap. I began to struggle at about 22 miles and had to let Neil and Greg go, which left me with the other Russian for company, but after a few more laps he went ahead. I passed

50Km in 3-16-00 and gradually pulled back the Russian. I got some assistance when Nigel Robinson in the 10 X 10Km relay came past at the start of the back straight and I was able to tuck in behind him and get shelter from the easterly wind for half a lap.

Greg was about 7 or 8 minutes ahead of me when Neil dropped out. I kept on pushing, but the wind was becoming stronger and I was finding it increasingly difficult to run into it up the back straight. By then the sun was shining from a cloudless sky and conditions were becoming rather warm as I passed 50 miles in 5-31-31. Eventually I reached the finish, very tired, happy that it was all over and satisfied to be 2nd. I wore a new photo of Sai Baba on the back of my watch and called for assistance from my guardian angel during the race.

Carolyn Hunter Rowe ran very well in such adverse conditions to improve her British and Commonwealth records. Carolyn and I were the winners of the Road Runners Club championships.

Greg Dell finished in 6-58-50 and I recorded 7-09-40 for 2nd and 1st V45, with Paul Taylor 3rd in 7-47-04. Carolyn Hunter Rowe was 1st lady in 7-34-54, ahead of Sue Ashley with 8-46-20. There were 49 finishers from the 96 starters.

John Legge arranged for a taxi to take me to the East Midlands airport and from there I returned by 'Business Air' via Dundee to Aberdeen. I got a taxi to Dyce rail station and then a train to Elgin. Izzy met me at Elgin rail Station at 23:19 and drove me home. It was a change to be home so quickly again.

Being a perpetual optimist I had entered the National 24-hour championship, which started the following Saturday. I had only 5 days to recover from the 100Km and my sunburn.

On Friday the 28th of May Izzy picked me up from college and drove me to Inverness airport where I caught the flight to London Heathrow. Anna was quite unwell with a bad cold in her chest. John Lamont met me at Heathrow and drove me to his home in Guildford. After a vegetable curry I went to bed at about 22:00.

On Saturday, the 29th of May, John drove me to 'Thames Water', Kempton Park Works, Feltham for the **AAA of England and British Athletics Federation 24-hour championships**, organised by Feltham Puffers, which was scheduled to start at 10:00. Eleanor Robinson and I took the lead at a very sedate pace, but almost immediately after this Sam Moore came scuttling past.

We settled down to a comfortable pace, but I began to feel that I was working too hard, running with Eleanor, so I eased back. The sun broke through, conditions became rather warm and there was a fairly stiff breeze blowing. Eleanor made a pit stop after about one and a half hours, so I found myself in the lead and continued at a comfortable pace, putting on more sun cream as the temperature continued to rise.

Mick Francis arrived, back from a stage race in France, and took over from John as my second, allowing John to go home for a break, before returning the following day. I was taking 200mls of grape flavoured Leppin Enduro booster of 10% concentration every 20 minutes and a banana every hour after 3 hours and Mick continued looking after me very well.

I became conscious of pain at the top of my right quads, near where it met my pelvis. I realised that it might have been an error not to run during the previous 5 days, because running would have indicated this problem and I could have received appropriate treatment from Malcolm.

As the sun shone from a cloudless sky the afternoon became very warm despite the breeze. I began to slow as both my quads were now painful and Mike Aris began to unlap himself and I could do nothing to respond.

In due course he moved into the lead, following my 15 hours in this position and continued his progress with running and 'walkies' as he called his race walking sections. I struggled on with the insides of my knees scuffing together as I shuffled along and this caused them to bleed. This was the first time that I had experienced this and I realised later that this was probably because I was compensating for, in particular, my right quads problem. I had to make two toilet stops, before going in for a massage, which was quite comforting but did not help my quads.

I had been feeling nauseous for some time and, following my massage, when I began to jog, I promptly vomited several times, which made me feel rather depressed. I got going again, but started walking again soon after. With about 5 hours remaining I decided to walk for the remainder of the time as Mike and Hilary Walker were both walking and neither of us could improve our positions. I was now fully hydrated, as I had to pee almost every lap, but this may have been due to the tea, with one spoon of sugar and milk, that I had started drinking.

Eventually it was over and I could sit down and relax, which was something that I had been looking forward to for several hours. Mike Aris ran and walked very well and appeared to be a man inspired. He achieved 142 miles 1205 yards and I covered 129 miles 932 yards in 2nd and Hilary Walker achieved 126 miles 68 yards in 3rd place. **I should have been happy with 2 British championships silver medals within a week, but I had been aiming for 2 wins.**

After the medals presentations, John drove me back to his home in Guildford where I had a bath and then lay down for an hour. John and Vera prepared a meal, which I enjoyed.

John drove me to Heathrow to catch the 19:45 flight to Inverness, but this flight was delayed because there was no cabin crew available due to some runway closure earlier that day. We got underway at about 20:25 and on reaching Inverness there was fog on the ground and the pilot made two approaches to land, but had to overshoot on both attempts because he could not see the landing lights. He diverted to Aberdeen, but was not allowed to land as the airport was closing down for the night. The pilot then diverted to Edinburgh airport, where we landed at 23:00. I managed to telephone Izzy from there at the 3rd attempt. She had been waiting at Inverness airport, had heard the aircraft trying to land and had just got home.

We passengers now had a choice: either we went to a hotel in Edinburgh and then fly to Inverness at 10:00 the following day; or take a bus to Inverness. The Hotel option was attractive, but I had a class at 09:00 on Monday so I opted for the bus journey. Two buses were provided and we departed for Inverness at just after midnight. At 03:10 we arrived in Inverness and I got off at the rail station, where I talked with a fellow traveller, Steve Wilkinson, who also lived in Lossiemouth. He offered me a lift back there as his wife was driving through to pick him up. We had a long wait in the cold station until 04:20, when Mrs. Wilkinson arrived. I was very fortunate to be getting a lift home and arrived there at 05:25. I went to bed for 1.5 hours to warm up and doze.

On Tuesday, Malcolm began treating my right quads problem and repeated this twice more that week. By early June Malcolm had got my right leg sorted out, which was a great relief. I had another infected tooth removed, so I was approaching the 'Roy Fowler condition'. (Roy was the toothless English warrior who won the International Cross Country title back in 1963.)

I had been invited to the **Lake Saroma 100Km race in Japan** and, although I knew that I was not in top condition, I readily accepted this offer.

On Wednesday the 23rd of June, after my 15 miles Calcots loop I caught the 09:02 train for Aberdeen, got off at Dyce and walked round to the airport terminal. I caught the flight at 11:40 to London Heathrow and on arrival made my way to Terminal 3 where I checked in for my flight with 'All Nippon Airways' (ANA) flight at 18:00. In the departure lounge I met Ramon Alverez from Santander and Huguet Joualt from France. The aircraft was a Boeing 747 and departure was on schedule. A video projection system showed a map of our flight path and the aircraft's current position, with information on distance to destination, distance to next major city, outside temperature, altitude and speed. I had never seen this system before. Our route was over Holland, Denmark, Estonia, Russia, the Russian federation and Siberian plain, then over a mountainous region before crossing the Sea of Japan.

We arrived at Tokyo Narita airport on Thursday afternoon after a flight of about 11 hours for the 6,452 miles (10,381Km) route. Our tour assistant, a charming Japanese girl called Makiko Suzuki, met us and escorted us by bus to the Haneda Tokyu Hotel on Tokyo Bay. The time in Japan was 8 hours ahead of British summer time. Stefan Feckner from Canada arrived later and he was to be my roommate. We had dinner at about 19:30 local time and then, after a short walk in the hotel garden I went to bed.

On Friday after a Japanese breakfast we got taxis to Haneda airport, the domestic airport and there we were introduced to Souhei Kobayashi of 'Sports World Inc', who was to travel with us. Our fight departed at 11:00 for Memanbetsu airport in the Island of Hokkido and we arrived there at 12:50. There were many Japanese runners on this flight.

Osamu Nohira of 'Runners Inc' took us for lunch and then drove us in a small mini-bus, for about an hour, to the 'Saromako Tokyu Resort', where we were to stay. The hotel was by the seashore of a sea loch. Once we had settled in and picked up Patrick Macke, who had arrived the day before, we were taken around the 'Lake Saroma' 100Km course in the mini-bus. I did not get round to running, although the air was fresh and the temperature of around 20°C was much better than in Tokyo.

Saturday morning was taken up by interviews with Fuji Television. Each of the 5 invited runners was interviewed separately, in front of the hotel near the water's edge. Occasionally the interviews had to be interrupted as fishing boats headed out, with their outboard motors roaring. After lunch we had a press conference for a couple of hours, in the sports centre where the race was to finish.

NO JOKE IN JAPAN

On Sunday the 27th of June, at around 04:50 we set off for the beginning of the race at Yubetsu Gymnasium and we arrived there in good time for the 06:00 start. Leaving our shoes just inside the entrance door, we were shown to a room where we could relax. I managed a final toilet visit before heading for the start along with around 1500 others!

We got underway and the pace appeared to be fine, so I continued with the leading group. I passed 10Km in a shade under 40 minutes but, shortly after the turn around on the pier, where enormous drums were being beaten, I began to feel the pace. I lost contact with the group and began to fall behind. Rain began to fall, which I enjoyed initially and I caught and passed 2 runners and began to feel a bit happier. On the hills, which followed I caught a couple more, and was soon through 50Km. There was further climbing to about 60Km and by then I was beginning to feel rather cold because of the incessant rain and slight breeze. Runners now began to pass me as I slowed down. At around 73Km I noticed a display showing time and temperature alternatively, which indicated the temperature was 14°C. A few more passed before I reached 80Km and began the undulating dogleg through the dunes. I became exhausted and could only progress at a very slow pace. I saw the leaders coming back as I headed out to the turn point at just before 90Km. Many runners passed me on this section, but once I reached the main road, I was able to run slightly better. Eventually I reached the finishing area, where we had to squelch for a lap around the muddy baseball field. On finishing my legs would hardly move, so I was assisted to the medical tent, where a doctor put some plasters on my skinned toes. In the sports hall there were gas fuelled turbo heaters and there I was wrapped in a blanket and massaged back up to temperature. I gradually recovered and was able to eat some hot food.

We were taken back to the Hotel for some time and then taken back to the Tokoro Citizen Centre for the awards ceremony. This lasted for about two hours and afterwards we were returned to the Hotel while the rain continued to fall.

Toshiro Kashihara (Japan) won in 6-43-14, from Narihisa Kojima (Japan) 6-48-31 and Patrick Macke (GB) 6-49-59. Ramon Alverez (Spain) had run very well to finish 4th in 6-51-34 and Stefan Feckner (Canada) finished 6th in 7-13-52. I found that I was 14th in an embarrassing personal worst of 8-02-38.

In the evening, at the hotel, there was a reception for the invited runners, foreign dignitaries and those involved in helping with the run. There was a wonderful selection of foods and drinks available and I tried as many different foods as possible including raw fish. Malcolm Campbell had to make a short speech in his capacity as President of the I.A.U.

Once the reception finished Stefan and I went to our room, but we were pleasantly surprised when Patrick Macke knocked on our door and invited us to a party at the guesthouse where he had stayed prior to this hotel. The staffs of 'Runners Inc' were staying there and the party with Karaoke was in full swing when we arrived. We joined in, eating grilled fish, including squid and washing it down with Sake, drunk from a small wooden box, traditionally used instead of a glass. I was given one of these and a large bottle of Sake as a gift. Near the end Tee shirts and later bare backs were autographed with marker pens. This party was a very enjoyable get-together and I particularly liked being able to mix informally with some Japanese.

On Monday, 28th June, Stefan, Ramon, Huguet and I borrowed bicycles from the hotel and set off for a spin. We cycled into the nearby town, and around the harbour, where there were hundreds of fishing boats, all fairly new and made from fibreglass. We then crossed the bridge to the nature reserve and spent some time at the centre there, before cycling on the roads through the dunes. This was the area in which the last 20Km of the race route passed through. We had a very enjoyable outing and then returned to the hotel to quickly pack, ready for departure to the airport.

Our driver and guide, Osamu, got lost a couple of times en-route to Memanbetsu airport, but we arrived there in ample time for our flight to Haneda airport in Tokyo. On arrival there Malcolm, assisted by Osamu, arranged to take our luggage to the hotel where we were to stay. Our guide Makiko met us and escorted Stefan, Ramon, Huguet and me to downtown Tokyo. Patrick also came as he was making his way to stay with friends.

We had a train journey followed by 3 underground train sections, which was interesting, before we reached the area of the city that Makiko intended us to visit. Some time was spent looking at shops, where Ramon made a lot of purchases, then a temple, before having a meal. Following this we were guided to the 'Akasaka Tokyu Hotel'. This was a very plush hotel and we were given cards like credit cards to open our room door locks, which was entirely new to me.

The following morning, the 29th of June, after an early breakfast, Huguet, Ramon and I, accompanied by Makiko and Malcolm, set off for the Central railway station by taxi. On the way to the station we passed the grounds of the Imperial Palace, which looked attractive. At the station Makiko purchased our tickets for the express train to Narita airport. The train ticket was also our seat reservation on this train, which was very clean, comfortable and quite fast.

At the airport we had a snack before saying farewell to Makiko, who had been a very attentive, sympathetic guide. We then paid our airport tax and headed through passport control to the departure lounge.

Our ANA flight departed on schedule and, as the journey was in daylight and the visibility was good, I could see the ground over Eastern U.S.S.R, then Siberia and then Western Russia. I thought that I could pick out Helsinki and Stockholm as we passed over the Baltic Sea. We arrived in Heathrow after twelve and a half hours in the air.

I said farewell to Ramon and Huguet and caught the B.A flight to Aberdeen where I was pleasantly surprised to meet Ronnie Maughan on this flight. He moved seats and we were able to have a good 'blether' on the way up. At Elgin, George met me and drove me home. As ever, it was good to be home.

On Saturday the 3rd of July, Isobel, Anna and I set off on our summer holiday, driving to South Shields, stopping at (Isobel's cousins) Wilma and Ted's in Perth and at 'Run and Become' in Edinburgh to see Adrian Stott. We arrived at Bill and Yvonne's in the early evening. Jean and Doug Hellyer, Yvonne's parents, were also there, so it was nice to meet them all again. On Monday we drove to Edit and Roy's home in Westcott near Dorking. On Tuesday Roy drove us to Heathrow where we caught our Singapore Airlines flight to Bombay. It was on this flight we celebrated our 10th wedding anniversary and my 49th birthday.

I had been selected for the GB team to run in the IAU 100Km World Challenge at Torhout on the 8th of August, so it was essential that I maintained adequate training.

On Wednesday, 7th July, Sampat, an Indian friend of Isobel's, took me from the hotel to Juhu Beach by auto rickshaw. I ran there for over 40 minutes in the warm humid weather and incorporated a couple of efforts. At one end of the beach there was a river flowing into the sea and a shantytown on the other bank. I was surprised to see that people used the beach as their toilet, so I had to watch where I placed my feet.

On Thursday, 8th July we took a domestic flight from Bombay to Bangalore and booked into the 'Ashraya' Hotel. The following day I ran mainly in Cubbon Park and because Bangalore is on a plateau at about 3000 feet the temperature and humidity were not a problem. I felt very lethargic, but did 2 efforts of one minute each and covered about 9 miles in the run.

On Saturday, 10th July, we travelled from Bangalore to Puttaparthi and Sai Baba's Ashram, where we were allocated accommodation in a 'Round house', which was minimally furnished. We had to go to the local shops to purchase mattresses and mosquito nets and settled in. We had a disturbed night with Anna, who had a fever and a sore head and did not fall asleep until 01:00. Poor Anna vomited at 07:20 and again at 10:30

HEALTH CHALLENGES IN INDIA

On Sunday I ran a road circuit around by the beautiful 'Super Speciality' hospital designed by Keith Critchlow. I had suffered diarrhoea before starting and I had to make a stop during my run. I included 1, 2 and 1 minutes efforts, but the whole run was an effort because of the hot windy, but overcast weather. The locals were amused to see me running.

My waking pulse was up to 54 on Monday and I felt rather weak and had a slight sore head. I ran at midday, but after 14 minutes I had to make a toilet stop and noticed that there was blood in my urine, I turned back and my run lasted less than 30 minutes. I felt rather 'washed out'. I had noticed before my run that I had some pain around the region of my kidneys. I began taking Co-Trimoxazole to combat a possible urinary infection. The rest of that week was a struggle with health issues, but I did get in some 9-mile runs incorporating effort sessions, but my total for the week was a modest 28.5 miles.

The following week was even worse, as I had a fever and my total running amounted to 19 miles.

On Thursday, 22nd of July, we travelled from Puttaparthi to Bangalore by Taxi and on the way we saw the upsetting sight of a girl of perhaps 13 years lying dead on the road with her head badly damaged, just like a rabbit road-kill back home. The taxi driver did not stop; he just swerved to avoid her.

Sai Baba had moved to Brindavan at Whitefield, so we had afternoon darshan there. I did not run because I had intestinal problems again. I managed a couple of runs in Bangalore before we moved to Madras, where we stayed in the Hotel 'President'. The following morning, Sunday, 25th of July, I ran from there, mainly along the Marina. The weather was very humid and hot at 35°C.

On Monday morning I ran for over an hour on the marina and the beach. I had to dodge people doing their morning toilet in the sand and the evidence of completed toilet functions. There were hundreds of people, who had slept on the beach. I got 2 more decent training runs done before catching a flight to Bombay and checked into the ''Kohinoor'' Hotel. Running was not practical from there because of the traffic, people, no pavements and poor road surface at the edges.

On Friday, 30th of July, we returned to London by a Singapore Airlines flight and stayed overnight at Edit and Roy's at Westcott. I ran from there on Saturday morning for over an hour, taking in the 12% hill and the 18% hill, which took me 7 minutes to get up on weak legs.

We made our way driving home with stops to visit friends at Baldock and South Shields and arrived home on Tuesday the 3rd of August. I then ran my 15 miles Calcots loop in 1-34-52, with a cold, pains in my intestines. Next day I ran the same loop with Mick, but 6 minutes slower. My stomach was painful and I had a blood taste in my mouth.

Although I was not in good condition I decided to go to Torhout, and on Thursday the 5th of August I travelled to Brussels from Aberdeen airport to Amsterdam and then by train. At Brussels I met Mick Francis and Trudi Thompson and a person from the race organization. He drove us in his large Citroen to Torhout and to the race headquarters at St Joseph's school, which was also serving as the 'Athletics Village'. He then drove me to Wilfried and Rita's, with whom I was to stay again and then took Mick and Trudi to the hotel about 10Km towards Bruges, where the rest of the British team were staying. I ran a lap of the course with Wilfried and Rita's son, Jurgen, but did not feel very fresh.

On Friday afternoon I participated in the opening ceremony for the I.A.U 100Km World Challenge. I was given the honour of carrying the Union Jack, along with Carolyn Hunter Rowe carrying a smaller Union Jack. This ceremony was well done and was an important symbol of the developing status of the 100Km championships.

The race had originally been scheduled for the 7th of August but, because of the death of the Belgian King, whose funeral was being held on that day, the race was rescheduled for the 8th.

On race day I planned to rise at 05:00 and had set my watch alarm for this time, but I did not hear this alarm and Rita woke me at 05:30. I got ready and walked to the start, which was not far from Wilfried's home. John Legge gave me my race number and Tony Jones took my personal drinks.

TORTURE IN TORHOUT

The **100Km World Challenge at Torhout** got underway at 07:00, with 10 loops of 10Km through Kaastel d'Aertrycke grounds and surrounding roads and paths on the northwest edge of Torhout ahead of us. I ran cautiously, aiming for 41 minutes for the first 10Km and passed this marker in 41-38. I increased my effort a little on the 2nd lap and passed the leading lady, Bagmanova (Russia), and the 20Km mark in 80-something, so I was back on my schedule. By 25Km I began to experience pain in both groins and also began to feel very tired and slowed badly, which was disturbing. Runners started passing me as I struggled on. Then during the old railway line section, I had to make a toilet stop and I saw Eleanor Robinson, Carolyn Hunter-Rowe and Mick passing by during my stop.

I carried on, to see if I could recover, but I did not and the leaders lapped me before I reached 50Km. I decided to abandon the race at 50Km, which I reached in 3-58. Massage was available at the finish so I had a massage to see if the groin pains could be helped. The masseur was good and showed me a new stretching exercise to help my groin problem and also suggested that I have my back checked.

Mick McGeoch also dropped out, at 60Km and Erik Seedhouse had a groin injury and abandoned the race at 50Km. Neil Featherby was running very well, although very tired and was unfortunate to collapse at 91Km. Stephen Moore ran a solid race and Mike Hartley finished despite having a rough time.

Carolyn ran very confidently and won, but only by 20 seconds in a personal best of 7-27. All the ladies finished apart from Eleanor, with Trudi running a personal best and our women were 2nd team. My training pal, Mick Francis ran well and finished in 7-56-00. In the evening the reception/ awards ceremony started about an hour late and it did not finish until about 22:15. We went for a meal after this.

On Monday, 9th of August, Rita drove me to Torhout rail station where I caught a train to Bruges and from there a train to Brussels Central. I found where the train for the airport departed from, before depositing my luggage and going on a mini foot tour in the city. Later I caught the train to Brussels airport, a flight to Amsterdam and then a flight to Aberdeen. I got a train for Inverness and fell asleep and I was fortunate to be wakened in Elgin, rather than in Inverness, by Izzy banging on the carriage window.

A week later I had an X-ray with a tracer injected, at Dr Gray's Hospital, to check my kidney function.

I had entered the **Two Bridges Race** and was due to stay at Trudi Thompson's overnight, but on Friday I had a painful throat. I felt extremely fatigued, had kept falling asleep during the day and my left groin was also painful. **In view of these symptoms and the 'feeling' I had that I should not go to the race, I decided to withdraw**, and telephoned Trudi, to let her know that I would not be coming.

On Saturday morning the 29th of August, for some reason I began looking at the sole wear on my Reebok Racer-X shoes. From the wear pattern I could see that my right leg was stronger and doing more work than my left. I compared the wear on similar shoes from the previous year, and I was surprised to find that my left leg had been stronger then. Because I had experienced long-term left quads problems since July 1992, this probably accounted for these changes

On the 2nd of September, after about a mile of my run to work, I was aware of a pain in my right buttock, which became more intense, so I stopped to try some stretching. As this was ineffective I decided to make my way back to our house. Once I had stopped I found it was extremely difficult to get jogging again, but I reached home and cycled to and from work. Malcolm Morgan diagnosed my problem as sciatic nerve pain, and it proved very difficult to get rid of, despite his best efforts, including acupuncture. Training in September was ruined, so my total for that month amounted to 35.5 miles.

By late October my sciatic nerve problem began to ease and I accumulated 109 miles by the end of that month. In November there was further improvement and I began to build up my training again. Midway through the month I had my front left incisor tooth extracted, which was my 7th tooth extraction that year.

In December my sciatic nerve problem finally cleared, so I was able to start building my base mileage again. During this month I had a further 2 infected teeth extracted, making a grand total of 9 for the year. I finished the year with flu, throat infection and sinusitis. **Despite a couple of reasonable performances, it had not been a good year, perhaps due to racing ultras when I was neither fit nor healthy. Was age having an effect as well?**

At the end of the month I found that I had a total training and racing mileage of 4928 miles, reduced from previous years' due to injury, illness and our holiday in India. My average per week was 94 miles.

1994

January 1994 passed without any major problems, so I achieved a substantial training load of 546 miles for that month. Training in February went well and I accumulated 552 miles.

My first race in 1994 was the Inverness half marathon on Sunday the 13th of March, my first race since the 7th of August the previous year. I finished 40th in 79-02, a personal worst. I felt quite rough afterwards with an upset tummy and I was also coughing up yellow phlegm. My left quads began giving trouble on Monday, so I had to seek Malcolm's help once more.

Work on the **'Ritchie Foundation'** (see appendix 1) **Speyside Way 50Km** had come to fruition and a good entry had been received. 'Bell's' whisky were very generous sponsors and their 'United Distillers' office in Elgin handled all my race mail.

On Friday the 1st of April Mick Francis (who had been elected some time previously as 'Race Director') and I marked the course on the Speyside Way, up from Carron. The following day we completed the course marking, aided by Graham Milne and Noel McPartlin.

On Sunday morning, the 3rd of April, Alan Barclay of United distillers sent 81 runners on their way in the first 'Bell's Speyside Way 50Km' trail race from Ballindalloch to the Spey bay Hotel. A cold following wind aided us initially as I ran with a group of 8 until we began the climbing on Ben Aigen.

I found the uphill running rather hard and my left quads became tight again, but they recovered on the downhill sections.

On the road section down to Fochabers I picked up 3 places and on the last stretch to Spey Bay I moved into 6th. I was pleased with my run, especially as I was running quite strongly towards the end. I drank 500mls of 10% solution 'Hi Five' at each of the 4 aid stations.

Fraser Clyne won in 3-02-07, fron early leader Alan Reid, 3-15-00 and Erik Grant 3-19-28. Simon Lund was 4th in 3-24-49, Mike McCulloch was 5th in 3-25-22 and my time in 6th was 3-31-06, just a minute ahead of V50 winner Charlie Love in 7th of the 77 finishers.

Three weeks later, on the 24th of April, Mick Francis drove us down (and picked up Andy Farquharson in Inverness) for the 11th edition of the Lochaber Marathon.

I started cautiously, running the 1st mile in 6-05, which prompted me to speed up and I joined a group that was going along at 6 minutes a mile pace. I passed 10 miles in 60-10 and 20 miles in 2-02-18 and I caught Andy at just before 26 miles, but my token sprint-finish was not sufficient to beat him.

I was pleased enough with this run, especially as I had been unwell with some form of flu the previous weekend. I ran for the 100Km Association and we finished 2nd team.

Fraser Clyne won in 2-25-17, which was a course record, from Andy Stirling (V40), 2-36-45 and John Durnin 2-37-00. Mick Francis was 4th in 2-40-34 and I was 7th in 2-42-54.

My next race was to be in the European 24-hour championships as part of the Great Britain Team along with my training partner Mick Francis, Ian Gunn and James Zarei. The race was to be held in Szeged in southern Hungary.

On Wednesday the 18th of May, Mick Francis and I caught a B.A flight from Inverness airport to Heathrow. We met the rest of the G.B. team there and boarded the B.A flight to Budapest, where we arrived at almost 9 pm. We were then driven in a mini coach to Szeged and witnessed a spectacular electrical storm on the journey. Our driver told us that the temperature there was 35°C during the day. We arrived in Szeged on Thursday at 01:30 and booked into the Hotel 'Hungaria', where I shared a room with Mick.

Later that day we ran for about 3 miles in rather warm weather. The temperature rose to 30°C, as we did some sightseeing in the city. I was surprised to encounter swarms of mosquitoes, which were keen to sample our blood and so became very annoying.

The following day we walked a little in the city, rested and provided urine samples for our team manager, John Walker, so that he could check our hydration levels.

HUNGARY: A WALK IN THE PARK

On Saturday the 21st of May, the 3rd edition of the **European 24-hour championships** began at 10:01 in Nepliget Park. The route was a 1000 metres rectangle up and down either side of an avenue in the Park. An Antinov biplane, the largest biplane in the world, flew low over the park, spraying insecticide to try and kill off the mosquitoes. I was not very happy at having to breathe in these chemicals.

I made a cautious start, aiming for 13Km, or at least 12Km per hour. There was a 12-hour race, taking place simultaneously with the 24-hour, so the route was quite crowded. The temperature rose to 30°C in the bright sunshine, but we were mostly shaded by the trees. The lap recorders appeared to be High School students and they were located on a trailer from an articulated lorry, at the bottom end of the lap.

Various activities were underway or took place in the Park: Two parachutists landed nearby; white smoke from the landing markers covered part of the course; there were two beer tents; a disco type set-up; and a live group playing at one time; as well as a Judo demonstration; and cycling proficiency through an obstacle course.

I felt nauseous after about 3 hours, but taking some dioralite cured that. I passed 100Km in 8-20, which was right on schedule. However, by about 120Km I began to get pain in my left knee, initially near the centre of my patella. I had some freeze spray applied to it and also to my back, which was aching and pressed on.

At twilight the relative humidity became very high and I had difficulty breathing. My knee problem did not improve and I was now having a pain at the front, near the top of my tibia.

I decided to have a massage to see if this would help alleviate this problem. The masseur asked, 'What is this?' He was pointing to a lump to the left of my left knee. This alarmed me as it looked like a half-submerged pigeon's egg. John Walker gave me a tubigrip bandage to put on, which I did and started walking. I tried to jog a couple of times, but on each occasion the pain from my knee was too intense to allow me to get started. I was rather despondent, but I decided that the only thing that I could do was walk for the remaining 13 hours. Time passes much more quickly when one is running compared to walking, so it was a long, long night.

Janos Bogar was still running quite strongly, despite his extravagant speed earlier in the race, but his earlier challengers had all paid the price for their ambitious pace, and were either retired or running very wearily.

Mick Francis collapsed twice, and on the 2nd occurrence, Diane, John Walker's helper, made him lie down in the tent, where he fell asleep, and was wakened 3 hours later. Eleanor had joined Mick in the tent for some time, but they both rejoined the race and began to run quite strongly again.

A runner from the previous 12-hour race, who now had a 24-hour number on, was pacing Bogar! James Zarei was running steadily as was Ian Gunn, and Sandra Brown was keeping up her schedule of walking and running, while Marianne Savage was plugging away and looking exhausted.

Eventually the end approached and we were able to stop at 10:02:30, on Sunday, so the run was 24 hours and 1.5 minutes. Due to some mistake I was credited with 48Km during one of my walking hours! John Walker estimated my distance as 110 miles, so I was very surprised when the official results, which I did not see until a few months afterwards in Malcolm Campbell's I.A.U newsletter, placed me 9th with 222.353Km. John and Dianne did a magnificent job looking after us all.

Janos Bogar (Hun) had covered 261.122Km, ahead of J-P Guyamarch (Fra) 254.013 Km, and V Klement (Ger) 252.110Km. James J Zarei (GB) finished 6th with 243.34Km and Mick Francis (GB) achieved 210.735Km in 15th place.

On Monday the weather was again very warm at 30°C. The hotel manager drove us to the airport at Budapest, where we caught a flight to London Heathrow. After a long wait Mick and I caught the 20:15 flight, to Inverness, where Izzy met us and I and drove us home where we arrived before midnight.

Malcolm Morgan examined my left knee and leg on Tuesday and found an acute gastrocnemius strain, which was causing the knee pain. As the origins of this muscle are at either side at the back of the knee, he gave me pulsed currents through 4 pad electrodes. He repeated this treatment 4 days later and gave me acupuncture on a painful region deep in my right buttock. He also freed my sacroiliac joint, which was always a shock and then stretched my quads and hamstrings, so this was quite a physiotherapy session. Malcolm thought that I probably had this back problem before going to Hungary. I decided that **it would be sensible to have a check over from Malcolm prior to my next important race to ensure that I was not carrying any potential injuries or any minor injuries.**

Malcolm had cleared my problems by the following week, so I was able to resume my training schedule.

SLIPPING ALONG THE WEST HIGHLAND WAY

I agreed to participate in the **West Highland Way race** again along with John Diffey and on Friday the 17th of June, John called for me at 5 pm and drove us to Milnegavie, where we arrived soon after

9 pm. John was going to run the West Highland Way to raise sponsorship for his brother who was suffering from cancer. Noel McPartlin was already there and, along with Graham Milne, would crew for John. We also met Sandy McDonald from Forres Harriers. We had a meal in a Chinese restaurant, where Graham Milne joined us. Later we all tried to sleep in Graham's VW camper van in the rail station car park, as steady rain fell.

I rose at 02:00 and began preparing for the start of the race as rain continued to fall. I made a cautious start, running carefully in the dark with the aid of my head torch. As it became light I began to move through and by the first checkpoint I was just behind John Whitehead. I caught and passed him in the forest section before Conic Hill, but I had to make a toilet stop there. My chest was tight and I had a wheeze, which was disturbing! By Balmaha I was with the leaders, including John Whitehead, who had caught me on the descent from Conic Hill.

My Air Mariah shoes were not very suitable for the wet conditions. I took the lead briefly before John caught up again on one of the rough sections. By Rowardennan he was about 400 metres ahead, but on the forest road I caught him and went ahead. He was not in sight as the forest road ended and the footpath began. I had trouble on this twisty slippery footpath and I was soon caught and passed by John and some time later passed by 2 others. They were soon out of sight as I picked my way along the path, attempting not to slip excessively.

Mick Francis ran in from Inverarnan to meet me with drinks and a banana, He and Adrian Stott were my support crew and they proved very attentive.

There was water everywhere: all the streams were torrents; and all the paths were streams. I began to feel cold as the route became higher and the wind became gale force, so I put on my Gore-Tex top and tracksters, which helped a good deal.

I had a bad fall, cutting my right knee, thigh, shoulder and my right temple, which gave me quite a shock and shook my confidence. I was able to continue, but I fell again on the descent to Inveroran. I crossed the Rannoch Moor section with a combination of jogging and walking. I would jog until my quads protested too much, at which point I would walk for 30 paces and then resume jogging. This worked quite well, but I was becoming cold on this elevated section, so it was important that I kept working to maintain my body heat. The weather had deteriorated even more so there was now some sleet mixed with the rain.

Adrian and Mick met me before the end of this section and informed me that the race was to be terminated at Kingshouse Hotel because of the appalling weather. In particular there was mist on the 'Devil's Staircase' and there was a report from walkers who had come from Kinlochleven that the stream that had to be crossed in the gully in the traverse to Kinlochleven was a raging torrent. This would be a potentially lethal obstacle for tired runners to negotiate. I was quite pleased to stop but was surprised to see that I was coughing up green phlegm.

Once I had changed my clothes, Mick drove us to Fort William, where we showered and got sorted out in the sports centre there. We ended up seeking a B&B at 21:50 after a poor meal at 'Luigi's'. Fortunately, we were successful in finding accommodation and we shared a room. I had to wrap a tee shirt around my head to stop blood going onto the pillowcase and sheets. It had been quite an adventure!

Brian Davidson was first in 13-41, ahead of Tom McPake (V40) 14-16 and I was 3rd and first V45 in 14-46. John Diffey finished 19th in 17-52. Sue Ashley was first lady in 16-23 ahead of Isobel Clark in 16-48.

On Sunday morning the weather in Fort William was beautifully sunny and warm, so after breakfast we drove up Glen Nevis. Adrian and Mick walked up the Ben Nevis path some way, while I pottered around near the river. We saw the village that had been built as part of the set for 'Braveheart', the film about William Wallace. The bridge across the River Nevis there had been swept away by the spate. After the prize giving Adrian got a lift back to Glasgow and Mick drove us back to Lossiemouth.

I entered a new Veteran category on Wednesday the 6th of July, when I celebrated my 50th birthday and also our 11th wedding anniversary.

On Monday the 11th of July we began our summer holidays, and Izzy, Claire, Anna and I began our journey to India by travelling to the 'Ambassador' Hotel near Slough. The following day we caught our flight to Bangalore and booked into the 'Ashraya' Hotel.

Over the next 3 days I trained in Cubbon Park and included some 800 metres efforts on the cinder track there. However, I thought that my sciatica problem was starting again, so I reduced my interval session to 8 X 400 metres with 200 metres recovery the following day.

The Scottish Athletics Federation (S.A.F) had selected me to represent Scotland in a 100Km team race in Victoria, Canada, in conjunction with the Commonwealth Games being held there in late August. In view of this I wanted to maintain a reasonable training mileage while in India.

I decided that I should try running from the Ashraya to Sai Baba's Ashram in Brindavan. Sai Baba was spending some weeks there rather than at his Ashram in Puttaparthi and the UK group of children, which included Claire and Anna, were rehearsing there daily, to perform a play for Baba.

On Monday the 18th of July at 5am I departed from the 'Ashraya' Hotel in Bangalore and ran the 15 miles to Baba's Ashram at Brindavan in 1-50-54. There were minimal streetlights, but enough to see my way, but once clear of the city it was pitch black. I carried a small torch to warn approaching cyclists with no lights, and to identify my route, which I had memorised from taxi trips to Brindavan. It was quite peaceful at such an early hour, but as dawn broke, people began stirring and road traffic increased. The taxi with Izzy, and the girls would pass me near Brindavan and when I reached the parked taxi our driver would give me the toast and jam that Izzy had taken for my breakfast.

Over the next 6 days I repeated this run and ended the week with a satisfactory total of 105 miles. I ran this route on another 6 mornings, the following week, before we moved to Madras on Saturday 30th July, where we stayed in the Hotel 'President'. A 10 miles run from there on Sunday morning, in humid conditions gave me 100 miles for that week.

After 3 days exploring Madras and surrounding area, we used our Indian Airlines unlimited flights package to move on to Agra on Wednesday the 3rd of August. We stayed in Hotel 'Amar' and, the following day during my morning run in very humid conditions, I took in the Red Fort and the Taj Mahal. On Friday morning the weather was again very humid and hot and I felt very tired on my run over a different route.

Our next flight was to Delhi, where we stayed in the 'Hans Palace' Hotel. On my first morning run from there on Saturday, 6th of August, I took some time to find a good route. I ended up in a large green area around the Presidential building and other Government buildings. I took the wrong road back and got lost, so I had to retrace my steps to find the correct road. As a result, I was out for over 2 hours.

After breakfast I began to get intestinal pains and I felt nauseous and generally unwell. At Gandhi's Museum I had to rush to the toilets in the grounds. I began to feel rather weak and all I wanted to do was lie down in a cool place and close my eyes.

During our city tour I had to ask the taxi driver to stop as I felt a vomit coming and, as he did so, I vomited twice. I had picked up some bug, perhaps from the water I drank after my run, from the fridge in our room. Although it was bottled, but opened, I assumed it would have been filtered etc. Perhaps the culprit was the fresh fruit (papaya, peaches, pineapple and sweet lime) that I had at breakfast, although I had peeled the peaches.

Later at the Domestic airport I vomited 3 times as we walked to board our aircraft. I survived the flight to Jaipur. On arriving there and getting a taxi to our hotel and checking in, I went straight to bed. I had flu-like symptoms, aching muscles and sensitive skin. I took antibiotic and anti-diarrhoea tablets, but my diarrhoea continued and I also had a headache.

By Sunday my diarrhoea had stopped, but I had no appetite and only ate 2 bananas during the day. I was too weak to run. The following day I felt a lot better, but I still felt weak and had muscle soreness. Izzy was unwell with dehydration symptoms. We did manage, with the aid of a local taxi driver, to see the sights in and around Jaipur.

Our next flight on Monday, 8th of August, was to Aurangabad, at an altitude of 1907 feet, where I felt much improved, but my right quads were still painful. We did some walking at the nearby 'Ellora' carved caves. Anna became unwell, so she and Izzy were confined to the hotel all day. I did some walking at the Ajanta caves. On Thursday I felt sufficiently recovered to try a run at 5am from the 'Ajanta Ambassador' Hotel in Aurangabad. The weather was hot and the humidity was sufficient to stop my digital stopwatch from operating, but I managed about 45 minutes slow running.

Later that day we caught a flight to Delhi and transferred, on the tarmac because our plane had been delayed, to the flight we had booked to Goa. On arrival we got a taxi to our hotel, the 'Holiday Inn, Leela Beach'. On Friday morning I managed one and a half hours running on the beach and had some company, as some local lads started to run with me. I repeated this run on Saturday in a downpour of warm rain; and again on Sunday; and this gave me 45 miles for the week.

In the afternoon we caught a flight to Bombay to get ready for our journey back to London. We checked into the 'Golden Manor' Hotel near Juhu beach. I ran from there onto Juhu beach on the following two mornings, covering at least 10 miles on each occasion.

Later on the 2nd day, Tuesday, 16th August, we boarded our flight back to London and then continued to Aberdeen. The following morning, I was pleased to run my 'Boars Head' 21 miles course in 2-26-58, wearing Reebok 'Racer X' shoes to see if they would be suitable for the 100Km in Victoria. The following day, Thursday, I resumed running to and from work.

A week later, Wednesday the 24th of August, I woke with a stiff neck and, on my run to work, I was conscious of pains in my abdomen and, on reaching College, certain parts were very sensitive when pushed or prodded. I could not walk upright because of the discomfort and I could not take deep breaths. As the day wore on I developed a headache and began to have flu-like symptoms. At 13:20 I telephoned the Laich Medical centre and luckily I was given an appointment for 16:10. After work I ran, with great discomfort, down the old railway line to the Medical centre, where Dr McLean gave me a good examination, but she could not find anything specifically wrong, but said that it was not my appendix, which I had suspected, so that was a relief. She did not prescribe anything and suggested that I contact a doctor when I arrived in Victoria.

On Thursday I rose at 04:00 and I felt a good deal better, but I still had pains in my neck muscles and abdomen. I did my final packing and got ready to leave for Glasgow airport with Scottish teammate Mick Francis at 05:00. He drove us there with no difficulty and deposited his car in the airpark compound.

Our flight, on board a United Airlines Boeing 767, departed at 12:15 for Washington, Dulles Airport, where we arrived at 15:05 local time. I felt better as the day went on, which was a great relief. Our next 2 flights were also with United Airlines, to Seattle in a DC10 and on to Vancouver arriving at 21:10, which was as far as our tickets allowed. I noted that our return tickets cost the Scottish Athletics Federation £811 each.

There was no one to meet us, so I telephoned the race organiser, Bob Reid to find out what the possibilities for continuing to Victoria were. As the last ferry departed at 22:00, we could either purchase a flight to Victoria or spend the night in the airport and get a ferry the next day.

Fortunately, we had enough money and chose the flight option and bought tickets for the 22:15 on a 'Dash 8-300' to Victoria. Bob Reid, the president of 'Prairie Inn Harriers' and his wife Susan met us there and drove us to Bob's parent's home, where we were to stay with our third team member, Norrie Williamson, who had already arrived. As we had been travelling for about 25 hours we were very glad to get to bed.

The following day, Friday the 26th of August, Norrie, Mick and I went to the Commonwealth Games and enjoyed a good afternoon's sport. Later we met Bob Reid, who drove us to the 100Km race location, where we ran one lap of the 8.25Km course, which we would have to complete 12 times on race-day. I tried to pick up the pace, but soon began to struggle and falter, and had to hang onto the rest as they maintained the pace that I had initiated. Later we walked to the inner harbour in Victoria and watched the spectacular fireworks display at the end of the evening.

On Saturday morning we ran down to the marathon course to see the women's marathon, which started at 07:00 and, once the leaders had passed, we ran to different parts of the course to watch the runners. In the afternoon we went to the Games stadium, where the temperature reached 30°C. After the Games, Bob drove Mick and I to Elk/Beaver Lake, where we ran for 43 minutes around it on trails. I got dropped when Bob increased the pace and although Mick hung on for a bit, Bob got away fairly easily.

The following morning, we ran down again to watch the men's marathon. There had been an electrical storm so conditions became rather wet. Afterwards we went to the final day of the Games, but left before the closing ceremony started. The fireworks display in the evening was excellent. Prince Edward closed the event at 23:30.

A SOLID RUN FOR SCOTLAND IN CANADA

Three days later, it was 'race-day', Wednesday the 31st of August. We rose at 04:30 and got ready for our 100Km race. Susan picked us up at 05:00 and drove us to the start at Stelly's Secondary School, where we used the facilities and left our kit. It was just becoming light as we started the '**Prairie Harriers' 100Km 'International Championships'** at 06:00. I started cautiously, but my 10Km time was a little on the slow side, so I increased my pace accordingly. I moved through the field and took the lead of the second group.

Andy Jones, who was expected to win, Maciej Cieplak and Stefan Feckner were ahead and pulling further away. By 40Km Andy was being pulled back and by 50Km, reached in 3-18-21 he dropped out, due to a pulled hamstring, so I was then 3rd and passed 50Km in 3-34-26. Mick and Norrie were running well and not far behind me. By 12:00 the temperature was rather warm, so I got my hat and used wet sponges given to me by Brian Kennedy, Mary Morgan's coach, at the 4Km point on each lap. After 7 laps of the 12-lap course, Mick was beginning to have problems and Norrie was losing ground to me although still maintaining 4th place. I began to feel the effects of the concrete pavements on my feet and legs, but I was not distressed and was delighted to finish comfortably in 3rd place in 7-29-46, also 1st Over-50.

I drank a 330mls bottle of 10% solution; grape flavour 'Leppin Enduro Booster' at the completion of each lap, so I drank 3.3 litres in all and this seemed to be adequate.

Norrie finished 4th in 7-42-25 and Mick was 8th man in 8-05-01. He collapsed on finishing, so he had to be carried into the shade to recover. **Our Scottish team, the first ever in a 100Km race, was 2nd to the Canadian team, which was very satisfying**. Mary Morgan set an Australian's woman's record of 7-48-13 in finishing 6th overall. Stefan Feckner (Canada V40) won in 6-54-31, from Maciej Cieplak (Poland) 7-09-26. There were 40 finishers from the 63 starters.

On Thursday morning we went into Victoria to attend to some business and to exchange some shoes, which were given as prizes by 'Front Runner' sports shop. Later we soaked in a hot tub at 100°F at Bob Reid's, before having a meal and a very memorable party, at which Brian Kennedy was the star singer.

The following morning Susan drove us, along with Mary and Brian, to catch the 09:00 Ferry to Vancouver. This was a very pleasant sail and the scenery was a bit similar to the West Coast of Scotland. At the ferry terminal in Vancouver we caught the bus to the city, but missed our stop and had to get a trolley bus back to where we wanted to meet Norrie, who had flown across earlier.

Once we had left our bags in lockers at the bus station, we took the 'Sky train' down to 'Gas town' and walked around sightseeing. A trip up to the observation floor of a skyscraper gave us a wonderful view of the city.

On returning to the Bus Station I was nominated by our group to arrange possible overnight accommodation with one of the runner contacts given to us by Bob Reid. I telephoned Ean Jackson, but he was out, so I then telephoned Ken MacLeod, who answered from his work number. Ken came to pick us up in his Jeep and drove us to his home, which he and Heidi had just moved into after their recent marriage. It was a beautiful house on a hillside with a magnificent view.

Ken took Mary, Mick and I for a run along by the shoreline and up over some hilly trails near the University of British Columbia. I got dropped on the climb and Mick just managed to stay with Mary, who was an amazingly strong hill runner. After this, Ken, Heidi, Ean Jackson and Greg cooked a lovely meal for us and provided a party. We went to our respective sleeping places at 02:00; Mick and I were on the landing at the top of the stairs, with our alarms set for 04:30. I did not sleep because Mary wanted to 'talk' to Mick and I!

Later that morning, Saturday the 3rd of September, Ken drove us to the airport as promised and then took Mary and Brian to catch the ferry to USA. Mick and I were soon checked in and on our way to Chicago at 06:40 and on to Dulles, Washington on a Boeing 747. We found that our flight to Glasgow was to be delayed for 3 hours. This upset our plans to run in the Moray marathon on Sunday.

We arrived back in Glasgow at 07:55 and after collecting our luggage, Mick collected his car from the airpark and drove home very well. We saw the Moray marathon runners at Burghead and we reached Lossiemouth at midday. After lunch, Izzy and I went to Cooper Park to see the later marathon runners finish.

I did not race in September, but concentrated on consistent training with a view to running in the Sri Chinmoy 24-hour race at Tooting Bec on the 22nd of October.

My training went well and, on Friday the 21st of October, Izzy dropped me off at Inverness airport on her way to visit her Mum. There I joined Mick Francis, Allan Stewart, Andy Farquharson and Mick's Dad, Roy. We all caught the 12:21 flight, delayed from 11:35, to Heathrow, to participate in the 24-hour race next day.

From Heathrow I went to Waterloo Station, where I left my bag, and then went to Oxford Circus to find the camera repair shop listed in 'Amateur Photographer' magazine. I located the shop and gave them Izzy's German camera for repair. I bought myself a modern camera from Dixon's in Oxford Street on my way back to Waterloo Station. I caught a train to Guildford, where John Lamont met me at 19:20. We had rice and chilli mince at about 21:00.

24 HOURS: OVERCOMING PROBLEMS IN WET WEATHER

On Saturday John and I left at 10:15 for the **Sri Chinmoy 24-hour race** at Tooting Bec and we arrived there in plenty of time. There had been showers all morning and the wind was getting stronger. John parked his car on the grass alongside the track and pitched his tent alongside.

We got underway at 12:08 and were subjected to showers of rain and a strong wind and there were some quite large puddles on the top bend of the track, which we had to splash through. Mick, Allan Stewart, Alan Young and Geoff Oliver ran with me for about an hour and then gradually eased off, except Allan Stewart, who stayed with me for around 4 hours.

We changed direction every 4 hours, which is good as it equalizes the stress on one's legs. I wore my Nike 'Duellist' shoes with one pair of lightweight socks turned inside out to avoid rubbing from seams. These seemed fine for several hours, but I began to get backache and pains in both my groins. I decided to change into Nike 'Air Mariah' shoes, which on reflection was a crucial move. I became very fatigued well before 10 hours and lost my lead to Mick Francis. I was pleased that he was running so well and that he appeared likely to win.

In desperation I asked John to arrange physiotherapy or a massage for me. I had a massage, which helped a great deal, although the masseur found nothing in particular wrong. I had a brown bread jam sandwich at this time with some 'Staminade' as I thought that I might be suffering from some dehydration, although this appeared unlikely given the wet conditions. Following this I ran well for about 2 hours.

My insides began giving me problems and I had to make 7 visits to the toilets. I also began to feel nauseous, but that excellent German paste, which Helmut's wife had given to me during the Barcelona to Madrid race in 1992, cured this.

Mick began to have problems with his quads and he had to go for physiotherapy treatment, but this did not benefit him. I went for another massage session, but this time I found that it made little difference. Perhaps the 5 minutes lying on my back helped as much as anything. Mick had to withdraw from the race at 106 miles, which was a real shame. Many others gave up the fight and the numbers on the track got fewer and fewer. A torrential rain shower occurred, just like a monsoon shower, so I was glad that John had my Gore-Tex jacket handy. Gradually I began to feel better and was able to maintain a reasonable trot to the finish.

I had taken 200mls of 10% solution 'Leppin' 'Enduro Booster', every 20 minutes, after one hour, alternating grape flavour and vanilla flavour, which I found a bit sickly. After 2 hours, I alternated a banana and 2 fig rolls on the hour. The fig rolls were too dry to eat properly after several hours so I replaced them by a banana. At 6 hours John made my 'Smash' with beans and I had 2 yoghurt cartons of this, which seemed to go down well. In addition, every 2 hours after 14 hours, I had coffee with two spoons of sugar and with a little milk, made up to 200mls I found that the brown bread and jam began to irritate my mouth after a while, so bananas were used instead.

I was delighted to be able to complete the race and also to finish first. Of the 40 starters only 17 finished the 24 hours.

My final distance achieved was 147 miles 314 yards, with R. Littlewood (M40) 2nd with 135 miles 808 yards and Stephen Till 3rd with 133 miles 291 yards and Geoff Oliver (M60) 4th with 127 miles 1624 yards. Sharon Gayter was first woman in 5th place overall with 127 miles 314 yards ahead of Marianne Savage in 6th with 124 miles 1474 yards.

There were no suitable races during the remainder of October or November, so I maintained a relaxed one hundred miles per week schedule. I had decided to avoid cross-country league races, feeling that I had done my share of these for the Club in the past.

Towards the end of November, I was surprised to see a large red scratch on top of my left calf muscle, with a painful region around it, which was hot, with considerable swelling. Malcolm said that I had some sort of infection, which made sense, because this problem was becoming progressively worse without exercise. Malcolm advised me to start taking antibiotics. At the Laich Medical centre I saw a doctor who did prescribe a course of 'Amoxycillin', 250mg capsules. These cleared the problem over the next 5 days.

December was also race-less so I ended 1994 with a total training and racing mileage of 5910 miles, which was an average of 113 miles per week.

1995

I had my first race of 1995, when I ignored my decision to give up cross-country, and ran in the North District cross-country league races in Elgin on the 14th and 28th of January and on Saturday the 25th of February, when I drove to Hawick for the Scottish Veterans cross-country championships. The course was good, but a little hilly for my liking, I finished 63rd.

On Friday, the 3rd of March, I cycled to and from work and after dinner I drove to Aviemore, where I picked up Andy Farquharson and then continued to Edinburgh and to Adrian and Lynda Stott's home, where we were to spend the night.

AGE GROUP RECORDS ON A WINDY WELSH TRACK

Andy and I departed from Adrian's just after 8am on Saturday morning for Barry, south Wales and arrived in late afternoon. We found 'Jenner Park', and then the B & B, 'Barbarce'.

On Sunday morning, the 5th of March, we made our way to Jenner Park and got ourselves ready for the 'Barry 40'. By the start at 10:00, there was a wind and showers of rain, so conditions were not great. Robin Gardner took the lead from me after the first bend, so I was quite happy to run behind him, especially into the wind on the back straight.

Malcolm Griffiths joined us and we ran together up to 2 hours. We passed 5 miles in 30-34, 10 miles in 61-16, 15 miles in 1-32-12 and 20 miles in 2-03-46. By this time, I was finding the pace too difficult to maintain, and I had to ease back as I began to struggle and the leaders lapped me. I managed to recover somewhat, passing the marathon in 2-45-20, and at 30 miles, reached in 3-10-15, I had improved the over 50's record by 2-38. My 50Km time was 3-17-21, an improvement of 2-11 on the previous record.

Malcolm Griffiths began to have difficulties, so I was able to catch him and then unlap myself and begin to hold the gap to Robin constant. The wind strength increased during the race and was sufficient to blow some marker cones across the track.

I was very pleased to finish 2nd and to achieve, another over 50's record, taking 4-32 off the previous best held by George Kay. I drank 200mls of 10% concentration solution of 'Leppin' every 20 minutes after 40 minutes and I wore my Reebok Racer X shoes.

Robin Gardiner won in 4-17-45, while my time was 4-21-34 and Malcolm Griffiths was 3rd in 4-24-04. Andy Farquharson finished 7th in 4-58-22. There were 13 finishers from 17 starters.

After the awards ceremony I drove back home by Inverness to drop Andy there. I arrived home at 4am on Monday, in plenty of time for my 9am class. Since I left home on Friday evening I had driven 1217 miles. It was a relief to get home and receive a welcome from Izzy.

Later Mick McGeoch sent me, along with the results and my lap times, a cheque for £50 from Les Croupiers Club towards my travelling expenses, which was a welcome surprise.

A week later, the 12th of March, in the Inverness half marathon, I felt quite good initially, passing the first mile in 5-42, but by 8 miles I felt exhausted. I passed 10 miles in 59-54. I was quite pleased with my run, being first over 50 in 79-10, which was only 8 seconds slower than the previous year. I wore my Nike Niobe shoes, which gave me quite hot feet by the end.

My next race was to be the London Marathon and for some reason, I think financial, I decided to travel down by bus. On Friday the 31st of March, after work, Izzy drove to College with my kit and then drove me to Elgin bus station, where I caught the bus to Inverness. The overnight bus to Victoria Coach station in London arrived at 06:20 next morning. Joan Cameron of Moray Road Runners and Gerald Box, Inverness Harriers, were also travelling on this coach for the London marathon. I went to Olympia to register and see the exhibition. I met: Malcolm and Marilyn Campbell, John Walker, Graham Milne and Colin Youngson. Following this I went to Waterloo Station and caught a train to Guildford, where John Lamont met me. The weather was rather warm at 70°F. John drove me to his home and I got my first view of John and Vera's baby daughter, Maria. She had Vera's eyes.

John made fish pie for our evening meal, which we had rather late at 22:00, so I ate sparingly, conscious of the closeness of the race next morning. I went to bed at 22:30.

On race-day, Sunday the 2nd of April, John drove me to Tower Bridge station where I caught a train to Blackheath, along with several hundred other runners. I got an excellent position at the start in about the 5th row back. I did not feel very good once I started running, my first mile was 5-48 and I maintained this pace through 3 miles. My 10Km time was 36 something, Allan Stewart and Willie Sichel passed me soon after. I began to struggle after 10 miles, which I passed in 59-something. By the halfway point, reached in 78-38, I was jogging. My left quads were hurting quite a lot. Graham Milne came past and then my weekend training partner Mick Francis and then Alan Ross. The temperature was now over 70°F, which made conditions uncomfortable.

At a drinks station at about 15 miles I coughed while trying to drink causing my top dental plate to come flying out of my mouth. I failed to catch it, so I had to stop and retrieve it from among the discarded empty and partially empty water bottles. I ran the rest of the race clutching my denture plate in my left hand!

My condition did not improve and 20 miles was passed in 2-04-something, but at around 24 miles I did begin to pick up and finished fairly strongly, passing Alan Ross and Colin Youngson. My time of 2-46-45 was rather poor and gave me 551st place. After finishing I was coughing up yellow mucus again. I received a massage before meeting up with the Les Croupiers Team, who kindly let me use their hotel rooms for the afternoon and early evening before going for some beers. My return bus to Inverness departed at 23:00.

Following the London marathon, we were on our Easter holiday, so we took our caravan to Haughton House Caravan Park at Alford, for 3 days. I enjoyed morning runs over some familiar routes there. We moved to Blair Atholl Caravan Park for 3 days. Again my morning runs were up Glen Tilt to the wooden footbridge and back, or further, to past Forest Lodge by a good way, before returning.

Several months earlier Mick Francis and I decided to organise the 2nd edition of the Bell's Speyside way 50Km race. Mick took on the task of race director, and I produced and distributed entry forms, secured the S.A.F permit, sourced folding tables for the feed stations and enlisted helpers for all the tasks that had to be attended to on the day and much else. On Friday and Saturday, Mick and I marked the Speyside Way Race route.

On Sunday the 16th of April, in the second edition of the **'Bells Speyside Way' 50Km trail race**, Allan Stewart, Andy Farquharson and I took the lead, but a short while later Allan took off. Andy and I ran together up and over Ben Aigen, but I began to struggle on the climb back up to the 'Moss of Cairnty' and lost contact with Andy. I caught up going down to Fochabers, but lost contact again on the next climb. Soon after this Peter Baxter caught and passed me and went on to run with Andy. I began to lose ground on the rough track once we left the road and lost more as I slowed on the uneven surface, steps and twists. On the last section I was surprised to catch Allan and easily pass him because he was a spent force. My time was 4-41 faster than last year's, which was pleasing.

I drank 330mL of 10% concentration of Leppin Enduro booster at each of the four feed stations. Izzy made a video recording of this race.

Peter Baxter won in 3-23-11, from Andy Farquharson 3-23-21 and I was 3rd and 1st V50 in 3-26-25. There were 62 finishers, which was satisfactory.

The following Sunday, the 23rd of April, Mick, Allan, Andy and I travelled to Fort William for the Lochaber marathon, which incorporated the Scottish Marathon Championships. The start and finish of the course had been changed so, instead of going into town for a loop, the route now went through Inverlochy village and past Inverlochy Castle before joining the old route. I never expected to be running a marathon, which passed the place where I lived as a pre-school child! The old cottage, where we had lived, had been demolished and replaced by a bungalow.

I felt quite tired from the start and found it difficult to maintain 6 minutes-a-mile pace, but I managed to join a group that was running at a pace that I could handle. We caught Mick Francis, who was suffering by 5 miles and we reached half way in 1-19-15. On the return journey we faced a head wind and, as I was not strong enough to lead the group, I was content to let others do so. On a few occasions I tried to do my share at the front, but I lacked the strength and dropped back. We passed 20 miles in 2-02-55 as our group broke up, and Jackie Stewart of Metro Aberdeen pulled away from Mick and I, leaving us to help each other. We passed Allan Stewart at about 22 miles and encouraged him to keep going for the team. Mick kept the pace going until the last mile, when he faltered. I was pleased to catch two in the last mile, especially as one was Bobby Young of Clydesdale Harriers. I finished 9th in 2-42-47, while Mick finished an exhausted 12th in 2-43-47 and Allan a tired 16th. We were delighted that our team, Moray Road Runners, had won the team prize.

John Duffy of Shettleston Harriers won in 2-31-19, from Alan Reid (Peterhead), 2-35-52 and Ritchie Davidson (Dundee RR), 2-35-59. Davie Fairweather was 1st V50 in 4th with 2-36-02. There were 120 finishers from 124 starters.

On Wednesday the 3rd of May my right foot was rather painful on my morning run to work. Malcolm Morgan examined it and formed the opinion that there was a crack in my second metatarsal shaft, which is the one going to the second smallest toe. He gave me laser treatment, which helped reduce the discomfort. I feared that I would have to stop running and rest for 4 to 6 weeks to allow healing of the bone. Malcolm advised me to stop running until the weekend. He estimated that there was a 70% chance that the cracked metatarsal would be healed by the 27th of May, when I had been selected to represent G.B. in the European 100Km Championships. Vigorous cycling should be sufficient to maintain my condition, so I cycled to and from work each day at a hard effort and received daily laser treatments from Malcolm.

On Saturday, 13th May 1995, Izzy and I drove over to the A9 and met Richard Brown on his L.E.J.O.G, on the old A9 north of Kingussie. He was in excellent spirits and walking strongly and aiming to cover 80 miles a day by combining running and fast walking. I cycled with him until beyond Slochd Summit. There was quite a heavy snow shower on the section after Aviemore. His support team consisted of two camper vans, with the following crew in one: Doug Aitken, the organiser/ route finder and driver, Cyril the cycling attendant and James the physiotherapist, who also looked after the cooking and meals. In the other van were: Don Thompson (1960 Olympic gold medallist in 50 km Walk), Amos Seddon and another walker/cyclist.

The two vans worked in 4-hour shifts and Richard had an attendant walker or cyclist with him at all times to carry drinks of 'Leppin' and provisions. The on-duty van continually leapfrogged Richard from one lay-by to the next convenient grass verge, so that they were never more than half a mile away. In this way Richard could get food on request and any additional clothing required to cope with the changing weather.

Richard was sleeping in his fresh kit and rising at 04:00 so that he could get out on the road by 04:15 and did not take a break until 12:00, when he would take 40 minutes or an hour for lunch. He then continued without a break until 23:30! During this time, he alternated race walking with running. While I was there he did a little jogging before his lunch break, but after that he only walked because he was worried about a knee problem. However, his walking pace of 4.25 to 4.5 miles an hour was sufficient to meet his schedule. I expected that he would reduce my end-to-end record by several hours and should be close to ten days. There was some talk that Richard and his wife Sandra, who had also embarked on her own L.E.J.O.G., had received some financial assistance from the distributors of the film 'Forrest Gump', but I forgot to ask Richard about this.

Since my 'JOGLE' run in 1989 there had been some road improvements and one major advantage was that there was a bridge over the Dornoch Firth, which removed the need to climb over the 'Struie' and the loop through Bonar Bridge, as well as saving ten miles.

Richard Brown completed his Land's End to John o'Groats journey in 10 days 2 hours and 25 minutes, which was an improvement of 13 hours on my time of 1989.

Gradually my foot improved thanks to Malcolm's efforts, so I gingerly tried running 3 miles on the golf course each morning before my cycling to and from work. My foot accepted this, which encouraged me, but Malcolm continued with his treatments, by then twice weekly. I noticed a wheeze developing and I wanted to find out if I had any congestion in my lungs and if necessary, get it cleared up before the European 100Km Championships in 8 days time. I was fortunate to get a cancelled appointment at the Laich Medical centre and my lungs were found to be clear but I got a prescription for antibiotics in case I needed them.

On the weekend before the 100Km I tried two longer runs of 12 and 15 miles in my Nike 'Air Mariah' shoes and I was delighted that my right foot was OK although slightly uncomfortable.

The following Wednesday, 24th of May, George picked me up at 15:40 and drove me to Inverness airport, where I caught the 17:35 flight to Heathrow. I got the transfer bus to Gatwick and walked by a circuitous route to the Gatwick Moathouse Hotel, where the G.B. team were staying. I was sharing a room with Dave Lacey, another 50-year-old, who had run 2-28 in that year's London Marathon.

On Thursday we caught the 08:20 flight to Nantes, where an official of the race organization met us and took us by coach to Chavagnes-en-Paillers, to our accommodation. This was in a 'College', dormitory, like an early university or a boarding school. In the afternoon we ran for about 6 miles on quiet roads.

On Friday I slept between breakfast and lunch, which I seem to have needed. We attended the opening ceremony for the championships at 18:30 in the square at Chavagnes-en-Paillers Town Hall. I had a fairly light dinner at about 20:30. The food was plentiful and good.

EUROPEAN OVER-FIFTY CHAMPION IN FRANCE

On Saturday the 27th of May, we rose at 03:50 and got ready for the 05:00 start of the **European 100Km championships, which was incorporated in the 8th edition of the 'Vendee 100Km'.** As we started in darkness the 2.4Km lap in town was dangerous, but I managed to avoid being tripped in the rush and fairly quickly the field settled into a steady tempo. We then had to complete 4 laps of 24.4Km. I joined a group with 3 Poles, 3 Russians, 3 Belgians and a few others. Our time at 10Km was 42-something, so I was a little concerned about the pace, but it gradually began to increase and our group began to break up. On lap 2 I had to make a toilet stop.

My marathon time was 2-50-21 and 50Km was passed in 3-23-something. On lap 3, I was catching Stephen Moore and I finally caught him at drinks station on lap 4. I moved ahead of him, but he came past again with a runner from Hungary. I began to struggle more and more as my legs became less and less able to keep functioning. The last 15Km were particularly difficult, but I managed to continue and finished 18th in 7-16-17. Our team of Stephen, Robert Gardner, and I finished 5th behind: Russia, Poland, France and Belgium. Lynn Harding ran very well in her debut 100Km to finish 2nd and this helped our ladies' team finish 2nd behind France and ahead of the Germans.

I drank 10% concentration 'High Five', about one litre per 24Km lap and also 3 X 200mls of 'Dioralite'. I wore my Reebok 'Racer X' shoes, which were good. I was delighted to learn that I was **European V50 champion** and also very relieved that my right foot was all right. This was **my 8th G.B. vest**. The organisers provided an excellent post race meal and party in the evening after the awards ceremony, in the large sports hall.

J. Janicki (Pol) won in 6-28-36, from I. Riabov (Rus) 6-30-04 and A. Magier (Pol) 6-35-37.

I. Olive (Fra) won the ladies race in 7-43-14, from Lynn Harding (GBR) 7-52-23, with D. Geoffroy (Fra) 3rd in 7-54-10.

My next race was the West Highland Way on Saturday the 17th of June; so on Friday evening I travelled by train to Edinburgh, getting off at Haymarket. Adrian Stott met me and drove me to his home, where Linda prepared some pasta before I went to bed at 22:30.

THE WEST HIGHLAND WAY AGAIN

My alarm went at 1am to get me up for the race, which was due to start at 3am in Milnegavie. We arrived there at 2:30am and rain was pouring down as we started, so I was glad of my Gore Tex jacket. As we splashed along the stony path through Mugdock wood, our torches picked out the occasional frog, which I took care not to step on. The rain eased as dawn broke and then stopped. I took the lead when we reached the road at Gartness Waterfall and felt quite good. Jimmy Shaw chased me and we were together at Drymen School. In Garadhban Forest I had to make a toilet stop. As I climbed Conic Hill I entered the mist and on the steeper section I walked to save energy. On the descent, Dave Wallace came past and was soon out of sight. He stopped in Balmaha car park to change into shorts, so he was within catching distance again. On the tracks along loch Lomond side I lost ground to Dave and at Rowardennan I was surprised to learn from Adrian that Brian Davidson was also ahead of me. He had not passed me, so I assume that he must have found a better route. On the forestry road I caught Dave, but once this finished I slowed on the tracks that followed. At Inverarnan Adrian informed me that I was 20 minutes down on the leader, but I had decided to stop racing and concentrate on getting through this run without injuring myself. The weather improved and by then the sun was shining brightly. I mentioned to Adrian that I **had been made an M.B.E. in the Queen's birthday honours list**, but he knew already and had not let on.

By Tyndrum I was rather tired, although I was fairly content, but by Bridge of Orchy my quads hurt a lot. My run across 'Black Mouth' was easier this year as I was in better condition. Approaching Kingshouse the weather had deteriorated and we had wind and rain to contend with. At the Kingshouse Hotel, I put on tracksters and Gore Tex jacket, hat and gloves. I also changed my shoes from Racer X to Reebok Infernos. It was difficult running into the wind and rain, so it took longer than expected to cover the 2 miles to Altnafeadh. There I had another toilet stop before ascending the 'Devil's Staircase'.

On the way across to Kinlochleven, conditions worsened and I began to feel cold and I was glad to lose altitude and then meet Adrian on the track near Kinlochleven. I could smell the pollution in the air from the Aluminium smelter as I approached the town. Soon after this I was climbing up the other side of the valley, heading for the old military road. This road is very stony and I had to take care not to trip and fall.

Adrian met me again on the track near Lundarva with drinks, a banana and torch. The next section over to Glen Nevis seemed to take a long time. On reaching the forest road in Glen Nevis it was much easier to jog along. At 23:46 I finally arrived at the Leisure centre in Fort William, and the finish, happy to complete the route again, a good way to celebrate my M.B.E. Adrian had done a very good job as my handler.

Dave Wallace won in 17-43-30, from Brian Davidson 20-34-20 and I was 3rd in 20-46-43.

Sue Ashley was first lady in 6th place in 23-29-53.

Adrian and I slept, or tried to, in sleeping bags on the floor of the leisure centre overnight. On Sunday morning Adrian drove us to the car park at the very top of the Glen Nevis road, where he went for a run along the path towards Rannoch Moor, while I walked a little way along and back on this path.

After the prizegiving that afternoon, Adrian dropped me at Dalwhinnie Rail Station on his way home to Edinburgh and I got a train at 16:22 to Inverness at no cost, because there was no conductor to collect fares. Izzy met me at Inverness station at 17:35 and drove me home.

The following Sunday, on a visit to Rachel Hollas's at Tollcross in Edinburgh, Izzy and I went to a service in Barclay Church at Tollcross, where I was surprised to meet former Scottish cross-country champion, Andy McKean, who was an elder there.

On Saturday the 15th of July we set off on our summer holidays in our new to us caravan, which was more modern than the previous one. We set up at Culloden Moor Caravan Park for a few days. I had a chance to explore some quiet roads from there on my morning runs. Our next stop was at the Caravan Park at Invernahavon. From there I had an enjoyable run along a picturesque side road towards Laggan Bridge and then towards Loch Laggan, before retracing my steps. Scone Palace Caravan Park was our next stop, then Lizard Lane Caravan Park in South Shields, where we stayed for 4 days. On our way home we stopped at Lochlands Caravan Park near Forfar, for 2 days, which gave us a chance to explore Forfar and the surrounding countryside on my morning runs. On Wednesday the 26th of July we were back in Lossiemouth to find the temperature unusually high at 28°C.

WRONG DRINKS IN THE SCOTTISH 100 KM

On Saturday the 29th of July, I drove down to Edinburgh, picking up Andy Farquharson at Aviemore on the way. Izzy and I stayed in the guest flat at Rachel's building at Tollcross.

On Sunday I ran in the **4th edition of the Scottish 100Km championships**, which also incorporated the British Championships, at Heriot Watt University campus. Stephen Moore set a reasonable pace and I followed him accompanied by Andy Farquharson, but Willie Sichel dropped back. Even at 07:00 the sun was well up and the temperature rose. I decided to let Stephen go after about 5 laps, hoping that he would slow as he had done in France in May. I passed the marathon in 2-48-50, 50Km in 3-22-35 and as these were encouraging times, I began to think in terms of a 7 hours time. However, some time after passing 50 miles I began to get cramp in my left calf muscle and then in my right calf. This got increasingly worse and I was reduced to a hobble on the last 2 laps. Willie passed, running strongly, near the end of lap 29. I was relieved to get finished.

Izzy gave me my drinks and did some video recording and enjoyed her day in the sun.

I wore Reebok 'Racer X' shoes without socks, which was OK apart from some cuts and blisters on both my big toes. I drank 500mL of 10% concentration Leppin Enduro Booster 2 hours before the start; 200mL-five minutes before the start and took a Voltarol tablet. During the race I drank 150mL of the Enduro booster every lap, so I drank a total of 4.2 Litres during the race. To avoid the cramps I experienced I should have alternated the Leppin with an electrolyte replacement drink such as Isostar or Gatorade. Dioralite might have been a better alternative. I had learned this lesson before, but for some reason forgot to implement this strategy on this occasion. My lap times ranged from 12-44 to the last at 20-38, 'Oooch!' as Adrian Stott commented on my lap record sheet.

My team, **Moray Road Runners, was first team**, which was pleasing. Izzy and I walked around a lap, once my cramps had settled, with Robert Young, a real character, who said that he had raised £72,000 for charity. Because of this we missed the awards ceremony.

Stephen Moore won in 7-17-47, from Willie Sichel 7-28-18, while I took 7-34-30 to finish in 3rd and **1st V50**. Hilary Walker was 1st lady in 8-26-28, which was a new ladies' course record. There were 30 finishers.

On Sunday the 3rd of September in the Macallan Moray marathon I was quite pleased to finish 8th in 2-43-51. My left quads were troublesome, as they tightened and began to inhibit my pace. I wore my Nike Duellist shoes. Izzy gave me my drinks of 200mL of 10% concentration 'Leppin' at prearranged places.

Alan Reid won in 2-34-43 ahead of George Sim, 2-34-45 and Dave Lancaster 2-35-30.

A week later I ran my Monaughty 50Km route in 3-37-04 wearing Duellist shoes. Because of heavy overnight rain there were flooded sections of road 80 metres long and up to 5cm deep. This was my glycogen depletion run, so I would follow a low carbohydrate diet until Wednesday morning.

On Thursday, the 14th of September I began my journey to Winschoten to represent Great Britain in the IAU 100Km World Cup. I rose at 04:00 to get ready to catch the 05:43 train from Elgin to Aberdeen, but due to severe flooding no trains were running between Forres and Inverurie and buses were being used to transport passengers from Forres to Elgin, Keith, Huntly and Inverurie. Izzy drove me to Elgin train station, where I joined a lady in the waiting room, but no bus arrived. After some telephoning the ticket office attendant found out that there would be no bus because the bus driver had slept in. Further phone calls resulted in a taxi being summoned and the driver detailed to transport us to Aberdeen. I had gladly paid the £11 for the single ticket to Aberdeen and about one hour and 20 minutes later I was dropped off at Aberdeen airport, with £66 on the taxi's meter. I was in plenty of time for my 10:30 flight to Amsterdam.

My insides were quite painful from eating so much bread and the sudden change in diet had given me the 'runs'. I managed to settle down and mark an O.U. T292 (Instrumentation), student assessment, which had arrived just outside the deadline date, but I decided to mark it and post it off to Walton Hall, rather than disappoint my student.

As Willie Sichel did not appear for this flight, I assumed that he had been fogbound in Kirkwall. At Schiphol I made my way to the trains and met Simon Lund and Jane, Sharon and Bill Gayter and Eleanor Robinson. We ended up travelling in a carriage, which became very crowded, as the whole train appeared to be, as it made its way northeast. A lot of the passengers were smoking, which was annoying. An accident on the line caused us to be delayed by an hour. Initially we had to vacate the train, but then we were told to go back onboard, so we lost our seats in this exercise. The rest of the journey was spent standing in the spaces between carriages. The train pass, costing BAF £34 for each of us, did not guarantee a seat, only transportation.

On arriving in Winschoten we were met by John Legge and his wife Helen and he escorted us to 'De Klinker' the race headquarters, where we met the rest of the GB team. Greg Dell and I got a lift to Dennenweg 14, where our host family, De Boer, welcomed Greg and me for the second time. I went to bed at 22:00 feeling rather tired, unsurprisingly.

On Friday we had a team meeting at 10:30 in the De Klinker and then toured the course loop in a van. After lunch I slept until 17:00 and then I had a massage from my old Birchfield Harriers teammate Len Cullen.

At 7pm the team met for dinner at 'Geppeto's'. I ordered spaghetti vegetarian, but by the time it was presented and I had eaten the meal it was around 10pm, which is rather late for me, with a race at 2pm the following day. I then walked to Sharon Gayter's host family to get enough 'High Five' to prepare my drinks for the race. I took a Voltarol tablet in the morning and at night.

The following morning, Saturday the 16th of September, Greg and I prepared our drinks, knowing that there were 2 drinks stations per lap at 4.2Km and 9.3Km. I called these A and B and decided to alternate, 200mL of 10% concentration 'High Five' and 200mL of 'Dioralite'. I planned 'Dioralite' on A2, A3, A4, A5, A6, A7, A8 and A9, and 'High Five' on B3, B4, B5, B6, B7, B8 and B9. I added 15gm of branched chain amino acids to the 'High Five' drinks as evenly as I could.

There was a team parade with national flags at 12:30 and after that I found a quiet area to prepare for the coming race.

IAU 100KM WORLD CUP IN HOLLAND: FIRST OVER FIFTY

By start time the temperature had risen to 26°C, which felt quite warm. I tried to run 40 minutes per 10km pace, but I found it difficult to get it right and completed the first 10Km in 40-43. I found myself running with Patrick Macke and we were both rather staggered when Ann Trayson passed us as we approached 20Km. Shane Downes and Greg Dell were ahead of us and after about 30Km Mike Hartley, Simon Lund and Robin Gardner came past with a group of others, going at a slightly ambitious pace.

As I had suspected after the late meal the previous evening, I had to make a toilet stop at around 45Km. During my stop, Willie Sichel passed and he was soon 100 meters ahead. My 50Km time was 3-26-something, which was disappointing. I began to feel better and able to run more quickly. I caught Willie and then passed him and then Patrick and got some way ahead of him. I caught Robin before Patrick caught me and pulled away at around 80Km. I caught Mike Hartley on lap 8. Nunes (Brazil) lapped me as he sped on to victory and I was very pleased to see him run so well. Voglin (Russia) passed me just before the end of the lap and I started my last lap at 6-21-something. I tried to push on, but my legs would not work any harder. Denis Gack (France) and Kevin Stenes (USA) came past just before 95Km.

I was pleased to finish and was quite satisfied with my time of 7-09-49, which was my best since May 1993, when I had run 7-09-40. I was 2nd counter for the GB team behind Greg Dell, who had leg and stomach problems and finished 30th in 7-03-05. Patrick, who was not in the team, was 25th in 7-00-30, just 17 seconds ahead of Ann Trayson. I found that I was 37th and Mike Hartley was 43rd in 7-13-25, with Willie Sichel, 46th in 7-17-39, which was a personal best for Willie by over 11 minutes. I think that my carbohydrate loading helped, as did the branched chain amino acids. I wore Nike Duellist shoes.

Valmir Nunes (Brazil) won in 6-18-09, ahead of Alexey Voglin (Russia), 6-20-44 and Tom Johnson (USA), 6-30-11.

The awards ceremony was at 10am on Sunday, and it was good to see the individual and team winners being presented with their medals. I was **first in the V50 category**. There were 221 finishers and 134 abandoned the race including Shane Downes and Simon Lund.

After lunch we watched the 'Great North Run' on TV. Sjoerd and Janny drove me to Groningen, where I caught the 15:37 train to Schiphol airport. I arrived there in good time for the flight to Edinburgh/Aberdeen. Izzy met me at Aberdeen airport and I drove home arriving there at 11pm and received a good welcome from all.

Three weeks later I ran the Monaughty route as my glycogen depletion run for a 100km the following weekend. I wanted to see if I could break the existing record for a 100Km Track race by an over 50-year-old. I would use, with the organisers' approval, the Sri Chinmoy 24-hour race at Tooting Bec as the venue.

On Friday the 13th of October, after work I picked up my kit, and Izzy and I set off for Inverness airport, arriving in good time for the 17:35 flight to Heathrow. I caught a bus to Woking Station, where John Lamont met me at about 21:00 and we were back in his home in Guildford by about 21:30.

AGE-GROUP WORLD RECORDS ON TOOTING BEC TRACK

On Saturday the 14th October, I rose at 08:00 and started preparing drinks for the race. Although this was a 24-hour race at Tooting Bec, I was aiming to improve the over 50 world records for 50 miles and 100Km on the track. Harry Arndt of Germany, held both with 5-40-06 and 7-12-26 respectively. I did not take any breakfast before John, drove me to Tooting Bec, arriving there at about 10:45. I met Adrian Stott and his daughter Elizabeth, who was going to be seconding both of us. I gave my drinks schedule to her along with my drinks and 200mL bottles for decanting my prepared drinks. I planned to take my first drink after 40 minutes and then every 20 minutes from then, using 200mL of 10% concentration 'Leppin', with 18gm of branched chain amino acids added to three litres. On the hour I would take 'Dioralite' until 5 hours and then use 'Leppin' only.

The race started at 12:00 and I aimed to run 1-40 per lap, which would give me a final time of 6-56-40. It was quite a warm day and when the sun broke through the temperature reached 22°C. I felt quite comfortable as I trundled round, but my pace was slipping, so after my first 10Km in 42-05, I had to speed up a little and recorded 41-25 for my next 10Km. I went on like this until 4 hours, when I started pushing for the 50 miles record, as I knew that it would now be a close thing if I managed to break it. I managed to pick up my pace and reached 50 miles in 5-37-17 to improve Harry's record by 2-49.

My pace slumped after this and I got a jolt when Elizabeth informed me that my next 10Km split was 46 minutes. I began pushing again towards the 100Km and I was delighted to finish in 7-07-29 to take 4-57 off Harry's record. I ran another lap just in case there was a mistake in the lap counting. I then ran another lap at a slower pace, became aware of the aches in my legs and withdrew from the race at 100.8Km, emotionally drained. Adrian stopped momentarily from his race to give me a hug, which I really appreciated.

Tony Lenagan was running well in 2nd place, 10 miles behind as I retired. Chanakya from New York was there, so it was a nice surprise to meet him again. It was a shock when he told me that his mother in Birmingham had been murdered 2 weeks previously and that the lodger had been arrested for this crime. Andy Farquharson and Josephine arrived to watch as I was preparing to leave. John came to pick me up after I had telephoned Vera and we were back in their home by 10pm.

Sunday was spent relaxing with John, Vera and their daughter Maria. We went for a walk on the army training ranges near Aldershot. Later John drove me to Heathrow, where I caught the 20:15 flight to Inverness. Izzy met me there and I drove us home.

My next race was on Saturday, 25th of November, in the North District cross-country championships at Forres on my least favourite Cluny Hill course. I was pleased that my right knee and right groin, which had been troublesome since my last 100Km effort, held out on this demanding route. I finished 56th and 2nd over 50 to Ray Williby. Graeme Bartlett won from G Herbert and J Brooks. Keith and District were first team ahead of Moray Road Runners.

On Saturday the 2nd of December, Izzy, Claire, Anna and I travelled to Edit and Roy's at Westcott, where we were to stay for a few days before my MBE investiture. The following morning, we caught the train to London to be shown around the Houses of Parliament by Margaret Ewing's secretary. We then met Christina, did some shopping and also met Andy Farquharson.

MEMBER OF THE BRITISH EMPIRE: PRESENTED BY THE QUEEN

On Tuesday the 5th of December, Edit drove us to the station to catch the 08:20 train to London and from there we got an underground train from Victoria Station to near Buckingham Palace. We walked to Buckingham Palace for the Investiture, where the Queen presented me with the M.B.E, when my turn came. We all enjoyed the occasion. Anna was pleased to see Peter Banks and Claire was thrilled to see Elaine Paige. When the Queen spoke to me, all I responded was 'Yes Mam.' She had been briefed about my JOGLE Charity run and observed that it must have been 'jolly hard work'.

December was devoid of races, so I just maintained my base mileage. I found that my training and racing mileage for 1995 amounted to 5211 miles, which was an average of 100 miles per week.

1996

On Monday the 15th of January my right knee and leg were quite painful on my run to work. After work on my run back, on a downhill section the pain at the back of my right knee became much worse. The pain became so acute that I could not continue running. I walked rather disconsolately home from there and arrived at 7pm.

The following day Malcolm Morgan examined my leg and found that a muscle, which was part of the right hamstring, had developed a problem and was very tight. He used the inferential machine and then stretched it by pushing on the part affected, which was a rather uncomfortable experience. I cycled to and from work for the rest of the week.

Despite Malcolm's best efforts my injury persisted and the weeks of no running soon became a month. Towards the end of February, I felt improvement and began trying some short runs on the golf course. During this 'off' time I learned that the IAU World Cup 100Km scheduled for Athens on the 13th of March was cancelled as the organisers had withdrawn from their commitment. I had dental work done by Tim Griffiths, but he could not get a tooth root out, so later that day the broken tooth root was duly removed at Dr Gray's Hospital.

In the first week of March I was able to resume running to work by my old railway line route and getting a lift back after work. My right knee was still hurting, but it did not become worse and would recover by the following morning, which encouraged me.

On the 12th of March, as Malcolm was giving me treatment on my right hamstring, he informed me that, because of restructuring, he would be retiring as Head of the Physiotherapy Department at Dr Gray's Hospital. He would be a great loss to the department and to the many patients he treated. He would work in private practice from then on.

I was able to increase my running gradually, back to my base of 100 miles a week by the 3rd week in March. On Sunday the 24th of March I was just thinking how good my right knee was becoming, when my right foot caught on a rock in the cliff path and I went sprawling on the path. This fall made my right knee pain considerably worse, but this pain wore off as I continued to jog. I was out for over 2 hours on a glorious spring morning. Following this run I iced my knee and noticed that I was passing blood in my urine so I would require treatment for a urinary tract infection. I noted that my goal race, the BAF 100Km championship, was in 8 weeks time, so I had to keep trying to get fit for this race.

On Sunday the 7th of April in the Moray Road Runners 10Km road race my right knee was painful from the start. As the pain appeared to have eased off, after I stopped to massage the back of my knee joint, I continued around the course. With about 2 miles remaining the pain recurred, causing me to stop again briefly to massage the region once more. I jogged to the finish in 110th place in 47-58. I was rather disappointed by this latest setback.

On Monday Malcolm Morgan came to our home and gave me treatment and said that the problem was coming from my right hamstring, which was rather tight. He massaged it and applied ultrasound. He also put a small acupuncture needle on a patch onto the right side of my knee to try to stop the pain there.

On Friday Izzy drove me to Ballindalloch, where I cycled with our dog Muffin down the Speyside Way route, marking the route. The cycle over Ben Aigen was quite hard work. We marked the next section of the route to Fochabers.

On the following day Izzy and I marked the remainder of the Speyside Way Race route from Fochabers to the finish in Spey Bay.

While Izzy and I were marking the course near Fochabers on Friday afternoon, Simon Pride came running past at a rapid pace and I remember thinking that he looked very good. Simon's wife Linda worked at Moray College in the catering department and she told me several months before the Speyside Way Race that Simon wanted to run in it, and he had asked Linda to ask me for advice on preparing for this 50Km race. Simon had not raced further than a half marathon, so I advised that he maintain a consistent weekly mileage of around 70 miles and include a long run of at least 2 hours each weekend. I also emphasised the need to prepare suitable energy replacement drinks and use these at appropriate points in the race.

I had lost my pal, training partner, near neighbour and Speyside Way Race director, Mick Francis, so I was now race director in addition to being race organiser. Since the 100Km in Victoria Mick had been corresponding with Mary Morgan, and had gone to Australia to visit her and then they both ran a 100Km race in New Zealand. Fairly soon after this Mick and Mary got married and settled in Bunbury, a town south of Perth in Western Australia.

On Sunday the 14th of April I rose at 05:00 and delivered tables, water, bananas, biscuits and cups to the locations for the refreshment stations on the **Bell's Speyside Way 50km** course and put up two more direction signs. Later I decided to run in the race and, as my knee was hurting, I started cautiously, but after about 10 minutes felt able to pick up my pace. I was not running smoothly and by Aberlour my right knee and hamstring were quite painful, so I decided to abandon my run at Craigellachie.

I was then free to observe the race unfold. Simon had established a lead as he approached Fochabers and was running strongly. After going under the bridge, which carries the A96 over the Spey there was a section of the course on road, before rejoining the path on the bank of the Spey. This point was about 25 miles after the start, so one would expect runners to find getting up the short bank to the path difficult, but Simon was like a gazelle as he bounded from the road up the bank onto the path. At that moment I realised that Simon had the potential to be a great 100Km runner.

Simon Pride won in 3-11-00, from Rab Brown, 3-19-29 and Brian Scally, 3-21-01. Sharon Gayter was the first lady in 17th place overall in 3-56-06. There were 45 finishers. My old friend

Colin Youngson had complained that marathons seemed to be giving him up. Although delighted to come in 6th and 1st M45 in 3.29.27, he admitted that only a very helpful tailwind had allowed him to finish in a reasonable time.

On the following morning running was not an option, so I was back cycling to and from work and on Tuesday evening I attended the Sports Injury clinic that Malcolm had been instrumental in setting up. The opinion of the doctor who examined me was that I had injured the lateral ligaments. I received physiotherapy from Gordon Turner, who used ultrasound. The charge was £12. My next session at the clinic was on Thursday, when I received physiotherapy from Gordon Turner at the reduced charge of £6. My weekly mileage was zero and the following week was the same.

There appeared to be something wrong with the tendons and ligaments in the back of my right knee joint. I did not think that the cause of the pain had been properly diagnosed yet, which was frustrating. I got notification that I would receive physiotherapy treatment through the NHS and my first session began on Wednesday the 1st of May from Alison in Dr Gray's. She said that my quads were tight and that might be contributing to my problem. She applied laser treatment to the back of my right knee joint and then stretched the ligaments or what was attached to them using her elbow. She then stretched my right quads. Before this treatment I had 'cycled' for 10 minutes (4Km) at a load of 3, to warm-up my muscles.

The following day, on returning from a short run along the beach, I noticed that my foot pattern on the wet sand showed that my right foot was tending to point right instead of straight ahead.

By the 20th of May Alison was pleased with my progress, so I was discharged. Over the weeks my knee pain gradually diminished as I used the exercises that Alison had shown me and increased the length of my runs in stages. I began running to and from work that week and could then concentrate on getting some good ultra distance training done. I decided to aim for the West Highland Way again.

I told Simon Pride that I thought that he could become a great 100Km runner if he wanted to. He was rather dubious, so it took some time for him to agree to see what he could achieve at 100Km. He was persuaded to come over to our home for a Sunday run over the Monaughty 50Km route with Allan Stewart and me. I was pleased that he handled this run perfectly well, so I suggested that he incorporate such a run each Sunday from his home in Fochabers, using the forestry roads. I contacted Adrian Stott, who was on the selection panel for the Scottish team in the Anglo Celtic plate 100Km race in August and suggested that Simon be included on the basis of his Speyside Way win and my opinion of his potential. Simon was included in the Scottish team, which prompted David Strachan to write a letter to 'Athletics Weekly' (AW), suggesting that this was not fair as Simon was Welsh. Simon responded with a letter to AW, which was included in the letters section of the 27th of November 1996 issue. He stated that he had been born in Swansea and had represented Wales as a junior, but on leaving the army he had been resident in Scotland for the past 8 years and could represent Scotland on residential grounds. His final sentence was: 'I hope to continue to run well and, with plenty of hard work, determination and support, who knows, perhaps one day I may be considered for the British Ultra team'.

STRUGGLE ON THE WEST HIGHLAND WAY

On Friday the 21st of June after cycling to and from work and after dinner, Izzy and I set off for Milngavie, where the **West Highland Way Race** was due to start at 03:00. As we drove down I noticed that the sky was becoming clear at about Stirling, so I expected good weather for the race. We arrived at Milngavie in plenty of time at about 01:45.

When we got going I joined the leaders and felt good. I upped the pace a little on reaching a tarred road section and had Ian Donnelly and Richard Townsend for company. At the first checkpoint at Drymen, reached in 1-40-00, Izzy was there with my bum-bag and drinks. My time there was 9 minutes faster than the previous year.

I found that I was in the lead, so I pressed on through the forest section. On Conic Hill, Ian Donnelly passed me on the climb and Townsend and Dave Wallace passed me on the way down. At Balmaha I regained the lead, but Dave caught up and I had to let him go. I had quite a bad wheeze and my chest felt quite tight. Douglas Walker passed me on the section to Rowardennan, but we were joint 2nd at the checkpoint there, which we reached in 4-10, one minute faster than the previous year.

On the forestry road I felt quite weak and walked up the hills and along Loch Lomond side. No one passed me until nearly the end when Tom McPake and Jim Carruth came past. I caught and passed Tom to reach Inverarnan 4th in 7-27, which was 11 minutes slower than my time the previous year. Here Izzy put sunscreen on my exposed skin, as the sun was shining from a cloudless sky.

On the next section, Steven Bell passed and by Tyndrum he was 16 minutes ahead. I reached this checkpoint in 10-17, which was 24 minutes down on my time the previous year. Izzy had bought me an iced lollie there, which I enjoyed. Tom McPake passed again before Bridge of Orchy, which I reached in 11-52, 44 minutes down compared to last year. I revived a bit going over the 'Black Mouth' and closed on Tom and at Kinghouse, reached in 14-36, I passed him again.

After the 'Devil's Staircase' I found it impossible to run on the stony paths and Tom came past again and the path down to Kinlochleven seemed to go on for ever! My time at the checkpoint there was 17-14, which was 46 minutes down on the previous year. The next section over to Lundarva was as difficult as always and I was pleased to see Izzy there. Unfortunately, she was badly bitten by midges there. I had already put on my Gore Tex suit because the weather had become much cooler. By then it was twilight and I needed to use a head torch quite a bit. I began to imagine that I could see figures and hear voices. At one point I heard something and glanced around and saw the figure of a young boy on the path. I thought of asking him what he was doing out here at this time of night, 11pm. I glanced back a couple of times, but the apparition had gone. Later I thought that I saw a girl kneeling with a collie dog, directly in front of me on the path. Various other hallucinations followed and I had difficulty balancing.

Charles MacLeod passed me near the top of the pass into Glen Nevis. I was unable to jog on the paths in the poor light and my motivation was much reduced. I shuffled down the forestry road until I met Izzy and Linda Stott. I walked with them down to the Glen Nevis road and then jogged to the finish, while Izzy drove our car, slowly behind me.

There were people climbing Ben Nevis as part of the Three Peaks Challenge and it was quite a spectacle seeing the lights from their head torches bobbing along the path. I was pleased to be finished, as was Izzy, who had done very well supporting me.

Dave Wallace won in 18-56-22, from S. Bell, 20-21-55 and Tom McPake 21-03-00. I had finished 7th in 22-11-24 and Isobel Clark in 13th place was 1st lady in 25-13-00.

On Sunday, following a good night's rest in our bed & breakfast, Izzy and I went for a walk from the car park at the top of the Glen Nevis road.

My next race was to be the **British Athletics Federation (BAF) and Scottish Athletics Federation (SAF) 100Km championships**, on Saturday the 20th of July. Izzy and I drove to Edinburgh and on to Rachel's. At 16:30 we went to 'Run and Become' and there we met most of the English team and Norrie Williamson, his wife Karen and Andy Farquharson. Andy came back to Rachel's with us and we went to get an Indian carry out. I had a portion of steamed rice and a vegetable curry side dish, which I thought should be through by tomorrow morning.

On Sunday Izzy and I rose at 05:00 and started to get ready for the 100Km Championships and Anglo-Celtic Plate race at Heriot Watt University campus. We ended up in a bit of a rush and we arrived 15 minutes before the start.

SILVER SUCCESS IN THE BRITISH AND SCOTTISH INTERNATIONAL 100 KM

I had the honour of being made team captain of the Scottish team, consisting of: myself, Norrie Williamson, Andy Stirling, Andy Farquharson and Simon Pride. The first 3 finishers of each team would count for the Anglo-Celtic Plate competition.

The 'Anglo-Celtic Plate' 100Km, (for two silver salvers), was started by John Foden in 1995 and is a competition between the 4 nations of the United Kingdom plus the Irish Republic. From the outset, the event was combined with the British Championships. An exception is made every 5 years when the Irish Republic is asked to organise the event. The purpose of the 'Plates' are: 'To further friendly competition between ultra distance athletes living in all parts of the British Isles and to encourage British runners to improve by first earning a Home Country vest and thus strengthen the pool from which the British team is chosen'. Initially the team size was: 4 men with 3 to count and 3 ladies with 2 to count. Later the men's team was increased to 5 with 3 to count.

Stephen Moore led from the start, running at sub seven-hour pace and I settled down running with Neil McGregor at 14 minutes per lap. This pace proved too ambitious, so I slowed and Mark Guichard joined me as Neil dropped back. My marathon time was 2-58 and my 50Km was around 3-32. These times were a lot slower than I had anticipated, but it was the best that I could manage.

By then I was in clear 2nd, but was having periodic stomach pains and a couple of laps later a toilet stop was necessary. I had pain in the ball of my left foot and under the heel of my right heel, like a blister was forming. I was wearing my 'Duellist' shoes, which were rather 'well-worn' and the many turns on this course made these problems worse. I also developed tightness and pain in my right hamstring, which was annoying.

Nevertheless, I was delighted to finish 2nd and delighted for Simon finishing 3rd. Izzy was a very attentive handler, giving me my drinks and also making a video recording of the race. I drank 4 litres of the energy drink with branched chain amino acids supplied by Dr Newsholme. My drinking schedule was: 500mL of 10% concentration Enduro booster 1 hour, 45 minutes before the start, 250mL of the same 15 minutes before the start. During the race, from the end of lap two I drank 150mL of the energy drink for 3 laps and then 200mL of Dioralite on the 4th and repeated this sequence to the end, but from lap 13 I increased the energy drink to 200mL. This worked well as I had no stomach problems and did not become depleted of glycogen or dehydrated. I also took a Voltarol tablet before the start and another on laps 15 and 23.

Simon performed extremely well and was very pleased, as was his wife Linda, who was supporting him. Andy Stirling finished strongly. Norrie Williamson, who had been on antibiotics during the week, had to abandon the race as did Andy Farquharson. The weather conditions had been good, but the relative humidity was fairly high and the temperature reached 25°C. I was surprised when Norrie informed me again that the total climbing in this 100Km course amounted to 3000 feet.

Stephen Moore (Eng) won in 7-17-16, I was 2nd in 7-38-15 and Simon Pride (Sco) got the bronze medal in 8-01-38. Andy Stirling was our 3rd counter in 6th in 8-21-20. Eleanor Robinson (Eng) was first lady in 9-02-45 ahead of Kate Todd (Sco), 9-06-45 and Hilary walker (Eng) 9-23-08. There were 47 starters and 25 finishers. England was 1st team with 23-42-23, and Scotland was 2nd with 24-01-13

On Monday I put an ice pack on my hamstring problem region, which appeared to be clearing. The physiotherapist at Heriot Watt after the race said not to stretch it until 2 days had elapsed.

Two days later, the 24th of July, I drove Izzy and the girls to Glasgow and booked into the Forte 'Post house' Hotel, close to Glasgow airport. The following morning, I ran for over 40 minutes from the Hotel and found my right hamstring was a little uncomfortable. We caught our flight with 'Airtours' to Orlando, Florida. On arrival there I picked up our hire car, a Chrysler 'Neon', and managed to drive it and eventually found our Motel the 'Days Inn Motel' on Chancellor drive, off

International Drive, in the twilight. Over the following 8 days we visited all the attractions: Disney's 'Magic Kingdom', Disney's 'Typhoon Lagoon', 'Disney-MGM Studios', 'Epcot', 'Gatorland', Universal Studios. I was surprised to meet Shettleston Harrier Bill Scally at the E.T. experience at Universal Studios. Other attractions visited were: 'Blizzard Beach', 'Pleasure Island' and 'Florida Mall'. We all enjoyed the experience of eating at the 'Ponderosa' buffet style restaurant.

I found it quite difficult to run because of the high relative humidity of 75% and the warm conditions of 85°F at 8am. I met Steve Leggat from Burghead, who recognised me on my second day's morning run so we had a brief chat.

Once our time in Orlando was up I drove to St Petersburg beach on the Gulf of Mexico, where we checked into the Radisson 'Sandpiper' Hotel, where we were to stay for 7 nights. We enjoyed visiting the Salvador Dali museum, which contained the world's largest collection of Salvador Dali's works. A boat trip on the Gulf of Mexico allowed snorkelling to be tried and some 'sand dollars' collected from the seabed in a shallow region. I ran each morning over an estimated nine and a half miles road and beach course. The temperature at 7am when I started running was 85°F and the relative humidity was usually 75%. Later the temperature rose to 95°F.

On Thursday the 8th of August I drove back to Orlando airport, returned the hire car and caught the overnight flight back to Glasgow. We landed at Glasgow at 06:45 and, once we had our luggage, we collected our car from the 'Post House' Hotel. We then drove to South Shields to Bill and Yvonne's, where I ran my usual route from Brandling Court.

On the 12th of August I was notified that I was selected for the G.B. team (my 10th G.B. vest) to run in the European 100Km championships in De Cleder on the 25th of August.

I attended Dr Gray's Hospital, two days later to take a glucose tolerance test as I was suspected to have developed 'type two' diabetes.

On Thursday the 22nd of August, I met with Dolina Watson, who was the treasurer of the Elgin branch of the Cancer Research Campaign, Scotland and George Runcie of United Distillers in their offices at Trinity Road in Elgin. Les Parker, the photographer for the Press & Journal newspaper arrived to take a photograph of me presenting a cheque for £500 to Dolina, which was the money raised from the 'Bell's Speyside 50Km race' on the 14th of April. Les then wanted some photographs, 'artistic shots' of me running on Ladyhill. Following this I rushed home and finished packing and then grabbed something to eat. George drove me to Elgin, where I got the train to Dyce station and got a taxi across to the airport, where I met my G.B teammate, William Sichel.

At Heathrow I set out for Margaret and Alex Vose's home near Bromley. The Victoria tube line was out of action, so I had to use the buses provided, which caused a very lengthy journey. Eventually, three hours after leaving Heathrow, I got to Bromley South rail station where Alex met me and drove me to his home, where after a nice meal with them I got to bed at 23:30.

On Friday morning Alex drove me to the station, where I caught the 06:14 fast train to Victoria and there got a train to Heathrow. I used the courtesy bus to the Holiday Inn, Crowne Plaza, where I met the rest of our G.B. team and departed in our coach for Plymouth at 09:00.

At Plymouth we boarded the afternoon Brittany Ferry to Roscoff, which was a 7-hour crossing. As we had reserved 3 cabins I was able to get a good sleep. In France we drove for about 5Km to our overnight stop at a small Hotel, where I shared a room with William Sichel.

After our breakfast on Saturday we completed our journey to the region of Finistere and to Cleder, where we registered for the race and moved into our accommodation, which was about 10Km away near the beach. We had excellent bungalows at a camping site. In the afternoon the parade of national teams through the town took place, followed by speeches, and the public supported all this very well. Before this I was rushing to prepare my drinks for the race, as these had to be deposited with the race officials by 16:00. At 18:00 I had my last meal, which was plain pasta and then two halves of cantaloupe melon. Because we had to rise by 03:00, we all headed to bed early that evening.

EXHAUSTED AT THE EUROPEAN 100KM

On race-day, Sunday the 25th of August, we boarded our coach just after 4am for departure to Cleder. **The IAU European 100Km Championships race** started with fireworks at 5am. As it was dark, each runner had been issued with a torch on entering the start pen. The pace was brisk at the start, so I settled down, running with Willie as we headed out of town, having completed a loop there. A tractor marked each junction with its warning light flashing and its headlights indicating the direction to follow.

As dawn broke Martin Eccles joined us and we ran on together. At about 20Km I was aware of discomfort under my right heel, like a blister was forming. I was wearing my Asics 'Bordin Racer' shoes, which I had tested over 50Km, so this was an unexpected problem. I also began to feel tired and I had to let Martin and Willie go and my heel was becoming worse. I passed the marathon in 2-56-53 and the end of lap one, 50.177Km in 3-33-45. I stopped there and changed my shoes to Reebok Racer X. While I was sitting down doing this, Patrick Macke passed me. On resuming I felt better initially, but by 60Km my pace was slowing a lot. I could see Stephen Moore only 60 metres ahead, having a rough time, but I could not catch him. My form continued to deteriorate and I felt completely drained. I was receiving all my planned drinks of 200mL of 'Pripps', Dr Newsholme's drink, approximately every 5Km, so this was not the reason. My glucose intolerance might have had some bearing on my lack of strength as perhaps the glucose in my blood stream was being excreted rather than being converted to glycogen to be used or stored. Other possibilities that I thought of were that perhaps I had not recovered from the training week beginning on the 12th of August or climbing Ben Rinnes 'off path', through the deep heather on the 18th of August.

I struggled on, being passed at about 80Km by the first four ladies, who were led by Carolyn Hunter Rowe. I began to take coffee and chocolate from the general refreshment stations and eventually I reached the finish in 8-11-20.

Our Team manager, Mick McGeoch, took me to the medical facility to get treatment for my right heel. A medic examined my heel and then she carefully cut away valuable hard skin until she reached the blood blister and cut through to relieve the pressure and the burning sensation. There appeared to be quite a bit of blood on the cotton wool swab. I was mentally asking my guardian angel for help during the cutting and I was very relieved when she put the dressing on my heel.

About an hour later I went for a massage, but one of the girl medics noticed that blood was seeping through the dressing, so she said that it required changing. Before putting on a new dressing she probed with a syringe needle to releases any other blood and again I was very relieved when she had finished.

At the awards ceremony it was great to see Carolyn going up to receive the ladies winning trophy and the G.B. ladies team were 3rd team. I was pleased to be 2nd over 50, behind Roland Vuillemenot, who was 50 the previous week and who ran 6-43-33, a new age group best. I received a pair of Reebok 'Boston Road' shoes, a tee shirt and a cup. A reception and wine tasting followed the awards ceremony. There had been 1062 entries for this race.

J. Janicki (Poland) won in 6-33-39 ahead of J. Jelinek (Czech), 6-38-15 and A. Magier (Poland) 6-39-49.

On Monday we departed from our accommodation at about 07:20, heading back to Roscoff and the ferry back to Plymouth. We had an uneventful journey back to the Holiday Inn Crowne Palace Hotel at Heathrow, where we said our goodbyes to most team members.

At Heathrow airport, after we had checked in and eaten a snack, Colin Donald came over and introduced himself after seeing our G.B. shell suits. He was the club coach who had got me started with Aberdeen AAC way back in 1962 and I had not seen him for approximately 26 years, so we had a good chat.

Willie and I shared a taxi from Aberdeen Airport to Dyce station where I caught the 21:45 train for Inverness. Willie was staying in a B & B in Dyce and would catch a flight to Kirkwall the following day. Izzy met me at Elgin station. It was a real pleasure to be home once more.

My leg muscles were too painful to allow running for the next 4 days, but I managed a short run on the golf course and beach on Saturday.

I started in the Macallan Moray marathon the following morning, 1st September, running cautiously to begin with. At about 2 miles I felt a muscle in my right hamstring go 'ping' and from then on I had quite a lot of discomfort in the lower right side of my right hamstring. This began to affect my running action and I became even slower. I stopped to massage the region and tried to stretch the muscle, but this did not help. Because of this I decided to abandon the run at about 4 miles. Izzy picked me up and we drove around the course encouraging the runners. It was really good to see Allan Stewart win the race.

Malcolm Morgan came to examine and treat my right hamstring and found two problem sites. One was in the belly of the muscle and the other was around the tendon towards the back of my knee. I resumed running two days after Malcolm's treatment and although my right hamstring hurt a little I continued increasing the lengths of my runs. On my weekend runs it became progressively more painful, not the muscle but the tendon region behind the right knee joint. There seemed to be some misalignment of my right leg.

Malcolm gave me treatment and advised me that my hamstring and Gluteus strain would not cope with a 24-hour race, as it would probably last only 2 hours before tightening up again.

Consequently, I telephoned John Legge to tell him that I had to withdraw from the G.B. team for the European 24-hour Championships.

I did not attempt running for the next six days and then started 4.5 miles morning runs on the golf course and beach before cycling to and from work. My next step was to run to work and get a lift home or vice versa.

By the last Sunday in September I was pleased that my right hamstring appeared to be OK on a 2-hour run along the coastal path to beyond Hopeman and back. To err on the side of caution I continued with my one way run to or from work.

DIABETES DIAGNOSED

On the 9th of October I attended the diabetic clinic at Dr Gray's Hospital where I saw Dr Thomason. **She told me that I had type-2 diabetes, also known as maturity onset diabetes**. After an examination and a blood sample extraction I was given a self-test kit to check my blood glucose, medication and relevant information. **I expect that this was a result of an over-worked pancreas due to at least two decades of a high carbohydrate diet.**

During the 2nd week of the 'October break', I increased the length of my daily runs to reach 100 miles for the week, with no apparent adverse effect on my right hamstring. Then I cut back during the following two weeks to prevent overloading my hamstring.

On the last Saturday in October Izzy and I drove down to Edinburgh and Rachel's, to attend, as invited guests, the Sri Chinmoy 'Peace Concert' at Murrayfield that evening.

On Sunday morning I ran from Rachel's at Tollcross with Norrie Williamson, who took me along the Edinburgh to Glasgow canal towpath and then up an old railway line, which was a very pleasant route.

Another problem occurred a few days later with a pain in the top of my calf muscle at the back of my right knee joint. I could feel some tendons clicking during the knee bending movement of running.

On the following Tuesday evening, as my right knee joint was rather painful, I went to the Sports Injury Clinic. Malcolm was on duty and found a problem on my right calf muscle.

I thought, rather optimistically, that my injury problems were behind me and for the remainder of November I trained normally. However, on my long run, my right knee joint became progressively more painful, but I managed to jog home on it.

Malcolm found the problem to be a strain in my right calf muscle. I was back cycling to and from work again and then one-way runs. My injury was still annoying so Malcolm gave more treatment. He also sorted out a left hamstring 'short heads' problem. I decided to avoid running for a week to let my hamstring recover.

On the 27th of December I went for a jog around Lossiemouth, but I ended up extending my run by going up the old railway line and back. I was pleased that my legs appeared to cope with this. I increased the lengths of my runs on the remaining days in December and my hamstring and calf appeared to cope. On the last day of December, I ran an extended 'Ponds' course of 15 miles with our Springer Spaniel, Muffin, and my right leg felt good; a big relief.

On checking my training diary, I found that during the year I had a total of 32 physiotherapy treatments: 25 from Malcolm Morgan, 4 from Alison, 2 from Gordon and one at Heriot Watt following the BAF/SAF 100Km. Because of a succession of injuries, my total training and racing mileage for 1996 was well down on previous years at 3595 miles, which was an average of 69 miles per week.

1997

MENTORING SIMON PRIDE

My injury troubles had appeared to clear by January 1997, so I was able to train to my usual schedule with no interruptions. February was also trouble-free, so I was happy to put an entry in for the 'Barry 40'. I had advised Simon Pride to enter some weeks earlier. I felt the next step in Simon's 100Km running career would be to get selected to represent Great Britain. To get the attention of the selectors, primarily John Legge, he should run in the 'Barry 40'.

Since Simon had won the Speyside Way 50km Trail Race I had gradually become a mentor to him. One of the first things that we discussed was consistency of training, which Simon was lacking because of his job as a steel fabricator. His work could be near or far from home, working long hours, for a few weeks at a time. I suggested that he seek employment near home with regular hours. He did this and worked in a sawmill workshop in Elgin, which constructed wooden crates and pallets. Unfortunately, one of his workmates was careless with a nail gun, which brushed against Simon's thigh, triggering the gun and a four-inch nail was fired into Simon. Luckily no artery or vein was punctured. In an interview to a newspaper reporter, 29-year old Simon, said: '*It went right through my thigh bone*'. '*It was pretty nasty at the time and shook me up quite badly*'. The X-ray photograph of the nail in the leg was quite a souvenir and I think that Simon must be quite proud of it. The nail was duly removed and Simon made a complete recovery and the incident had no adverse effect on his subsequent running.

Simon did not return to working with nail guns, but instead became a postman, which was an excellent choice from a training point of view. Although he had a very early start to his round, he was normally finished just after midday and he could then train in the afternoon. This was particularly beneficial throughout the winter months, as he could train in daylight.

On Saturday the first of March I began my drive to Barry and stopped in Edinburgh, where I ran at an easy pace for about 50 minutes with Norrie Williamson. He took me around a newly paved route for walkers and cyclists, which would be good for a 100Km race or a 24-hour event. I drove to Barry from Norrie's in six and a half hours, having covered 636 miles from home. Simon had gone down earlier to visit his parents in Swansea, so we met later at the B & B we had booked into, where we shared a room.

HARD WORK IN THE BARRY 40-MILES TRACK

On race-day the weather conditions for the Barry 40 miles track race were good with only a slight wind and some sunshine. I started easily, but soon found that I had to run quite hard to catch up the group going at the pace at which I wanted to run at. This group consisted of: Robin Gardner, Jim Redfern, Mark Guichard, Simon Pride and Greg Dell. Stephen Moore had gone straight to the front and had established a lead of about 200 metres.

Our group ran together until about 7 miles, when Greg began to chase after Stephen. I urged Simon to go with Greg, which he did. Simon caught Greg and carried on past to catch Stephen. The remainder of our group: Jim, Mark and I passed 10 miles in 60-25 Shortly after this Simon moved into the lead, followed by Greg.

By 20 miles, which I passed in 2-03-19, my feet were hurting quite badly, especially my right heel. I was wearing my Nike Niobe shoes, which were proving inadequate for this length of race on a hard track. My right hamstring began to feel tight and twitched a couple of times as I began to struggle quite badly.

Every 20 minutes from 40 minutes, I drank 200mL of 10% concentration Leppin Enduro Booster'. Perhaps, because of my diabetes I was not metabolising this properly. Simon continued to run very strongly and actually increased his pace as the race progressed.

As I approached 30 miles, I was informed that I was close to my over 50 record, so I put in an effort for two and three-quarter laps, but I missed it by 13 seconds. I then had a go at my 50Km record and just missed that by 2 seconds, passing in 3-17-23. I stopped to change my shoes on the next lap to Asics 'Bordin Racers'. These were some improvement, but I did not feel like pushing harder because of the pains in my feet and my grumbling right hamstring.

I was surprised to see Greg withdrawing from the race, as did Allan Stewart, who had blood blisters under the balls of his feet. Meanwhile, **Simon was flying and finished with a track record of 3-54-24, which put him eighth on the World All-Time list**. Stephen Moore was 2nd in 4-05-18 and Jim Redfern 3rd in 4-17-48. I finished 5th in 4-23-28 and the first lady was Hilary Walker in 5-05-58. There were 39 starters and 22 finishers.

I set off for home at 17:30 and weather conditions were good until the Drumochter region where it began snowing and the road was covered. I arrived home at 03:30 on Monday, having driven 1232 miles in George's Vauxhall Astra.

I cycled to and from work and continued this for the remainder of the week. My feet were rather painful and there appeared to be a blood blister or bruising under my right heel.

This did not improve and it felt like there was an infection starting there. At the Medical centre the nurse was of the opinion that there was no infection there and used a needle to drain some fluid off. My right heel became very painful by Wednesday the 12th of March and I could not bear to put any weight on it. There was indeed an infection there and Dr White got some pus out of my heel and prescribed a 10-day supply of the antibiotics. I felt flu-like symptoms because of the poison circulating in my system. However, I continued cycling to and from work, but my heel was not improving. My G.P prescribed Flucloxacillin to combat my heel infection. **He said that because I was diabetic, this injury would take longer to heal. I made a mental note to take more care of my diet.** Six days later Dr Sabiston cut away the dead skin over the blister and prescribed another antibiotic, 'Klaricid' and said that I now had a '**diabetic ulcer**' rather than a blood blister. By pulling my right leg up by my ankle, I could see the ulcer slightly larger than a five pence coin.

On Friday the 2nd of April I cycled over most of the Speyside Way race route, with Izzy's help, to mark the course. On Sunday in the 4th edition of the 'Bell's Speyside Way 50Km trail race we had 77 starters. Simon Pride ran brilliantly finishing in 2-59-18, to take 2-49 off Fraser Clyne's course record. Allan Stewart was 2nd in 3-19-06, followed by Brian Scally, 3-29-00, who held off Peter Shirley, 4th in 3-29-52. Helene Diamantides won the ladies race in 3-44-42, improving Sharon Gayter's course record by 11-22, ahead of Kate Todd, 4-08-09 and Hilary Spencley, 4-10-53.

I was having my heel dressing changed by a nurse at the Medical Centre every 2nd day, so I was unable to run at all in April. The ulcer was reducing in size until it eventually healed over.

On Saturday the 22nd of May I jogged for 17 minutes on the golf course and my right heel appeared to be OK. It had been 11 weeks and 4 days that I had been disabled by this injury.

From then on I tentatively increased my mileage, taking care to protect the healed ulcer, which was rather sensitive and tender. On Sunday the 1st of June, I ran my 15 miles 'Ponds' course on a beautiful summer morning. My right heel was slightly uncomfortable and rather tender afterwards. I ran one lap at the Rotary 'Bell's Marafun' – the lap of honour – in Elgin.

Simon Pride was running for Great Britain in the IAU 100Km World Cup over the Del Passatorie course the previous day. I heard that he had run well and was second counter for the team. This justified my letter to John Legge some months before, where I said that I felt that Simon would be a great asset to the GB 100km team. John was reluctant to pick Simon because of the hill climbing and descending in the Passatorie, but decided to take a chance on him.

I found that the Asics 'Gel 111' shoes caused least discomfort to the callus (scar tissue), which had formed over the healing ulcer on my right heel, so I used these shoes for most runs. Despite this my right heel was often uncomfortable on my run home from work.

In the 2nd week of June my next injury developed, as I experienced a pain in my left heel near the base of my Achilles tendon, almost on the bone. I reduced my run lengths in the hope that my heel would recover, but this proved a vain hope, as the discomfort increased and I was back at zero-miles per week.

Malcolm could not find the real cause of the pain after giving a thorough examination to the painful region. I thought that the problem was the periosteum because, when I tapped the heel bone with my finger, this produced quite a painful result in a fairly localized region. After some weeks it seemed to improve, so I began to run hopefully again, building up the mileage.

On Sunday the 6th of July, my 53rd birthday, on my 18 miles run through Innes House grounds with Muffin, my left heel problem became quite acute after an hour and 20 minutes and my right heel was also giving me discomfort.

On Thursday the 17th of July Dr Sabiston agreed to give me a cortisone injection into my left heel at the sensitive area. This was quite unpleasant, but I was desperate to be free from the persistent heel pain.

IN TOO MUCH PAIN TO FINISH A 100KM

Three days later, the 20th of July, I started in the **BAF/SAF 100Km championships as part of the Scottish team for the Anglo-Celtic Plate** competition over the Heriot Watt University course. My initial pace was quite restrained, but after about 3 laps my right heel callus began to hurt. I was wearing my Nike Mariah shoes with heel pads and this might have allowed too much movement of my heel. On lap 4, I stopped and put a sheet of Spenco adhesive knit over my right heel. This helped for a while, but I had to stop and change my shoes to Asics DS racers on lap 7.

I felt much better with these shoes, but by lap 14 I had to take 'Nurafen' and Voltarol tablets. My right heel became extremely painful, so I stopped and changed into my Asics 'Gel 111' shoes. These were so heavy that my legs could hardly move them and my right hamstring began to tighten up. I stopped again on lap 17 for a massage to try and relieve this. I decided to try my DS racers again after lap 19. This helped a bit, but on lap 21 my right heel was so painful that I decided to abandon the race.

On inspecting my right heel, I was relieved to see that there was no additional damage. My left heel problem was not seriously affecting my running although I was still conscious of some discomfort. Izzy looked after me very well and she was certainly kept busy.

Stephen Moore ran very well to win the title for the 3rd time in 7-04-22. Simon Pride also ran a good race, finishing 2nd in 7-14-13, but I felt that he should have been able to win the race. Allan Stewart withdrew, suffering from the effects of his recent Brechin 24-hour race. Andy Farquharson managed to carry on past 50 miles, but did not reach the end. John Sneddon did well to finish.

On following Friday, I noted in my training diary that *'both heels felt fine'* on a fifteen miles run.

On Sunday, 27th of July we set off on our summer caravan holiday, making stops at: Perth, Edinburgh, South Shields, Scotch Corner, Wetherby, Birmingham and Alderstead Heath near Redhill. From there we visited: Mark Pickard, Andy Farquharson, Edit and Roy Richards, John and Vera Lamont, and Margaret and Alex Vose.

We returned home with stops at: Hatfield, Cambridge, Stanford on Avon, Stockton on Tees and Perth.

Each morning during that holiday I ran for a minimum of one hour, using an Ordnance Survey atlas of the UK to get a rough plan of my routes. This proved to be quite satisfying, especially as both heels were only giving minimal discomfort and I was able to run between 70 and 80 miles a week during this time.

On Sunday the 7th of September in the Macallan Moray marathon, the pace required was rather a shock and I had to work hard to stay with my chosen group. I could see from my recently acquired heart rate monitor, that my heart rate to maintain this pace was 150 beats per minute. Approaching Burghead, I lost five places as I was inhibited by right hamstring tightness. It seemed to ease and I pulled back 2 places before Lossiemouth and was heading to catch Raymond Farquhar when a 'pull' occurred in my right hamstring. I had to stop immediately and was extremely disappointed at having to drop out.

Malcolm Morgan gave me treatment on my right hamstring and repeated this a week later, which combined with no running, but cycling, appeared to allow recovery. On Wednesday the 17th of September, I jogged for 15 minutes on the golf course at a very cautious pace and my right hamstring appeared to be OK. I then cycled to and from work. I repeated this for the rest of my working week, but increased the morning runs to 7 miles. On Sunday I tested my right hamstring by running my 27 miles, Garmouth/Kingston route with Muffin in 3-04-02. I was delighted that my hamstring was healed.

My next problem occurred on Friday the 3rd of October, when at 06:48 I set out on a run before driving to Aberdeen for my O.U. T401 (Project) student, Ian Wood's 'viva' (oral presentation). In the darkness I tripped on a protruding stone on the farm track to Oakenhead Farm, fell and banged my right knee and cut my left elbow. Later in the day my right knee began to swell and stiffen, but after 3 days the swelling was reduced and the stiffness became less, so I decided to attempt the 24-hour run that weekend.

FIGHTING BACK IN THE 24 HOURS TRACK

On Friday the 10th of October, Izzy, Claire and I caught the 09:35 flight from Inverness airport to Heathrow in preparation for the **Sri Chinmoy 24-hour, B.A.F championships** on 11/12 of October. On our arrival at Heathrow we made our way by underground and bus, to the 'Barclay Court Hotel' in Hafer Road. Anne O'Leary, the joint owner, was a Sri Chinmoy disciple. Claire's room had a nail in the door to serve as a doorknob and the door was not a proper fit. In the afternoon we went in to London and in the evening we went to the theatre to see 'Grease', which we enjoyed.

On Saturday rain began falling as we came out of Tooting Bec underground station, so the weather forecast was correct. On arrival at the track we set up our base in a corner of the lounge area of the clubhouse and I got ready for the start at 12:00.

Rain was still falling and would continue for the next 18 hours, as 40 of us got underway. Martin Eccles set the initial pace but Jaroslav Kocourek and I soon led and passed 50Km in 3-59-54. Izzy and Claire gave me drinks every 20 minutes as per my schedule. At 6 hours I was 3rd, but I had to stop and go into the clubhouse to attend to my feet. I was wearing my DS Racer shoes without socks, but because of the rain, sand from the long jump pit was being thrown up by runners and some found its way into the sides of my shoes, causing rubbing and eventual bleeding. I put plasters over the cuts and also socks and resumed running. By 18:26 my right hamstring began to give trouble, so I went to the physiotherapist for some treatment.

Andy Farquharson and Josephine arrived at about 18:15 to give encouragement. I became exhausted and was reduced to walking and jogging and at 21:40 I returned to the physiotherapist in the hope that he could revive me and I was there until 22:00, when I resumed the struggle. At 22:40 I took a 'Co-codamol' tablet.

My left leg became extremely painful on the top left just down from my knee. I could not put any weight on it so jogging was impossible. I visited the Physio again and took another 'Co-codamol' tablet and put some freeze spray on my painful leg region. I still could not run, so I walked until 03:00, when I visited the Physio once again. This time Jackie John was on duty and she did a lot of work on the muscles around my left knee. This helped a bit, but I still could not run. I walked on until 07:00, when I realised that my left leg was sufficiently recovered to allow me to resume running. At this time, I was 14th with 85 miles covered.

I was delighted with my recovery and began to enjoy working my way back up the leader board. I took another Co-codamol tablet at 10:40. Also I had half a Gliclazide tablet, for insulin production, crushed between two spoons on about 4 occasions. I was pleased that I had recovered and managed to complete the event, not only for myself, but also for Izzy, Claire and Andy, who was very positive in his support. My right heel gave me no trouble throughout the run, which was very encouraging.

Jaroslav Kocourek (Czech) won with 150 miles 1727 yards, from Lucio Bazzana (Ita) with 146 miles 1331 yards and Richard Brown with 128 miles 1333 yards. Sharon Gayter was first lady in 5th place with 120 miles 357 yards and I finished 9th, with 112 miles 1490 yards.

Training for the remainder of October was uneventful apart from an infection, which on investigating, I found to be a cut on my right heel, from the 24-hours over two weeks before. The scab came off easily and pus oozed out. I was healthy in November, but developed sinusitis in December.

I finished 1997 having had 6 physiotherapy treatments from Malcolm, which was quite an improvement on 1996. My total training and racing mileage for the year cane to 3808 miles, which was an average of 73 miles per week. **I could only hope that 1998 would be a better running year.**

1998

January started well, but by the 2nd week my right hamstring was causing discomfort again, although this was reduced when I started doing the buttocks exercise that Malcolm Morgan reminded me of when I telephoned him. This was not sufficient, so Malcolm had to give me treatment on my right buttock and right calf muscle, which was also giving trouble.

I experimented with taking half a Gliclazide tablet, (40mg) 20 minutes before starting long runs to see if the increased insulin production would produce a beneficial effect. I could not notice any benefit and found the same when a crushed Gliclazide tablet was included in a 330mL bottle of 10% concentration 'Leppin' and consumed during my longest training run.

In early February my right hamstring began to twinge badly, I stopped, very disappointed, and began cycling to and from work again. Malcolm provided appropriate treatment again.

Mike McCulloch telephoned to tell me that fellow runner, Alan Ross, had died of cancer. Two days later I attended his funeral in Newtonmore. The church was packed and people had to stand in the isles. Alan, only 32 years old, was very well liked and respected.

On Sunday the 8th of March in the Inverness half marathon I was pleased to get through without any problems in 1-20-23. The weather was beautiful with brilliant sunshine. One hour before the start I drank 500mL of 10% concentration Leppin and one 80mg Gliclazide tablet. The last time that I ran this race had been in 1995, when my time was 1-19-10.

As the evenings became lighter, towards the end of March, I introduced twice weekly effort sessions in my runs home from work.

My next unfortunate incident occurred on the 1st of April, when nearing the end of my 18-mile run, I managed to trip over a paving slab, which had a raised edge, I went sprawling, cracking my chin and bashing my nose on the paving slabs. Luckily my legs and knees were OK. I lay there for about a minute trying to recover and holding my nose, which I knew was going to bleed. I walked for a while, dripping blood and once my nosebleed had subsided I jogged home.

On Saturday the 4th of April, I drove Izzy and Claire to Aberdeen airport as they started their journey to Berlin for a week's holiday, based in the 'Berlin Hilton' in one of the 2 rooms allocated to Izzy's brother Bill, an airline pilot with TUI (Thomson's) and his wife Yvonne, an air hostess, also with Thomson's. I then drove to Edinburgh Zoo members' house, for the Open University T401 (Project) day. I drove back by the A9 in bad weather.

On Sunday in the Moray Road Runners 10Km road race I became alarmed as my heart was fibrillating, causing my heart rate monitor to go beyond the maximum threshold of 180 beats per minute. I had to slow and after about 3 miles my heart rate began to settle down at around 154-158 beats per minute. I was pleased to get through this test without injury or heart failure. I finished 34th in 39-25 and 2nd over 50, to Graham Milne who was 17th in 36-32.

The following Friday and Saturday I spent marking the Speyside way 50Km course, helped by George Stewart, who drove between access points. On Sunday I rose at 05:30 and set off, to set out the tables, water and food for the feed stations. There had been more snow overnight and the northeast wind was still very strong. I completed my tasks by 09:45, when I arrived at Ballindalloch.

Linda Pride did an excellent job of registering the runners and Graham Milne did the announcing, welcoming the runners and issuing instructions about the arrangements regarding personal drinks, kit transport to the finish and registration.

FIRST OVER FIFTY IN THE SPEYSIDE WAY 50 KM

Once I started the race, I soon found that my Asics DS racers were not very suitable on the snow and mud and I had not worn socks. My heart rate monitor kept going over-limit, probably due to inadequate skin contact. I never felt great, but persisted, hoping to feel better.

By Craigellachie I was running with Neil McGregor, Andrew Sneddon and Carolyn Hunter-Rowe. I got dropped on the road hill and fell further back in the forest roads over Ben Aigen. Coming off Ben Aigen, the path was slippery and potentially dangerous, so I picked my way down, losing more ground. On the road section I began to run a bit better and passed three before Fochabers. Over the last section to Spey Bay, I had great difficulty running, despite trying hard and this effort made me nauseous. I finished 10th in 3-58-32 and first over 50.

Despite the rather difficult conditions, 71 of the 75 starters completed the course and no one got injured, which was a big relief. Simon Pride won in 3-19-59, from Allan Stewart, 3-30-22 and Dave Hurst, 3-38-15. Carolyn Hunter-Rowe was first lady in 5th overall in 3-47-09 ahead of Kate Jenkins, 11th in 4-02-24.

Izzy and I had agreed to help the fund raising event for McMillan Cancer relief, organised by May and Jim Gilchrist. The trans-Scotland event offered sponsored walkers or mountain bikers the opportunity to make the journey from Ullapool in the West of Scotland to Bonar Bridge in the East of Scotland. My task was to open up the deer gates on the last third of the route. On Sunday the 3rd of May, Izzy and I drove up to Bonar Bridge and picked up the key for opening the deer gate locks. We then drove up to Croik and then along the rough track to Lubacoinnich. We pressed on to the first gate and after opening it, Izzy turned the car as the track became too rough to drive on. I ran on to open the 2nd and 3rd gates, about two miles further up the glen. The mountain bikers and walkers would then have a clear passage.

We drove back to Croik, parked our car and began our 11-miles walk down Strath Connon to Bonar Bridge, which we enjoyed. Jim Gilchrist then drove me in his van up the glen to the shepherd's lodge. As the last walker was now through I ran up to the furthest deer gate, locked it and locked the others on the way back. After that I ran back to our parked car and, in all, I estimate that I covered around twelve miles. Finally, I drove back to Bonar Bridge and the Bridge Hotel where we were staying along with several of the walkers. A singsong was underway as I joined the company and the group had an enjoyable evening.

I had been selected to represent Scotland in the Anglo Celtic Plate 100Km race on the 12th of May, as had fellow Moray Road Runner, Allan Stewart. On Saturday the 11th I picked up Allan and drove to Inverness airport, where we caught the 07:00 flight to Gatwick. We caught a train to Kidbrooke, where the race was to be held. On arrival we walked in the warm sunshine from the rail station to our accommodation, the 'Weston House Hotel', 8 Eltham Green, Eltham. Once we had signed in and paid £21 for a room sharing with Dave Murrie, William Sichel's advisor, I relaxed for a while.

I walked up to Eltham centre to get bottled water for making up my drinks, and telephoned Izzy on the way. The weather was quite warm at 23°C. I began mixing my drinks, as the 'Pripps' powder took some time to dissolve. I also snacked on raisins, dates, grapes, whole-meal bread and 20% concentration 'Enduro Booster'. Between times I dozed off. My roommate Dave turned up about 6 pm, Adrian Stott and Norrie Williamson popped in to say hello and then William Sichel arrived.

LAP COUNTER MISTAKE IN THE ANGLO-CELTIC PLATE 100 KM

On race day morning we walked down to Sutcliffe Park, where the **National B.A.F 100Km Championships and the Anglo-Celtic Plate race** was to be held. Alan Young, our team manager, procured a table and we set up our base on and around it. As usual I drank 250mL of 10% concentration Leppin 'Enduro Booster' 15 minutes before the start.

The race, organised by the 100Km association, got underway at 07:30 in warm sunshine and we had to complete 4 laps of the tartan track and then 52 laps in the park of 1.892Km each. I made a cautious start, running with Walter Hill, (Eng) and Jeff Rees (Wal) in joint 3rd. We continued running together for over 20Km and then I began to move ahead of them and was pleased that I felt OK.

Stephen Moore (Eng) was running very well and lapped me a couple of times and Willie Sichel (Sco) also lapped me at about 50Km. Mikk Bradley (Eng) was running strongly, but later he began to take walking breaks. I lapped Walter and Jeff and felt comfortable. As I approached the 50 miles timing point, Stephen lapped me for the 3rd time. I was surprised that, 3 laps later when I passed this point, the timekeeper informed me that 'next lap would be 50 miles completed', as I thought that I had already passed 50 miles.

By then I was becoming quite tired and my legs and feet hurt and in addition I started to get concerned about my 'missing lap'. Stephen lapped me for the 4th time on the track section, just before he began his last lap. I should then have had 5 laps to run, but on enquiring I was told that I had to complete 6 more laps. I asked Alan Young to sort out this mistake. As the laps were completed I became more frustrated as the lap recorder insisted that my lap count was correct. Willie, who was one lap and one lap of the track ahead of me, began his last lap and I was told that I had to complete another 3 laps. I duly did this under protest and lacking motivation.

Because of this Brian Davidson was given 3rd place and I was given 4th. Brian informed Graham Ives, the race director, that I was coming up to lap him with 4 laps remaining and that he had never passed me.

The weather during the race was warm with the temperature reaching 23°C, with sunshine and a breeze. I remained fully hydrated using the drinking schedule that I had prepared. I drank every 3rd lap, alternating Dioralite and Leppin and then replaced the Leppin with Pripps from lap 20. Apart from William and myself, our other Scottish team members were: Norrie Williamson, 10th in 8-25-

36, Robert Sharp, 11th in 8-35-20, Allan Stewart dropped out. I was pleased to get through this run without any problems. Stephen Moore (Eng) (V50) won in 6-57-32 from William Sichel (Scot), 7-26-33, I was duly given 3rd in 7-41-28 and Brian Davidson (Scot) 4th in 7-42-57.

England won the Anglo Celtic plate with 22 hours, 48 minutes, 44 seconds, a new record time. Scotland was second with 23 hours, 33 minutes, 37 seconds and Wales third with 26 hours, 34 minutes, 2 seconds. Hilary Walker (England) was the first lady in 9-00-59.

There were 80 starters and 48 finishers. Dave Beattie of Crawley gave me a lift to Gatwick Airport, which I greatly appreciated.

TOUGH TIME AT TORHOUT

As a result of my run in the Anglo Celtic Plate / National 100Km I was selected as part of the Great Britain team for the I.A.U. European 100Km championships in Torhout, Belgium on the 19th of June. My training had been going well and I averaged 140 miles a week with pyramid effort sessions, peaking at six minutes on Tuesdays and Thursdays, 8 times 6 minutes on Saturdays and 50Km on Sundays. Because of this I expected to perform well in Torhout.

On Thursday the 18th of June Izzy met me at College, after my class and drove me to Inverness airport for my flights to Gatwick and on to Brussels. The same person who had met me in 1991 met me and he drove me to Torhout to where the Great Britain team were staying, in a sort of Church/ retreat called 'Ter Loo'. The environment was very tranquil. We ate in the evening at a nearby café.

On Friday morning at the team meeting, Norrie Williamson, Ros Young and Dave Walsh gave us all the information we required. Following this I made up four litres of 'Pripps' drinks and went to bed for about 4 hours and slept quite well.

At 6:30 pm we went to Torhout and to the start area, where Ros found my cyclist and I gave him my drinks and arranged to meet me at 9Km. Before the start I drank 300mL of 10% concentration Leppin with half a Gliclazide tablet dissolved in it. By start time the temperature was down to 25°C, but there was still bright sunshine.

The start was rather chaotic, as the 10Km and marathon runners started behind us, so there was quite a stampede into the narrow streets and I could not get a clear run for quite some time. As I worked through the field I was pleased to meet Wilfried, who was running in the marathon. I had stayed with Wilfried and Rita during my three previous visits for this race.

I passed 10Km in 39-34, which was quicker than I had aimed for and. by about 15Km I began to feel a little stressed, so I eased back, but still going at a good pace. I passed 50Km in 3-30-40, feeling quite tired. I had had a lot of pain from my right heel callus and I began to worry that it would become blistered and ulcerated as before, as this would ruin the rest of this year's running. I pressed on and caught a few tired runners before heading back from Ostende. Gradually I became weaker and slowed considerably after 65Km. Some parts of the route were extremely dark and my cyclist had no lights, so I had to run cautiously.

I was very relieved to complete the route. My time of 7-59-38 was quite poor, but I was 3rd over 50, behind Stephen Moore (G.B) and Roland Vuillemenot of France.

Grigoriy Murzin (Russia) won in 6-23-29 from Dmitriy Radiuchenko (Russia), 6-34-40 and Nikolay Buskarov also from Russia in 6-40-45. Stephen Moore was the first of the Great Britain team, finishing 11th in 6-55-48, Simon Pride finished 13th in 6-57-28, William Sichel, 28th in 7-21-31, Brian Davidson 51st in 8-02-37, Ian Anderson, 82nd in 9-02-18 and Walter Hill finished in 10-23-31. In our ladies' team, Sharon Gayter finished 83rd in 9-02-38 and Kate Todd 97th in 9-30-59. There were 153 finishers.

On Sunday morning, 21st of June, a coach picked us up and took us to Brussels airport. As the flight to Glasgow for Simon Pride, Kate Todd and I was not departing until 2:20 pm, we had quite a long wait. In the departure lounge I met Niall Bairamgalin and most of the Russian team, who invited me to share the beer that they had bought at the 'duty free', so I had an enjoyable 'chat' with some of them.

At Glasgow Simon and I had a wait of 5 hours before our flight to Inverness, but this was delayed and we did not depart until 8:40 pm, in a Shorts 360, 'Skyvan'. At Inverness airport, Simon's wife, Linda met us and drove me home. Naturally, it was good to be home.

HERIOT-WATT NIGHTMARE

My next 100Km race was to be the Scottish championship on the Heriot Watt University course on the 19th of July 1998. I was surprised at how much weight I had gained, as I was 6 pounds heavier than when I started carbohydrate loading.

The day before the race, Saturday, Izzy and I drove down to Edinburgh, were to stay with Sai Baba devotees, Chandima and Shyama de Silva. I had difficulty sleeping that night.

We got underway at 7am on Sunday and Mark Guichard went straight into the lead, I followed him and we completed the first lap in 14-14. I was a little concerned that I was not finding this pace comfortable, but the next lap at the same pace seemed a little easier. On lap three Andy Bottomley joined us and I began to struggle at this pace, so they pulled away and Barry Hards was fairly close behind me.

I set a pace, which I thought was appropriate and settled into 3rd place. As the race progressed I developed severe pains in the outside of both hamstrings and also my quads began to hurt. In addition to this I was conscious of a wheeze when I exhaled. My time at the marathon was a slow 3-09-25 and soon after this Barry Hards came past. I passed 50Km in a poor 3-50-13 and at the end of lap 15 I stopped to have physiotherapy on my hamstrings and quads, to see if this would ease my discomfort. The race was turning into a real nightmare for me. I got going again after my physiotherapy session, but I felt quite weak and I noticed that my heartbeat was irregular. On completing 18 laps I stopped with the intention of receiving more physiotherapy, but the St Andrews Ambulance Medic felt my pulse and said that it was 'racing' and he advised me to stop my race.

I was quite glad to have this 'out', as there was obviously something wrong with me. Later I was coughing up yellow phlegm, so I assume that I had picked up a lung infection.

Mark Guichard won in 7-50-35 from Barry Hards, 7-54-26 and Andy Bottomley, 7-54-56. There were 13 finishers from the 23 starters.

Two weeks later I felt back to normal and resumed my training schedule. In the 'Unison' half marathon at the Nairn Highland Games on the 15th of August, the 130 starters got off at a brisk pace and I began to struggle with the early pace, so I eased back and as George Mitchell caught me, I decided to run with him. Just after the turn, George put in an effort, which broke me. I had to battle the wind myself, while George managed to catch a strong runner and sit behind him.

After a few miles on my own a group of three caught me, which was a great help, as I could get some shelter from the wind. I ran with this group back to the track, where I finished 16th in 1-23-54. I was 2nd over 50 behind George, who was 14th in 1-21-49.

Brian Fieldsend won in 1-16-26 from Steve Reeve, 1-16-32 and Kenny Riddell, 1-16-33.

A week later, following my Monaughty 50Km route I began tapering for the European 24-hour championships the following weekend. By Tuesday I had developed a 'raw throat', which thankfully did not become any worse in the following days. On Thursday the 27th of August, Izzy picked me up outside the College at 10am and drove me to Inverness airport. On leaving Forres we gave a lift to a 'hitch hiking' couple and their two children, all from the 'Findhorn Foundation' The man informed us that he was an excellent chess player and that he could play three others at chess while blind-folded! He predicted that I would run 150 miles in the 24-hour race that I was travelling to.

I caught the flight to Gatwick and a flight to Paris Charles de Gaulle, (C.D.G) airport. I located the ticket office for the trains and purchased return tickets to 'Little Europe' (Marquette, Lille,

France) and took the shuttle bus to the rail station. My train arrived in Little Europe at 10:19pm, but Ros Young, our team manager, was not there to meet me as arranged, so I waited outside the station until she arrived. A friend of the race organization drove us the 8Km to the 'Nuits d'Hotel, actually further than this, as she got lost a few times. I got to bed at about midnight.

On Friday morning my resting pulse was still elevated, at 56, when I rose. I had breakfast with the rest of the Great Britain team, but this was rather Spartan, so I ate some of the provisions that I had brought with me. I returned to bed and slept until lunchtime. We walked to the 'Pizza Hut' restaurant, where we all enjoyed our various meals. Again I slept for some time after this food and then at around 6 pm I walked to a supermarket and had a look around. Our dinner, provided by the race organisers was at 8 pm in a hall at a community centre. I ate salad and rice and was pleased to notice that my throat was improving.

On Saturday morning, 'race day' I ate a very light breakfast of two slices of bread with honey at 7am and then prepared for the race. We were taken from our hotel to the sports hall 'The Forum', where we set up our drinks station, as we were to run through this hall on every lap. After the presentation of National teams, we were transported by bus to the start, 3.5Km away from the 'Forum'.

DECENT RUN DESPITE A BAD STOMACH

The I.A.U 24-hours European Challenge got underway at 11am in fairly warm weather with intermittent sunshine and there were approximately 160 runners on a 1.6176Km loop. Taelman from Belgium went into an early lead and he was soon lapping runners. I decided to run comfortably, using my heart rate monitor as an indicator of my effort and kept my pulse rate in the range 118 to 125. Things went well and I was delighted with my running and how I felt. I was eating and drinking to the schedule that I had prepared. After about 17 hours I began to suffer from bad stomach pains, which eased when I slowed and almost disappeared when I walked. Later I discovered that I was bleeding either in my stomach or in my small intestine. Richard Brown gave me soft cheese on bread to try to combat this. My last 7 hours were rather poor as I walked quite a lot. I stopped for a massage and had blistered feet tended to by Nigel Robinson, who did an excellent job on them. Once I had my feet done I could not continue in Asics 'DS racers', as they were now too tight, so I wore Air Max shoes, which were rather heavy. I eventually finished 11th with 145 miles 804 yards (234.083Km).

Lucien Taelman (Belgium) won with 267.626Km, with Tomas Rusek (Czech) 2nd, with 263.144Km (M50 age best) and Michael Maier (Germany) 3rd with 259.067Km. Alain Prual (France) was 4th with 253.912Km and Lubomir Hrmo (Slovakia) 5th with 251.908Km. There were 121 finishers.

Our G.B. team of James Zarei 30th, Martin Eccles 36th and I, were 5th team behind: France, Germany, Czechoslovakia and Slovakia. Our Ladies team, Sharon Gayter, 25th and Sandra Brown 37th were 2nd team behind France.

After the race I felt quite bad, because of my stomach pains. I vomited twice before lying curled up on the grass outside trying to recover. After the presentations of awards, we were given a post race meal by the organizers in a sort of Church Hall, but due to stomach pains I could not eat. I did have some wine as an alternative and this did help alleviate the pain. We were then taken back to our Hotel to rest, but before I entered I had to vomit again. I could not sleep, so I went for a gentle walk.

In the evening Per Lind from Norway interviewed me, before we all went to the 'Pizza Hut' to eat at 8pm. Following this Len Cullen, James Zarei, Neil Speirs and I went to the 'Three Brasseurs' microbrewery Pub, which was interesting.

Monday, 31st of August was spent returning from Lille, via Paris C.D.G airport, Gatwick and on to Inverness airport by a delayed flight. I arrived there at 10:20 pm, but my bag did not, so I had to go to report this problem. Izzy was there to meet me and drove me home.

I was shocked to learn that my cousin, Brian Ferguson, had been killed in a motorbike accident at a crossroads between Rothienorman and Inverurie. Brian was a helicopter pilot with Bristow's, flying oil workers to various rigs and platforms, from Aberdeen airport.

On the following Sunday, despite having a cold and not being fully recovered from the 24-hour race, I decided to go ahead with my plan to run in the Macallan Moray marathon, assisted by Izzy on a beautiful sunny and warm day. I started cautiously, keeping my heart rate at 140 or less and I was comfortable until about 20 miles. After this I had to work harder to maintain my heart rate at 140 beats per minute. I finished 16th in 3-08-54.

TOO SOON TO RACE AGAIN

The IAU 100Km Veterans World Championships was to be at Winschoten on the following Saturday. On Friday after morning classes I quickly made my way to the rail station, caught the train for Aberdeen, got off at Dyce, got a taxi to the airport and caught the KLM flight to Amsterdam. I caught the next train to Winschoten; arriving there at about 11pm. John Legge was there to meet me and escorted me to where he and Charles Avis, the masseur and I were staying. The lady, who was our host, was called Helen Van Vuren.

On Saturday morning, 11th September I prepared for the race, then walked to De Klinker, where I met the other team members and gave my drinks to Charles Avis. The men's G.B. team were: David Beattie, Mikk Bradley, Walter Hill, Stephen Moore, Donald Ritchie and William Sichel. The Ladies team were: Jackie Leak, Eleanor Robinson and Hilary Walker.

The race was started at 1pm by race director Harm Noor, in light rain, and I set off intending to run 42 minutes for the 10Km laps, for as long as possible. Soon after the start I ran with a group of 7 in joint 6th place and we completed the first 10Km lap in 41-28, which was OK. However, on the 2nd lap the pace increased slightly as they began to close on William Sichel. I drifted off the back of this group and at the completion of the lap my time was 1-22-04. I began to slow during the next lap, but thought that I would be able to keep a reasonable pace going. My time at the marathon was 3-01-06, almost 8 minutes faster than the previous Sunday's Moray marathon. Rain continued to fall as it had done from the start.

By 50 Km, passed in 3-40-15, my legs were painful and quite tired and from then on I deteriorated until I could barely put one foot past the other. I shuffled wearily around the route in the rain. Having taken over an hour for the last 10Km lap, I finally reached the finish. I asked for a massage, but the Medics insisted on taking my body temperature and blood pressure and informed me that I was suffering from hypothermia. They also took a blood sample from my ear lobe to check my blood glucose, as they could not get any from my white fingers. The blood glucose figure of 7.2 was satisfactory. After two hot teas and some food, my body temperature rose to near normal.

The massage I received was excellent and would assist recovery. Ros Young walked me back to my lodgings. John Legg, his wife Helen and Charles were still up when I arrived just before midnight. We relaxed, chatting for some time before going to bed.

I learned that I had finished 37th in a very poor 8-53-10. Probably I had not recovered from the 24-hour race two weeks previously.

Next morning, we went to De Klinker for the awards ceremony and although I was not a counting member of the G.B team, I was thrilled to receive a winning team medal. Later I also got a cup for being 4th in the over 50 years category.

A Magier (Poland) won in 6-59-50, from Stephen Moore (GBR) and 1st M50, 7-05-11 and S. Lavrenyuk (Ukraine), 7-11-40. There were 124 finishers.

I walked back to the Hotel by the railway station with Hilary Walker, where we had a drink with John. Charles gave me an excellent massage before escorting me to the station to catch the train for Amsterdam along with Willie Sichel. On the train we met an interesting ultra runner who had been the Dutch 5000 metres champion 18 years before with a best of 13-56-40 and his best marathon was 2-21. Following our flight to Aberdeen I got a taxi to Dyce railway station, caught the train for Inverness. Izzy met me in Elgin and drove us home.

I was surprised, especially at 54 years old, perhaps the oldest ever, to be selected for the Great Britain team for the IAU 'World Challenge' to be incorporated in the River Shimanto 100Km in Japan on 18th of October 1998.

Izzy and I had arranged to go to Puttaparthi, India, for the 'Paduga Ceremony' in the Ashram of Sai Baba during the week before this race, so I would have to travel to Japan from there. We arrived on the 5th of October and were given accommodation in the Ashram

Each morning that week I ran from the Ashram gates, on a loop around to the 'super speciality' hospital, turning at the staff quarters. The weather was quite warm and humid, most of the run was at 500 metres altitude and I covered 54 miles for the week. My 'Polar' heart rate monitor/stopwatch ceased functioning, which I think was due to the high relative humidity or sweat ingress.

I caught a flight from Puttaparthi by Indian airlines to Bombay (Mumbai), on Tuesday 13th October and transferred from the domestic airport to the International airport. My next flight with Korean Air, departed on Wednesday, at 1:10am to Bangkok, in business class, which was a first for me. From there I flew with Thai Airways at 9:15 am to Osaka and on arrival there, Norrie Williamson met me and took me to the All Nippon Airways, (A.N.A), Gate Tower Hotel. Once checked in I ran for 5 miles at an easy pace with Hilary Walker. On Thursday morning we caught a flight from Osaka, south to Kochi on the large island of Shikoku and from there we had a 3-hour coach trip to Nakamura over severely undulating roads.

On the following morning, I ran for 35 minutes with my Great Britain team-mates from the 'New Royal Hotel Shimanto' in Nakamura. Later we were taken to Towa village at the 40Km point on the course for an excellent 'self service' lunch in a school hall. Next we moved on to Nishitosa Village at the 62Km point on the course, for the signing ceremony for the **1999 World Challenge**. At 4pm we all attended the flag Parade and then we went to a welcome event in the Tenjinbashi Shopping Arcade, which included Hata-Kagura dancing, Koto performance and a tea ceremony. We all rested on the following day as a typhoon approached, preceded by torrential rain and wind, which was due to pass close by overnight.

PAINKILLER AGONY

On Sunday the 18th of October the start of the **River Shimanto 100Km** was delayed by half an hour to allow some extra clearing up time following the passing through of the edge of the typhoon overnight. Daylight was just beginning as we set off. I felt good as we followed a river valley up into the hills and I was running in a group of 2 Germans, a Mexican and an American.

At the first special drinks station I managed to dislodge my wedding ring and I heard it strike the roadway. I turned back and luckily managed to spot it and retrieve it. As we progressed the gradient increased and so did the number of runners catching me and passing me, but I tried to avoid going too hard, so I held back.

On reaching the top of the pass at 21Km, at a height of 650 metres, I began to run down the other side quickly, passing many runners, but I must have run too quickly as my quads became quite weak and painful. I found it difficult to stride out because I could not bring my legs through properly. At the first 'handling' point I got a massage on my quads from Norrie and changed my shoes from Magic racers to DS Racers. I decided to do this because the downhill section had started to make my right heel callus hurt and I did not want it to develop into a major problem. I took 2 'Ibuprofen' tablets and 2 for later pinned to my shorts.

For a while I ran along fairly comfortably, despite being unable to stride out, but the next hilly section just before 60Km finished off my legs and I almost had to walk down the hills on very painful legs. At 62Km I had another massage and took more painkillers. I struggled on, becoming gradually weaker, until I had to alternate jogging and walking. I drank at every refreshment station, taking water or 'Pocari Sweat' an electrolyte replacement drink. For my personal drinks I was taking 'Pripps 11'.

My right heel became very painful as the temperature built up. The only relief I could get from this was to stop, remove my right shoe and let the inside of the shoe and my heel cool down. I had to repeat this about every 20 minutes. By then there was bright sunshine and it became very warm, so at times I became uncomfortably hot, but I decided that I had to complete this run; I had not travelled all the way to Japan to drop out.

I began to experience stomach pains and realised that I had taken 9 Ibuprofen tablets, so this was probably the cause. I continued jogging and walking towards the finish, which I eventually reached in an exhausted condition in 10-43-42, a huge personal worst. After some time lying down, I began to recover and with assistance from Len Cullen, got the bus back to the hotel. The course had been beautiful, but I had been too distressed to appreciate this.

Simon Pride ran very well to finish 6th in 6-59-38, but Stephen Moore and Greg Dell dropped out, leaving Simon, Willie Sichel, (7-46-26) and myself as the counting members of the Great Britain team, which finished 9th of 15 teams entered. Later I found that I was 48th of the 50 finishers in the IAU event. I made **a promise to myself not take painkillers in a race again.**

Russians filled the first 4 places: Grigori Mourzin, 6-30-06, Igor Tioupine, 6-34-10, Ravil Kasharov, 6-36-33 and Anatoli Koredanov, 6-38-02. Carolyn Hunter Rowe (G.B.) won the women's race in 8-16-07, ahead of Lilac Flay (N.Z), 8-19-11 and Maria Auxuliadora (Brazil), 8-21-55. The Great Britain women's team were 4th.

On Monday we caught a flight from Kochi to Osaka and then returned to the A.N.A Gate Tower Hotel to stay overnight. My leg muscles were very painful. The following morning our flight from Osaka followed a 'Great circle' route over Siberia to Heathrow. A flight to Aberdeen, a taxi to Dyce rail station, a train to Elgin where Izzy met me completed my journey. It was particularly good to be home again, after such a tough experience.

Two weeks of cycling to and from work, with some jogging on the second week, allowed recovery from my disturbing 'River Shimanto' experience. I was able to resume running properly on the 1st of November.

There were no suitable races to tempt me in the remainder of 1998, so I continued my base training schedule, through November and December. My total training and racing mileage for the year was 5768 miles, which was an average of 111 miles per week.

Obviously, age was affecting my performance; and diabetes was probably responsible for some extra problems during races. However, I was still determined to continue trying hard, for as long as participation in my sport was possible.

1999

On the first day of 1999 I ran my 27 miles, Garmouth/Kingston route accompanied by my weekend and holidays running companion, our Springer Spaniel, 'Muffin'. She got badly cut on her belly near her right back leg. I did not know when it happened, but I first noticed her lifting her back right leg on the forest road section on the way back with about 7 miles remaining. When I began washing her on returning home, I discovered the rip in her flesh, exposing about 2 inches of muscle. This was covered in mud and was completely black.

An emergency appointment was arranged for her with the Vet's in Elgin and Izzy and I took her up at 1pm. The vet examined her and advised that she would need a general anaesthetic so that he could clean out the wound and stitch it up. Izzy and I picked her up at 7:30 p.m. The Vet had sown her up nicely and had put in a drain to allow the wound to discharge fluid resulting from the anticipated infection. She had a cone fitted to her collar to prevent her from licking her wound.

SUFFERING IN WALES

My first race of 1999 was to be the **Barry 40 miles track race** on the 7th of March. I prepared well with 575 miles in January and 533 miles in February, which included at least one effort session each week.

On Friday evening, the 5th of March, I drove down to Adrian and Linda Stott's home in Edinburgh, where I stayed overnight. The next morning, as I began my drive to Barry, snow was falling, but soon melting. I stayed at 'Barbaree' B&B again, sharing a room with Simon Pride. Hilary Johnson was there with Tony Jones and it was good to meet them again. Shane Downes was also staying there and he was looking fit. Next morning from the 10am start Simon set off at 5-40 per mile pace or perhaps faster and was certainly on schedule to break my record of 3-48-35. Shane Downes gave chase, followed by Jan Vandendriessche (Belgium) and Stephen Moore. I sat behind Mark Guichard for several laps before deciding that I could not hold that pace. Following this I ran with a group consisting of Walter Hill, Brian Davidson, Allan Stewart, Andy Bottomley and Jeff Rees.

I was alarmed to find that, by 5 miles, I began to struggle with the pace, and I had to drift off the back of this pack, which quickly moved away once I had relaxed my effort. I had no energy and my quads and hamstrings began to ache. My drinks of 200mL of 10% solution Leppin, every 20 minutes did not improve things, so I ran on hoping for an improvement, but none came, only a further slowing in my pace.

My right heel callus began to hurt badly, so before 20 miles I changed shoes. My condition continued to deteriorate and every 20 minutes I would walk to take my drink. In addition to this I began to have a nosebleed.

Things got worse as I got a severe pain on the outside edge of my left knee and it felt like a nerve being pinched. This caused me to stop and try to eradicate it by stretching my quads, calf and massaging the tendons and ligaments around that region. This allowed me to continue, but the problem recurred every 3 or 4 laps, so I had a lot of stops and a lot of anxiety. **I suppose I should have abandoned the run when it first occurred, but I did not want to give up.**

I eventually finished 23rd in the very poor time of 5-19-56. Hilary Johnson gave me my drinks, so I should have had sufficient potential fuel available.

I tried to analyse what caused this poor run. My training in preparation had been good, but perhaps I over-trained by allowing insufficient recovery between sessions. My diabetic control was too lax in as much as, when I began increasing my carbohydrates on Wednesday evening, I was not taking sufficient Gliclazide, so I suspect the carbohydrates were not being converted to glycogen. I think that this would mean that they were being lost through urination. This theory was supported by the fact that my weight increased by two pounds from Wednesday to Thursday followed by a one-pound loss from Thursday to Friday. The remainder of the carbohydrates ingested after this may have gone the same way, so when I started the race I could have been in a near glycogen-depleted state. Also I learned that if one's blood glucose was 14 or above, and mine was, this caused the production of ketones and one was advised not to run with such levels.

In future I would have to monitor my blood glucose more frequently and also use Gliclazide daily and increase the dose particularly during any carbohydrate loading phase. My intermediate times were: 5 miles, 31-31, 10 miles, 64-35, 15 miles, 1-38-34, 20 miles, 2-16-20, 25 miles, 2-55-06, 30 miles, 3-37-04 and 35 miles, 4-19-05. My last 5 miles took me 60-51 to complete, which was awful.

Simon Pride won in the excellent time of 3-53-55, ahead of Stephen Moore, 4-03-37 and Mark Guichard, 4-18-51. Carolyn Hunter-Rowe was the first woman in 8th in 4-35-42.

I set off driving home with Simon at 5pm and it was a long haul home in our Volvo, but I eventually reached Fochabers, where I dropped off Simon, and reached home safely at 3:30 a.m. after 10.5 hours driving, and having driven 1238 miles since setting off on Friday. During the following non-running week I caught flu, which took a few weeks to fully recover from.

BETTER ON THE SPEYSIDE WAY

My next planned race was the **Speyside Way 50Km** on the 11th of April. On Friday the 9th of April I cycled from Ballindalloch marking the Speyside Way course with assistance from Izzy, as far as Bridgeton Farm. The next day I finished marking the Speyside Way route with Izzy and attended to other tasks relating to Sunday's race.

On race-day I began at 6am to deliver tables, water and food for the refreshment stations on the race route. The weather was pleasantly mild and on returning home, I began to prepare myself for the race. Izzy and I drove to Ballindalloch, where Linda Pride was handling the registration again and did this job magnificently and coped with 7 late entries.

I started cautiously in the record field of 97 and ran in a group of 5, including Carolyn Hunter-Rowe, through Carron and Aberlour. On the section going over Ben Aigen I lost 4 places. After Bridgeton Farm I picked up one place on the road, but the outside of my left knee began to give trouble and I could not take advantage of the downhill sections. Going through Fochabers I dropped another place to Robert Jardine. Over the last 5 miles I passed 3 and almost caught John Macrae of Lochaber AC. **I was pleased to finish first MV50 in 3-44-44** in 13th. Carolyn ran magnificently to break the women's course record by a whopping 12-43, with 3-31-59, finishing 7th overall.

Simon Pride won in 3-02-20, from Steve Reeve, 3-18-41 and Allan Stewart (V40), 3-25-32. 91 runners finished the course.

On the following 3 days I had so much to attend to that I cycled to and from work to generate a little extra time. On Thursday I resumed training, running to and from work.

Two weeks after the Speyside way race, on the 25th of April, I drove to Fort William for the Lochaber marathon. I started cautiously again at what I thought was a sensible pace and once we reached the Mallaig road I began to run quite well and moved up the field to about 15th. I reached the half way in 1-22-something, but on the return journey I began to struggle and my right heel callus began to hurt quite badly. I had put extra padding on after the 'Spenco' adhesive tape over my callus, but it appeared to be ineffective. Afterwards I discovered that the padding had compressed and so provided no extra cushioning.

I finished 15th in 2-55-17, which was quite a poor time, but it was the best I could manage. I was 3rd over 50. Simon Pride ran strongly to set a new course record of 2-24-24. I wore my Reebok racers but they gave me a cut on my left Achilles.

FIRST OVER-FIFTY IN THE SCOTTISH 50 KM

Next race on my schedule was the **Scottish 50Km Championship** at Glenrothes on the 9th of May. At 6am on the morning of the race I drove to Glenrothes in poor weather, with heavy rain and a lot of water lying on the roads. I arrived at the 'Fife Institute', which housed the changing rooms, at 9:05 am.

In the Scottish Athletics Federation (S.A.F) 50Km championships race I ran with the 'Metro' team from Aberdeen for the first 4 of the 14 laps. Moira Stewart, Allan's wife, gave me my drinks of 200mL of 'Isostar', at the end of laps: 2, 4, 6, 8, 10 and 12. In the drink at the end of lap six I had added 20mg of Glislazide, in an effort to aid carbohydrate metabolism.

I began to drop off the pace after about 8 laps and the race became quite a struggle. I had to stop for the toilet on lap 12. Eventually I finished 11th in 3-34-48 but first over 50. I wore my Reebok 3D racers with a heel pad for my right heel. This helped, but because of the wet conditions, both of my big toes developed blood blisters. My lap times ranged from 13-38, the first to 16-40, my 12th.

Alan Reid won in 3-12-48, from Clyde Marwick, 3-20-58 and Steven Mason, 3-21-46. There were 46 finishers.

On Sunday the 6th of June I ran a 'Lap of Honour' with Simon before the Rotary 'Marafun' relays in Elgin City centre. Later I ran the first leg for the 'Nifty Fifties' team. The weather was wet and miserable and I felt terrible on the first lap. I think that my warm-up was inadequate. By lap two I began to get going and I was running quite strongly by the 8th and final lap.

A BETTER RUN IN DUBLIN

I was pleased to be **selected for the Scottish team to run in the Anglo-Celtic Plate 100Km** in Dublin on the 19th of June. On Friday, 18th June, Izzy gave me a lift to Elgin train station, where I caught the 5:43 am train to Dundee, changed to a train for Glasgow Queen Street Station. I walked to Central Station and caught a train to Prestwick International airport, for the flight to Dublin. My teammates; William Sichel and Allan Stewart arrived about an hour after me. Our flight with 'Ryanair' was only 30 minutes, and on arrival we shared a taxi to our accommodation, the 'Sunnybank Hotel', Glas Nevin. This was a pleasant hotel, where I was shared a room with William. After a short nap we had dinner at about 7:30 pm. I chose vegetable curry on rice, which would be light enough to be digested before the race next day. Jim Taylor from Glenrothes and Alan Young from Arbroath were our team managers.

On Saturday the 19th of June, we got a taxi to Phoenix Park for the Anglo-Celtic Plate 100Km race, which was scheduled to start at 8am. We had to complete 37 laps of a 1.68- miles loop in the form of a triangle, with sharp turns at each corner.

From the start, Stephen Moore set off at a good pace and nobody went with him. Andy Bottomley and Willie Sichel were next and then Mikk Bradley and I. Mikk gradually increased his pace and I went with him, so we caught Andy and Willie. We went past and pulled away, but eventually I could not sustain the pace that Mikk was producing, so I had to ease back. I was wearing the new version of my Asics DS racers without socks and my feet were hurting badly, especially under the ball of my left foot. Willie caught me on lap 28 and on lap 31 I stopped to change my shoes. I put on my old DS racers and socks, to enable me to finish off in less discomfort. I also tried eating a few jelly babies and found them quite helpful.

Our teammate Brian Davidson came storming through during the last 7 laps to set an excellent personal best of 7-25-56. **I was pleased with my 5th place in 7-35-29, which was quite an improvement on the times that I had produced over the previous 3 years**. My lap times ranged from 11-21 to 16-07, the lap when I stopped to change my shoes. Allan Stewart abandoned the race after 17 laps.

Stephen Moore (Eng) won in 6-56-27, from Mikk Bradley (Eng), 7-16-52 and Brian Davidson (Sco), 7-25-27. There were 23 finishers.

After returning to the hotel I walked to the 'Gravediggers' pub to say hello to Eugene Cavanaugh, the owner, who I had run against in the 50Km at Douglas in the Isle of Man. We had a bit of a chat over a couple of pints of complimentary Guinness. In the evening a wedding reception was being held in the hotel and the 5 bars were fully used.

On Sunday morning I was surprised to see that the bar where breakfast was being served was still open, serving revellers from the previous night, so along with a full Irish breakfast Brian and I had a pint of Guinness. After that we shared a taxi to the airport, caught our flight to Prestwick. There Brian left us, so I continued with Willie and Allan by train to Glasgow Central. We walked to Queen Street station, where I caught the 5:55 pm train to Aberdeen and then on to Elgin, where Izzy met me at about 22:10.

INJURED IN EDINBURGH

Four weeks later, the 18th of July I was entered to run in the **SAF 100Km championship** on the Heriot Watt Campus course. On the day prior to this race I drove down to Edinburgh to stay overnight in the guest flat at Rachel's housing complex at Tollcross. I completed my eating by 5 pm, to minimize the chance of a bowel movement during the 100Km race next day and went to bed early at 8:45 pm.

My alarm woke me at 4:30 am and once I had finished taping my feet I drank 300mL of 10% concentration 'Leppin' as a pre-race food. I left Rachel's at 6:10 am, but I made a bad mistake at the roundabout crossing the City Bypass. For some reason I had forgotten the way to Heriot Watt University, and I ended up on the bypass, which meant that I had to drive down to the next roundabout so that I could come back on the other carriageway. Unfortunately, I missed the exit to the left, so I had to continue up to the junction for Carlisle before I could turn. Eventually I arrived at the race venue with 20 minutes to spare.

We got underway at 7 am and Shane Downes took the lead and began to pull away. William Sichel, Mark Foster, Ian Anderson and Stephen Mason and I ran in the following group. After some time, Ian Anderson speeded up and chased after Shane, who was now out of sight, but Ian caught and passed him to take the lead. Mark Guichard abandoned the race quite early, which was a big surprise. William and I ran together for quite a few laps and I passed the marathon in 3-00-06, with William about 7 seconds ahead of me. I did not try to close this gap, as I felt happy at the pace I was maintaining. My 30 miles time was 3-27-00 and I passed 50Km in 3-34-49, which I thought would be a good basis for a decent 100Km time.

On lap 16, while pushing off with my left foot going over a speed ridge in the road, I felt something 'go' on the outside of my left knee. The sharp pain caused me to stop immediately and I tried to massage the region and then attempted to carry on cautiously. I was able to get going again, but my left leg did not feel quite right. Approaching the end of lap 17 the problem recurred, on the incline to the finish point. Again I had to stop to massage the region and stretch my left quads. I could not run properly by then and I completed the lap limping.

Bob Campbell, the physiotherapist, gave me treatment and soon found the painful spot. He said that a ligament had been stretched, probably caused by an over-tight muscle in my left quads. I changed shoes and tried to resume the race, but could not push off with my left leg because the injury was causing pain when I tried. I decided that there was nothing to be proved by carrying on limping for the remaining 25 miles, so I decided to abandon the race at 36.24 miles in 4-06-44.

Bob Campbell gave me a general massage on both legs, which was excellent. Jim Watson from the Livingston club had a massage once a week from Bob, and this had made a big difference, as it improved his ability to race well and recover afterwards. **Bob suggested that I should get a massage three days before a major race to loosen off any muscles as necessary. I thought that this made good sense and I would do as he suggested before my next 100Km.**

The disappointment at having had to withdraw became more intense as time passed. This was **the 3rd year in succession that I had failed to complete this race**.

I waited to see the race unfold. Shane Downes appeared to have the race won, but he suddenly stopped at the end of lap 25. This allowed William Sichel to take the lead and he continued to run well to finish in 7-32-19. Ian Anderson was 2nd in 7-50-05 with Paul Gibb not far behind in 7-50-37. Mark Foster ran well to finish 4th in 8-07-56. There were 39 starters and only 18 finishers.

My drinks schedule worked well, but perhaps the level small teaspoon of salt per litre of 10% concentration Leppin was excessive as the drinks tasted quite salty. I had also added a dash of Ascorbic acid to each litre of drinks.

I determined to be positive and get the injury cleared, cut back on my food intake in an attempt to lose some body fat and then get back into steady running.

Bob Campbell had suggested that I avoid running for 3 days. My left knee became puffy with fluid. On the 21st of July, Izzy and I travelled to Bombay and on to Bangalore. Next day we travelled to Puttaparthi, registered in Baba's Ashram and were given accommodation. We were there as part of the United Kingdom Sathya Sai Education in Human Values (S.S.E.H.V.) group to attend the first Sri Sathya Seminar on Value Parenting from the 24th of July to the 27th of July.

I did not run for the remainder of the week because my left knee still felt a little painful in some positions. My change in diet did not appear to suit me, as I was constipated for over 5 days.

Following 9 days of no running, on the 28th of July I ran my usual 'Hospital' route from the Ashram in Puttaparthi. My left knee was painful when I started to push, but it appeared to settle down after a couple of miles. I ran the same route on the following 2 days On Friday we began our journey back home by departing for Bangalore. Our taxi driver ran out of diesel with about 24Km remaining, so he flagged down a passing car and set off with a can to get more fuel. We had to wait in the taxi until he returned on the back of a motorbike with the fuel.

We finally arrived home on Saturday the 31st of July, having been on the move since 11pm on Friday; so with the time difference taken into account, this amounted to 25 hours.

On the following Wednesday, 4th of August, I ran in the World Vets 10,000 metres track race at Monkton track near Gateshead. I was seeded into the 'C' race, but I found the initial pace quite hard and dropped off the group. This was a pity because the wind on the back straight was rather strong. I could only manage 39-45.5, which gave me 26th in the M55 category.

I stayed with Bill and Yvonne at Brandling Court in South Shields for 5 days and, 4 days after the 10,000m, the marathon was scheduled. Bill gave me a lift to Gateshead Stadium for the X111 World Veterans marathon. I got off to a reasonable start, but by about 5 miles I realised that my right heel callus was beginning to hurt very badly. I was wearing my Reebok 3D racers with a heel pad stuck in the heel cup of my right shoe. I had worn these for the Fife 50Km, where they had proved quite satisfactory. I had to favour my right heel and I was becoming quite concerned about what I would have to do. I could not complete a marathon with such discomfort, so I considered abandoning the race.

I stopped at about 7 miles, removed my right shoe and attempted to take out the heel pad from the shoe. As it had been glued in place I could not get it all out as it broke into pieces. Once most had been removed I put the shoe on again and rejoined the race. My heel was not so painful, so that was a relief. I continued to complete the run, favouring my right heel until about 22 miles. Then I was able to let go and finish strongly in 2-59-24 in 19th position and **5th M55**. On examining my right heel there appeared to be no major damage, but it was very tender to touch. This was a rather disappointing performance

After Sunday lunch with Jean and Doug Hellyer, Bill drove me to Newcastle Rail station. I caught a train to London, then the underground to the station nearest to Carole & Bob Alderman's in Pinner. I got a mini cab to their house, to join Izzy, who had been teaching S.S.E.H.V there.

On the following 6 days I ran from Carol and Bob's home, increasing my distances as my right heel became less painful. I found some good paths in Ruislip woods and on the perimeter of Pinner golf course and finally included a loop around Ruislip Lido.

We got back home on the 15th of August and I resumed high mileage training with weeks of 147 and 157 miles, before easing down for the Moray Marathon on Sunday the 5th of September. The 18th edition of the Macallan Moray marathon took place on a warm humid day with occasional strong sunshine, with the temperature reaching 26°C. I ran as hard as I could for as long as possible, but by 10 miles my legs were rather tired and they would not function very quickly. At about 20.5 miles I was surprised to be caught by Dave Tann. My quads were very fatigued, so I ran behind him for about 1.5 miles until the little hill, where Kate Jenkins caught us and I 'gave in' a little and they dropped me.

I was pleased to get finished and my 3-04-30 in 7th place was the best that I could manage. I supposed that my muscles were not recovered from the last 2 weeks of high training mileage. I wore my Asics DS racers, but the ball of my left foot and my right heel callus were giving me discomfort. **I appeared to need racing shoes with more forefoot protection**.

I drank 6 X 250mL of 10% concentration Leppin with a pinch of salt and a dash of vitamin C powder. Dave Lancaster won in 2-46-37, from Andrew Cruickshank, 2-56-43 and Tom Coyle, 2-58-44. Kate Jenkins was first lady in 5th place overall in 3-03-56.

I had been selected to represent Great Britain in the IAU European individual 24-hour track championships (Lupatotissima 1999), under the patronage of E.A.A.A, near Verona on 25th/26th September, so I maintained my high mileage for another 2 weeks after the Moray marathon.

On Thursday the 23rd of September, I observed the T402 oral presentations at the O.U. premises in Edinburgh. My student gave a very good presentation. Later I got a train to Aberdeen, where Bob met me. I slept the night at Annie and Bob's in Marcus Gardens.

On Friday morning Bob gave me a lift to Aberdeen airport, where I met my G.B teammate for the 24-hours race, Willie Sichel. We caught the 06:45 BA flight to Gatwick, where we waited in the departure lounge for David Murrie from Newcastle. David, who is Willie's coach, was to be our second in the 24-hour race. When he arrived we boarded the 12:55 B.A flight to Verona. The views as we flew over the Alps were magnificent. On arrival just after 4pm, the temperature was 28°C. We took a bus to Verona railway station and there, were met a race official and taken to the 'City Hotel' on the outskirts of Verona, quite close to the race venue. William and I shared a twin room, which William had kindly offered to pay for from his lottery funding. This was a much better option than trying to sleep in the school gymnasium, on a folding bed, with 'mattress, sheet, coverlet and pillow'. We had a few hours rest before going with all the other competitors, for dinner in a self-service restaurant. This did not take too long and we were back in our room by about 9pm.

On race-day, Saturday the 25th of September, we rose quite early and went in the bus provided to have breakfast at the track and to inspect the facilities there. After this we walked back to the hotel, stopping at a supermarket to buy some: bread, cakes, bananas and grapes. We rested for a few hours before completing our final preparations by 17:00, when we took a taxi to the stadium and got our drinks and food set up on a table, with David in attendance.

FIGHTING TO ACHIEVE A DECENT PERFORMANCE IN THE EUROPEAN 24 HOURS

The opening ceremony and parade of national teams started at 18:00 and the race began at 18:30. A couple of Russians, I think, and Yiannis Kouros set the pace from the start and began to regularly lap the rest of us. I started cautiously and felt quite happy with my progress in the early hours. A 'Champion Chip' system was in use and I was impressed by the organization of the event. We ran in lane 4 as there was a 24 X 1-hour relay being run on the inside lanes.

I began to 'pick up' after about 6 hours and enjoyed the feeling of running well. At 01:00 there was a good fireworks display. By half way I felt quite good, but I still had to urinate frequently despite sweating continuously. Later in the morning I gradually faltered as my strength drained away. I stopped and left the track to have a massage in the hope that this would improve the functioning of my legs. The massage was not done very deeply and I felt no benefit from it. Perhaps some appropriate stretching would have helped, but this did not improve matters. Eventually I could only jog and walk and I developed pains in my stomach: the usual ulcer type bleeding pain and taste.

I had moved through to 4th place and only two laps behind 3rd by 12 hours, with 318 laps completed (134.313Km) but, once I lost my strength, drifted back to 5th as Alain Prual of France moved through. I also had to make 3 lengthier toilet stops.

I was wearing my old Asics DS racers with holes cut for the ends of my big toes to poke through. My feet had been well taped as appropriate and I wore two pairs of 1000-mile socks, one inside the other. I still had some discomfort from my left foot, but this lessened after several hours. I developed a blister on the inside of my right big toe, which burst after about 6 hours, so I stopped to put a Comspeed plaster over it. Later I tried XLR8 shoes to see if they would give me more protection to my feet. They gave no noticeable advantage and after a few hours the ball of my left foot began to hurt so I returned to wearing DS racers.

For the last few hours I did a lot of walking and slow jogging, which was twice as quick as my walking. **I decided that if I ever did another 24-hour run I must keep walking to an absolute minimum.** I would also have to review my drinks/food schedule, having considered my comments on the schedule for this race.

For the last 10 minutes I jogged, but I stopped prematurely when a gun went, but this was to signal that there was one-minute remaining, so once I realised this I resumed jogging. It was just as well that I did, because Tomas Rusek collapsed onto me as the 24-hour gun went, so he was only one metre behind me! I did not know at that time that Thomas was actually one lap behind me. It was wonderful to be finished.

Later I was informed that I had been **awarded the bronze medal**, because Yiannis, who won was living in Australia, and had not been entered by the Greek Athletics authority SGAS; and Antonio Mazzeo, who finished 4th, had not been entered by the Italian Athletics authority, FIDAL.

Willie had to abandon the run after 17 hours because of 'shin splints' after a very courageous run. Dave Murrie proved to be a good handler but, because he was alone, he had to leave us to fend for ourselves for about 3 hours during the night, so that he could get some rest. My intermediate times were: marathon, 3-27-43, 50Km 4-06-04, 40 miles 5-17-25, 50 miles 6-48-53, 100Km 8-34-53, 150Km 13-44-47, 100 miles 14-50-31, 200Km 19-56-49. My average lap time was 2 minutes 44.2 seconds; and average speed 9.268Km/h.

On finishing I decided that this would be my last 24-hour event, but perhaps as my memory of the hardship faded, I might reconsider. The prize structure was, Men and Women: 1st 250 $US, 2nd 100$US, 3rd 75$US, over 180Km 50$US, over 220Km $75 $US, over 260Km 150$US, European record 200$US.

Yiannis Kouros (Greek guest) was first with 262.324Km, followed by Lubomir Hrmo (Slovakia) with 249.234Km and Alain Prual (France) 3rd with 234.823Km. Antonio Mazzeo (Italian guest) was 4th with 231.333Km; **I was 5th, representing Great Britain** with 222.454Km and Tomas Rusek (Czech Republic) 6th with 222.032Km.

In the ladies' race, Irtina Reutovich (Russia) won with 223.763Km, ahead of Helga Backhaus (Germany) with 209.678Km, and Rimma Paltseva (Russia) was 3rd with 202.082Km

On Monday morning I travelled home via Verona rail station, the airport, a flight to Gatwick and on to Aberdeen, but in total about 6.5 hours was wasted waiting for flights. At Aberdeen airport there were no taxis available to take the 50 plus potential customers waiting at the taxi rank. Because of this I missed the last train at 21:54 to Inverness. I telephoned my sister Annie to arrange a bed for the night. Scott picked me up and drove me to Marcus Gardens.

Annie gave me a lift to Dyce Railway station the following morning, where I caught the 06:35 train for Inverness. Izzy met me at the station in Elgin and drove me home, where I had half an hour to prepare for work, before getting a lift to College from Bill Liebnitz.

On the 13th of October Izzy and I received a phone call from Ward 9 in Dr Gray's Hospital at 01:50, informing us that Izzy's mother, Grandma Tait had passed away. She had been staying with us for 2 years before being admitted to hospital and was a well-loved member of our family. We drove up to see her; she was still warm, but now at peace.

On my morning run to work that day, a Jack Russell terrier bit me on the left calf. It was not a serious bite, but my skin was pierced.

I had no further races in 1999 but, with an eye on next year's Barry 40-miles track race, I introduced a Wednesday lunchtime session, from college, into my training in December. I ran down to Morriston and ran 8 X 800 meters around the neglected cinder track there, with a 400 metres jog recovery. Wednesdays became 'three sessions' days totalling 25 miles.

On totalling my training and racing miles for the year I found that I had accumulated 5797 miles, which was an average of 111.48 miles per week.

NEW MILLENNIUM

My first race of 2000 was the **Barry Track 40 miles** on the 5th of March. I tapered on Friday by cycling to and from work. Ominously, in the afternoon there was a heavy snowfall. In addition to my mid-week 800 meter repeats I had introduced my 'Hills session' on Saturday mornings and the Monaughty 50Km run on Sundays and weekly mileage was between 125 and 130 miles. I also experimented wearing different racing shoes and socks to find the optimum combination for the race. In view of this preparation I was anticipating a satisfactory performance On Friday evening the 3rd of March, I drove to Edinburgh, where I had arranged to stay overnight with Adrian and Linda Stott.

The following morning Adrian and I set off, in Adrian's car, for Cardiff and on arrival there, visited the new 'Run and Become' shop. I caught a train to Barry and walked up to my bed and breakfast at No 9 Lower Romelly Road. I met Jim Taylor as I walked and found that he had accommodation at No 1 on the same road. I did not eat a proper meal at night, but snacked on crunchy oats and coconut flakes with raisins and then sugar free 'Alpen' with sultanas. I relaxed and went to bed at 21:30.

At breakfast on Sunday morning I ate a small plateful of dry 'fruit and fibre' and drank two cups of black coffee. Jim Taylor gave me a lift to Jenner Park along with Kendra White.

OVERTRAINED FOR THE BARRY FORTY

We got underway at 10:00 in good weather conditions and I started quickly, aiming to get close to Otto Perkins' M55 30 miles and 50Km records of 3-11-01 and 3-17-26 respectively. However, after 5.5 laps I began to feel breathless, as my heart began to fibrillate and I had to slow right down. Once my heartbeat had settled down I pulled back to the group containing Mark Guichard, Brian Davidson and Jeff Rees. I felt quite comfortable passing 10 miles in 65-22, but after about 70 minutes my right heel callus began to hurt. I was wearing my Asics 'Bordin Racers', which had given me no trouble on three Monaughty training runs of 50Km. After some more laps I decided to stop and change shoes to my old DS racers. I got going again, but could not catch the group that I had been with.

I began to tire quite badly, needed to make a toilet stop and later had to repeat this. My legs hurt and I lacked strength. Eventually I finished 6th of the 35 starters in 4-44-09, well outside Bob Emerson's over 55 record of 4-31-36. **I was disappointed with my run and did not know what to do to improve. Perhaps I had trained too hard for this event. Perhaps I should have done more long steady runs. My preparation had not produced the desired effect.**

Hilary Johnson gave me my drinks, 200mL of 12% concentration Leppin every 20 minutes after 40 minutes. My 10-mile splits were: 65-22, 68-11, 73-11 and 77-25.

Chris Finill won in 4-21-57, from Ian Anderson 4-26-01 and Brian Davidson 4-32-29.

Adrian drove us back to his home and then I carried on to Lossiemouth, arriving at 03:45 on Monday and managed to get a couple of hours sleep before going to work.

My next race was the Moray Road Runners 10Km road race on the 26th of March. My heartbeat became quite irregular during the lap of Cooper Park at the start and I had to ease back. This problem recurred every time that I tried to increase my pace. By 3.5 miles my heartbeat settled down and I was able to run strongly. My time of 39-52 was disappointing and my heart malfunctioning was a concern. At the post-race tea my trusty helpers agreed to man feed stations on the Bell's Speyside Way race, in 2 weeks time.

On Friday the 14th of April, I cycled down the off-road parts of the Speyside Way race route, marking it. Izzy drove the Volvo and Muffin ran as I cycled. The condition of the course was quite bad with a lot of water on the first section and it was snowing heavily, so it took me an hour to reach Carron, which concerned Izzy. The total journey took us 6 hours.

M55 RECORD ON THE SLIPPERY SPEYSIDE WAY

On race-day, Sunday, 16th of April, I had my usual early start as I set out at 5am with the laden Volvo estate to set out the tables and food at the feed stations on the course. I got back about 3 hours later, ate a small plate of muesli, then Izzy and I drove to Ballindalloch.

Linda Pride handled runner's registration and the 10 late entries in an efficient manner. 89 started the 7th edition of the race in pleasant spring sunshine. I started cautiously and after about 2 miles, I began to increase my pace and ran with William Watson and at Carron we were joint 9th. Thankfully the course had dried out a great deal since I cycled over it 2 days previously. Some parts were messy and I tended to lose ground there.

Between Aberlour and Craigellachie, Ian Murphy and his dog passed us. I was pleased with my run with William Watson over Ben Aigen and we caught and passed Allan Stewart and caught Graeme Goodall. The section coming off Ben Aigen was very muddy and slippery, so I took great care not to fall, which meant that I slowed and lost contact with Graeme and William. The road section down to the 4th feed station on the outskirts of Fochabers was good, but my right heel callus began to hurt.

The next section off-road was muddy and slippery, made worse by the rain/sleet shower of the previous 20 minutes, so I had difficulty again and Allan Stewart caught and passed me. The new section of path after going under the A96 was extremely slippery, so I lost a lot of ground to Allan. I was pleased how I felt and was running strongly when the underfoot conditions would allow this.

Stephen Mason caught me with about 2 miles remaining and, as he was running very strongly, soon pulled away. I was pleased to finish 10th in 3-43-32, which was 1-12 faster than last year, when conditions were considerably easier. My time was a **MV55 course record**, which was also pleasing. 81 runners finished the course.

Alan Reid won in 3-12-20, ahead of William Sichel in 3-26-54 and Alistair Black in 3-27-10. Kate Jenkins was first lady, finishing 19th in 3-56-32.

Two weeks later I drove to Fort William for the Lochaber marathon in glorious weather, with the sun shining from an almost cloudless sky. At 12:00, the 17th edition of the marathon got underway with just over 240 runners, which was an excellent turn out.

I started cautiously, by 2 miles had settled into a good pace and by 8 miles had caught a group of 5, which included Dave Fairweather, my V55 opposition. At the drinks station at 10 miles I had to leave the road, to go to the drinks table, which was well off the roadside, to find my personal drink. This nuisance stop left me 30 metres behind the group that I had been running with.

At the turn Dave was 12th and I was 16th and now over 100 meters down. At the 15 miles drinks station I crossed the road looking for my drink, but I was then directed back to the other side where my drink was lying on the grass verge. I had to stop and bend down to pick it up, and this action caused a twinge in my left hamstring. At about 23 miles I passed Ruairidh Campbell of Arbroath Footers.

My time of 2-53-43 in 10th was 1-34 faster than the previous year. Dave Fairweather was first V55 in 9th place. I wore my Reebok 3D racers and my right heel callus was OK until about 18 miles, but it never became too bad. I drank 250mL of 10% concentration orange flavour 'Hi-Five' at drinks stations and liked the flavour and the consistency. I made a mental note to cut back on my food intake on the day before races.

Two weeks later, the 14th of May, I drove to Glenrothes for the **Scottish 50Km Championships**. About 50 runners got under way and I started well, running in a group of about six in joint 6th place, but after 4 laps I began to find the pace too hard, so I let the group go and concentrated on my own race, in the warm sunshine and easterly breeze.

Colin Mathieson came past and I was unable to go with him, since I was feeling tired by then, but towards the end I picked up 3 places, although I could not catch Colin on the last lap.

I was pleased to finish 7th in 3-33-04, which was 1-44 faster than last year (1999) and to receive a **S.A.F silver medal for second veteran**.

Bill Gayter, Sharon's husband, gave me my drinks of 250mL of orange flavour Hi-Five at 10% concentration every 2nd lap and found that this worked well. My fastest lap of the 14 lap course was my first at 13-38 and then I got progressively slower to my last at 16-13. **Moray Road Runners won the team prize** with members in 4th, 7th and 9th places.

Alan Reid won in 3-07-42, from Craig Marwick 3-19-05, and Kevin Tulloch 3-27-44. Sharon Gayter won the ladies in 3-58-04. 41 runners completed the course.

My next aim was to run well in the **100Km 'Nacht Van Vlaanderen' race in Torhout, Belgium** on the 16th of June. On Thursday the 15th I travelled to Torhout via Brussels where I met Yiannis Kouros and Edith Berces from Hungary. We then met a representative from the 'Night of Flanders' 100Km race, who drove two Russians and us to Torhout.

My host family (as on previous occasions, Wilfried, and Rita Viestraete) met me and drove to their home. It had been several years since my last visit, but Wilfried and Rita were just the same. Nathalie, their daughter, was then 16 years old. Their son Jurgen's was studying in Ghent for a Law degree at the university there.

I slept until about 11am on Friday and after a light lunch I began preparing my drinks, consisting of: 18 X 200mL of 10% concentration 'Hi-Five'. Jurgen drove me to the sports hall to place my drinks in the appropriate boxes for delivery to stations on the course.

SLIGHT FRUSTRATION IN FLANDERS: BUT FIRST M55

The combined races in the 21st edition of the 'Nacht Van Vlaanderen' were: 10Km, marathon and 100Km and they started simultaneously at 8:02pm. I ran carefully to avoid tripping in the crush of runners in narrow streets. After a 10Km loop in and around Torhout, the route headed out of town, and up a slight hill to start the first of three 27.5Km loops. On the first of these there was plenty of company, as we were mixed up with the marathon runners. Shortly after the start of the 2nd lap I was informed that I was 18th, which pleased me. By then it was quite dark, but there was a full moon, which helped in the country sections.

At about 65Km the leading lady, Edith Berces, caught me and I made the mistake of not increasing my pace slightly to go with her to take advantage of her company and the lights from the following vehicle. I was too comfortable in my own pace and decided to stick with it. Two more runners passed me, but I overtook three, so remained in 18th place.

My right heel callus began to hurt at about 65Km but, apart from that, the Reebok 3D racers appeared to be fine. I could not pick up my pace in the later stages as I had hoped to do, so my time of 8-05-10 was not very good. However, **I felt fine and my right heel was not damaged. On reflection I know that I should have tried to run harder earlier in the race**.

Wilfried, Rita, Nathalie and her friend met me at the finish and, after going to the sports hall to collect my clothes, drove me home. I went to bed at 5am, but had to rise on three occasions for toilet calls. I had to make three stops for calls of nature during the race, so **I must have been drinking too much and become overhydrated.**

Russians filled the first 3 places; Farid Ganiev won in 6-33-19, from Oleg Kharitonov, 6-45-12 and Alexander Massagirin, 6-46-24. Jan Vandendriessche was the first Belgian, 4th in 6-48-24. Edit Berces of Hungary was first lady in 17th overall in 7-52-16. There were 72 finishers.

Later on Saturday morning I cycled with Wilfried, round to visit his parents. His father showed me around the farm on which he raised about 600 pigs. He said that in six months they reached 1200Kg and were sent for slaughter.

In the afternoon we attended the awards ceremony in the sports hall and it was good to recognise quite a few familiar faces amongst the runners and officials. I learned that I was first in the MV4 (V55) category by 2 hours 20 minutes.

That evening we went for dinner at a traditional restaurant with friends of Wilfried and Rita's, called Alex and Heidi. Heidi made and sold candles as a side business, and it was interesting to see the equipment and the materials she used and also the finished products.

On Sunday, Wilfried drove me to Torhout rail station where I caught the 10:45 train to Brugge, but as the train was several minutes late in arriving, it would be tight to make the transfer to the Brussels train. Wilfried had briefed me that Brussels train would be on platform 9 or 10 and as the train I was on drew into the station, I could see the train for Brussels already at the platform. I ran down the steps and along the underpass and up the escalator to reach this train just before it departed.

At Brussels Central Station I transferred to the Airport Express train and duly reached the airport and could relax. The flight to Glasgow was on time and once there I made the reverse journey of the previous Thursday to Elgin, where Izzy met me and drove us home.

Two weeks after the 100Km in the 'Follow the Herring' 20Km road race from Portsoy as part of the 'Boat Festival' I made a cautious start because of a painful throat but, after about 1.5Km, I was able to increase my pace and start racing. I finished 13th of the 83 finishers, in 1-20-14. The atmosphere at the picturesque harbour, where the race finished, was very good.

Martin Flynn won in 68-04, from Eric Riddle, 68-13 and George Sim, 68-18.

In the Elgin Highland Games 10 miles road race on 15th July, my left quads became quite fatigued and painful. I finished 10th in a slow 65-37, despite my three effort sessions a week during the preceding weeks.

On Sunday the 20th of August, I drove from Marja and Charlie's home in Lochgilphead, after a visit and overnight stay, to Glasgow to participate in the marathon. The roads were quiet and there were some spectacular views as the sun shone on the hills and lochs. I parked about 2 miles from the start at Glasgow Green. I walked there and found the appropriate changing tent. I was in a rush by the time I had changed and toileted and did not do my pre-race stretches.

I made my way through the throng of runners to the start with about 5 minutes to spare. We got underway at 09:30. The 'Champion Chip' system was in use so as we crossed the sensor pads at the start our individual chips were noted. At about 6 miles I felt a twinge in my right hamstring, which rapidly became a permanent pain and I started to worry about the possible consequences of continuing. In Pollok Park I stopped at a bench and stretched my right hamstring and massaged it before continuing. I considered dropping out at halfway if it became any worse, but thankfully it did not develop into a pulled muscle.

I passed halfway in 1-23-something and began to settle down to the task of finishing. My time of 2-58-25 in 61st place was slower than I had expected, but I was pleased to finish. I wore my Reebok 3D racers without socks, but with appropriate taping, and this was satisfactory.

About one hour after finishing I had a 'fitness check', which gave the following results: weight 63Kg, height 177mm, lungs peak flow 500L/min, blood pressure 259/80.

I returned to our car and drove to Loch Lomond Youth Hostel and met Izzy and Anna there at the conclusion of their workshop. We drove to Culdees where we met Marisa, who showed us the farm, 'Borland Farm', which she intended to purchase to start a school.

Two weeks later on 3rd September, I ran in the 19th edition of the Macallan Moray marathon, which that year incorporated the Scottish Marathon Championships. My start was OK, but I soon became breathless as my heart began to fibrillate, so I had to ease back. By Brumley Brae normal heartbeat returned so I began to increase my effort. I almost caught Charlie Noble as I finished 11th and **first V55 in 2-57-18.**

Izzy gave me my drinks: 6 X 250mL around the course and did some video tape recording. Simon Pride ran very well to set a new course record of 2-21-17 and it was good to see Linda there supporting Simon. Martin Ferguson was 2nd in 2-35-49 and Nick Milovsorov 3rd in 2-40-04. I assumed that I would be recovered from this marathon in time for the 100Km in Winschoten, in six days time.

On the following Friday, 8th of September 2000, I travelled to Amsterdam by a KLM flight from Aberdeen. At Schiphol I met Peter Gledhill, a fellow 100Km runner, and we caught the train for Groningen. At Zwolle the train split and, after an announcement in Dutch, we realised that we were in the wrong part of the train and so we went to Leeuwaarden. There we changed to another train for Groningen and there, caught a train for Winschoten. I was pleased to find Allan Stewart on this train and on arrival we were taken to De Klinker by the transport provided.

After registering, we watched the parade of the National teams. Following this, our host's neighbour gave us a lift to our host family, who were: Jannie and Trijinko Pelgrim. They already had Ian Anderson and Chris Finhill staying with them and were expecting only one more. However, they managed to find an extra bed, which they put on the third floor, loft bedroom, which Allan and I shared. This was reached by two sets of spiral stairs. After some sandwiches we were in bed by 10pm.

I slept well and then lay in bed dozing until about 10:00 on Saturday. I decided against having breakfast and began preparing my drinks of 200mL 10% concentration plain Leppin, for every 5Km after 10Km. I prepared my feet by taping the vulnerable parts.

AGE GROUP CHAMPION IN THE WORLD VETERANS 100 KM

Allan and I were taken down to De Klinker in good time for the start, where we gave our drinks to Dave Walsh and John Legge, who were to be at the 5Km and 10Km feed stations respectively. **The IAU 100Km World Challenge incorporating the IAU Veterans World Challenge race and the Dutch Championships**, started on time at 1pm and I settled into a comfortable pace,

so I completed the first 10Km lap in 42-55 and kept this pace going for another 2 laps. I did not get my 40Km or 50Km split times, but I was on sub 7-30 pace. I wore my Reebok 3D racers, which appeared to be fine initially, but my right heel callus began to hurt badly in the usual place. The pain became so intense that I requested my Asics LD racers to change into. The discomfort became less noticeable as the race progressed and I began to slow.

The first lady, Edit Berces of Hungary, came past at about 60Km, going quickly. I felt comfortable, but I could not keep my pace going, yet I was pleased to finish **First V55 in 7-54-45** in 61st overall. After that I had a good massage, which would aid recovery. Then I collected my kit and walked up the course to encourage Brian Davidson and Hilary Walker. Our host arrived and drove us back to his home, where I ate some food and drank a few beers. I was pleased at how well I felt, although I had a pain in my right groin from about 30Km. There were 307 starters and 194 finishers.

1st V55 in the 2000 World 100Km Championships, Winschoten.

P. Fetizon from France won in 6-23-15, from D. Radiuchenko of Russia, 6-29-13 and O. Kharitonov, also from Russia, 6-29-29,

At the awards ceremony on Sunday, I was surprised when Georgs Jermolajevs from Latvia was awarded the 'gold' for first M55, although the results showed that he was third M55 with 9-32-23. The reason appeared to be that I was not in a national team, and this was the same for the second M55, Koos Rademaker in 8-57-25, who was not in the Netherlands national team. Georgs came to me and gave me the medal, which I gratefully accepted, but some time later he came back and asked for the medal back, as he had been talking to someone about it. It obviously meant a lot more to him than me so I gave him the medal back. **I had the satisfaction of actually being the IAU Veterans World Challenge M55 winner and also finishing ahead of two members of the GB team**: Brian Davidson and Alan Reid. Stephen Moore was the M50 champion with 7-20-55 in 38th.

After the awards ceremony, which lasted 2 hours, we walked to the rail station and caught a train to Groningen and on to Amsterdam. I travelled back to Aberdeen with Alan Reid on the KLM flight. At Dyce I caught a train for Inverness and Izzy met me at Elgin station and we were home by 11pm. From the very comprehensive results booklet, I found that my 10Km splits were: 42-55, 43-00, 43-13, 45-03, 50-05, (3-44-22 at 50Km), 42-40, 45-18, 53-19, 52-47 and 56-19.

FIRST M55 IN THE LEGENDARY LONDON TO BRIGHTON ROAD RACE

Three weeks after Winschoten 100Km, I tackled the R.R.C **London to Brighton** on the new and longer course, following a request from Ian Champion, the race director, to participate. On Saturday the 13th of September I caught the BA flight, from Inverness to Gatwick, where John Lamont met me with his children, Michael and Maria. He drove me to his home in Guildford and we ate at about 6:30pm: pasta with tomato sauce, onions and chicken.

I rose at 4:30am on Sunday, had a shower and began preparing for the race. John and I drove to the changing rooms and after registering and toileting, John drove me to the start on Westminster Bridge.

There was a large entry and the start at exactly 7am was a little confused. I could not get going for some time until the runners thinned out. I did not feel very sprightly and my breathing appeared to be laboured. I wore my Reebok 3D racers, but John had Asics LD racers in reserve in case I needed to change.

By 10 miles I had moved up the field to 12th, but was surprised at the slow time of 71-51. I had my first drink there: 350mL of 10% concentration plain Leppin with a little salt and I would have every 5 miles from then.

I felt the climb up 'Farthing Downs' hard work and did not like the downhill sections. On the Downs we were bathed in beautiful sunshine but, as we descended towards Redhill, we entered mist. I passed 20 miles in 2-24-11 and by 30 miles, reached in 3-36-36, I had gained three places, one being Greg Dell, who was walking. At about 32 miles I was surprised to be passed by Tom Glare, who was running strongly. I reached the 40 miles marker in 4-56-38, now in 7th place. After 45 miles Walter Hill caught me and went past, but climbing Ditchling Beacon, I caught him and passed him on reaching the top. Walter sat behind me to shelter from the wind and at 50 miles, reached in 5-25-51 he moved ahead again. I did not try to keep with him, because my quads and left knee were hurting.

The last 5 miles seemed never ending and, to my surprise, there was another climb and following this, the descent into Brighton became increasingly steep, which I did not like and I had to hold myself back. On reaching the flat, Danielle Sanderson caught me, and we ran together for a little while but then I managed to pull away over the last 100 metres. **I was pleased to finish 8th in 7-07-03 and first M 55.**

John escorted me back to his car and we drove to the rail station to meet Vera and the children. I showered and joined John, Vera and the children on the Front, for a stroll. The children each had a turn on a bungee-assisted trampoline, which they thoroughly enjoyed.

We went to the tea and awards ceremony in the Brighton Centre. This was a little difficult to follow because the public address system was not very effective. The presentations started late and became extended. Sarel Ackerman from South Africa won in 5-56-50, from Stephen Moore, 6-24-17 and, Danny de Chaumont also from South Africa, 6-33-26, Danielle Sanderson was first lady in 7-07-12, ahead of Karen Bradford from South Africa, 7-16-24 and Hilary Walker, 8-17-23. There were 146 finishers.

We left at 6:40pm for Gatwick, but the traffic was very heavy, so we were still in Brighton at 7pm and my flight was due to leave at 8pm. John drove as fast as possible in the traffic and got me to the North Terminal of Gatwick airport at 7:29pm. On checking in I was relieved to be told that the flight was delayed until 9pm because of fog in the morning. I duly caught this flight to Inverness and drove home, reaching there by 11:30pm.

I was selected for the Great Britain team for the European 24-hour championships at Uden in the Netherlands on the 21st-22nd of October 2000. On Thursday the 19th of October Bill Liebnitz gave me a lift to Elgin, where I caught the Bus to Aberdeen airport. After checking in, I did a quick interview with Robert Duncan for BBC Aberdeen. The British Athletics Federation had booked my flights to Amsterdam via Manchester. On arrival I purchased a return rail tickets to Oss. My two necessary changes went well, and I arrived in Oss at 18:28, but I was disappointed that team manager Dave Walsh was not there to meet me as arranged. After waiting about 40 minutes, I decided to telephone Nanette's mobile phone. I got Dave on it and he suggested taking a taxi to the stadium in Uden.

I did this and, on arrival at the stadium, I met the race organiser who took me to our accommodation, which was in the Scout hut. We had a room with camp beds and blankets, but no curtains on the windows. Dave, Nanette, Walter Hill and William Sichel came to pick me up and we went for a meal. During the night the temperature dropped and I had a rather disturbed sleep because of the cold, so more blankets would have helped.

TEAM BRONZE FOR GREAT BRITAIN IN THE EUROPEAN 24 HOURS

Dave Walsh managed to find a host family for William and I whom we joined at midday on Friday. In the afternoon William and I had a photo session with a photographer for the 'Sun' newspaper. We both went to bed later in the afternoon for a few hours. At 6pm we had a meal at the same restaurant, before going to the flag parade and opening ceremony of the **I.A.U. European 24-hour championships**. We finished by 9pm and returned to our hosts for an early bed.

At 10:30 the following morning we received a telephone call from John Forsyth, as arranged, preparing us for a live interview on the John Beattie sports programme on BBC Scotland.

After making up some drinks, William and I were taken down to the stadium, where we got sorted out for the race start at 2pm. I felt good and went with the leading group and maintained this for about four hours. By then I was through 50Km, but had decided to ease back my pace. By 5.5 hours I was a lap, 2.5Km, behind the leaders and somewhere between 8 and 9 hours I passed 100Km, but I was gradually slowing. **I do not think that this was due to lack of energy, but rather because of muscle fatigue, mainly in my quads.**

I drank about 150mL of 10% concentration Leppin or had 200mL of dioralite each lap and supplemented this with 'squeezes', parts of Neways 'extreme balance' bars and bits of bananas.

My quads just would not work properly any more, but my feet felt fine in Asics DS racers – even though they were old, they were comfortable. **Perhaps newer shoes would have given my leg muscles more protection from jarring on the road**. Richard Brown was looking after me again and he did a very good job. I tried some smash with cheese on a few occasions and some yoghurt.

I chugged on as best I could, cheered by the news that our team was in 3rd place, and encouraged by how well Adrian Stott was running. The last 30 minutes were on the track in warm sunshine and

L-R, Adrian Stott, Donald Ritchie, Walter Hill and William Sichel

after a few laps I became dizzy and decided to walk for the last 20 minutes or so. I was very glad to finish. During the race I had to make four toilet stops. I was exhausted, but revived a little following an excellent massage.

At the awards ceremony two of the French team, one man and one woman, fainted. Adrian and I, along with Walter Hill, were proud to receive **team bronze medals**, but Walter was too ill to stand on the podium long enough to receive his medal. My final distance was 136 miles 1636 yards, quite a way short of my target 155 miles.

Lubomir Hrmo Slovakia was first with 259.273Km, ahead of Andrei Kazanisev of Russia, 257.760Km and Alain Pruhal of France 255.510Km. Adrian Stott was our best finisher in 8th place with 230.667Km. I finished 17th with 220.220Km, and Irina Reutovich, from Russia, in 12th place with 225.518Km, was first lady. France won the team event from Russia and Great Britain. There were 121 finishers.

The next morning Thea, our hostess, drove William and I to the railway station at Oss, where I caught trains to Schiphol, caught a flight to Manchester, then a flight to Aberdeen. I caught a bus for Inverness and at Elgin Izzy met me to drive home.

I decided to have a rest from running after the 24-hour race. After 12 days of no running, I completed a 15.5 miles course with Mike McCulloch on a Saturday morning. It felt a little odd to be running again!

I had no more races planned for 2000, so training in November and December consisted of steady runs to work in the twilight and back from work in darkness. I could run confidently on quiet roads on the way back from work, but I had a head torch and a flashing armband, both of which I turned on when I saw a vehicle approaching. At weekends I would limit my runs to around 15 miles.

On totalling my training and racing mileage for 2000, I found that I had accumulated 5598.8 miles, which was an average of 115 miles per week.

I was fairly satisfied with my performances taking into account that I had reached 56 years half way through the year.

2001

My first race of 2001 was the RAF Kinloss to RAF Lossiemouth, Dave Johnson Memorial half marathon on Sunday the 25th of February. I started quite quickly, but my heart misfired quite badly, so I had to ease back until it settled down, which occurred after about a mile. From then on I was able to run strongly, passing 10 miles in 63-48, which was pleasing. I finished 11th in 1-23-38 for the course, which Dave McFarlaine the race organiser, informed me was 135 metres over distance. I was first over 50, as there was no V55 category. Eric Riddle won in 1-10-36, from Alan Reid, 1-13-02 and Raymond Hardie, 1-14-53,

The Barry 'Track 40' was scheduled for the following Sunday so on Friday, after work I drove to Banff to pick up Alan Reid and drove down to Edinburgh to stay with Adrian and Linda Stott. On Saturday I drove down to Port Talbot, where we stayed with Jeff and Sharon Rees.

On 'race-day', the 4th of March, my blood glucose reading at 8:20am was rather high at 22.4. The race got underway in very cold weather after a one-minute's silence in memory of John Legge. I started well and joined a group, consisting of Mikk Bradley, Walter Hill, Mark Farrell and myself, in joint fifth place. This group gradually broke up before 10 miles, which I passed in 65-52, which was on schedule, but I became slower and my target of 4-31-36 became impossible. My heart was fibrillating, not pumping properly so I lacked strength. I passed 20 miles in 2-15-08 and 30 miles in 3-31-06. Perhaps my high blood glucose had an adverse effect on performance. I was quite disappointed with my poor run, but was pleased that Alan Reid won in 4-11-45, with Ian Anderson second in 4-19-29 and Chris Finill third in 4-23-28. I finished 9th and first V55 in 4-53-07. There were 23 finishers from 33 starters. After the awards ceremony I drove the huge distance back up to Banff to deliver Alan home and then on to Lossiemouth.

The following Sunday, after a gradual warm up, to help my heartbeat settle into the effort required, I ran in the Inverness half marathon, finishing 81st in 1-25-13, which was disappointing. I was third MV55 behind G Smith of City of Edinburgh in 1-19-58 and Dave Stewart of Moray Road Runners, who finished in 1-23-27.

Early next Sunday, the 1st of April, I set off in tee shirt and shorts to run an extended Monaughty course. Because of the 'foot and mouth' restrictions I avoided the forest and continued on the road past Pluscarden Abbey and then up the long hill on the north side of the valley. At the top I turned right and climbed up and over the ridge and then joined a road, which eventually led me onto the last third of my Monaughty course. I felt quite good throughout the run and my last mile was 7-41. My running time was 4-26-57 and I estimated, from the Ordinance Survey map, that the distance was 37 miles.

Our two-week Easter holiday from School and College began on the 2nd of April and as I had to cancel the 'Bells Speyside Way' 50Km race, because of the 'Foot and Mouth' restrictions, we were free to take a holiday. Izzy, Anna and I decided to visit New York and flew there from Glasgow on Monday the 2nd of April. We stayed in the 'Metropolitan' Hotel on 51st and Lexington Avenue. This was fairly close to Central Park, so I ran there and completed at least one loop around each morning.

CHRONIC ACHILLES PROBLEMS

On the 4th morning, in Central Park, I ran several laps of the reservoir, so I was running for 1-46-28. During this run, my left Achilles tendon became very painful and I had to stop several times to try stretching my calf muscle. I noted in my training diary: *This is a very worrying occurrence.* Next day I wrote in my diary: *'Man proposes, but God disposes'. My training plan cannot now be implemented, as I had assumed it would be and my racing plans may also 'go by the board'. My left Achilles is swollen and I have difficulty walking.*

Running was not possible for the next 6 days, but it did not stop us continuing our sightseeing, including the 'Twin Towers'. Because the weather was favourable we were allowed out onto the roof to appreciate the magnificent views. Every evening we used the Subway system to visit Broadway and see a different show each night.

Adrian and Linda Stott and their family were staying, with members of the Sri Chinmoy group, in the district of 'Queens' during our stay in New York. Sri Chinmoy, via Adrian, invited us to visit him in Queens at the tennis courts. We had a lovely day there with Adrian Stott and family, Chanakya and Sri Chinmoy. Sri Chinmoy lifted Izzy, Anna and me, physically and spiritually, using a lifting frame.

My left Achilles injury became chronic and eventually the tendon ruptured, which required an operation to join the ends together again. This was carried out on the 1st of June; followed by several weeks with my leg in a cast. This was removed on the 23rd of July and I had to carry out exercises; start cycling to and from work; and finally was able to start jogging again on the 23rd of September, with a jog to the lighthouse and back in 34-55. My left Achilles tendon felt OK, but my quads and hamstrings were painful. In the following week I repeated this jog every morning and cycled to and from work on Monday through to Friday.

Because I had been chosen to be the Road Runners Club (RRC) President I felt that I should attend the London to Brighton race. Therefore, on Friday afternoon, the 5th of October 2001, I caught a flight to London. In the evening I attended the London to Brighton pre-race party, for overseas competitors at Hilary Walker's home. Roddy Fisher, the RRC secretary, with whom I was to stay over the weekend, drove me to his house in Eton School, where he was a teacher and housemaster. On Saturday morning, while Roddy donned his gown and headed off to teach a class, I walked about 6 miles in Eton and Windsor and also in Windsor Great Park.

On Sunday I jogged only the first 10 miles, as planned, of the course in some very heavy rain showers, which soaked us and caused the gutters to rapidly fill with running water. By the top of Ditchling Beacon the wind almost became a gale and with the rain made conditions very difficult. Some scaffolding was blown down, causing the road along the seafront to be closed.

By mid October I felt confident enough to resume running one way to work by my old railway line 9 miles course and get a lift home after work. I repeated this on the remaining workdays and ran on the golf course and beach at the weekend to accumulate 47 miles for the week, with no adverse reaction from my repaired Achilles tendon.

Over the following weeks I increased the distance of my runs to work and then ran to and from work, alternated with days of a four and a half miles run on the golf course and beach before cycling to and from work. Weekend runs on Saturdays and Sundays were extended to 10 miles. **By the end of November, I had reached 100 miles for the week and all was well.**

My first attempt at a race was on Sunday the 9th of December, in the R.A.F. Lossiemouth 10 miles 'Turkey Trot'. I found the pace required very hard to maintain, so I tried to settle at 7 minutes per mile pace. Mike McCulloch held back to run with me and we finished together in 70-59 in 38th and 39th places. During the remainder of December weekend runs were between fifteen and seventeen miles at a steady pace with Mike McCulloch.

My total training and racing mileage for 2001 was greatly reduced because of my left Achilles tendon rupture to 2753 miles, which was an average of 53 miles per week

2002

In January 2002, I began increasing my mileage again, planning to get fit for the Barry track 40 in early march. I was invited to the inaugural British Athletics Federation (BAF) ultra distance squad weekend meeting at St Mary's College in Twickenham on the 19th and 20th of January. On Saturday the 19th at Aberdeen airport, I met Ronnie Maughan, who was also going on the 08:25 flight to London to give a presentation at the ultra distance squad meeting.

Ron and I shared a taxi to St Mary's College and after the first session, in the afternoon we went for a short run to Bushy Park. I participated in a Paarlauf over 400 meters, with Dennis Walmsley, Ian

Anderson, Danielle Sanderson, Adrian Stott and Hilary Walker. This was rather hard, but quite good fun. I completed 7 X 400 metres.

I shared a room in the 'Park Hotel' in Twickenham with Adrian Stott, and on Sunday we ran at 06:45 to Regent's Park where we ran round the perimeter plus a bit extra before returning, with a running time of 2-23-39. On the agenda item of electing a coach for the 'Ultra Distance squad', someone proposed Stephen Moore, while Adrian and William Sichel proposed and seconded me. Alan Storey steered the resulting vote in favour of Stephen, which suited me, because I would not have the time to devote to make a success of this responsible position.

My first race of 2002 was on Sunday the 17th of February, was the RAF Kinloss to RAF Lossiemouth half marathon. After about 30 seconds I had difficulty running because my heart began fibrillating and consequently felt very weak. Following 3 miles of easy running my heart rhythm normalised and I began to increase my pace. I was surprised to learn that I was first over 55, despite my poor time of 1-31-22.

A DIFFICULT BARRY 40

I planned to run in the 'Barry 40' on the 3rd of March. On Friday the 1st of March, after work I drove to Banff to pick up Alan Reid and continued to Edinburgh, to stay overnight with Adrian and Linda Stott. On Saturday, Adrian, Alan and I departed in Adrian's car for Cardiff, where Jeff Rees picked up Alan and me at Pontyclun rail station. At Jeff and Sharon's, we had an excellent meal and relaxed for the remainder of the evening.

On race morning the weather was good with a temperature of 9°C and very little wind. I wore my Reebok 3D racers. The early pace was quite slow and I felt fine, but once Alan had made a move a few people got going and I began to struggle with the pace. I passed 10 miles in 68-30. My right heel callus began to hurt and I became anxious that I might damage my heel again. I think the discomfort was promoted by the rise in temperature caused by the synthetic material in my socks (85% coolmax, 10% polyamide, and 5% Lycra). I stopped to change to Mizuno 'Sonic racers', which I had been training in for weeks and they appeared to help initially.

I was forced to make a 'pit stop' since I had eaten too much, too late, the previous evening. My right heel pain became worse, so to alleviate this I went into the changing rooms and put 'Spenco' adhesive knit over my heel. By then I had lost a lot of enthusiasm but decided to plod on. I felt quite drained and had no energy to run faster than what felt like a jog. Perhaps I had been training too hard, or perhaps, because of my diabetes I was unable to store enough glycogen any more. Forty miles is a very long way when one is not running well, so I was glad to finish in 5-31-50 in 16th. Adrian finished in 5-37-03 in 19th and Alan had to drop out after 75 laps because he was not fully recovered from his recent injury.

We set off for home at 5 pm and arrived at Adrian's in Edinburgh at 00:50. I drove home via Banff to drop Alan off and arrived home at 04:50, which allowed me a couple of hours in bed before heading off to work. On my drive through Aberdeen I triggered a 30 mph, speed camera in Bucksburn, on a section of road where the speed limit drops from 40 mph to 30 mph, before returning to 40 mph. This occurred at about 03:40, when the streets were deserted, so I pointed this out when I wrote appealing against my fine. This of course was not taken into consideration, so I decided to pay the £60 fine and Alan insisted on paying half when he found out.

Two weeks later, the 17th of March, in the Inverness half marathon and, despite a cautious start, I began to experience an irregular heartbeat, which became worse as I tried to increase my pace. This settled down, but my pace deteriorated as the race progressed. I experienced a severe pain in my right heel under the callus. I passed 10 miles in 69-32, running awkwardly as I was favouring my right heel. I finished 134th and third V55 in 1-32-06, which was quite disappointing. I wrote in my diary; *perhaps I am still training too hard. My endurance seems to be suspect, as I did not pass many people after halfway as I normally can. At present the means do not justify the ends.*

The following morning, I was surprised to see that my weight had dropped to 9 stones and 4 pounds. I was aiming to have a reasonable run in the National 100Km championships on the 7th of April, and therefore continued with high mileage, including 2 effort sessions each week and a 50Km run on Sundays over my Monaughty course.

A week before the 100Km in the Moray Road Runners 10Km road race I felt weak, but after a mile I began to run more forcibly and finished 53rd in 43-30. I was probably tired from my 50Km Monaughty course run the previous day.

For several weeks I had been experiencing stomach pains and a taste of blood coming up. On the 5th of April I attended Dr Gray's Hospital for a stomach investigation, upper GI Endoscopy. The Doctor carrying out the procedure said that there was no sign of an ulcer in my stomach, but a biopsy sample was taken for analysis.

Later that day, Friday, I drove to Banff to pick up Alan Reid and continued down to Edinburgh, to stay overnight with Adrian and Linda Stott.

100 KM NIGHTMARE

The following morning, Adrian, Alan and I drove to Moreton-le-Marsh, where the National 100Km championships were to be held on Sunday. We continued to the National Fire Service Training College and booked into our accommodation there.

On race day, there was still a strong cold wind blowing. The course was 25 laps of 4Km around an old airfield, which was now used for various fire training exercises, and parts had a strange post-apocalyptic feel as we ran past burnt-out buildings and vehicles.

Soon after the second lap I began to feel 'washed out' and lacked strength, but decided to keep going in the hope that I would feel better later. My heart was palpitating and I had tightness across the top of my stomach, like my liver was a solid lump. In addition, I was breathless and wheezing. By half way my Asics 'Bordin Racers' were hurting my feet badly and I stopped to change my shoes and added some blister protection.

My feet hurt really badly again, so I stopped again and changed into my Asics 'Magic Racers', which were okay for some time, but I had to make another stop to put more protection on my feet. I could only manage 2 more laps before my feet became quite uncomfortable again. I was alarmed that the event was turning into a complete nightmare for me. I probably should have abandoned the struggle, but stubbornly carried on. I stopped again to put on 'comspeed' blister protection pads and put on 2 pairs of fresh socks. This appeared to help for a while, but once Adrian had finished I stopped and borrowed his Asics DS trainers to complete the final laps. I eventually finished in 11-12-15. The 'Red Bull' drink that I had been taking periodically in addition to my usual 10% solution carbohydrate drinks did not seem to have any beneficial effect.

It was good to see Alan Reid get the bronze medal after a brave front run for the first half. Later I wrote in my diary: *There must be something wrong with my health at the moment, because I had no strength, my heart was palpitating and I felt utterly exhausted.*

Dennis Walmsley overtook Alan at 70Km to win in 7-07-39, from Chris Finill in 7-23-57 and Alan Reid finished 3rd in 7-36-09. Sharon Gayter was the first lady, 7th overall in 8-53-17 and Adrian Stott finished 9th in 9-23-47.

The following Thursday because of my health concerns I decided to have blood tests done to check for any abnormalities/deficiencies.

Following 7 years of excellent sponsorship, United Distillers said that after the Bell's Speyside way race in 2000, they would not be continuing their sponsorship. The 2001 race was cancelled because of the 'Foot and Mouth' restrictions. The 8th edition of the race was the first with our new sponsor, 'Neways', who made a range of health and personal care products.

On Saturday, 12th of April, I marked the 'Speyside Way 50Km' race route with Izzy. On race day morning I put out the tables food, cups and water for the feed stations, then drove John McGrath, with my bike in the back of the Volvo, up to the start at Ballindalloch. John was to cycle behind the last runner and report any problems. Simon Pride, the 4 times winner of this race, and course record holder with a time of 2-59-18, asked if he could start 10 minutes after the official start to make his race more interesting. I agreed and arranged this with the timekeepers The former world 100Km champion used this 'Hares and Hound' approach to ensure that he would not have such a lonely run as in some previous years as he worked through the field of 60 runners.

The race went well which was, as always, a big relief. Simon Pride won for the fifth time in 3-07-27 from Ian Lewis, 3-24-43 and Charlie Noble, who almost broke my M50 course record with 3-26-44, only 5 seconds ahead of fellow M50 runner, James Watson. Kate Jenkins was first Lady in 13th in 3-58-48.

I had entered the **Lochaber Marathon** and on Sunday the 28th of April I met Alan Reid, Gail, their daughter Alana, Charlie Noble and his wife Dot, at Craigellachie. I got a lift with them to Fort William as arranged. Rain began falling well before Spean Bridge, which made conditions rather unpleasant by the start of the marathon.

I made a reasonable start, but soon began to struggle with he pace, but by Corpach I began to settle and ran with Dave Green for some time, but by 10 miles I was unable to maintain that pace and began drifting back. My time at the turn was 1-38-21. I stopped for a pee and was surprised how dark coloured my urine was, almost haemoglobin urine. This was despite drinking 200mL of 10% solution of Leppin every 3 miles or so. I eventually finished in 3-31-08 and was surprised to learn that I was 2nd over 55, behind Alexander Nicol, who had finished in 3-00-02. Charlie Noble was first over 50. Alan Reid did not feel good and jogged the 2nd half to finish in 3-16-20.

The results of my blood tests indicated that my kidneys, thyroid function, Vitamin B12 and iron levels were all OK. My liver function was not satisfactory, so my GP requested an ultrasound scan and wondered if I was having a reaction to the Glislazide tablets. He wanted me to have two more blood tests done, one for hepatitis studies and another to check my liver function again. I stopped taking Glislazide tablets that evening and would avoid alcohol.

SOME IMPROVEMENT

Just over a week later, on Sunday the 12th of May I left home at 05:45 and drove to Glenrothes for the **Scottish 50Km championships** and arrived in plenty of time for the 10:00 start. I started cautiously and then picked my pace up to run with Peter Baxter for nine and a half of the 14 laps. On the 10th lap I began to struggle, so Peter pulled away and Carol Cadger caught and passed me on lap 11. I passed the marathon in 3-24-40, which was 6-28 faster than my Lochaber effort. I felt a good deal better than in my last two long races, which was encouraging. I finished 11th in 4-05-49, first over 55 and 3rd over 50. Terry Mitchell won in 3-16-18, from Ian Anderson 3-16-39 and Jim McLaughlin, 3-23-58. There were 24 finishers. I had a good massage from Peter Baxter after the run.

In the 'Follow the Herring' 20Km road race from Portsoy on the 13th of June, I ran quite well up to 10Km and then began to fade. I finished 25th of the 93 finishers in 1-25-35, which was 5-21 slower than the last time I ran, in 2000. Alan Reid won in 70-12, from Charlie Noble, 72-50 and D Whyte, 74-02.

On the 3rd of July Izzy and I caught a flight to Gatwick on the first stage of our holiday in Canada. The hotel near the airport, where we stayed overnight, was actually on the road that I had run on during London to Brighton races.

The following morning, we caught a flight to Calgary, but Izzy's suitcase did not arrive off the plane. Reverend Aldeen MacKay, Izzy's cousin met us and drove us to her home in Fort Macleod, which is at an altitude of 3,300 feet and not too far from the foothills of the Rocky Mountains. The 'Fort', constructed entirely of wood housed the museum of the North-West Mounted Police.

We enjoyed the cloudless sky and the surprisingly high temperature of 30°C, but were not prepared for the hordes of mosquitoes that attacked you as soon as you stepped out of the house or car.

Aldeen drove us around, visiting: Waterton Lakes National Park, 'Crowsnest Pass', 'Frank Slide', 'Head smashed in Buffalo jump', Lethbridge, 'Indian Battle Park' and 'Fort Whoop-up'.

As the 'Calgary Stampede' was taking place during our visit Aldeen drove us up to Calgary, by the 'Cowboy Trail' through the very scenic foothills of the Alberta Rocky Mountains, reaching 7000 feet at its highest point. We spent an interesting day at the 'Stampede'.

We continued north to Drumheller, in the 'Bad lands', a region, rich in fossil deposits and home to the huge, Royal Tyrrell Museum with dozens of dinosaur skeletons, fossils and mammals.

On returning to Calgary we travelled through the spectacular, Rocky Mountains by 'Greyhound' Bus, to Kelowna in British Colombia to visit Izzy's cousin Hunt McKay, his wife Joan and their family.

On the 22nd of July we went to stay with Reg and Chloe Anderson. Chloe and Izzy were friends from their secondary school days at Inverness Royal Academy. We shared a log cabin, by the Athabasca River, near Jasper, for three days. We toured around from this base in Jasper National Park, enjoying the stunning mountain scenery thermal pools and sighting black bears.

Further visits were to: Columbia Icefield, the Athabasca glacier, Banff, spectacular Lake Louise and Moraine Lake.

On Monday the 29 of July we travelled by bus to Edmonton, to visit Phil and Cheryl Cruickshank. Phil was a running pal from Elgin, who emigrated to Canada, married Cheryl and settled in Edmonton. It was good to catch up with them and their two daughters. They showed us around Edmonton, including the 'West Edmonton Mall'.

We returned to Calgary on the 31st of July, to stay a further three days with Chloe and Reg before returning to the UK and home on the 4th of August. We had certainly packed a lot into our Canadian adventure. My morning runs were a minimum of one hour during this holiday.

I resumed my 'home' training schedule, which soon involved running to and from work again and 3 effort sessions in the week. On Sunday the 1st of September I participated in the 21st edition of the **Macallan Moray Marathon**. I felt tired from the start, probably due to enthusiastic running during the previous 3 weeks. By Hopeman my feet were hurting, particularly under my right heel callus, so I stopped at our home and changed from my Reebok 3D racers to my Asics DS racers. This was a big help and I was able to run in comfort to the finish in 28th, in 3-27-31. Moray Road Runners, with Graham Harcus from Orkney, Dave Green and I won the team event.

On Friday, 4th October, Izzy and I travelled to London and on to the Richmond Hill Hotel, where we booked in and prepared for the RRC 50th Anniversary dinner, organised by John Foden. We were seated with Roddy and Gina Fisher, Ted Corbitt and John Foden and we had an enjoyable evening once my President's speech was delivered. I did not know most of the members present, but it was good to meet James Zarie and Leslie Watson there.

On Saturday, we travelled into London and booked into the 'Mad Hatter's Hotel', near the changing accommodation for the start of London to Brighton race. Andy Farquharson joined us for dinner and we sampled Fuller's cask-conditioned 'London Pride', which was excellent.

SOLDIERING ON IN THE BRIGHTON

On Sunday John Foden drove us to the start along with Andy Farquharson. I set off steadily but, on the climb onto Farthing Down, realised that I was already tired. My breathing seemed to be restricted by my stomach/liver, which felt tight but I expected to run more freely later.

At the drinks stations at 20 miles and 30 miles my drinks were missing, which was a nuisance. John Foden and Izzy appeared between 30 and 35 miles, so I took Dioralite and a squeezy from Izzy. As the route undulated onwards, I found some of the climbs quite challenging. I had to make a toilet stop around 40 miles, so I still had not got my pre-race eating sorted yet. On Ditchling Beacon I had to walk up and at the refreshment station at the top I poured water over both my shoes to try to reduce the pain in my feet, which worked quite well. I did not like the long downhill into Brighton on painful legs. In the last 50 metres to the 'new' finish, no longer on the seafront, I had to increase my pace to avoid being overtaken by Margaret Swithenby the second lady.

I was very glad to finish and to learn that **I was first over 55 in 23rd place in 8-12-20**, over 2 hours behind the winner. My 50 miles time was 7-30-40. The volume of traffic on some parts of the route worried Izzy and I agreed that the traffic does spoil parts of the race experience.

Brian Hennessey of Crawley AC won in 6-00-57, from Greg Dell, 6-25-06 and Ian Anderson, 6-25-36; there were 115 starters and 102 finishers. The awards ceremony went well. Chris, the Crawley team manager, gave Izzy and me a lift to Gatwick airport, for our 20:00 flight to Inverness.

I had agreed some time before to participate in the 100 miles track race on Crystal Palace track, organised by John Foden with the help of the RRC and scheduled for Sunday, the 20th of October. This race was to be an attempt to break my world best performance (world record) time of 11-30-51, which was established in 1977 during a 24-hour race on the Crystal Palace track. As an incentive a prize of £5000 was promised to anyone who could break my record, which was an indication of how much has changed in athletics since 1977. Yiannis Kouros of Greece had expressed an interest in competing, but his request for £4000 appearance money surprised John Foden, who told him that there was no chance of this. Valmir Nunes of Brazil also wanted to participate, but arrangements for his flight and accommodation did not come to fruition.

On 19th of October I travelled via Aberdeen, Heathrow, underground and surface trains to Crystal Palace. I met John Foden and Raymond Hutcheson on my way to book into my accommodation at the Lodge. Later I met William Sichel, Pam Storey and Geoff Oliver.

AFTER 25 YEARS, MY 100 MILES WORLD RECORD IS FINALLY BROKEN

The next morning, I made my way to the track, where I met Konstantin Santalov, who gave me a hug. He and another fellow were managing the two Russian runners: Oleg Kharitonov and Denis Zhalybin. In the I.A.U European 100Km Championships in Winschoten on the 14th of September, Denis was runner up with 6-36-19 and Oleg was 3rd in 6-41-16. I knew that they would be making a serious attempt to break my record and win the £5000 put up by William Hill. I would have been grateful to receive the equivalent when I broke Cavin Woodward's record and I am sure Cavin would also have been pleased to receive such a sum, if on offer.

The two Russians sped off, leaving the remaining 12 of us to sort ourselves out. Ian Anderson went next in line followed by William Sichel. I began running at 2 minutes per lap, but after an hour this began to slip by a second or so. I stopped and changed into my Asics LD racers. These were good, and I felt comfortable. Mark Pickard had my drinks and food schedule and was seconding: me, Walter Hill and Andy Farquharson.

By 4 hours I had begun to struggle, mainly because I had not recovered from the 'Brighton', two weeks before, so my legs would not function very well. My pace dropped as my stride length became restricted. I had various leg pains, so took two Dihydrocodine tablets after 4 hours and at 4-hour intervals, but these did not appear to make any difference. Ian Anderson, Hilary Walker, Sharon Gayter and John Lucas withdrew. By 10 hours I began to walk and I had decided to walk until the cut-off time. The race doctor asked me to withdraw, which I agreed to do at 12 hours, having completed 245 laps (60 miles and 1574 yards).

Zhalybin led for most of the race, passing 50 miles in 5-35-04, 100Km in 6-58-36 and 150Km in 10-34-30, which broke my record by 2-12 and he was about 4 laps ahead of Kharitonov at this point. As the end neared Kharitonov increased his pace to six-minute miling, to catch and pass Zhalybin to reach 100 miles in 11-28-03, which was 2-48 inside my record. Zhalybin finished in 11-29-32. I witnessed the two Russians break my record and stopped my walk to congratulate them. William Sichel was 3rd in 15-17-47 and Walter Hill 4th in 16-34-28.

John Foden, in his report of the race wrote among his personal comments: *'From the time William Hill offered their inducement to beat Don's world record I have been worried that I was organizing something to break it, not celebrate its quarter century and honour him. Loyalty is the human characteristic most valued in the Services'.*

Three weeks later I attended the 'Ultra Distance squad' weekend meeting having driven down to Edinburgh to stay overnight with Adrian and Linda Stott on Friday evening. On Saturday morning, 9th November, Adrian drove us down to Penrith, where we met Steven Moore who drove us in his Range Rover to Sutton Coldfield and our accommodation for the weekend. I was pleased to be part of the squad, but felt that my performances barely justified inclusion.

On 8th of December, in the 'Turkey Trot', 10 miles road race from RAF Lossiemouth my usual heart fibrillation began and I had to slow. Once my heart rhythm settled I could increase my pace and finished in 69-24, which was 1-35 faster than last year. On totalling my training and racing mileage for the year 2002, I found that I had accumulated 5626 miles, which is an average of 108 miles per week. It had been a hard year, but at least I had struggled on and done my best in difficult circumstances.

2003

I was invited to participate in the 'Ultra Distance Squad' weekend at Teddington on the 1st of February. I was due to catch the 08:25 flight to Heathrow, but because of overnight snow at Heathrow this flight was cancelled. I should have gone home, but I decided to persist and I was put on standby for the 16:25 flight. I was accepted on this flight and on arrival I caught a bus to Teddington and walked to the 'Park Hotel'. I had arrived in time to join the Ultra Distance Squad members for dinner. It had been a frustrating day and I was glad to be there at last.

On Sunday morning I overslept and missed the start of the training session. I ran down to Bushy Park and joined in, just missing the last long effort. I found it hard to keep up on the following steady run and gradually fell behind. The flight back to Aberdeen was uneventful.

In the RAF Kinloss to RAF Lossiemouth half marathon, on the 16th of February, after the start my heart began fibrillating, so I had to slow as I became breathless and my legs became tired and heavy due to lack of oxygen. After about 4 miles I began to feel better and ran more freely and finished 83rd and third V55 in 1-32-59, which was 1-37 slower than last year. Simon Pride won in 1-11-25, from Frankie Barton, 1-11-51 and Brian Forman, 1-11-57. There were 214 starters and 180 finishers.

On Thursday prior to the 'Barry 40' race, after work I drove down to Glasgow, where Sye Murray and I had been booked into the Holiday Inn, in preparation for Scottish Qualifications Authority (SQA) meeting next day.

After the meeting I drove to Keswick, went to the 'Theatre on the Lake' to meet Steven and Cath Moore as arranged and stay overnight with them.

On Saturday morning, after Steven had run up 'Cat Bells' and back, he and I set off for Penrith, where I left my car in the 'Lakes Hotel' car park. I then joined Steven as he drove to South Wales, via Lytham St Anne's to visit his mother and Cath's Dad. Steve dropped me at PenCoed rail station where I got a train to Bridgend. Sharon Rees met me there along with William Sichel. At Sharon and Jeff's home, I was made most welcome again.

BARRY FORTY MILES

From the start I felt tired and had a stop after two hours to change my shoes, as my right heel callus was hurting. My pace gradually deteriorated, but I kept plodding on. eventually finishing 19th in

5-38-03 and second V55, a lap and a half behind first V55, Gary Hyatt (5-34-40). Brian Hennessey won in 4-13-10, from Chris Finill, first V40, in 4-19-49 and Stephen Pope, 4-41-00, with William Sichel, first V45 close behind in 4-41-40. Samantha Bertherik was the first lady, finishing 12th in 5-17-50. 28 of the 34 starters completed 40 miles.

After the presentations Steven and I set off and arrived back in Preston at 23:00. Steven waited until I had the engine of my car running and the car de-iced. I arrived home at 04:15, so I was pleased to get a couple of hours sleep before setting off for work.

The following Saturday, 9th March, after a week of no running, I ran in the Scottish Veterans cross-country championships in Forres. I managed to complete the 3-lap course around and over Cluny Hill and Grant Park. The local organization by Forres Harriers was excellent and the sun was shining. I finished 99th of the 111 finishers and 11th in the V55 category. *It was quite frustrating being beaten by so many that I used to be able to finish ahead of in races.*

A week later I participated in the Inverness half marathon and ran very poorly feeling completely drained after about 7 miles. My quads were painful and my legs felt like they were being restricted. I finished 266th of 931 finishers, in 1-36-23, which made me 14th V55. I wrote in my diary: *This experience confirms to me that I have over-trained and that I need to take a rest. I decided to alter my training schedule, and to cut back training volume, by introducing cycling days, which should aid recovery.*

Further thoughts from my diary were: *I think that I should have 'key sessions' such as a couple of long runs and two effort sessions each week. The rest of the days could be cycling.*

On the following Sunday I ran in the Moray Road Runners 10Km road race and finished 62nd of 157 finishers in 43-29. There was a fairly strong wind blowing fine sand off the fields, which made conditions quite unpleasant on one section of the course.

The following Wednesday, the 9th of April, I was reassured to learn that all the tests done on my latest blood samples were satisfactory. This meant that I could not link my poor running form to some blood disorder and would have to consider other reasons.

I did not feel fit enough to run in the 'Neways Speyside Way' 50Km race on Sunday the 14th of April. We had 88 starters and 84 finishers. Simon Pride again started 10 minutes after the runners set off and won again in 3-11-56, from Nigel Holl, 3-30-39 and John Kennedy, 3-31-49. First lady was Andrea Devine from New Zealand in 11th place overall in 3-48-39.

I experienced an unusual injury the following Sunday as I rose at 05:15 to get ready for my 50Km Monaughty run. I had put on my slippers and walked to the bathroom and, as I entered, I felt a stab under the instep of my left foot, so I thought that there must be a thorn in my slipper. When I removed the slipper to investigate I could see nothing, but I noticed a wasp crawling over the carpet after falling out of my slipper. My foot began to hurt quite badly so I returned to bed as running would not be possible and by mid-day my foot was still aching and accompanied by a burning sensation around the sting region. I resumed running the following morning.

On Sunday the 27th of April John McGregor drove us to Fort William for the 20th edition of the **Lochaber Marathon**. I felt quite good early in the race and ran at 7-minutes per mile up to 10 miles and reached the turn in 1-33-something. By 16 miles I was beginning to struggle and the first woman came past, followed by a group of 3 including Adrian Stott's daughter Elizabeth. I was quite satisfied with my time of 3-15-41, which was 15-27 faster than last year, but I knew that I could do better. John Duffy of Shettleston won in 2-41-22, from Jason Smith, unattached, 2-43-22 and Italian tourist Valentino Caravaggio, 2-45-03. Kate Jenkins, Carnethey was first lady in 3-05-44 ahead of Dhavala (Elizabeth) Stott, Sri Chinmoy AC, 3-08-48 and Denise Muir, 3-12-00.

Colin Youngson and Martin Walsh organised a JOGLE reunion for Saturday the 3rd of May in the Atholl Hotel, Aberdeen. Izzy and I drove to Aberdeen and to Martin Walsh and Freda's, where we were to stay the night after the reunion. The reunion was very well attended, so it was a pleasure to meet so many team members and drivers again and recall our 'adventures'. Peter and Rita Duffy were the furthest travelled, having come up from Oldham to be present. The event was very successful and enjoyable and a credit to the effort that Colin and Martin had put in to make it happen.

I had entered the **Scottish 50Km championships**, scheduled for the following week, so early on Sunday, race day, I drove to Banff, to pick up Alan Reid. He had gone to his street cleaning work at 04:30 to complete his 2 hours stint.

We arrived at the Sports Centre in Glenrothes in good time for the 10:00 start. At the beginning I felt heavy and I was soon dropping back, but after a couple of the 14 laps I began to settle down. On about lap 10 I had a stop to answer a 'call of nature' and I suppose that this cost me a minute or so. *I decided that I should not eat breakfast before an ultra race.*

I passed the marathon distance in 3-26-55, which was rather disappointing and my time at 30 miles was 3-59-50. I finished 14th of 31 finishers, in 4-09-02, which was 2-50 slower than the previous year. I felt that my strength was returning and I was catching runners towards the end. My left knee gave a few problems on lap 12 and I almost fell when my right knee tweaked in sympathy. I was 5th over 50. Dennis Walmsley won in 3-08-37, from Matthew Lynas 3-13-37, and Clyde Marwick 3-19-08.

On Saturday the 24th of May I finished my preparation for the **Apeldoorn 24-hour race** the following weekend by running my Monaughty, 50Km course in 4-15-07. I decided to try having the following 5 days as non-running days to see if this would enhance my performance in Apeldoorn.

On Thursday the 29th of May, I caught a bus to Aberdeen airport, caught a flight to Amsterdam and travelled to Apeldoorn by train. I was surprised that the temperature there was 29°C. I walked to the park where the 24-hour race was to be held next day. I met Sharon and Bill Gayter and Roy Bainbridge and his wife there, already 'set up'. I pitched my specially purchased one-man tent near theirs and settled down. Jim Taylor arrived soon after and then Ian Sutter along with his wife and two boys. Ian was a race walker, who had achieved 120 miles in 24 hours by walking and hoped to achieve the 220Km qualifying distance for GB team selection by adding running to his walking. I had difficulty sleeping because of the oppressive heat.

On Friday morning, the sun shone from a cloudless sky and there was no cooling breeze. By 2pm, when the race started the air temperature was 29°C. The boot shaped 1.65186 Km lap was beautifully smooth black asphalt, so as black surfaces are the best absorbers and radiators of heat, the surface temperature must have been well above ambient temperature. Bill Gayter would be too busy looking after Sharon, so he could not look after my drinks requirements. Ian Sutter's wife, and their sons, agreed to give me my drinks.

I started cautiously but I was soon drenched in sweat, which, because of the high relative humidity, was not evaporating to provide a cooling effect. Within a couple of hours my feet, particularly my right one, were burning. I was wearing Asics 'Tiger Paw' shoes, which I had raced 50Km in and done several 50Km, 4-hour runs in before with no problems. I wondered if the socks were causing extra friction or the Spenco tape on my right heel was causing trouble, but I suspect that it was just due to the high temperature of the black surface.

I stopped and changed into my old LD racers, which felt good for a while as they had better cushioning. After some time, they also caused my right heel to become extremely painful under the callus. I stopped again and made a pad with a hole in it for the callus, from some foam padding. I taped this to my right heel and put another piece of foam inside the heel of my right shoe. I tried this arrangement and it seemed to work fairly well initially, but the heel pain returned, as bad as ever. I decided that I could not continue jogging and began walking.

By this time Ian Sutter had retired, so I was responsible for my own refreshments, apart from what the organizers provided. Sharon Gayter also pulled out.

I decided to stop and take my shoes and socks off to let my heel and feet cool down to see if they would recover somewhat. I did this and crawled into my sleeping bag and fell fast asleep for nearly 6 hours. I put my LD racers on again and resumed the event and my right heel felt a bit easier. I did my first pee since the start and discovered that I was well on the way to dehydration, because my urine was quite dark. Jim Taylor was still going, but Ramona Thevenet-Smith had given up. Helga Backhaus arrived as promised. She was recovering from a serious injury, but had won this race on 6 previous occasions.

I struggled on, jogging and walking in the rising temperature, and by then my right heel and feet were burning again. I was very glad to hear the finishing shot. I had completed 79 laps and about 200 metres, which I found out was 130.9329Km. Etienne Van Acker, a M50, veteran from Belgium was first with an excellent 253.021Km, followed by Luciano Prado Dos Santos, from Brazil, 229.76Km and Jan Anderson, of Denmark with a national record of 227.816Km. Irina Reutovich from Russia was first lady in 4th place overall with 220.654Km.

Jim and I caught a train to Amsterdam airport as I felt quite nauseous and thought that I might vomit at any time. I caught the 8pm flight to Aberdeen, still in my shell suit and caught the Inverness bus and Izzy met me at Elgin. As she drove me home I realised that I had lost my bottom dentures. I had removed then on the bus journey, in preparation for an imminent vomit into a sick bag, but this did not happen, so I kept them in my shell suit jacket pocket for the next occasion I felt a vomit coming on. They must have slipped out of my pocket onto the seat without me noticing.

The following day I jogged a lap of the Rotary/Bells Marafun, the warm-up lap, with Simon Pride to lead the participants around. On Monday I cycled to and from work and felt frustrated that my quads felt good, but my feet and right heel hurt and I was still partly dehydrated. I telephoned the bus company to report the loss of my lower dentures, but they had not received them and they thought that they were unlikely to be handed in. I made an appointment with my Dentist, Tim Griffiths to arrange to have a replacement made. Until they were ready I had to persevere, delivering my lectures with a modified voice. I did not run for the following week and a half.

On the 9th of June, David Fraser, head podiatrist at Dr Gray's Hospital, removed some hard skin from the callus under my right heel and removed a corn from its centre, so it felt much easier after his treatment. I should have had this done before attempting the 24-hour run.

Izzy and I had arranged to visit Mick Francis and Val in Southwest Australia, near Perth, exchanging a Scottish summer for an Australian winter. During the next four weeks, amongst other things, we explored Fremantle; visited 'wineries' and small breweries, saw humpback whales. With our hired car we drove north visiting: Cervanties, Geraldton, Nambung National Park, Kalbarri Gorges, Shark Bay, Monkey Mia and Carnarvon.

A MARATHON IN AUSTRALIA

I ran with Mick quite a lot and also did some training on our travels. On Sunday the 6th of July 2003, I ran in the 25th edition of the **Perth Marathon**, on my 59th birthday and our 20th wedding anniversary. The race began at 07:30, just as it became light enough to see and the flat course used cycle paths in Parks and along the shoreline of the Swan River estuary. I was fortunate to be able to tuck in with a group at about 10 miles. We passed the half way in 90-38 and after the turn I had great difficulty making my legs work. At about 16 miles I began to catch a few, but more were passing me. I was glad to finish 62nd in 3-26-21, which gave me 6th in the V55 category. I had been surprised to see Danny Bird from Inverness Harriers, also on holiday, who finished first in his veteran category and 5th overall in 2-54-25. S. Burt won in 2-42-21, from C. Francis, 2-47-53 and J. Albrecht, 2-49-56. Mick was 7th in 2-55-11. There were 245 finishers. There was quite a party following the race in the clubhouse as friends and finishers made use of the bar facilities. After the presentations, Val and Mick drove us down to their home near Dunsborough, stopping off at Mandurah for 'Wedges and fish', a bit like fish and chips.

Home in Lossiemouth by the 29th of July, I eased back into my training schedule with tried and tested sessions. Following 4 weeks of good training, I ran in the 22nd edition of the **Macallan**

Moray Marathon, on 31st August. I joined the group containing: John McGregor, Gordon Cowie and Dave Green. My right heel began to hurt under my callus, which concerned me, so I stopped at the next refreshment station and poured a cup of water down the edge of the heel of my right shoe to cool my heel. I asked Anna to get my DS racer shoes ready for changing into when I reached our house. With 6 miles remaining I began to move better and passed quite a few before finishing 52nd in 3-32-27. Jamie Reid of Cambuslang won and Kate Jenkins was first lady.

I noted in my diary: *Possibly not taking breakfast was now a bad move, but I had thought that I had enough stored glycogen from the previous day. Perhaps being a Type 2 Diabetic caused problems with carbohydrate metabolism and glycogen storage. I drank about 300mL of 10% concentration 'Boots' carbohydrate / electrolyte mixture before the start. I did seem to benefit from the small portion of banana. However, I think the main reason for my poor run was that I was not fully recovering from the high volume of training that I had completed over the previous month.* **I will have to take care not to over-train again.**

I decided to try having a rest day on Tuesdays of each week, to counteract my tendency to over-train. On these days I would cycle to and from work in 'Moray College', Elgin.

My next race was to be a month later near Verona, so on Friday the 26th of September, Izzy and I rose at 03:00 to get ready for our flight at 07:00 from Inverness airport to Gatwick.

CELEBRATION IN VERONA OF MY 100KM TRACK RECORD

At Gatwick we met Malcolm and Marilyn Campbell who were also travelling to Verona for Lupatotissima 2003, the 100Km track race, 'Stars under the stars', **IAU '100Km World Track Trophy, to celebrate the 25th anniversary of my 6-10-20, offering a 1000-euro prize if someone broke my record.** On our flight to Verona the view as the aircraft flew over the Alps was magnificent. At Verona Airport I.A.U vice president, Gerard Stenger and two Italian girls, Erica and Valerie, who were to be our interpreters, met us. They took us in a mini-bus to the City Hotel in San Giovanni Lupatoto on the outskirts of Verona.

Izzy and I caught a bus into Verona and walked into the old city and were very impressed by the character of this city and agreed that we must return some time to explore properly. We returned to the hotel and got ready for the VIP dinner at the Stadium, followed by a 'Gala' celebration in the Astra Theatre, which was excellent. I was presented with a specially made 25th anniversary plate and also a plate from the local running club. Our invitation had come from Stefano Scevaroli, who was the organiser of the race and all the associated events. Once the Gala finished everyone enjoyed wine and a local specialty cake.

After breakfast on Saturday, Izzy and I went for a walk around the shops in the vicinity and bought some presents before returning in time to be taken to the stadium at 12:00. The weather was warm again with the temperature at 24°C.

A 24-hour relay race was underway, having started at 12:00, the ladies' 100Km started at 14:00 and the men's race started one hour later with 28 starters. I felt the pace quite difficult to maintain after a couple of laps, so I had to ease my pace and let the group pull away. Mario Ardemagni and Denis Zhalybin lapped me after only about 6 laps. I felt embarrassed to be running so slowly and in last place and with number one on my vest.

I changed my shoes after about one hour as my left big toe began to hurt badly and further changes were necessary in an attempt to alleviate my right heel callus pain.

Italian, Mario Fattorre, the 2002 World 100Km Champion, won the 50Km race staged in conjunction with the 100Km, in 3-06 and seemed still full of running. Denis Zhalybin from Russia was exhausted by trying to keep up with Mario and staggered to a stop soon afterwards. I pressed on and speeded up a little as I got close to my intended finish at 50Km. My time at 50Km point was 4-17-44, but by the time I knew that I had passed this distance I had run 2 extra laps. I was pleased to be finished. Mario Ardemagni, Italy won the 100Km in 6-41-49, a new National best track performance, from Vladimir Netreba, Russia, 6-48-39 and Igor Tyazhkorob, Russia, 6-49-53. Norimi Sakurai from Japan was first woman in 7-14-06, a new world best performance, beating the previous record set in 1996 by over nine minutes.

We enjoyed a meal in the Marquee by the track at 19:30 and then relaxed, enjoying the band that was playing. Izzy and I even managed a dance, fortified by local wine. We eventually got back to our hotel at 2 am on Sunday.

The electricity supply was cut during Sunday morning and extended over most of Northern Italy for about 3 hours. After breakfast we packed, left our luggage at the hotel and got a lift to the stadium, where we watched the last hour of the 24-hour relay, which was quite exciting. Again the weather was very pleasant for sitting and watching. After lunch in the marquee, the awards ceremony began at about 12:45, but we had to depart before it was completed to catch our flight to Gatwick, where we relaxed until our flight to Inverness.

My next race, the **Sri Chinmoy 24-hour at Tooting Bec track** was scheduled for 3 weeks time. On the Sunday before the race I decided not to train and to have a week of no running as my taper for the 24-hour race. I had not tried such a long taper before, so I was interested to see if this proved beneficial.

On Friday the 10th of October, after work Izzy drove me to Inverness airport, to catch the 17:30 flight to Gatwick. Mark Pickard had agreed to look after me in the race and he was waiting for me at 'Arrivals' as promised. He drove me to his home via the local Indian Take away as arranged. At Mark's home I was introduced to his Dad and Mum, who were 89 and 87 years old respectively. Mark gave up his bed for me in his bedroom, crowded with trophies and running-related materials. It would have been interesting to look at these in more detail.

The next morning, I had 2 soft-boiled eggs with 2 slices of white bread toast along with a cup of tea. I had a quick shower before we departed for Tooting Bec and we arrived there at 11:15 and began to get ready for the race.

GLAD TO WIN, BUT EXHAUSTED

The race got underway at mid-day in brilliant sunshine, with not a cloud to be seen. I wore my Nike Air Streak shoes, but after about 3 hours my right heel under the callus began to feel very hot. I stopped and changed into my old DS racers, which felt much better. However, after some time they also began to cause discomfort in my right heel, so I had to stop and put lubricant on my heels and the ball of my right foot. This lasted for 1.5 hours, so I had to stop to repeat this process. This practice was repeated every one and a half hours throughout the race, which was quite a nuisance. By midnight I was still on my schedule with 74 miles completed, but I began to get quite exhausted and had to jog the straights and walk the bends.

Mark's friend Tony arrived at about 1am and looked after me until 5am, so that Mark could get some sleep. My lead by then was 6 miles and thankfully Garth Peterson in 2nd was as tired as I was and he could not close on me, which was a relief.

I managed to maintain my lead and was very pleased to finish and to have won with a modest 189.126Km, (117 miles and 951 yards). Garth Peterson, finished 2nd with 183.407Km and Sandra Brown was 3rd with 179.842Km. Geoff Oliver finished 6th with 170.585Km, a very good performance for the 70-year old runner and his 100km time of 11-02-02 and 65 miles 1086 yards in 12 hours were M70 World Bests. My intermediate times were: 50 miles 7-39-31, 100 Km 9-57-30 and 100 miles, 19-08-54.

I was quite exhausted afterwards and just sat in the changing rooms, too weary to move and with a dazed expression on my face. Eventually I shuffled to the showers and then dressed. I was extremely tired and felt nauseous, so I was allowed to sit as Tony Smith presented the awards. Just after the presentations, I began to vomit and again, once Mark had found a stopping place, on the way back to

Mark's home. It appears that I was dehydrated, as this was a typical reaction that I have to dehydration when I try to rehydrate. I only had 3 pee stops during the race and I noticed that my urine was quite dark on the first occasion, so I drank more Isostar. On reflection I should take more Dioralite drinks rather than carbohydrate drinks. I wrote in my diary: *I will have to see if I can get my feet problems sorted out. The discomfort becomes quite intense, then when I stop, take my shoes and socks off and massage them, they recover and afterwards there is no permanent damage.*

Mark drove me to Gatwick, where I caught the flight to Inverness, where a delighted Izzy met me.

On the 14th of December, in the RAF Lossiemouth 10 miles 'Turkey Trot' I felt tired from the start and finished 62nd. I wrote in my diary: *I am uncertain about what I should do to improve my pace and endurance.*

This was my last race of 2003 and on totalling my training and racing miles for the year I found that I had accumulated 4130.5 miles, which gave an average of 79 miles per week

2004

On Friday the 6th of February, after work, I drove to Edinburgh airport and caught a flight to East-Midlands airport. Ron Maughan met me there as arranged and drove me to Loughborough University, where the **Ultra Distance Squad weekend** was to be held. Ron was to give a talk on 'Nutrition for Ultras' at the squad meeting next afternoon. Later Ron took me to sample some local beers and have a meal with Susan. William Sichel and I were sharing a room in one of the student's halls.

On Saturday morning, Danielle Sanderson navigated us to the canal, where we ran along the towpath for some way and back. On the way out I got dropped, so I turned when I met them on their return. Lacking strength I fell behind again, well before reaching the University.

The squad meeting was well worthwhile, but I felt that my talk on 'Preparing for an Ultra' could have been better, because I missed some points, as I only used my 'Buzan' diagram as a prompt.

On Sunday morning William and I ran for about 20 minutes as a warm-up for our track session. I felt like I had some weight in my abdomen, restricting my breathing and my legs were dead. The planned track session was: 200m, 400m, 800m, 1600m and down again with only one-minute recovery, was severe. Dennis Walmsley romped through it, but I abandoned this session after the first 400m. I doubted the relevance of this session to 100Km racing, where the aim is to maintain six minute miling pace for as long as possible. Following the track session, we all set out on a steady 10 miles run, but I soon fell behind, so I just did my own run. William and I got a lift to the East-Midlands airport and caught our flights north.

A week later, the 15th February, in the RAF Kinloss to RAF Lossiemouth half marathon I ran steadily with John Diffey. I began to get intestinal pains and realised that I needed to make a pit stop. My time of 96-19 was disappointing.

I had entered for the 'Barry 40' again, but could not face the long drive there and especially the drive back. I decided to take a flight from Edinburgh to Cardiff on Saturday the 6th of March. I caught the 09:05 flight to Cardiff, where Fran Williams met me and drove me to Jeff Rees's new home, which was up the valley from Port Talbot.

On Sunday morning, Jeff and I departed for Barry on a fine morning and I had decided to wear my new Asics 'Tiger Paw' shoes with the old DS insoles and no socks. During the week I had established which toes would get rubbed, so I taped these up and put Spenco adhesive knit over my right heel callus in an effort to protect it.

STRUGGLING AT THE BARRY FORTY MILES

I settled into a good rhythm, but soon began to fade and passed 10 miles in 76 minutes. My legs were dead and I lacked strength. My right heel began to hurt, so some time later I stopped and changed into my older 'Tiger Paw' shoes and put on socks. I eventually finished 17th of the 28 starters in 6-05-29 and 2nd V55. Brian Cole won in 4-08-16, from Herman Mulder, 4-13-50 and Chris Finill (V45) with 4-24-44. Siri Terjensen was first lady, finishing 11th in 5-15-35.

Fran drove me to Cardiff airport, where I caught my flight to Edinburgh and drove home safely.

Following this poor performance, I wrote in my training diary: *I am not sure how to progress from this depressing performance, but on reflection I think that I should try cycling to and from work every second day during the week. This should help strengthen my quads, while providing a respite from running. I should still do long runs on Thursday and Sunday mornings and two effort sessions a week, or one effort session and a hill session. I have to try something different to get some respectable form back.*

The following Sunday I ran in the 20th edition of the Inverness half marathon. I finished 301st out of 896 starters in 1-40-28. My right heel was hurting a lot under the callus despite the padding that I had applied.

Two days later I got a surprise when I took my shoes off after my run to work, when I found blood on the insole of my right shoe by the heel. I checked my right heel and I could see that it had been bleeding from the callus. At the Medical Centre, Christine put a dressing on my heel and arranged for me to have the dressing changed every 2nd day for two weeks.

On Sunday the 4th of April 2004, I resumed running on the golf course and the beach to the lighthouse and back by the golf clubhouse with our Springer Spaniel 'Muffin'. My right heel appeared to be okay on this 31-minute outing, but I was aware of some discomfort.

On Saturday, 10th April, Izzy and I marked the course for the 'Neways Speyside Way' 50Km race. I cycled from Ballindalloch to Craigellachie, the Ben Aigen section and finally the Section from Fochabers, checking the route and fixing markers. Muffin accompanied me on the cycling sections and thoroughly enjoyed the change of location.

On Sunday I delivered the water, food and tables for the refreshment stations on the course. I picked up Debbie Cox in Elgin as arranged and drove to Ballindalloch for race registration. Runners waiting to register and those wanting late entries soon overwhelmed me. We had 98 starters,

My team of helpers were excellent again. One runner, Kris Crowe from Dundee Road Runners missed a direction marker on Ben Aigen and became lost, which gave me a horrible sick feeling as I began to imagine various unfortunate scenarios. His wife was very upset and informed me that my organization 'sucked'. I did not know the meaning of this, but assumed it was derogatory. Thankfully he made it to the finish under his own steam. 94 finished, which was satisfactory. Simon Pride, Metro Aberdeen, won again in an excellent 3-02-15, ahead of Andy Eccles, Wigan Phoenix, 3-24-11, who set a V40 course record. Andy and Nigel Holl, unattached, ran in together for joint 2nd. First lady was Kate Jenkins, Carnethy, 14th in 3-58-23. I finished the majority of the post race tidying up by 01:00 on Monday.

On Wednesday, 21st of April I got the 'all clear' from the nurse, so no further dressing was required on my heel callus. In the following week I ran 4.5 miles on the Golf Course and beach each morning before cycling to work and back.

Before I could get my mileage back up I developed a swollen left knee, which was acutely painful to touch, and running was not possible, so my latest attempted comeback did not last long! Malcolm diagnosed a strained lateral ligament and found the painful point at the lower end of this ligament. He also found that my cruciate ligaments were strained. He worked his magic, and advised not to run for 3 days.

I cautiously increased my running sessions and after 6 weeks I got back to my base level of 100 miles in a week in mid June.

Tom McCook, the president of Birchfield Harriers, telephoned with the sad news that Roy Tilling, one of my regular training pals from my time in Birmingham, had died suddenly. I had a difficult journey down to attend Roy's funeral on 25th June, and stayed with Tom and Carol.

The funeral, at Aston Parish Church, was very well attended, with over 300 people there, and it was an emotional event as I remembered shared times with Roy and Mal Pickering, who sat next to me.

Afterwards it was good to meet old pals from my Birchfield Harriers days at the tea and sandwiches in the Birchfield Harriers clubrooms at the Alexander Stadium, Perry Barr.

John Graham, was as extrovert as ever and I was surprised to see how overweight he was. When I commented on this I think John said that he weighed eighteen stones! I travelled home the following day.

On Tuesday, 29th June Izzy and I drove to Glasgow airport for an overnight stay at the 'Express by Holiday Inn'. On Wednesday morning I ran along the road to Inshinnan and past the building where the tyre factory used to be. This was where Dad had worked during the Second World War and where he and Mum met, so I felt quite emotional. We flew to Philadelphia and onwards to Orlando. While there we attended a 'Time Share Apartment' demonstration; went to Disney world and Epcot. We drove to Fort Lauderdale; and decided to purchase a Time Share week at Palm Beach resort. We went on a cruise from Port Everglades to Nassau in the Bahamas, where Izzy went snorkelling at a coral reef. Later we visited Daytona Beach and Cape Canaveral. We returned home on 19th July and I resumed my 100 miles per week schedule, which included two effort sessions each week and my familiar routine was re-established when I returned to work on the 16th of August.

On 29th of August in the 23rd edition of the **Macallan Moray Marathon,** I finished 53rd and **first V60**, in 3-35-30. I wrote in my diary: *My high mileage training has taken its toll on my leg muscles, which are never fully recovering, but I was pleased that my strength was returning towards the end.*

REDUCED TO WALKING IN THE 24 HOUR RACE

I continued with my high mileage schedule, peaking at 153 miles, aiming to run well in the **Sri Chinmoy 24-hour race at Tooting Bec.** On Friday the 8th of October, with no running since the preceding Saturday, after work I drove to Inverness airport, caught the flight to Gatwick. On reaching Reigate, Mark came to collect me and drove me to his home. I was given Mark's room, which he had kindly vacated for me.

On Saturday, Mark and I arrived at Tooting Bec track at 11:00. I went to the briefing and met Hilary Walker and Helga Backhaus there and then got myself ready for the event.

I started cautiously and ran at between 6 to 7 miles per hour. After about 5 hours my left knee became painful and it became steadily worse, so that by 7 hours I was forced to stop running and walk to see if it would ease. After 9 hours I decided to try some physiotherapy in the hope that this would be beneficial. The physiotherapist was the 'Physio' for the English Rugby team and he was very good, but my knee still hurt and I still could not run. I continued walking, but I went back for physiotherapy after 15 hours and this time a lady was on duty. She put an ice pack on my knee, which by then was quite swollen and hot. Unfortunately, this treatment did not help either. I walked for another 5 hours before returning to the Physio for more ice treatment and a knee support. This knee support appeared to make the situation worse, so I removed it after a couple of hours.

Mark's friend Dave came to help again during the night so that Mark could get some sleep. The hours passed slowly, but eventually 12:00 on Sunday arrived. I had walked for about 17 hours and completed 84 miles 1504 yards in 19th place out of 30 starters. This was a very disappointing outcome for me, as I had prepared well for this race. Mark drove us back and I went to bed for a couple of hours.

The following morning, I got a taxi to Gatwick got the flight to Inverness and drove home ready to enjoy the rest of my 'Tattie holidays' October break.

On Tuesday Izzy and I drove to Aberdeen and caught our flight to Amsterdam and onto Prague. The Central Hotel, a 4 star, recently renovated hotel, would be our base for the next 4 days. We enjoyed exploring Prague, on foot and using the trams.

I returned to work on Monday, 18th October, but as my left knee was still puffy and stiff, I cycled to and from work and continued this for the week and the following week. On the following weekend I tried a jog on Saturday and I wrote in my diary: *My left knee is stiff and does not have the same range of bending as my right knee joint.* Another working week of cycling to and from followed and at the weekend I did two runs of 8 miles. I was disappointed to find that my left knee was not improving.

I decided to use the College Gym, so after my initiation session I was given a suitable exercise programme utilizing the various apparatus and machines by the supervisor. I fitted in a gym session every 2nd day during my lunch breaks. This was some compensation for not being able to run. My total weekend jogging miles in November amounted to a mere 74 miles. The time I gained by not running was put to good use as my work commitment had changed on being appointed Curriculum Leader for Electronics and Mechatronics.

I continued cycling to and from work in December, as my left knee was not improving. My GP arranged an appointment with Mr. Anderson at Dr Gray's Hospital for further investigation.

On the 22nd of December I began my journey to Bangalore and onto Puttaparthi, where Izzy had gone about a week earlier. I caught a bus to Blackburn, walked up to Annie and Bob's where I stayed overnight.

The following morning Bob gave me a lift to Aberdeen airport to catch the 06:30 Air France flight to Paris. I caught the Air France flight to Mumbai (Bombay), transferred to the domestic airport and caught the 06:30 flight to Bangalore. Modi's taxi driver drove me to Puttaparthi, where I arrived in time for afternoon darshan.

On Christmas Day, I rose at 03:45 to get into the lines at the Ashram by 04:15. Izzy was singing in the choir that morning. It was a very good experience being able to celebrate Christmas there. In the afternoon, following three speakers, Sai Baba gave a speech.

My training and racing mileage for 2004 amounted to 3616 miles, an average of 69.5 miles per week, because of my left knee problem during the last third of the year.

2005

I started to jog daily during my stay in India and I tried to continue this on returning home and back to work. On one week I reached 65 miles, but my left knee was swollen, stiff and painful, indicating that there was an underlying problem.

In late January Mr. Anderson at Dr Gray's Hospital examined my left knee and suggested I have a cortisone injection, and was surprised when he pushed the whole length of the stout needle under my patella. I had both knees X-rayed for comparison purposes and to inspect the left for signs of arthritis. Mr. Anderson examined my X-rays and said that he could not see any obvious fault. He wanted me to have an MRI scan in Aberdeen to see if I had damage to the meniscus (cartilage), which he suspected was the case.

The cortisone injection reduced the swelling and the pain in my knee, so I resumed running to and from work and ran up to 15 miles at weekends. My first race in 2005 was on Sunday the 27th of March in the Moray Road Runners 10Km road race, finishing in 47-57.

A few days later Izzy and I drove to Aberdeen airport, caught the flight to Copenhagen and made our way to the 'Savoy' Hotel, which was to be our base for a short holiday in the Danish capital. We enjoyed exploring this city on foot, often for several hours at a time.

Returning from Copenhagen on the 4th of April, I drove to Woodend Hospital to have the MRI scan on my left knee. I was informed that the machine was out of action and I could see technicians working on it with parts laid out along the corridor.

On Saturday, 9th April, I marked the Neways Speyside Way 50Km race route with the help of Mike McCulloch. On Sunday morning I did my usual delivery of tables and provisions to the feed stations on the route and went to Ballindalloch for the runners' registration for the 11th edition of the race. 61 runners were sent on their way by starter, Ken McKen. Simon Pride, the course record holder and winner on 6 previous occasions was not participating, so the race was 'wide open'. Simon was to cycle the course with his daughter, Morven, to raise funds for her playgroup in Fochabers. Carl Pryce, a newcomer, running for Cosmic Hillbashers took an early lead and continued to extend his lead to win comfortably in 3-45-11. Ritchie McCrae from Penicuik Harriers finished 2nd in 3-49-23. Carolyn Hunter-Rowe, the ladies course record holder moved through the field to a convincing 3rd win in 3rd place in 3-55-45. I was relieved to see 59 runners finish, and the two that abandoned the race were accounted for.

On Friday the 22nd of April I drove to Aberdeen in convoy with our College minibus, taking students on two industrial visits. After the first visit I went for my MRI scan on my left knee.

EVEN WORSE AT LOCHABER

Two days later, in the **Lochaber Marathon** I settled at just under 8 minutes per mile pace. At 6 miles I felt my left knee becoming painful and my right heel callus was starting to flare up. I stopped seven times at drinks stations to pour water into the heel of my right shoe in an attempt to cool/lubricate my heel and this appeared to help. I finished 241st from 382 starters and I was 4th V60 in a poor 4-06-32. My left knee was badly swollen and stiff; depressing.

On 4th May Mr. Anderson said that the MRI scan of my left knee showed that the anterior cruciate ligament was ruptured. He said that arthroscopy surgery would be used to remove the ends of the ligament. I agreed to go ahead with this procedure, which, would probably be in September. A six weeks period of recovery would be necessary after surgery.

I decided to continue with some running because my knee was not going to get any worse by using it and I could accept a certain level of discomfort.

On Sunday the 5th of June I ran the warm-up lap of the 'Marafun' in Elgin with Simon Pride and the children. I found it difficult to run up Batchen Street because my heart rate would not increase to cope with the demands of running up the gradual rise.

That summer we flew back to India, arriving in Mumbai soon after midnight and were taken to the 'Holiday Inn' at Juhu Beach. This hotel was flooded 3 weeks later during the devastating floods, when 99.6 cm of rain fell in 24 hours.

Next day we caught our flight to Bangalore, for an overnight stay. The following morning our driver, Venkatesh, drove us to Mysore, where we arrived in time to have a conducted tour of 'Mysore Palace. Izzy had booked the 'Hotel Metropole', a renovated colonial building with a central courtyard, for our night's stay, as a treat for my 61st birthday.

I felt nauseous the following morning and could not eat my breakfast and had to make a quick dash for the toilets. Later at a stop on the way to Ooty I had another close call, just making it to the traditional Indian toilet.

I had some sort of fever with flu-like symptoms, as my muscles were aching and my heartbeat was irregular. In addition, I had a headache and I felt weak. After a long journey on poor roads and a multi double bend climb we arrived at our accommodation for the week in the Sterling Resort at Fernhill, in the 'Hill Station' of Ooty. The resort was at 7600 feet and the weather was cold and damp. I began to feel better in succeeding days, as we did some sight seeing in and around Ooty. I started running, covering about 3 hilly miles each morning.

Following our week at Ooty we moved on to 'Sterling Yercaud', a cliff top resort about 600 feet above the plain below. My daily morning runs from there were estimated as 4.5 miles.

On the 21st of July we returned to Bangalore and next morning we travelled to Puttaparthi. I tried running the same route as last January, and found it very difficult because of the high temperature and high relative humidity, but managed to complete the 5 miles route. I continued my 5-mile runs and also two ten-mile Hospital' loops', during our stay in Puttaparthi.

On Saturday the 12th of August we began our journey home: taxi, to Bangalore, flight to Mumbai, where Sampat and his boys met us. They had been flooded out of their home and they were in temporary accommodation: one room, kitchen, shower and a toilet in a high rise-block. We caught our flight at 02:30 to Frankfurt, which was completely full, so Izzy and I had seats several rows apart. On arrival we caught our flight to Edinburgh, collected our car and reached home by 6 pm.

I returned to work on the 17th of August, cycling to and from work. A week later, having completed one mid-week run I ran in the 10Km road race, part of the Moray marathon group of races. Anna, our daughter, was also taking part in her first race. I started easily, but I still had 'pins and needles' in my upper arms. My time of 53-01 was disappointing, but at least I felt that I was running a little better towards the finish. On jogging back, I was delighted to see Anna crossing the Lossie Bridge and heading to the finish. She ran well to finish in 64 minutes and very importantly she enjoyed the experience.

On the 12th of September I received a message that there had been a cancellation in the knee surgery waiting list and I could have my operation done on the following Tuesday the 20th of September. I was taken through to the theatre at 09:30, where I met Dr Taylor, the same anaesthetist, who looked after me when I had my ruptured left Achilles rejoined two years earlier. He was apologetic about the epidural anaesthetic that he had given me then and said that, as I had been agitated then, he would give me a general anaesthetic on this occasion.

Izzy came to pick me up and drove me home. My left knee felt quite good, but by evening there was some blood leaking from below the pressure bandage.

During the night I woke and felt something wet around my knees and was shocked to see that the bandage around my left knee was soaked in blood and there was a large patch of blood through the sheets and blanket on our bed. I had been slowly bleeding to death! When I rose I was dripping blood everywhere, so I wrapped a towel tightly around my knee. Izzy drove me to Dr Gray's Accident and Emergency at around 4:30am. A Doctor inspected my knee and squeezed it to see that there was no more blood inside the knee joint. I was squirming during this process. He decided that the wound required stitching and he gave me a local anaesthetic before putting in two stitches. We were home by 8 am and spent the rest of Wednesday with my left leg elevated, while Izzy changed our bed sheets and blankets and debated if we needed a new mattress.

Soto Rojas had invited me to **travel to Santander to receive a 'gold medal' to celebrate my contribution to the annual 100Km race** he organizes there. I accepted his invitation before I knew about my knee surgery date, but I decided to make the journey. On the 31st of September, 10 days after my knee surgery I drove to Aberdeen airport, caught a flight to London, then a flight to Bilbao. There, Hemma and her driver drove me to Santander, where I met Soto Rojas, Luth Mari and their son, Jose, who was now a grown man.

On Saturday morning, I walked up to the start/finish of the 100Km race, which was well underway. I walked around the 10Km loop, which runners had to complete 10 times. Following lunch, I returned to my hotel room and did not realise that I had forgotten to put my watch one hour ahead, so I was still on UK time and late for my presentation. At 5:10pm Spanish time I was presented with a **gold lapel medal of the organization along with a framed inscribed metal plate and also a photograph in a frame of Malcolm Campbell and I in the Crystal Palace 100Km, when I set the record of 6-10-20.** In the evening I attended an excellent dinner for the runners, officials and helpers.

On Sunday morning the same driver who had met me on Friday arrived at the hotel to take two Argentineans and me to Bilbao airport. This drive was now so much shorter than in the old days, when it was a 4-hour tortuous drive. Now there was dual carriageway all the way.

I caught my flight to Madrid, then to London, Heathrow. I don't know how it happened, but I saw Aberdeen on the departures board and I followed the instructions to wait in Gate 8. I only saw one flight to Aberdeen at this time. When the flight was called and I presented my boarding pass I was told that this was a BMI flight and that my flight was with BA from Gate 5. It was then 19:42 so I rushed to Gate 5, but I could not get on the aircraft as the doors had been closed as the flight was due to leave at 19:45. I had made a bad and expensive mistake and I could have kicked myself.

I had to get a hotel for the night, the 'Thistle' Hotel using the shuttle bus to get there and back in the morning. On Monday morning I caught the 07:30 flight to Aberdeen, picked up our car and drove to my work, arriving at 10:30.

I received the sad news that 'Magic' Malcolm Morgan had died of a brain tumour. Izzy and I attended his funeral on the 7th of October at Watson's funeral parlour and then at the Moray Crematorium. He had been a very great help to me over the years and we were good friends.

My first jog, almost 6 weeks after my knee surgery, was on 29th of October, when I jogged to the furthest edge of the golf course and back with Muffin, covering 2.5 miles. My left knee hurt on the right side, but I hoped that this would wear off.

. From then on I gradually increased my running, sometimes doing a 4-mile morning run before cycling to work and on other days running one way to work by my shortest route and then getting a lift home from colleague Willie Friend. By the end of November, I had regained confidence in my left knee and my weekly mileage reached 70 miles.

I participated in the **RAF Lossiemouth 10 miles 'Turkey Trot'** on Sunday the 18th of December. I had a disheartening experience as my legs refused to work properly at the pace I wanted to achieve. During the rest of December, I continued to train with the hope that I would recover some of my previous fitness.

My total training and racing miles for 2005 was, because of my injury, much lower than previous years at 1953 miles, which was an average of 37.5 miles per week.

2006

In January I was back to running each day, but still not showing any signs of improving my fitness.

I accepted an invitation from Norman Wilson to attend the UK Athletics Ultra Distance Squad weekend as part of a panel, at Tigworth, near Gloucester. On Friday the 20th of January I caught a flight from Aberdeen to Bristol, caught a bus to Bristol and a train to Gloucester, where Anne Wilson picked me up and drove me to Tigworth.

I began a run with the squad the following morning, but could not keep up and ran by myself for over 2 hours. The meeting was worthwhile, but I felt that more benefit could have been derived from the panel, question and answer session on 'Planning/Racing 100Km and 24-hours', which was restricted by time constraints.

On Sunday morning Norman Wilson gave me a lift, through the fog, to Bristol Airport, where I later caught my flight to Aberdeen and drove home.

My right heel callus had been giving trouble and an infection started under it, which required a course of Ampicillin to fight the infection. At my appointment on the 26th of January, with Hospital Podiatrist, David Frazer he showed me, with the aid of a mirror, the ulcer under my heel, which was about 1.2 cm in diameter. He then very skilfully opened up the ulcer and cut away the dead skin with a scalpel and showed me the result again with the mirror. He made an elaborate dressing, which gave a lot of protection to the affected region. I felt much happier after this treatment. He inspected the ulcer on the following day and was very pleased by the healing progress.

Several weeks of no running followed as my heel recovered, but by March I had resumed daily running. I could not establish any consistent training as my left knee and my right heel appeared to be taking turns at causing problems, which restricted the distances that I could run. Tripping on a wire, covered by snow on the old railway line in late March, on my run to work and bashing my left knee was a setback.

At my appointment at Dr Gray's for the Diabetic clinic on 20th February, I was advised that I should start injecting insulin, because my Glislazide tablet dose was at maximum.

As part of my preparations for the 12th edition of the Neways Speyside Way 50Km I learned that the company, which owned the Spey Bay Hotel was declared bankrupt and that the hotel was no longer operating, so I had to cancel the race. The hotel and the attached caravan park shower block were vital to provide finishing facilities, changing, showers, food and presentation of awards, for the runners.

During the first week of my Easter vacation from work Izzy and I went to Amsterdam for a week's holiday and stayed at the 'NH Central' Hotel. I jogged about 3 miles for 2 mornings and then gave up, but we did do a lot of walking around Amsterdam.

Izzy and I decided to participate again in the **Cross Scotland Walk or Cycle**, for MacMillan Cancer Relief. The event, organised by May Gilchrist, encourage participants to raise sponsorship for their effort in getting from Ullapool on the west coast to Bonar Bridge on the east. On Saturday the 29th of April Izzy and I drove to Bonar Bridge and then cycled the last quarter of the route from Lubacoinnich to Bonar Bridge. We then joined the other walkers and cyclist on the hired bus to transport us to Ullapool and our overnight hotel stay.

The following morning, we began our cycle over the route, which was quite straightforward until we reached the higher ground. We had to follow one or other side of a Landrover track with numerous water-filled sections and streams to negotiate. Izzy fell twice and had to withdraw on Doctor's advice at the Scout camp after 14 miles of these rough tracks and streams. I continued, knowing that Izzy would be taken out by 'SCOTAN' in their four-wheel drive vehicles. I arrived in Bonar Bridge in a quite depleted state, having used my emergency rations. I was reunited with Izzy at the post event accommodation in the Portmahonack Hotel. I was pleased to see that she had recovered, but was still in pain from her worst fall.

In the **Forres Harriers 10Km road race** on Saturday, 13 May, I made it around the course with little energy in a poor 57-35. On Sunday morning I tried running, but after one minute I had to stop because I became breathless and felt tightness in my upper arms. I thought that I might have a recurrence of the virus that I had a few weeks previously.

For the rest of May and most of June I continued running one way to work or cycling and got a lift home. My weekly mileage seldom exceeded 30 miles and I was continually feeling tired. One morning, I fell onto the A96 when I started to cross as my left foot caught on the kerb. I was shocked to sprawl on the road and thankfully there were no oncoming vehicles nearby. I was not injured, just rather shaken. I also had to deal with a recurrence of sciatica, which persisted for several weeks.

I received an invitation via Soto Rojas to attend as a **guest at a six-hour track race in Madrid, where runners would be attempting to better my six-hour record of 97.2Km.** I accepted and asked if Simon Pride could be invited to compete, as I felt that he had the potential to get close to my distance. The organiser agreed and Simon was keen to participate and asked me how he should prepare for it. I told him to train, as for a 100Km race and that I would be his second during the race.

I wrote the following report on the race for the RRC Newsletter:

THE SIX HOURS INTERNATIONAL TRACK RACE IN MADRID, 24TH JUNE 2006

A six-hour track race was organised by Paco Rico and his team of helpers, in a suburb to the North of Madrid, called San Sebastian de los Reyes. The aim of this race was to improve on my record of 97.2Km set at Crystal Palace during the RRC 100Km track race on 28th October 1978.

The first prize was to be a Chevrolet 'Matiz' car, or 5000 euros, with smaller amounts of prize money, down to 28th place. As an incentive, if my record were broken, the winner would receive a Chevrolet 'Lacetti' or 7000 euros.

To avoid high temperatures and sun the race was scheduled to start at 10pm.

In February I received an invitation to be a guest at this race and readily accepted. I asked Simon Pride if he would be interested in participating in this event, in which I thought he could do very well. He decided to accept the challenge and within a few weeks began to prepare for this race as though it were a 100Km event.

Simon and I duly arrived, in mid afternoon, at Madrid airport on the 23rd of June and were met by a member of the race organisation, who drove Jaroslaw Janicki and us, to a hotel about 4km from the stadium. Janicki was regarded as favourite to win the race, despite having run in the 'Comrades' the previous weekend finishing 6th.

The six-hour race was part of the 3rd edition of the 'Athletics festival', which began at 8:15 pm with a 3000m race for youngsters over 15 years old. Races for children followed, ranging in distance from 1200m to 110m, for different age categories. Other activities on the programme were: 'Jazz Ballet', acrobatic Gymnastics, Tae-Kwon-Do exhibition and entertainment from a music group.

We arrived at the Stadium at 9pm; where there was a good atmosphere generated by the several hundred, perhaps over a thousand, spectators.

By the start of the 6-hour race, weather conditions were fairly good with a temperature of about 20° C, but there was a breeze against the runners, in the home straight.

Jose Posado Perez of Spain set the early pace and was soon half a lap ahead of the chasing group, including Simon. His pace was well inside record schedule, so I wondered how long he could sustain this intensity. His pace started to slow after about one hour and Simon began to close on him and pull away from Jorge Martinez of Spain and Janicki of Poland. By one and a half hours, Simon caught and passed Posado Perez and was running well and inside record schedule pace. However, after 2 hours, Simon began to slow and informed me that he was experiencing stomach cramps and could not keep any of his drinks down. Martinez and Janicki soon caught and passed Simon as he continued to have problems. We tried some alternative drinks, but to no avail so Simon's condition did not improve and he decided to abandon the race.

Relieved of my seconding duties I sampled the barbecue, which was free, along with soft drinks, to all spectators.

Only the first 4 lanes were used for the 6-hour race, so that lanes 5 to 8 could be used for other events. There were elimination races for women and men, with a maximum of 8 in the women's race and 10 in the men's race. A similar race called, 'Deil Tak the Hindmost', (Devil take the last one), is held in some Highland games in Scotland. The last person at the completion of a lap is eliminated, so as you can imagine, there were some dramatic pace changes, before and after a lap is completed.

Another novel event was a relay race between 4 teams composed of a runner and a cyclist. The runner completes one lap and hands over to the cyclist who completes 2 laps and hands over to the runner again. This repeated four times.

At midnight a 3-hour race began, using these outer lanes. Both the 3-hour and 6-hour races used the 'Champion Chip' monitoring, recording and displaying system.

In the 6-hour race, Janicki and Martinez passed through 50Km in a little over 3 hours, 9 minutes and were about 2 laps ahead of the 3rd runner. As the race progressed Janicki pulled away from Martinez and established a gradually extending lead. As Martinez faded other runners, notably Alexei Belosloudtsv of Russia and Ferenc Biri of Hungary, began to run more strongly.

By now running conditions were excellent, with not a breath of wind and a cool temperature.

As the race neared its conclusion, Janicki slackened his pace and ran in a group of lapped runners, knowing that he had several laps of a lead. He finished with 91.7Km and Alexei claimed 2nd from a tired Martinez.

The awards ceremony was held at about 4:50am, to end a very well organised event.

Results: 1) Jaroslaw Janicki (Pol) 91.270Km,

2) Alexei Belosloudtsv (Rus) 89.486 Km,

3) Jorge Martinez (Esp) 89.097Km,

4) Ferenc Biri (Hun) 88.551Km

I was concerned that my persistent tiredness and lack of strength may be due some ailment or deficiency, so I arranged to have blood samples taken for analysis to identify any unusual parameters. A week later Dr Barclay said the results showed no abnormalities. I had to accept the fact that I appeared to be ageing rather rapidly, compared with the expected gradual decline in abilities.

Izzy and I had arranged to return to India and visit some different regions. On the 2nd of July we flew from Aberdeen to Paris and then overnight to Bangalore. Later that day we travelled to Mysore and went sightseeing in and around Mysore the following day.

After two nights in Mysore we travelled to Conoor to stay at the 'Taj Garden Retreat Hotel', which was in the hills at just over 6000 feet. Next morning, my 62nd birthday and our 23rd wedding anniversary I felt unfit on my run and only covered about 2 miles. We had a memorable journey down the mountainside to the plain below on the old winding narrow gauge railway in ancient carriages connected to a vintage steam train engine.

Following our three-day stay at Conoor we travelled to Madurai, where we stayed for three days and a local guide took us around the various impressive temples and sights.

We returned to Bangalore on the 10th of July and the following day travelled to Puttaparthi. I set out to run the ten-mile loop, but struggled with the heat and almost had to walk the last 3Km. For the following three weeks I settled into a daily early morning 4-mile run routine, so that in the last week in July I reached my biggest weekly mileage for several months with 65 miles.

We returned to the UK and home on 2nd August, two weeks before returning to work.

My right foot 5th metatarsal head started giving trouble again and was rather painful, as did the callus under my right heel. By trying various shoes and different padding arrangements and insoles I was able to persevere with my attempt to improve my fitness level. My left knee began hurting also, which combined with my right heel and 5th metatarsal head troubles caused me rather a lot of frustration.

On 3rd September, in the **Moray half marathon I** finished 181st of 254 finishers in a disappointing 2-01-37. John Goodall won in 1-15-35, from Martin Ferguson, 1-16-02 and George Sim, 1-16-40.

A week later in the **Speyside 10** from Ballindalloch to Aberlour on the Speyside way, with about two miles remaining I became very weak as my atrial fibrillation was debilitating. I had to stop and walk until my heart started beating more regularly. I became concerned that I would experience a heart stoppage and end up collapsing on the track. I finished without this happening in 1-29-57, which was 20 seconds slower than last year.

The following Sunday, after a non running week, I tackled the 'Dava Way', multi-terrain 15 miles race, which I had wanted to run in since its inception a few years previously. By about 6.5 miles I was favouring my left knee and my right heel and the usual metatarsal head, all of which were hurting. I had difficulty on a forest path section and had to walk on the down hills to protect my left knee on the rough twisty track.

By then my blood glucose must have been rather low, or I had become depleted of glycogen, so my run was more of a shuffle and, as I had not taken any emergency carbohydrate items with me, I could not improve my condition. I reached the welcome sight of the finish in 33rd in of the 36 finishers. T. Christie was first home in 1-33-36, from Paul Rogan, 1-35-26 and Robbie Paterson, 1-40-57.

A week later in the **Dyke 10Km road race** at a left turn at a junction after about a mile, I felt something pop in my left foot, followed by a sharp pain, which caused me to stop immediately and I could not continue, so I walked back to the start. On consulting Peter Sperryn's book at home, I decided that the peroneal tendon was damaged. Three weeks of no running, but cycling to and from work allowed my left foot to recover and I resumed some short jogs.

During October my attempts at establishing a daily running routine were curtailed by my recurrent right heel pain and fifth metatarsal head pain in the same foot and a twinging left Achilles tendon. By mid November I had debilitating pain in both my heels, which prevented running and even walking, was painful.

I contacted David Frazer the Podiatrist at Dr Gray's Hospital, who surprised me by diagnosing **chilblains**. He gave me advice on how to treat these chilblains: 'keep your feet dry and warm, e.g. two pairs of socks, change from damp socks/shoes immediately, daily use of chilblain cream or moisturizer and don't 'toast' your feet in front of a fire'.

My chilblain pains gradually receded, but my running through the rest of November and December was minimal, with weekly mileages ranging from 7 miles to 9 miles.

On Saturday the 16th of December I was relieved and delighted to pass my Institute of Advanced Driving (I.A.M) test.

As 2006 came to an end and I found that my very poor running year had amounted to a total of 1615 miles, an average of 31 miles per week.

2007

By January I resumed daily running and, during my working week I ran 8 miles to work. After work my colleague and fellow curriculum leader, Willie Friend, would give me a lift home. On Saturdays and Sundays, I would fit in slightly longer runs.

In the **RAF Kinloss to RAF Lossiemouth half marathon** on the 18th of February Izzy saw me with 400 metres remaining and noticed that I was running very lopsided. My last 3 miles were poor and I finished in 2-04-23. Doug Cowie, a marathon running adversary from an earlier time, commented that 'he would retire from running, well before he became as poor as Don'. Doug was still running well several years later, which confirmed my belief that we grow old at different rates.

My next run was the **Moray Road Runners 10Km road race** along with our daughters Claire and Anna on 25th March. My heart fibrillation problem returned, which was alarming as I became quite breathless. I finished 211th in 57-24. I was pleased to see both Claire and Anna finishing well on no preparatory training. Claire had raised £200, for the Fordyce 'Toddlers' group.

During my Easter vacation from work Izzy and I travelled to Tenerife for a week's holiday and enjoyed the experience of exploring the island. On our return I became extremely tired and this persisted for several weeks, during which I could only try the occasional jog. By June I was able to resume daily running, one way to work as before.

In early July Izzy and I returned to India and onto Puttaparthi. I started running after a few days there, but only on alternate days in an attempt to minimise my tiredness.

Izzy had developed sciatica and got treatment from a Tibetan doctor, Dr Gedun. He used acupuncture, cup therapy and moxa therapy on her every second day until her condition was relieved. At the same time, I had acupuncture on my right foot, with 9 stout needles inserted in an attempt to eradicate the discomfort from the callus under my right heel. Unfortunately, this did not have the desired effect, despite 4 sessions. However I did find the Tibetan music playing in the background quite soothing.

On the 8th of August we returned home and I decided to have my irregular heartbeat and recurring atrial fibrillation investigated. At the cardiology section in Dr Gray's Hospital in Elgin, following an ultrasound heart scan and a stress walking test on a treadmill I was fitted with a monitor to record occurrences of my heart fibrillations over a 5-day period.

I participated in the Moray Half Marathon, wearing the recorder. I had to start recording when I felt my heart beginning to fibrillate or beat irregularly. I made three recordings during my run, when I felt that I was beginning to experience a heart malfunction. My right heel became unbearably painful with about 2.5 miles to the finish, so I was forced to stop, remove my shoe and the dressing I had put over the callus to protect it and then refit my shoe. I suppose this stop cost me about two minutes. I finished in 198th. I returned my monitor to the cardiology department at Dr Gray's hospital for analysis and awaited feedback.

Two weeks after the half marathon and with minimal running I ran in the **Dyke 10Km road race**. I finished 139th in 55-26 out of 160 finishers. My time was 2 minutes faster than my previous 10Km in March.

During the October break from College, Izzy and I went to Benalamadena on the Costa del Sol, staying in the 'Sunset Beach Club' for a week's holiday. I was surprised to meet Eric Fisher, of Edinburgh A.C, who I had run against in marathons in the 1970s. I had met him a few years previously at the Scottish Boys' Brigade Cross Country championships, which were held in Buckie that year, when I was asked to present the awards.

In late November I attended a surprise 60th birthday party for Graham Milne, my running pal from earlier years, in the Elgin Golf Clubhouse. It was a very enjoyable evening, meeting so many of our mutual running pals, spanning 3 decades at least. The following morning, I jogged up to the clubhouse to pick up my car. This boosted my weekly mileage to 55 miles.

The rest of November and December were uneventful as I continued with less enthusiasm to run and cycle alternately, hoping to feel resurgence in my energy level.

I finished 2007 with a total of 1717 miles run, which was an average of 33 miles per week

2008

Dr Garg, the cardiology consultant from Aberdeen Royal Infirmary (ARI), asked for further tests, so in early January I drove to ARI for a radionuclide heart scan. The gamma ray emitting substance was injected into a vein in my arm, to act as a tracer and the gamma rays would be detected by a scanning gamma camera. Computer processing of the signals produced a three-dimensional image of the blood supply to my heart.

I had a second heart scan, this time a heart stimulant along with the radioactive tracer was added to my bloodstream.

January passed with only 106 running miles recorded, evidence that I had given up my effort to regain my lost ability.

In mid February I decided to participate in the **Kinloss to Lossiemouth half marathon**. I felt fairly okay until around 6 miles; when I lacked any energy and I could barely move my legs. I felt like I was in the later stages of a 24-hour run and wanted to stop and walk. My heels hurt and I was taking very small strides. I felt embarrassed by my poor performance, finishing 196th, with only 5 others behind me.

Despite my very erratic training, with weekly mileages never exceeding 30 miles, I decided to participate in the **Moray Road Runners 10Km road race** on 30th of March, along with Claire, raising funds for Fordyce toddlers group along with Anna and Angie. I stupidly tripped on the edge of a speed bump in Cooper Park and fell heavily, cutting my right knee, ankle and the top of my right femur, plus both hands. Someone stopped to help me up and I got going again. I jogged steadily around the route, but did not feel comfortable.

Claire accompanied by her friend Dianne, did very well off no training and she was pleased at how good she felt and raised £230 through her effort. Anna jogged/walked around the course with Angie, who raised over £200 in sponsorship.

A couple of days later, Charlie and Marja Greenlees, Tapio and Kerttu Pekola, from Finland arrived to visit us and stay overnight. We all enjoyed the get-together. Tapio went to bed with my training diaries, which he perused and made notes from, while everyone else slept. He planned to use the information gleaned to write an article in 'Juoksija', the running magazine that he produced in Finland.

During my Easter vacation, Izzy and I enjoyed some warm weather on a holiday in Tenerife. I lacked the urge to run, during and after this holiday, so recorded two weeks of zero miles.

On the 19th of April I attended A.R.I for cardiac catherisation. Access was through my right wrist artery and after the catheter was in place a radioactive tracer was injected to show the blood supply to my heart muscle. I was able to see some of the pictures obtained on the monitors. This procedure had to be stopped to allow an emergency case from Raigmore hospital in Inverness to be treated. I was wheeled out of the theatre and had to wait in the recovery room for a couple of hours, before being wheeled back into the theatre, for Dr Garg to complete the procedure. **He fitted a bare metal stent in my right coronary artery to open it up, as it was narrowed to about 15% of its original diameter.**

After another week of zero miles I started to run and was disappointed that, despite having the stent fitted (angioplasty), I felt no benefit and my running was as laboured as before.

At the start of my summer vacation Izzy and I travelled to Bangalore and on to Puttaparthi. I decided to try another comeback effort and ran a 10 miles loop on our third day there. I managed a few more of these following rest days and shorter 3.5 miles loops. During our stay in India I received the sad news that Ron Hindley, the founder of the 100Km Association had died. Unfortunately, I could not attend Ron's funeral in early July. On the 6th of August we travelled back to the UK.

I resumed some sporadic running sessions and participated in the **Moray half marathon** on the 7th of September finishing 245th of the 274 finishers.

Another week of no running was necessary to allow my recovery from a chest infection.

The following week also yielded zero miles because of a lack of motivation and travelling to and from a Scottish Qualifications Authority (SQA) subject network meeting in Glasgow including an overnight stay. **My lack of motivation extended for a further 5 weeks, when even cycling to and from work was replaced by driving a scooter there and back.**

I resumed cycling to and from work in early November and on the 2nd day on my cycle home I crashed when joining the cycle path opposite the Buccaneer Garage on the outskirts of Elgin. I had approached the small kerb at too acute an angle and my front wheel just slid along it and, as I was travelling quite quickly, I crashed off. I banged the left side of my face along the tarred pavement, but nothing was broken. A lady runner, who had just passed me, heard the crash and came back to assist me, which was good of her. Later I found that I had cuts on my knees, my left hand and left shoulder.

I was invited as a guest to attend the World and European 100Km championships, being held in Italy. Two days after my crash I drove after work to Blackburn to stay overnight with Annie and Bob prior to catching the 06:30 Air France flight to Paris the following morning.

I travelled to Paris, caught a flight to Rome, where three girls who were representatives of the race organization met me. They took me to a minibus and we set off for Tuscania but we made a detour up some dirt roads and made a stop for 20 minutes at a hilltop house. I was not informed what the reason was as the driver retraced his route there and rejoined the road for Tuscania. Once there I was taken to the square, where the opening ceremony for the IAU 100Km World challenge and European 100Km championships was taking place. I was introduced to the assembled teams of runners and officials and several runners from different countries came to greet me. Yiannis Kouros was already there and we met each other later.

Inspired, I went for a jog from the hotel that I was staying in, up the hill to where the race was to finish. I soon had to walk as the hill was very steep and I was not fit.

I joined Soto Rojas, his wife Luth Mari, their son Jose and Ramon Alverez for dinner in the hotel and this was a very pleasant occasion. I had wild boar as my meat course.

Although I had been invited to the race, I was not taken to the start next morning, which was in another city at 10:30, so I had plenty of time to explore Tuscania. This ancient town was interesting, but I found the day long despite spending quite a while in the museum.

There was a good atmosphere at the finish and an Italian was wildly cheered as he won from Janicki of Poland and a Russian won the ladies race. It was good to see the expressions of relief and joy as runners crossed the finish line. The awards ceremony was a long drawn out affair, but I remained in the vicinity of the finish until everything was finished.

Back in the hotel, I was invited to have dinner with the IAU officials at a very late 23:30. Norman Wilson, recently appointed as vice president of the IAU, and I adjourned to the lounge with some wine and chatted until the early hours.

Later that morning I caught the minibus to the airport and arrived in plenty of time for the flight to Paris Charles De Gaul airport. My flight to Aberdeen got me there, where my car was iced up, but it started okay. I arrived home safely at 23:30and discovered that the bottle of vodka from the Russians had not been securely sealed and the contents had leaked into my kit and clothes in my bag.

My motivation was short lived and several non-running weeks followed and meetings in Glasgow, were also a distraction, so my mileage for November was 2 miles and for December it amounted to 27 miles. For the year, 2008, my total mileage was 956 miles, an average of 18 miles per week.

2009

My intended training plan was thwarted in the first quarter of 2009 by a recurrence of chilblains in both feet, so my mileages for January, February and March were 27 miles, 28 miles and 37 miles respectively. Podiatrist, David Frazer, arranged weekly appointments for me to eradicate the chilblain problem, which we succeeded in doing by the end of March.

In mid February our Springer Spaniel, Muffin, had become quite unwell and on taking her to the vets in Elgin we were informed that she had cancer that had started in her shoulder and spread to her lungs. After work next day Izzy picked me up and took me to the vets, where Muffin was to be put to sleep because her cancer was inoperable. This was a very sad event and afterwards Izzy drove us home and we buried Muffin at the bottom of our garden.

Muffin had been a happy running companion to me for over 10 years and probably ran about 10 thousand miles at weekends and during holiday times with me. She would complete my longest Sunday runs of 50Km enthusiastically and then, after some water and food, lie contentedly, stretched out on the floor for several hours. She loved running, but did renege on a few occasions, during one summer vacation from work, when I was running at least 20 miles each day. She was almost 15 years old and was a dog of great character and was loved by all the family.

During my Easter vacation Izzy and I caught a fight to Malaga and picked up our rental car and drove to 'Crown Resort Marbella' in Calahonda. The resort was on a hillside, so my daily morning run was uphill for a couple of miles and then returning. By the end of our week's holiday I was showing some improvement in my uphill running ability.

During the rest of April and in May and June I tried to get back into a weekly running routine, but I never succeeded in maintaining a regular schedule for various reasons, including waning motivation. **On Friday the 16th of June I ran a symbolic 8 miles old railway line route for the last time, on my last day of work at Moray College Technology Centre.**

I retired from work just a few weeks before my 65th birthday. Celebrations got underway at lunchtime with tea and a cake and a presentation from the Technology Centre staff. My colleagues were curiously coy in avoiding the subject of going to the pub as was usual at end of terms/semesters. That evening Izzy drove me to the 1629 Restaurant in Lossiemouth for a meal. It was a wonderful surprise to find that the meal was a retiral dinner and it was a great pleasure to see so many colleagues there along with running pals, friends and my sister Annie and her husband Bob. My colleague Jenny McKenzie had planned this dinner for several months in advance to make it the very memorable night it became. I will always be grateful to Jenny for all the effort that she put in preparing for this: 'Don's Retiral Do'.

On Wednesday the 12th of August, Izzy and I drove to Glasgow to meet Anna and stay overnight at her flat, then continued to Norfolk to stay with Roy and Edit Richards near Saxmundum. On Friday we drove on to Harwich to join the 'Thomson Spirit' ship for the Baltic Capitals Cruise. This was the day when my colleagues at Moray College were to resume work, so my thoughts were with them as I began my retirement lifestyle.

Five laps of the promenade deck were equal to one mile, so each morning, unless the deck was roped off because of windy and wet weather, I ran these 5 laps. One other passenger also did a morning run and although he did not look like a runner, he was moving more quickly than I was.

On 13th September in the **Moray Marathon 10Km**. having jogged to the start from home as a warm-up. I enjoyed participating in the event, despite being unable to raise my pace.

On the 15th we enjoyed the train journey from Glasgow Queen Street Station on the West Highland Line to Fort William, on to Mallaig and return. This was excellent and was something that I had wanted to do for a long time.

Norman Wilson, chairman of the executive committee organizing the inaugural **Commonwealth ultra-distance and Mountain running Championships,** in Keswick invited me to attend as a VIP guest. On the day after our West Highland Line trip we drove to Keswick and checked into our bed and breakfast accommodation at 'Clarence House', where we were to stay for five nights. I saw the start of the 24-hour race in the park the next day and I was delighted to see my old training partner, **Mick Francis, running for the Australian team**. I watched for several hours and returned before midnight so that I could wish Mick a happy 50th birthday just after midnight. Unfortunately, it was not a happy birthday because on a poorly lit part of the loop in the park Mick veered off the edge of the path, fell over and damaged his left hamstring. After some strapping was applied he continued as best he could for some time before being forced to abandon his race. Martin Fryer of Australia won with 255.9Km ahead of Joe Blake, also of Australia with 249.1Km and John Pares, Wales with 244.37Km. Sharon Gayter, England, won the ladies race with 226.48Km from M Skelton, England, 212.68Km and S Jamieson, Australia, 206.9Km.

In the 100Km road race, England secured a 1-2-3 finish, with Jez Bragg winning in 7-04-01, from Matt Giles, 7-05-28 and Matt Lynas, 7-09-52. Grant Jeans, the son of my Moray Technology Centre colleague, Bill Jeans, was first of the Scottish team finishing 6th in 7-24-05. Jackie Fairweather, Australia, won the ladies race in 7-41-23, from E Gooderham, England, 8-04-09 and Lucy Colqhoun, Scotland, 8-08-19.

My training pal from my Birchfield Harriers days, Mal Pickering, came to meet me, along with Sally his wife and their children on the day of the last mountain race. Later in the evening the awards ceremony for all the races was held in a large marquee and followed by the closing ceremony. This initiative was very successful and an important development towards, hopefully, incorporating these events into the Commonwealth Games.

On arrival back form Keswick, I managed to establish a daily running routine of at least 6 miles each day and anticipated an improvement in my running ability. Sadly this was not evident, as my muscles failed to adapt to the training stimulus. I think that I read somewhere a long time ago, the theory that one's body has a finite amount of 'adaptation energy', so perhaps I had used up my quota.

Towards the end of October 2009, Izzy and I returned to India, flying to Bangalore and then by pre booked taxi to Puttaparthi, where we were to stay for 5 weeks. My proposed daily running was delayed by tiredness and bouts of bad diarrhoea and vomiting. On recovering I ran a 3.5 miles loop on most mornings and then tried my 10 miles 'Hospital loop', which I found very hard and very tiring. I reverted to daily morning 3.5 miles loop and maintained this for three weeks. We returned to Aberdeen on the last day of November to a temperature of +1°C, which was quite a shock to us.

Running during the last 2 weeks in December was difficult due to snow, ice and sometimes, slushy roads and pavements.

My total running in 2009 amounted to a modest 1015 miles, an average of 19.5 miles per week, which reflected my restricted running due to lack of strength and falling motivation.

2010

In January, ever hopeful of running well again I increased my running distances and completed 163 miles by the end of that snowy and icy month.

On the 6th of February, I started in the **Scottish Veterans cross-country championships** in Grant Park and on Cluny Hill in Forres. I lacked pace, had no strength in my legs and could not move through the field, so I was soon second last, just ahead of Willie Russell (M75). I decided to give up after the first big lap. I was rather disheartened and at a loss to know what to do about my very poor condition.

A week later Izzy and I travelled to Bangalore and on to Whitefield to stay at the Sai Renaissance Hotel, to be convenient for Izzy's dental treatment.

On my second morning run there, a boy on a bicycle with a full water pot at either side of his back wheel drew alongside and said; 'Good running' and 'How many Kilometres have you run?' I replied about 4Km, to which he replied 'That is awesome' and then continued to say 'At such an age it is a miracle' and cycled ahead, leaving me to ponder how old and decrepit I must have appeared. I found running very difficult and on some mornings my leg muscles would hardly respond and on other mornings I was too tired to run.

After three weeks at Puttaparthi, we travelled to Bangalore caught a flight to Delhi and on to Srinagar in Kashmir. We were stay a week with Farook's extended family. I did not attempt running because it was rather inconvenient and I was concerned about becoming lost in the warren of narrow streets.

Farook's friend, Airshad, was hired to drive us around, using his people carrier. Srinagar. 'The Lake City' is at an altitude of 1530m and we visited: the Mughal Gardens, the old city and Dal Lake and spectacular Sonamarg, 84Km from Srinagar at 2730m, with huge surrounding mountains. Other excursions were to: Pahalgam, 90Km distant and at 2130m, the upland meadow was surrounded by jagged snow-capped mountains, Gulmarg at 2730m and 56Km from Srinagar, a ski resort. We took the gondola up to the mid station at an altitude of just over 4000m to enjoy the views.

Our week in Kashmir passed quickly and on 28th of March we travelled back to Bangalore. After a few days back in Puttaparthi, I felt very weak on my morning run and later I became ill with my skin feeling very sensitive and I ached in most regions. I went to bed and slept for 21 hours. I was surprised to see that my morning weight was down to 9 stone 5 pounds, at least 9 pounds below my usual weight.

Back home I got into regular running again and averaged 30 miles for several weeks before Izzy and I went to Northern Portugal on a package holiday. From Oporto, we and our fellow guests were taken to our week's accommodation in the 'Santo Andre Hotel', which was located next to the sea shoreline. There was a boardwalk from the hotel to the nearest village and then a section of road to the next village further up the coast, so each morning I ran there and back, about 3.5 miles.

Daily bus tours enabled us to see quite a lot of the surrounding region, including one long trip to Santiago de Compostela, the capital city of Galicia in northern Spain. The cathedral there was very impressive and a UNESCO World Heritage Site and is the finishing point of the 'Way of St James' pilgrimage, a long distance pilgrimage walk of at least 5 days on the shortest route in northern Spain.

On returning from Portugal I pottered along through the rest of May, June and July, rarely attempting to run further than 5 miles, and usually with one rest day, so my weekly mileages were in the range of 20 miles to 30 miles. Izzy happened to drive past as I was nearing the end of one of my 5-mile runs and commented later that I was not really running, but shuffling along. **I should have realised by then that, despite my optimism that I was not going to recover sufficient ability to make running enjoyable again.**

Izzy and I arranged to take our oldest grandson, Sunny, for a week's holiday in Benidorm in early August. Our self-catering apartment was on the 10th floor of the Flamingo Playa building, about half a mile up a fairly steep slope from the promenade.

My morning shuffles were down to the Prom and then alternately left and right, along to the end and back, about 3 miles. Evening meals were at the 'Dennis The Menace' Pub/restaurant. Sunny enjoyed learning to play Pool there and was quite a confident player by the end of the week.

On the 5th of September, I participated in the **Moray Marathon 10Km** with Anna and her friend Irene Buchan. Anna came trotting past me about halfway and finished 219th in 59-04, which pleased her. I finished in 63-29 for 261st and Irene in her first race finished 305th in 80-23. I felt quite dispirited by my poor performance.

Back in India in October for five weeks, I felt too tired to run for five days, but then I began morning runs/jogs around my 3.5 miles loop. I averaged 20 miles per week over the last 3 weeks.

We returned to Aberdeen on the 6th of December and after an overnight stay at Annie and Bob's arrived home next morning to deal with the unpleasant after-effects of a burst water pipe upstairs.

The remainder of December was occupied with clearing snow, redecorating the room affected by the burst pipe and some running when the underfoot conditions were suitable. I found, from my diary that in 2010, I had run 1262.7 miles, an average of 24 miles per week.

2011

In January and February, I began to re-establish a daily running routine, but this was interrupted by snow, icy surfaces and gastric flu, so my weekly mileage never exceeded the 30 miles covered in the 2nd week of January.

On the 10th of March, Izzy and I returned to Bangalore and on to Puttaparthi, to complete Izzy's dental treatment in Whitefield. Four days after arriving I began morning shuffles around the by-pass loop, a distance of 3.5 miles. On some mornings my legs would not respond well and I did not enjoy struggling round. I could not run/jog/shuffle faster than 10-minute miles and I felt that continuing my daily shuffling was pointless, so I decided to stop trying after my Puttaparthi by-pass shuffle on the 5th of April. My previous month's mileage amounted to 69 miles.

Sai Baba was unwell while we were in Puttaparthi and following two weeks in hospital he left his bodily form on the 24th of April. On the following days thousands of devotees arrived to file past Baba's body. On our taxi journey to Bangalore airport, we saw a continuous stream of buses bringing more devotees to pay their respects to Baba.

I did one more shuffle when I went around the Lossiemouth loop with Anna on the 4th of June. The remainder of 2011 was shuffle free, so my total mileage for the year was 228 miles, which was an average of just over 4 miles per week. At last I had decided to stop running completely, because my body was not responding to the training stimulus and I was not happy shuffling along at about 12 minutes a mile.

REFLECTIONS

I had always liked to run, but at school this was limited to the annual sports day where the short race was from the bottom goal posts to the top goal posts of the football pitch and the long race was from the bottom goals, around the top goals and back. Annual Inter- Boys-Brigade-and-Scouts Sports also provided the opportunity to race over 100 and 200 yards.

Nobody suggested that we should practise (train) for such events, so we raced on natural ability.

When I joined Aberdeen Amateur Athletic Club in 1962 I participated in twice weekly club training nights and also began running from home, but with inappropriate shoes: 'gutties'. The club coach suggested that I concentrate on 440 yards racing, but after several months he decided that I did not have enough 'fire in my belly', so I happily moved on to cross-country league races in winter, athletics league races and highland games in summer. Longer races seemed to suit me and I enjoyed improving at cross-country, in road races and hill races.

Giving up my job and taking up full time further education allowed me to progress academically and to train, usually twice a day in daylight. Inspired by my club mate, Alastair Wood, I ran my first marathon, having reached the required minimum age of 21 years in 1966 and showed some promise. The following year I was delighted to finish second to Alastair in the Scottish marathon championship. At university I continued to improve and produced some good performances in cross-country and on the track. In 1970 I ran in the 36 miles 'Two Bridges' race for the experience of running beyond the marathon but, although I finished seventh, I did not see this as my future forte.

My choice of employment on finishing university was influenced by my running ambitions, so I moved to Birmingham to work for Lucas Aerospace. By joining Birchfield Harriers, I hoped that training with Ian and Peter Stewart would provide the stimulus to enable me to make the Scottish team for the international cross-country championship. As I had been 13th in the Scottish cross-country championship the previous year, I thought that I could make the necessary improvement. The standard in the Birmingham cross-country league races was extremely high and I made minor improvements. I was delighted to finish 6th in the Warwickshire cross-country championship to gain selection for my one and only inter-counties cross-country match.

During my time in Birmingham, in 1974 I ran the 'Two Bridges' again and followed this a month later with the London to Brighton 53 miles race and was surprised to finish third. I realised that I was not going to make the grade in cross-country and track running and felt a need to return to Aberdeen. My work there as a satellite navigation engineer in 1975, involved in the dynamic positioning of semi submersible oil exploration rigs meant working offshore for periods. Because of this I had given up the desire to be a good runner and opted to be a recreational runner.

Surviving a dunking in the Norwegian sector of the North Sea changed my outlook on life and I enrolled for a secondary teacher-training course to allow me to teach physics and combined this with a Diploma in Education at Aberdeen University. The latter allowed me to compete for the university again and I decided to take my running training very seriously.

My first teaching post, at Lossiemouth High School in 1976, was challenging but rewarding and allowed me to meet my future wife, Isobel. I lived in Elgin and began running to and from work by various courses, which proved to be very beneficial in improving my fitness. The following year I was delighted to set world best performances for: 50Km, 150Km and 100 miles and won the London to Brighton. A year later in my first 100Km race in Finland I was extremely pleased to set a world best road performance of 6-18-00. Thankfully my good form continued and I won the London to Brighton again in the fastest average time over a longer course. Four weeks later in the R.R.C 100Km track race I ran especially well to establish world best track performances at 6 hours and for 100Km with 6-10-20.

My 100Km performance led to invitations to events, and I thoroughly enjoyed the 'Runners World Running Week' in Palo Alto, south of San Francisco, where I met several great runners. I accepted several invitations and enjoyed racing and winning 100Km races in Italy and Spain. A 100 miles road race in Flushing Meadows, New York was difficult because of the heat, but I was delighted to win in a new world best performance of 11-51-11. Over the following years I was pleased to set world best performances at 40 miles, 50 miles and 200Km. In 1983 I finally broke 2-20 for the marathon with 2-19-35 in the London marathon, finishing 90th.

My desire to run the length of Great Britain became strong enough for me to plan an attempt to run from Land's End to John o'Groats for April 1987. This attempt failed when I suffered a tibia stress fracture near Hereford. A second attempt in April 1989 from John o'Groats proved very stressful and unpleasant, but successful, completing the journey in a record time of 10 days 15 hours and 27 minutes.

The profile of Ultra Distance Running was enhanced with the introduction of a National 100Km championship in 1989, thanks to the efforts of John Legge. Malcolm Campbell established, with the help of Andy Milroy and Dan Brannen, the 'International Association of Ultra runners' (I.A.U) in 1987 and worked with the IAAF and the European Athletics Federation to establish World and European championships at 100Km and later 24 Hours. I was past my best by then, but I was pleased to take second place behind Domingo Catalan of Spain in the first IAU 100Km World challenge in Belgium. John Foden introduced the 100Km 'Anglo Celtic Plate' competition to stimulate 100Km running in the home nations and the Republic of Ireland, which motivated runners to achieve the required standard to gain team selection and national vests.

Great Britain vests were not awarded for international ultra-distance races until 1990, when I received my first G.B team kit for the 100Km World Challenge in Duluth.

I loved racing and had a tendency to race too frequently, when not fully recovered from a previous race or not totally fit. This was the case in 1990 when I ran six 100Km races, winning four, but running below expectations in the last, which was 21 days after the penultimate 100Km. I had also run four marathons, a 50 miles race, the Two Bridges race and an indoor 24-hours world best that year. My mind expected too much from my body on a number of occasions and also I was prone to developing chest infections when my immune system was depressed following a hard 100Km. Picking up infections was partly an occupational hazard of being a teacher.

I over-trained occasionally, but usually recognised the symptoms and had the sense to ease back. In later years, atrial fibrillation started to develop, which was alarming initially and debilitating when it occurred in races. My irregular heartbeat was present from about 1986, but did not present a problem until 2008 when I required angioplasty in my right coronary artery. Atrial fibrillation became permanent, but cleared again after two years. In 1996 I developed Type Two Diabetes, which I believe was caused by the high carbohydrate diet, which fuelled my training for over three decades. I should have planned my diet more carefully to avoid this disease, with potentially serious complications.

By the new millennium, my strength was declining, but I could get under 3 hours for the marathon and under 8 hours for 100Km, which was considered okay for a 55-year-old. My ability deteriorated significantly over the decade and, although I continued to train, my body would not respond to the training stimulus and eventually I could not exceed ten-minute miles. My running was no longer enjoyable, as a run became a jog and then more of a shuffle, and this prompted me to abandon trying to run, as I had appeared to have exhausted my quota of 'Adaptation Energy'.

Looking back, I am satisfied with my lengthy running period of 48 years, with races ranging from 100 yards to 24-hours. I had no idea when I started that, at 39 years old, I would represent Scotland, and on a further ten occasions, in marathons (5 vests) and 100Km races (6 vests). I was delighted to be selected for Great Britain international teams on 17 occasions: 11 for 100Km championships, and 6 for 24-hour championships, the last when I was 56 years old. I was very fortunate to be able to continue running long enough to get selection for these international World and European championships. I felt sad that great British runners, such as Cavin Woodward, Martin Daykin and Mike Newton missed out on selection opportunities.

I felt fulfilled that I was able to establish world best performances on the track at: 50 Km, 40 miles, 50 miles, 6 hours, 150Km, 100 miles and 200Km. In addition, I was delighted to achieve World bests for a road 100 miles and an indoor 24-hours.

Being awarded an M.B.E., and receiving this from the Queen in Buckingham Palace, was special, and Isobel, Claire, Anna and I enjoyed the occasion.

Running has taken me on an interesting journey, with many unexpected twists of fate, and took me to places/countries that I never expected to visit and allowed me to meet many interesting people. I did my best, which is all that can be asked of anyone.

APPENDIX

APPENDIX ONE: THE RITCHIE FOUNDATION

THE RITCHIE FOUNDATION

During an early morning training run from their homes in Longside, Aberdeenshire, John Diffey, mentioned to Graham Milne, 'Don Ritchie's entry in the 1990 Guinness Book of Records for his John o'Groats to Land's End solo record run'. He told Graham that, 'for many months I have been considering how best to celebrate Don's colossal achievement'.

One of John's ideas was to collect and publish a short collection of North East running anecdotes. 'It would contain an account of Ritchie's epic run, plus funny events about other runners which we have all enjoyed and forgotten, but which I now propose should be used to raise money for Ritchie's Run charities'. Graham grasped the idea, 'Go ahead with your idea' urged Graham. By the end of their run that chilly St Andrew's Day, John had decided to implement his idea and called it his 'St Andrew's Day Pledge'.

John was convinced that a trust, known as 'The Ritchie Trust', should be set up so that funds could be gradually built up while I was still in a 'prominent and influential position within the sport'. 'To this end it is proposed that a group of trustees be selected by Donald to decide certain issues: areas that the trust might support, methods of fund raising and administration of the fund'.

The following trustees were appointed: Noel McPartlin, Chairman, Graham Milne, Vice-Chairman, John Diffey, Secretary, Donald Ritchie, Treasurer and Isobel Ritchie. It was decided to call the trust 'The Ritchie Foundation' and the inaugural meeting was held in Elgin on the 14th of November 1990. John Diffey would produce a letterhead to include the phrase: 'To help charities by celebrating Don Ritchie's athletic achievements'. Noel McPartlin would use his legal training to prepare a constitution. Graham Milne would take on the role of publications editor and I would produce a list of potential contributors, who would be asked for anecdotes relating to me along with their own potted biography. Glen Elliot and Raymond Wood were to receive minutes of our meetings.

To minimise travel for John and Noel, meetings were often held in the 'Banff Springs Hotel'. Responses to the requests for material for the proposed publication were disappointing with only 22 received from 62 requests and Graham indicated that 'editing into a publication would not be easy'.

At the meeting in February 1992 it was decided to investigate the staging of a local ultra-distance race. I thought that 50Km would be an appropriate distance and Noel suggested using the Speyside Way. It was decided to investigate the route by bicycle, so Noel, Graham and I, accompanied by our daughter Claire, set off from the old Ballindalloch railway station. Claire stopped at Aberlour, where we had our pub lunch and we continued, suitably fortified, to the Spey Bay Hotel. We agreed that the course was suitable for running and quite challenging, especially the climb over Ben Aigen. The route was modified to avoid a dangerous road crossing and carefully measured from OS maps by Jim McWilliam and the start line arranged at Ballindalloch so that the estimated distance was 50Km. Mike Francis joined our group as a trustee, as we planned the race. It was decided to plan for the race to be on Easter Sunday, the 3rd of April 1994.

Sponsorship for the race was obtained from Isobel Ritchie, Gleaner Oils, United Distillers, both Elgin-based, the Coasters running club, Banff and Badenoch & Strathspey Enterprise. The race finish would be at the Spey Bay Hotel, where post race refreshments would be served and the Caravan Park showers made available. Mick Francis agreed to be race director, with all race entries being sent to him. A pre-race pasta party staffed by Moray Road Runners helpers was to be held in Lodge Moray.

In this inaugural race, Fraser Clyne finished first in the excellent time of 3:02:03, ahead of Alan Reid and Eric Grant and the remainder of the 81 starters. Everyone involved with this event agreed that it was a success. Once all the expenses had been dealt with and all donations summed, including £62.32 raised by our nine-year-old daughter, Anna, who played her violin for two hours outside the Lossiemouth Co-op supermarket, £1247.82 was donated to the Elgin and District Cancer Research Campaign.

Mike Francis and I were keen to have this race continue as an annual event, despite some Trustees being unable to commit their time to future events. We decided to proceed with a trimmed down version, with Mike as race director and I would organise the event. United Distillers, 'Bells', were main sponsors, along with Moray Badenoch & Strathspey Enterprise', plus help from Gleaner Oil and Gas and the Co-op. The 1995 race on the 16th of April had 62 finishers from 70 starters.

This arrangement continued for the race in 1996, when Simon Pride started his winning sequence setting the course record of 2:59:18 the following year and winning in 1998 and 1999. When Mike Francis emigrated to Australia, I took over as race director and organiser. As Simon turned to marathon racing, Alan Reid became the winner of the 2000 race. Because of the foot and mouth epidemic the 2001 race was cancelled.

'Neways' a health and personal care company, sponsored the 2002 race, along with help from Gleaner Oil and Gas and the Co-op. Simon won again in 2002 and 2003. The 2006 race had to be cancelled when the Spey Bay Hotel ceased operating, went into receivership, closed and remained in this state, so the original 'Speyside Way' race was consigned to history. No other fund raising events were organised by the Foundation, so with the agreement of the trustees the 'Ritchie Foundation' was closed and, on the 21st of June 2011, the 'Gold Deposit account' with RBS was closed, having raised £8737 for cancer research charities. Approximately a third of this was raised by sponsorship of John Diffey running in the 95 miles, West Highland Way Race in June 1994.

APPENDIX TWO: TRAINING

In 1987 I wrote the following for the 'Training for Ultras' booklet, edited by Andy Milroy and published by the Road Runners Club.

When I was asked to write down some of my thoughts on training I was a bit apprehensive. Sometimes when things are going badly and I am not running well, I think then that I know nothing about proper training methods. At times like that an advisor/mentor, or coach may be useful, to talk things over, as he may see the reason for your difficulties quite clearly, while you are baffled. There are other periods when running is going well and you think you know exactly what training is good for you.

I have never had a coach and my training developed by empirical methods to what seems to suit me. There is no one 'right' way to train as success has been achieved by many combinations of methods.

The important thing is to believe in the training you are doing, so that your confidence and expectations of success improve along with your physical condition.

As I see it the object of training is to submit your body to stressful situations similar to those likely to be encountered in a race, so that it can adapt to handle the race situation better. It is important to apply the stress in small doses with adequate recovery between applications, so that adaptation can take place.

Too much stress, training too hard, or inadequate rest, will cause deterioration of condition. Also, increasing the stress too quickly can lead to problems. When building up to a high weekly mileage you should listen to the feedback from your body, and run accordingly. You get plenty of warning signals from your muscles/body as you approach the 'overdose' condition: it is then time to back off somewhat, remember you are training, not straining. The idea then is to keep the stress level high enough to promote adaptation, but not high enough for breakdown.

It is also important to have consistency in training and a fairly regular lifestyle. For example, it is better to run 10 miles every day, than two tens every second day. Consistency also, in my experience, tends to prevent injuries and I find the 'safest' period is when I have established a steady mileage of 110 miles a week.

Most of my injuries have occurred when there has been some dramatic change in training, e.g. starting effort sessions or hill runs, or building up to a plateau again, following a rest of more than four or five days. I also consider roads as the 'safest' training surface.

I have found that I respond best to a fairly high mileage and average 100 miles a week, but this can be between 20 miles and 160 miles per week, depending on the circumstances. I also benefit from fartlek, on grass and forest roads and from efforts of one minute to five minutes duration on the roads. If you are a person who does not put on weight easily (I do) then I think it is unnecessary to train so heavily.

To run an ultra-marathon, you need a good training background, and a suitable mental attitude, i.e. you must be a little crazy.

I like a ten-week build up to an important race, increasing my mileage from 100 miles a week to perhaps 160 miles per week. Hopefully this will ensure that you can tolerate the discomfort a 100Km race can inflict on you.

A certain type of mentality seems to be advantageous. I think you require to be a calm, determined, patient person with a high tolerance for prolonged discomfort and with a high capacity for delayed gratification.

It is important to stress the value of the weekly long training run. In my opinion this is a key session and should be of at least two hours duration but not too long, otherwise enjoyment is lost and it becomes a drudge. I found my Sunday 31 miles course on roads and Forestry tracks suited me and

I tried to do this twice or three times a month. Longer training runs were too time consuming and I did not think they contributed any more to improving one's condition.

I have been running since 1962 with only injury induced rests, so I must enjoy it. I think it is very important to make training varied and enjoyable. We are very fortunate in the area where I live that we have undulating forestry roads, beach, golf courses, disused railway lines and quiet roads. Consequently, runs of 20 to 31 miles can be very pleasurable.

I alter my training throughout the year, changing the emphasis on the type and intensity to prevent boredom. Up to mid May I normally worked towards a marathon, then varied training to aim at a 100Km, before easing back in the summer holidays. Then I raced every week at 10 miles or half marathon. In August I started working towards a 100Km again. That variety keeps my enjoyment going.

My normal training programme would involve running twice a day, Monday to Friday, with single runs on Saturday and Sunday. Usually the pace was 10 miles per hour, or quicker and nearly all was done alone. If I was trying to improve my pace, I would include three 'effort' sessions per week. I would do a 10-mile run, broken up by alternating one and two minute hard runs, with equal time recoveries; a 15-mile run, incorporating: 1-2-3-4-5-4-3-2-1 minutes hard, with equal time recoveries, then repeating until the run is completed; a further session on hills would be the third effort session

Appendix Three is an extract from my training record for a period preparing for my first and second 100Km races in 1978 and illustrates my training schedule during that period.

My training in recent years has been on similar lines but with a lower total mileage, as I did not run so far to and from work or train with the club twice a week. During this period, I managed to get under two hours twenty minutes for the marathon twice (2-19-34and 2-19-58) through cutting back on mileage and trying to run my effort sessions faster. I also raced in shorter races in my area, treating them as speed-endurance training.

Sometimes I used the carbohydrate loading diet, but I am not convinced of its effectiveness after several uses. Done strictly, it can cause extreme weakness and lower resistance to infections, when in the low carbohydrate stage. I have had some bad experiences in the early days, on the strict diet. Now I just eat more vegetables, cutting out bread and jam and most carbohydrates for the initial three days following my glycogen depletion run, then I ate a lot of carbohydrate-rich foods during the 48 hours preceding the race.

Usually I took two days of no running prior to the race, but sometimes tapered down to five miles on the day prior to the race. During marathons and ultras, I took 'Electrolyte, Replacement & Glucose' (ERG) drinks and a long chain glucose polymer drink that I concocted myself, and alternated these drinks every 5Km, consuming 200ml of each.

I regard stretching as extremely important in reducing the risk of muscle injury. Before training I did not stretch, but began at a slow pace and gradually picked it up. Following a run, I spent about five minutes stretching my calfs, quadriceps and hamstrings. I did this sequence before a race also.

Perhaps a general diet has an influence on performance. My diet was high in carbohydrates and fibre with little meat and quite a lot of fish. This is what I 'felt' like eating and it suited me.

Ultra-marathons, I think, will become more popular in future as runners seek a greater challenge than the marathon. Times will improve as faster runners tackle them. I do not know what the optimum training for a 100Km might be, but it may be interesting to see what could be achieved with training in excess of 200 miles per week.

FURTHER THOUGHTS

A very important part of preparation is planning, which could be long-term or medium-term plans. A long-term plan would set some goals or targets for two to four years ahead. A medium-term plan could be for the year ahead, where you select the three or four races in which you want to run well. Based on this race selection an appropriate training programme can be planned to achieve an optimum performance. If you are not familiar with some race, such as a championship in Europe or elsewhere, then some research can be done to find out about the nature of the course and likely weather conditions. This will allow you to modify your training to try to adapt to the type of course and the likely weather conditions.

Having a training diary and recording your race results is important, as this can be consulted in future, when planning your training schedule.

Tapering before an important race is necessary and I found that easing down on training for three days suited me, but this may not be sufficient. You have to try to find what length of taper is optimum for you and it is better to err on the side of caution.

Another important part of planning is preparing a race plan in as much detail as possible, including a schedule for your drinks and food in 100Km and 24-hour events. This schedule can then be used by your second to supply you with your requirements. For example, I would alternate 200mls of 10% concentration glucose polymer with 200mls of 'Dioralite' every 5Km in a 100Km and the same for a 24-hour, plus some food every two hours, but I never got my 24-hour nutrition optimised.

Consideration should also be given to: motivation, mind, nutrition and lifestyle. Motivation is essential and there can be many sources of motivation such as a desire to achieve a particular standard or a personal best. Achieving the standard necessary to gain selection for a G.B. team in a 100Km or 24-hour championship was a great motivating factor for me.

To train well, your mind has to be free from potentially distracting thoughts or worries, so that you are in the right frame of mind and happy with life. Visualisation can be used in training runs as part of your mental preparation.

It is vitally important to get adequate nutrition to ensure that glycogen stores are replaced and damaged tissues and muscles are repaired. Sufficient carbohydrates, preferably 'complex' must be included in your diet along with adequate protein. A multi-mineral and multi-vitamin supplementation may be beneficial.

As part of a long term-plan it might be worth changing your lifestyle to maximise your chances of becoming the very best runner you can be. This could mean changing your work situation or modifying your social life, at least for a few years, to find out what you can achieve. I became a teacher in 1976, after working in industry for several years and found this very beneficial for my training and performance.

APPENDIX THREE: 1978 TRAINING FOR TWO 100 KM RACES

	Preparation for my first two 100Km races			
Date	**Session**	**Day's Total**	**Comments**	**Week's Total**
01/05/78	22 miles road & forest in 2-15.	22 miles		
02/05/1978	12 miles road in 1-16 & 5 miles with club	17miles		
03/05/1978	8.5 miles road back from school in 50 mins	8.5 miles		
04/05/1978	8.5 miles road to school in 52 mins, 6.5 miles back		Knee felt O.K.	
	& 8 miles hard with club at night	23 miles		
05/05/1978	6.5 miles to school in 39 mins	6.5 miles		
06/05/1978	22 miles road in 2-16-20.	22 miles	Knee felt O.K.	
07/05/1978	No run	0		99 miles
08/05/1978	14.5 miles back from school in 1-27	14.5 miles		
09/05/1978	7 miles to school in 39 min, 17.5 miles back	24.5 miles		
10/05/1978	8.5 miles to work 52 min, 14.5 miles back 1-28-30	23 miles		
11/05/1978	7 miles to school in 38 min, 7 miles back 38 min & 8 miles with club	22 miles		
12/05/1978	7 miles to school in 36-30	7 miles		
13/05/1978	21 miles on forest paths in 2-20	21miles		
14/05/1978	15 miles with friends	15 miles		127 miles
15/05/1978	12 miles road in 1-11	12 miles		
16/05/1978	7 miles back from work & 7.5 miles hard at Club	14.5 miles	Club 7.5 race?	
17/05/1978	8.5 miles to work 49-30, 20 miles back in 2-06	28.5 miles	Felt good	
18/05/1978	14.5 miles to school in 1-27-07, 7 miles back in 38-00 & 8.5 miles with club at night	30 miles		
19/05/1978	14.5 miles to school in 1-29, 12 miles back in 73-42	26.5 miles		
20/05/1978	23 miles Kellas route in 2-18	23miles	warm day	
21/05/1978	23 miles Monaughty Forest route in 2-13	23miles	Hard run	157.5 miles
22/05/1978	20 miles back from school in 2-00-10	20miles		
23/05/1978	8.5 miles to work 52, 7miles back & 7miles hard			
	with club in 35-00	22.5 miles		
24/05/1978	12 miles to school in 1-19, 20 miles back in 2-03-32	32 miles		
25/05/1978	14.5 miles to school in 1-31, 7 miles back & 8 miles with club at night	29.5 miles	Stomach pains	

Preparation for my first two 100Km races				
Date	Session	Day's Total	Comments	Week's Total
26/05/1978	7 miles to school, Colitis diagnosed	7 miles	Colofac Tablets	
27/05/1978	13 miles easy	13 miles	feeling better	
28/05/1978	10 miles road race, 2nd in 54-53	13 miles	Stomach tight	137 miles
29/05/1978	20 miles back from school in 2-02	20miles	Stomach tight	
30/05/1978	14.5 miles to school in 1-28-30, 7miles back &			
	8 miles with club at night.	29.5 miles		
31/05/1978	14.5 miles to work; 1-28-30, 14.5miles back; 1-32-30	29 miles		
01/06/1978	14.5 miles to school in 1-32, 7miles back & 8 miles			
	with club at night.	29.5 miles	very tired	
02/06/1978	12 miles to school.	12 miles	very tired	
03/06/1978	31 miles road in 3-07-3,1 to try racing kit	31 miles	satisfactory	
04/06/1978	22 miles road & forest	22 miles	felt well	173 miles
05/06/1978	24 miles road at night in 2-23-50	24miles	Felt good	
06/06/1978	7 miles to work & 7miles back, 8miles with club	20 miles		
07/06/1978	14.5 miles to work in 1-34, 14.5 miles back in 1-30.	29 miles		
08/06/1978	14.5 miles to work in 1-30, evening 6 miles race, 7th. & 2.5 miles warm up/down	24 miles		
09/06/1978	14.5 miles to work; 1-28-30, 22 miles Monaughty			
	course in evening in 2-14-20.	36,5 miles		
10/06/1978	23 miles Kellas route in 2-17-57.	23 miles	Felt good	
11/06/1978	31 miles route road in 3-20-14.	31 miles	very windy	189.5 miles
12/06/1978	24 miles road at night in 2-20-32	24 miles	Felt good	
13/06/1978	14.5 miles to school in 1-28-30, 7miles back &			
	6 miles hard with club at night.	27.5 miles		
14/06/1978	12.5 miles to work; 14.5 miles back.	27 miles	very tired	
15/06/1978	14.5 miles to school in 1-27-30, 7miles back &			
	8.5 miles with club at night.	30 miles		
16/06/1978	14.5 miles to school in 1-33.	14.5 miles		
17/06/1978	31 miles route road in 3-03.	31 miles	Best for route	
18/06/1978	22 miles Monaughty route & 5.5 miles later	27.5 miles		179.5 miles
19/06/1978	24 miles road at night in 2-21-30	24 miles		
20/06/1978	14.5 miles to school in 1-31, 7 miles back.	21.5 miles	Left calf pains	
21/06/1978	14.5 miles to work in 1-28-30, 20m back in 2-03-30	34.5 miles		

	Preparation for my first two 100Km races			
Date	Session	Day's Total	Comments	Week's Total
22/06/1978	14.5 miles to work in 1-29-30, 14.5 miles back in 1-25	29 miles		
23/06/1978	14.5 miles to school in 1-28.	14.5 miles		
24/06/1978	20 miles in 1-50-40.	20 miles	Depletion run	
25/06/1978	15 miles with friends & 12.5 miles later in 1-19	27.5 miles		171 miles
26/06/1978	23 miles Kellas route in 2-25-40.	23 miles	Felt good	
27/06/1978	20 miles course in 2-11-50.at 04.20	20 miles	Depart for London	
28/06/1978	10.5 miles in 1-02-42, in Helsinki	10.5 miles	Carbo Loading	
29/06/1978	At world Games with Tapio Pekola & Charlie.	0 miles		
30/06/1978	To Hartola; 100Km start at 22.00 hr; set pace from 10Km; mar = 2-31-30, 50Km = 3-01-00 100Km in 6-18-00. World Road Best Second = Gennari (Italy) 6-53		World best; lost ~ 2 min by misdirected 250m past junction	
31/06/1978		62.25 miles		
01/07/1978	No run	0 miles		
02/07/1978	10 miles in forest	10 miles		126 miles
03/07/1978 to 09/07/78	recovery run; bad blisters - one infected		treatment sports clinic	
		83 miles		83 miles
10/07/1978	17.5 miles in 1-54-00; infection clearing	17.5 miles		
11/07/1978	No run	0		
12/07/1978	4 miles in morning, 12 miles in evening in 67-00	16 miles		
13/07/1978	12 miles in morning, 12 miles in evening	24 miles		
14/07/1978	20.5 miles in morning, 12 miles hard in evening	32.5 miles		
15/07/1978	12 miles easy	12 miles		
16/07/1978	22.5Km road/forest race, PUTAJA, 2nd in 1-14-06	14 miles	felt weak	116 miles
	1st was 1-13-36			
17/07/1978	20.5 miles in 2-07; became ill in evening-like flu	20.5 miles	Rest, pulse 85!	
18/07/1978	No run, ill	0		
19/07/1978	10 miles easy, recovering	10 miles		
20/07/1978	6.5 miles including 2 x 1 minute efforts	6.5 miles		
21/07/1978	Travel to JAKOBSTAD; 5hr, train north	0		
22/07/1978	JAKOBSTAD; marathon, 9th 2-29-39.	26.25 miles	1-11-50 at half, but slowed	
23/07/1978	13.5 miles easy	13.5 miles		77 miles

Preparation for my first two 100Km races				
Date	**Session**	**Day's Total**	**Comments**	**Week's Total**
24/07/1978	12 miles road, Helsinki	12 miles		
25/07/1978	14 miles road, Helsinki	14 miles		
26/07/1978	15 miles, Helsinki, return to London	15 miles		
27/07/1978	10 miles, Wanstead Park, London	10 miles		
28/07/1978	No run, resting	0		
29/07/1978	Woodford to Southend 40 mile race. 2nd 3-59-35		struggled from 5 miles	
	Cavin Woodward 1st in 3-50-14		stiff legs	
30/07/1978	5 miles easy	5 miles		96 miles
31/07/1978	Return, London to Elgin			
01/08/1978	12 miles in morning, 11 miles in evening, Ulapool	23 miles		
02/08/1978	18.5 miles in two runs, Stornaway with Ron & Y.P	18.5 miles		
03/08/1978	No run, bad weather	0		
04/08/1978	No run, bad weather	0		
05/08/1978	22 miles Monaughty route in 2-06-00	22 miles		
06/08/1978	22.5 miles Forest route	22.5 miles		86 miles
07/08/1978	23 miles Kellas route in 2-16, best for course	23 miles	resume training	
08/08/1978	No run, car repairing	0 miles	felt sick/weak	
09/08/1978	Jogged in mountains for 6hr; 6 Munros! With Ron & Co	10 miles		
10/08/1978	23 miles Park bridge route in 2-12-54	23 miles		
11/08/1978	17 miles with Alastair Wood in 1-43	17 miles		
12/08/1978	Nethy Bridge 9.5 miles road race, 1st; 49-44			
	& 5 miles after,	15 miles		
13/08/1978	22.5 miles; 20 mile time of 1-56-30.	22.5 miles		110.5 miles
14/08/1978	22 miles Monaughty route in 2-09	22 miles		
15/08/1978	23 miles Kellas route in 2-14-24, best for course			
	7,5 miles in 46-44, with club at night	30.5 miles		
16/08/1978	No run; busy in Aberdeen	0 miles		
17/08/1978	24 miles in forest in 2-24 & 8 miles at night	32 miles		
18/08/1978	23 miles Kellas route.	23 miles		
19/08/1978	Extended Monaughty route in 2-30-30	25.5 miles		
20/08/1978	31 miles course in 3-04-21	31miles	Depletion run	164 miles
21/08/1978	20 miles back from work in 2-04-54	20 miles		

Preparation for my first two 100Km races				
Date	**Session**	**Day's Total**	**Comments**	**Week's Total**
22/08/1978	14 miles to work; 1-28-58, 14 miles back; 1-32	28 miles		
23/08/1978	14 miles to work; 1-32, 14 miles back; 1-32	28 miles	Legs puffy	
24/08/1978	12 miles; early morning in 1-19-30	12 miles	Carbo Load 08:10	
25/08/1978	No run	0 miles		
26/08/1978	Two Bridges race, 5th in 3-32-49; 4-15 slower than	36 miles	Poor run; tired from start	
	last year!			
27/08/1978	10 miles in 1-10 with Pete Duffy	10 miles		
28/08/1978	14 miles back from work in 1-27-40	14 miles		
29/08/1978	7 miles to work, 14 miles back; 1-24-30	21 miles		
30/08/1978	14 miles to work; 1-28-30, 14 miles back; 1-24-42	28 miles		
31/08/1978	14 miles to work; 1-30, 8.5 miles back; 50-12 &			
	11 miles hard in 64-00, with club	33.5 miles		
01/09/1978	14 miles to work; cold starting during day	14 miles		
02/09/1978	No run; cold worse	0 miles		
03/09/1978	No run; recovering	0 miles		110 miles
04/09/1978	2.5 miles with school club, 20 miles back; 1-55	22.5 miles		
05/09/1978	14 miles to work; 1-25, 8.5 miles back; 50-26 &			
	8.5 miles with club, second half hard	31 miles		
06/09/1978	14 miles to work; 1-31, 14 miles back; 1-30	28 miles	very tired	
07/09/1978	14 miles to work; 1-31, 8.5 miles back; infection in			
	left foot	22.5 miles		
08/09/1978	No run; treatment for infection & antibiotics	0 miles	aching muscles	
09/09/1978	No run; treatment for infection & antibiotics	0 miles		
10/09/1978	No run; treatment for infection & antibiotics	0 miles		104 miles
11/09/1978	4 miles with school club, 14 miles back	18 miles		
12/09/1978	7 miles to work, 8.5m back, 5.5miles hard with club	21 miles		
13/09/1978	14 miles to work; 1-27-30, 14 miles back; 1-29-40	28 miles	felt better	
14/09/1978	14 miles to work; 1-29-10, 8.5 miles back; 49 &			

Preparation for my first two 100Km races				
Date	Session	Day's Total	Comments	Week's Total
	2 miles with club	24.5 miles		
15/09/1978	7 miles to work,	7 miles		
16/09/1978	7.5 miles course in Aberdeen	7.5 miles		
17/09/1978	18 miles hard with Aberdeen Lads, 12miles in afternoon	30 miles		132 miles
18/09/1978	8 miles course in Aberdeen	8 miles		
19/09/1978	8.5 miles back from school in 45-00	8.5 miles	Felt good	
20/09/1978	14 miles to work; 1-25-10, 20 miles back; 2-05-19	34 miles		
21/09/1978	14 miles to work; 1-28-20, 8.5 miles back; 53-12			
	8.5 miles with club	31 miles		
22/09/1978	14 miles to work; 1-30-10, 12 miles back; 67-30	26 miles		
23/09/1978	No run; very tired	0 m		
24/09/1978	31 miles course in 3-00-48; best for course	31 miles	Depletion run	138.5 miles
25/09/1978	3.5 miles school club, 14 miles back in 1-33-40	17.5 miles		
26/09/1978	14 miles to work; 1-32-40, 8.5 miles back; 54-02	22.5 miles		
27/09/1978	14 miles to work; 1-29-40, 14 miles back; 1-26-30	28 miles	Felt good	
28/09/1978	14 miles to work; 1-32-30, 8.5 miles back; 55 min			
	3.5 miles with club; start carbohydrates at 20:30	26 miles		
29/09/1978	No run; resting	0 miles		
30/09/1978	No run; travel to London, resting	0 miles		
01/10/1978	London-Brighton 1st 5-13-02: fastest average pace record Cavin Woodward 2nd in 5-18-30; 10 miles = 55-31	53.5 miles		147.5 miles
02/10/1978	No run; legs and feet too painful	0 miles		
03/10/1978	No run; legs and feet too painful	0 miles		
04/10/1978	8.5 miles to work; 56, 14 miles back; 1-43	22.5 miles	Legs painful	
05/10/1978	7 miles to work; 8.5 miles back; 7.5 miles with club	23 miles	Legs less painful	
06/10/1978	14 miles to work; 1-27-31, 12 miles back; 73-30	26 miles		
07/10/1978	Alves-Forres 5.9 mile race, 5th in 29-01	8 miles		
08/10/1978	Extended Monaughty route in 2-35-30	25.5 miles	Felt tired	117 miles
09/10/1978	18.5 miles with friends in 2-03	18.5 miles		
10/10/1978	10.5 miles with Graham & Peter in 1-17	10.5 miles		

Preparation for my first two 100Km races				
Date	**Session**	**Day's Total**	**Comments**	**Week's Total**
11/10/1978	31 mile course in 3-09-08; best for course	31 miles		
12/10/1978	24 miles in forest at Counteswells	24 miles		
13/10/1978	23 miles Park bridge route in 2-22	23 miles		
14/10/1978	North Dist X, Country League race 6th	8 miles		
15/10/1978	26.5 miles road & Forest roads in 2-37	26.5 miles		141.5 miles
16/10/1978	3.5 miles with school club; 20 miles home in 2-02	23.5 miles		
17/10/1978	14 miles to work; 1-31-40, 8.5 miles back; 49-40, 5.5 miles hard with club	28 miles		
18/10/1978	14 miles to work; 1-28-40, 20 miles back; 2-03-20	34 miles		
19/10/1978	14 miles to work; 1-29-20, 8.5 miles back; 52-10, & 7.5 miles with club	30 miles		
20/10/1978	14 miles to work; 1-31-20, tummy upset	14 miles		
21/10/1978	North Dist X-Country relay Champ Leg 1 in 13-42	7 miles		
22/10/1978	26 miles Forest & road.	26 miles	Depletion run	161.5 miles
23/10/1978	6.5 miles with school club; 14 miles home in 1-32	20.5 miles		
24/10/1978	14 miles to work; 1-33-30, 14 miles back; 1-34-10	28 miles		
25/10/1978	14 miles to work; 1-34-30, 14 miles back; 1-31-20	28 miles	very weak	
26/10/1978	14 miles to work; 1-31-30, carbohydrates at 06:30	14 miles		
27/10/1978	No run; travel to London, resting	0 miles		
28/10/1978	100Km in 6-10-20. RRC Crystal Palace	62.5 miles	last 12 miles very hard average pace under 6 min/mile	
	10km=34-06, stop ~ 16 miles for toilet, 1.5 laps behind Cavin & Mick Molloy! 50Km = 2-59-59 in 2nd, 40miles = 3-52-55, 50miles = 4-53-28 World Best			
29/10/1978	Return, London to Elgin	0 miles		

APPENDIX FOUR: TRAINING FOR A 24-HOUR RACE

	Preparation for Milton Keynes indoor 24-hours race				
Date	Session	Days Total	Comments		Weeks Total
06-Nov-89	10.5 miles to work; 66-30, 10.5 miles back; 66-01	21 miles			
07-Nov-89	11miles, Kintrae Brae; 1-17-25, 9.5miles back; 58-13	20.5 miles			
08-Nov-89	11miles, Kintrae Brae; 1-18-19, 9.5miles back; 59-46	20.5 miles			
09-Nov-89	11miles, Kintrae Brae; 1-19-20, 9.5miles back; 58-54	20.5 miles			
10-Nov-89	15 miles ponds route; 1-32-45	15 miles			
11-Nov-89	North Dist X-Country League; 36-28	8 miles	poor run; tired		
12-Nov-89	12 miles social run in 1-12-53	12 miles			117.5 miles
13-Nov-89	11miles, Kintrae Brae; 1-18-10, 9.5miles back; 58-12	20.5 miles			
14-Nov-89	11miles Kintrae Brae; 1-18-34, 9.5miles back; 58-34	20.5 miles			
15-Nov-89	11miles Kintrae Brae; 1-16-00, 9.5miles back; 58-24	20.5 miles			
16-Nov-89	11miles Kintrae Brae; 1-18-33, 9.5miles back; 58-34	20.5 miles			
17-Nov-89	15 miles ponds route; 1-32-45	15 miles			
18-Nov-89	Hill session: 5x long 2-18 average & 5x short 1-33 av	7 miles			
19-Nov-89	31 miles Monaughty route in 3-21-29	31 miles			135 miles
20-Nov-89	11miles Kintrae Brae; 1-21-32, 9.5miles back; 59-25	20.5 miles	cold developing		
21-Nov-89	11miles Kintrae Brae; 1-17-05, 9.5miles back; 60-50	20.5 miles	chest cold		
22-Nov-89	11miles Kintrae Brae; 1-17-43, 9.5miles back; 60-30	20.5 miles	Ampicillin		
23-Nov-89	11miles Kintrae Brae; 1-19-59, 9.5miles back; 57.50	20.5 miles			
24-Nov-89	15 miles ponds route; 1-35-07	15 miles	Eve Dinner dance		
25-Nov-89	North Dist X-Country Champs; 20th 43-00	10 miles	tired		
26-Nov-89	15 miles ponds route; 1-37-15	15 miles			122 miles
27-Nov-89	11miles Kintrae Brae; 1-21-51, 9.5miles back; 59.54	20.5 miles			
28-Nov-89	11miles Kintrae Brae; 1-18-30, 9.5miles back; 60.03	20.5 miles			
29-Nov-89	11miles Kintrae Brae; 1-19-42, 9.5miles back; 59.22	20.5 miles			
30-Nov-89	11miles Kintrae Brae; 1-19-34, 9.5miles back; 59.03	20.5 miles			
01-Dec-89	15 miles ponds route; 1-37-15	15 miles			
02-Dec-89	5 miles easy	5 miles			

Preparation for Milton Keynes indoor 24–hours race				
Date	**Session**	**Day's Total**	**Comments**	**Week's Total**
03-Dec-89	31 miles Monaughty route in 3-26-48	31 miles		133 miles
04-Dec-89	11miles Kintrae Brae; 1-20-50, 9.5miles back; 58.25	20.5 miles		
05-Dec-89	11miles Kintrae Brae; 1-21-48, 9.5miles back; 59.02	20.5 miles		
06-Dec-89	11miles Kintrae Brae; 1-21-14, 9.5miles back; 59.57	20.5 miles		
07-Dec-89	11miles Kintrae Brae; 1-20-04, 9.5miles back; 59.39	20.5 miles		
08-Dec-89	15 miles ponds route; 1-34-45	15 miles		
09-Dec-89	22 miles Boars Head route in 2-27-06	22 miles		
10-Dec-89	31 miles Monaughty route in 3-29-34	31 miles		150 miles
11-Dec-89	11miles Kintrae Brae; 1-22-36, 9.5miles back; 59-43	20.5 miles		
12-Dec-89	11miles Kintrae Brae; 1-19-36, 9.5miles back; 61-55	20.5 miles	snow at night	
13-Dec-89	11miles Kintrae Brae; 1-21-00, 9.5miles back; 60-13	20.5 miles	snow and ice	
14-Dec-89	11miles Kintrae Brae; 1-20-36, 8.5miles back; 56.06	19.5 miles		
15-Dec-89	15 miles ponds route; 1-34-45	15 miles	moon; crisp snow	
16-Dec-89	15 miles ponds route; 1-34-45	15 miles		
17-Dec-89	31 miles Monaughty route in 3-21-22	31 miles		141.5 miles
18-Dec-89	11miles Kintrae Brae; 1-25-00, 9.5miles back; 57-26	20.5 miles	Gale	
19-Dec-89	11miles Kintrae Brae; 1-22-32, 8.5miles back; 57-00	19.5 miles		
20-Dec-89	11miles Kintrae Brae; 1-19-38, 9.5miles back; 56-13	20.5 miles		
21-Dec-89	11miles Kintrae Brae; 1-20-54, 9.5miles back; 58-05	20.5 miles		
22-Dec-89	11miles Kintrae Brae; 1-22-50, 13.5miles back;	25.5 miles		
23-Dec-89	Forres Harr X-Country Christmas H'cap	4.5 miles		
24-Dec-89	31 miles Monaughty route in 3-30-02	31 miles		140 miles
25-Dec-89	15 miles ponds route; 1-32-20	15 miles		
26-Dec-89	22 miles Boars Head route in 2-22-53	22 miles	beautiful weather	
27-Dec-89	27 miles Garmouth/Kingston route in 2-54-34	27 miles		
28-Dec-89	22 miles Boars Head route in 2-25-22	22 miles		
29-Dec-89	27 miles Garmouth/Kingston route in 2-50-28	27 miles		
30-Dec-89	15 miles ponds route in 1-31-03	15 miles		
31-Dec-89	31 miles Monaughty route in 3-24-34	31 miles		159 miles
01-Jan-90	22 miles Boars Head route in 2-24-13	22 miles		

Preparation for Milton Keynes indoor 24–hours race				
Date	**Session**	**Day's Total**	**Comments**	**Week's Total**
02-Jan-90	8 miles social run with club & 10.5 miles back home	18.5 miles		
03-Jan-90	21.5 miles Boars Head route in 2-19-11	21.5 miles	detour to avoid shoot	
04-Jan-90	22 miles Boars Head route in 2-23-45	22 miles		
05-Jan-90	15 miles ponds route; 1-31-02	15 miles		
06-Jan-90	22 miles Boars Head route in 2-27-01	22 miles		
07-Jan-90	31 miles Monaughty route; 3-15-25; best for route	31 miles	best for Mick Francs	152 miles
08-Jan-90	11miles Kintrae Brae; 1-21-51, 9.5miles back; 59-28	20.5 miles		
09-Jan-90	11miles Kintrae Brae; 1-20-25, 9.5miles back; 58-51	20.5 miles		
10-Jan-90	11miles Kintrae Brae; 1-23-21, 9.5miles back; 57-11	20.5 miles	heavy rain/ sleet	
11-Jan-90	11miles Kintrae Brae; 1-18-34, 9.5miles back; 58-18	20.5 miles		
12-Jan-90	15 miles ponds route; 1-31-02	15 miles		
13-Jan-90	North Dist X-Country League; 18th	10 miles	left quads tight	
14-Jan-90	31 miles Monaughty route; 3-19-58	31 miles		138 miles
15-Jan-90	11miles Kintrae Brae; 1-23-43, 9.5miles back; 56-56	20.5 miles	chest cold	
16-Jan-90	11miles Kintrae Brae; 1-20-50, 9.5miles back; 59-46	20.5 miles		
17-Jan-90	11miles Kintrae Brae; 1-24-52, 9.5miles back; 58-39	20.5 miles	ampicillin x 4/day	
18-Jan-90	11miles Kintrae Brae; 1-21-16, 9.5miles back; 58-39	20.5 miles		
19-Jan-90	15 miles ponds route; 1-38-24	15 miles	strong wind	
20-Jan-90	15 miles ponds route; 1-36-28	15 miles		
21-Jan-90	31 miles Monaughty route; 3-18-32	31 miles	ampicillin finished	143 miles
22-Jan-90	11miles Kintrae Brae; 1-23-02, 9.5miles back; 58-05	20.5 miles		
23-Jan-90	11miles Kintrae Brae; 1-22-18, 9.5miles back; 58-58	20.5 miles		
24-Jan-90	10.5miles Calcots; 1-09-06, 9.5miles back; 57-43	20 miles		
25-Jan-90	10.5miles Calcots; 1-07-38, 9.5miles back; 61-44	20 miles	Gale	
26-Jan-90	15 miles ponds route; 1-33-27	15 miles		
27-Jan-90	31 miles Monaughty route; 3-26-35	31 miles	Sporanox throat infection	
28-Jan-90	15 miles ponds route; 1-33-27	15 miles	142 miles	
29-Jan-90	8.5 miles in 56-58 & 8.5 miles back in 54-37	17 miles	easy runs	
30-Jan-90	8.5 miles in 54-13	8.5 miles		

Preparation for Milton Keynes indoor 24-hours race				
Date	**Session**	**Day's Total**	**Comments**	**Week's Total**
31-Jan-90	8.5 miles in 55-35 & 8.5 miles back in 53-17	17 miles	now rest	
01-Feb-90	8.5 miles cycle	0 miles		
02-Feb-90	8.5 miles cycle & travel to London	0 miles		
03-Feb-90 to 04-Feb-90	Start Milton Keynes Indoor 24hr World Challenge		1.5hr traffic jam M25	
	I arrived 5 minutes before the start, agitated 100Km = 7-04, 100 miles=12-56-13, World best		put kit on in back of John's car at 90 mph	
	200Km=16-31-08. World best 24hr = 166 miles 429 yds; World Best Indoors			200.5 miles

APPENDIX FIVE: YEARLY TRAINING AND RACING MILEAGE

Yearly training & racing mileage		
Year	Mileage	Comments
1962	92.5	
1963	1499.5	440/880 yards runner
1964	2013	440/880 yards & 1 mile races
1965	2556	Ben Nevis race, 49th
1966	3867	1st marathon 2-43-28
1967	4372.25	2nd in Scottish mar 2-27-48
1968	4130	2nd in Scottish mar 2-32-25
1969	3852.5	Harlow marathon in 2-24-38
1970	4866.75	First ultra, Two Bridges, 7th
1971	5120	One-hour track, 19241.8 m
1972	4688.5	First marathon win 2-24-26
1973	4858.25	20 miles track, Bristol, 1-46-32
1974	4988	3rd in London Brighton 5-24-54
1975	4235.6	C-C v Queens U, New U, 1st
1976	3034.25	fractured left foot metatarsal
1977	5168.5	100 miles in 11-30-51
1978	5735.75	100Km in 6-10-20
1979	5721.5	50Km in 2-50-30
1980	3782.75	100Km Turin-St Vincent 6-35-00
1981	3935.5	50Km in 2-52-25, Niort
1982	5003.5	40 miles world best, 3-48-34.7
1983	6011.25	200Km in 16-37-30, world best
1984	6047	50 miles Ed-Glasgow 5-03-44
1985	5225.5	1st V40, Dundee Mar, 2-28-35
1986	5407.5	100Km Turin-St Vincent 6-36-02
1987	5650	100Km Torhout, Bel, 60-40-51
1988	5054.5	fractured left patella
1989	6472.75	J.O.G.L.E , 10d 15h 27min
1990	6121.75	24hr indoor, 166.25 miles
1991	6592.5	1st, West Highland way 95 miles
1992	6114.5	100Km Brit Champ 1st 6-51-54
1993	4928.25	100Km Brit Champ 2nd 7-09-04
1994	5910	24-hr Brit Champ 1st 147 miles
1995	5211.75	100Km Winschoten 7-09-49, V50
1996	3595	Type-2 diabetes diagnosed
1997	3808.25	Barry 40 miles, 4-23-28
1998	5768	24-hr Europe champ 145.5 miles
1999	5797	24-hr Europe champ 222.45Km
2000	5988.5	24-hr Europe champ 136.9 miles

Yearly training & racing mileage		
Year	Mileage	Comments
2001	2753.5	Left Achilles tendon rupture
2002	5626	poor racing
2003	4130.5	24-hr London, 1st 117.5 miles
2004	3616	Left knee injury
2005	1953.5	Left knee cruciate surgery
2006	1615.5	many personal worsts
2007	1717.5	more personal worsts
2008	956.5	Heart angioplasty
2009	1015	no strength
2010	1262.7	more personal worsts
2011	228.5	retired from running
Total	208100.8	

POSTSCRIPT

My decades of running have not protected me from some serious health issues, of which diabetes is the most significant long-term condition. Diabetes may have contributed to plaque deposits in my arteries, which led to angioplasty in 2008. My irregular heartbeat and atrial fibrillation are probably the result of decades of high mileage running. In July 2013, I experienced three Transient Ischaemic Attacks (TIAs). An ultra sonic Doppler Carotid Arteries investigation in August showed a narrowing of the arteries. A head CT scan indicated that my left Carotid artery, which provides blood to the left side of my brain, was 95% blocked.

A Carotid endarterectomy was carried out on this artery in Aberdeen Royal Infirmary on the 10th of September 2013. I made a slow recovery and since then I have had no further TIAs.

Now in November 2015, I continue to enjoy life.